HAZARDOUS WASTE MANAGEMENT

McGraw-Hill Chemical Engineering Series

Building the Literature of a Profession

Fifteen prominent chemical engineers first met in New York more than 60 years ago to plan a continuing literature for their rapidly growing profession. From Industry came such pioneer practitioners as Leo H. Baekeland, Arthur D. Little, Charles L. Reese, John V. N. Dorr, M. C. Whitaker, and R. S. McBride. From the universities came such eminent educators as William H. Walker, Alfred H. White, D. D. Jackson, J. H. James, Warren K. Lewis, and Harry A. Curtis. H. C. Parmelee, then editor of *Chemical and Metallurgical Engineering,* served as chairman and was joined subsequently by S. D. Kirkpatrick as consulting editor.

After several meetings, this committee submitted its report to the McGraw-Hill Book Company in September 1925. In the report were detailed specifications for a correlated series of more than a dozen texts and reference books which have since become the McGraw-Hill Series in Chemical Engineering and which became the cornerstone of the chemical engineering curriculum.

From this beginning there has evolved a series of texts surpassing by far the scope and longevity envisioned by the founding Editorial Board. The McGraw-Hill Series in Chemical Engineering stands as a unique historical record of the development of chemical engineering education and practice. In the series one finds the milestones of the subject's evolution: industrial chemistry, stoichiometry, unit operations and processes, thermodynamics, kinetics, and transfer operations.

Chemical engineering is a dynamic profession and its literature continues to evolve. McGraw-Hill and its consulting editors remain committed to a publishing policy that will serve, and indeed lead, the needs of the chemical engineering profession during the years to come.

The Series

HAZARDOUS WASTE MANAGEMENT

Charles A. Wentz

Argonne National Laboratory

McGraw-Hill, Inc.

New York St. Louis San Francisco Auckland Bogotá
Caracas Lisbon London Madrid Mexico Milan
Montreal New Delhi Paris San Juan Singapore
Sydney Tokyo Toronto

This book was set in Times Roman by the College Composition Unit
in cooperation with General Graphic Services, Inc.
The editors were B. J. Clark and John M. Morriss;
the production supervisor was Janelle S. Travers.
The cover was designed by Carla Bauer.
Project supervision was done by The Total Book.
R. R. Donnelley & Sons Company was printer and binder.

HAZARDOUS WASTE MANAGEMENT

67890 DOCDOC 943

ISBN 0-07-069291-2

Library of Congress Cataloging-in-Publication Data

Wentz, Charles A.
    Hazardous waste management.

    Includes index.
    1. Hazardous wastes—Management. 2. Hazardous
wastes—Law and legislation—United States. I. Title.
TD1030.W46 1989   363.7'28   88-13593
ISBN 0-07-069291-2

ABOUT
THE AUTHOR

CHARLES A. WENTZ is the technology assessment manager at Argonne National Laboratory in the field of hazardous waste management, including waste minimization systems, innovative waste treatment processes, site remediation, and technology transfer programs. Dr. Wentz was formerly manager of waste management at the University of North Dakota Energy Research Center and Professor of Engineering Management where he was responsible for research projects on thermal destruction; biological, chemical, and physical treatment; and asbestos programs. He has taught hazardous waste management to both undergraduate and graduate students. His prior industrial experience includes the presidency of ENSCO in Arkansas, the presidency of Newpark Waste Treatment in New Orleans, and various executive positions with Phillips Petroleum in oil shale, chemicals, polymers, federal government relations, and investor relations. He received his B.S. and M.S. degrees in chemical engineering from the University of Missouri-Rolla, his Ph.D. in chemical engineering from Northwestern University, and an M.B.A. from Southern Illinois University. He has been active in the New York, Chicago, Bartlesville, and St. Louis AIChE sections and has been chairman of numerous environmental sessions at national AIChE meetings. He has organized and presented conferences and workshops dealing with hazardous waste management. He is a member of a number of business, honorary, and technical organizations, author of technical papers, and is a consultant on environmental matters.

CONTENTS

PREFACE

The primary purpose of *Hazardous Waste Management* is to integrate a broad field into a single book that deals with all phases of this important subject. Hazardous waste management as a field has grown so rapidly that technology transfer has had difficulty keeping pace with ambitious regulatory programs.

This textbook has been written at a level suitable for the senior undergraduate or the beginning graduate student who has knowledge of the basic fundamentals of science and engineering. While this book is intended primarily as a textbook, managers, engineers, and scientists should find it a useful reference in dealing with the varied and complex problems of hazardous waste. Additionally, government officials, lawyers, and the concerned public may also find this book helpful in gaining an overview of the field.

The material brings together legislation, regulation, technology, and business matters relating to hazardous waste management. In order to understand this dynamic field better, numerous case studies have been provided, which should assist the reader in relating to actual environmental situations.

McGraw-Hill and the author would like to thank the following reviewers for their many valuable comments and suggestions: Greg Boardman, Virginia Polytechnic Institute and State University; Harold Cota, California Polytechnic Institute; Ernest Johnson, Princeton University; David Marks, Massachusetts Institute of Technology; and Duane Rollag, South Dakota State University.

The author also wishes to acknowledge the assistance of Gloria Pederson, Ursula Smith, and Sylvia Warren, who were particularly helpful in the preparation of this textbook.

Charles A. Wentz

INTRODUCTION TO HAZARDOUS WASTE

DEFINITION OF HAZARDOUS WASTE

In the United States hazardous waste has been defined by Resource Conservation and Recovery Act (RCRA) legislation as "a solid waste, or combination of solid wastes, which because of its quantity, concentration, or physical, chemical, or infectious characteristics may (1) cause, or significantly contribute to, an increase in mortality or an increase in serious irreversible or incapacitating reversible illness or (2) pose a substantial present or potential hazard to human health or the environment when improperly treated, stored, transported or disposed of or otherwise managed." While the definition refers to "solids," it has been interpreted to include semisolids, liquids, and contained gases as well.

The U.S. Environmental Protection Agency (EPA) has defined a waste to be hazardous under the legislation if it meets one or more of the following conditions:

- Exhibits characteristics of ignitability, corrosivity, reactivity, and/or toxicity
- Is a nonspecific source waste (generic waste from industrial processes)
- Is a specific source waste (from specific industries)
- Is a specific commercial chemical product or intermediate
- Is a mixture containing a listed hazardous waste
- Is a substance that is not excluded from regulation under the Resource Conservation and Recovery Act, Subtitle C.

THE MAGNITUDE OF THE PROBLEM

The National Screening Survey of Hazardous Waste Treatment, Storage, Disposal, and Recycling (TSD) Facilities conducted by the EPA was designed to estimate the total quantity of hazardous waste managed by TSD facilities and to identify hazardous waste management processes, their commercial availability, and the general waste type managed at each facility. This 1985 EPA survey identified 2959 facilities, regulated under RCRA, which managed a total of 247 million tons of wastes.[7] An additional 322 million tons of hazardous waste was handled by units exempt from RCRA reporting requirements.

A 1981 EPA survey of hazardous waste (Table 1-1) indicated that approximately 90 percent of the hazardous wastes were generated by manufacturing operations. The chemical and petroleum industries accounted for 70 percent of this, the metal-related industries for 22 percent, and other types of manufacturing for the balance.

The Chemical Manufacturers Association (CMA) conducted a survey to determine hazardous waste generation by its member companies. The results for 1985, shown in Table 1-2, cover 681 industrial plants and 47 percent of the CMA member companies.[14] The total waste generated was 213.2 million tons, of which 98 percent was wastewater. It has been estimated that the CMA results, which cover only a partial representation of the CMA membership, actually account for only 48 to 68 percent of the total national hazardous waste generation.[13]

Another estimate of hazardous waste generation, made by the Congressional Budget Office, was based on assumptions that specific industries generate hazardous wastes at a known rate and that the overall quantity of wastes produced varies with process technology and production efficiency. This procedure led to an estimate that the hazardous waste generation in 1982 was 223 to 308 million tons; the statistical confidence was reported to be 95 percent.

TABLE 1-1
1981 EPA SURVEY OF HAZARDOUS WASTES HANDLED BY MANAGEMENT FACILITIES

Type of waste	Quantity, millions of tons
Spent halogenated and nonhalogenated solvents	11.9
Electroplating and coating wastewater, treatment sludges, and cyanide-bearing bath solutions and sludges	9.7
Listed industry wastes from specific sources	48.4
Off-specification or discarded commercial chemical products and manufacturing intermediates	10.8
Acutely hazardous waste	0.7
Ignitable waste	5.2
Corrosive waste	122.7
Reactive waste	11.9
Extraction procedure (EP) toxic waste	41.3
Unspecified (including state-regulated and self-defined hazardous waste)	43.5
Total	306.1

Source: U.S. Environmental Protection Agency.

TABLE 1-2
1985 SURVEY OF HAZARDOUS WASTE GENERATED

SIC code	Description	Solidwaste, tons	Wastewater, tons
281	Industrial inorganic chemicals	243,208	24,456,702
282	Plastic materials and synthetic resins, synthetic rubber, synthetic and other manmade fibers except glass	226,051	23,092,523
283	Drugs	269,263	8,293,092
284	Soaps, detergents, and cleaning preparations; perfumes, cosmetics, and other toilet preparations	6,374	6,380
285	Paints, varnishes, lacquers, enamels and allied products	90,833	34,888
286	Industrial organic chemicals	1,782,271	112,000,970
287	Agricultural chemicals	152,129	7,970,867
289	Miscellaneous chemical products	122,613	2,156,785
2800	Chemical manufacturing, general	38,054	32,237,299
Total		2,930,796	210,249,506

Source: Chemical Manufacturers Association.

Finally, the Office of Technology Assessment used data from state hazardous waste surveys, together with estimates for nonreporting states, to arrive at a figure of 255 to 275 million tons of hazardous wastes in 1983.

The 1985 EPA Survey results have been generally viewed as the most accurate, since they are based on legally required reporting results.[9] The CMA survey is considered to provide the most detail on the chemical industry.

The United States also generates approximately 450,000 tons per day of municipal solid waste, the typical composition of which is shown in Table 1-3.[10] There are hazardous materials in municipal waste.[11] Problems connected with leaching of heavy metals and other toxic materials from municipal waste landfills have led to concern that the hazardous material content of municipal solid waste may be higher than previously thought and may constitute a serious threat.

Industrial activity generally takes place in areas of high population density. However, through the application of local zoning ordinances, most industry is separated from residential areas. Despite this regulation of land use, industrial effluents and hazardous waste may still reach populated areas. Most instances of this arise from poorly controlled waste dump sites and/or illegal dumping of hazardous materials, resulting in contamination of groundwater.[1]

A major hazardous waste problem is the large number of old dump sites that have been abandoned by their owners but still contain large quantities of hazardous wastes.[2] The magnitude of the problem is so great that a special Superfund has been set up by the U.S. Congress under the Comprehensive Environmental Response, Compensation and Liability Act (CERCLA) to finance the cleanup of these old sites.[17]

TABLE 1-3
TYPICAL MUNICIPAL SOLID WASTE

Waste material	Percent by weight
Paper	43.0
Plastics	3.0
Rubber, leather	2.0
Wood	3.0
Textiles	3.0
Yard waste	10.0
Food	10.0
Fines	10.0
Glass, ceramics	9.0
Metals	
Ferrous	6.0
Aluminum	0.7
Other nonferrous	0.3
Total	100.0

The Stringfellow site in California is a classic example of the improper disposal of hazardous wastes. The following case study illustrates many of the complex issues related to long-term management of hazardous wastes.

CASE STUDY
The Stringfellow Site

The Stringfellow acid pits site near Glen Avon, California, was used as a surface impoundment from 1956 to 1972; during this time over 30 million gallons of various liquid hazardous wastes were disposed. The events at Stringfellow resulted from incorrect analysis of the site's hydrogeology.

Original geological studies concluded that the site was on impermeable bedrock and that once a downstream concrete barrier had been installed, there would be no potential for groundwater contamination. Therefore, the canyon site was legally sanctioned as a hazardous waste facility. Subsequent information and events revealed that the site was unsuitable for such a facility and that there had been substantial surface and groundwater contamination over a period of years. In fact, the site was located over the Chino Basin aquifer, a major source of drinking water for 500,000 people.

Early findings of groundwater contamination in 1972 were wrongly interpreted to be a result of surface water runoff rather than groundwater contamination. The same mistake was made by other consultants in 1977. One lesson to be learned from Stringfellow is that having many different consultants, contractors, and government agencies involved in cleanup studies and decisions can lead to trouble. The record reveals problems resulting from inadequate overseeing of work by qualified government people, redundant activities, and conflicts among various local, state, and federal agencies.

In 1977, it was estimated that total removal of all contaminated liquids and solids from the site—the preferred option—would cost $3.4 million. Two years later, after heavy rains, no action had been taken. Total removal was still the preferred option, but the estimated cost was four times higher. A state agency then chose a lower-cost option based on containment, which involved removing contaminated liquids and some contaminated soil, on-site neutralization of soil with kiln dust, placement of a clay cap, and installation of monitoring and interceptor wells to deal with groundwater. Both before and after this approach was implemented, 800,000 gallons of contaminated water from the site flowed into the downhill area of Glen Avon and 4 million gallons of contaminated water were disposed of at considerable expense in a BKK-land disposal site in West Covina. This site was subsequently found to be leaking and was closed. The Casmalia Resources landfill, which now receives 70,000 gal/day from Stringfellow, was fined recently by EPA for inadequate monitoring of groundwater. Thus, Stringfellow illustrates the inadequacy of a solution based on transferring risk from one community to another when cleanup is based on removal of wastes to land disposal sites.

About $15 million has already been spent at the site, and all concerned acknowledge that no permanent cleanup has been achieved. The permanent-cleanup option still being studied by EPA would be costly; the state estimates that it would be $65 million. A program for on-site treatment of contaminated groundwater is now under way, but this is not a permanent solution. The unfavorable hydrogeology of the site—fractured bedrock and underground springs—has frustrated all containment attempts. As long as the materials remain in the ground, it will be necessary to extract contaminated water and treat it at considerable cost to the state. Even so, because extraction is not likely to be completely effective, there may be further spread of contaminated groundwater in the surrounding aquifer.

The moving plume of contamination in the groundwater will eventually enter the main flow of the Chino Basin aquifer. Down-gradient wells 1 mile and more from the site have revealed substantial contamination by toxic chemicals in concentrations sufficient for decertification of the supply of drinking water. Drinking water from another source is being supplied to some local residents.

As time passes, costs will continue to mount. And, if there is widespread contamination of additional soil and groundwater, it may not be possible to effect total cleanup, in which case alternative actions will have to be considered. Because measures taken so far have been impermanent, there is a high probability that much more money will be spent in the future for more permanent cleanup, for expensive groundwater monitoring of the aquifer, and possibly for cleanup of the West Covina disposal site. Whatever the final costs, they will far surpass what they would have been had the hazardous materials been removed and treated when the problem was first discovered.

CHEMICALS, LIFESTYLES, AND THE ENVIRONMENT

Since 1950 there has been a tremendous increase in the production of organic chemicals to satisfy our demand for consumer goods, as well as an increased demand for valuable heavy metals. The result of these and other factors has been that the average American is responsible for the generation of 2400 pounds of hazardous organic and inorganic wastes per year.

As we enjoy the benefits of consumer goods, we must also learn to deal with the challenges that go along with them. The production of all the desirable products that sustain our living habits generates hazardous waste. For example, our nation's farmers have increased their crop yields with the aid of agricultural chemicals. The use of pesticides, herbicides, and insecticides as well as a broad range of fertilizers has helped make United States farm productivity the envy of the rest of the world. These farm chemicals are used in enormous quantities, and their applications must be managed so as not to affect the environment adversely. Unregulated use of agricultural chemicals has sometimes harmed the environment and endangered human health. The existence of harmful residues in fish and wildlife has raised questions from all concerned parties. Progress has been made to lessen the potential problem from these contaminants, but much work remains to be done.

The chemical industry has produced a wide variety of products that have improved our standard of living and generally increased human life expectancy. However, associated with these benefits is the risk of accidents that can endanger human health and the environment, as demonstrated in the following case study.

CASE STUDY
Dioxin Cloud at Seveso

The town of Seveso, located in northern Italy, is known for dairy products and furniture craft. In the late 1960s a subsidiary of the Swiss pharmaceutical manufacturer Hoffman-La Roche selected Seveso as the site for a chemical manufacturing plant. The plant was built and operated by Hoffman-La Roche's subsidiary Industrie Chemiche Meda Societa Aromia (ICMESA). On July 10, 1976, the ICMESA plant had one of the worst dioxin accidents ever recorded.

Dioxin is a general term given to a group of polychlorinated dibenzodioxins (PCDD). Chlorine atoms in PCDD compounds produce up to 75 isomers, which vary greatly in toxicity. The isomers with the highest activity and greatest potential toxicity are those having 4 to 6 chlorine atoms, particularly in the lateral (2,3,7,8) positions. 2,3,7,8-Tetrachlorodibenzo-*p*-dioxin (2,3,7,8-TCDD) (see Figure 1-1) has the greatest acute toxicity. (The term *acute toxicity* refers to toxic effects that have a rapid onset, a short course, and pronounced symp-

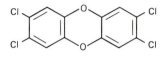

FIGURE 1-1
2,3,7,8-Tetrachlorodibenzo-*p*-dioxin.

toms. In contrast, *chronic toxicity* refers to effects that persist over a long period of time.) 2,3,7,8-TCDD was first identified in 1955 by Karl Schultz, a West German physician, while treating workers from a Boehringer pesticide plant at Ingelheim who had contracted a skin rash called chloracne.

At room temperature, 2,3,7,8-TCDD is a colorless crystalline solid. It has a melting point of 305°C and a low vapor pressure and is soluble in common solvents and water. The fear of the effects of 2,3,7,8-TCDD is understandable because its oral LD_{50} can be as low as 600 ng/kg (for guinea pigs). (LD_{50} means *median lethal dose,* that is, the dosage level at which 50 percent of the subjects given a substance die.) However, its effects vary greatly in different species of test animals. Several studies have shown that dioxin is a powerful carcinogen (cancer-causing agent) in many species. Rats and mice, for example, have developed malignant tumors when fed dioxin.

One well-documented effect on humans of 2,3,7,8-TCDD exposure is chloracne, a disorder the symptoms of which range from an eruption of blackheads to reddening of the skin.

Most chemical carcinogens tend to be organ-specific and produce one particular type of tumor. Dioxin, however, seems to produce different tumors in different organs. These data have led some researchers to speculate that dioxin is a promoter rather than an initiator of carcinogenicity. Whether dioxin is a carcinogenic promoter or a carcinogenic initiator is a controversial question. Test results are open to interpretation by researchers attempting to establish cause-and-effect relationships in cases involving carcinogenic agents. It has been demonstrated beyond doubt that dioxin is extremely toxic to certain animals, but scientists are just beginning to understand the nature of its toxicity and exactly how it affects humans.

Most of the studies of dioxin toxicity in humans have been of victims of industrial accidents or of people exposed to dioxin-contaminated materials. The Seveso accident stands out because as many as 37,000 people in and near the Seveso plant were exposed to measurable amounts of dioxin.

The most common toxic effect on humans of the Seveso dioxin exposure was chloracne. There were 134 confirmed cases of chloracne, most of them in elementary school children. Chloracne by itself is not considered serious because it clears up when the victim is no longer exposed to dioxin. The most significant finding from the Seveso data was that humans are much less sensitive than guinea pigs to the immediate toxic effects of dioxin.

In another study of dioxin exposure, undertaken by Dow Chemical in the United States, the study group consisted of 2192 employees who had some degree of exposure to dioxins while working with chlorinated phenols and derived products. Fifteen percent of the group exhibited chloracne, and the study included a separate analysis of the mortality rate for that group. In both groups, the general mortality rate and the cancer mortality rate were below normal.

Explosion at ICMESA

The ICMESA plant was located in the small town of Meda, near Seveso in northern Italy, 12.5 miles north of the heart of Milan. It produced 2,4,5-trichlorophenol for use in making disinfectants, deodorants, cosmetics, and herbicides. Like other factories in the region, ICMESA expelled foul and odorous fumes from time to time, but residents in the area had become accustomed to the ill-smelling fumes.

The accident occurred shortly after noon on July 10, 1976, when shift workers at the ICMESA plant allowed a reactor in which trichlorophenol was being processed to overheat. The ensuing chemical reaction produced 2,3,7,8-TCDD, which ruptured a safety valve and escaped into the atmosphere. After the contents of the reactor overheated, expanded, and blew rupture disks, 1 kg of dioxin was discharged into the air above the plant.

The dioxin cloud traveled southward toward Milan, spreading over thousands of acres. The area nearest the factory, in Meda and Seveso, had the heaviest concentrations of dioxin contamination; lesser concentrations were found in the neighboring towns of Desio, Cesano Maderno, and Barucanna. Three contamination zones were established. Zone A, covering about 285 acres, was the most highly contaminated area, with 95 percent of the contamination. Two weeks after the explosion, 730 residents were evacuated from this zone. To control the spread of contamination, the area was sealed off and the farm animals were slaughtered. The dioxin levels in zone B, covering an area of over 500 acres, were lower. The 4280 residents of this area were warned not to eat home-grown fruits and vegetables, but no one was evacuated. The residents of the third zone, which covered an area of 3500 acres outside of zones A and B, were also ordered not to eat any of their crops or animals. The region has many waterways and streams which contribute to the groundwater reserves of the Milan area. The Cartesa stream cuts through zone A and joins the Seveso stream, which flows into the Po River, the largest river in Italy. Dioxin particles settled on rooftops, were carried into drains, and were subsequently carried into the groundwater. Contamination was also spread in the dust on the superhighway that connects Milan with Como and runs through zone A.

Sociopolitical Reaction and Short-Term Health Effects

Immediately following the explosion, workers at the ICMESA plant were told to take showers, and the plant remained in operation. One day later, a local doctor and one of the directors met with the mayor of Seveso. People were told that some trichlorophenol—a herbicide—had escaped and that they should not eat local fruits and vegetables. The accident was not represented as serious. Plant and soil samples were sent to Geneva by the mayor of Seveso.

In the days following, trees began to lose their leaves. Dogs, birds, and rabbits were dying. Within 5 days after the explosion, some of the children in the area developed chloracne on their faces and other parts of their bodies. Adults suffered from nausea and diarrhea.

On July 16, workers called a strike and refused to go back to work. On July 23, the company finally admitted that the area comprising zone A was badly contaminated. Residents were evacuated and were prohibited from taking clothing and personal effects with them. Children with skin and liver troubles were confined for observation, pregnant women were told that they might bear deformed babies, and men were told that their genetic material might have been damaged.

Fear of bearing malformed babies created a heated debate in predominately Catholic Italy. Doctors in Seveso warned that if they found fetusus with signs of deformation, they would recommend abortion. The archbishop of Milan insisted that women must bear their children under any circumstance and that if parents were not willing to raise children who were deformed, the Church would find other people willing to take care of them. In the end, the Church agreed that abortion could be performed if a woman's psychological or physical health was threatened.

The Cleanup of Seveso

Cleanup of the Seveso site was complicated by the magnitude of the task, by the complex social and political interactions involved, and by a general sense of uncertainty on the part of all concerned. Previous dioxin accidents had been limited to contamination of factories. In those cases, the factories were decontaminated and dismantled, and the dismantled factories and the decontaminating instruments were entombed in concrete and placed in old mine shafts. This procedure was an effective way to dispose of limited quantities of dioxin-contaminated materials, but was not appropriate for Seveso. Cleanup of the contaminated ICMESA factory and the surrounding area required a technically safe plan that was massive in scope. The area of maximum contamination contained 12 ICMESA factory buildings and 100 houses. Dozens of plans for decontaminating the area—such as using flamethrowers to burn off the area or soaping it down with chemical foams—were considered and rejected.

Italian authorities finally concluded that incineration and on-site burial would be reasonable. The advantage of incineration was that it would permanently destroy the dioxin-contaminated material. However, Seveso residents eventually rejected this idea, not because of the uncertainty of the destruction method but because they feared that other areas in Europe would want to use the incinerator to destroy their toxic wastes.

Burial of the contaminated material was finally accepted. There was considerable concern that trucking the waste to an off-site burial dump might spread contamination. As a result, the final plan called for burial of the wastes in two protected on-site pits. The contaminated land was cleared of vegetation, and possessions were removed from the houses. Workers wearing protective suits razed 27 buildings, including the now-closed ICMESA plant. The work crews then removed the top 2 inches of topsoil. Some 500,000 tons of soil, vegetation, building materials, and contaminated cleanup tools were placed in the two pits, which were lined with bentonite and polyethylene sheets and sealed with impermeable caps. A layer of soil and grass has changed the partly buried dump into artificial hills, and the area around them is now parkland. The cleanup at Seveso has cost Hoffman-La Roche about $200 million, including compensation for crops that could no longer be grown and purchase of the parkland.

It is now some 10 years since the accident, and the burial process is nearly complete. Because it took so long after the accident to dispose of the contaminated materials, a major concern was protection of the surface water and groundwater. Normal rainfall, with subsequent runoff and groundwater recharge, could move dioxin into the supply of drinking water. Many soil particles with dioxin attached could be swept into surface waterways and contaminate other areas far from Seveso.

Not all the dioxin-contaminated materials remained on-site at Seveso. In June 1982 local officials shipped 41 drums of contaminated material for off-site disposal. The drums were removed from Seveso and transported to unspecified destinations by two one-employee trucking firms. The wastes were labeled ''aromatic hydrocarbon derivatives'' rather than dioxin, and the point of origin was listed as Meda rather than Seveso. Rumors abounded: The drums had been shipped to the United Kingdom for incineration, to East Germany for landfill disposal, to West Germany for burial in salt mines. After 9 months of frantic searching, the drums were found hidden in a French slaughterhouse. At this point, Hoffman-La Roche stepped in and had the wastes shipped to Switzerland, where they were incinerated in November 1985, 2½ years after being removed from Seveso.

The Seveso accident and the ''missing drums'' made it clear that each European country, as well as Europe as a whole, needed regulations for governing hazardous waste. The European Economic Community set up a waste control program for handling chemical wastes within its member countries and for monitoring the transport of hazardous substances across borders. Cradle-to-grave regulations covering toxic wastes from producer to final disposal were established.

Chronic Health Effects and Liability

One of the important aspects of Seveso will involve determining whether dioxin exposure has long-term consequences for human health. Short-term effects such as headaches, nausea, and chloracne were reported soon after the accident; but so far no human deaths have been attributed to dioxin exposure.

In April of 1983 five former ICMESA employees were tried in an Italian criminal court for their part in the accident at Seveso. The engineer who designed the plant testified at that time that the plant had been modified from his original design after his departure in 1971 and that the accident could not have happened if the plant had not been modified. The five defendants were found guilty of criminal negligence.

As stated above, the costs of cleanup have so far totaled a staggering $200 million. Although no long-term health effects have been demonstrated, this may change as the children affected by the accident reach childbearing age. The trials of former employees after the Seveso accident are illustrative of the rapid growth in the litigation of cases involving injury and illness caused by hazardous substances. Protecting themselves from the potential liability of dealing with hazardous wastes has become a problem of major proportions for businesses. If the courts establish a presumption that the levels of dioxin to which people have been exposed are harmful, the focus of attention will undoubtedly shift to compensation. Lawsuits of mammoth proportions may well be the result.

Hazardous waste is generated both by big industries, such as automakers and computer manufacturers, and by small businesses, such as neighborhood cleaners and photo labs. About 10 to 15 percent of all wastes generated in the United States are hazardous. Many of our favorite activities depend on products the manufacture of which creates hazardous waste. While the harmful effects on humans of the existing levels of toxic contaminates have not been quantified, the mere presence of hazardous waste is reason for concern. Since we are not about to shut down our domestic industries or give up our lifestyles, we must ensure that wastes are managed safely and at the same time cope with the results of past negligence. It is a job that will require the skill, determination, and patience of government, industry, and the public cooperating together.

The public has demanded clean air and water. In response to this demand the government has enacted laws and promulgated regulations to bring about desirable reductions in pollutants. Industry has removed considerable quantities of potential pollutants from air and water. Many of the gains have been achieved because of procedures that favor recycle, reuse, and recovery whenever feasible. This is particularly true in the chemicals, metals, and food-processing industries. Many desirable environmental improvements have been attained, but not without massive costs to the pollution-producing sources. The management of air and water pollution has created new industries and often forced the development of new technology. Achieving lower levels of pollution has also increased the costs of goods and services to consumers, but the benefits of cleaner air and water have more than offset the added expense.

PUBLIC AND GOVERNMENT AWARENESS OF HAZARDOUS WASTE

Until the mid-1970s, the government and the general public lived in a dream world, unaware that there *was* a hazardous waste problem.[6] Solid waste management of garbage, trash, and other refuse consisted mainly of burial in landfills. This world was shattered forever when the disposal practices of the past resulted in environmental disasters like Love Canal. In the United States, burial had long been regarded as the "ultimate" disposal method, and the nation was unprepared to deal with such shocking revelations. Even as past hazardous waste *mis*management practices were coming to light, the U.S. Environmental Protection Agency (EPA) did not know where the hazardous waste generators were, what was in their waste streams, how much hazardous waste there was, how dangerous it might be, or where it was going. In contrast, when the federal government decided to take a leading role in air and water pollution control in the early seventies, it was able to build on decades of industry and state government experience.[4]

The general public is very concerned about hazards from toxic chemicals.[5,16] There are frequent reports in newspapers and on television and radio about new discoveries of hazardous chemicals in drinking water, about cases of unauthorized chemical dumping, and about potential environmental and health threats from new factories.

Because of the structure of the environmental assessment process, which requires public hearings when a new facility is planned, the public has an opportunity to influence decisions on the location and operation of hazardous waste treatment facilities.[8] Frequently local populations object strongly to the location of treatment plants in their neighborhoods.[18] A phrase frequently used to describe the public's attitude is the "not-in-my-backyard (NIMBY) syndrome." It refers to the general acknowledgment that while waste treatment facilities are necessary, no one wants to live near one.

The emergence of hazardous waste as a major issue has forced us to rethink our entire environmental control program. We cleaned up the air and the water and landfilled the resultant waste products as if they were household garbage. We thought the land could be used as a bottomless sink, not realizing that the hazardous wastes involved are toxic and that, unlike biodegradable materials, their toxicity persists for a very long time. Strategy that ignores this toxicity, and its persistence, is shortsighted and ill-conceived, and such strategy has caused many of the hazardous waste problems we now face. Irresponsible dumping is no longer an option, a factor that has changed the economic picture for many important industries. Some years ago, a respectable industrial or disposal firm could buy a farm in the backwoods country, dig a trench on it, and forget about what they dumped there. Those days are gone forever.

INDUSTRY PERSPECTIVE

Industry is reluctant to let any wastes, hazardous or otherwise, out of the plant gate. Concern about the public health consequences of waste disposal, bolstered by fears of long-term legal liability and adverse publicity, has made generators of hazardous wastes improve on-site control.

Historically, the priorities of industry for the management of hazardous wastes were in accordance with the following ranking, which favors land disposal.

1 Land disposal and storage
2 Treatment
3 Reduction of waste generation
4 Recycle and recovery
5 Incineration

Land disposal (see Figure 1-2) has been the dominant alternative for hazardous waste disposal because it is less expensive than incineration, neutralization, stabilization, or other non-land-based options. Further, environmental statutes such as the Clean Air Act, which place stringent controls on air emissions from incineration, have encouraged land disposal of hazardous waste. However, the true costs of land disposal often have not been fully recognized by the generator or disposer of the wastes. As shown in Figure 1-3 land disposal of hazardous waste has contaminated ground and surface waters, resulting in possible adverse effects on human health, the closing of drinking water wells, displacement of communities, and occasional fish kills.

Although land disposal facilities are now regulated by more stringent controls, all land disposal sites, even under the best conditions, will probably eventually leak. In the future, surface impoundments containing hazardous wastes will be required to install two or more liners and a leachate collection system and to monitor groundwater. Operators of existing surface impoundments will have to meet these requirements, cease operation, or seek a waiver. The law now discourages the disposal of hazardous wastes in underground in-

FIGURE 1-2
Hazardous waste disposal in 1981 in the United States. (*Source*: U.S. Environmental Protection Agency.)

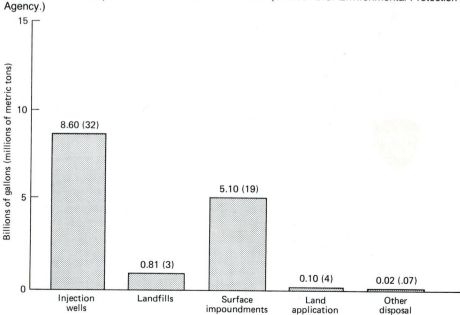

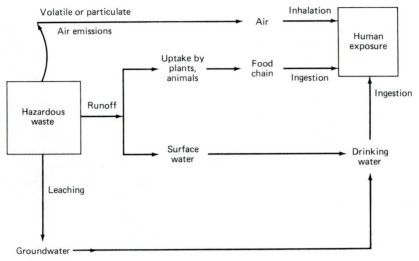

FIGURE 1-3
Human exposure pathways for hazardous waste.

jection wells, land treatment facilities, and waste piles, because these pose potential dangers to groundwater supplies.

GOVERNMENT PERSPECTIVE

The U.S. Environmental Protection Agency and the Resource Conservation and Recovery Act have set the following priorities for the management of hazardous wastes:

1 Waste minimization
2 Recycle and recovery
3 Treatment and incineration
4 Land disposal

Clearly, this order of priorities differs from historical industry practices. As long as land disposal techniques cost significantly less than other alternatives and were allowed under existing regulations, industry was motivated to use them.

Land disposal of hazardous waste is still the lowest-cost of the available technologies. However, there is growing economic incentive to use recycle and recovery techniques. Processes that produce large quantities of waste have been modified or abandoned in favor of those that produce less waste and are hence more cost-effective in the long run. While it is possible to reduce the volume of hazardous waste in manufacturing, it is simply not possible to eliminate it entirely because of continued and varied demand for goods and services.

Waste exchange–reuse procedures offer potential disposal solutions for many industries. However, a major stumbling block to large-scale adoption of waste exchange has been the lack of means to match supply and demand, such as a centralized information service. Secrecy and competitiveness in industry have also hampered the free flow of information and have caused regulatory backlash.

Any strategy for disposal of hazardous waste must take into account all the costs of the numerous components in the cradle-to-grave route to ultimate disposal:

- Generator handling and storage costs prior to treatment
- Transportation to the treatment process
- Operation of the treatment process
- Handling and storage of the waste treatment residue
- Transportation of residues for final disposal
- Final disposal

There is a need for improved long-term planning in the management of hazardous waste. While secure land disposal is the least-desirable alternative for managing hazardous waste, there will always be a need for some disposal of residual hazardous waste in the environment. And land disposal techniques, no matter how well engineered and designed, are ultimately vulnerable to various types of failure that can release contaminants into the environment. The planning process must ensure that the design of short-term treatment and disposal techniques is compatible with the technologies that will be used to minimize failure of the ultimate disposal sites. Minimization, incineration, recovery, and treatment offer the greatest growth potential for hazardous waste management in the future.

THE HAZARDOUS WASTE MANAGEMENT INDUSTRY IN THE UNITED STATES

In the future, the hazardous waste management industry is likely to be restricted to fewer but larger firms. Firms with full-service transportation, storage, treatment, and disposal capabilities are more profitable than those with specialized operations. Third-party liabilities put increased financial demands on aspiring entrants and increase their risk. Secure landfills and high-temperature incinerators are capital-intensive facilities with high entry costs. Strict federal, state, and local regulations further limit ease of entry for new firms.

A number of factors are significant in determining the success of firms in the hazardous waste management industry, which is relatively labor-intensive. Transportation expenses are often a significant part of the total cost. The most successful firms are often those nearest the sources of waste generation. Corporations with greater access to financing have been able to obtain a larger share of the market. The most successful firms historically have been those with access to inexpensive means of ultimate disposal, such as landfills or injection wells.

Local resistance to the prospect of new waste disposal sites has made it difficult to obtain permits and has added significant costs and uncertainty to the siting process. As a result, expansion or replacement of existing facilities has been closely tied to a firm's ability to gain public confidence.

There are numerous firms in the hazardous waste management industry. It is estimated that commercial hazardous waste management companies will experience above-average revenue growth. Those firms that have strengths in groundwater management, incineration and chemical treatment techniques, analytical services, and remedial site cleanup are in a favorable growth position. Companies in these areas should achieve high growth rates in this rapidly expanding, dynamic industry.[12,15]

THE EUROPEAN INDUSTRY

In contrast to United States practice, the disposal of hazardous waste in Europe has, historically, favored destruction and treatment rather than landfill. Europe is thus well ahead of the United States in this important environmental area.[3]

Denmark Throughout the 1970s, incineration was Denmark's preferred disposal alternative, and that country's centralized hazardous waste treatment incineration operation is the model for similar facilities in other European countries.

In 1972, Denmark enacted the Disposal of Oil and Chemical Waste Act, which gave the minister of the environment the power to regulate waste disposal throughout the country. Under this legislative umbrella, the National Agency of Environmental Protection enacted regulations designed to prevent pollution caused by hazardous oil and chemical wastes. These regulations cover all types of storage, transportation, and disposal of hazardous waste. To implement this program, in the late 1970s Denmark established 21 inter-municipal transfer stations, which feed waste material to Kommunekemi, a publicly owned hazardous waste treatment plant located in Nyborg. The transfer stations, which are under the jurisdiction of their local municipalities, segregate both household and industrial wastes. Kommunekemi's treatment techniques are based upon rotary kiln incineration and various types of physical and chemical treatment processes. There is also a nearby secure ultimate landfill that is used for disposal of Kommunekemi's incineration ash and treatment sludges, waste from oil and gas exploration, and used batteries.

France In France environmental legislation enacted in 1975 empowered SARP Industries, near Paris, to provide incineration of liquid hazardous waste and such physical and chemical treatments as neutralization and reduction and fixation processes. Since then, SARP has established incineration plants in the Bordeaux and Brittany regions and physical and chemical treatment plants near Lyon and Lorraine.

Sweden Sweden has a single central hazardous waste treatment and disposal facility at Norrtorp which is operated by Svensk Avfallskonvertering AB (SAKAB). The majority of the SAKAB operation is owned by the Swedish government. Services provided by SAKAB include rotary kiln and liquid injection incineration, physical and chemical treatment, and an aboveground secure landfill.

Switzerland Switzerland has a government-owned hazardous waste rotary kiln and liquid injection incineration near Geneva for the thermal destruction of hazardous wastes. This facility also offers treatment services for both organic and inorganic liquid wastes.

Finland In 1980, Finland enacted legislation creating a central system for collection, transportation, treatment, and disposal of hazardous wastes. In 1984, EKOKEM OY AB at Riihimaki began to operate a rotary kiln incinerator, an inorganic waste treatment plant, and a secure storage facility. EKOKEM is jointly owned by the Finnish government, private industry, and Finnish municipalities.

Belgium In 1985, a private company, INDAVER, N.V., was chartered to treat and dispose of most of the hazardous chemical wastes in the Antwerp region of Belgium.

Spain In 1986, when Spain joined the European Economic Community, legislation was enacted that obligated Spanish industry to manage hazardous waste disposal through procedures in accordance with established practice in other EEC countries.

THE FUTURE FOR THE UNITED STATES

While new and proposed U.S. legislation and EPA regulations seem to be leaning toward European practice, until appropriate economic disincentives are in place, we will continue to create more domestic Superfund sites—that is, sites in need of massive remediation. And shortsighted domestic disposal practices of the past will continue to haunt industry and government alike as the public demands solutions to this perplexing problem.[19]

QUESTIONS

1 Define the following terms as they relate to hazardous waste management.
   Acute toxicity
   Chronic toxicity
   Carcinogen
   Persistence

2 In what sense is the creation of hazardous wastes a product of our lifestyles?

3 Identify and discuss the areas of hazardous waste management that offer the greatest growth potential for individual companies.

4 Discuss the probability that hazardous waste management in the future will be restricted to a few large companies.

5 Discuss the differences between historical hazardous waste management priorities in Europe and those in the United States.

6 What should be the future priorities for hazardous waste management?
7 How have industry and government perspectives on hazardous waste management differed?

BIBLIOGRAPHY

1 Bhatt, H., R. Sykes, and T. Sweeney: *Management of Toxic and Hazardous Wastes,* Lewis Publishers, Chelsea, Mich., 1985.
2 Boraiko, A. A.: "Storing Up Trouble...Hazardous Waste," *National Geographic,* vol. 167, no. 3, 1985.
3 Dawson, G. W., and B. W. Mercer: *Hazardous Waste Management,* Wiley, New York, 1986.
4 *Directory of Commercial Hazardous Waste Management Facilities,* U.S. Environmental Protection Agency, Office of Solid Waste, Washington, 1987.
5 Dominguez, G. S., and K. G. Bartlett: *Hazardous Waste Management,* vol. I, *The Law of Toxics and Toxic Substances,* CRC Press, Boca Raton, Fla., 1986.
6 *Environmental Progress and Challenges: An EPA Perspective,* U.S. Environmental Protection Agency, Office of Management Systems and Evaluation, Washington, 1984.
7 *Hazardous Waste Treatment, Storage and Disposal Facility Report for 1985,* U.S. Environmental Protection Agency, Washington, 1985.
8 *Hazardous Waste Treatment, Storage, and Disposal Facility Report for 1987,* U.S. Environmental Protection Agency, Washington, 1987.
9 "Hazardous Waste, Uncertainties of Existing Data," Government Accounting Office Report No. GAO/PEMD-87-11BR, Washington, February 1987.
10 Hickman, H. L.: *Thermal Systems for Conversion of Municipal Solid Waste,* vol. 1, Rep. No. ANL/CNSV-TM-120, Energy and Environmental Systems Division, Argonne National Laboratory, Argonne, Ill., May 1983.
11 Hickman, H. L.: "Why We Have a Hazardous Waste Problem," *EPA Journal,* vol. 10, October 1984.
12 McIlvaine, R. W.: "1987 Market Outlook for Air Pollution Control and Hazardous Waste Management," *JAPCA,* vol. 37, no. 3, 1987.
13 Matey, J. S., and L. F. Tischler: "Chemical Manufacturers Association 1984 Hazardous Waste Survey," *JAPCA,* vol. 36, no. 6, 1986.
14 *1985 CMA Hazardous Waste Survey,* Chemical Manufacturers Association, Washington, April 1987.
15 Shelton, Robert D.: "Hazardous Materials Management Markets," SRI International, Business Intelligence Program, Rep. No. 752, Fall 1987.
16 Suess, M. J., and J. W. Huismans: *Management of Hazardous Waste,* World Health Organization, Copenhagen, 1983.
17 Thomas, L. M.: "EPA Fights Hazardous Wastes," *EPA Journal,* vol. 10, October 1984.
18 White, D., and B. Burke: "Choices in Disposal of Hazardous Waste," *EPA Journal,* vol. 10, October 1984.
19 Young, A. D., Jr.: "Underground Storage Tanks: Management's Latest Challenge," *JAPCA,* vol. 38, no. 1, 1988.

RISK ASSESSMENT

This section, except for the case studies, was adapted from the report titled *Risk Assessment of Hazardous Chemical Systems in Developing Countries*, by Kirk R. Smith, Richard A. Carpenter, and M. Susanne Faulstich, Occasional Paper No. 5, Environment and Policy Institute. Honolulu, HI; East-West Center, 1988. Excerpted by permission of the authors and the East-West Center.

INTRODUCTION

Rapid growth in chemical technology and an increasing dependence on chemicals are characteristic of industrialized nations.[5] The widespread availability of chemicals has brought benefits to almost all sectors of the economy, but experience has shown that there are significant hazards associated with some of these chemicals. Strategies for avoidance or mitigation of hazards related to chemical technology should be integrated into all plans for use of chemicals. If this is done, countries can avoid repeating the mistakes that have in the past resulted in human illness, degradation of the ecosystem, and the necessity for costly cleanup efforts.[18]

Effective regulation of the vast and growing array of chemicals, processes, and types of facilities and disposal sites will be a difficult task.[1,2,11,12] Quantitative, standardized techniques—keeping systematic inventories, performing comparisons that are statistically meaningful, and carefully monitoring control measures to ensure that they are effective—are necessary if risk assessment is to be meaningful.[14]

Various risk assessment techniques are in place or are being adopted by government agencies in the United States and elsewhere to provide consistent quantitative frameworks for evaluating hazards associated with waste disposal and to offer options for minimizing the dangers of these hazards.[10,15,16] These techniques are sometimes difficult to apply because of the enormous amount of data needed to implement them properly.[17] In some cases, assessment of risk involves analyzing traditional hazards (e.g., poor sanitation) and modern hazards (e.g., pesticide runoff) that exist side by side at the same site. In addition, a number of economic, technical, administrative, educational, and political barriers stand in the way of effective implementation of modern risk assessment and risk management techniques. Despite these problems, risk assessment should be a valuable tool in hazardous waste management.[19,20]

THE PROCESS OF RISK ASSESSMENT

Risk assessment should be viewed as a process, not a one-time activity. This process involves collecting, analyzing, and communicating scientific and economic information for use in policy formulation, decision making, and risk management.[4,6] The objective is to use risk assessment as a tool for arriving at decisions that will best result in gaining the benefits of chemicals while avoiding their hazards.[18]

Most chemicals are not hazardous except in cases of extreme misuse.[3,8,9] Several million different chemical compounds are known. Of these, 60,000 to 70,000 have some use, but a mere few hundred account for 99 percent of the total tonnage currently manufactured. Still fewer—perhaps 50 to 100—chemical compounds that are used widely and manufactured in large amounts may be hazardous. Avoidance or reduction of risk by simply minimizing the use of hazardous chemicals is an important management option.[13] Using technologies that do not rely on hazardous chemicals, as well as substitution of less hazardous compounds, appears to be an effective way to manage the future growth of chemical industrialization.

Risk assessment techniques include environmental impact assessment, systems analysis, cost-benefit analysis, and probability analysis. In some ways risk assessment is really based upon environmental impact assessment in that it quantifies the potential hazards of economic development and technological change. Environmental impact assessment is already accepted and practiced in many countries. In the same way, risk assessment should be readily assimilated into the risk management process rather than being regarded as another new concept to be introduced with caution and greeted with skepticism. In fact, risk assessment is performed today in most management situations, even though in some cases it is intuitive, qualitative, and unstructured.

There are several steps in the risk assessment process. Systems boundaries are established and all assumptions are explicitly stated. Uncertainty is calculated, explained, preserved in sequential analysis, and communicated in the final report. Risks are quantified and compared. The role of value judgment is recognized in the perception and acceptability of risk. Alternative management actions—including no action—for mitigating each risk are identified and ranked using parameters such as lives saved, morbidity and ecological damage avoided, cost effectiveness, degree of uncertainty, and "acceptability" (i.e., how acceptable to various affected groups will the action be). Decisions about whether additional research and monitoring are necessary are made in terms of potential improvement in decision-making procedures and reduction of uncertainty.

The term "risk" refers to the likelihood, or probability, that a particular event will have an adverse effect, direct or indirect, on human health and welfare. Risk is expressed in time or unit activity, e.g., worker days lost per year from illness due to drinking contaminated water, or cancer cases per pack of cigarettes smoked. Assessment of risk must take into account the cumulative effects of all instances of exposure. For example, in assessing the risk that a person will suffer adverse effects from air pollution, both indoor and outdoor pollution must be taken into account.

In making risk assessments, the fact that not all segments of the human population or of a community of organisms will be at the same degree of risk from a given contaminant must be taken into account. In addition, in assessing the risk associated with a particular type of event, both the likelihood that the incident will occur and the severity of the consequences must be considered.

Very-low-frequency–high-consequence events: The Bhopal chemical disaster is an example of this type of risk. It was catastrophic, but disasters of this type have occurred infrequently.

Moderate-frequency–moderate-consequence events: Events involving fires in chemical warehouses or chemical transport almost always result in several deaths, but such events are relatively rare.

Low-level–chronic-consequence events: The effect of low-level but widespread environmental contamination may not be immediately apparent, but the cumulative effects on the people affected may be serious.

RISK ASSESSMENT AND RISK MANAGEMENT

Many observers feel that it is important to make a distinction between risk assessment and risk management. The goal of risk assessment is to estimate the excess incidence over some ''normal,'' or background, level of the potential adverse effect on an individual or population (e.g., cancer, fish kill) of a given agent or condition (e.g., dioxin leak, toxic waste disposal in a city's river system).[18]

Recently, a standard procedure for risk assessment has evolved (Figure 2-1):

1 *Hazard identification*: This involves recognizing the existence of a potentially harmful condition or substance.
2 *Hazard accounting*
   a *Establishing the boundaries of the system*: This involves analyzing the technological system containing the hazard. It may entail describing each of the steps in a chemical flow cycle, including extraction, processing, use, and disposal. In other circumstances, however, only one step in the flow cycle may be evaluated. The choice will depend on the risk management option being considered.
   b *Environmental pathway evaluation*: This involves delineating chemical movement from the release point to the point of impact on humans or ecosystems in terms of emissions, concentrations, exposures, and doses. This step may involve evaluation of each of the steps in the technological flow cycle.

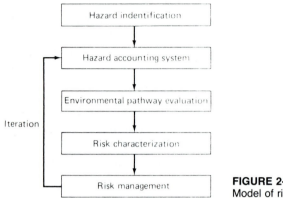

FIGURE 2-1
Model of risk assessment.

3 *Risk characterization*: Here the degree of harm per unit of exposure—i.e., the dose-response relationship—is determined. Often, quantitative dose-response data are not available. In such cases, less direct relationships between dose and response must be relied on to approximate the hazard. The use of hazard indices already developed in some industries is helpful here.

4 *Risk evaluation*: The extent of exposure and the risk of harm are evaluated.

Once the results of risk assessment have been presented as clearly as possible—stated several different ways and with all uncertainties made clear—the next stage is risk management. Whereas risk assessment ideally consists of objective, quantifiable determinations, risk management involves such unquantifiable factors as perceptual, cultural, economic, and political influences.[18]

If, after an initial evaluation, the risks of a particular operation seem unacceptable, various alternative solutions will be formulated by management, ideally in collaboration with statisticians, engineers, and scientists familiar with the problem. Different points within the flow cycle may be targeted for control, for example, changing the site of a facility, training the users of a toxic substance in safe application methods, and intercepting toxic emissions. The feedback line in Figure 2-1 connecting risk management and hazard accounting suggests that the design of a given risk assessment procedure depends on the type of question being asked. There is, therefore, no "universal" risk assessment method. In some cases the risk management question may dictate a procedure in which assessments are made of, say, amount of emissions and of exposure levels but not of projected overall health effects. For example, in many cases in developing countries, lack of data will require that analysis be truncated in some way.

The risk assessment procedure is usually not a once-through system, but rather an iterative loop around which the risk assessor may travel several times. If the initial cycle has led to qualitative indicators of risk only and at the management stage it is determined that these indicators are inadequate to an-

swer the questions of concern, the loop can be reentered at the hazard accounting stage. Then whatever additional measurements and calculations are
necessary to achieve quantification can be made. Another reason for reenter-
ing the cycle is to evaluate the changes in risk resulting from various control
measures being considered at the risk management level. Other reasons for it-
eration might be to change the system boundaries (e.g., to include a new transport link that did not exist when the system boundaries were first set) or to
redo the risk characterization calculations on the basis of new information on
occupational health hazards. Obviously, such changes could result in substantial changes in the overall risk assessment.

The goals of risk assessment procedures are twofold: to organize and analyze risk indicators and to indicate the degree and type of remaining uncertainties. In both cases, the information provided should be quantitative wherever
possible, but in many situations it will not be possible to gather exact data.
When conclusions are based on assumptions rather than quantifiable data, this
should be explicitly stated in the final report. Too often, the assumptions underlying the choice of particular system boundaries or the selection of data to
use in evaluation of pathways is not stated, with the result that persons relying
on the information as presented have unrealistic expectations regarding the reliability of that information. In addition, no matter how the report is going to
be used, it should be subject to peer review and revision.

The flowchart shown in Figure 2-2 shows the factors affecting the hazardous waste risk assessment procedure, beginning with identification of the
waste itself and of the laws and regulations which pertain to that waste. Once
the waste has been identified, its toxicity and persistence must be calculated in
order to evaluate the risk of exposure for both humans and the environment.
No matter how beneficial a chemical is from an economic standpoint, if it is
dangerous to human health and safety or potentially detrimental to the environment, controls must be established to regulate its use in industry, its distribution, and its use by the consumer.

The control of hazardous substances is partially achieved by providing for
penalties—financial or otherwise—to be imposed on users who fail to comply
with the laws and regulations that apply to each link in the cradle-to-grave
chain of hazardous waste procedures. Thus producers of hazardous wastes

FIGURE 2-2
Factors affecting the risk assessment of hazardous waste.

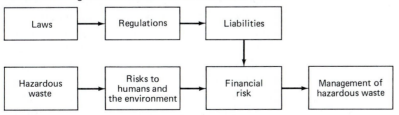

face financial risk in two areas: (1) legal—penalties for noncompliance with regulations; (2) environmental—the costs of cleaning up accidents and paying for the damage caused by the accidents.

Clearly, meaningful assessment of the risks of hazardous wastes is essential, and decision making in this area must involve input from all concerned parties: industry, government, and the general public. Although risk assessment is not an exact science, it does provide a reasoned approach to making accurate cost-benefit analyses and to sorting out various management alternatives. Risk assessment is a vast improvement over past methods, and as our experience and database grow, we will further refine and improve the ways in which we manage hazardous wastes and protect human health and the ecosystems that make up our environment.

The following case study illustrates how concepts of risk assessment and risk management were applied to the environmental control of a widely used pesticide, ethylene dibromide. It is adapted from the Fifteenth Annual Report of the Council on Environmental Quality.[7]

CASE STUDY
EDB and the "Vanishing Zero"

Ethylene dibromide (EDB) became a household word in late 1983 and early 1984 when a variety of flours, cereals, and cake mixes were withdrawn from the shelves of supermarkets across the nation because residues of EDB had been discovered in certain food products. As a result of the EDB experience, greater emphasis has been placed on systematic testing for pesticides in groundwater, improvements in the way tolerance levels are set for pesticide residues in food crops, and open communication to the public of information about these and similar risks.

The Toxicity of EDB

EDB is a relatively simple molecule, $C_2H_2Br_2$, that has long been used as a soil, fruit, and grain fumigant to control nematodes in the fields, fruit flies in citrus crops, and weevils in stored grain and milling equipment. In the late 1970s and early 1980s, however, traditional toxicological animal tests showed that EDB was inherently more toxic than had previously been estimated. Hazard identification data on laboratory animals showed that EDB is a carcinogen that produces multiple malignant tumors—with short latency periods—in both male and female animals. The fact that there was only a small number of people with a history of exposure to EDB ruled out an epidemiological approach to determining its carcinogenic potential for humans, and data from the animal studies were used by the EPA to generate a dose-response assessment. In the process, the agency utilized innovative techniques that took advantage of the fact that EDB tumors appear in animals in a relatively short time following administration.

Environmental Pathway Evaluation: The Persistence of EDB

For many years it was assumed that EDB, a volatile compound, would leave no measurable trace in the soil or food crops to which it was applied and that it would not migrate in the environment. In the early 1970s, however, advanced techniques in analytical chemistry detected trace amounts of EDB in fruit, grain, and grain products which had previously been analyzed as having "zero" EDB. The "case of the vanishing zero" was testimony to the technological advances that allow us to answer the question, "What's in this stuff?" at a much more sophisticated level of sensitivity. On the other hand, detection methods, no matter how advanced, do not help us answer the companion question, "So what?"

In early 1984, EPA received information from a variety of sources that EDB residues were being reported in grain products on grocery store shelves. Once the first data became available, many researchers, including those in other agencies and industrial groups, moved to expand the database. The additional data were generally consistent with the first reports. It was clear that human exposure to EDB in grain products was greater than had been anticipated—again, greater than zero. Studies were then made of the effect of food processing and preparation on the levels of EDB that actually remained in the food when it was eaten. The residues of EDB in "food as eaten" were considerably lower than the residues in unprocessed food, as a result of the removal of the outer portion of the grain in processing and the heating and subsequent vaporization of EDB caused by baking.

It had also been assumed that the small quantity of EDB used to control nematodes could never reach groundwater. It had been expected that most of the EDB incorporated into the soil during application would slowly vaporize into the atmosphere and that any of the chemical that remained would bind to soil particles and eventually be decomposed by physical, chemical, or biological processes. Data gathered in the 1970s, however, strongly suggested that EDB could persist in the soil and leach into groundwater. Later, following up on a 1982 report that found EDB in localized groundwater in the south, EPA initiated a large effort, aided by the South Carolina government and U.S. Geological Survey personnel, to validate the initial reports. Within 2 months, the data had been confirmed.

Risk Characterization and Risk Management

The pathway, dose-response, and exposure evaluations were then combined in the risk characterization step. It was clear that the existence of EDB—a hazardous substance—in groundwater and in food products meant that risk existed where none had previously been expected. The question to be answered in the risk management portion of the decision-making process became, "Was the risk acceptable or unacceptable?" Here a variety of nonrisk factors had to be considered, including the following:

The benefits associated with use of the chemical
The availability, effectiveness, and toxicity of any substitutes
The availability and feasibility of any control measures designed to reduce exposure
The economic impact of any proposed regulatory action, for example, crop losses

Once this information was assembled, the decision makers had to weigh the risk and nonrisk factors and reach a judgment on whether the risks outweighed the benefits, i.e., whether the risk was unacceptable. If it was determined that the risk was unacceptable, an analysis had to be made of the various control options available, including the following:

Restricting the availability of EDB to personnel specially trained in its use
Restricting the use to geographic areas where groundwater contamination was not likely
Eliminating certain uses entirely
Applying special warning labels to the chemical
Banning the substance

Groundwater Contamination It was known that lifetime exposure to EDB-contaminated groundwater constituted a significant health risk. Therefore, in the risk management step, EPA considered the following factors:

Availability and cost of methods for cleaning up contaminated groundwater
Availability, effectiveness, and costs of potential substitutes for EDB as a soil fumigant
Effectiveness of limiting, but not banning, the use of EDB as a soil fumigant

After carefully considering the risks and nonrisk factors, EPA concluded in late 1983 that nothing short of banning the soil-injection use of EDB would adequately address the problem of groundwater contamination. The agency took the unusual action of issuing an "emergency suspension." This effected an immediate ban on use of EDB for soil fumigation. Cancellation, the alternative to suspension, involves a more elaborate review process and would have delayed the removal of EDB from the market.

Fruit and Grain Contamination

Before the EDB ban could be fully implemented, the data concerning EDB in grain products and citrus fruit were reported. Risk characterization data and data on residues in food-as-eaten were analyzed, and an assessment was made of the risk associated with consuming grain products already in the food distribution network.

In reaching the risk management decision for EDB as a fumigant on fruit and grain, a process which was more complex than the groundwater decision-making process, a number of factors were considered, including the following:

Alternatives to using EDB for citrus fumigation were not readily available, although some were under development, for example, temperature treatment and gamma irradiation.

The United States had assisted Latin American countries in developing a citrus export industry that utilized EDB fumigation.

EDB substitutes for fumigation of stored grain were available, although there were questions about the efficacy and toxicity of some of them. Among the alternatives were methyl bromide, which was under study in the Netherlands to determine its carcinogenic potential, and carbon tetrachloride, which has a long history of acute and chronic effects in other industrial uses.

The public and political attention given to the issue appeared to be greater than the actual level of risk warranted.

Workplace practices could be altered to reduce the risks for workers handling fumigated fruit, but it would not totally eliminate their exposure.

These factors, together with risk assessment data for the various uses, were analyzed. The risk management decision regarding the pesticidal uses of EDB included the following measures:

Immediate suspension of certain uses of EDB as a soil fumigant

Immediate suspension of uses of EDB as a grain fumigant and as a "spot" fumigant in grain milling facilities

A phaseout over one growing season on the use of EDB as a fumigant for citrus

Establishment of recommended maximum acceptable EDB residue levels for raw grain, milled grain, and finished ready-to-eat products that were still in the food distribution network

These risk management actions fed back to earlier considerations in the risk assessment portion of the decision-making process. The inherent toxicity of EDB and the risks associated with exposure to it remained unchanged. Banning the use of EDB as an agricultural chemical would eventually eliminate the risk. At the same time, it would create the problem of finding adequate cost-effective substitutes. Projections were that the new regulations would cost users up to $50 million. In addition, some questions about citrus fumigation would be unresolved. But given the magnitude of the possible risk and the intense public interest in the issue, the costs were not judged to be excessive.

The next case study, involving leaded gasoline, illustrates how cost-benefit analysis can be used in the risk assessment process to achieve environmental goals in a cost-effective manner. It is adapted from the Fifteenth Annual Report of the Council on Environmental Quality.[7]

CASE STUDY
The EPA Lead Phasedown

The phased reduction of lead in gasoline in the United States illustrates the valuable role that risk management techniques, such as cost-benefit analysis, can play in identifying and defining solutions to health and environmental problems. Throughout the phasedown period, which began in 1972 and continues today, EPA regulation of leaded gasoline in the United States represents a case in which quantitative analysis pointed the way to significant action in the absence of statutory deadlines or public pressure.

In the 1920s, refineries began adding lead to gasoline as an inexpensive way of boosting octane. (To meet octane requirements without lead, refineries must use aromatics or other octane builders, which raises costs, or additives that are more expensive and potentially more toxic than lead.) In 1973, in recognition of the health hazard posed by leaded gasoline, EPA promulgated regulations designed to reduce the amount of lead in gasoline. In subsequent years, EPA conducted exhaustive cost-benefit studies which ultimately brought a "final" ruling: On March 3, 1985, EPA ruled that lead in gasoline had to be reduced to 1.1 grams per leaded gallon by July 1985 and to 0.1 gplg in January 1986.

Phase 1
1973 to 1982

The 1973 rules were meant to reduce lead in gasoline by about 65 percent—to a level of 0.5 percent. They also required that refineries make available unleaded gasoline for 1975 and later model light-duty vehicles. EPA thought that these two sets of regulations would result in acceptable lead reduction by the mid-1980s.

The regulations were based on a "pooled standard" method, wherein each refinery was able to divide its quarterly lead usage by total gallons produced to arrive at a figure to be used by EPA in determining whether the refinery was complying with the regulations. This meant that a refinery producing a large percentage of unleaded gasoline could make leaded gasoline with a higher percentage of lead than 0.5 and still be in compliance.

Phase 2
1982–1985

In 1982 EPA became concerned about the effectiveness of the 1973 regulations and undertook a complete review. This review resulted in a new set of regulations being promulgated on August 18, 1982. The pooled system was super-seded by a system requiring all domestic and foreign refineries to meet the same standard—1.10 gplg. EPA estimated that this system would result in a real reduction in overall lead use in the period 1983–1990 35 percent greater than would have been achieved using the 0.5-gplg standard.

In addition, the 1982 regulations allowed a system of lead allocations, under which refiners who were not in compliance with the quarterly standard could obtain lead rights from refineries that had complied and had produced gasoline below the permitted maximum.

The 1983 rules resulted in a substantial decrease in total mass of lead used in gasoline. In 1984 it was estimated that lead use in gasoline was about 20 to 25 percent of what it had been during the peak lead-use years of the late 1960s and early 1970s. Leaded gasoline comprised about 40 percent of the total prod-uct sold, and each gallon had about half the lead that it would have had prior to the regulations.

Phase 3
The Phasedown Is Accelerated

Three major areas of concern led EPA, in 1985, to promulgate new—more stringent—regulations for control of lead in gasoline:

New findings about the adverse effects on human health of exposure to lead
The continued practice of fuel switching
The effectiveness of the regulations in the areas of vehicle maintenance and fuel economy

Health Effects   The continuing concern about the harmful effects of lead on human health caused EPA to reopen investigation of this issue several times. Initially, there was some question about whether lead in gasoline was a significant source of lead in the blood. However, the Second National Health and Nutrition Evaluation Survey demonstrated a startling correla-tion between blood lead levels and total lead used in gasoline (see Figure 2-3). In addition, in early 1985, the Centers for Disease Control issued new figures regarding the level of blood lead in children above which further screening and follow-up treatment is necessary—from 30 µg/dl to 25 µg/dl. This change tripled the number of children requiring treatment because of excessive blood lead levels.

Fuel Switching   Fuel switching, the practice of using inexpensive leaded gasoline in vehicles designed to use unleaded gasoline, continued to be a per-sistent problem despite EPA enforcement efforts. EPA estimated that 16 per-cent of vehicles that should have been using unleaded gasoline were using leaded gasoline. The major reason for fuel switching was (and is) the price dif-ferential between regular grades of leaded and unleaded gasoline—between 2 and 12 cents per gallon.

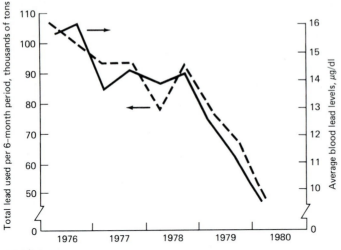

FIGURE 2-3
Lead used in gasoline production and lead in the blood. (*Source*: U.S. Environmental Protection Agency.)

Fuel switching poisons a vehicle's catalytic converter, causing increases in hydrocarbons and carbon monoxide, and, in newer vehicles equipped with three-way catalyst converters, in NO_x. In addition, the practice of fuel switching made it unlikely that EPA recommendations for overall lead use in gasoline could ever be achieved.

In the early 1980s, EPA instituted an aggressive enforcement program designed to reduce fuel switching. The measures included direct investigations of violations and notices issued to noncomplying gasoline stations by both EPA and state personnel; encouragement of states to institute anti-fuel switching programs in their regular inspection and maintenance programs; and campaigns to raise public awareness of the fact that fuel switching results in increased maintenance and replacement costs that outweigh the savings in cost per gallon. These measures were only partially successful.

Alternatives for Continued Phasedown

It was clear to EPA that lead levels in gasoline were too high. The first alternative considered was the elimination of lead in gasoline altogether. The primary problem with this approach had to do with valve recession in certain gasoline engines. In addition to being an octane booster, lead serves as a valve seal lubricant, and it seemed likely that some engines could not do entirely without lead. The need for lead appears to be a function of engine operating speed and the load on the engine. The higher the speed-load factor, the more likely the need for some lead. Certain laboratory studies suggested that a lead level of 0.04 to 0.07 gplg would be necessary to meet the lubrication needs of all vehicles; others, that a zero lead level would be feasible for all but the heaviest-duty requirements (large-engine boats, heavy-duty farm equipment and trucks). EPA decided that until more conclusive evidence was gathered regarding the feasibility of setting zero lead levels, reduction would remain the preferred course of action.

Cost-Benefit Analysis

The cost-benefit analysis described below led EPA to determine that despite the fact that substantial lead reductions had been achieved through regulations promulgated between 1973 and 1975, further tightening of the lead limit would yield major health gains, with benefits far in excess of costs.

Costs   Using a model of the refining industry, EPA estimated the cost of the proposed rule requiring a reduction from 1.1 gplg to 0.5 gplg by July 1985 and to 0.1 gplg by January. The model represented individual processing units by a series of equations which showed how varying inputs could be transformed into outputs at varying costs. The equations also took into account constraints on industry capacity. Given a set of final products, the model determined the least-cost method of production.

EPA first ran the model specifying the 1.1-gplg limit and computed the cost of meeting demand for refined petroleum products. It then reran the model, specifying a tighter lead limit. The difference between the results of the two sets of equations was the estimated cost of the tighter standard.

On the basis of this analysis, EPA's best estimate was that the rule would cost $96 million the second half of 1985 (when the standard would be 0.5 gplg) and just over $68 million in 1986 (the year the 0.1-gplg standard would take effect). The results also showed that demand for gasoline and other petroleum products could be met with existing refining equipment and without any increase in imports.

EPA also conducted extensive sensitivity analyses that tested for the effects of more pessimistic assumptions, such as unexpectedly high demand for high-octane unleaded gasoline, increased downtime for refining equipment, and reduced availability of alcohol additives. The analyses showed that the 0.1-gplg rule would be feasible unless many adverse conditions occurred simultaneously—an extremely unlikely possibility.

Benefits   Assessment was made of potential benefits in the following areas:

Health
Vehicle maintenance and fuel economy
Reduction of emissions through reduction of fuel switching

For each benefit category, EPA first estimated the impact of reduced lead in physical terms. To estimate the effect on children's health, for example, it used statistical studies relating gasoline lead to blood lead to project how the reduction in gasoline lead would affect the number of children with elevated blood lead levels. To estimate the impact of reduced fuel switching on emissions of hydrocarbons, nitrogen oxides, and carbon monoxide, EPA combined data on the prevailing extent of misfueling, and the increased emission rates in misfueled vehicles, with a projection of miles driven by different types of vehicles.

Leaded gasoline, even with scavengers added to prevent excessive lead deposits in engines, corrodes engines and exhaust systems. On the basis of several studies comparing vehicles using leaded gasoline with vehicles using unleaded gasoline, EPA estimated the impact of the proposed rule on the frequency of exhaust system replacements, oil changes, and spark plug changes.

Assessment of the rule's effect on adult health involved first estimating the relationship between blood lead and blood pressure. Looking at those estimates together with studies that related amounts of gasoline lead to lead levels in the blood, EPA was able to predict the impact the proposed lead reduction would have on adults with high blood pressure and on hypertensive adults. Data from large epidemiological studies of cardiovascular disease were then used to estimate the effect of lead reduction on the number of heart attacks and strokes and deaths from all causes related to elevated blood pressure. Because the best data were available for white males aged 40 to 59, the estimates were restricted to that group. Table 2-1 summarizes several important nonmonetary benefits of the phasedown that were projected for the years 1985 to 1987.

The next step was to give the benefits a dollar value. For benefits in some areas this was easy. For example, one dollar benefit in the area of maintenance

TABLE 2-1
NONMONETARY BENEFITS OF THE LEAD PHASEDOWN

Benefit	1985	1986	1987
Reduction in number of children with blood lead levels above 25 µg/dl	64,000	171,000	156,000
Reduction in tons of emissions of conventional pollutants			
Hydrocarbons	0	244,000	242,000
Nitrogen oxides	0	75,000	95,000
Carbon monoxide	0	1,692,000	1,691,000
Reductions in blood-pressure-related effects in males aged 40–59			
Hypertension	547,000	1,796,000	1,718,000
Myocardial infarctions	1,550	5,323	5,126
Strokes	324	1,109	1,068
Deaths	1,497	5,134	4,942

Source: U.S. Environmental Protection Agency.

TABLE 2-2
COSTS AND BENEFITS OF LEAD PHASEDOWN (millions of dollars)

	1985	1986	1987
Benefits			
Children's health	$ 223	$ 600	$ 547
Pollution reduction	0	222	222
Vehicle maintenance	102	914	859
Fuel economy	35	187	170
Total benefits (excluding blood pressure)	360	1923	1798
Total costs	96	608	558
Net benefits (excluding blood pressure)	264	1315	1240
Adult blood pressure benefits	1724	5897	5675
Total net benefits (including blood pressure)	$ 1988	$ 7212	$ 6915

Source: U.S. Environmental Protection Agency.

was obtained by estimating the difference between the number of oil changes necessary when leaded gasoline was used and the number necessary when unleaded gasoline was used and multiplying that difference by the average cost of an oil change.

For the other benefit categories, however, valuation was much more difficult. How much is it worth to prevent a child from having a dangerously high level of blood lead? How much is each case of reduced hypertension worth? What is the dollar value of stroke prevention?

EPA took a conservative approach toward evaluating the cost benefits of reduced blood lead levels in children. The number of cases in which blood lead levels had been brought below 25 µg/dl were calculated and that number was multiplied by the cost of recommended medical tests and treatment for children above the 25-µg/dl level. The costs of treating a subset of cases over the 25-µg/dl level, consisting of children who suffer significant losses in learning as a result of excessive blood lead levels, were also assessed.

EPA made two estimates of the benefits of reduced emissions of conventional pollutants. The first involved direct estimation of the benefits to health associated with reduction of these pollutants. An estimation was also made of the cost per ton controlled of the emission control equipment destroyed by inadvertent misfueling. The final calculation of estimated and total net benefits was made by averaging the results of these two assessments.

Estimations of benefits related to reduced blood pressure were made by putting a dollar value on the medical costs of blood-pressure-related hypertension and on wages lost because of illness. There is a wide range of estimates in the literature of the dollar value of reducing the risk of death. EPA's Regulatory Impact Analysis (RIA) guidelines suggest a range of $400,000 to $7 million per statistical life saved, with an average estimate of $1 million per life.

Table 2-2 shows the estimates of monetary costs and benefits of lead phasedown for 1985 to 1987. Note that the benefits exceed the costs by 3 to 1 if the preliminary blood-pressure-related benefits are not included and by better than 10 to 1 if they are included.

The estimates in Tables 2-1 and 2-2 were based on the assumptions that the 0.5-gplg rule would not have an impact on fuel switching and that the 0.1-gplg rule would eliminate 80 percent of fuel switching.

Whether or not the assumptions about fuel switching were justified, and regardless of whether blood-pressure-related benefits were included, EPA concluded that net benefits would be maximized when the tightest of the alternative standards was put into effect—0.1 gplg for 1986 and subsequent years.

The lead phasedown case study illustrates the role that cost-benefit analysis and other risk management techniques can play in helping EPA and other agencies design regulations concerning hazardous wastes that will yield the greatest benefits for human health and the environment. Although EPA took many factors into account in establishing its timetable for lead phasedown, it is clear that the estimates of the tremendous health gains to be realized from drastically reducing the lead content of gasoline expedited the regulatory process by hastening public acceptance of the new rules and were an important factor in EPA determination that phasedown should be achieved as rapidly as possible.

QUESTIONS

1 Define risk.
2 Discuss the process of risk assessment.
3 What is the goal of risk assessment?
4 Describe the model for risk assessment.
5 Describe the systems approach for risk assessment for hazardous waste.
6 Discuss the concept of zero-risk hazardous waste management.

BIBLIOGRAPHY

1 Andelman, J. B., and D. W. Underhill: *Health Effects from Hazardous Waste Sites,* Lewis Publishers, Chelsea, Mich., 1987.
2 Brown, H. S.: "Management of Carcinogenic Air Emissions: A Case Study of a Power Plant," *JAPCA,* vol. 38, no. 1, 1988.
3 Calabrese, E. J.: "Animal Extrapolation," *Environmental Science and Technology,* vol. 21, no. 7, 1987.
4 Conway, R. A.: *Environmental Risk Analysis for Chemicals,* Van Nostrand, New York, 1982.
5 Dawson, G. W., and B. W. Mercer: *Hazardous Waste Management,* Wiley, New York, 1986.
6 Deilser, P. F., Jr.: "The Risk Management–Risk Assessment Interface," *Environmental Science and Technology,* vol. 21, no. 1, 1988.
7 Fifteenth Annual Environmental Quality Report, Council on Environmental Quality, Washington, 1984.

8 Gough, M.: *Dioxin, Agent Orange: The Facts,* Plenum, New York, 1986.
9 Grisham, J. W.: *Health Aspects of the Disposal of Waste Chemicals,* Pergamon, New York, 1986.
10 Hallenbeck, W. H., and K. M. Cunningham: *Quantitative Risk Assessment for Environmental and Occupational Health,* Lewis Publishers, Chelsea, Mich., 1986.
11 Lincoln, D.: "The Assessment of Risk at Superfund Sites," *Environmental Progress,* vol. 6, no. 4, 1987.
12 Long, F. A., and G. E. Schweitzer: *Risk Assessment at Hazardous Waste Sites,* American Chemical Society Symposium Series, Washington, 1982.
13 Newill, V. A.: "Reducing Risk in Hazardous Waste Management," *JAPCA,* vol. 37, no. 7, 1987.
14 Rowe, W. D.: *Evaluation Methods for Environmental Standards,* CRC Press, Boca Raton, Fla., 1983.
15 Severn, D. J.: "Exposure Assessment," *Environmental Science and Technology,* vol. 21, no. 12, 1987.
16 Sielken, R. L., Jr.: "Cancer Dose-Response Extrapolations," *Environmental Science and Technology,* vol. 21, no. 11, 1987.
17 Silbergeld, E. K.: "Five Types of Ambiguity: Scientific Uncertainty in Risk Assessment," *Hazardous Waste and Hazardous Materials,* vol. 4, no. 2, 1987.
18 Smith, K. R., Carpenter, R. A., and Faulstich, M. S.: *Risk Assessment of Hazardous Chemical Systems in Developing Countries,* East-West Environment and Policy Institute, Honolulu, 1988.
19 Travis, C. C., et al.: "Cancer Risk Management," *Environmental Science and Technology,* vol. 21, no. 5, 1987.
20 Yosie, T. F.: "EPA's Risk Assessment Culture," *Environmental Science and Technology,* vol. 21, no. 6, 1987.

CHAPTER 3

ENVIRONMENTAL LEGISLATION

INTRODUCTION

We live in a world in which the existence of chemical carcinogens, mutagens, and teratogens is taken for granted. [A mutagen is an agent that alters DNA in such a way as to cause a mutation; a teratogen is an agent that causes a physical defect in a developing embryo.] Both the acute and chronic toxicity of these chemicals, as well as their persistence, need to be understood so that a meaningful legislative and regulatory program can be developed that will protect the environment but will not put an unreasonable burden on industry or on individual taxpayers.

The numerous state and federal laws designed to protect human health and the environment from hazardous wastes have been enacted over a period of many years. In order to adequately assess environmental risks, industry, government, and the general public must have a thorough understanding of these laws and regulations.[4]

RIVERS AND HARBORS ACT

The first of the many laws which have had an impact on the environment was passed in 1899. This act, the Rivers and Harbors Act, prohibited the disposal, in waterways, of solid objects that would create a hazard to navigation. It also prohibited the creation of any object that would interfere with the navigability of any United States waterway. It was illegal to build a wharf, pier, breakwater, jetty, or any similar structure without federal permission. It also became illegal to alter a waterway's course, location, condition, or capacity without government approval. The act established a permit system that applied to dredge-and-fill projects and to projects that involved possible obstructions to navigation. The Rivers and Harbors Act marked the beginning of the regulation of solid wastes in the United States; amazingly, it remained the only significant source of environmental legislation until the mid-1950s.

ATOMIC ENERGY ACT OF 1954

The Atomic Energy Act of 1954 was a revision of the Atomic Energy Act of 1946, which had created the Atomic Energy Commission for the purpose of regulating the atomic energy industry in the United States. The new act provided for civilian participation in such programs as research and development and production of nuclear power, and the scope of the AEC's power was broadened to include the regulation of all programs involving the use of atomic energy, for example, the mining and milling of uranium, the construction of nuclear power plants, medical and scientific research, and medical treatment. Such peacetime uses of nuclear energy are of tremendous benefit to the general public. At the same time, they generate radioactive wastes which, unregulated, would be a serious hazard for human beings and for the environment. The AEC and the Nuclear Regulatory Commission draft and enforce laws that govern all uses of nuclear power—military and civilian.

THE NATIONAL ENVIRONMENTAL POLICY ACT

On January 1, 1970, President Richard Nixon signed into law the National Environmental Policy Act (NEPA), ushering in a decade of legislative activity in the field of environmental protection that ended on December 11, 1980, when the Carter administration passed the Superfund law. A key passage in the act states.

> It is the continuing policy of the Federal Government, in cooperation with state and local governments, and other concerned public and private organizations, to use all practicable means and measures, including financial and technical assistance, in a manner calculated to foster and promote the general welfare, to create and maintain conditions under which man and nature can exist in productive harmony, and fulfill the social, economic, and other requirements of present and future generations of Americans.

Responsibility for coordinating the implementation of the various provisions of NEPA was given to a new executive branch agency, the Council on Environmental Quality. Under the terms of NEPA, any federal branch or agency proposing a project that might have a significant effect on the environment had to prepare a detailed statement that included the following:

A description of all potential impact the project might have on the environment, including any seemingly unavoidable adverse effects

Alternatives to the proposed action

A discussion of the project's short-term usefulness and long-term productivity

A list of any resources that would be irreversibly depleted during the lifetime of the project

TABLE 3-1
ENVIRONMENTAL IMPACT STATEMENTS FILED 1978–1984

Agency	1978	1979	1980	1981	1982	1983	1984
U.S. Department of Agriculture	225	172	104	102	89	59	65
U.S. Department of Commerce	56	54	53	36	25	14	24
U.S. Department of Defense	...	1	1	1	1	1	0
Air Force	5	8	3	7	4	6	5
Army	16	40	9	14	3	6	5
U.S. Army Corps of Engineers	182	182	150	186	127	119	116
Navy	6	11	9	10	6	4	9
U.S. Department of Energy	43	28	45	21	24	19	14
Environmental Protection Agency	77	84	71	96	63	67	42
General Services Administration	27	13	11	13	8	1	0
U.S. Department of Housing and Urban Development	263	170	140	140	93	42	13
U.S. Department of the Interior	91	126	131	107	127	146	115
Interstate Commerce Commission	9	8	5	2	2	2	1
Nuclear Regulatory Commission	25	19	17	47	31	11	11
Regional River Basin Commissions	6	12	8	8	2	0	0
Tennessee Valley Authority	6	9	6	4	...	2	1
U.S. Department of Transportation	288	277	189	221	183	169	147
Other federal agencies, commissions	30	59	14	18	20	9	9
Total, all federal agencies	1355	1273	966	1033	808	677	577

Source: U.S. Environmental Protection Agency.

For every project that may affect our environment, and hence needs a federal permit for operation, NEPA requires an *environmental impact statement* (EIS). The EIS is meant to quantify the anticipated environmental impact as well as the potential benefits of the proposed activity, as well as to describe and compare alternatives. The EIS is an integral part of all siting procedures, as Table 3-1 illustrates.

Since NEPA was passed, the courts have broadly interpreted its regulations to cover virtually every activity that affects the environment and at the same time requires a federal permit or uses federal lands or funding. Many states have enacted legislation similar to NEPA to cover projects not covered by the federal regulations.

NEPA has been the basis for numerous environmental lawsuits. In 1963, 146 NEPA suits were filed in federal court (see Table 3-2); 21 of these resulted in injunctions. The Department of the Interior was sued 36 times; other executive departments that were sued a significant number of times include the departments of Transportation, Agriculture, and Defense (Army). The most frequently sued independent agencies were the Federal Energy Regulatory Commission and the Nuclear Regulatory Commission; each was named as defendant five times. Table 3-3 shows the number of NEPA suits brought by different types of plaintiffs: individuals or citizen's groups filed the most suits

TABLE 3-2
NEPA LAWSUITS FILED AGAINST FEDERAL AGENCIES IN 1983

Federal agency	Number of lawsuits
Department of the Interior	36
Department of Transportation	24
Department of Agriculture	18
Department of the Army	14
Department of Commerce	8
Department of Housing and Urban Development	8
Environmental Protection Agency	7
Department of Justice	6
Federal Energy Regulatory Commission	5
Nuclear Regulatory Commission	5
Department of the Navy	4
Department of the Treasury	3
Interstate Commerce Commission	3
Department of the Air Force	1
Department of Energy	1
Federal Communications Commission	1
Department of Health and Human Services	1
National Aeronautics and Space Administration	1
Total	146

Source: U.S. Environmental Protection Agency.

(57), followed by environmental groups (55), state governments, business groups, and directly affected property owners or residents (17 each).

Table 3-4 lists type of complaint in order of frequency. In 1983, the most frequently litigated NEPA issue was that a department or agency had failed to prepare an EIS in a situation in which one was required. As the table shows,

TABLE 3-3
PLAINTIFFS IN NEPA CASES IN 1983

Type of plaintiffs	Number of cases
Individuals or citizen groups	57
Environmental groups	55
State governments	17
Business groups	17
Directly affected property owners and residents	17
Local governments	13
Indian tribes	5
Legal foundations	2
Total	183

Source: U.S. Environmental Protection Agency.

TABLE 3-4
TYPES OF NEPA COMPLAINTS IN 1983

No EIS when one should have been prepared	63
Inadequate EIS	58
Inadequate Environmental Assessment	14
Other	25

Source: U.S. Environmental Protection agency.

63 lawsuits were based on that complaint. The allegation that an agency's EIS was inadequate was the basis of 58 suits, and 14 cases involved a claim that an environmental assessment was inadequate.

OCCUPATIONAL SAFETY AND HEALTH ACT

The Occupational Safety and Health Act of 1970, which is implemented by OSHA (the Occupational Safety and Health Administration) was enacted to protect the health and safety of employees in the workplace. Among its provisions is one requiring employers to maintain up-to-date health records for all employees who are exposed to chemical substances.

MARINE PROTECTION, RESEARCH, AND SANCTUARIES ACT

The Marine Protection, Research, and Sanctuaries Act of 1972 was enacted to prevent or limit ocean dumping of any wastes that would adversely affect human health or welfare or the marine environment. Under the terms of the act, a permit is required for the transportation of all wastes that are to be dumped at sea. Permits are not issued for radioactive or chemical or biological warfare wastes. States are not permitted to enact their own regulations governing activities covered by this act.

The management of ocean, estuarine, and coastal contamination is not an easy matter for a number of reasons. Oceans and coastal waters are sources of food, oil, and minerals, and are utilized for waste disposal, recreation activities, and as a means of transportation. It is estimated that at some time in the near future, more than 75 percent of the U.S. population will live within 50 miles of the coastline. The development associated with this population growth will put increasing stresses on ocean and coastal ecosystems. In addition, conflicts over how to use coastal areas—for example, deciding whether a particular wetland should be preserved or be developed for recreational use—will increase.

Coastal and marine environments receive a variety of contaminants from multiple sources, including runoff from the land via streams and rivers, atmospheric fallout, point-source discharges into the coastal zone, ocean dumping of dredged materials and other wastes, operational discharges from ships and offshore platforms, and accidental spills. While many of these contaminants are generated by human activities in the coastal zone, others are derived from sources far removed from the marine environment. Some contaminants persist in the environment for long periods and are relocated and mixed through the action of currents, the deposition of sediments, and resuspension. This multiplicity of sources, and the complicated dynamics of mixing, add to the difficulty of managing the marine environment.

Another problem is that marine ecosystems are subject to stress and modification caused by such noncontaminant factors as changes in weather and climate, alterations in food supplies, and human modification of marine habitats. Examples of the latter are the dumping in and diversion of rivers, which may affect fish migration routes and limit access to spawning or nursery grounds, and the draining, dredging, and filling of marshlands or shallow submerged habitats, which may eliminate protective cover and modify the normal food supplies of resident estuarine organisms.

Finally, the complex functional dependencies among different organisms and their ecosystems and the natural variability of marine systems make it impossible to assess the potential significance of a marine pollution problem simply by measuring water quality. Water-quality readings cannot be used to estimate long-term effects, and pollution problems often go unrecognized until they have become severe. As a result, data that might be used to predict long-term effects of a contaminant on marine environmental quality are generally available only for cases in which problems have already occurred. The relationships between environmental quality measurements and potential effects on marine ecosystems are often unclear. Predictions regarding the probable effects of contaminants on the marine environment are made on the basis of data obtained from experimental laboratory results.

For all these reasons, assessing the short- and long-term impact on the marine environment of human activities and the pollutants they produce is a formidable task. Continued research and monitoring are necessary if we are to be able to make informed decisions regarding the best use of our coastal areas— that is, to obtain optimum economic yield from our natural resources while preserving the integrity of coastal and marine environments.

FEDERAL INSECTICIDE, FUNGICIDE, AND RODENTICIDE ACT

The Federal Insecticide, Fungicide, and Rodenticide Act of 1972 (FIFRA), as amended in 1978, established regulations for the storage and disposal of pesticides and requirements for informative and accurate labeling. Pesticides are classified as *general-use* or *restricted-use,* and restricted pesticides require user certification. FIFRA also specified acceptance tolerance levels for certain pesticides and mandated the premarket clearance of pesticides so as to prevent unreasonable hazards.

Pesticide contamination of groundwater is emerging as a significant environmental issue as investigators find pesticides in private and public drinking water wells in more and more areas of the country. Most of the reported cases of contamination are at trace levels, and so do not appear to present an immediate health risk. In some instances, however, special treatment systems have had to be installed or alternative water supplies found.

Using the authority granted to it by FIFRA, EPA has accelerated the collection of information on those pesticides suspected of being pollutants and is requiring that some manufacturers conduct extensive field-monitoring studies. Two pesticides—ethylene dibromide (EDB) and dibromochloropropane (DBCP)—have already been withdrawn from the market. Advisory label statements and geographic restrictions on use are required for several others. As more data become available, many other pesticides will no doubt be subject to similar regulation.

EPA is also establishing educational and technical assistance networks, such as those provided by the U.S. Department of Agriculture, to inform pesticide users about potential problems and to implement practical methods for reducing the risk of leaching.

AIR QUALITY

The Clean Air Act

The Clean Air Act of 1970 consisted of amendments to previous legislation dealing with air pollution standards. It was further amended in 1977 to allow more realistic attainment deadlines. Under the Clean Air Act, EPA has the responsibility for identifying air pollutants that are potentially hazardous to public health and welfare, establishing National Air Quality Standards that set the permissible levels for those pollutants, and, in cooperation with state governments, enforcing the terms of the act.[1,5]

The act originally designated six air quality hazards which represented a serious enough threat to public health and welfare as to require immediate action: total suspended particulates (TSP), sulfur dioxide (SO_2), carbon monoxide (CO), nitrogen dioxide (NO_2), and ozone (O_3). In 1987, airborne lead (Pb) was added to the list. Table 3-5 gives the health threats posed by the seven pollutants now covered by the Clean Air Act.

TABLE 3-5
HEALTH THREATS POSED BY THE SEVEN MAJOR AIR POLLUTANTS

Pollutant	Health concerns
Ozone	Respiratory tract
Airborne particulates	Eye and throat irritation
Carbon monoxide	Cardiovascular, nervous, and pulmonary systems
Hydrocarbons	Various compound-specific health hazards
Sulfur dioxide	Respiratory tract
Nitrogen dioxide	Respiratory illness and lung damage
Lead	Retardation and brain damage in children

Source: U.S. Environmental Protection Agency.

TABLE 3-6
NATIONAL AMBIENT AIR QUALITY STANDARDS (NAAQS)

Pollutant	Primary (health-related)		Secondary (welfare-related)	
	Averaging time	**Concentration**	**Averaging Time**	**Concentration**
Particulates	Annual geometric mean	75 μg/m³	Annual geometric mean	60 μg/m³
	24-h	260 μg/m³	24-h	150 μg/m³
Sulfur dioxide (SO₂)	Annual arithmetic mean	(0.03 ppm) 80 μg/m³	3-h	(0.50 ppm) 1300 μg/m³
	24-h	(0.14 ppm) 365 μg/m³		
Carbon monoxide (CO)	8-h	(9 ppm) 10 mg/m³	Same as primary	Same as primary
	1-h	(35 ppm) 40 mg/m³)	Same as primary	Same as primary
Nitrogen dioxide (NO₂)	Annual arithmetic mean	(0.053 ppm) 100 μg/m³	Same as primary	Same as primary
Ozone (O₃)	Maximum daily 1-h	0.12 ppm (235 μg/m³)	Same as primary	Same as primary
Lead (Pb)	Maximum quarterly average	1.5 μg/m³	Same as primary	Same as primary

Source: U.S. Environmental Protection Agency.

The act set *primary standards,* which represent the level at which a given pollutant is dangerous to human health, and *secondary standards,* which represent the level at which the same pollutant is a threat to public welfare. As Table 3-6 shows, secondary standards differ from primary standards only for sulfur dioxide and TSP.

The Clean Air Act also provided for control of five airborne hazardous chemicals that are known to present risks at relatively low concentrations: asbestos, benzene, beryllium, mercury, and vinyl chloride. Table 3-7 presents a summary of health concerns related to those pollutants.

Although the air quality standards mandated by the Clean Air Act have not been universally achieved, definite improvements have been made in the quality of the air we breathe. As Table 3-8 shows, the National Ambient Air Quality Standards have been met, in most areas of the country, for sulfur dioxide, total suspended particulates, nitrogen dioxide, and lead. Carbon dioxide is still

TABLE 3-7
HEALTH THREATS OF SELECTED HAZARDOUS AIR POLLUTANTS

Hazardous air pollutants	Health concerns
Asbestos	Lung cancer
Benzene	Multisystem cancer
Beryllium	Lung disease
Mercury	Brain, renal, and gastrointestinal disease
Vinyl chloride	Lung and liver cancer

Source: U.S. Environmental Protection Agency.

TABLE 3-8
NATIONAL AMBIENT AIR POLLUTANT CONCENTRATIONS, 1975–1983

Pollutant	Measurement units	No. of sites	YEAR								
			1975	1976	1977	1978	1979	1980	1981	1982	1983
Total suspended particulates: annual geometric mean	µg/m³	1510	60.8	61.7	61.2	60.4	61.1	62.6	58.4	49.5	48.7
Sulfur dioxide: annual arithmetic mean	ppm	286	0.015	0.015	0.014	0.013	0.012	0.011	0.011	0.010	0.010
Carbon monoxide: 8-h average	ppm	174	11.89	11.22	10.61	10.00	9.57	8.87	8.78	8.00	7.91
Nitrogen dioxide: annual arithmetic mean	ppm	177	0.027	0.027	0.028	0.030	0.030	0.029	0.027	0.026	0.026
Ozone: 1-h average	ppm	176	0.154	0.154	0.153	0.153	0.139	0.142	0.128	0.126	0.141
Lead: annual maximum quarterly average	µg/m³	61	1.00	0.97	1.02	0.91	0.69	0.49	0.43	0.40	0.33

Source: U.S. Environmental Protection Agency.

a problem in a few metropolitan areas. Ozone is the most pervasive problem, but the downward trend in ozone levels over the past decade has been significant. Federal controls on automobile emissions (see below), controls on stack gas emissions, and modifications in industrial practices have contributed to these improvements. Further improvements in the levels of the six criteria pollutants should, for the most part, be achieved without additional federal controls.

Motor Vehicle Emissions

Since a major source of carbon monoxide pollution is motor vehicle emissions, federal programs for the control of such emissions have contributed significantly to its decline. Establishing stringent emission standards for late-model vehicles, equipping earlier models with emission-control devices, and phasing down the use of leaded gasoline have had a significant effect in reducing pollution.

The reduction in carbon monoxide pollution was brought about by the Federal Motor Vehicle Control Program, which, since 1967, has set progressively more stringent emission-control standards for all new vehicles.

The Pollutant Standard Index

The Pollutant Standard Index (PSI) was developed by an interagency committee in 1976 to provide a common index of air quality. This index represents daily measured concentrations of the air pollutants for which National Ambient Air Quality Standards have been established. Table 3-9 shows the relationship between measured air pollution levels, the PSI index number, health effects, and warning statements to the public made at each level. As the table shows, the cautionary statements issued at PSI levels over 100 are designed to protect the health of the most sensitive segments of the population. The PSI index can be used to analyze trends in urban air quality and to make comparisons between different areas of the country.

Since 1976, the Council on Environmental Control has used the PSI index in its annual reports on air quality. The Clean Air Act amendments of 1977 made use of the PSI index mandatory for all air pollution control agencies in the United States.

The EPA Air Pollutant Study of 1984

In 1984 EPA concluded a comprehensive study designed to assess the extent of the nation's air pollution problems and to identify the dominant contributory sources. The assessment was not meant to be the basis for new laws, but was intended to educate policymakers on the nature and magnitude of the problem and to stimulate discussion of alternative strategies for handling the risks associated with toxic air pollutants. The study has been helpful not only in the area of air quality but in other areas of environmental control as well.

TABLE 3-9
POLLUTANT STANDARD INDEX (PSI) STANDARDS

PSI index value	Air quality level	Pollutant levels					General health effects	Cautionary statements
		TSP (24-h) µg/m³	SO₂ (24-h) µg/m³	CO (8-h) µg/m³	O₃ (1-h) µg/m³	NO₃ (1-h) µg/m³		
500	Significant harm	1000	2620	57.5	1200	3750	Premature death of ill and elderly. Healthy people will experience adverse symptoms that affect their normal activity.	All persons should remain indoors, keeping windows and doors closed. All persons should minimize physical exertion and avoid traffic.
400	Emergency	875	2100	46.0	1000	3000	Premature onset of certain diseases in addition to significant aggravation of symptoms and decreased exercise tolerance in healthy persons.	The elderly and persons with existing diseases should stay indoors and avoid physical exertion. General population should avoid activity.
300	Warning	625	1600	34.0	800	2260	Significant aggravation of symptoms and decreased tolerance in persons with heart or lung disease; widespread symptoms in the healthy population.	The elderly and persons with existing heart or lung disease should stay indoors and reduce physical activity.
200	Alert	375	800	17.0	400	1130	Mild aggravation of symptoms in susceptible persons; symptoms of irritation in the healthy population.	Persons with existing heart or respiratory ailments should reduce physical exertion and outdoor activity.
100	NAAQS	260	365	10.0	240	NA		
50	50% of NAAQS	75	80	5.0	120	NA		
0		0	0	0	0	NA		

Source: U.S. Environmental Protection Agency.

Unfortunately, the lack of quantitative data available on toxic airborne substances significantly limited the scope of the analysis. For example, only cancer and direct inhalation were covered. It was not possible to consider quantitatively acute or chronic noncancer effects, nor was the impact of indoor exposure, stratospheric contamination, and emissions from nontraditional sources such as hazardous waste disposal included. In addition, many of the procedures and assumptions were necessarily conservative. The values used to estimate the carcinogenic potency of the pollutants covered in the study assumed nonthreshold effects, and generally only plausible upper-bound estimates were available for unit risk values.

Because of the uncertainties associated with quantitative risk assessment for environmental cancers, the results of the EPA analysis must be used with great care. Some of the more interesting findings presented in the study (appropriate caveats are also detailed in the report) are:

1 Additive lifetime individual risks of cancer in urban areas due to simultaneous exposure to 10 to 15 pollutants ranged from 1 chance in 1000 to 1 chance in 10,000. These risks did not appear to be related to specific point sources, but rather represented a portion of the total risks associated with complex mixtures typical of urban ambient air.

2 Both "point" and "area" sources appeared to contribute significantly to the problem of toxic airborne substances. Heavy point-source pollution was associated with many high individual risks. Area sources appeared to be responsible for most of the increases in aggregate risk.

3 Using plausible upper-bound values for unit risks, it was estimated that the annual incidence of cancer due to exposure to the pollutants and sources studied was from 1600 to 2000. (Approximately 440,000 deaths from cancer from all causes occur in the United States annually.)

4 The problem of airborne toxic substances appeared to be very diverse. No source category or specific pollutant dominated the analysis. Organic particulates that are products of incomplete combustion, which were represented by benzo-*a*-pyrene in the study, accounted for 45 percent of the incidence; volatile organics, 30 percent; and metals, 25 percent.

5 For those cities with sufficient data for analysis, large city-to-city and neighborhood-to-neighborhood variation in pollutant levels and sources was found. However, the database used was inadequate for analyzing most local problems related to toxic airborne substances.

6 Over the past decade, programs designed to control the criteria pollutants covered by National Ambient Air Quality Standards have reduced risks associated with toxic airborne substances more than have programs designed to control specific toxic compounds. This seems reasonable considering the widespread sources of air pollutants, the multipollutant nature of the problem, and the relative intensity of regulatory programs for criteria pollutants, especially those for ozone and particulate matter.

WATER QUALITY

Federal Water Pollution Control Act

The Federal Water Pollutant Control Act of 1972 (Clean Water Act), as amended in 1977 and 1981, has given EPA and the states broad authority to deal with water pollution. The primary goal of the act was to restore and maintain the chemical, physical, and biological integrity of the waters of the United States. It also set as an interim goal the restoration of the nation's waters to "fishable and swimmable" conditions. Numerous programs for reducing the volume of pollutants that can enter surface waters have been put in place. EPA has established limits on the quantities of pollutants that may be discharged into surface water by industries and municipalities.[6] All industries and municipalities that discharge wastes into domestic waters must have permits from EPA or appropriate state authorities. (States have the right to establish standards which are more stringent than those promulgated by EPA.) If a source is not in compliance, appropriate enforcement actions are taken. Appendix A lists the 129 priority pollutants that have been identified by the Clean Water Act as fitting into the general category of hazardous wastes.

In the period just after 1972, regulatory activity concentrated on establishing or improving permit programs to limit municipal and industrial point-source discharges to surface waters. Attention during those years focused on pollutants that had been known to harm water quality or public health. Later in the decade and into the 1980s, the focus broadened to include nonpoint sources of pollution and toxic pollutants from point and nonpoint sources. In addition, many states which had previously concentrated their attention on streams and rivers expanded the scope of their regulatory programs to include lake water quality and groundwater.

State and local governments have conducted studies to evaluate the extent of nonpoint sources of pollution and have emphasized education and demonstration projects to promote use of the best management practices available to reduce or prevent runoff. Agricultural nonpoint pollution is generally being addressed through voluntary programs. In a few instances, states have adopted legislation enabling or requiring urban localities to manage their storm-water runoff, with the state agency providing technical assistance. Nonpoint pollution sources from mining and from construction activities are the only categories commonly subject to state-initiated regulation, although federal mine land reclamation programs are being used to deal with drainage from abandoned mines.

The states and the EPA are also developing approaches that go beyond the Clean Water Act's regulations that mandate use of the best available technology to reduce or eliminate the toxicity of discharges to surface waters from industrial and municipal sources. EPA has developed an integrated regulatory strategy through which it will use both biological and chemical methods to achieve this end.

The discharge of pollutants into the nation's water is prohibited unless a permit is obtained under the National Pollutant Discharge Elimination System

(NPDES). There are about 50,000 industrial and 16,000 municipal NPDES permits at the present time. These permits must be renewed every 5 years. The NPDES permit records effluent limits and spells out requirements for monitoring and recording. The restrictions on the amount of specific pollutants that a given facility may discharge into surface water are, in general, based on national effluent guidelines. However, depending upon local water requirements, the national guidelines may be modified on a case-by-case basis. Periodically, the facility must monitor the discharge effluent and report the results to the EPA and the appropriate state authority.

Sources of Water Pollution

About one-half of the surface water pollution in the United States is caused by nonpoint sources, that is, multiple diverse sources of pollution, rather than point sources, for example, discharge from a single pipe at a facility. An example of a nonpoint source is storm-water runoff—from farmland, forests, or mining and construction projects. Pollutants from nonpoint sources include soil and other sediments, agricultural chemicals, fertilizers, gasoline, motor oil, bacteria, and viruses. There are also numerous spills of oil and other hazardous substances each year in the United States. The incidence of such spills has been decreasing, but they remain an important contribution to pollution.

Municipalities are the source of about 25 percent of the stream pollution in the nation. Municipal wastewaters are principally from toilets, sinks, showers, and other domestic sources. Municipal sewage contains considerable quantities of organic compounds, nutrients, soil, bacterial, and viruses as well as toxic household chemicals including motor oil, paint, kitchen cleaners, and pesticides. Municipal storm water is normally combined with sewage. To compound the problem, the discharges of industrial facilities are often tied into municipal systems (see Case Study: The Biocraft Spill, Chapter 5).

Following nonpoint sources and municipal discharges, the next largest source of stream pollution in the United States is industrial point sources. Industrial processes produce significant quantities of wastewater, which must be treated to remove toxic substances, the extent of which is typically greater than in municipal wastewater.

Water Quality Trends since 1972

Water quality trends since 1972 indicate that although the degradation of the nation's surface waters has been arrested since enactment of the Clean Water Act, the statutory goal of restoring the nation's waters to "fishable and swimmable" conditions has not been achieved everywhere. The challenge ahead is to identify those water quality measurement techniques that are most effective in assessing the true health of the nation's waters and to design policies that effectively control the remaining significant sources of degradation.

TABLE 3-10
STREAM WATER QUALITY IN 1972 AND 1982

Use category	1982		1972	
	Miles	%	Miles	%
Supporting uses	488,000	64	272,000	36
Partly supporting uses	167,000	22	46,000	6
Not supporting uses	35,000	5	30,000	4
Unknown	68,000	9	410,000	54

Source: Association of State and Interstate Water Pollution Control Administrators.

In 1983 the Association of State and Interstate Water Pollution Control Administrators issued a report comparing the quality of the nation's surface waters and publicly owned lakes and reservoirs in 1972 with that in 1982. The report evaluated data on 758,000 stream miles (42 percent of the nation's streams) and 16,320,000 acres of lakes and reservoirs (nearly 50 percent of the nationwide total). Of the streams evaluated, 47,000 miles improved in quality, 296,000 miles maintained the same quality, 11,000 miles degraded, and changes for another 90,000 miles were unknown. Of the lakes evaluated, 390,000 acres showed improved water quality, 10,130,000 acres maintained the same quality, 1,650,000 acres were degraded, and 4,150,000 acres were unknown or not reported.

The Clean Water Act establishes as a goal fishable and swimmable water quality, that is, waters that provide for "the protection and propagation of fish, shellfish, and wildlife, and for recreation in and on the water...wherever attainable." Most of the nation's surface waters have these uses designated as their ultimate quality targets.

Over 120,000 stream miles are designated for uses more stringent than fishing or swimming, such as drinking and food processing. Only 32,000 stream miles are designated for less stringent uses. Tables 3-10 and 3-11 show that in

TABLE 3-11
LAKE WATER QUALITY IN 1982

Use category	1982	
	Acres	Percent
Supporting uses	13,800,000	84
Partly supporting uses	1,700,000	10
Not supporting uses	400,000	3
Unknown	400,000	3

Source: Association of State and Interstate Water Pollution Control Administrators.

1982 the majority of surface waters assessed fully supported the uses for which they were designated, including 84 percent of the lakes and reservoir areas and 64 percent of river and stream miles. An additional 22 percent of rivers and streams and 10 percent of lakes partly supported the uses for which they were designated.

Table 3-12 shows the progress, in 19 states, toward achieving the Clean Water Act goals of providing for the protection and propagation of a balanced population of fish and allowing recreational water activities. The percentage of total river miles that meet one or both of these standards varies widely from state to state, but in some cases the variations may be attributable to different assessment techniques rather than actual differences in water quality.

Wastewater Treatment and Discharge

The decade from 1972 to 1982 saw enormous advances in managing the problems associated with the discharge of sewage and other wastewaters. In 1982:

TABLE 3-12
STATES REPORTING PROGRESS TOWARD THE FISHABLE-SWIMMABLE GOAL OF THE CLEAN WATER ACT

State	Total river miles	Assessed river miles	Percent fishable	Percent swimmable	Percent swimmable-fishable
Arkansas	11,202	11,202	94	53	...
Delaware	...	491	...	...	43
Maine	31,806	2,652	...	...	66
Maryland	9,300	7,440	...	...	92
Massachusetts	10,704	1,630	...	...	47
Minnesota	91,871	2,708	94	39	...
Mississippi	10,274	10,274	...	...	90
Missouri	18,750	18,670	99	21	...
Montana	19,168	17,251	95	96	95
Nebraska	24,000	7,152	74	19	...
New Hampshire	14,544	14,544	...	...	93
New Mexico	3,500	3,500	100	...	...
North Carolina	40,207	37,378	...	...	81
Ohio	43,919	4,949	...	...	62
Oregon	90,000	3,500	...	...	74
Rhode Island	724	724	...	...	81
South Carolina	9,679	2,489	...	...	57
Texas	80,000	16,120	...	...	90
Vermont	4,863	2,325	...	...	93
Virginia	27,240	4,964	81	46	...

Source: U.S. Environmental Protection Agency.

141 million people (of a total population of approximately 224 million) were served by secondary treatment facilities that met the standards set up by the Clean Air Act, representing an increase of 57 million from 1972.

Approximately 23 million people were served by facilities that provided less than secondary treatment.

The number of people served by sewer lines carrying raw wastewater to streams had dropped by 4 million (from 5 million to 1 million) from the 1972 figure.

The number of people requiring but not receiving public sewage collection and treatment had dropped from 21 million to 14 million.

About 44 million people did not need municipal sewage systems because they were adequately served by on-site disposal systems.

Upgrading the level of sewage treatment produced direct benefits by reducing pollutant discharges to waterways. The most widely used measure of municipal pollution was the extent to which the treated waste's organic content depleted the receiving water's dissolved oxygen, reducing the oxygen availability to fish and other aquatic life. Between 1972 and 1982 municipal organic pollution decreased dramatically. During those years, the amount of oxygen-demanding pollutants entering the nation's sewage plants grew by 12 percent but the amount released into waterways dropped by 46 percent. If improved treatment facilities had not more than compensated for the growth in population—and sewage—during those 10 years, the 1982 discharges might have been as much as 191 percent greater than they actually were.

Industry has responded positively to the mandates of the Clean Water Act. Industrial dischargers have invested heavily in the means to reduce water pollution. Under the act, industries must meet discharge limits based on the "best practicable" and "best available" treatment technologies as defined by EPA. One key measure of industrial progress is the greatly increased level of compliance with state or federally established discharge limitations. Between 1972 and 1982, the compliance of municipal facilities improved from 33 to 76 percent, and that of industrial facilities from 36 to 78 percent.

The treatment of wastewater from point municipal and industrial sources may produce large quantities of sludge which contain concentrated levels of pollutants that have not been destroyed in the water treatment processes. Since this sludge may contain toxic hazardous wastes, it must undergo additional treatment or be carefully landfilled. This has resulted in the use of land-disposal alternatives for the acceptance of hazardous waste products from water-related sources. Through the Clean Air and the Clean Water Act, Congress shifted the entire burden of ultimate disposal to land-based facilities. This course of action, coupled with the abundance of available low-cost land in the United States and the low initial disposal costs at land facilities, has resulted in numerous and massive contaminated disposal sites throughout the United States. Attempts are now being made to rectify this situation by more strictly regulating land-disposal programs, making the initial costs associated with such alternatives higher, and educating industry and the public about the seriousness of the long-term liabilities that result from land disposal.

Toxic Pollutants

Figure 3-1 lists the water pollution problems most widely reported as statewide concerns. As the figure shows, the most frequently cited concern is bacteria, followed by biochemical oxygen demand (BOD), nutrients, and total suspended solids.

In 1984 the National Water Quality Inventory identified pollutants that may have an adverse impact on human health or the aquatic environment at relatively low concentrations. This group, called *toxics,* includes some of the metals, pesticides, and other synthetic organic pollutants that contaminate water, fish tissue, and bottom sediments. Thirty-seven states reported high levels of toxics in their waters, and an additional eight states had detected the presence of toxics. Nineteen states considered toxic pollution as a special concern. Table 3-13 lists the number of states that reported elevated levels of specific toxics. The Food and Drug Administration, EPA, and the states have established "action levels" for these toxics—that is, the concentration of toxic chemicals in fish tissue at which there is potential for harmful human health effects if the fish is consumed. In 1984, 33 states reported detectable levels of toxic pollutants in fish tissue; 21 reported the occurrence of concentrations ex-

FIGURE 3-1

Water pollutants most widely reported by stages. (*Source:* U.S. Environmental Protection Agency.)

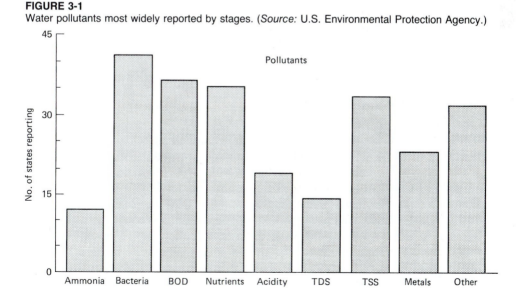

TABLE 3-13
PROBLEM POLLUTANTS IN VARIOUS STATES

Pollutant	No. of states reporting
Metals	
Mercury	21
Copper	16
Zinc	14
Lead	13
Cadmium	11
Chromium	11
Arsenic	6
Nickel	5
Silver	4
Selenium	3
Pesticides	
Chlordane	15
DDT and its metabolites	8
Dieldrin	7
Other organics	
PCBs	22
Phthalate esters (e.g., di-*n*-butyl-phthalate)	6
Halogenated aliphatics (e.g., carbon tetrachloride)	5
Phenols	5
Monocyclic aromatics (e.g., benzene)	4
Dioxin	3

Source: U.S. Environmental Protection Agency.

ceeding FDA action levels. As illustrated in Table 3-14, most toxic pollutants can enter the aquatic environment from a variety of point and nonpoint sources.

SOLID WASTE DISPOSAL ACT AND RESOURCE RECOVERY ACT

The Solid Waste Disposal Act of 1965, while recognizing that solid waste management was essentially a local issue, was the first federal effort to improve waste disposal technology. Its principle aim was regulation of municipal waste. Increasing concerns over protection for human health and the environment led to amendments of the 1965 act, and in 1970 the Resource Recovery Act was passed. This act greatly expanded federal involvement with the management of solid waste; it encouraged waste reduction and resource recovery and created a system of national disposal sites for hazardous wastes. This legislation was the forerunner of the Resource Conservation and Recovery Act of 1976, which is discussed later in this chapter and in Chapter 4.

TABLE 3-14
SOURCES OF POLLUTION

Pollutant	Source
BOD	Municipal wastewater treatment plants, sewage, pulp and paper mills, natural sources
Bacteria	Municipal wastewater treatment plants, sewers, urban runoff, feedlots, pastures and rangeland, septic systems, natural sources
Nutrients	Municipal wastewater treatment plants, agriculture, septic systems, sewers, construction runoff
TSS	Agriculture, urban runoff, silviculture, construction runoff, mining sewers
TDS	Agriculture, mining, urban runoff, combined sewers
pH	Atmospheric deposition, mine drainage
Ammonia	Municipal wastewater treatment plants, sewers
Other	Industries, municipal wastewater treatment plants, agriculture, land disposal of wastes, silviculture, urban runoffs, spills, sewers

Source: U.S. Environmental Protection Agency.

SAFE DRINKING WATER ACT

The Safe Drinking Water Act of 1974, as amended in 1977, set minimum national drinking water standards and put in place mechanisms to protect groundwater from potential pollution sources. Under the regulations that have been promulgated by this act, maximum containment levels have been developed for coliform bacteria, and other hazardous wastes. Supplies of public drinking water are periodically monitored to assure compliance.

All naturally occurring water contains some microbes, and treatment processes must include controls for these organisms in order to protect the public from their associated disease. Chlorination is the most widely used, cost-effective means of controlling microbes in drinking water. However, it has been shown that in some treatment processes, chlorination, while producing the beneficial effect of microbe control, may also chlorinate trace organic chemicals that are sometimes present in water destined for drinking by the general public. These chlorinated trace organics could cause chronic toxicity effects in humans. Various municipalities have responded to this potential health problem by revisions and modifications to their drinking water treatment processes, including using oxidizing media other than chlorine and absorption with activated carbon. Most modifications of treatment processes have produced their own solid and liquid wastes that must eventually be disposed of in land-based alternatives.

TOXIC SUBSTANCES CONTROL ACT

The Toxic Substances Control Act of 1976 (TSCA), which will be discussed in more detail in Chapter 4, was enacted to regulate the introduction and use of new hazardous chemicals. Under TSCA regulations, industry must furnish data on the anticipated production, usage, and health effects of all new chemical substances and mixtures before they are manufactured for commercial distribution. TSCA also regulates the manufacture, processing, use, and disposal of all chemical substances by requiring the testing of potentially harmful chemicals. The manufacture, processing, and distribution of products containing polychlorinated biphenyls (PCB) have been banned under TSCA, and TSCA has required that EPA promulgate regulations covering the storage and disposal of PCB-contaminated products and wastes.

RESOURCE CONSERVATION AND RECOVERY ACT

Up to 1976 the laws and regulations restricted the disposal of hazardous wastes into the atmosphere or bodies of water. These rules and regulations, coupled with the economics of disposal, greatly favored the use of land disposal and deep-well injection of hazardous wastes. In order to close the environmental loop of air, water, and land disposal, the Resource Conservation and Recovery Act (RCRA) of 1976 was enacted to protect the quality of groundwater, surface water, the air, and the land from contamination by solid waste.[2,3] It established the first comprehensive federal regulatory program for controlling hazardous waste and provided grants and technical assistance to the states to help improve their waste management techniques. Initially, federal efforts focused on establishing the regulatory framework for hazardous waste management: standards for identifying and listing hazardous wastes, for generators of hazardous waste, for transporters, for hazardous waste managers awaiting administrative disposition of their permits, and for managers with permits. Among RCRA's most important features are the following:

Wastes may be hazardous because they possess certain characteristics, EPA lists them as being hazardous, or generators declare them to be hazardous.

Generators must identify their hazardous wastes; obtain EPA identification numbers; comply with the uniform hazardous waste manifest system if they send their waste off-site for management; follow good housekeeping standards, which require labeling and marking of wastes; keep complete records; and file biennial reports with EPA.

Transporters of hazardous waste must obtain EPA identification numbers, comply with manifesting requirements, deliver waste only to the facility the generator selects, and clean up spills or discharges immediately.

Managers of hazardous waste facilities who are waiting for a final permit must evidence good housekeeping, record keeping, and reporting activities; obtain EPA identification numbers; prepare and follow closure and postclosure plans; show that they have sufficient funds available to close the facility if necessary; provide insurance following closure for care of land disposal facilities; monitor their groundwater if they are land disposal facilities; and comply with technical standards covering specific waste management practices.

Managers of facilities with permits must comply with all of the requirements for facilities without permits. In addition, they must comply with a far more stringent set of technical standards. They are required to provide liners for land disposal facilities, to destroy 99.99 percent of the organic wastes in the feedstock for incinerators, and to clean up any groundwater contamination that has been caused by land disposal facilities.

Since RCRA was passed, amendments have been added that further encourage and implement the goals listed above. RCRA emphasizes conservation and recycling of wastes whenever practical. It also sets standards for the handling of hazardous wastes within a cradle-to-grave framework that originates with the generator and goes on through handling, transporting and treatment, and final disposal.

THE HAZARDOUS AND SOLID WASTE AMENDMENTS OF 1984

The scope of the RCRA regulatory framework was significantly broadened by Congress through amendments that became law in November 1984. A major theme of the Hazardous and Solid Waste Amendments of 1984 (HSWA) is the protection of groundwater through the following requirements:

New technological standards for land disposal facilities including double liners, leachate collection systems, and groundwater monitoring

New requirements for the management and treatment of small quantities of hazardous waste, such as those generated by auto repair shops or dry cleaners

New regulations for underground tanks that store liquid petroleum and chemical products

Upgraded criteria for disposing of municipal solid waste in landfills.

Restrictions on the future land disposal of many untreated hazardous wastes

Groundwater is increasingly seen as a vulnerable resource because it is used so widely for drinking water and, once contaminated, is extremely costly to cleanse. According to the U.S. Geological Survey, groundwater provides approximately 50 percent of the drinking water and 20 percent of all water used in the United States. In addition to measures to protect groundwater from chemical contamination, the HSWA brought several other waste disposal activities under federal regulatory control, for example, the blending of hazardous wastes with fuels that fire industrial or commercial boilers.

COMPREHENSIVE ENVIRONMENTAL RESPONSE, COMPENSATION AND LIABILITIES ACT

RCRA and HSWA focused on existing and future hazardous waste management practices but failed to deal with serious historical pollution problems— the numerous existing inactive hazardous waste disposal sites that endangered public health and safety and the environment. The Comprehensive Environmental Response, Compensation and Liabilities Act (CERCLA), also known as the Superfund Act, provided for liability, compensation, cleanup, and emergency response in connection with the cleanup of these sites. The primary focus of CERCLA was to establish funding procedures for obtaining the billions of dollars that will be required to clean up these substandard sites. Additionally, CERCLA established a Postclosure Liability Trust Fund to interact with RCRA to ensure adequate financial coverage for the ultimate closure of present and future hazardous waste management operations.

The Superfund Amendments and Reauthorization Act of 1986 (SARA) provided additional funding to continue the cleanup effort begun under CERCLA.

QUESTIONS

1 Discuss the federal legislative history for management of gaseous, liquid, and solid wastes.
2 What is the focus of the Resource Conservation and Recovery Act?
3 Why was the Toxic Substances Control Act passed by Congress?
4 Why was the Comprehensive Environmental Response, Compensation and Liability Act of 1980 necessary?
5 Discuss the federal laws other than RCRA, TSCA, and CERCLA that have an impact on hazardous waste management.

BIBLIOGRAPHY

1 *Air Quality Handbook,* ERT, Concord, Mass., 1986.
2 Dawson, G. W., and B. W. Mercer: *Hazardous Waste Management,* Wiley, New York, 1986.
3 Dominguez, G. S., and K. G. Bartlett: *Hazardous Waste Management,* vol. I, *The Law of Toxics and Toxic Substances,* CRC Press, Boca Raton, Fla., 1986.
4 *Fifteenth Annual Environmental Quality Report,* Council on Environmental Quality, Washington, D.C., 1984.
5 40 Code of Federal Regulations, Parts 50–87, July 1, 1987.
6 40 Code of Federal Regulations, Parts 104–149, July 1, 1987.

CHAPTER

PROMULGATION OF TSCA, RCRA, AND CERCLA

In the mid-1970s, when Congress was debating proposed legislation for toxic chemicals and hazardous waste, an environmental disaster occurred in Hopewell, Virginia, that unleashed widespread pollution. The incident that set the stage for the enactment of some important pieces of federal environmental legislation is discussed in the case study below.

CASE STUDY
The Kepone Disaster

Hopewell, Virginia, is the self-proclaimed "chemical capital of the south." It was here that one of the most costly chemical disasters in United States history occurred. In 1973 Allied Chemical subcontracted the production of the pesticide Kepone to Life Sciences Products, a small company operating out of a converted gas station near the James River. Life Science Products, which had been formed by two former Allied employees, both of whom had been involved in Kepone production at Allied, was to purchase the raw materials from Allied and sell the finished product back to Allied almost at cost.

Sixteen months after Life Science began production of Kepone, health problems among its employees resulted in investigations by OSHA, EPA, and the state of Virginia. The investigations uncovered the fact that Life Science had violated numerous employee health and safety regulations and that both Allied and Life Science had illegally discharged Kepone into the James River, which empties into Chesapeake Bay.

59

Background

Kepone was developed by Allied Chemical in the early 1950s. Production was contracted to Hooker Chemical during the 1950s and early 1960s. But because of market demand, Allied then began production of the pesticide itself, though Hooker continued to be a major supplier of the raw materials. The market grew steadily; annual output increased from 36,000 pounds in 1965 to 400,000 pounds in 1972.

Allied produced Kepone in their Hopewell plant, where they also made polymers used in coating electric wire. In 1973 Allied decided to contract out Kepone production to make room for their expanding polymer production. The lowest bid came from Life Science Products. Contracting to Life Science seemed a safe strategy for Allied. The owners of the firm, Virgil A. Hundtofte and William P. Moore, both had worked for Allied in Hopewell. Hundtofte was an engineer who had been director of research for the agricultural division for several years and had helped in the development of Kepone. And when they awarded the contract, Allied also provided Life Science with a detailed production manual that included operational procedures for maintaining employee safety.

Pollution Problems

Life Science did not live up to Allied's expectations. In March 1974, only two weeks after full production began, periodic surges of white, foamy, pungent wastewater came through the city sewer system and into Hopewell's sewage treatment plant. Within 2 months, this water had killed the bacteria in the plant's vital digester system. Hopewell contacted EPA and the Virginia State Water Control Board, the agencies responsible for setting the limits on Kepone levels in effluents. Their response was to raise the control limits, but neither agency moved to monitor the discharge from the Kepone plant. The situation was compounded when the Hopewell public works department began, illegally, to landfill the undigested sewage materials.

Later in the year a former worker at Life Science filed a complaint with OSHA, complaining of the presence of fumes and dust during Kepone production. Because of "insufficient evidence," OSHA declined to act and no investigation followed. However, the Virginia Health Department did begin to investigate the Life Science plant after one of the workers was diagnosed as having Kepone poisoning. Blood samples taken from employees showed Kepone levels ranging from 2 to 72 parts per million (ppm); the previously highest documented level of Kepone in a human had been 5 ppm. Thirty-one of the employees tested were hospitalized. The health department closed the plant in July 1975 and joined OSHA in an inspection of the facility.

What was found inside the plant was far worse than could possibly have been imagined. Kepone dust covered the floor, several inches deep in some places, and filled the air in the plant. Employees stated that they had complained to their supervisors about the deplorable working conditions, but Life

Science management had shown no concern, despite the fact that the surrounding neighborhood was also being affected by lack of any safety precautions. Air emissions often halted nearby traffic, and the neighboring ice distribution plant complained of Kepone contamination and of vapors that irritated the eyes and skin of their employees.

In August 1975, after OSHA had completed their investigation, Life Science was fined $16,500 for violations of employee safety precautions. OSHA cited the company with "willfully failing to use feasible engineering control measures to prevent harmful levels of exposure and with willfully not providing or maintaining personal protective equipment such as impervious clothing and respirators." In response to these charges, Hundtofte stated, "we feel there is no factual basis for these citations, and we are going to meet immediately with OSHA to review these charges and results of their investigations." Hundtofte also claimed that the illnesses "related to plant modifications that were made to meet water effluent standards."

By the end of August, EPA had also become involved. Files from the Virginia State Water Control Board indicated that the Life Science plant had been discharging wastewater with 500 to 600 parts per billion (ppb) of Kepone, greatly exceeding the 100-ppb limit. EPA investigated samples of drinking water, air, plant life, and municipal waste in Hopewell and analyzed samples taken from area rivers. Sludge near Hopewell's sewage treatment plant contained 200 to 600 ppm of Kepone; fish and shellfish in the nearby James River, 0.1 to 20 ppm; and water in the James River, 0.1 to 4 ppb. In some areas, Kepone was found to compose up to 40 percent of the total particulate matter in the air.

State officials determined that the plant should be dismantled because of the severity of the contamination. Life Science was financially unable to pay for such an operation, so the state attorney general's office asked Allied to assume responsibility for detoxifying the plant site. Initial estimates put cleanup costs at $175,000, but conditions proved so bad that dismantling the plant eventually cost Allied $394,000. Allied's chairman was conciliatory: "Whether or not we had legal responsibilities, we at least had the moral responsibility to resolve the damages and to help the people who had been injured."

The results of the EPA investigation prompted the U.S. attorney to ask a federal grand jury to investigate the formation and operation of Life Science Products. The grand jury investigation was only the beginning. At the end of December, negligence charges were filed in a $29.1 million lawsuit brought against Allied and Hooker Chemical by 12 former Life Science workers. These charges alleged that Allied had withheld toxicity information from Life Science and that the shipping labels used by Allied in transporting Kepone did not indicate that the pesticide was poisonous to humans. More legal action ensued; 120 commercial fishermen filed suit, seeking $2.8 million in damages, when the James River was closed to fishing. They claimed that chemical waste had affected all marine life in the James River and that Kepone had effectively destroyed their market.

As allegations against Allied and Life Science mounted, top officials from both companies began to point the finger at one another. Allied denied charges that they had hired Life Science to avoid the environmental and occupational hazards involved in Kepone production, stating that they had been required by contract to pay for any capital costs involved in improving the Life Science plant for environmental, health, or safety reasons. Rather, they laid blame on Hundtofte and Moore for the Kepone poisoning of the Life Science workers. Allied officials had visited the plant on several occasions, they claimed, and had observed the "sloppy conditions" there. When they had stated their observations and objections to Moore and Hundtofte, they were assured, they said, that appropriate action would be taken. On the other hand, Moore, a former Allied chemist, stressed that he had not known the toxicity of Kepone. Against that claim, an Allied official testified that when Moore was involved with Kepone production at Allied, he had "insisted that the plant be kept clean at all times and that safety equipment such as rubber gloves and face masks be worn."

The U.S. Senate itself opened hearings on the case, and while the grand jury investigation continued, more former Life Science workers sought compensation. At the end of February 1976, three new suits, seeking a total of $83 million, were filed by former workers and their families. Two of the suits, totaling $66.5 million, were filed against Allied and Hooker, alleging that they had not informed Life Science Workers about the dangers of Kepone. The third suit sought $16.5 million in damages from Life Science, claiming operational negligence.

The Disposition of the Case

After 4 months of investigations, the federal grand jury handed out 1094 indictments against Allied. Of the indictments, 314 were misdemeanor counts of washing Kepone down the drain and into the James River, while 626 counts alleged that Allied had discharged other industrial wastes into the river. Of the remaining 154 indictments, 153 included misdemeanor counts of aiding and abetting the discharges from the Life Science plant and the other was a felony charge alleging that Life Science and Allied had conspired in the discharge of Kepone. These charges could have cost Allied up to $17.1 million in fines. The grand jury also brought charges against Life Science, Hundtofte and Moore, four supervisory employees at Allied's facility in Hopewell, and the city of Hopewell itself.

The 940 misdemeanor charges levied against Allied for discharge into the James River could be directly linked to Hundtofte. In 1971 federal legislation had been enacted requiring permits for the discharge of effluents into waterways. During their investigation, EPA discovered an omission in an application for a discharge permit filed by Allied. On the application, Allied had failed to mention that both Kepone and polymers were produced in their Hopewell plant. In effect, Allied was discharging these chemicals without a permit.

Hundtofte was the Allied plant manager. During questioning, Hundtofte claimed that the form he filed did not seem to require the listing of discharges that were only temporary, and since Kepone was being produced only during 2½ months of each year, he considered its production "temporary." However, Hundtofte's claims were refuted when the government found a memo he had written to other executives at Hopewell in 1972, indicating that Kepone had been deliberately left off the form to avoid the cost of installing $700,000 worth of filtration equipment. Hundtofte indicated in the memo that the effluent might go unnoticed by EPA until the city's new water treatment plant was completed in 1975. The discovery of this memo forced Allied to plead no contest to the charges. The U.S. district court judge subsequently fined Allied $13.24 million, the maximum penalty and the largest ever assessed in a federal pollution case.

Virgil A. Hundtofte was charged with felony conspiracy and with 79 misdemeanor counts, all dealing with the illegal Life Science discharge of Kepone into the James River. In order to reduce the felony conspiracy charge, Hundtofte plea-bargained with the U.S. attorney and agreed to assist the government in preparing a case against others indicted by the grand jury. He pleaded guilty to a lesser misdemeanor charge of conspiracy and entered a no contest plea to the 79 other charges. He was sentenced to 5 years of probation and fined $25,000.

William P. Moore, the other Life Science owner, was charged with felony conspiracy and 153 counts of illegally discharging Kepone. He pleaded innocent, but was found guilty on all counts. He was fined $25,000 and given a 5-year suspended sentence.

The charges levied against Life Science itself dealt with conspiracy with Allied and with illegally discharging Kepone. The firm pleaded no contest to all counts and was fined $3.8 million, though the U.S. attorney was quoted as saying that the fine would never be paid since at the time of its assessment, Life Science was worth only $32.

The grand jury indictment of the city of Hopewell brought expressions of surprise and dismay from city officials. Hopewell was accused in three counts of "willfully, negligently, and unlawfully" failing to notify EPA of the large amounts of Kepone waste that were being discharged from Life Science into the sewage treatment plant. In the end, the city was fined $10,000 in what EPA felt was a very important case. The agency believed that many cities, in order to keep local industries happy, were overlooking toxic discharges and other pollution violations. Cities "can't ignore pollution without stepping into the breach themselves," said EPA's deputy assistant administrator for water enforcement. "There are likely to be a lot more administrative and judicial actions against cities."

The judge allowed Allied to reduce their record fine if they could find a way to keep the money in Virginia. In response, Allied donated $8 million to establish the Virginia Environmental Endowment, a trust fund now used to finance conservationist projects, and the judge lowered the fine to an amount equivalent to the donation. Allied was then able to take a tax deduction on the donation, reducing their total net cost from $13 million to $8 million.

Even after the criminal charges against Allied had been settled, the company faced several suits in civil court. At that point, Allied decided to try to settle out of court. Suits settled included charges brought by former Life Science workers, fishermen, and an Allied shareholder, who alleged failure "to use reasonable and ordinary care, skill and diligence in conducting the business of Allied" and breach of fiduciary duty in making and handling the pesticide Kepone. In addition, Allied paid $5,250,000 to settle claims brought by the state of Virginia and by the town of Hopewell for damages that had occurred when Allied was dumping its effluent into the James River. This money was used to cover the cost of repairing Hopewell's sewage plant, cleaning up areas that had been subjected to air pollution from the Life Science plant, and patrolling the James River to make sure that fishermen were not violating the fishing ban.

In March 1977, the Securities and Exchange Commission filed a precedent-setting suit by claiming that Allied had failed to tell shareholders that it faced potential financial liability from its discharges of Kepone. This was the first time the SEC had charged a company with failure to disclose potential environmental liability. At the same time, Allied agreed to conduct an independent investigation of the "material environmental risk and uncertainties in connection with its business" and to keep the commission informed about procedures used to ascertain and assess environmental risks. Allied also agreed to a permanent injunction barring it from future violations of the antifraud and reporting provisions of federal securities laws.

Environmental Considerations

In its prime, the Life Science plant operated 24 hours a day, 7 days a week, and manufactured 3000 to 6000 pounds of Kepone per day. When the situation was first seen to be serious, an EPA air-monitoring station was located about 200 yards from the Kepone manufacturing site. Between March 1974 and April 1975, the station found the Kepone content of the particulates to be as much as 40 percent.

Water pollution from the plant's operation exceeded air pollution. Life Science had been the only large industry in Hopewell to receive permission to discharge directly into the city's sewage system. It was the effluents from the plant that put Hopewell's sewage treatment plant out of operation, since the Kepone content inhibited the normal bacterial action required for sewage treatment. Untreated sewage-plant discharges then polluted a large part of the nearby James River and associated waters.

In August 1975, the Virginia Health Department asked the EPA research laboratory in North Carolina to assist in determining whether environmental contamination had, in fact, occurred. Sample collections were initiated on August 16, 1975. The samples were analyzed by gas chromatography interphased with mass spectroscopy for positive identification. The data assembled by EPA showed widespread dissemination of Kepone in the James River and Chesapeake Bay areas. In August 1975, the concentration of Kepone in the James River water was 0.1 to 4 ppb. All of the fish samples taken from the river contained Kepone at levels above federal health guidelines of 0.1 ppm. Contamination appeared to be spreading up the western shore of Chesapeake Bay. Once Kepone precipitated out of the flowing water, it tended to cling to fine sediment on the river bottom. The pesticide-coated particles were then actually moved upstream by the tides.

Nearby sediment from the Bailey's Creek area and wastewater from the sewage treatment plant and landfill areas contained 100 to 100,000 ppb Kepone. Sludge samples taken from the holding pond and from landfill areas near the Hopewell sewage treatment plant contained 200,000 to 600,000 ppb Kepone. Soil around the Life Science plant had values as high as 1 to 2 percent (10 million to 20 million pbb). As noted earlier, air samples collected near the plant from March 1974 to April 1975 ranged from 0.2 to 50 μg of Kepone per cubic meter of air. However, as late as June 1976, 0.025 μg of Kepone per cubic meter of air was recorded. EPA considered removal or burial of polluted soil around the plant site, and the James River was closed to fishing in December 1975 because of dangerous concentrations of Kepone.

Since the discovery of Kepone in the James River, numerous studies have been conducted to determine its potential effects on biota. Chronic effects on mammals are evident and found at various levels of activity. Tests on mammals with Kepone levels ranging from 5 to 80 ppm have demonstrated serious side effects. In the early 1960s the Medical College of Virginia had exposed test animals to Kepone and studied lethal and sublethal doses. Kepone was administered orally in single doses to discover the median lethal dose, or LD_{50}. Kepone's LD_{50} was 65 mg/kg of body weight in rabbits, 95.5 mg/kg in rats, and 250 mg/kg in dogs.

Kepone is a *cumulative* poison, meaning that toxic levels are reached after small amounts are taken over a long period of time. In tests that ran for 80 weeks, 70 percent of male rats fed 24 ppm Kepone developed cancer, as did 22 percent of female rats fed 26 ppm, 88 percent of male mice fed 23 ppm, and 47 percent of female mice fed 40 ppm. Abnormalities in cell growth were mainly liver lesions, some cancerous, but abnormalities were seen in other organs as well.

Waterfowl that wintered on the James River and water birds that were permanent residents accumulated Kepone in their tissues. The concentration reached by the various species reflected their feeding habits. Canadian geese which fed mainly in cornfields showed the lowest concentration of Kepone, while fish-eating blue heron had the highest contamination levels.

Aquatic organisms were also affected by Kepone exposure. Because of its large molecular weight and relatively low water solubility, Kepone tends to settle in aquatic bodies, causing adverse effects on unicellular algae at low concentrations ranging from 0.35 to 1.0 ppm. In addition to being highly toxic to various aquatic invertebrates, Kepone was also found to cause chronic effects in these organisms, such as reduced shell growth, loss of equilibrium, and impaired reproductive capacity. Bioconcentration through feeding or exposure to contaminated sediments was high. For example, the average concentration of Kepone in blue crabs was 0.3 to 3.0 ppm; average concentration in fish were 0.04 to 2.0 ppm. Species-specific variability of impact caused a range of adverse chronic effects in invertebrate species at low levels of exposure. Experiments with fish indicated that Kepone had low acute toxicity in some species, while in others it could be highly toxic at relatively low exposure concentrations.

The Chemistry of Kepone

Kepone is the registered trade name for an organic chemical that belongs to a family of insecticides including mirex, aldrin, dieldrin, and heptachlor. Kepone is readily soluble in acetone, lower aliphatic alcohols, aqueous sodium hydroxide, and organic solvents such as benzene, toluene, and hexane; it is slightly soluble in water. Another property of Kepone which exacerbated the contamination at the manufacturing site is its high affinity for particulate matter. Kepone is produced by reacting hexachlorocyclopentadiene with SO_3 in the presence of a catalyst. All these chemicals are highly toxic.

Kepone Contamination at the Plant

Early in the development of the pesticide, Allied had contracted with the Medical College of Virginia to study the acute and chronic toxicity of Kepone in several animal species, but all the information was kept confidential. Only later was it disclosed that the effects of Kepone contamination in rats and mice were similar to effects experienced by Life Science factory workers, effects which included tremors, skin changes, blurred vision, loss of memory, coordination difficulties, and joint and chest pain. The Life Science plant experienced a 400 percent employee turnover rate, largely due to physical problems and poor working conditions. The workers were subject to Kepone-contaminated dust, slurries, dirt, and toxic Kepone-precursor chemicals. Nor were the workers adequately informed of the toxic nature of the chemicals or of the proper safety procedures in handling them.

Ten days before the Life Science plant shut down in the summer of 1975, a local doctor diagnosed a factory worker as suffering from neurological symptoms caused by occupational exposure to Kepone. The blood sample of this factory worker showed 7.5 ppm of Kepone. In July of 1975, the month the factory closed, 150 plant employees were evaluated by the Virginia state epidemiologist. Of these employees, 70 showed Kepone toxicity symptoms and 30 required immediate hospitalization or medical treatment. Families of several workers were also exposed to Kepone from the dust and dirt carried home on clothes. Oil samples removed by acetone-soaked gauze pads from the foreheads of hospitalized workers showed 0.2 to 0.3 μg of Kepone in each sample, while samples from the nonhospitalized workers showed 0.05 to 0.8 μg. Since no detectable amounts of Kepone were found on the foreheads of the normal population, these findings became a basis for determining the level of exposure to Kepone.

The Cleanup

Although production at Life Science was halted in July of 1975, the problem of the Kepone and Kepone-contaminated materials already produced was yet to be addressed. The first task was to detoxify the Life Science plant, which was laden with Kepone dust and constituted a health hazard to everyone in the neighborhood. With Life Science about to go bankrupt, Allied agreed to pay $394,000 for the remediation of the site. Because normal detoxification procedures were determined to be inadequate, the plant was systematically dismantled, the pieces were wet-vacuumed, and the refuse was buried in a huge plastic-lined pit. The top 6 to 12 inches of soil underneath the plant was also buried in the landfill. The 200,000 gallons of Kepone-containing water recovered from cleaning out Life Science's facilities was passed through portable carbon filtration units provided by EPA until it was of drinking-water quality.

Another problem to be dealt with was the "Kepone lagoon" at the Hopewell sewage treatment plant, a concrete impoundment holding about 1.5 million gallons of liquid containing 3 to 5 percent sludge from the plant and grounds. The liquid portion had 2 ppm Kepone, while the sludge contained 200 to 600 ppm. The sludge was dewatered and placed in sealed containers, and the water was passed through carbon filtration units. The lagoons were filled and a permanent marker was placed on the site.

Also requiring disposal were 655 drums of debris from the dismantled plant. Plans to incinerate the Kepone wastes—decomposition of Kepone takes place when it is exposed to 900°C for approximately 1 second—aroused the resistance of local citizens who feared that the process would not destroy the Kepone or would release equally hazardous compounds into the air for even wider dispersion and contamination. The drums were eventually shipped to West Germany to be deposited in a deep underground salt mine used for toxic waste disposal.

The last problem to be addressed was the James River. In 1975 the Virginia Health Department asked EPA to assist in determining if the river had been contaminated. The data collected by EPA showed widespread dissemination of Kepone in the river and in Chesapeake Bay. On December 18, 1975, Virginia closed fishing in the James River and its tributaries from Richmond to a point 80 miles downstream where the river entered Chesapeake Bay. The question of what to do with the river sediments remained. The U.S. Army Corps of Engineers had routinely conducted dredging operations for navigational purposes, and it was feared that the dredging might stir up the Kepone-containing sediments on the bottom of the river. A temporary moratorium on dredging was declared in March of 1976. In July of the same year, the moratorium was lifted to allow experimental dredging to take place. The results of this dredging suggested that Kepone has a strong affinity to both colloidal and particulate matter and that the release of Kepone into the river after settling occurred would be small. Based on these conclusions, the Army Corps of Engineers resumed normal dredging of the James River in 1978.

Since 1976 the Virginia State Water Control Board has been responsible for collecting fish, sediment, and water samples from the river. Their results have been encouraging. The yearly Kepone average for fish in the Hopewell area peaked in 1978 at 0.55 ppm; in 1986 that average had decreased to 0.17 ppm. The Federal Action Level for Kepone is 0.3 ppm for fish in the James River, and as of 1983, some of the restrictions on fishing had been lifted, though currently the James River is still closed to fishing for migratory fish such as trout and striped bass.

The Lessons Learned

Many individuals and organizations, public and private, contributed to the Kepone disaster in Hopewell. Management at Allied did not adequately inform themselves of actions taken by the former Allied employees who sacrificed safety for profit. Regulatory agencies such as EPA and OSHA failed to act on individual complaints. The city of Hopewell ignored environmental concerns when it landfilled sludge from its disabled sewage treatment plant.

The events in the Kepone disaster indicated problems in government at the local, state, and national levels. The city of Hopewell paid a fine for its irresponsible action, a penalty that should deter other cities from such action in the future.

Virginia, like other states, seemed inclined to allow the federal government to handle environmental problems. Now states will have to take more responsibility for the regulation of industries within their borders as the government continues to reduce funding for the implementation of federal regulations.

On the national level, communication channels between regulatory agencies must be opened. The problems at Life Science may have been detected earlier if OSHA and EPA had investigated initial complaints or had questioned each other about improprieties concerning Life Science. Regulatory agencies must avoid the tendency to define a problem too narrowly to fit existing categories and available solutions.

The Kepone disaster also emphasized the need for regulating the production of chemicals and associated waste disposal. In 1976, in the aftermath of the Kepone incident, Congress approved the Toxic Substances Control Act (TSCA). The Resource and Conservation and Recovery Act (RCRA) soon followed.

Industry practices were changed by the Kepone incident. Companies began concentrating on social and environmental responsibilities to avoid the potential costs of legal actions. For example, Allied established new incentive compensation programs which downgraded profitability as a measure of performance and focused on the manager's concern for the environment.

The association between Allied and Life Science brought into question the legal ramifications of tolling outside production. In the case of the Kepone disaster, Allied voluntarily accepted the financial responsibility for the cleanup and for the health care of former Life Science employees, even though the courts had determined that Allied's tolling relationship with Life Science did not make them legally liable. Even so, the court's decision could encourage large corporations to use tolling as a method to avoid legal liability in the production of toxic chemicals. This could be avoided by legislation requiring a company that produces toxic chemicals to have some minimum level of assets.

Attitudes of the general public need to focus on preserving the environment and on protecting human health. Citizens of Hopewell ignored the problems at Life Science because they wanted to keep the plant in operation; some even protested the fines against Allied and Hopewell because they felt that the legal action would eliminate jobs.

In sum, the Kepone disaster illustrated that changes needed to be made in the attitudes of government, private industry, and general public in order to protect the environment and human health.

In the preceding chapter, we studied the numerous and far-reaching laws that form the basis of environmental legislation in the United States. Each of these laws interrelates with the others and impacts upon hazardous waste management. Federal environmental laws prior to 1976 were not sufficiently comprehensive to control hazardous wastes, but since that time, Congress has enacted three major laws that have given the U.S. Environmental Protection Agency much broader and more far-reaching control in matters of hazardous waste management. These three laws are the Toxic Substances Control Act (TSCA), the Resource Conservation and Recovery Act (RCRA), and the Comprehensive Environmental Response, Compensation and Liability Act (CERCLA). This broad legislation, which places hazardous waste in a special category apart from municipal refuse, has given the Environmental Protection Agency the tools to more fully address the regulation of hazardous wastes, and most of the present regulatory emphasis is based upon these three laws.

TSCA regulates the production and commercial introduction of chemical substances that pose a reasonable risk to human health or the environment. RCRA allows EPA and the states to follow the trail of hazardous wastes from their initial generation through final deposit. CERCLA provides EPA with the ability to manage damage, long-term hazards, and spills at historic or abandoned waste sites.

TOXIC SUBSTANCES CONTROL ACT (TSCA)

The creation of chemicals and their manufacture form the basis of the very heart of our industrialized society. Chemicals of various nature and in various forms protect our health; clothe, shelter, and feed us; and can be found in virtually every product used in our homes and businesses. Without these chemicals, our standard of living would be far less desirable than it is today.

The chemical industry plays a key role in our domestic economy, contributing approximately 5 percent of our nation's gross national product and employing well over a million people. The United States produces 60,000 different commercial chemicals today, and about 1000 new chemicals are introduced into commerce each year. Most chemicals present little if any danger to the environment or to human health when properly used. However, some do have the potential to cause significant harm.

In 1971 the United States Council on Environmental Quality initiated a legislative proposal for managing the problems being created by toxic substances in our environment. This proposal and the public hearings and debates it occasioned caused a great deal of concern within the domestic chemical industry. It was generally believed by all companies engaged in the manufacture of chemicals that extensive legislation improperly conceived could stifle technological innovation and place the domestic chemical industry in a disadvantaged position compared with both European and Japanese competitors. As a result, the industry, working through the Chemical Manufacturers Association, lobbied extensively to develop evenhanded legislation that would not have undue impact on the domestic chemical industry. Through the joint participation of Congress, the chemical industry, EPA, other special interest groups, and the general public, the Toxic Substances Control Act was passed in 1976.

TSCA established new requirements and authorities for identifying and controlling hazardous chemicals in the environment.[2,5] EPA was given the authority to gather basic information on the inherent risks in the manufacture of chemicals. Under TSCA the toxic effects of new chemicals have to be evaluated by EPA before chemicals are manufactured for commercial distribution. Existing chemicals can also be tested for toxic effects by EPA under this legislation. Should EPA determine that a chemical presents an unreasonable risk to human health or the environment, distribution and use of the chemical can be restricted, with controls ranging from a warning label to an outright ban on its manufacture and use. Product categories exempted from TSCA include tobacco, pesticides, nuclear substances, firearms and ammunition, food, food additives, drugs, and cosmetics. These product categories were exempted by Congress because in most cases they were already regulated under existing federal laws.

Under TSCA, EPA can require testing of existing chemicals by manufacturers whenever there is insufficient information to form a reasonable risk assessment, when a chemical substance presents a possible risk to human health and the environment, or when a chemical is produced in large enough quantities to result in significant human exposure or environmental release. EPA may implement these testing requirements only after following a procedure that includes a public hearing. EPA also coordinates interagency participation in its testing program, receiving advice from representatives of the departments of Labor, Commerce, and Health and Human Services, from the National Science Foundation, from the Council on Environmental Quality, and from EPA.

With the enactment of TSCA, a major thrust in the industry became the premarketing risk assessment of new chemical substances. EPA now requires manufacturers or importers of new chemicals to provide a 90-day advance notice of intent to manufacture or import. When an existing chemical is going into a significant new use which may increase exposure to humans or the environment, EPA also requires 90-day advance notification.

For purposes of TSCA, a "new chemical" is one which is not on the EPA inventory list of existing chemicals. A major challenge for EPA under the TSCA program then involved the development of a means to identify all old or existing chemicals and to devise a list of such chemicals. Working closely with industry, EPA published an initial chemical inventory that was scrutinized by all interested parties and revised according to their comments. This list provided, for the first time, an overview of chemicals used for commercial purposes in the United States. Since there are over 5 million known chemical compounds, most of which are noncommercial and used only in research and development, the inventory required considerable effort from government, industry, special interest groups, and the general public. The list eventually published was all-encompassing and has been used as the basis for identifying the "new" chemicals which are subject to the premanufacturing notification requirement of EPA.

Chemicals which are produced in small quantities solely for research and development are automatically exempted from the premanufacture notification and significant-new-use requirements. And TSCA also allows test marketing of unsanctioned new chemicals in order to allow quantities of new chemicals to be produced and distributed for purposes of market development.

But TSCA gives EPA the ultimate authority to limit or even prohibit the manufacture, processing, distribution, or disposal of a chemical substance that presents an unreasonable risk to human health or the environment. In this regard, EPA is required to coordinate its activities with other federal agencies and programs, including the Consumer Product Safety Commission, the Food and Drug Administration, the Department of Agriculture, the Occupational Safety and Health Administration, and the Department of Health and Human Services. TSCA does not affect the authority of state and local governments to establish regulations in dealing with chemicals, so long as these regulations are at least as protective of human health and the environment as are TSCA regulations.

No chemical may be imported into the United States if it is in violation of TSCA, and a new chemical may not be exported from the United States without prior notification to EPA, which then has the responsibility of notifying the importing country's government regarding the chemical in question.

All health and safety information submitted to EPA under TSCA is subject to public disclosure. However, EPA treats all such information as confidential unless the agency determines that the information is not entitled to such protection.

In order to implement the provisions of TSCA, EPA can inspect any operation where chemicals are manufactured, processed, or warehoused. Persons who fail to comply with the rules and regulations of TSCA may be subject to civil penalties of up to $25,000 a day. In addition to these civil penalties, anyone who knowingly violates the law may also be subject to criminal penalties of $25,000 a day and imprisonment for up to 1 year.

Two Special Cases: PCB and Asbestos

During the enactment of TSCA, Congress identified polychlorinated biphenyls (PCBs) for immediate regulation and phased withdrawal from the marketplace and directed EPA to prohibit the manufacture, processing, distribution, and use of PCBs except for those applications in areas that are totally enclosed. EPA was also authorized to require adequate PCB labeling and the safe disposal of those PCB applications still in use.

PCBs had been produced in the United States since 1929. Their excellent heat stability and heat-transfer properties had made them ideally suited as a heat-transfer medium in electric transformers and capacitors. But tests on laboratory animals showed that PCB can cause skin lesions and tumors. And it is highly persistent in the environment; animals can absorb PCB from their surroundings and concentrate it in their fatty tissues.

Although the manufacture of PCB ceased in 1977 under TSCA, considerable quantities of this substance are still being used within the electrical industry. An estimated 77,000 PCB-filled transformers are presently in use in the United States. Most of these transformers belong to building owners; only about 18,000 transformers are owned by utility companies.

Those PCB transformers and capacitors still used in buildings will be removed through an EPA-managed withdrawal program. The most widely accepted technology for PCB destruction is incineration. EPA regulations for the process require certain operating parameters; the material must be maintained at $1200 \pm 100°C$ for a 2-second residence time, with 3 percent excess oxygen in the stack gas—or as an alternative, $1600 \pm 100°C$ for a 1.5-second residence time, with 2 percent excess oxygen in the stack gas. The destruction and removal efficiency (DRE) must be at least 99.9999 percent.

To assist the general public with PCB questions, each regional EPA office has a designated PCB contact person.

While asbestos was not identified for regulation under TSCA, EPA has since used its authority to promulgate regulations for this hazardous chemical substance. In the mid-1960s, an American Cancer Society study showed an increased incidence of asbestosis and mesothelioma-type cancer in workers who were exposed to asbestos insulation materials. As a result, the Occupational Safety and Health Administration (OSHA) began to regulate the use of asbestos in 1971.

The magnitude of the asbestos problem in the United States is serious. Many buildings constructed throughout the 1960s and early 1970s contain significant quantities of asbestos-based fireproofing and insulating material. Through recent building demolition, remodeling, and normal degradation, these fibers are being released into the work, school, and home environment.

In an attempt to protect their employees and the public, many organizations are considering asbestos removal or various abatement programs. But before a thorough asbestos abatement program can begin, a comprehensive assessment of the presence and potential hazards at each site must be performed. This assessment includes locating and identifying the specific type and relative abundance of asbestos-containing material.

Asbestos is a naturally occurring family of fibrous mineral substances. The typical size of asbestos fibers is 0.1 to 10 μm in length, a size that is not generally visible to the human eye. When disturbed, these asbestos fibers may become suspended in the air and produce long-term exposure for people in the vicinity.

Most of the asbestos used in the United States is mined in Canada, California, and Vermont. There are numerous types: White asbestos, or chrysotile, and blue asbestos, or crocidolite, are the two most common forms of this hazardous substance. Historically, asbestos-containing products used in commerce have included vehicle brake and clutch linings, gaskets, roofing felt, floor tile, protective coatings, cement pipe, insulation, and decorative coatings. These products represent substantial liabilities to people who are exposed to them and must be factored into any risk assessment.

The disposal of asbestos is best handled by landfilling because previously mined asbestos fibers are virtually immobile in soil. Other disposal techniques such as incineration or chemical treatment are not recommended because of the unique properties of asbestos.

RESOURCE CONSERVATION AND RECOVERY ACT (RCRA)

Prior to the twentieth century, the United States produced minimal amounts of solid wastes. But industrial revolution and changes in our lifestyle caused accelerated growth in the volume of solid wastes produced by our society. The Solid Waste Disposal Act of 1965 addressed the enormous problem of how to safely dispose of huge daily volumes of municipal and industrial solid wastes. Its purpose was to protect human health and the environment, to reduce wastes and conserve natural resources, and to limit the generation of hazardous waste as expeditiously as possible. But by the mid-1970s, Congress and the general public recognized that additional regulations were needed to ensure that solid wastes would be managed properly in the future. These concerns resulted in the passage of the Resource Conservation and Recovery Act of 1976 (RCRA), which was enacted as an amendment to the original waste disposal act of a decade earlier.

RCRA has revised our nation's solid waste management practices and greatly expanded provisions for the management of hazardous wastes.[1,3,7,8] For example, Subtitle C of RCRA is a framework for the hazardous waste management program; Subtitle D relates to the solid waste program; and Subtitle I regulates underground storage tanks. Each of these programs has broad and far-reaching implications in the environmental field.

TSCA and RCRA were enacted at about the same time, but whereas TSCA was a product of broad-based participation by all concerned parties, the 1976 version of RCRA was passed by Congress without significant input from industry, EPA, or the general public. In part, this was because there was much more concern about the possible impacts of TSCA than of RCRA, which was perceived to be of concern only to the commercial trash and garbage disposal business. Even so, since its enactment, and as subsequently amended, RCRA has become the single most important legislative vehicle for management of hazardous solid wastes. The objectives of the act have evolved in a dynamic fashion, and Congress has twice amended RCRA to reflect those changing needs, once in 1980 and again in 1984. Particularly significant were the 1984 Hazardous and Solid Wastes Amendments, which expanded the regulatory scope of RCRA.

Subtitle C of RCRA established a program to manage hazardous wastes from cradle to grave. It first identified the solid wastes that are hazardous and then established requirements for the facilities that generate, transport, treat, store, or dispose of such wastes. The objective of the program has been to ensure that hazardous waste management is accomplished in a manner that protects human health and the environment. This Subtitle C program is the most comprehensive legislation EPA has ever promulgated. Specifically, hazardous waste generators, transporters, and treatment, storage and disposal (TSD) facilities all fall under its purview. In 1985 EPA had records for about 56,000 generators, 12,000 transporters, and 5000 TSD facilities. The regulations for each TSD facility serve as a basis for developing and issuing required permits. This permitting process allows either the federal EPA or its state counterpart to apply RCRA technical standards to the facility.

Designation of Hazardous Wastes under RCRA

The RCRA definition of solid waste is extremely broad and has been interpreted by EPA to include virtually any type of waste. By congressional definition, hazardous waste is any waste or combination of wastes which, because of its quantity, concentration, or physical, chemical, or infectious characteristics may (1) cause, or significantly contribute to, an increase in mortality or an increase in serious irreversible or incapacitating reversible illness or (2) pose a substantial present or potential hazard to human health or the environment when improperly treated, stored, transported, or disposed of, or otherwise managed.

Solid, semisolid, liquid, and gaseous materials resulting from industrial, commercial, agricultural, and community activities may all be regulated. But in addition to defining hazardous wastes in RCRA, Congress required EPA to develop a regulatory framework that would identify wastes that must be managed as hazardous wastes under the Subtitle C program. In developing that framework, EPA has defined a waste as hazardous if it:

Exhibits any of the characteristics of a hazardous waste defined by standard analytical test protocols and procedures

Is listed as a specific hazardous waste (under Subtitle C, RCRA)

Is a mixture that contains a listed hazardous waste and other wastes

Has not been excluded from RCRA regulations as a hazardous waste

Is a by-product from the treatment of any hazardous waste (unless specifically excluded under RCRA)

There are numerous attributes that might be appropriately used in defining the characteristics of hazardous wastes. They would include toxicity, flammability, explosivity, reactivity, corrosivity, bioaccumulation, carcinogenicity, radioactivity, teratogenicity, mutogenicity, and irritation to skin and human senses. It could be argued that each of these properties could be legitimately incorporated into the characterization of hazardous waste. However, many are difficult to scientifically quantify and relate to human health and environmental hazards, and some are surrounded by controversy in the scientific community and would therefore be difficult to regulate in an objective manner.

It was initially decided by EPA that hazardous waste characteristics must be definable in terms of physical or chemical properties that would cause the material to meet the RCRA definition of hazardous wastes. The second criterion adopted by EPA was that these physical or chemical properties must be measurable by standard test protocols. Since the primary responsibility for identifying hazardous wastes rests with the generators, who need standardized and practical methods for determining the characteristics of their solid wastes, EPA recognized that their RCRA-promulgated characterization system had to be kept simple in order for it to work properly at the generators' facilities. Because of this "keep-it-simple" approach, EPA did not incorporate biomedical testing in defining RCRA characteristics. Biomedical test protocols were judged to be too complex, controversial, or dependent upon expert personnel and sophisticated laboratory equipment. Further, the resulting health data would have required the establishment of quantitative threshold levels that have not been sufficiently developed within the scientific community.

In the end, EPA assigned four characteristics as the criteria for determining whether a waste should be identified as hazardous under RCRA:

- Ignitability
- Corrosivity
- Reactivity
- Toxicity Characteristic

As mandated under RCRA, EPA also developed three lists of hazardous wastes. (The lists are found in Appendixes B, C, and D.) The lists categorize the wastes according to their derivation:

1 *Nonspecific source wastes*: These are generic wastes which might commonly be produced by industrial processes; representative wastes are spent halogenated degreasing solvents and sludge from treatment of electroplating wastewater.

2 *Specific source wastes*: These industrial wastes are identified with the industry of origin, such as petroleum refining and organic chemical production. Sludges, wastewaters, and spent catalysts are representative.

3 *Commercial chemical products*: This list contains specific chemicals such as organics, pesticides, and acids.

However it is classified, each waste on the EPA lists meets either the RCRA definition of hazardous wastes, is acutely toxic or hazardous, or exhibits one of the four characteristics of a hazardous waste set forth above.

Normally, hazardous wastes do not consist of a single, discrete chemical but rather are made up of a variety of chemicals that form a waste mixture. Often these waste mixtures contain substances that may be identified as RCRA-listed hazardous wastes and substances identified under RCRA as being nonhazardous. EPA faced an extremely complex issue in trying to determine when such a mixture was hazardous and when it was nonhazardous. Since even a small amount of listed hazardous wastes in an otherwise nonhazardous mixture could endanger human health and the environment, EPA concluded that any mixture containing a listed hazardous waste should be considered a hazardous waste mixture and must be so managed under RCRA. In making this determination, EPA prohibited hazardous waste generators from circumventing the Subtitle C regulatory requirements of RCRA by commingling listed hazardous wastes with nonhazardous wastes.

In promulgating regulations regarding this complex issue though, EPA did make several exclusions to the mixture rule. Mixtures of nonhazardous wastes and hazardous wastes would not be considered hazardous if the resultant mixture did not exhibit any of the hazardous waste characterizations. Also, wastewater with low concentrations of a listed hazardous waste would not be considered a listed hazardous waste itself unless the wastewater mixture exhibited one of the RCRA hazardous characteristics. Of course, the wastewater exception would still be subject to discharge regulations under the Clean Water Act (see Chapter 3).

When Congress enacted RCRA, certain types of wastes were specifically excluded from being identified as hazardous under Subtitle C. These exclusions were generally large-volume wastes that either did not present a significant threat to human health or the environment or were managed under other environmentally related programs. Included in these legislative exclusions were wastes from households, from municipal resource recovery operations, from agriculture, and from mining overburden that was returned to the mine site. Later EPA amended this congressional exclusion list, adding certain chromium-containing wastes and laboratory samples. Further exclusions were made in 1980 when Congress temporarily exempted wastes from oil and gas exploration and production, mining operations, fossil fuel combustion, and dust from cement kilns. These 1980 exclusions are now being studied by EPA for possible regulation under RCRA, Subtitle C.

In order to allow some degree of flexibility in hazardous waste characterization and listing, the EPA created a *delisting* process that allows exceptions on a case-by-case basis. The burden of proof for delisting is borne by the individual or organization who is petitioning EPA. Should a waste be delisted for one facility under this procedure, it is not automatically delisted at other such facilities.

The Cradle-to-Grave Concept

Under RCRA, a cradle-to-grave chain of hazardous waste management was established. This cradle-to-grave concept, illustrated in Figure 4-1, includes hazardous waste generators, transporters, treatment plants, storage facilities, and disposal sites in the management scheme, as well as EPA and its state counterparts. A *generator* is defined as the creator of the hazardous waste who must analyze all solid wastes produced to ensure compliance under Subtitle C of RCRA. Under that subtitle, the generators are required to test and identify any wastes produced and transported to an RCRA treatment, storage, or disposal (TSD) facility.

There are numerous small-quantity generators of hazardous wastes in the United States. In order to effectively implement RCRA, EPA recognized that if all small generators were forced under the Subtitle C regulation system, it would be virtually impossible implementing the program. Also, many small businesses did not have the financial and legal capabilities to comply with the strict interpretation of RCRA regulations. As a result, EPA exempted small-quantity generators of hazardous wastes from most of the Subtitle C regulations, even though the small-quantity generators were still required to analyze their wastes, store them properly, and dispose of any hazardous waste at approved facilities. In 1980 EPA defined a *small-quantity generator (SQG)* as a facility that produced less than 1000 kg of hazardous wastes on-site per month

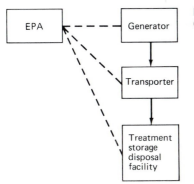

Figure 4-1
Cradle-to-grave hazardous waste management.

or accumulated less than 1000 kg of hazardous wastes at any given time. The small-quantity generator was also defined as one that produced less than 1 kg of *acutely* hazardous waste per month or accumulated less than 1 kg of *acutely* hazardous wastes at any given time.

Since numerous entities qualified as small-quantity generators under this ruling, there was a growing concern that this hazardous waste exemption could result in harm to human health and the environment. In 1984 Congress therefore amended the small-quantity-generator definition by reducing the ceiling from 1000 kg to 100 kg of hazardous waste per month. In order not to place an undue burden on those businesses previously exempted as small-quantity generators, EPA was given authority to modify their regulation requirements so long as human health and the environment were protected.

The RCRA hazardous waste generator must obtain an EPA identification number, a system which enables the agency to monitor and track all hazardous wastes produced. EPA identification numbers are also required for transporters and TSD facilities. Generators are forbidden from furnishing their hazardous wastes to any transporter or TSD facility that does not have an appropriate EPA identification number.

To ensure that the generator properly handles hazardous wastes before they are transported, EPA adopted the regulations used by the U.S. Department of Transportation (DOT). The DOT regulations include proper packaging to prevent leakage of hazardous wastes during transport and use of labels or placards to readily identify the dangers of the wastes being transported. These DOT regulations apply only to generators shipping their hazardous wastes offsite. A generator may accumulate hazardous waste on-site for up to 90 days, as long as it is properly stored and under the supervision of personnel who have been properly trained in the handling of such wastes.

In order to track and manage the RCRA cradle-to-grave hazardous waste management system, a *uniform hazardous waste manifest* was created. This manifest system, shown in Figure 4-2, is based upon an EPA format that was published in the *Federal Register* in May 1980. The combined manifest form contains information on the waste generator, transporter, and TSD facility

Figure 4-2
Manifest system to track hazardous waste.

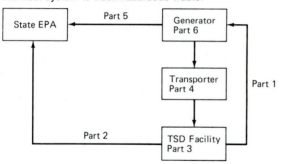

destination in addition to a characterization of the hazardous waste being transported. The multiple-copy form is initially completed and signed by the hazardous waste generator. As is typically the case, the generator retains part 6 of the manifest, sends part 5 to the appropriate state EPA regulatory agency, and gives the remaining parts of the manifest to the transporter. At this point, the state EPA has been notified of the shipment of the hazardous waste by the generator through the transporter. The transporter retains part 4 of the manifest and gives the remaining parts of the manifest to the TSD facility upon arrival. The TSD facility retains part 3 and sends parts 1 and 2 to the original generator and the state EPA, respectively.

By using such a manifest, the generators and the state EPA can track the movement of the hazardous waste from its generation (cradle) to the point of ultimate disposal (grave). As noted, these manifests contain the name and EPA identification number of the generator, the transporter, and the TSD facility as well as a qualitative and quantitative description of the hazardous waste being transported. Additionally, each manifest must certify that the generator has used its best practical technology to reduce the volume and toxicity of the hazardous waste. Further, each manifest must certify that the TSD facility chosen by the generator is the best practical method to minimize risk to human health and the environment. (Manifests are not required for generators who have their own TSD facility on-site.) The manifests must be properly prepared and processed so that the generator, who is ultimately responsible for the hazardous waste disposal, is able to track the cradle-to-grave system with a high degree of reliability. Throughout this management system, the hazardous waste is generally considered to be in the custody of the last signatory on the manifest.

Generators are required to obtain part 1 of the manifest form within 35 days from the date the hazardous waste was accepted by the initial transporter. Otherwise, the generator must contact the transporter or the TSD facility to determine the status of the hazardous waste in the manifest system. If part 1 of the manifest has not been received by the generator within 45 days after it was initially accepted by the transporter, the generator must file an exception report with the EPA regional office. The exception report must detail the efforts of the generator to locate the waste.

The transporter of a hazardous waste is an important link between the generator and the ultimate TSD facility. Since the DOT has had a long history of regulating transportation, EPA worked closely with the DOT to promulgate transportation regulations for hazardous wastes that would not cause conflict between the two agencies.

The *transporter,* under RCRA Subtitle C, is any person engaged in the domestic off-site transportation of hazardous wastes. (Regulations do not apply, however, to the transportation of hazardous wastes *within* a TSD facility.) The transporter must have an EPA identification number and comply with the appropriate manifest system. The transporter cannot accept hazardous wastes from a generator who does not have an EPA identification number. The transporter must deliver the entire quantity of hazardous wastes to the TSD facility listed on the manifest. Transporters must retain their copy of the manifest for 3 years following acceptance of the hazardous wastes by the TSD facility. (See Chapter 9 for full discussion of transportation regulations.)

The final link in cradle-to-grave hazardous waste management is the *treatment, storage,* and *disposal facility,* which involves three functional areas:

Treatment: Any process that changes the characterization or composition of a hazardous waste so as to render it less hazardous or that is capable of volume reduction or resource recovery

Storage: The temporary holding of hazardous wastes prior to treatment or disposal

Disposal: The deposit of a hazardous waste so that it might either safely reenter the environment or be safely and securely disposed.

Under RCRA, there are two categories of TSD facilities: those that have a full permit and those that do not hold a regular permit but have an interim-status-facility permit. TSD facilities operating under interim status must meet only a portion of those requirements of a permitted facility. Interim-status permits primarily ensure that the TSD facility is following good housekeeping practices. The standards for fully accredited TSD facilities, on the other hand, are based upon the design and operating criteria specified in the TSD facility permit. A number of facilities are exempted completely from meeting the TSD regulations, including:

- Farmers who dispose of their pesticides
- Totally enclosed treatment facilities
- Neutralization or wastewater treatment units of the facility
- Operations to clean up hazardous waste spills or discharges
- Operations that reuse or recycle hazardous wastes
- Transporters who store manifested hazardous wastes for less than 10 days
- Facilities that are regulated by state programs

An RCRA operating permit is obtained by all TSD facilities through a standardized process:

- Submittal of the permit application
- Regulatory review of the application
- Preparation of the draft permit
- Request for public comment
- Permit finalization
- Maintenance and termination of permit

The TSD facility is required to submit a permit application that covers the design, operation, and maintenance of the facility. This permit application is divided into parts A and B. Part A requests general information, including a description of the activities to be conducted at the facility. Part B requires highly detailed and technical information, such as analyses of hazardous wastes to be managed at the facility. Facilities existing on or before November

18, 1980, may submit only part A upon application for interim status, with submission of part B required in a timely manner. Should the facility delay in filing part B, it could lose its interim status and be closed down. Facilities established after November 18, 1980, are ineligible for interim status and must submit parts A and B simultaneously, at least 180 days prior to commencement of construction.

The administrative review process initially focuses upon the completeness of the permit application. Once the application has been deemed complete, a review process by EPA determines either approval or denial of the application. This lengthy process may take as long as 3 years.

After the application has been approved, a draft permit which incorporates technical operating requirements and other conditions is prepared to ensure compliance. When the draft permit has been completed, EPA is required to solicit written public comments for 45 days. A public hearing may be held during this same time period. Following the public comment period, EPA issues the RCRA permit decision.

Issuance and maintenance of the permit is based upon compliance with numerous federal laws, including the Endangered Species Act, the Wild and Scenic Rivers Act, the National Historic Preservation Act, the Fish and Wildlife Coordination Act, and the Coastal Zone Management Act.

Each TSD facility must have an EPA identification number. These facilities must also properly identify and handle their wastes and ensure that operations are according to standard and that personnel are properly trained in hazardous waste management. The TSD facility must conduct waste analysis prior to treatment, storage, and disposal of the material. The TSD facility must have security barriers in place to prevent people from unauthorized entry into the facility. Employee training must be provided to reduce the potential for operational errors that might threaten human health or the environment. All ignitable or reactive wastes must be protected in such a way as to remove that cause for concern.

Drums and other containers which are used for waste storage eventually may corrode and pose threats to human health and the environment. In order to minimize this potential problem, EPA promulgated container regulations which include using only containers in good condition, ensuring the compatibility of the waste with the container, and preventing the mixture of incompatible wastes in containers. The use of tanks to store or treat wastes must be done in such a way as to avoid leaks, ruptures, and corrosion. Storage tanks should be diked to contain leaking liquid wastes.

Surface lagoons and other impoundments present serious potential problems for groundwater contamination. Prior to the Hazardous and Solid Waste Amendments of 1984, regulations for surface impoundments were inadequate to protect against groundwater contamination. But the 1984 amendments increased the level of protection by requiring double liners, leachate collection systems, and adequate monitoring for groundwater contamination. Hazardous waste piles must comply with the RCRA requirements for landfills. Landfarming or land treatment of hazardous wastes has been regulated so as to render the wastes less hazardous. Monitoring of surface water and groundwater is required when using this hazardous waste management approach. RCRA regulations prohibit the growing of food-chain crops on land that has been previously treated with hazardous wastes containing arsenic, lead, cadmium, mercury, or other such hazardous constituents.

Another aspect of RCRA involves regulation of underground storage tanks, which are defined as any tank with at least 10 percent of its volume buried underground, including any pipes that are an integral part of the tank's system. There are 1.5 million underground tanks in the United States containing hazardous wastes; an estimated 200,000 of these are leaking and polluting underground water supplies. This groundwater contamination caused Congress to create a new management program under the 1984 RCRA amendments. Future installations of underground storage tanks will be heavily impacted by these 1984 amendments. All owners and operators of underground storage tanks must have methods for detecting leaks, maintain records, take corrective action when leaks occur, and provide for final closure of the tanks. The 1984 amendments also provided a ban on new unprotected storage tanks, requiring that all tanks be well protected from corrosion through the use of proper construction materials and protective coatings or linings.

New TSD facilities must be in compliance with all local, state, and federal standards. Further, the TSD facility must retain complete and accurate records of its operations so that the appropriate regulatory authority may assess compliance with the appropriate hazardous waste regulations. General standards applied to TSD facilities cover three major areas: (1) groundwater monitoring, (2) closure and postclosure processes, and (3) financial accountability.

Groundwater monitoring is necessary to determine the impact of the TSD facility. The monitoring of groundwater is required for landfills, land treatment, surface impoundments, and certain waste piles. In all cases, the monitoring must be conducted for the life of the facility, and for up to 30 years after closure. In developing and installing a monitoring system, RCRA requires that four wells be installed. One of these wells must be up-gradient from the TSD facility and three must be down-gradient. Baseline uncontaminated groundwater data are provided from the up-gradient well. The three down-gradient wells must be placed so as to monitor any released waste that might be migrating from the TSD facility. Comparison of the groundwater data from the up-gradient and down-gradient wells gives an indication of potential contamination from the TSD facility. After installation, these wells are monitored for 1 year to establish background data for potential chemical contamination. This background monitoring provides the database for future monitoring information. Once the background levels have been established, the groundwater is routinely monitored semiannually for contamination. Should contamination be suspected, a groundwater program must be implemented to determine if hazardous waste is, in fact, entering the groundwater, the magnitude of contamination, and the rate of its migration. The TSD facility must submit a ground-water quality report to the EPA regional administrator within 15 days of conducting this assessment.

The period of closure begins once the facility no longer accepts wastes. During this period, TSD facilities must completely process all on-site wastes and place a final cover over the landfill. The equipment, structures, and soil of the facility must either be disposed of or decontaminated. In order to ensure proper closure of a TSD facility, operators are required to develop a closure plan that must contain the schedule for closure, an estimate of the amount of wastes the facility will handle, a description of the closure process, and an out-line of necessary decontamination procedures. Though the closure plan may be amended during the active life of the TSD facility, once that plan has been implemented, the operator must certify its authenticity.

Following closure, a 30-year postclosure period commences, during which time the TSD facility must continue groundwater monitoring and any mainte-nance activities necessary to preserve the integrity of the site. These closure and postclosure requirements minimize the need for long-term maintenance and en-sure control of any potential leakage of contaminants into the environment.

TSD facilities are required to prepare both closure and postclosure cost es-timates, which should be adjusted for inflation, and to provide financial assur-ance of ability to implement the closure and postclosure plan. There are nu-merous methods by which the TSD facility may guarantee financial ability to adequately fund closure and postclosure activities; such methods include trust funds, surety bonds, letters of credit, insurance policies, corporate guarantees, and financial tests that demonstrate the availability of sufficient funds.

The facility must also provide adequate liability coverage to compensate third parties for bodily injury and property damage caused by accidents related to the operation. The liability coverage is necessary to demonstrate financial responsibility for sudden accidental occurrences such as explosion and fires as well as nonsudden accidental occurrences over time such as groundwater and surface water contamination.

TSD facilities are closely monitored and inspected. The EPA has an en-forcement program to ensure compliance with RCRA laws and regulations. If a solid waste disposal facility fails to comply with the RCRA criteria to protect human health and the environment—that is, fails to meet minimum technical standards and criteria based upon protection of floodplains, surface water and groundwater, air, endangered species, and land used for food production—that facility may be classified as an *open dump*. An open dump classification re-quires the operator to either upgrade the facility or close it. Once a facility has been classified as an open dump, the state places it on an Open Dump Inven-tory Report that is sent to the U.S. Bureau of the Census, with the information also forwarded to EPA.

In any case where noncompliance is detected by EPA, legal action may be taken. The use of administrative orders and civil or criminal lawsuits may fol-low, depending upon the severity of the problem.

At one time, EPA estimated that only 10 percent of hazardous waste was being managed in an environmentally sound manner. The remainder was being transported, treated, and disposed of in a way that potentially threatened human health and the environment. It was this problem that led to the enactment of the 1980 RCRA amendments. Then the increasing production of hazardous wastes and the continued nonmanagement of these wastes resulted in the 1984 Hazardous and Solid Waste Amendments. This, in essence, is the history of RCRA.

COMPREHENSIVE ENVIRONMENTAL RESPONSE, COMPENSATION AND LIABILITIES ACT (CERCLA)

The Comprehensive Environmental Response, Compensation and Liabilities Act was created to respond to "sins of the past." Until passage of CERCLA, EPA was able to regulate hazardous waste management only at active and properly closed facilities. New legislation was therefore enacted by Congress in 1980 to address environmental and public health problems caused by the prior uncontrolled handling and disposal of hazardous substances or by otherwise unregulated waste management. The heart of CERCLA is Superfund, which is in essence a pool of money generated by special taxes to ensure that funds are available for cleanup efforts in accordance with RCRA requirements.[4,9,10,11] Under CERCLA, EPA was granted the authority to take any necessary short-term and emergency steps to address any hazard to human health and the environment triggered by burning, leakage, or explosion of hazardous substances, imminent contamination of food chains, or pollution of a drinking-water source.

Under CERCLA, EPA can also undertake long-term actions, those carried over more than 6 months, at complex hazardous waste sites. Each of these sites is selected on the basis of a risk assessment. In order to be eligible for remedial cleanup under CERCLA, a site must be placed on the National Priority List (NPL), which identifies the hazardous wastes sites in the United States. Sites are placed on the NPL following evaluation through the *Hazard Ranking System* (*HRS*), a model which assesses the relative risk to public health and the environment from hazardous substances in groundwater, surface water, air, and soil. There are probably at least 10,000 potential Superfund sites throughout the United States, though the present NPL names less than 1000. The majority of the estimated 10,000 sites that are presently uncontrolled and in need of remedial action will have to be negotiated between EPA and the respective state offices. Most of these sites are closed solid waste management facilities. Additionally, there are numerous operating hazardous waste facilities that will probably require groundwater cleanup.

The reasons for the wide disparity between the actual number of identified cleanup sites and estimates given by state offices are found in the fact that EPA does not include surface impoundments and closed industrial landfills in its evaluations, nor does the agency apply the more stringent 1984 amendments in risk assessment.

One of the major issues regarding uncontrolled hazardous waste sites is the identification and quantification of risks to human health and the environment. The lifestyle promoted by our society results in our daily exposure to hazardous and toxic substances in our homes, work environment, and other areas of daily contact. This broad-based exposure makes it difficult to pinpoint the cost and attribute the cause of contamination to any one source. It is virtually impossible to precisely quantify risk in relation to levels of liability at hazardous waste sites.

The "how clean is clean" issue is a complex one, requiring consensus of government, industry, and the general public. We cannot assess the ultimate needs in cleanup until clear, concise, mutually agreeable goals are supported by all concerned parties. From a human health and environment perspective, the entire approach should be to require restoration of the sites to their original condition or to apply the best available technology at whatever cost to achieve conditions that are commensurate with nearby background locations. Since each Superfund site offers somewhat unique pollution problems, cleanup policies for these sites would appear to be best served by making remedial site cleanup a case-by-case consideration. Cost-benefit analyses must enter into each of these case considerations. Environmentally effective cleanup goals must be established for each site, and a cost-effective response implemented to achieve these goals.

EPA has the authority under Superfund to take action whenever there is an actual or potential release of any hazardous substance into the environment. EPA also has the authority, under Superfund, to take appropriate action wherever there is actual or potential release of *any* pollutant or contaminant that would pose an imminent and substantial danger to public health. But EPA may implement remedial action only at those hazardous waste sites identified on the National Priority List.

There are two types of response actions that may be taken by EPA. The agency may require removal of the dangerous substance and immediate cleanup at the surface of the site or possibly a stabilizing action at the site until a permanent solution can be identified and implemented. Such removal actions are generally short-term efforts to address imminent danger. The other response EPA may implement is that of remedial action at the site. Such an action would be an attempt to provide a permanent solution to threats posed by hazardous substances at the location. All wastes which are produced through Superfund site cleanup efforts must be treated, stored, or disposed of in accordance with RCRA regulations.

Part of EPA's remedial action process involves the identification of the responsible parties. These responsible parties may be historic owners or operators of the site, generators of the hazardous substances that have polluted the site, or the transporters who brought the hazardous wastes to the site. Ideally, all responsible parties should be liable for cleaning up polluted sites. The courts have recognized the concept of "jointly and severally liable" in cleaning up sites which involve multiple polluters. This judicial action clearly places the ultimate financial burden on the *generator* of the hazardous wastes. The enforcement process may now proceed with greater assurance of identifying at least one responsible party to pay for the cleanup costs.

EPA would prefer that the responsible parties perform the appropriate response actions themselves, but whenever the responsible parties do not respond, EPA is empowered to use money from the Hazardous Substances Response Trust Fund to pay for the cleanup. EPA may then take whatever steps are necessary to recover the costs from the responsible parties. CERCLA also provides resources for present and future remedial site cleanup and response actions through the Postclosure Liability Trust Fund, which was established as an assessment against the appropriate responsible parties. The Postclosure Liability Trust Fund provides financial guarantee against all possible postclosure remedial costs for up to 30 years after site closure.

SUPERFUND AMENDMENTS AND REAUTHORIZATION ACT (SARA)

The Superfund Amendments and Reauthorization Act (SARA) of 1986 is an extension of the CERCLA program to clean up hazardous releases at uncontrolled or abandoned hazardous waste sites.[6] SARA has $8.5 billion in funding but imposes more stringent remedial standards that increase the cost of site cleanup. It allows the government to take immediate action and seek reimbursement later. It also provides money for cleaning up sites where no responsible party with sufficient funds can be found.

Funding under CERCLA comes from tax on petroleum and 42 listed chemicals. Funding under SARA comes from:

- Taxes on petroleum and chemicals
- A corporate environmental tax
- General appropriations
- Parties responsible for site cleanup
- Superfund penalties

SARA also imposes on EPA a schedule for site investigations, feasibility studies, remedial action, and establishes "Community right to know" provisions.

POLLUTION PREVENTION

The Pollution Prevention Act of 1990 reaffirms the high priority of pollution prevention and waste reduction as discussed in Chapter 6.

QUESTIONS

1 Describe the premanufacturing and significant-new-use notification requirements imposed under TSCA.
2 Discuss the validity of the statement "PCBs are carcinogenic, mutagenic, and teratogenic to humans."
3 What are the EPA incineration criteria for PCB destruction?
4 What are the major RCRA goals?
5 Discuss the RCRA hazardous waste characteristics.
6 Describe the criteria covered under RCRA for classification of hazardous waste disposal facilities.
7 The initial Superfund tax was levied mainly upon crude oil and petrochemical producers. Discuss the equity of this tax.
8 During congressional discussions on the Superfund reauthorization, it was proposed that the following sources might provide major funding revenue. Discuss the merits of these proposed taxes as they relate to hazardous waste generation and reduction:
   (*a*) General corporate revenues
   (*b*) Petroleum industry feedstocks
   (*c*) Hazardous chemical disposers
   (*d*) General federal treasury funds

BIBLIOGRAPHY

1 Dawson, G. W., and B. W. Mercer: *Hazardous Waste Management,* Wiley, New York, 1986.
2 Dominguez, G. S., and K. G. Bartlett: *Hazardous Waste Management,* vol. I, *The Law of Toxics and Toxic Substances,* CRC Press, Boca Raton, Fla., 1986.
3 40 Code of Federal Regulations, Parts 240–280, July 1, 1987.
4 40 Code of Federal Regulations, Parts 300–306, July 1, 1987.
5 40 Code of Federal Regulations, Parts 702–799, July 1, 1987.
6 Hedeman, W. N., Jr., P. E. Shorb III, and C. A. McLean: "The Superfund Amendments and Reauthorization Act of 1986: Statutory Provisions and EPA Implementation," *Hazardous Waste and Hazardous Materials,* vol. 4, no. 2, 1987.
7 *RCRA Handbook,* ERT, Concord, Mass., 1986.
8 *RCRA Orientation Manual,* U.S. Environmental Protection Agency, Office of Solid Waste, Washington, 1986.
9 *Superfund Factbook,* U.S. Environmental Protection Agency, Office of Public Affairs, Washington, September 1985.
10 *Superfund Handbook,* ERT, Concord, Mass., 1987.
11 *Superfund Strategy,* U.S. Congress, Office of Technology Assessment, Washington, April 1985.

HAZARDOUS WASTE CHARACTERIZATION AND SITE ASSESSMENT

INTRODUCTION

A clear definition of hazardous waste is obviously necessary in order to promulgate meaningful regulations. Yet defining hazardous waste is a complex process, since many factors are potential contributors to the hazardous nature of a waste, and what can be viewed as hazardous to one individual may not be hazardous to another. For instance, the unsafe handling and transportation of waste products or substances can result in their becoming hazardous. And a waste may have a low degree of toxicity and yet be highly flammable, explosive, or reactive. Those wastes which have a tendency to bioaccumulate are more likely to produce undesirable chronic effects than highly flammable or explosive materials, so an assessment of the acute versus chronic toxicity of waste is also needed in any attempt at definition. But once the factors that enter into a consensus definition of hazardous waste have been determined, the defining attributes can then be used to generate solutions for the environmental problems caused by hazardous waste.

Over the years, numerous attempts have been made by government, industry, and the general public to define hazardous waste. In the process of developing its environmental legislative program, the United States Congress has given us several meaningful definitions.[3,10] For example, the Federal Water Pollution Control Act defines hazardous substances in terms of toxic pollutants and identifies 129 priority pollutants (see Appendix A).[9] The Resource Conservation and Recovery Act (RCRA) further defined hazardous waste and gave the United States Environmental Protection Agency the right to characterize these wastes in such a way that they would be identifiable. Under RCRA, hazardous waste is specifically defined as a waste that can cause or contribute adversely to human health and the environment. Other definitions of hazardous waste from trade associations such as the National Solid Waste Management Association and the European Economic Community are also based on the concept of risk to human health and the environment. But since RCRA is the driving force behind the management of hazardous waste in the United States, it is their definition that has become the generally accepted version, and the one on which we base our discussion here.

DEFINITION OF HAZARDOUS WASTE UNDER RCRA

In the Resource Conservation and Recovery Act of 1976, Congress defined the term "hazardous waste" as a waste, or combination of wastes, which because of its quantity, concentration, or physical, chemical, or infectious characteristics may (1) cause, or significantly contribute to, an increase in mortality or an increase in serious irreversible or incapacitating reversible illness or (2) pose a substantial present or potential hazard to human health or the environment when improperly treated, stored, transported, or disposed of.

Although Congress defined the term "hazardous waste" in RCRA, EPA was left to develop the regulatory framework that would identify those wastes that must be managed as hazardous wastes under Subtitle C. In 40 Code of Federal Regulations Part 261, EPA then specified that a solid waste is hazardous if it meets any of four conditions:

Exhibits any of the characteristics of a hazardous waste based upon analysis
Has been listed as a hazardous waste
Is a mixture containing a characteristic or listed hazardous waste and a nonhazardous waste, unless the mixture is specifically excluded or no longer exhibits any of the characteristics of the characteristic hazardous waste
Is not specifically excluded from regulation as a hazardous waste

Furthermore, the by-products of the treatment of any hazardous waste are also to be considered hazardous unless they have been specifically excluded.

In establishing these criteria for the identification of a hazardous waste, EPA selected four characteristics as inherently hazardous in any substance:

- Ignitability
- Corrosivity
- Reactivity
- Toxicity Characteristic

EPA used two criteria in selecting these characteristics. The first criterion was that the characteristic be capable of being defined in terms of physical, chemical, or other properties.[11,12] The second criterion was that the properties defining the characteristic be measurable by standardized and available testing protocols. The second criterion was adopted because the primary responsibility for determining whether a solid waste exhibits any of the characteristics rests with the generators. EPA believed that unless generators were provided with widely available and uncomplicated methods for determining whether their wastes exhibited the characteristics, the identification system would prove unworkable.

Largely because of this second criterion, EPA refrained from adding carcinogenicity, mutagenicity, bioaccumulation potential, and phytotoxicity to the characteristics. EPA considered the available test protocols for measuring these characteristics to be either insufficiently developed, too complex, or too highly dependent on the use of skilled personnel and professional equipment. Additionally, given the current state of knowledge concerning such characteristics, EPA did not feel that it could define with any confidence the numerical threshold levels at which wastes exhibiting these characteristics would present a substantial hazard.

As testing protocols become generally acceptable and confidence in setting minimum thresholds increases, more characteristics may be added. To date, the properties of wastes exhibiting any or all of the existing characteristics are defined in 40 Code of Federal Regulations, Sections 261.20–261.24.

Characteristic of Ignitability

Ignitability is the characteristic used to define as hazardous those wastes that could cause a fire during transport, storage, or disposal. Examples of ignitable wastes include waste oils and used solvents.

A waste exhibits the characteristics of ignitability if a representative sample of the waste has any of the following properties:

1 It is a liquid, other than an aqueous solution containing less than 24% alcohol by volume, and has flash point less than 60°C (140°F), as determined by a Pensky-Martens Closed Cup Tester (using the test method specified in ASTM Standard D-93-79 or D-93-80) or by a Setaflash Closed Cup Tester (using the test method specified in ASTM Standard D-3278-78).[1]

2 It is not a liquid and is capable, under standard temperature and pressure, of causing fire through friction, absorption of moisture, or spontaneous chemical changes and, when ignited, burns so vigorously and persistently that it creates a hazard.

3 It is an ignitable compressed gas as defined in the 49 Code of Federal Regulations 173.300 DOT regulations.

4 It is an oxidizer as defined in the 49 Code of Federal Regulations 173.151 DOT regulations.

A waste that exhibits the characteristic of ignitability but is not listed as a hazardous waste in Subpart D of RCRA has the EPA hazardous waste number of D001.

Characteristic of Corrosivity

Corrosivity, as indicated by pH, was chosen as an identifying characteristic of a hazardous waste because wastes with high or low pH can react dangerously with other wastes or cause toxic contaminants to migrate from certain wastes. Examples of corrosive wastes include acidic wastes and used pickle liquor from steel manufacture. Steel corrosion is a prime indicator of a hazardous waste since wastes capable of corroding steel can escape from drums and liberate other wastes.

A waste exhibits the characteristic of corrosivity if a representative sample of the waste has either of the following properties:

1 It is aqueous and has a pH less than or equal to 2 or greater than or equal to 12.5, as determined by a pH meter using an EPA test method. The EPA test method for pH is specified as Method 5.2 in "Test Methods for the Evaluation of Solid Waste, Physical/Chemical Methods."

2 It is a liquid and corrodes steel (SAE 1020) at a rate greater than 6.35 mm (0.250 inch) per year at a test temperature of 55°C (130°F), as determined by the test method specified in NACE (National Association of Corrosion Engineers) Standard TM-01-69 and standardized in "Test Methods for the Evaluation of Solid Waste, Physical/Chemical Methods."

A waste that exhibits the characteristic of corrosivity but is not listed as a hazardous waste in Subpart D has the EPA hazardous waste number of D002.

Characteristic of Reactivity

Reactivity was chosen as an identifying characteristic of a hazardous waste because unstable wastes can pose an explosive problem at any stage of the waste management cycle. Examples of reactive wastes include water from TNT operations and used cyanide solvents.

A waste exhibits the characteristic of reactivity if a representative sample of the waste has any of the following properties:

1 It is normally unstable and readily undergoes violent change without detonating.

2 It reacts violently with water.

3 It forms potentially explosive mixtures with water.

4 When mixed with water, it generates toxic gases, vapors, or fumes in a quantity sufficient to present a danger to human health or the environment.

5 It is a cyanide- or sulfide-bearing waste which, when exposed to pH conditions between 2 and 12.5, can generate toxic gases, vapors, or fumes in a quantity sufficient to present a danger to human health or the environment.

6 It is capable of detonation or explosive reaction if subjected to a strong initiating source or if heated under confinement.

7 It is readily capable of detonation or explosive decomposition or reaction at standard temperature and pressure.

8 It is a forbidden explosive as defined in the 49 Code of Federal Regulations 173.51, or a Class A explosive as defined in the 49 Code of Federal Regulations 173.53, or a Class B explosive as defined in the 49 Code of Federal Regulations 173.88 DOT regulations.

A waste that exhibits the characteristic of reactivity but is not listed as a hazardous waste in Subpart D has the EPA hazardous waste number of D003.

Characteristic of Toxicity

The test, toxicity characteristic leaching procedure (TCLP), is designed to identify wastes likely to leach hazardous concentrations of particular toxic constituents into the groundwater as a result of improper management. During the TCLP, constituents are extracted from the waste to simulate the leaching actions that occur in landfills. If the concentration of the toxic constituent exceeds the regulatory limit, the waste is classified as hazardous.

If the extract from a representative waste sample contains any of the contaminants listed in Table 5-1 at a concentration equal to or greater than the respective value given, the waste exhibits the toxicity characteristic. Where the waste contains less than 0.5 percent filterable solids, the waste itself is considered to be the extract. A waste, that exhibits the toxicity characteristic but is not a listed hazardous waste, has the EPA hazardous waste number

TABLE 5-1
MAXIMUM CONCENTRATION OF CONTAMINANTS FOR RCRA TOXICITY CHARACTERISTICS

EPA hazardous waste number	Contaminant	Maximum concentration (mg/L)	EPA hazardous waste number	Contaminant	Maximum concentration (mg/L)
D004	Arsenic[a]	5.0	D036	Hexachloro-1,3-butadiene	0.5
D005	Barium[a]	100.0			
D019	Benzene	0.5	D037	Hexachloroethane	3.0
D006	Cadmium[a]	1.0	D008	Lead[a]	5.0
D022	Carbon tetrachloride	0.5	D013	Lidane[a]	0.4
D023	Chlordane	0.03	D009	Mercury[a]	0.2
D024	Chlorobenzene	100.0	D014	Methoxychlor[a]	10.0
D025	Chloroform	6.0	D040	Methyl ethyl ketone	200.0
D007	Chromium	5.0	D041	Nitrobenzene	2.0
D026	o-Cresol	200.0	D042	Pentachlorophenol	100.0
D027	m-Cresol	200.0	D044	Pyridine	5.0
D028	p-Cresol	200.0	D010	Selenium	1.0
D016	2,4-D[a]	10.0	D011	Silver[a]	5.0
D030	1,4-Dichlorobenzene	7.5	D047	Tetrachloroethylene	0.7
			D015	Toxaphene[a]	0.5
D031	1,2-Dichloroethane	0.5	D052	Trichloroethylene	0.5
D032	1,1-Dichloroethylene	0.7	D053	2,4,5-Trichlorophenol	400.0
D033	2,4-Dinitrotoluene	0.13	D054	2,4,6-Trichlorophenol	2.0
D012	Endrin[a]	0.02			
D034	Heptachlor (and its hydroxide)	0.008	D017	2,4,5-TP (Silvex)[a]	1.0
			D055	Vinyl chloride	0.2
D035	Hexachlorobenzene	0.13			

[a]Formerly EP Toxicity Contaminants.
Source: U.S. Environmental Protection Agency.

specified in Table 5-1. The TCLP test replaced the EP toxicity test in September 1990 and added 25 organic compounds to the eight metals and six pesticides, that were subject to the EP toxicity test.

PROHIBITIONS ON LAND DISPOSAL

The HSWA land ban created land disposal restrictions (LDRs) to prohibit disposal of hazardous waste in or on the land unless the waste meets the specific RCRA treatment standards. The LDRs should control migration of and exposure to hazardous waste constituents. The EPA requires treatment to reduce toxicity or mobility in the wastes prior to land disposal using best demonstrated available technology (BDAT).

Specific BDAT treatment technologies should be used to treat hazardous waste based upon the toxic concentrations in the waste TCLP extract, the RCRA listed waste codes, and the concentration of hazardous constituents in the waste itself (40 CFR 268.41-268.43). The LDRs should better protect human health and the environment, while significantly increasing waste disposal costs for generators.

THE CONCEPT OF TOXICITY

A toxic waste on contact with a living organism is capable of killing, injuring, or otherwise impairing that organism. These poisonous substances are hazards in that there is risk depending upon the exposure and the manner in which such a waste is handled.

Adverse effects such as carcinogenicity, mutagenicity, and teratogenicity are generally linked to contact with toxic substances. These intrinsic properties define toxic materials and may also be used as criteria in a listing of hazardous wastes. However, the terms "toxic" and "hazardous" are not interchangeable. Hazardous substances may have both intrinsic and extrinsic properties. For example, the extrinsic properties of explosivity, ignitability, and reactivity are not related to chemical toxicity. In sum, *toxic* denotes the capacity of a substance to produce injury, while *hazardous* denotes the probability that injury will result from the use of (or contact with) a substance.

Acute toxic wastes may injure humans or other mammals when inhaled or ingested or upon contact with the skin. *Acute toxicity* is typically measured in terms of lethal dose concentrations (LD_{50}) in which 50 percent of the test population will die from exposure to a particular substance under prescribed conditions. LD_{50} toxicity measurements have been standardized on the basis of whether the contact is by ingestion, inhalation, or skin and are generally accepted by the scientific community as reliable indicators.

Long-term exposure, or *chronic toxicity,* measurements are not nearly as standardized as acute toxicity measurements. The inability to maintain humans and other mammals under long-term controlled test conditions makes reliable chronic measurements virtually impossible. The scientific community is faced with having to subjectively relate acute toxicity data to expectations in chronic cases. Testing of short-lived laboratory animals is often used to develop information on chronic toxicity. Based upon life expectancy, these laboratory animal data are then studied for possible relationships to humans and other mammals.

Exposure to radiation may cause severe acute and chronic health hazards. Such exposure to radioactivity has been shown to have potential carcinogenic, teratogenic, or mutagenic effects if improperly managed. On the other hand, the human population has benefited significantly from the use of radioactive materials in the medical community, in biological fields, and in the electrical power industry, and properly managed, these benefits can far outweigh the potential risks.

Infectious wastes contaminated with disease-producing substances or agents can also be hazardous to human health and the environment, creating hazards to personnel who handle their disposal as well as to the general public. At the same time, it is generally recognized that disease-causing organisms are everywhere in our environment, being present at various levels in all substances. The medical field itself is the major producer of these hazardous wastes, which are inevitable by-products of numerous beneficial advances in science. In any event, the disposal of medical hazardous wastes must always be done in such a manner so as not to endanger human health or the environment.

Toxic properties are also evident in irritants that produce roughened, reddened, or inflamed skin. Proper management of such wastes is necessary to minimize human contact wherever possible, and medically recognized procedures should be followed if such contact does occur.

Bioaccumulation of less than toxic levels of wastes can, upon chronic exposure, exceed the threshold level and create a hazard to human health. Some toxic substances can be concentrated in a single organism and be passed through the food chain.[4] Heavy metals such as mercury and lead and a few select hydrocarbons such as polychlorinated biphenyls (PCBs) and carbon tetrachloride are known to bioaccumulate in human beings. Hence proper management of these wastes is necessary to avoid their release into the environment.

Some hazardous wastes may alter the genetic base of humans and other mammals. Such wastes produce a variation in organisms that could have long-term adverse effects on human health and the environment. The potency of hazardous wastes to alter genetic activity, either from acute or chronic exposure, has not been quantified. In most if not all incidences of such exposure though, it is reasonable to assume the existence of some threshold value which triggers an appropriate adverse response. Lack of consistent exposure data on laboratory animals and the difficulty of obtaining reliable data regarding human exposure have made this area of hazardous waste management highly controversial within the scientific community.

Figure 5-1 presents a model of the threshold theory. This theory holds that exposure to low concentrations of chemical substances is not harmful to human health until some threshold exposure level has been exceeded. It even can be argued that prior to achieving such a threshold level, trace amounts of otherwise hazardous inorganics such as certain heavy metals can be highly ben-

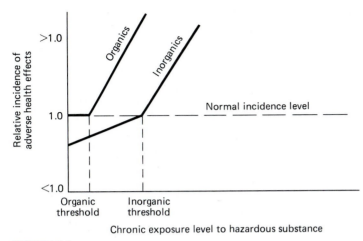

FIGURE 5-1
Threshold theory of long-term exposure to toxic substances.

eficial in diets of humans and other mammals. But the threshold theory is not universally accepted. For instance, the Delaney Amendment, which forbids the addition of any known carcinogen to food products in even the lowest concentrations, argues implicitly against it.

THE CRITERIA APPROACH TO DESIGNATING HAZARDOUS WASTES

The threshold theory offers a quantitative methodology that compares hazardous waste characteristics to a predetermined threshold value. If the threshold is violated, the waste is designated as hazardous. This technique based on intrinsic properties may be applied to all present and future wastes, though it is easily seen that it is more costly to administer because of the considerable laboratory work required in testing wastes. And testing for chronic exposure in most situations is prohibitive in cost.

The responsibility for determining if a particular waste is hazardous falls on the generators. They must either test their waste using standard methods or have sufficient knowledge about their waste to assess whether it exhibits any of the characteristics used to define a hazardous waste. The tests must be done with representative samples to obtain results that adequately characterize the nature of the waste.

If the waste does exhibit one of the four characteristics established by EPA, then it is hazardous and must be handled accordingly. Tests must be applied to each individual waste and cannot be used to assess a type of waste other than to define the waste generically as hazardous. This provision was established to prevent a company with several locations from making one waste determination locally and using that result nationwide to mask potential regional variations.

EPA-DESIGNATED HAZARDOUS WASTES

Use of the RCRA criteria of extrinsic characteristics in identifying hazardous wastes has been supplemented by publication of official lists of designated hazardous wastes. The designation procedure used by EPA has involved risk assessment techniques described in Chapter 2. The EPA lists (see Appendixes B, C, and D) contain numerous examples of hazardous wastes that require careful handling and treatment in a cradle-to-grave management system. This listing of hazardous waste has greatly simplified the identification and enforcement procedures for all concerned parties, giving generators and regulatory authorities alike a clear understanding of the status of all waste materials. A listed waste may be categorized without costly laboratory testing. But the lists pose problems too. They may be so well-defined that they become inflexible and cannot accommodate special situations on a case-by-case basis. Another drawback involves their currency; generation of new wastes, pontentially hazardous, means either constantly revising the lists or else compromising their integrity.

Three lists of specific hazardous wastes have been promulgated by EPA:

1 *Nonspecific source wastes (Appendix B)*: These are generic wastes, commonly produced by manufacturing and industrial processes. Examples from this list include spent halogenated solvents used in degreasing and wastewater treatment sludge from electroplating processes.[5]

2 *Specific source wastes (Appendix C)*: This list consists of wastes from specifically identified industries such as wood preserving, petroleum refining, and organic chemical manufacturing. These wastes typically include sludges, still bottoms, wastewaters, spent catalysts, and residues, e.g., wastewater treatment sludge from the production of pigments.[6]

3 *Commercial chemical products (Appendix D)*: The third list consists of specific commercial chemical products or manufacturing chemical intermediates. This list includes chemicals such as chloroform and creosote, acids such as sulfuric acid and hydrochloric acid, and pesticides such as DDT and Kepone.[7]

EPA developed these lists by (1) examining different types of wastes and chemical products to see if they exhibited one of the characteristics of a hazardous waste, (2) met the statutory definition of hazardous waste, (3) were acutely toxic or acutely hazardous, and/or (4) were otherwise toxic.

One of the questions that EPA faced when setting the conditions for identifying hazardous wastes was how to classify a waste mixture that contains both a listed hazardous waste and a nonhazardous waste. EPA decided that any waste mixture containing a listed hazardous waste should be considered a hazardous waste and should be managed accordingly. This applies regardless of what percentage of the waste mixture is composed of listed hazardous wastes. Without such a regulation, generators could evade RCRA Subtitle C requirements simply by commingling listed wastes with nonhazardous waste. Most of these waste mixtures would not be caught by Subtitle C because they would contain wastes which lacked the specific characteristics cited by EPA, yet which should be listed for other reasons—e.g., they are acutely toxic. Allowing this situation would leave a major loophole in the Subtitle C management system and create unacceptable inconsistencies.

There are, however, a few exceptions permitted to the mixture rule outlined above:

If a wastewater discharge subject to regulation by the Clean Water Act is mixed with low concentrations of a listed waste, the resultant mixture is not considered a listed hazardous waste. Of course, if such a mixture exhibited one of the four EPA-designated characteristics, it would nevertheless be deemed hazardous.

Mixtures of nonhazardous wastes and wastes listed because they exhibited one of the characteristics are not considered hazardous if the mixture no longer exhibits any of the characteristics.

Congress decided that certain types of waste should not be considered "hazardous" under Subtitle C. These include a number of common wastes that either do not present a significant threat to human health or the environment or else are currently managed under other programs in a way that minimizes any threat. The exempted categories include household wastes, municipal resource recovery wastes, agricultural wastes, and mining overburden returned to the mine site. EPA added to this list certain chromium-containing wastes and laboratory samples.

In 1980 Congress temporarily excluded oil and gas wastes, mining wastes, waste from the combustion of coal or other fossil fuels, and cement-kiln-dust waste. To find out if these wastes should be regulated at all, Congress directed EPA to conduct studies and report on whether the results indicated that the wastes should be regulated under Subtitle C. Since then EPA has generally recommended that these large-volume wastes continue to be excluded from regulation under Subtitle C.

EPA recognized that its procedures for listing hazardous wastes might not be applicable in all cases. To provide for these cases, the agency created a process called *delisting* that allows any person—whether waste handler or member of the general public—to petition EPA to exclude a listed waste from regulation under Subtitle C. For a petitioner to get a waste delisted he or she must prove to EPA that the waste is not hazardous because of facility-specific variations in raw materials, processes, or other factors. In evaluating a delisting petition, EPA considers factors including constituents other than those for which the waste was listed, if there is reason to believe that such additional factors could cause the waste to be hazardous. If, upon evaluation, it is determined that because of conditions at the facility the waste is not hazardous, that waste is removed from the Subtitle C regulatory jurisdiction. It is important to note that delisting is done on a case-by-case basis. Therefore, if a waste is delisted at one facility, it is not automatically delisted at other facilities.

Early in the development of the RCRA program, EPA recognized that the hazardous waste regulations would impose a substantial burden on the regulated community. Further, it recognized that if all small generators were brought entirely within the Subtitle C regulatory system, their numbers would far outstrip the resources available to achieve effective implementation of the program. Thus, in issuing waste regulations, the EPA first focused on large generators who produce the greatest portion of hazardous waste. The initial EPA regulations, published on May 19, 1980, exempted small-quantity generators (SQGs) from most of the hazardous waste requirements. A *small-quantity generator* was defined as a

Generator who produced less than 1000 kg of hazardous waste at a site per month (or accumulated less than 1000 kg at any one time)

Generator who produced less than 1 kg of acutely hazardous waste per month (or accumulated less than 1 kg at any one time)

Concern subsequently arose that hazardous wastes exempted from regulation because of the SQG exclusion might be causing environmental harm. Therefore in the Hazardous and Solid Waste Amendments of 1984 (HSWA), Congress amended the definition of a SQG, reducing the cutoff point from 1000 kg to 100 kg. Thus the new definition establishes the SQG as a

Generator who produces less than 100 kg of hazardous waste at a site per month (or accumulates less than 100 kg at any one time)

Generator who produces less than 1 kg of acutely hazardous waste per month (or accumulates less than 1 kg at any one time)

These small-quantity generators do have to meet some minimum management requirements; for instance, they have to test their waste, store the waste properly, and dispose of it at approved facilities. SQGs are also required to maintain the same records as the larger hazardous waste generators, obtain an EPA permit number, and use the EPA standard manifest form.

ASSESSMENT OF HAZARDOUS SITES

In determining the risk presented by a potentially hazardous waste site, it is necessary to perform a site assessment. These site assessments must determine the source of contamination, provide a qualitative characterization of the transport mechanisms by which the contaminants are migrating, and determine the consequences likely to be associated with the contaminants and their effect on human health and the environment. Initially, the site assessment process must determine the location, the quantities, and the sources of public contamination. This information might be found in industry and government records. (It should be noted, however, that prior to 1970 such data were generally not maintained by operators of hazardous waste disposal facilities.)

Once the existing records have been studied, additional information will usually be needed and must be obtained to complete the assessment. A visit to the site to be assessed is necessary to conduct actual field sampling and analysis. Field sampling is generally accomplished by drilling core holes in the site area. A well-designed pattern of core holes along with subsequent core analysis will help reveal and confirm the dimensions and quantities of hazardous waste present at the site. It should be noted that core sampling is both expensive and may be hazardous to operators. To lessen the potential exposure of personnel to hazardous waste, remedial site operators rely heavily on geophysical techniques that were developed primarily for geological surveys and for oil and gas exploration.

It is extremely important to properly select representative sampling locations and obtain an appropriate number of samples to ensure representative data. If the sample locations are improperly selected, the data obtained will produce erroneous information about both the level of the contamination and its distribution throughout the site. The more heterogeneous the site, from a topographical and geological viewpoint, the more complex the site sampling program. A sufficient budget must be provided to ensure an accurate picture of the site contamination during the assessment program, since major dollar expenditures for remedial site cleanup depend on the accuracy of the site assessment program.

The following case study illustrates the complexity and the need for accurate site assessment information so as to allow sound management decisions regarding hazardous waste site remediation. It is adapted from a case study by the U.S. Environmental Protection Agency.[2]

CASE STUDY
PCB Contamination at GE

The General Electric site occupied about 24 acres in an area in the southwest section of Oakland, California, which is east of San Francisco Bay. An estimated 20,000 gallons of polychlorinated biphenyls (PCBs) and petroleum-based oil were spilled onto the property at various times during the production and repair of transformers from 1927 to the late 1970s. PCB-oil was found on-site in soils at various depths and within subsurface sand and gravel lenses. Of the initial 12 on-site monitoring wells sampled, two were found to contain PCBs in the water at levels of 0.63 and 15.0 ppb. PCB-contaminated groundwater was not found off-site, but the large volume of the PCBs on-site caused concern within state agencies about the off-site migration potential. Virtually all unpaved soil in the storage and loading areas had PCB concentrations of greater than 5 ppm, and in some locations 11,000 ppm PCBs were found.

Background

Spills, leaks, and disposal of PCB-contaminated material occurred throughout a 50-year period at the Oakland GE site. Use of the insulating fluid Pyranol, consisting of equal portions of PCBs (Aroclor 1260) and trichlorobenzenes, be-

gan in the early 1930s and peaked in the mid-1950s. In 1968 transformer production at the site ceased, and thereafter only a minimal amount of Pyranol
was used on-site in the repair of transformers. The use of PCBs at the facility
was terminated in 1975, when the last drum of Pyranol was delivered.

Sources of site contamination during the 50-year period included:

Leaks in tanks that sometimes went undetected
Trench burial of liquid PCBs and contaminated solids
Pyranol spills from a mobile filtering unit
Discharges from a lab sink that emptied onto the ground

The total amount of Pyranol beneath the site was estimated at about 20,000
gallons in 1979 when a complaint from a GE employee about mishandling of
PCBs brought the attention of the California Department of Health Services to
the situation. Subsequent discoveries led to a site study by GE and the immediate mitigation measures that followed.

Site Description

The site is located in a coastal region characterized by subdued topography.
Elevations across the site range from 20 feet on the northeast boundary at East
14th Street to approximately 8 feet along the northwest boundary with the
railroad line (Figure 5-2). In general, the drainage across the site is southerly,
with surface runoff eventually emptying into San Francisco Bay. The entire
GE facility was located within a 100-year floodplain, with flooding a result of

FIGURE 5-2
GE facility in Oakland, California.

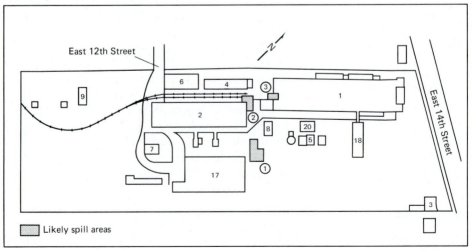

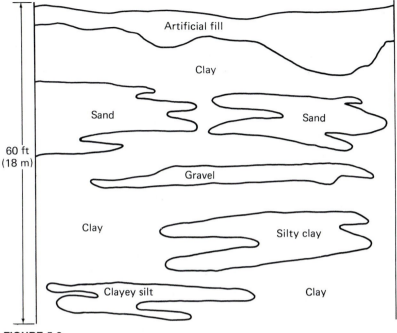

60 ft
(18 m)

FIGURE 5-3
Typical geological cross section of the GE site.

runoff from high-intensity precipitation in the Berkeley Hills to the east. The facility property was bounded on the southwest and southeast by industrial development. The northwest and northeast sides were bounded by residential and commercial properties, respectively.

The native soils on-site consisted of dense alluvial deposits of silt and clay materials. Overlying the native soil across much of the site was artificial fill composed of a mixture of sand, gravel, building debris, and crushed rock. This fill material ranged up to 5 feet in depth.

On-site stratigraphy is a complex sequence of tightly packed silty clay and sand and gravel lenses. The depth to the nearest aquifer is 230 feet. A typical geologic cross section of the site area to a depth of 60 feet is shown in Figure 5-3.

To simplify the discontinuous nature of the strata beneath the site for the purpose of calculating average vertical and horizontal permeabilities and groundwater flow rates, the groundwater flow system in the area was defined as a single homogeneous unit extending to a depth of 60 feet. The average vertical permeability for material between 0 to 60 feet was found to be 5×10^{-8} cm/s. The average horizontal permeability was established at 3×10^{-4} cm/s. Nearly all groundwater flow appeared to be occurring horizontally, with the average flow velocity in the range of 5×10^{-4} and 5×10^{-3} cm/s. The direction of groundwater flow within the upper 60 feet of material tended to be away from a groundwater mound identified at the northernmost corner of the tank farm (seen in Figure 5-4). Large fluctuations had been noted in levels of the groundwater mound between December (dry season) and April (rainy season). It is likely that the mound had been produced by collection of rainfall in the diked tank farm area, followed by slow infiltration.

Groundwater levels in the site area varied between approximately 5 and 30 feet below the ground surface. The shallowest groundwater levels were identified in the southwest area of the site, while much deeper groundwater levels were found in the northern section. The amount of infiltration directly affected groundwater levels across the site area, the difference being attributed to surface coverage by either buildings or asphalt pavement.

Operations History at the Site

The General Electric Oakland facility began operating in 1927 and underwent numerous modifications during its history. One of the more critical expansions at the facility, coming in 1930, involved the installation of two aboveground

FIGURE 5-4
Groundwater flow at the GE site.

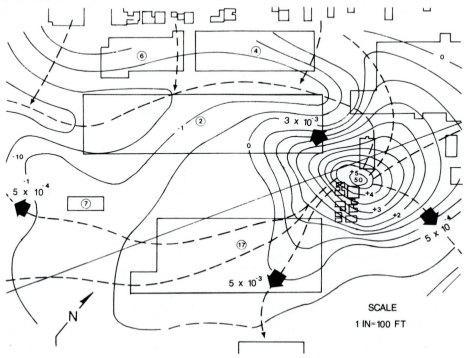

tanks for the storage of Pyranol. The growth of the Pyranol-filled-transformer market paralleled the growth of industry in the region. However, as the Oakland facility's total capacity increased over the years, the levels of Pyranol usage there actually decreased, largely because of increased efficiency in the manufacturing process. The production of Pyranol-containing transformers was finally terminated at the Oakland plant in 1968. However, the facility continued to service units under warranty until the transformer manufacturing plant was closed in 1975.

Monsanto was the facility's sole Pyranol supplier. Their shipments of Pyranol to GE between 1954 and 1975 varied from a high of 9245 gallons in 1959 to a low of 55 gallons in 1975. During the operation, Pyranol was pumped from 5000-gallon tank cars into the two 5000-gallon aboveground storage tanks. From these tanks the Pyranol was transported through an underground system to the rear of building 1 (Figure 5-2). After 1975 the Pyranol tanks were used for waste oil storage; the tank farm itself, located near the northern corner of building 17, consisted of 11 tanks when the facility closed down in 1975. Three of those had been used for a petroleum-based thinner and the remaining eight held mineral oil.

Over the years, disposal of both solid and liquid wastes had taken place at the facility. Prior to 1940 when the facility manufactured a number of products, a significant amount of solid waste resulted from the production of motors. This waste accumulated and was eventually buried in a trench that was excavated in the general vicinity of what is presently building 17, area 1, and in a second trench in area 2. The burial of solid waste ceased in the mid-1960s.

Liquid waste at this facility consisted primarily of waste mineral and Pyranol oils. Area 3 received small quantities of both mineral and Pyranol oils, as they were both brought to the quality control laboratory for testing. The laboratory sinks, into which oil samples were emptied, initially drained into a septic tank. However, this septic tank eventually collapsed and the sink then drained directly onto the ground surface. This practice ceased in the early 1960s when 55-gallon drums were provided for test sample disposal.

The main location where most waste oils were disposed of was a trench between areas 1 and 2. The trench was excavated in the late 1940s for the purpose of waste burial after attempts to burn mineral and other waste oil in plant boilers were unsuccessful. But waste oil burial practices ceased in the early 1950s when it became plant policy to store the oil in drums and tanks and sell it regularly to oil disposal contractors. Until the mid-1950s, there was no attempt made to separate the Pyranol from the waste mineral oil. The waste oils were accumulated together in tanks and drums located in the tank farm. Then around 1955, the disposal contractors asked that the two types of oils be kept separate and GE agreed to the request.

Liquid waste spills most likely occurred where the waste oil was handled, i.e., pumped, filtered, or transferred, in significant volumes. Three areas where these types of activities were undertaken, shown in Figure 5-2, are described below.

Area 1 comprised the tank farm. It was a diked, unpaved enclosure which consisted of 11 tanks and associated pumping, mixing, and filtering equipment. This was the area where the majority of the spills occurred.

Area 2 included the ground surface in vicinity of the two 5000-gallon Pyranol tanks and the forward end of the pit where rail tank cars were unloaded by pumping.

Area 3 consisted of the northwest end of building 1, the least likely area to have had significant oil spills. However, minor leakage could have occurred during operations inside the building.

The Problem Surfaces

On July 20, 1979, a representative from the Hazardous Materials Management Section of the California Department of Health Services (DHS) visited the GE facility in response to a complaint made by a GE employee concerning improper handling of PCBs at the site. At that time, the DHS representative found no reason to believe PCBs were being mishandled. The GE employee who initially contacted the DHS was not satisfied with this conclusion and requested that a second inspection be conducted. Ten days later, the field inspector from the DHS conducted a second inspection of the Oakland facility. This time soil samples of two oily areas were found to have 63 and 170 $\mu g/g$ PCB. Upon interviewing the plant manager, who had worked at the site since the late 1940s, the DHS representative learned that no Pyranol was presently stored in bulk. Two 1000-gallon tanks had once been used to store Pyranol on the east side of building 2, but they had been removed in 1976.

Because soil samples collected across the site had indicated the presence of PCBs, the DHS directed GE, in a November 29, 1979, letter, to remove all PCB-contaminated soil from the site for disposal at a landfill.

In January 1980, GE hired Brown and Caldwell Consulting Engineers to assess the problem. That firm conducted a four-part investigation:

1 In a preliminary investigation the operational history of the facility was developed, existing geotechnical information was reviewed, and the regulatory agencies involved were identified.

2 An ensuing field investigation yielded soil and groundwater samples that established a three-dimensional distribution of on-site PCBs.

3 Laboratory analyses of samples collected in the field investigation followed.

4 In the final phase, evaluation of contamination problems took place and several corrective programs were suggested.

As a result of the Brown and Caldwell study, it became apparent to both GE and the state that the contamination problem at the site was more extensive than had been initially believed and would require more than soil removal. On December 5, 1980, the state of California issued a Cleanup and Abatement Order (CAO), which directed GE to (1) reduce PCB oils and oily material and other wastes on the site; (2) provide additional data on the contamination by January 1981; (3) submit a plan to control and remove the oil and to contain runoff; and (4) submit a long-term mitigation plan for final site cleanup.

Investigation
Phases I and II

In accordance with the CAO, the site was divided into three areas, based on the type and extent of contamination, and two investigative phases were initiated. Phase I entailed predominantly surface sampling techniques, such as shallow soil borings and seismic refraction. Surface sampling, however, did not adequately define the extent of contamination in the three areas. Areas 2 and 3 required additional investigative work (phase II). This second investigation involved deeper sampling and use of multicased wells and borings. Figure 5-5 shows the soil boring and monitoring well locations for both investigative phases within the three areas previously identified in Figure 5-2.

In area 1, surface PCB concentrations ranged between 0.1 and 220 ppm. The higher PCB levels were restricted to pockets near the surface and generally decreased to nondetectable levels by a depth of 5 feet.

The contamination in area 2 was much more extensive. PCB concentrations generally ranged from 0.33 to 1900 ppm; however, "hot spots" with concentration levels up to 14,000 ppm were identified. All concentrations generally decreased with increasing depth. In addition to surface and subsurface soil contamination, area 2 contained high concentrations of PCBs in the form of free oil located beneath the water table at the clay-sand interface. Oil contamination existed in shallow-to-intermediate soils up to 32 feet beneath the tank farm. The total quantity of oil in the contaminated area was estimated to be 20,000 gallons, with the oil layer in monitoring wells being a maximum of 8 inches thick. The extent of the oil plume is shown in Figure 5-5.

Following the first field investigation, the extent of PCB contamination in area 3 was estimated. Subsurface PCB contamination within the saturated soil zone was identified in the southern portion of the area.

The state concurred that additional data would be necessary in order to fully define the problems in both areas 2 and 3. The information needed on site conditions would be required during a phase II field investigation, which was to be restricted to these two areas. The phase II field activities involved the installation of additional groundwater monitoring wells and the collection of both additional groundwater and soil samples.

In the vicinity of building 7, detectable PCB concentrations decreased to nondetectable levels (\1 ppb) at a depth of 15 feet.

Along the northern boundary of the site, near building 4, the maximum PCB concentration level identified was 510 ppm. Near buildings 17 and 2, detectable PCB concentrations extended to a depth of 35 feet, but levels were less than 1 ppm below 10 feet.

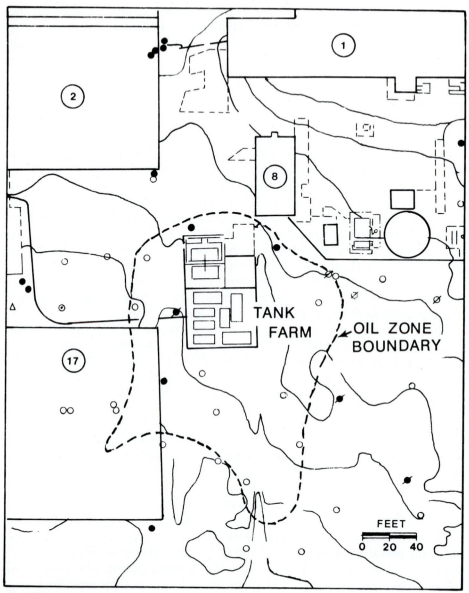

FIGURE 5-5
Locations of soil borings and monitoring wells.

The highest PCB concentrations measured during the phase II investigations were from soils located between buildings 1 and 2. From the ground surface to a depth of 11.5 feet, values of 3800 to 5500 ppm were measured. Between 15 and 25 feet concentrations ranged from 900 to 1400 ppm, and below 33 feet concentration values decreased to nondetectable levels. In addition to defining the extent of surface and subsurface soil contamination, results from the phase II activities confirmed the extent of the free oil plume presented in Figure 5-5.

Groundwater samples were collected and analyzed from monitoring wells during both phase I and phase II field investigations. The samples were analyzed for PCB, oil, and grease using the Freon extractable method. If a sample was found to have detectable PCB levels (>0.3 ppb), it was filtered to remove suspended solids and reanalyzed. Because PCBs in oil tend to absorb onto fine-grained soil particles, the removal of suspended solids ensures that the detected PCB concentrations are within the fluid itself and not a result of PCB absorption onto suspended solids.

In addition, fluid samples collected were analyzed for all isomers of dichlorobenzene, trichlorobenzene, and tetrachlorobenzene. The resulting concentrations from the chlorobenzene analyses ranged from nondetectable (<0.001 ppm) to 11.7 ppm.

Final PCB analyses conducted on groundwater samples collected from areas 2 and 3 during the phase I investigation revealed nondetectable concentrations after filtering. PCB analyses conducted on samples collected during the phase II study revealed unfiltered PCB concentrations ranging from 0.36 to 1.8 ppb. Filtered concentrations were all less than the detectable limit of 0.3 ppb. Oil and grease concentrations ranged from 6 to 10 ppm.

The field investigations concerning the extent of groundwater contamination concluded that (1) detectable concentrations of PCBs were not in the groundwater and (2) the vertical migration of PCBs in shallow soils was insignificant.

Regulatory Considerations

In the November 29, 1979, letter, the California State Department of Health Services directed GE "to remove all PCB contaminated soil...to a Class I disposal site for immediate burial" and to sample the site area to determine the extent of contamination. This directive to excavate and remove the PCB-contaminated soil was made because under state law PCBs are defined as an extremely hazardous waste, and the law requires that "any hazardous material disposed of to the land, accidentally discharged to land or accidentally spilled on to the land be managed as a hazardous waste." After reaching an agreement with the DHS on an engineering survey plan, GE retained Brown and Caldwell in January 1980 to prepare a detailed problem definition and correction plan. Their draft report dated June 1980 found a much larger volume of contaminated soil than was initially expected. For this reason the June 1980 report discussed a variety of site response options, aside from excavation, including the immediate correction plan eventually carried out. It consisted of installation of a French drain and treatment system and surface sealing with runoff control.

Aside from the legal mandate on hazardous waste disposal that compelled the state to issue the directive to GE, there were three general reasons for the state to seek action at the site. There was concern about:

The migration potential of the PCB oil under the tank farm

Direct contact by workers with contaminated surface soil

A potential threat to surface waters and water resources in the San Francisco Bay Area, since a dry soil sample from an on-site drainage ditch with 100-ppm PCB portended bioaccumulation in edible shellfish in the bay

In their December 5, 1980, Cleanup and Abatement Order, the DHS noted that there were "surface and subsurface soil and water contamination with PCBs...which create a serious threat of contamination to surface and ground waters of the State, to aquatic life and to public health." The site cleanup activities were accomplished in 1981.

The Biocraft Laboratories case study that follows provides another illustration of site assessment and the way leaking underground storage tanks can pollute both surface water and groundwater. It is adapted from a case study by the U.S. Environmental Protection Agency.[2]

CASE STUDY
The Biocraft Spill

Biocraft Laboratories is a small synthetic penicillin manufacturing plant located on a 4.3-acre site in an industrial park in the town of Waldwick, New Jersey. Sometime between 1972, when the plant opened, and 1975, when the pollution problem was discovered, two pipes leading from the plant to underground waste solvent storage tanks leaked their contents into the ground, contaminating an area 360 feet × 90 feet × 10 feet thick. The waste solvents seeped into a storm sewer, which flowed into a nearby creek, and also contaminated a shallow aquifer. The town's drinking water well was less than a quarter mile away from the site and drew from a deep aquifer. City officials were concerned that the high level of pollution would eventually contaminate the well, and local health officials suspected the spill was responsible for a fish kill in a pond fed by the contaminated creek.

Background

As noted above, sometime over a 3-year span between 1972 and 1975 two pipes connecting underground waste solvent storage tanks belonging to

Biocraft leaked an undetermined amount of butanol, acetone, and methylene chloride into the ground. The amount of leaked waste solvents is unknown, but it could have been as much as 33,000 gallons, assuming that the gauging system would not have detected less than 50 gallons per transfer of lost solvent and that about 660 transfers were made prior to discovery of the problem. The waste solvent traveled through a storm sewer that ran through and in front of the site and led into Hohokus Brook, a tributary of Allendale Brook. Wastes from Biocraft were suspected of having been responsible for a 1973 fish kill in a pond into which Hohokus Brook empties. The mayor of Waldwick was concerned about the lack of a report from the Fish and Game Commission about the fish kill and about the health of the children who played in the brook.

In the spring of 1975 the director of the Northwest Bergen Regional Health Commission (NWBRHC) called the New Jersey Department of Environmental Protection (DEP) to report an "Obviously...degraded ecological condition" in Allendale Brook and its tributary.

On June 2, 1975, a representative of the Passaic-Hackensack Basin Element of the DEP and two NWBRHC officials performed a preliminary investigation of the Biocraft site for possible discharges into the Hohokus. A storm sewer was reported to be discharging contaminants into the brook, based on observations of "a strong pungent odor...in the brook and in the sewer pipe" and a "grayish-black growth covering the entire bed of the tributary down to its junction with Allendale brook" and coating the inside of the storm sewer. The odor and discharge flow were traced back to the storm sewer junction leading from the Biocraft plant site; a water sample was taken at the junction. An inspection of the storm sewer grates showed no discernible flow above the pipe leading from Biocraft. And a dye test of the sanitary-industrial waste sewer revealed no leaks into the storm sewer, nothing to suggest the presence of an underground leak or an unknown connection. It was a study subsequently performed by Biocraft's consultant that revealed that a leak in the lines to underground waste solvent storage tanks was responsible for the discharge.

Site Description

The Biocraft site, as shown in Figure 5-6, is located in a small industrial park in the Borough of Waldwick, Bergen County, New Jersey. The Biocraft property is about 4.3 acres in size and lies in a relatively flat area with slopes from 0 to 3 percent. The original topography of the surrounding area has been somewhat modified by regrading for buildings, parking lots, and streets. Three basic soil types were found to occur in the vicinity: gravelly loam, silt loam, and muck. Drainage for these soil types ranges from very good to poor. Ponded areas, indicating shallow groundwater, were observed near the southern property boundary.

The western property boundary was located about 350 feet east of a small creek that flows toward the southwest. The creek received storm-water runoff from the Biocraft site and from other plant sites in the industrial park before

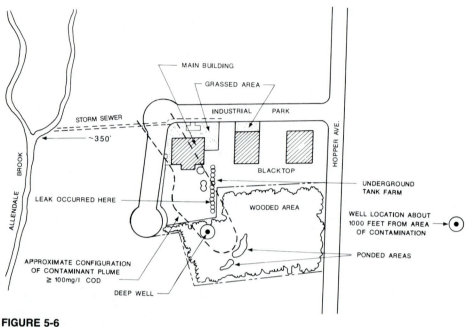

FIGURE 5-6
The Biocraft site.

emptying into Allendale Brook, which drains into Hohokus Creek. Allendale Brook and Hohokus Creek are designated by the state of New Jersey as "FW-2 Nontrout, suitable for potable, industrial, and agricultural water supply; primary contact recreation; and maintenance, migration, and propagation of natural and established biota." A municipal groundwater well was located about 1000 feet southeast of the contaminated area. Biocraft also operated a deep well to supply water to their chemical manufacturing operation; the well was directly under the contaminant plume.

The Biocraft facility is located in an area of unstratified and stratified drift deposited by the glaciers during the Pleistocene Epoch of the Quaternary Period. Figure 5-7 shows a geologic column of the underlying substrate at the site. Thin layers of silt and gravel found at the surface can be up to 3 feet thick in the area, presumably because of earlier stream deposition. In addition, regraded soils due to construction activities can be found near the surface.

Glacial till underlies the surface at a thickness of about 3 to 15 feet. It is a poorly sorted mixture of boulders, cobbles, pebbles, sand, silt, and clay. Some stratification occurs within the till layer because of glacial meltwater deposition, which is believed to have caused large permeability differences around the site. Permeabilities (hydraulic conductivities) have been calculated for five monitoring wells from slug tests and have been found to range from 0.02 to 36 gal/(day)(ft^2).

0–3 ft* silt and gravel

3–15 ft glacial till
          and stratified drift

40 ft* semiconsolidated
       silt and fine sand

>60 ft* Brunswick shale

* Formation Thickness

FIGURE 5-7
Geologic column for the Biocraft site.

Approximately 40 feet of semiconsolidated silt and fine sand underlies the till layer. Visual inspection of the material in this deposit suggests very low permeability, but no actual testing was conducted on this strata. This formation was considered to be an aquiclude.

Brunswick shale of the Triassic Newark Group underlies the site at a depth of 50 to 60 feet and has a thickness of several hundred feet. The Brunswick formation is the primary water supply aquifer for the area, yielding an average of 125 gal/min for 29 wells in the area, with an average well depth of 320 feet. Primary groundwater flow occurs in the interconnecting fractures, vertical joints, and faults in the shale, while little or no yield is obtained in the rock. Most of the wells of substantial yield have been drilled to great depths in order to contact a sufficient amount of water-bearing fractures.

Groundwater elevations, flow rates, and directions were calculated by Geraghty & Miller, Inc., in March 1979. Twenty-two wells with continuous level recorders were used to define the groundwater regime. As can be seen from Figure 5-8, groundwater flow is somewhat irregular in this area, being affected by heterogeneous geology, surface cover, and possibly other factors. The configuration is not constant but can change substantially with the season and the amount of precipitation.

A noticeable groundwater mound is present, corresponding to the south and east ends of the blacktopped area. This has been explained by the consulting geologists to be an area of groundwater recharge due to higher relative permeabilities in the area of well 22 and to surface characteristics conducive to recharge.

Groundwater flow from the mound is omnidirectional, with the major flow regimes moving toward the northwest, northeast, and south. In November 1980, the predominant flow direction was to the south, confirming the variable flow regime.

A distinct groundwater flow regime trough occurs in the northwest corner of the property, corresponding to an area of surface coverage and higher permeability. As shown by the flow direction lines in Figure 5-8, a contaminant plume emanating from the leak area would tend to flow northwest toward the trough area. It is also possible that the plume could travel toward the northeast and south, given the changing nature of the groundwater configuration and the fact that the area of subsurface leakage is inside the highest isopleth in this particular plot.

Available monitoring-well data indicate that the average groundwater depth ranges from zero to about 9 feet, depending on seasonal fluctuations. Average groundwater temperature ranges from 50 to 54°F. Groundwater velocities were

FIGURE 5-8
Groundwater elevation at the Biocraft site.

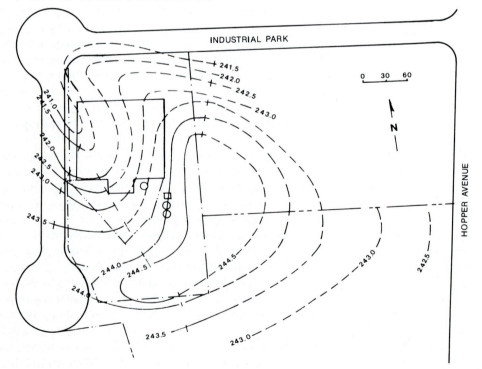

calculated by Biocraft's consultants based on the monitoring well data found at the site. Flow velocities were calculated to range from a maximum of 1.5 ft/day to a minimum of 0.0002 ft/day. Average flow velocities in the more permeable zones were calculated to average about 0.4 ft/day. This value indicates that the time required for groundwater to travel from the leak area to the eastern property boundary collection point would be about 1.5 years.

Waste Disposal History

The Biocraft facility was a bulk manufacturing plant that produced a wide variety of semisynthetic penicillin products, including 6-aminopenicillanic acid, ampicillin trihydrate, amoxicillin trihydrate, sodium oxacillin monohydrate, and sodium cloxacillin monohydrate. A number of organic and inorganic raw materials were used in the process. Organic feedstocks included potassium penicillin G, methylene chloride, n-butyl alcohol, acetone, methyldichlorosilane, dimethylaniline, ethylene glycol, and ethyl chloroformate. Inorganic chemicals used on-site include phosphorus pentachloride, liquid nitrogen, ammonium hydroxide, and hydrochloric acid.

Ten 10,000-gallon underground storage tanks were located at the southeast corner of the building. Seven tanks stored virgin and recovered n-butyl alcohol, acetone, and methylene chloride. The eighth tank held process wastewater which was periodically shipped to Earthline Services, Newark, New Jersey, for pretreatment. The ninth tank held spent solvents and centrifuge cake washings from penicillin cleavage and contained the following identified substances: acetone, methylene chloride, dimethylaniline, n-butyl alcohol, phosphorus acid, ethyl alcohol, methanol, and ammonium chloride. The tenth and last tank stored spent solvents from ampicillin processing, including acetone and methylene chloride. Stored liquids from the last two storage tanks were trucked about twice a week to Chemical Pollution Systems for solvent recovery services.

Description of Contamination

The leaking transfer line was discovered as a result of an underground tank and pipe testing program initiated by Biocraft after they were issued a Cease Administrative Order by the New Jersey Department of Environmental Protection because of the degraded condition of Allendale Brook. The leaking pipe led to storage tank 9, which held spent solvents and centrifuge cake washing liquors. It is not known when the underground line started leaking; however, an estimate of the amount of material discharged from the time the plant opened in June 1972 to November 24, 1975, the date when the lines were replaced, was made on the basis of (1) the actual number of 660 transfers to the storage tank during the above period; (2) a tank gauge accuracy of 50 gallons, i.e., discrepancies under 50 gallons could not be detected; and (3) the average

TABLE 5-2
ESTIMATED ORGANICS DISCHARGED AT THE BIOCRAFT SITE

Substance	Quantity, lb
Methylene chloride	181,500
n-butyl alcohol	66,825
Dimethylaniline	26,300
Acetone	10,890
Water and trace substances	10,890

composition of the mixture. Biocraft itself estimated quantities discharged into groundwater for the major components of the mixture; the estimates are shown in Table 5-2 and reveal that about 300,000 pounds of solvents and other organic substances may have leaked into the subsurface. The leaking transfer line was discovered as a result of an underground tank and pipe testing program initiated by Biocraft after they were issued a Cease Administrative Order by the New Jersey Department of Environmental Protection because of the degraded condition of Allendale Brook.

Trace substances included phosphorus acid, ethyl alcohol, methanol, and ammonium chloride. Other trace substances, later detected in the groundwater, which were not clearly associated with Biocraft's processes, were heptane, octane, dissobutylene, chloroform, trichloroethylene, tetrachloroethylene, benzene, toluene, m-p-xylene, and dichloroethane.

The contaminant plume flowed predominantly north and northeast toward the eastern edge of the property and the storm sewer, and also south toward the southern property boundary. Data from sampling of the flow in the sewer indicated that concentrations of methylene chloride, n-butyl alcohol, and dimethylaniline were as high as 114, 343, and 32 mg/l, respectively. Chemical oxygen demands were found to be as high as 7539 mg/l. Contaminated flow from the sewer was finally attributed to joint infiltration of grossly polluted groundwater emanating from the Biocraft site.

Six groundwater-monitoring wells were installed on-site in January 1976 under the supervision of Princeton Aqua Science. These were 2-inch well points with depths ranging from 10 to 15 feet. The maximum depth corresponds to refusal resulting from contact with the semiconsolidated layer of silt and fine sand. Monitoring data from February 1976 to June 1976 for the six wells established the ranges of concentrations of general pollutant parameters shown in Table 5-3.

In the period from June 1976 to early in 1979, 16 additional wells were installed for monitoring and selective pumping of contaminated groundwater. Geraghty & Miller used the 22 wells for its investigation of hydrology and contamination at the site. Eight of the 22 wells were drilled specifically for the Geraghty & Miller investigation early in 1979. No wells were drilled into the semiconsolidated layer of silt and fine sand, since this was not required by the NJDEP.

TABLE 5-3
RANGES OF INITIAL DATA FROM
MONITORING WELLS AT THE BIOCRAFT SITE

Parameter	Range
pH	5.2–7.5
BOD	2–21,000 mg/1
COD	8–31,000 mg/l
TOC	2–9625 mg/l
Chloride	5–6246 mg/l

Monitoring data from 1977 to 1978 indicated that chemical oxygen demand (COD) was the best parameter for showing levels of pollution in the groundwater. Geraghty & Miller plotted COD isopleths for the 1000- and 100-mg/l levels; the plots were based on levels found in the wells on March 5, 1979. Figure 5-9 shows the COD isopleths along with COD levels in the various wells. The north-south flow components of the contaminant plume are easily distinguishable from this plot. Some wells outside the main plume boundary also

FIGURE 5-9
COD isopleths and COD levels in groundwater at the Biocraft site.

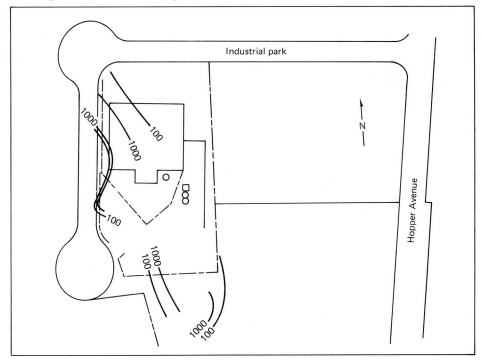

had elevated concentrations of COD. Geraghty & Miller stated that these areas were contaminated during periods when the water table had a different flow configuration.

On July 1, 1981, before the groundwater decontamination operation began, a test well was installed on-site, up-gradient from the pollution source. Chemical analysis of samples taken from this well revealed 85,000 µg/l acetone, 55,000 µg/l methylene chloride, and 648 mg/l COD.

Because of the complex nature of the contamination found at the Biocraft site, a number of treatment technologies were utilized for cleanup.

QUESTIONS

1 Describe the attributes that might be considered in defining a waste as hazardous.
2 Describe the characteristics of an RCRA hazardous waste.
3 List eight heavy metals related to the toxicity characteristic.
4 Define a toxic waste and compare that with the definition of a hazardous waste.
5 Discuss the "threshold theory" for hazardous waste toxicity.
6 What does LD_{50} mean when applied to hazardous waste?
7 How does the Delaney Amendment affect food processing?
8 Discuss criteria that you believe would be useful in developing a list of designated hazardous wastes.
9 What are the principal tasks of a site assessment plan that would be used to perform risk assessment?

BIBLIOGRAPHY

1 *Annual Handbook of ASTM Standards,* part 31, *Water,* American Society for Testing and Materials, 1987.
2 *Case Studies 1-23: Remedial Response at Hazardous Waste Sites,* U.S. Environmental Protection Agency, Washington, March 1984.
3 The Clean Water Act, PL 92-500, Section 307, 1977.
4 Erickson, M. D.: *Analytical Chemistry of PCBs,* Butterworth, Boston, 1986.
5 40 Code of Federal Regulations, Part 261.31, July 1, 1987.
6 40 Code of Federal Regulations, Part 261.32, July 1, 1987.
7 40 Code of Federal Regulations, Part 261.33, July 1, 1987.
8 *RCRA Orientation Manual,* U.S. Environmental Protection Agency, Office of Solid Waste, Washington, 1986.
9 Shields, E. J.: *Pollution Control Engineer's Handbook,* Pudvan, Northbrook, Ill., 1985.
10 *Standard Methods for the Examination of Water and Wastewater,* American Public Health Association, Washington, 1980.
11 Verschueren, K.: *Handbook of Environmental Data on Organic Chemicals,* Van Nostrand, New York, 1983.
12 Weast, R. C.: *CRC Handbook of Chemistry and Physics,* The Chemical Rubber Company, Cleveland, 1975.

WASTE MINIMIZATION AND RESOURCE RECOVERY

INTRODUCTION

Waste management is an all-encompassing term. It can be used to describe several distinct processes: the elimination or reduction of waste; the recycling or reuse of waste material; the treatment or destruction of waste, i.e., physically destroying, chemically detoxifying, or otherwise rendering waste permanently harmless; and waste disposal, or depositing the material into the air, water, or land. Environmental regulations have not necessarily channeled industry efforts toward the optimum choice of waste management techniques—waste minimization. Rather, recycling, reuse, and treatment seem to be industry's preferred waste management options, even though such methods pose more environmental risks than waste minimization.[4] Any time waste must be handled, stored, or transported, accidents can happen, threatening workers and sending hazardous wastes into the environment. Often what is called "treatment" of waste is simply removal and transfer.[5] For example, evaporation ponds and air-stripping columns used for treating liquid wastes purposefully put volatile toxic chemicals into the air, and adsorption materials used to remove toxic chemicals from liquids and gases are generally land-disposed. Statistics for industrial pollutants in waste streams sent to publicly owned water treatment plants indicate that only about half the pollutants are permanently altered. Those remaining are released into the air as volatile emissions, discharged into surface waters, or put into the land as sludge, from which they can migrate into groundwater. There are also concerns about air emissions of unregulated toxic chemicals from incineration of hazardous wastes.

Among all the techniques of waste management, waste reduction is the commonsense solution to the prevention of future hazardous waste problems.

By using materials more efficiently, industry can reduce the generation of waste and achieve the desirable protection of human health and the environment. At the same time, the costs of waste management and regulatory compliance can be lowered and long-term liabilities and risks can be minimized.[11]

But industry has generally not taken advantage of opportunities to reduce waste. There are many reasons for this. For one, reducing waste involves more than buying a black box, reading the directions, and plugging it in. Even a simple step toward waste reduction can seem difficult to a company with few technical resources. Then too, though there are clear pressures from government and the public to *reduce* waste, those pressures are not as immediate nor as compelling as the pressures to meet existing government-imposed requirements to *control* waste. The attention and resources industry must give to hazardous waste treatment necessarily limit the amount of energy, time, and money that can be devoted to hazardous waste reduction. Before industry as a whole can be moved toward all-out efforts at waste reduction, it must be seen as an attractive alternative; industry must see that waste reduction can pay for itself relatively quickly, especially when compared with the investment in time and resources needed to comply with existing programs regulating waste disposal. There are peripheral economic benefits to be realized: waste reduction can generate new waste-derived products, opening up a whole new market for a company; potential markets also exist for technical services in waste reduction, services developed by a company in managing its own waste stream.[6,1]

Federal law explicitly states that waste reduction is the preferred antipollution method, but government actions often send a different or ambiguous message to waste generators.[15,17] Currently, this country's environmental protection efforts emphasize control and cleanup of hazardous substances after they have been generated, served their purpose, and become pollutants. Such hazardous industrial wastes are often destroyed by subsequent pollution control methods, but they are also often put back into the land, water, or air where they remain to eventually disperse and migrate. The cost of controlling all of this waste involves many billions of dollars annually.[12]

As the costs of administering environmental programs and the costs of compliance mount, the economic and environmental benefits of reducing the generation of hazardous waste at its source have become more compelling. But paradoxically, it is these same regulatory requirements and the costs of complying with them that make it difficult for industry to give waste reduction the priority and resources it deserves if it is to have broad implementation. In practice, waste reduction is all too frequently subordinated to pollution control, even though reducing waste can be the most effective way to prevent environmental risk. The domination of pollution control over waste reduction is not new. It has occurred over a long period of time and it will not be reversed overnight.

GOVERNMENTAL POLICY ON WASTE REDUCTION

Federal policy in regard to waste reduction was promulgated in the 1984 amendments to RCRA:[13]

The Congress hereby declares it to be the national policy of the United States that, wherever feasible, the generation of hazardous waste is to be reduced or eliminated as expeditiously as possible.[3]

So saying, the United States government set waste reduction as the ideal waste management option. Though the concept has been universally embraced, the option has not been vigorously implemented. A look at the budget helps tell the story. EPA and state agencies together spend about $5 million annually on activities related to waste reduction. This is less than 0.1 percent of total government spending on pollution control programs. The Department of Defense, on the other hand, has committed larger sums of money for waste minimization, but DOD includes waste treatment in its definition of waste minimization, and its figures reflect that anomaly.

Historically, despite official policy, government agencies have never heavily promoted waste reduction as a method of environmental protection, though their regulatory programs have provided some indirect economic incentives for waste reduction by increasing the cost of compliance with waste management regulations and by increasing insurance costs and costs of cleaning up toxic waste sites through Superfund levies. However, these efforts have been weakened by uneven enforcement of regulatory programs and by different levels of regulation for specific wastes. And indirect incentives are not always the most effective means of encouraging attempts at waste reduction. Such incentives are not pertinent to many firms, while other firms lack the technological and economic resources to respond to them.

BENEFITS OF HAZARDOUS WASTE REDUCTION

The national debate on the environment is beginning to move away from traditional discussions about how to make pollution control regulations effective and toward discussions about how to use pollution prevention to complement pollution control.[8] Frequently, inadequate information makes it difficult for waste generators to assess the benefits of a one-time, up-front investment for waste reduction versus the costs of ongoing pollution control efforts. Because pollution control measures constitute a familiar operation, while waste reduction implies innovation—perhaps new equipment, certainly new processes—control measures seem to lend themselves more readily to cost-benefit analysis. Uncertainty and reticence on the part of industry in implementing waste reduction practices also arise because waste reduction, as a measure of materials productivity, is inevitably subordinated to other measures of the efficiency of industrial operations, such as labor productivity and energy consumption.

As a result, waste reduction, which can both save money for industry and protect the environment, is being implemented in an uneven and largely undocumented fashion. Yet those companies that have implemented waste reduction effectively see it as a way to improve profitability and competitiveness.[14,16] Statistical documentation of the amount of waste reduction that has already occurred nationwide would almost certainly remove the doubts that some representatives of industry and government have about its near-term feasibility. One of the country's leading companies, Minnesota Mining and Manufacturing Company (3M), has articulated the case for pollution prevention through waste minimization:

> Pollution controls do not solve problems. They only alter the problem, shifting it from one form to another. The form of the waste may be changed, but it does not disappear. It is apparent that conventional methods controls, at some point, create more pollution than they remove and consume resources out of proportion to the benefits derived. What emerges is an environmental paradox. It takes resources to remove pollution. Pollution removal generates residue. It takes more resources to dispose of this residue and in the process create more pollution.
>
> The combined total of 1,900 3M projects has resulted in eliminating annually the discharge of 110,000 tons of air pollutants, 13,000 tons of water pollutants, and 260,000 tons of sludge of which 18,000 tons are hazardous, along with the prevention of approximately 1.6 billion gallons of wastewater. Cost savings to 3M have been more than $292 million. These cost savings are for pollution control facilities that did not have to be built, for less pollution control operating costs, for reduced manufacturing costs, and for retained sales of products that might have been taken off the market as environmentally unacceptable.

Industry already spends significant sums on waste reduction, possibly a much greater percentage of its total environmental spending than the government figures would indicate. But waste reduction tends to lose out to waste management in the press of immediate concerns, such as siting waste management facilities, developing alternatives to land disposal, and determining safe levels of emissions. Little recognition is given to the fact that effective waste reduction methods can lessen these needs.

For companies and industries that are expanding production, waste reduction is an obvious way to offset the economic and environmental costs of managing the increasing amounts of wastes.[2] Waste reduction also minimizes the economic inefficiency of abiding by pollution control regulations that force the spending of more and more money for increasingly smaller increments of environmental protection.

Waste reduction as applied to emissions, discharges, and disposal is the best means of achieving pollution prevention.[18] However, because we now have an entrenched pollution control culture, developing a complementary environmental protection strategy based on waste reduction would represent a major shift in the thinking of most people; the shift would certainly be a substantial challenge for industry and government.

The traditional emphasis on pollution control and the viewpoint that substantial waste reduction is a long-term goal, not a realizable short-term strategy, constrain the consideration of alternatives by waste generators. Another inhibiting factor is concern about risking product quality by tinkering with or changing an industrial process solely for the purpose of reducing waste. Only slowly is American industry coming to see that waste reduction poses no inherent threat to product quality.

In order for waste reduction to be successful, it must result in an environmental benefit through the prevention of pollution and an industry cost savings that will result in an economic improvement. With both the environment and economics benefiting, all concerned parties are satisfied.

APPROACHES TO HAZARDOUS WASTE REDUCTION

Waste treatment is essentially an addition to the end of the industrial process, while *waste reduction,* or *waste minimization,* is intricately involved in all aspects of the production process. People with "end-of-pipe" pollution control jobs are not motivated to unilaterally reduce waste; such efforts must involve upstream workers and facilities, for waste reduction succeeds only when it is part of the everyday consciousness of all workers and managers involved with production rather than only of those responsible for complying with environmental regulations.

Almost all industrial processes have some potential for promoting or hindering waste reduction, but the options are rarely examined explicitly. Waste reduction is seldom seen as a criterion to measure job performance or performance in meeting government environmental requirements, developing production technologies, and setting research goals. Offering rewards and incentives for both workers and managers who find ways to reduce waste can be an especially important strategy.

Some generators believe they have already reduced their wastes as far as is feasible and view further waste reduction as a long-term ideal rather than an immediate and practical route to pursue. This appears to be primarily a consequence of resource commitment to and familiarity with pollution control rather than of any real technical constraints.

Successful waste reduction efforts have generally been a consequence of attempts to increase the efficiency of industrial operations. Most commonly, waste reduction has been a by-product, not a focus of altered industrial processes. For example, minimization of waste often comes as a result of efforts to conserve materials that may be scarce, strategic, or expensive.

Many of industry's statements about waste reduction—that there are few if any remaining waste reduction opportunities—are reminiscent of 1970s statements about industrial energy conservation. What this means is that to a significant extent, waste reduction may be blocked by individual attitudes based on limited information and experience rather than on lack of effective technology. Industrial leaders should explore many questions to determine if they have achieved optimal waste reduction in their operations.

Are managers, engineers, researchers, and workers familiar with all the technical means to reduce waste?

Have they examined all waste reduction opportunities?

Does the organization adequately reward waste reduction efforts?

Have the managers been able to see the economic value of a waste in terms of its raw material worth, its cost as a pollutant to be managed, and its potential long-term liability?

Do environmental engineers who are trained in and preoccupied with end-of-pipe management consider instead front-end process changes?

Are the engineers technically equipped to recognize waste reduction opportunities in all phases of the industrial process?

Are traditional mass balance or material balance calculations, which some companies perform to describe inputs and outputs, sensitive enough to reveal small amounts of waste that may be of economic and environmental significance?

Do managers consider reducing all wastes, even those that are currently unregulated or are being released into the environment according to the statutory limits?

There are substantial opportunities for waste reduction. The challenge is to persuade and assist most American waste generators to do what some companies have already discovered is in their own economic self-interest.

Waste reduction should be viewed as a criterion to assess all industrial processes and operations rather than as a unique type of technology, or even as a specialized field of expertise. The technological means to reduce waste are imbedded in all aspects of the production system. Therefore, the phrase "waste reduction technology," although it is convenient to use, can lead to confusion. There are several approaches to waste reduction:

Recycling a potential waste or portion of it on the site where it is generated

Improving process terminology and equipment that alter the primary source of waste generation

Improving plant operations such as better housekeeping, improved materials handling and equipment maintenance, automating process equipment, better monitoring and improved waste tracking, and integrating mass balance calculations into process design

Substituting raw materials that introduce fewer hazardous substances or smaller quantities of such substances into the production process

Redesigning or reformulating the end products

Recycling is usually the step before pollution control, which may make it the easiest option to recognize and implement.[9,10] But there are important economic limits to recycling, and many times there are other waste reduction opportunities that offer greater benefits even though they are not as easy to identify.

In spite of concerns about product quality, improvements in process technology and equipment appear to be a viable means for waste reduction. Such improvements are important because often an entire waste stream can be eliminated. This method depends, however, on the type of industry. Mature industries that use continuous processes are likely to have fewer opportunities for change in process technology, but they may still have waste reduction opportunities.

Improvements in plant operations can be accomplished by every waste generator, typically with minimal capital investment. Substantial waste reduction may be accomplished, for example, through selected raw material changes.

From the perspective of the plant operator, waste reduction efforts that require significant capital and human resources will always have to be weighed against expenditures related to pollution control requirements and against traditional corporate uses of resources to maintain or improve competitiveness and profitability. Thus, it becomes important to define and understand the technical means to implement waste reduction and to evaluate all alternatives on a cost-benefit basis.

It is difficult to generalize about what can be done technically within a specific plant at any particular time. Equipment, physical plant layout, control instrumentation, raw materials, product specifications, and volume of output may vary significantly from plant to plant, even for operations making the same product. These factors will affect the ease of implementing any specific means of waste reduction. The requirements of R&D, testing, capital investment, and time are unique from plant to plant; thus the effectiveness of any given approach to waste reduction will vary among plants, even though they may use the same process technology or produce the same product. The choice of one alternative might eliminate an entire waste stream, while in another operation it might not.

There is a fundamental antipathy in industry toward government involvement in the front end of production, where waste reduction most readily takes place. There is a strong belief that the voluntary approach to waste reduction based upon economics is the proper one. However, because any waste management facility poses environmental risks that require effective government regulation and enforcement, some believe that government ought to require waste reduction just as it requires pollution control measures. On the other hand, there are those who believe that waste reduction should remain a voluntary effort on the part of industry, that the site-specific character of waste reduction best lends itself to management by the individual waste generator. They assert that if government were to require waste reduction, it would face major difficulties in determining what is technically and economically feasible or practical for a specific industrial operation. It is recognized by all, however, that there must be a flexibility in meeting common goals, and that rigid government and industry product specifications already in place should, wherever feasible, be made more flexible to allow for product substitution and process modification that address environmental concerns.

Many in industry want to reduce wastes but do not know how to start or how to move into the complexities of implementation. Others believe that they have accomplished all the waste reduction they can and that if more opportunities present themselves they will respond in any way that is economically feasible. It is not clear whether they are considering the reduction of all hazardous wastes or only those regulated under RCRA. Often industry sees waste reduction as something that must take its own course, that will be accomplished when the time is right. This attitude has been a significant barrier to waste reduction.

PRIORITIES IN HAZARDOUS WASTE MANAGEMENT

Experience in the United States and elsewhere indicates that waste reduction is a near-term practical option, even though it is not possible to estimate accurately the upper limit of how much is technically and economically feasible. Because it is the most certain means of preventing environmental risk and because it is also preferable to most other waste management practices, leading as it does to lower direct costs and higher indirect benefits, waste reduction should be given priority over other means of waste management in industry, and the allocation of public and private resources should reflect that priority.

RCRA legislation is a clear statement of national priorities in hazardous waste management; the 1984 amendments, while emphasizing waste destruction, recognize the need to reduce the volume of hazardous waste and to recover and recycle valuable resources in the process. Such management practices are lauded as the most reasonable way to conserve the nation's supply of raw materials and at the same time to reduce the amount of hazardous pollutants that are otherwise discharged into the environment.

Under this scenario, the first priority, as shown in Figure 6-1, should be to reduce the generation of hazardous waste at the source. The ideal situation would be to completely eliminate the production of hazardous waste by what-

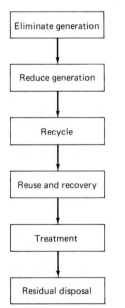

FIGURE 6-1
Hierarchy of priorities in hazardous waste management.

ever practical means possible. Since it is normally impractical to completely eliminate the production of hazardous waste from an industrial process, the minimization of waste volume is a realistic and desirable goal. A reduction in volume will lessen the environmental impact, lower the operating cost, decrease the complexity of waste management, and reduce the potential liability of the hazardous waste. Waste reduction may be accomplished through improved plant housekeeping and process control. Changes in the process itself may be possible to reduce the amount and toxicity of the wastes generated.

Though it is recognized that corporations and employees alike have been reluctant to change manufacturing processes that have historically operated well, modifications in the manufacturing operation should be seriously considered in a waste management program. Substitution of raw materials and intermediate materials in the production process has the potential to reduce, if not eliminate, many hazardous wastes. Often it may be necessary to completely redesign a process to eliminate waste generation. Economics should be the motivating factor in all of these considerations.

The needs of the marketplace also must enter into waste management decisions. Customers will be reluctant to adopt a product substitute without an economic incentive. Marketing personnel will be equally reluctant to promote a substitute product because of potential loss of an existing account.

A properly designed inventory audit can be an important part of the management information system for industrial waste materials. The inventory should list both wastes that are in storage and wastes that are being produced from operations. With such inventories, hazardous wastes should be readily identifiable and strategies more easily devised to mitigate their environmental impacts. For example, some wastes may be produced only because of occasional malfunctions beyond the normal control of operations personnel, but the repetitive production of undesirable wastes may reveal processing problems. Correction of these problems can often be accomplished with minimal investment and, at the same time, can forestall enforcement penalties for noncompliance with environmental regulations.

An inventory carefully carried out should provide the opportunity for a critical examination of plant process design and material flow that can be used to improve hazardous waste management. On the basis of this inventory, a strategic plan may be developed for the management of these wastes that will optimize both economic and environmental benefits. The facility will have an opportunity to design strategies for long-range planning based upon risk assessment of hazardous waste management. The selection of process technology and innovative techniques may then follow to allow a tradeoff between the waste management costs and generation. Raw materials that may be candidates for substitution should be identified. This inventory may also be used to study alternative methods for recycling waste streams into the process or for by-product markets. It can form the basis for industrywide technology and waste reduction and be used to quantify the potential for employee incentive programs by targeting goals in waste reduction programs. As all personnel begin to focus on the waste inventory, innovative ideas should ultimately result in the elimination or minimization of many waste streams.

DEVELOPMENT OF A TRACKING SYSTEM

A goal of waste reduction is to minimize the need for waste treatment. In contrast to waste treatment, which is essentially an addition to the end of the process, waste minimization in an industrial process requires detailed knowledge of all aspects of the specific production process. A properly designed tracking system can be an important part of a management information system. The tracking system should include an inventory of raw materials, wastes that are in storage, and wastes that are being produced from operations. Based upon this inventory, hazardous wastes should be readily identifiable and strategies can be devised to mitigate their environmental impacts. Proper utilization of a tracking system can allow personnel to focus on waste prevention or waste minimization and on the most cost-effective use of raw materials, rather than placing priority solely on waste treatment and disposal.

Tracking system designs should be dynamic and have the flexibility to change in response to changes in the need for information. In the initial stages of designing a waste minimization strategy, there typically is insufficient information on process and waste stream flows under various operating conditions. Thus, to construct an optimal waste minimization system, a somewhat intensive data collection program may be required. (It is critical in maintaining the support of the operations staff who will be affected by the data collection procedures that the tracking system designers should avoid collecting detailed data that have no apparent or relevant use in the system.) The initial data collection will provide a baseline for designing or reevaluating the objectives and procedures for the waste minimization system, and each design or reevaluation should include consideration of information from ongoing data collection.

The tracking system should provide a means to determine when changes are occurring that have an impact on quantities and types of waste generated. Processes that have frequent changes in operating parameters or in materials input may benefit economically from significantly larger data collection efforts. For processes with nearly constant operating parameters, there may be little need for collection of data beyond that necessary for initial characterization.

Disclosure statements for public companies are beginning to reflect the awareness of both shareholders and government in hazardous waste management. Tracking systems will greatly assist in compiling and reporting these statements and also trigger recognition of reporting requirements. Additionally, no corporation can afford to ignore public relations in dealing with the environmental concerns of the community. A well-designed inventory of wastes can provide management awareness of potential environmental problems before they become common knowledge. This provides management with the opportunity to make early remedial corrections to diffuse any potential community relation problems.

Waste Flow Diagram

A fundamental objective for the creation of a waste tracking system is the development of a *waste flow diagram*. Such a diagram provides a quantitative mass balance for the inputs and outputs of the process operations and is necessary to establish the basis for any meaningful waste minimization program. Without such a diagram, the final tracking system will be inaccurate and possibly inappropriate. The development of the waste flow diagram requires a thorough understanding of the process engineering, the chemical and physical properties of production materials, and the flow characteristics of the system that will be undergoing waste minimization.

Because it is highly unlikely that all of the necessary data and information for the process system to be analyzed will be initially available, a sequenced approach is recommended for developing the waste flow diagram. This approach, shown in Figure 6-2, begins with research involving operations, maintenance, environmental, procurement, and other personnel who manage the day-to-day activities of the facility. Based upon historic records, conversations with plant personnel, and site visits, an accurate qualitative flowchart can be produced that gives at least some preliminary quantitative information.

Normally, additional quantitative information must be monitored throughout the process to achieve a high level of confidence for the resulting system. This high degree of confidence will be reached with closure on the significant mass balances within the process. It will probably be necessary to conduct an additional monitoring program in order to develop the needed process information for closure of the subsequent waste management model that will be used to develop minimization alternatives. Achieving complete closure within

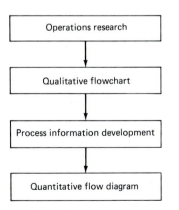

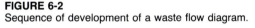

FIGURE 6-2
Sequence of development of a waste flow diagram.

the system may be so difficult and time-consuming that its attainment would not be cost-effective. Therefore, practical judgment must be exercised to maintain a reasoned approach to closure. Because development of process information could be a substantial portion of the overall tracking system, it will be necessary to educate and possibly train plant personnel to ensure their commitment to the tracking system. Obtaining this commitment requires that plant personnel understand the benefits to be gained from the information that they will be gathering. Without this commitment, it will be virtually impossible to reach closure on the waste management model.

The relationship of the flow of wastes throughout a facility should be critically examined on the basis of the process design and plant layout. Management of these wastes should focus on such a flow diagram to optimize solutions to environmental problems. This audit is particularly useful in identifying technologies and other innovative techniques for generation and cost optimization. Certain raw materials may be more likely to generate hazardous wastes and potential alternatives should be considered.

Once a reliable quantitative flow diagram—showing all incoming, intermediate, and outgoing streams at the facility—has been achieved, it forms the basis for developing the relationships within the waste management system shown in Figure 6-3. Incoming materials are obtained by procurement or purchasing per-

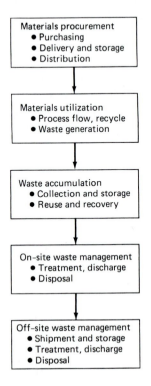

FIGURE 6-3
Relationships within the waste management system.

sonnel according to predetermined specifications and competitive economics. Following delivery, the materials are generally placed in storage vessels or warehoused, depending upon their physical and chemical properties. (The needs for tracking before and after this intermediate storage may vary significantly and may thus include separate, but compatible, systems.) The materials are then distributed from storage to be utilized in plant processes as needed.

As these incoming materials undergo physical and chemical process changes, products are created, streams are recycled, and wastes are generated. This is the critical operations area for any successful waste minimization program. The process waste that is generated is then accumulated through a collection system and placed in storage, pending further disposition. Economics should be the primary driving force in determining the potential for either reuse or recovery from the generated wastes. Some of the wastes may be reusable in the process following physical or chemical treatment. Wastes may also be further processed to be recovered as valuable by-products.

At this point in the evaluation, most of the process potential for waste minimization has been completed. The remaining steps involving waste management must focus on waste treatment to reduce the waste generated and minimize its discharge and disposal costs, whether the treatment takes place on-site or off-site.

It is of paramount importance that the waste tracking system obtain closure for each of these process steps. Innovative process engineering, based upon a reliable tracking system that scrutinizes every process step, can usually achieve significant waste minimization.

Waste Management Model

With the establishment of both the origin and quantities of the wastes and other process substances, the waste management model can now be designed, as shown in Figure 6-4. This model, which is derived from the information in Figures 6-2 and 6-3, represents the preliminary waste tracking system—a system that may reveal the need for additional data collection. This model should result in mass balances that have the general form of the following relationship:

Inputs = products + materials recovery + waste discharge + waste disposal

Mass balance relationships should be developed for each process step in the waste management model. These relationships should achieve closure, wherever it is economically practical, to reduce sources of error in the system and in the subsequent waste minimization alternatives. Using process relationships, the waste minimization system will serve as an important tool itself for collecting data necessary for the development of subsequent waste minimization alternatives and their selection for implementation, as shown in Figure 6-5. Optimal waste minimization should be a realizable objective if it is based

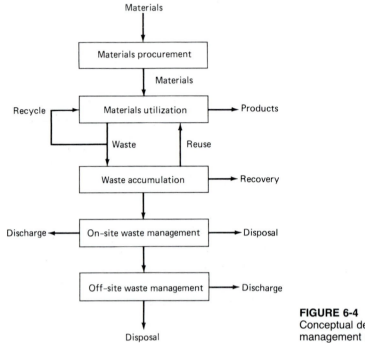

FIGURE 6-4
Conceptual design of the waste management model.

upon a sound waste tracking system. The design of this dynamic tracking system must be continually reworked to reflect process changes in the waste management model over time.

Potential Applications

The waste management model can be successfully applied to several field cases, each of which should be of general interest to the chemical engineering and environmental engineering communities. Each illustrates the principles involved in waste minimization or reduction.

The first case involves a waste management model for a lubricating oil system. The processing sequence, shown in Figure 6-6, includes shipment of the oil to the installation, utilization in vehicles and processes, and waste oil accumulation, treatment, and disposal. The treatment operations for re-refining include such processing steps as filtration followed by vacuum distillation, solvent extraction, or chemical treatment with hydrotreating. Both the vacuum distillation and solvent extraction steps generally involve the addition of clays (to remove mercaptans and other contaminants and to improve color characteristics) or acids (for extraction of metals, aromatics, asphalt, and other impurities). Typically, these re-refining processes have a product yield of 70 to 80 percent. The resulting re-refined oils perform as well as virgin oils. Treatment

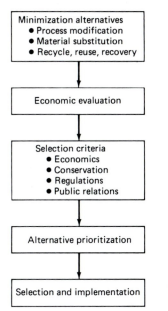

Minimization alternatives
- Process modification
- Material substitution
- Recycle, reuse, recovery

↓

Economic evaluation

↓

Selection criteria
- Economics
- Conservation
- Regulations
- Public relations

↓

Alternative prioritization

↓

Selection and implementation

FIGURE 6-5
Selection process in hazardous waste minimization.

FIGURE 6-6
Conceptual waste management model for a lubricating-oil system.

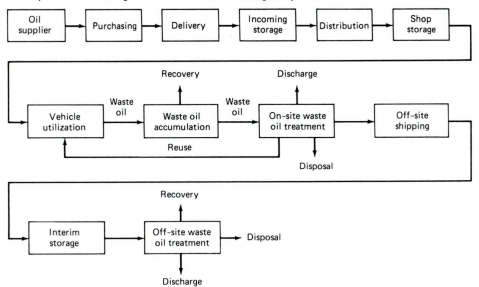

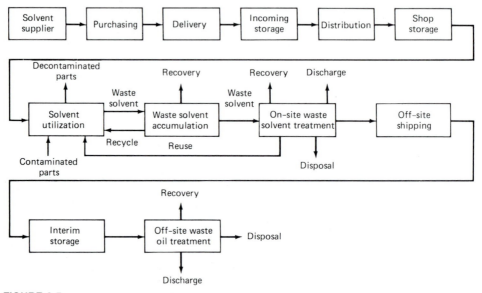

FIGURE 6-7
Conceptual waste management model for a solvent system.

operations associated with reprocessing to prepare the waste oils for either incineration or disposal include sedimentation, centrifugation, and/or filtration. The sequence steps of primary interest for waste minimization in this system are with the oil supplier (in choice of lubricants), incoming storage, shop storage, waste oil accumulation, and on-site and off-site waste oil treatment. The focal points involve recycle, reuse, and recovery to accomplish the waste minimization objectives.

The second case involves a waste management model for a solvent system, beginning with shipment from the solvent supplier through off-site treatment and final disposal of the sludges and residuals (Figure 6-7). Both on-site and off-site treatment usually involve distillation operations, and factors affecting selection of the appropriate distillation system include solvent boiling point, degree of separation desired, throughput requirements, contaminant type and characteristics, and distilled solvent specifications. The areas of greatest importance for waste minimization modeling include solvent supplier, incoming storage, shop storage, solvent utilization, waste solvent accumulation, interim storage, and treatment processing.

The last case involves a waste management model for plating operations. Plating operations are often performed as a means of reducing corrosion potential or of improving the properties of metals. Figure 6-8 shows a typical processing scheme, beginning with shipment of the plating materials from a supplier through the ultimate disposal of system wastes. Plating operations are generally preceded by a degreasing step to remove oils and greases. The metal-laden wastewaters are usually treated by hydroxide precipitation. When chromium is present, reduction of the solution is accomplished with sulfur dioxide, ferrous sulfate, metallic iron, or sodium metabisulfite prior to hydroxide treatment. To reduce hexavalent chromium to trivalent chromium, chrome-bearing streams are generally segregated and treated separately. Waste reduction or minimization is possible at several points in the process. For example, by segregating the wastes and employing selective precipitations, significant waste reductions are possible in the wastewater treatment phase. Recovery and re-use of the precipitated metals can be achieved by proper selection of the solution pH and sulfide dosage, use of chelating agents, and liquid extraction. Treatment with super triple phosphate produces a sludge that is considered nonhazardous. Other phases which can yield significant waste reductions are

FIGURE 6-8
Conceptual waste management model for a plating system.

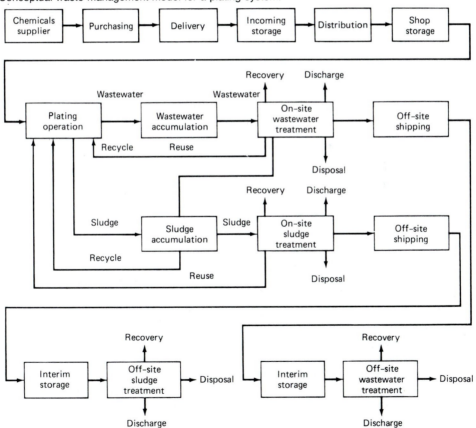

the supply stage (with choice of plating materials), the plating operation itself, and ultimate disposal of the sludges and residuals.

SELECTION OF THE WASTE MINIMIZATION PROCESS

The selection of the actual minimization process should take into account all factors that fit into the overall program goals. There are numerous ways to reduce the generation of hazardous wastes, whether organic and inorganic compounds, including compounds containing heavy metals, cyanides, and halogenated substances. The ease of treating these wastes, the raw materials costs, and the amount of wastes generated are all important factors that could influence on-site reduction and treatment by the generator. Also to be considered is possible conversion to end-use products.

In order to make an intelligent decision on the selection of the proper waste minimization approach, it is necessary to first develop potential waste minimization alternatives, based on knowledge of the waste management model seen in Figure 6-4, and to obtain participation of the facility personnel who will be involved in the program. Their opinions and judgments should be given careful consideration because they will ultimately have to implement the minimization process selected.

At this stage of the program, it is important to recognize all potential minimization alternatives and to accurately define the associated variables so that a realistic economic evaluation can be performed on each alternative. Selection criteria should be determined to permit an objective decision based upon those criteria. In addition to economics, the selection criteria might include such diverse items as ease of procurement, conservation of materials or energy, environmental regulations that force technology, and the need to maintain a desirable public relations image. The alternatives should then be prioritized and reviewed by all concerned parties before the selection of the best alternative. All of the key facility personnel must then commit to implementation of the alternative selected in order for it to be successful. If successful, implementation of the initial minimization process will greatly ease acceptance of any subsequent alternatives that may be recommended at that facility. Hence, a desirable waste minimization strategy would be to first select an alternative with a low risk of failure and a high benefit potential.

Identification of problem hazardous wastes being produced in significant volumes can encourage research and development efforts and can foster cooperation among personnel who come together to seek solutions through coordinated efforts.[7] Waste minimization considerations should be given priority in market development activities. A new chemical or product under commercial consideration should be assessed early in its development for potential waste by-products that would minimize or possibly eliminate waste production. Substituting a raw material or modifying the end product may also eliminate a hazardous waste or possibly change a waste to a less hazardous form. This process substitution necessitates careful evaluation of other potential waste products that might result as well as the impact on the production process and the marketplace.

Once goals have been established, the reduction in the on-site generation of wastes can proceed according to the opportunities that exist. By improving the plant housekeeping and maintenance of equipment, considerable reduction of production-process wastes can be achieved. Through periodic operator training, the production of off-specification material can be reduced. The modification or adjustment of operating procedures may also reduce wastes. Usually material balances for each production process can aid in the detection of both production losses and their potential contribution to waste reduction. A management information system for cost analysis will normally be an effective management tool in determining the feasibility of process changes.

As the final disposal of hazardous wastes becomes more strictly regulated and expensive, the recovery of waste energy and valuable materials will become more common. Hazardous wastes themselves may yield materials that might be useful to the generator. For instance, many hazardous wastes that contain hydrocarbons have considerable fuel value that could be recovered with modest additional investment. But hydrocarbon wastes may contain other contaminants that could cause operating problems during their thermal destruction, and it is not unusual for severe corrosion, erosion, and fouling problems to increase maintenance costs when a waste stream is being used to generate and recover energy. Hazardous wastes do not have the same high-quality assurance criteria that most commercial feedstocks do. This makes both their quality and quantity subject to fluctuations that may be difficult to manage in the operation of a commercial recovery facility.

Economics will always be the driving force for an industry to choose between resource recovery of desirable materials from hazardous wastes and their disposal. The recovery of these materials has often been unprofitable, a factor that has prevented many industries from adopting resource recovery techniques. The unavailability of process technology to accomplish resource recoveries within budget constraints has also hindered the development of this environmentally desirable goal.

In order for waste reduction and recycling to work in an effective manner, corporate management must have a strong commitment to support such a program, for it will demand resources and time if it is to be successful. Everyone in the organization, but particularly lower and middle management, must focus on this important issue, for only when people devote time and effort to accomplish desirable environmental goals are innovative solutions achievable.

It should be recognized that many waste reduction projects will involve considerable up-front investment of capital resources. In addition to the initial investment, there will be operating and maintenance costs that could make the return on these projects unattractive vis-à-vis historic economic evaluation parameters. But by working closely with research, production, and marketing, industry should be able to redesign or reformulate products to remain cost-effective even as their impact on the environment is lessened.

Still, commitment of management to such a program will probably be most strongly tested when marketplace and production concerns need to be addressed. Management support will help alleviate many of these concerns, and proper planning can create empathy among personnel, vendors, and customers and acceptance of mutually beneficial goals. Risk assessment can play an important role in helping to define strategies while not placing an undue burden on either production or marketing personnel. Market development activities can be enhanced with proper knowledge of customer waste management problems, and strategies can be devised to satisfy their needs.

Industry should benefit in the future by close cooperation of all personnel in trying to develop processes and products which minimize environmental impacts. Considerable savings could result from a modest investment that may pay for itself in a short time period. Those industries that appear to be adaptable to waste reduction techniques include chemical manufacturing, fabricated metal products, primary metal production, paper manufacturing, food processing, and petroleum production and refining. These industries produce large quantities of hazardous waste, and it is not surprising that they would be the leaders in reducing their hazardous waste volumes.

The case study that follows is an example of the effective use of process modification and market development in an effort to minimize hazardous waste production while producing a marketable brine for sale as an oil-field completion fluid. It is adapted from an industrial case history.[19]

CASE STUDY
By-product Recovery from Hazardous Waste Incineration

Incineration is used to destroy various chlorinated hydrocarbon liquids and solids, wastes including contaminated solvents, heat transfer fluids, plastics, and other discarded materials. Often they will be in combination with other liquids or solids that either become part of the incineration process or pass through as noncombustible residuals. Such residues may include metals and various types of ceramics, which then become part of the by-product solid waste mixture.

When chlorinated hydrocarbons are incinerated in the presence of oxygen, the following reaction occurs.

$$\text{Chlorinated hydrocarbons} + O_2 \rightarrow CO_2 + H_2O + HCl$$

Typically, under the regulations of the Resource Conservation and Recovery Act (RCRA), incineration takes place at 1500 to 2000°F and slightly less than atmospheric pressure. The process is illustrated in Figure 6-9. When polychlorinated biphenyls (PCBs) are incinerated, operating temperatures exceeding 2192°F are required by regulations from the Toxic Substances Control Act (TSCA). Either of these incineration conditions will ensure high thermal destruction and removal efficiencies (DRE) exceeding 99.99 percent (under RCRA conditions) or 99.9999 percent (with TSCA conditions). The carbon dioxide and water produced by the incineration process may be safely exhausted into the atmosphere. However, the hydrochloric acid (HCl) produced by incineration is an environmental problem that must be dealt with prior to the discharge of the other gaseous products. HCl is highly corrosive and if improperly discharged could endanger human health and the environment; its emissions affect air quality conditions, harm house and car paint, damage trees and shrubbery, and cause respiratory problems.

HCl emissions are highly regulated and must be handled in accordance with RCRA and TSCA guidelines. Typically, HCl is neutralized with a base such as lime or caustic. The choice is an economic decision, one based upon chemical costs and availability, processability, by-product handling and disposal, and by-product recovery potential.

Development of Production Processes

This study was based upon a hazardous waste incineration process that utilized lime to scrub the HCl. In this case, a major factor in the selection of lime over caustic to accomplish the neutralization reaction was the possible marketability of the resulting by-product. The use of lime results in the formation of calcium chloride, according to the following reaction:

$$2HCl + Ca(OH)_2 \rightarrow CaCl_2 + 2H_2O$$

The resultant by-product, calcium chloride brine with a mixture of residual noncombustible contaminants, was then stored in a nearby lagoon to await fur-

FIGURE 6-9
Hazardous waste incineration process.

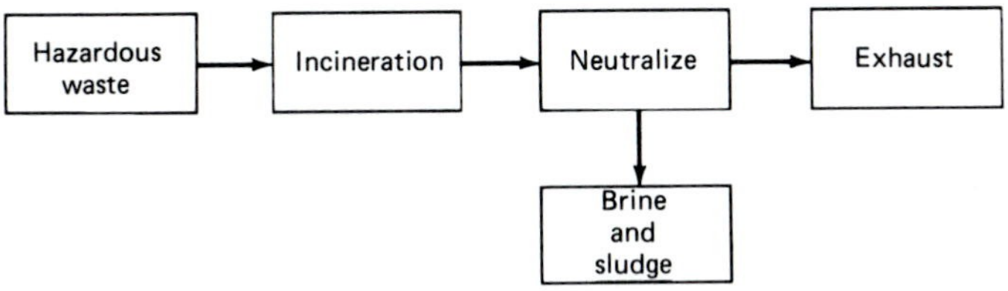

ther processing and management decisions on final disposal. The lagoon provided surge capacity, concentrated the calcium chloride by water evaporation, and allowed a more uniform composition of the by-product.

The by-product brine had a number of potential commercial applications, each involving separation from the accompanying sludge that contained the residual noncombustibles. Possible commercial applications for calcium chloride that were considered included use as a road deicer, as a dust depressant, and as an oil-field completion fluid. The residual noncombustibles in mixture with the brine consisted of several contaminants, the removal of which would be necessary to produce a marketable product:

Carbon, a sootlike product of partially complete combustion
Heavy metals, predominantly finely divided lead
Silicates, a powderlike material from refractory sources
Lime and hydrochloric acid, a carryover of incomplete neutralization products

It was found that the brine, along with the accompanying residuals, contained 3 to 10 percent suspended solids and had a specific gravity in the 1.4- to 1.5-g/cm^3 range and a pH of 5 to 9.

With the waste lagoon characteristics defined, preliminary laboratory tests were run, and they indicated the potential viability of the process separation technology. The project focus shifted to the market development of the calcium chloride brine. Use as a road deicer was rejected because of its seasonal nature and because the plant was situated a long distance from markets in the north-central states. Dust depressants are also seasonal, and the firm did not have a broad market of prospective customers. Oil-field completion fluid seemed to offer the best potential, and the process technology was at that point designed to target the brine by-product for that market.

The oil-field fluid would not require a long, involved market development program; it could enter a large established market with known product specifications, and a considerable market was located within a few hours' drive from the lagoon. The transportation advantage promised a desirable cost benefit over other competing sources. It would only be necessary to meet or exceed product specifications and to demonstrate an economic advantage over the competition to gain market acceptance for the valuable brine.

The specifications (Table 6-1) could easily be achieved:

1 High specific gravity was achievable by operating the lagoon at or near calcium chloride saturation. Water evaporation from the lagoon and the continuous recycling of the hot brine solution from the lagoon to the neutralization process would allow the brine to concentrate and reach equilibrium.

2 Slightly basic pH could be accomplished by the addition of ammonia. Ammonia addition was a standard oil-field practice that could be readily applied to this situation.

3 Low heavy metals content, particularly of lead, a prominent residual noncombustible, was an important parameter that had to be met to ensure compli-

TABLE 6-1
SPECIFICATION FOR CALCIUM CHLORIDE BRINE OIL-FIELD COMPLETION FLUID

Property	Specification
Specific gravity	1.39 g/cm³ (minimum)
	11.6 lb/gal (minimum)
pH	7.2 to 8.0
Lead content	5 ppm (maximum)
Particle size	10 μm (maximum)
Color	Water-white to straw
Toxic contaminants	None

ance with RCRA hazardous waste characteristics; failure to meet this requirement would make the brine unsaleable. But the specific level could be achieved with NaSH precipitation.

4 Low levels of solid particles and minimum particle size were desirable to lessen damage to the downhole formation. Both were attainable through filtration.

5 A clean, nearly colorless, fluid was achievable through clarification and filtration and gave the image of a quality product.

6 Absence of toxic hydrocarbon contaminants would be dependent on the efficiency of the waste incineration process and general plant operations. Because of its origin of production, the brine would have to undergo rigorous examination in the marketplace.

The marketplace had now been defined and the economics appeared attractive. Competitive brines were produced in other domestic regions, making their transport expensive and time-consuming. The lagoon location offered a distinct savings advantage. The next step was to determine the feasibility of process technology to achieve the product specification. Following preliminary laboratory testing, the calcium chloride brine recovery process scheme in Figure 6-10 was envisioned. The overall process flow diagram having been drafted, the firm was now ready for pilot-scale testing in an actual field location. Laboratory jar tests to determine optimum polymer types, concentrations, and pH settings were used extensively throughout this project. Since polymer chemistry remains somewhat of an art rather than an absolute science, multiple jar tests involved a lot of trial and error in determining process development. The brine and residual noncombustibles were pumped from the sludge lagoon to the clarifier at the rate of 35 gal/min. NaSH was fed at a rate of 0.2 gal/min to precipitate lead sulfide. Then the pH was reduced to 5.0 with HCl in order to ensure optimum enhancement of the polymer flocculation in the clarifier on the basis of preliminary laboratory screening and field testing. The nonionic polymer at 0.5 gal/min was particularly effective in attracting and holding colloidal-sized particles at the polar sites of the polymer molecule.

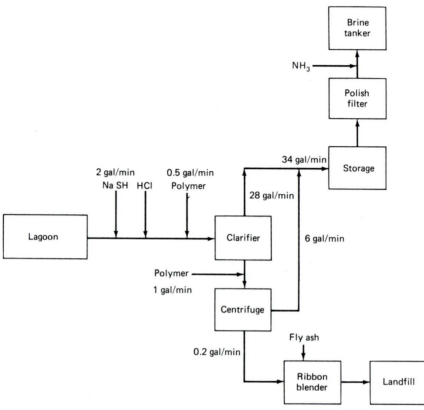

FIGURE 6-10
Calcium-chloride-brine recovery process.

This mixture was fed into a clarifier with a 20-minute residence time, which allowed good liquid-solid separation.

The clarified brine, which still contained some finely divided residual solid particles, was pumped to a surge storage tank. Here, settling of most of the remaining particles took place. This further reduced the solids loading on the subsequent and necessary polish filtration step. The overflow from the storage tank was pumped through a series of polish cartridge filters which were mounted in two separate housings. The initial filtration step consisted of a 35-μm guard filter, which served to protect the final filter. The 10-μm final filter housing was dictated by the stringent specifications of the oil-field completion fluid product. The marketplace would accept only a clean brine. At this point in the process, the product was a high-quality calcium chloride brine, whose pH was then upward adjusted with ammonia to meet the oil-field completion fluid criteria.

The underflow from the clarifier consisted of a flocculated residual solids-brine slurry. These clarifier bottoms were then dewatered by centrifugation in order to recover additional brine and reduce the solids volume. However, the fragile flocs from the clarifier slurry by themselves would not hold together sufficiently in the centrifuge. Therefore, a second and different polymer had to be introduced into the system to allow the centrifuge to be effective in separating and dewatering the solids. On the basis of laboratory screening and field testing, a cationic polyacrylamide polymer flocculant was chosen to accomplish this task. The cationic polymer contained polar groups that promoted small flocs and had a high molecular weight, which provided long bridges between the small flocs. The cationic polymer was fed at the rate of 1.0 gal/min to the centrifuge for dewatering the clarifier solids, and the brine centrate was then pumped to the surge storage tank, where it was held prior to further processing in the polish filter step.

The product brine was produced on a sustained basis at rates above 500,000 gal/month. Although the oil-field market had been depressed by low crude oil prices, the brine was marketed successfully in the $0.05 to $0.10 per gallon range, a range that made recovery of the valuable by-product economically attractive.

The dewatered centrifuged solids, which contained 20-weight percent liquid, were nearly dry enough to be landfilled. In order to ensure continuous production of a solid waste material suitable to landfilling, 5-weight percent of pozzolanic fly ash was uniformly blended with the dewatered solids in a continuous mixing process in a ribbon blender.

Conclusion

The process chemistry and unit operations to produce a high-quality calcium chloride brine from waste lagoon sludge have been developed. The process technology has been demonstrated and offers significant potential for recovery of a valuable waste by-product, calcium chloride, that is inherent in many waste incineration processes to destroy chlorinated hydrocarbons. There is also significant potential to transfer this process technology to other waste liquid and sludge streams that might otherwise become long-term disposal problems. However, because of the complexities of process technology, by-product specifications, and the needs of the marketplace, it is unlikely that this study represents a general solution for all brine waste lagoons.

On the other hand, the study did demonstrate a somewhat unique combination of many of the priority considerations of an effective hazardous waste management program. The concepts of waste recycle, waste minimization, and by-product recovery were achieved to the benefit of all concerned parties. The protection of the environment was enhanced through recovery of brine rather than its disposal in a landfill, and the firm realized reduced disposal costs and reduced long-term liability.

It has to be recognized, of course, that, because of economic or process technology limitations, some wastes generated in the industrial process cannot be utilized on-site or recycled. At the same time there is the need to recognize that one corporation's wastes can be another's valuable resource. The greatest potential for waste recovery may not necessarily be on the generator's plant site or even within the industry. Should the generating industry have the foresight to assess and evaluate outside waste streams, the potential for the utilization rather than the disposal of wastes could be found to be an attractive arrangement for all concerned parties. Waste exchanges involving solvents, lubricating oils, acids, bases, catalysts, and hydrocarbon fuels are certainly feasible. Once again, the criteria of economics and available technology play an important role in the development of any waste exchange program. But such programs offer so much potential that any manufacturing operation might wish to institute quality assurance–quality control procedures to protect their waste streams.

While waste exchange might be of interest to numerous industries, this field has received only minimal acceptance in industry as a whole. The primary factors for this are lack of communication, the guarding of trade secrets and proprietary process know-how, the fear of government retaliation, and the lack of economic incentives. As these potential drawbacks are eliminated or reduced, waste exchanges should become more commonplace.

Although reduction or elimination of waste generation is certainly the most desirable of all hazardous waste management strategies, there are constraints—imposed mainly by economics, process technology, and the creativity and innovativeness of all concerned parties—that guarantee that some treatment and ultimate waste disposal will probably be necessary in most waste management scenarios. However, as industry, government, and regulatory authorities focus on hazardous waste minimization, creative solutions to problems will become commonplace throughout all production and manufacturing operations.

Once all practical alternatives have been examined to reduce the generation and to maximize the recycling and reuse of hazardous wastes, the next priority should be to treat the hazardous waste to render it harmless and reduce its volume. Treatment may cover a wide range of alternatives from physical, chemical, and biological technologies to thermal destruction processes. The treatment process ideally should convert the hazardous wastes into substances that can be recycled and reused, properly converted and safely returned to the environment.

The final priority should provide secure land disposal for those hazardous wastes remaining from the reduction, treatment, and recycling processes. Virtually every hazardous waste treatment process will result in some residuals that will be subject to final disposal. Government, industry, and the general public alike need to recognize that it is impossible to completely eliminate all hazardous waste generation and disposal. There will always be a need for secure landfill capacity to accommodate these residuals.

These environmental priorities are counter to historic hazardous waste management practices in the United States. At the present time, the domestic waste management industry is still emphasizing the more economical disposal of hazardous wastes on land rather than minimization, treatment, and recycling. Large quantities of hazardous wastes are being disposed of in surface impoundments, landfills, and injection wells. Until the economic and regulatory climate changes, and generators are forced toward treatment and incineration rather than land disposal, waste reduction and resource recovery will not receive their desirable high priorities in hazardous waste management. As more stringent land disposal regulations come into effect, emphasis should shift toward waste reduction and resource recovery. It would also seem desirable to legislate prohibitive taxes on waste at the end of the discharge pipe. Such taxes would send a strong economic signal that would act as a disincentive to the generation of such wastes and, at the same time, be a strong incentive for volume reduction and cost-effective waste treatment.

Responsible generators will no longer be using short-term solutions to hazardous waste management that merely shift the costs and liability risks into the distant future. Corporate responsibility and the pressure of public opinion will help force the solution of this issue toward the side of protection of human health and environment.

QUESTIONS

1 Discuss the priorities of managing hazardous wastes.
2 What are the factors that determine the ability to recover and reuse hazardous wastes?
3 Describe the industries that offer the greatest potential for the reduction of hazardous waste and discuss their opportunities.
4 Describe the types of energy recovery that are possible from the thermal processing of hazardous waste.
5 Why has the concept of waste exchange among industries not been generally accepted?
6 Discuss why pollution control does not necessarily reduce the waste to be managed.
7 Discuss industrial waste minimization from the perspective of a large hazardous waste treatment company.
8 How could tax incentives be used to encourage hazardous waste minimization?

BIBLIOGRAPHY

1 Foecke, T. L.: "Hazardous Waste Minimization: Part II. Waste Minimization in the Electronics Products Industries," *JAPCA*, vol. 38, no. 3, 1988.
2 Gardner, L. C., and D. Huisingh: "Alternative Approaches to Waste Reduction in Materials Coating Processes," *Hazardous Waste and Hazardous Materials*, vol. 4, no. 2, 1987.
3 The Hazardous and Solid Waste Amendments of 1984, U.S. Congress, Washington, 1984.
4 Henz, D. J.: "Cofiring Hazardous Waste Fuels in Industrial Processes," *JAPCA*, vol. 36, no. 10, 1986.

5 Hirschhorn, J. S., and K. V. Oldenburg: "Hazardous Waste: Prevention or Cleanup?" *Environmental Science and Technology,* vol. 21, no. 6, 1987.

6 Hollod, G. J., and R. F. McCartney: "Hazardous Waste Minimization: Part I. Waste Reduction in the Chemical Industry—DuPont's Approach," *JAPCA,* vol. 38, no. 2, 1988.

7 National Research Council, *Management of Hazardous Industrial Wastes: Research and Development Needs,* NMAB-398, National Academy Press, Washington, 1983.

8 National Research Council, *Reducing Hazardous Waste Generation,* National Academy Press, Washington, 1985.

9 Noll, K. E., C. N. Haas, and J. W. Patterson: "Recovery, Recycle, and Reuse of Hazardous Waste," *JAPCA,* vol. 36, no. 10, 1986.

10 Noll, K., et al.: *Recovery, Recycle, and Reuse of Industrial Wastes,* Lewis Publishers, Chelsea, Mich., 1985.

11 Overcash, M. R.: *Techniques for Industrial Pollution Prevention,* Lewis Publishers, Chelsea, Mich., 1986.

12 *Report to Congress, Minimization of Hazardous Wastes,* EPA/530-SW-86-033, U.S. Environmental Protection Agency, Office of Solid Wastes, Washington, 1986.

13 Resource Conservation and Recovery Act, PL94-580, 1976.

14 Sarokin, D. J., W. R. Muir, C. G. Miller, and S. R. Serber: *Cutting Chemical Wastes,* Inform, New York, 1986.

15 *Serious Reduction of Hazardous Waste: For Pollution Prevention and Industrial Efficiency,* U.S. Congress, Office of Technology Assessment, OTA-ITE-317, Washington, September 1986.

16 Tavlarides, L. L.: *Process Modifications for Industrial Source Reduction,* Lewis Publishers, Chelsea, Mich., 1985.

17 *Technologies and Management Strategies for Hazardous Waste Control,* U.S. Congress, Office of Technology Assessment, OTA-M-196, Washington, March 1983.

18 Thompson, F. M., and C. A. McComas: "Technical Assistance for Hazardous Waste Reduction," *Environmental Science and Technology,* vol. 21, no. 12, 1987.

19 Wentz, C. A.: "Byproduct Recovery from Hazardous Waste Incineration," *Hazardous Waste and Hazardous Materials,* vol. 4, no. 2, 1987.

CHEMICAL, PHYSICAL, AND BIOLOGICAL TREATMENT

INTRODUCTION

While waste minimization goals are both necessary and desirable, most manufacturing operations will still create waste products that will ultimately need to undergo treatment to either destroy the wastes or render them harmless to the environment. There are numerous treatments applicable to hazardous wastes that can typically be categorized as chemical, physical, or biological in nature.[1,12,37] Many such processes are already widely used to manage hazardous wastes and have broad acceptance from government, industry, and public alike.[6,9] Combinations of these treatment technologies are often utilized to develop the most cost-effective and environmentally acceptable solutions to waste management problems.[10,13,14,15,16,17,33,34,36,39]

Treatment processes may also be used to advantage in by-product recovery processes and in the volume reduction of wastes that ultimately must be disposed of. All "end-of-the-pipe" wastes should first be surveyed and characterized to determine the applicability of various treatment and destruction processes.

CHEMICAL TREATMENT

Chemical treatment involves the use of reactions to transform hazardous waste streams into less hazardous substances. Chemical treatment can be useful in promoting resource recovery of hazardous substances. In that it can be employed to produce useful by-products and residual effluents that are environmentally acceptable, chemical treatment is a far better method of waste management than is the traditional method of disposal at a landfill. Although landfill disposal methods have historically been less expensive than chemical treatment, as landfill disposal costs rise and regulations become more restrictive, chemical treatment should become a more widely accepted practice.[20]

There are many different forms of chemical treatment used in the management of hazardous wastes.[3,26] Chemical reactions can be used to reduce wastes in volume or to convert wastes to a less hazardous form.

Solubility

Hazardous wastes may be either organic or inorganic substances, containing various chemical elements and structural configurations. Water, which is known as the universal solvent, will dissolve many of these substances, while others have only limited solubility. Generally, sodium, potassium, and ammonium salts are soluble in water, as are mineral acids. Most halogenated inorganics except fluorides are soluble, while many carbonates, hydroxides, and phosphates are only slightly soluble. Alcohols are highly soluble, but aromatic and long-chained petroleum-based organics have low solubility.[40]

In any event, the solubility of a substance will be the critical factor in any chemical treatment process.

Neutralization

The neutralization of acidic and alkaline waste streams is an example of the use of chemical treatment to mitigate wastes that have been characterized as corrosive, and therefore hazardous, under the RCRA guidelines. Neutralization of an acid or base is easily measured by pH, and acid-base reactions are among the most common chemical processes used in wastewater treatment.

Neutralization of a waste that is an acid or base involves the addition of a chemical substance to change the pH to a more neutral level—in the range of 6 to 8. Frequently, industrial wastewaters may be acidic or basic and may require neutralization prior to any other treatment or prior to release to a municipal sanitary sewer system. Sometimes it is feasible to mix an acidic waste stream with a basic waste stream and then use a constant-level equalization basin as a neutralization tank. Normally, however, it will be necessary to neutralize acid wastes with a base and to neutralize high-pH wastes with an acid, according to the equation

$$\text{Acid} + \text{base} \rightarrow \text{salt} + \text{water}$$

Acidic wastewaters may be neutralized with slaked lime [$Ca(OH)_2$], caustic soda ($NaOH$), or soda ash (Na_2CO_3). Since slaked lime is less expensive than other bases or soda ash, it is the most commonly used chemical for acidic neutralization. The slaked lime is added to the acidic wastewater in an agitator vessel that has a pH sensor to control the slaked lime feed rate.

Alkaline wastewaters may be neutralized with a strong mineral acid, such as H_2SO_4 or HCl, or with CO_2. The reaction with mineral acids is rapid; here too agitator vessels are used with pH sensors that control the acid feed rate. Neutralization of alkaline wastewaters with CO_2 usually consists of bubbling CO_2 in the bottom of the neutralization tank, thus creating carbonic acid (H_2CO_3), which reacts with the alkaline substances. Flue gas is frequently available as a source of CO_2, making the neutralization process more economical.

These neutralization reactions are exothermic and require systems similar to that seen in Figure 7-1 to avoid excessive high temperatures that could produce unsafe operating conditions and damage process equipment.

Precipitation

Often undesirable heavy metals will be present in liquid waste streams. If the concentrations of the heavy metals are sufficiently high to cause the waste stream to be designated as hazardous according to the RCRA EP toxicity characterization, the metals must be removed. The usual method for removal of inorganic heavy metals is chemical precipitation.[29] The metals will precipitate at varying pH levels, depending upon the metal ion, resulting in the formation of an insoluble salt. Hence the neutralization of an acidic waste stream can cause precipitation of heavy metals and allow them to be removed as a sludge residue by clarification, sedimentation, or filtration.

The hydroxides of heavy metals are usually insoluble, so lime is commonly used for precipitating them. The carbonates or sulfides are less soluble than the hydroxides but may also be precipitated. Economics may justify partial precipitation with lime to the solubility level of the hydroxide, followed by a secondary treatment with sulfide for further reduction.

FIGURE 7-1
Chemical neutralization treatment system for waste management.

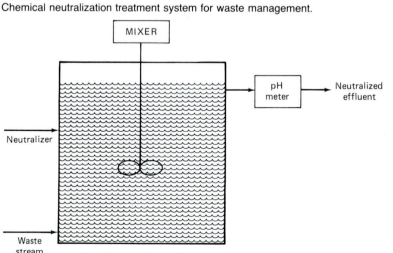

The choice of the reactant is the first consideration in the precipitation of heavy metals; the second consideration is solubility, since precipitation depends upon the solubility product of the undesirable compound, the metal that is to be removed. Because solubility is affected by temperature, it too is an important factor in precipitation reactions. Temperature will also influence the selection of the treatment equipment.

The valence state of the metal is also important in the process of precipitation. For example, ferrous iron is considerably more soluble than ferric iron, making treatment with an oxidizing agent to convert ferrous iron to ferric an essential part of the iron-removal process. Another example is hexavalent chromium, Cr^{6+}, which is considerably more soluble than the less hazardous trivalent form. Chromates must be reduced before removal of trivalent chromium by a precipitation process. Also, one must consider the possibility of formation of complex ions when dealing with wastewaters containing ammonia, fluoride, or cyanide as well as heavy metals. For example, iron may be complexed as the ferrocyanide ion, which is rather soluble, and will remain in solution unless the complex can be broken by chemical treatment.

Precipitation of heavy metals can also be achieved by the addition of sulfide chemicals such as sodium sulfide (Na_2S) or sodium bisulfide (NaHS). The addition of these soluble sulfide compounds must be carefully controlled to minimize odor and potential toxicity problems. During sulfide precipitation there is the potential of generating hydrogen sulfide, which is a severe health and safety hazard that has the potential to kill employees if the process is not properly controlled. To minimize this danger, slightly alkaline pH should be maintained.

One final factor in the precipitation process is the liquid/solid state of the waste. Generally the size of a precipitated particle increases if the chemical reaction is allowed to occur with previously precipitated particles. Because of this phenomenon, precipitation processes ideally should introduce the precipitating chemicals into a waste that contains solids.

Coagulation and Flocculation

The precipitation process of heavy metals can be greatly enhanced through addition of various water-soluble chemicals and polymers that promote coagulation and flocculation. Coagulation and flocculation are used to separate suspended solids from liquids when their normal sedimentation rates are too slow to provide effective clarification. These are two different but related mechanisms in clarification and dewatering.

Coagulation is the addition and rapid mixing of a coagulant to neutralize charges and collapse the colloidal particles so they can agglomerate and settle. Colloidal species in wastewater include clay, silica, heavy metals, and organics. Colloids require coagulation to achieve an effective size and settling rate when insufficient settling time is available in a treatment plant to remove suspended solids. Hydrophilic colloids may react with the coagulant used in the treatment process and hence require more coagulant than hydrophobic colloids, which do not chemically react with the coagulant.

The determination of the nature and strength of the particle charge is needed to define how closely particles in the colloidal system can approach each other. *Zeta potential* is a measurement of this force. For colloids in water with a pH range of 5 to 8, the zeta potential is generally -14 to -30 mV. This zeta potential must be reduced so that the particles may coalesce. As the zeta potential diminishes, the particles approach more closely, increasing the likelihood of collision. In a conventional clarification system at a pH of 6 to 8, coagulants provide the positive charges to reduce negative zeta potential. Coagulation usually occurs at a zeta potential which is still slightly negative, so complete charge neutralization is not usually required. Zeta potential is determined from observing particle motion under a microscope. However, for selecting the best coagulant, zeta potential estimates should be supplemented with results from jar tests because these tests best reflect the actual situation (see below). Alum $[Al_2(SO_4)_3]$, ferric chloride $(FeCl_3)$, and ferric sulfate $[Fe_2(SO_4)_3]$ are common coagulants used in treating aqueous waste streams.

Mixing is required to supplement addition of a coagulant to destroy stability in the colloidal system. For particles to agglomerate they must collide, and mixing promotes collision. High-intensity mixing which distributes the coagulant and promotes rapid collisions is most effective. The frequency and number of particle collisions are important in coagulation. In a low-turbidity water, the addition of solids such as clay or the recycle of previously settled solids may be required to increase the number of particle collisions.

The use of water-soluble organic polymers is often more effective than the use of alum or iron salts in promoting coagulation. These coagulants also promote *flocculation,* which is the agglomeration of the colloidal particles that have been subjected to coagulation treatment. Flocs are promoted by slow mixing of coagulated colloidal particles under controlled pH conditions to produce large particles, thereby improving the efficiency of subsequent dewatering steps.

Flocculation requires gentle agitation to allow bridging of the flocculant chemical between agglomerated colloidal particles to form large settleable flocs. A flocculant gathers together particles in a network, bridging and binding the individual particles into large agglomerates.

Flocculation is promoted by slow mixing, which brings the flocs gently together. High mixing speeds that would tear them apart are undesirable because they would seldom re-form to their optimum size and strength. Flocculation not only increases the size of the floc particles but also permits faster dewatering rates of sludges and slurries because of the less gelatinous structure of the flocs.

Alum and iron salts, which are widely used in water clarification, in fact, function as both coagulants and flocculants by forming positively charged species in the 6 to 7 pH range that is typical for clarification. This hydrolysis reaction produces insoluble gelatinous aluminum or ferric hydroxide, and the metal coagulants form flocs which trap the destabilized colloids. However, the sludges produced are usually difficult to dewater, and alum and iron salts are often not desirable in improving efficiency of centrifuges, filter presses, and other dewatering devices. Metal coagulants are particularly sensitive to pH and alkalinity. If pH is not in the proper range, these coagulants rarely induce adequate clarification.

Aluminum sulfate is employed more frequently than iron salts in water treatment clarification because it is usually cheaper, but iron salts are effective over a wider pH range. In the lime-soda softening process, lime serves as a coagulant to produce a heavy precipitate consisting of calcium carbonate and magnesium hydroxide, which has coagulating and flocculating properties.

The principal factors affecting the coagulation and flocculation of wastewater are suspended solids, pH, and the dosage and nature of the coagulant. The wastewater must be alkaline for aluminum sulfate to produce aluminum hydroxide:

$$Al_2(SO_4)_3 + 3Ca(HCO_3)_2 \rightarrow 2Al(OH)_3 \downarrow + 3CaSO_4 + 6CO_2$$

If the wastewater does not have sufficient alkalinity to react with the alum, it must be added in the form of calcium hydroxide (lime) or sodium carbonate (soda ash):

$$Al_2(SO_4)_3 + 3Ca(OH)_2 \rightarrow 2Al(OH)_3 \downarrow + 3CaSO_4$$

$$Al_2(SO_4)_3 + 3Na_2CO_3 + 3H_2O \rightarrow Al_2(OH)_3 \downarrow + 3Na_2SO_4 + 3CO_2$$

Ferrous sulfate treatment also requires alkalinity in the wastewater. Lime is usually added to raise the pH above 9.5 where ferrous ions are precipitated as ferric hydroxide:

$$4FeSO_4 \cdot 7H_2O + 4Ca(OH)_2 + O_2 \rightarrow 4Fe(OH)_3 \downarrow + 4CaSO_4 + 26H_2O$$

Ferric sulfate and ferric chloride may also be used:

$$Fe_2(SO_4)_3 + 3Ca(OH)_2 \rightarrow 2Fe(OH)_3 \downarrow + 3CaSO_4$$

$$2FeCl_3 + 3Ca(OH)_2 \rightarrow 2Fe(OH)_3 \downarrow + 3CaCl_2$$

Polyelectrolytes   While activated silica significantly improves the performance of alum and iron salts as coagulants and flocculants in water clarification, the development of organic polymers called polyelectrolytes was an even more important contribution to water treatment technology. Polyelectrolytes are polymers of large water-soluble organic molecules. They are organic compounds, whose ionic nature plays a major role in their performance. They usually have ion exchange sites which give the molecule an ionic charge. Those having a positive charge are cationic; those with a negative charge are anionic;

others may be neutral, or nonionic. These molecules react with colloidal material in the water by neutralizing the charge and by bridging individual particles to form flocs.

The performance of polyelectrolytes can be tailored to the colloidal matter to be removed from the water by modifying their molecular weight and ion exchange capacity. The cationic polyelectrolytes are either polyamines or copolymers containing acrylamide, which hydrolyzes according to the following:

$$\underset{R'}{\overset{R}{>}} NH + H_2O \rightarrow \underset{R'}{\overset{R}{>}} NH \cdot H^+ + OH^-$$

At a high pH, the reaction is forced to the left, and the polymer may become nonionic. The anionic polymers of acrylates incorporate a carboxyl group in their structure and ionize as follows:

$$R - COOH \rightleftharpoons R - COO^- + H^+$$

Anionics become nonionic at a low pH because the hydrogen ion forces the reaction to the left. Nonionic polymers are typically polyacrylamides.

By tailoring structures and molecular weights, it is possible to design a polymer for coagulation or flocculation problems, since organic polymers overcome many of the problems inherent in the use of alum or iron salts.

The polarity of nonionic bonds in the molecule, molecular size, and molecular geometry also play a role in polymer performance. Hence, high-molecular-weight nonionic polymers may be effective flocculants in many systems because of their ability to attract and hold colloidal particles at the molecular polar sites. They can also bridge together many small particles.

Jar and Cylinder Tests The flocculant that works best in any system can be determined only through experimental screening called *jar tests,* which are often used to select the proper coagulant and flocculant as well as the dosage level required for clarification for most waste streams. The cylinder test is similarly used for sludges and slurry streams, e.g., coal and mineral processing wastes and the sludge resulting from a primary clarification.

The jar test simulates the types of mixing and settling conditions found in a clarification plant; test results are sensitive to chemical dosage, mixing energy, and mixing time. The coagulant is added and stirred rapidly to disperse it in the water and promote increased frequency of collisions. A polymer flocculant, if required, is added during the last few seconds of the rapid mix. In the slow-mix period which follows, floc building proceeds until the floc becomes large enough to begin to break apart, which limits the size of the floc.

After slow mixing for an optimum period of time, the jars are allowed to settle. Jars with different chemicals or the same chemical at different dosages are run side by side and the results compared. Floc settling rate, final clarity or suspended solids, and volume of sludge produced are contrasted between jars. Although clarity can be judged by the eye, the more accurate standard measurement is made with a turbidimeter. Other quality control tests such as pH, biochemical oxygen demand (BOD), color, chemical oxygen demand (COD), and soluble metals may be used to establish performance standards.

The cylinder test, designed to indicate how fast the suspended solids will settle, employs a 500-ml stoppered graduated cylinder, stopwatch, and labware for dosing the chemical being evaluated. The slurry sample is placed in the cylinder, the chemical is added, and the cylinder is gently inverted several times. Mixing is much less severe than in the jar test because solids are present at much higher levels, causing frequent collisions to occur with less mixing energy. After mixing, the cylinder is set upright, and the interface between the water and the settling solids is observed. Time and solids level are recorded, and the data are plotted. A rapid settling rate is usually the primary goal. By running coagulants and flocculants at different dosages and comparing settling rates, the most effective polymers and dosage are selected.

The jar test protocol of rapid and slow mixing, which works best for clarification, is duplicated on the plant scale. In-line hydraulic mixing and high-speed mixing in a small mixing basin usually follow addition of the coagulant. Flocculation mixing occurs in gently stirred compartments with variable-speed motors. In the clarification plant, the lower the suspended solids in the process stream, or the higher the required effluent clarity, the more critical to the final results is the mixing.

Oxidation and Reduction

The chemical processes of oxidation and reduction can be utilized to convert toxic pollutants to either harmless or less toxic substances. *Oxidation* is a chemical reaction with an increase in valence from a loss of electrons. Oxidation must be accompanied by reduction. *Reduction* is a reaction with a decrease in valence from a gain of electrons. Chemical reactions that involve both oxidation and reduction are known as *redox reactions*.

Hexavalent chromium is highly toxic and its presence in a waste requires careful management to avoid harm to human health and the environment. Once hexavalent chromium is reduced to trivalent chromium, it then can be precipitated as chromic hydroxide, as shown in the following reaction which utilizes sulfur dioxide and lime:

$$SO_2 + H_2O \rightarrow H_2SO_3$$

$$2CrO_3 + 3H_2SO_3 \rightarrow Cr_2(SO_4)_3 + 3H_2O$$

$$Cr_2(SO_4)_3 + 3Ca(OH)_2 \rightarrow 2Cr(OH)_3 + 3CaSO_4$$

The reduction of hexavalent chromium to the trivalent state through process techniques similar to the above produces a chromium-containing compound that is much less toxic and more acceptable for either subsequent recovery or final disposal, depending upon the economics of the situation.

A common method for treating aqueous cyanide wastes is alkaline chlorination. In this process, the cyanide is initially oxidized to a less toxic cyanate and then to carbon dioxide and nitrogen in the following reactions:

$$NaCN + Cl_2 + 2NaOH \rightarrow NaCNO + 2NaCl + H_2O$$

$$2NaCNO + 3Cl_2 + 4NaOH \rightarrow 2CO_2 + N_2 + 6NaCl + 2H_2O$$

Both these reactions are sensitive to pH. The first reaction requires a pH greater than 10 to produce sodium cyanate. The second reaction proceeds more rapidly at a pH of about 8. This alkaline chlorination process can also be accomplished with hypochlorite bleach, as well as with peroxides and ozone, to achieve nearly complete destruction of the undesirable cyanide waste products.

Color Removal

An aqueous waste effluent may have difficulty meeting a low color specification. The chemical composition of the substance that is contributing to the color problem of an aqueous stream is sometimes difficult to determine in organic systems. If the chemical composition of such a color producer can be determined, it may be possible to modify upstream processing conditions to eliminate the color-producing contaminant. However, if this is not possible, then a suitable color removal process must be developed. Typically, color removal processes from aqueous systems may involve carbon adsorption, coagulation, and flocculation, or chemical oxidation with chlorine or other strong oxidizers.

Disinfection

The purpose of disinfecting drinking water is to destroy organisms that cause diseases. Most pathogenic and other microorganisms are removed from water by conventional treatment processes of coagulation, sedimentation, and filtration, but chlorination is often used in wastewater treatment to ensure satisfactory disinfection of potable water supplies. The disinfecting ability of chlorine is due to its powerful oxidizing properties, which oxidize those enzymes of microbial cells that are essential to their metabolic processes.

Chlorine is the most widely used disinfectant because it is effective at low concentration, is highly cost-effective, and forms a residual if applied in sufficient dosage. But chlorine addition must be a highly controlled process. Chlorine is a poisonous, yellow-green gas at room temperature and atmospheric pressure. Moist chlorine gas is extremely corrosive, and therefore piping and dosing equipment must either be nonmetal or be made of special alloys. Chlorine vapor causes respiratory and eye irritation, and high concentrations can cause physiological damage. Chlorine feeding rooms and storage areas should be kept cool and well ventilated.

Chlorine gas is soluble in water and forms hypochlorous acid:

$$Cl_2 + H_2O \rightleftharpoons HOCl + H^+ + Cl^-$$

Hydrolysis goes virtually to completion at pH values and concentrations normally experienced in waste treatment operations.

Hypochlorous acid ionizes according to the following equation:

$$HOCl \rightleftharpoons H^+ + OCl^-$$

The dissociation rate from hypochlorous acid to hypochlorite ion is sufficiently rapid so that equilibrium is maintained even though the hypochlorous acid is being continuously consumed.

The same equilibria are established whether elemental chlorine or hypochlorite is used for chlorination. Since hypochlorites are more expensive, liquid chlorine is applied in most water treatment plants in the United States.

Chlorine is a strong oxidizing agent capable of reacting with many contaminants in water. Chlorine reacts with ammonia to form three different chloramines:

$$HOCl + NH_3 \rightarrow NH_2Cl(monochloramine) + H_2O$$

$$NH_2Cl + HOCl \rightarrow NHCl_2(dichloramine) + H_2O$$

$$NHCl_2 + HOCl \rightarrow NCl_3(trichloramine) + H_2O$$

These chloramine compounds have biocidal properties.

Ammonia can be destroyed chemically by chlorination. The initial reaction forms chloramine, and when this material has been completely broken down, a free chlorine residual will be produced:

$$NH_3 + Cl_2 \rightarrow NH_2Cl + HCl$$

$$2NH_3 + 3Cl_2 \rightarrow N_2 + 6HCl$$

Ammonia cannot always be destroyed in this fashion, however, since many wastewaters contain organic materials that react with chlorine in preference to ammonia. These organics must be destroyed before sufficient excess chlorine is available for reacting with the ammonia.

Chlorine gas, hypochlorous acid, and the hypochlorite ion remaining after the chlorine demand is satisfied are collectively termed "free chlorine residuals." The chloramines and other reactive chlorine forms remaining after the demand has been satisfied are referred to as "combined chlorine residuals." Free chlorine residuals are faster acting than combined residuals, and, for the same concentration and time, the free chlorine residuals have much greater disinfecting capacity than combined residuals, especially for viruses.

Hydrogen sulfide may also be destroyed chemically by oxidation with chlorine:

$$H_2S + Cl_2 \rightarrow S + 2HCl$$

$$H_2S + 4Cl_2 + 4H_2O \rightarrow H_2SO_4 + 8HCl$$

Oxidizing biocides such as chlorine, hypochlorites, and organochlorine materials will kill all organisms in the system quickly if the free chlorine comes into direct contact with the organisms long enough and at a strong enough dosage level. These biocides also retain their effectiveness because organisms cannot adapt to or become resistant to chlorine.

In chlorination, increased time of contact results not only in greater destruction of microorganisms but in an increased amount of various chlorinated by-products. Chlorine and other disinfectants can react with trace organics found in many wastewater sources; the by-products may be objectionable in taste or odor, and some, like chloroform, may be harmful. Because of concern for the potentially adverse toxic effects of these chlorinated by-product compounds, regulatory agencies often restrict chlorine consumption in large effluent flows.

An efficient chlorination system provides rapid initial mixing of the chlorine solution in the wastewater and contact time in a plug-flow basin for a minimum of 30 minutes. Rapid blending can be accomplished by applying the chlorine in a pressure conduit under conditions of highly turbulent flow, or in a channel immediately upstream from a mechanical mixer. Adequate plug flow can be achieved by a baffled contact chamber. A well-designed chlorination unit provides adequate disinfection with a dosage of 8 to 15 mg/l.

Control of chlorine dosage is extremely important for proper operation. Automatic residual monitoring and feedback control are necessary to prevent both inadequate disinfection and excessive chlorination. To protect receiving streams, some regulatory agencies have specified maximum chlorine residuals in undiluted effluents of 0.1 to 0.5 mg/l.

While disinfection may take various forms, chlorine application to a detention basin providing at least 15 minutes reaction time has usually been used for this purpose. In some cases, dechlorination may follow to remove any trace amounts of residual chlorine that might be toxic to stream organisms. Because of concern for the production of chlorinated organics, which might also be toxic, other methods of disinfection are gaining popularity.

Ozone is used in certain municipalities in the United States for disinfection of potable water.[43] It is also used in certain waste treatment applications to avoid the residual chloramines that result from chlorination of wastewater effluent. Ozone is a powerful oxidant, more powerful than hypochlorous acid. In aqueous solution it is relatively unstable, having a half-life of 20 to 30 minutes in distilled water at 20°C. Ozone must be produced on-site because it cannot be stored like chlorine. Ozone is usually produced by an electric corona discharge through air or oxygen.

Ion Exchange

Ion exchange is a reversible exchange of ions between liquid and solid phases. Ions held by electrostatic forces to charged functional groups on the surface of an insoluble solid are replaced by ions of similar charge in a solution. Ion exchange is stoichiometric, reversible, and selective in removal of dissolved ionic species. Ion exchange materials should have ion-active sites throughout their entire structure, high capacity, selectivity for ionic species, capability of regeneration, chemical and physical stability, and low solubility.

Ion exchange is useful in treatment of hazardous wastewater. Some common applications are desalting, ammonia removal, and treatment of heavy-metal wastewaters, where through the ion exchange process, the heavy metallic ions become concentrated in the spent regenerate. Softening of water by the exchange of sodium ions for calcium and magnesium is commonly practiced in water treatment, and ion exchange is used for partial demineralization of wastewaters in tertiary treatment.

The earliest ion exchangers were inorganic sodium aluminosilicates called *zeolites*. These materials have relatively open structures with channels and interconnecting cavities available for ion movement. The lattice carries a negative electric charge balanced by cations which can be replaced by other cations. Some aluminosilicates also exchange anions.

Synthetic ion exchangers impart better characteristics into the resin than those of naturally occurring zeolites. The organic ion exchange resins are the most important synthetic resins. Typical of these are gels with a matrix of hydrocarbon chains that carry ionic groups capable of being exchanged. Cross-linking is accomplished by carbon-carbon bonding, giving the resin good chemical, thermal, and mechanical stability. The ion selectivity can be controlled by the fixed ion groups attached to the matrix. Synthetic resins are available that have both cation and anion exchange capabilities. Synthetic organic cationic resins have a high ion exchange capacity and have reactive groups, such as the sulfonic, phenolic, and carboxylic groups, that may be charged with exchangeable cations. Synthetic anion exchange resins have ionizable groups like quaternary ammonium or amine groups that may be charged with exchangeable anions.

Most commercial ion exchangers are synthetic polymers that are essentially insoluble in water. The ion exchange has a limited exchange capacity for storage of ions and eventually will become saturated. It is then washed with a regenerating solution to replace the accumulated undesirable ions, thereby returning the exchange material to a usable condition. This operation is a cyclical process, which includes the in-service ion exchange, backwashing, regeneration, and rinsing. Most ion exchange units contain a bed of ion exchange resin that is operated downflow. The unit is in service to a predetermined leakage level, first backwashed by upflow and then regenerated by downflow chemical elution. The resin bed is then rinsed downflow.

The solution feeding the column exchanges ions and the exchange region will move through the column until the entire bed is exhausted. The column is then backwashed with water to remove retained solids and to reclassify the resin bed particles. During the regeneration period, regenerant solution flows through the bed, displacing undesirable ions and restoring the resin to its original condition. A waste stream will be generated during this phase and will require disposal. In the rinsing operation, water displaces spent regenerant remaining in the bed. This water effluent is discarded as long as any contamination exists from the regenerant. For continuous product water, several ion exchange columns must be cycled, so that at least one column is always in service.

A significant concern in the selection of any ion exchange process is the waste created by regeneration of the ion exchange bed. The waste may be reusable, or it may present a disposal problem, as does spent acid from regeneration of a cation exchanger. The proper treatment of these wastes requires that the flow of the waste from the regeneration step and the concentration of contaminants be determined. Spent caustic from regeneration of a strong anion exchanger may be used to regenerate the weakly basic anion exchanger. Cation exchanger rinse following acid regeneration may be used as cooling tower makeup to provide alkalinity reduction. If spent regenerants cannot be reused, they must be treated to produce effluent that will not upset the waste treatment system.

To determine the performance of an exchanger resin with a particular ion in a solution, sorption tests should be performed. The column breakthrough curve test to measure the uptake of the particular ion is an experimental procedure. The breakthrough curve for an ion exchange column is similar to that for an adsorption column. An experimental breakthrough curve is required to show the ion concentration in the effluent as a function of the throughput volume. Test columns should be regenerated with the desired regenerate ion, and then an in-service test run should be performed until exhaustion. Then following resin regeneration, the design breakthrough curve should be determined.

The design of ion exchangers should be based upon the following relationship:

$$\ln\left(\frac{C_o}{C} - 1\right) = \frac{kC_s m}{Q} - \frac{C_o V}{Q} \qquad (7.1)$$

where C_o = solute influent concentration, g/l
$\quad C$ = solute effluent concentration, g/l
$\quad k$ = reaction rate constant
$\quad C_s$ = maximum concentration of sorbed solute in solid phase, g/l
$\quad m$ = adsorbent, g
$\quad Q$ = flow rate, 1/h
$\quad V$ = flow volume, l

Typical ion exchangers contain 0.4- to 0.8-mm beads, have a 2- to 8-foot bed depth, and operate at 2 to 6 gal/(min)(ft²). The height-to-diameter ratio is typically about 2 to 1, and the height should be sufficient to allow for expansion of the bed during backwashing, since zeolites expand about 25 percent and polymers may double in depth. Exchanger capacity is usually expressed as milliequivalents per milliliter (meq/ml).

Exchangers Defined Exchangers with negatively charged sites are cation exchangers because they take up positively charged ions. Anion exchangers have positively charged sites and attract negative ions. Cation exchange resins having strong acidic reactive sites, such as sulfonic groups ($-SO_3H$), readily remove cations. Weak-acid cation exchange resins having carboxylic groups ($-COOH$) remove cations such as Ca^{2+} and Mg^{2+} but have limited ability to remove Na^+ and K^+. Strong-base anion exchange resins have quaternary ammonium groups that readily remove all anions. Weak-base anion exchange resins have amine groups and remove mainly anions from strong mineral acids such as SO_4^{2-}, Cl^-, and NO_3^-.

Ion exchange resins have a finite number of exchange sites. A generalized equation for cation exchange by a resin has the following relationship:

$$C_1^+ + X \cdot C_2 \rightleftharpoons C_2^+ + X \cdot C_1 \tag{7.2}$$

where C_1^+ and C_2^+ are cations and X is the exchange resin. The equilibrium constant is represented as

$$K = \frac{(X \cdot C_1)(C_2^+)}{(X \cdot C_2)(C_1^+)} = \left(\frac{C_1}{C_2}\right)_{resin} \left(\frac{C_2}{C_1}\right)_{solution} \tag{7.3}$$

where K = equilibrium constant

$\left(\dfrac{C_1}{C_2}\right)_{resin}$ = equilibrium concentration for the resin

$\left(\dfrac{C_2}{C_1}\right)_{solution}$ = equilibrium concentration for the solution

K represents the relative preference of the resin to attract and hold cation C_1^+ as compared with cation C_2^+. The equilibrium constant is directly proportional to the preference for the ion by the exchanger. Cation exchanger resins generally prefer higher-valence cations that react strongly with the resin exchange sites and are less prone to form complexes. For strong resins, the selectivity preference ranking for common cations is:

Ba^{2+}
Pb^{2+}
Sr^{2+}

Ca^{2+}
Ni^{2+}
Cd^{2+}
Cu^{2+}
Co^{2+}
Zn^{2+}
Mg^{2+}
Ag^{+}
Cs^{+}
K^{+}
NH_4^{+}
Na^{+}
H^{+}

For example, the selectivity of cation exchange indicates that Pb^{2+} has a preference over Mg^{2+}.

Weak cation exchangers can improve the utilization of regenerant acid with a carboxylic exchanger, which reacts with the alkalinity of the incoming water. The strong exchanger then reacts with the balance of the cations. The advantage of the carboxylic resin is that it represents a cost reduction because of improved acid efficiency. The carboxylic unit operates at close to theoretical efficiency.

Anion exchangers are polymers, which include weak-base and strong-base exchangers. The functional group of an anion exchanger is an amine. Weak-base exchangers contain a secondary or tertiary amine group which can absorb strong acids. Strong-base exchangers contain a quaternary amine.

Weak-base anion exchangers are able to remove only strong mineral acids— for example, HCl, H_2SO_4, HNO_3—and have minimal exchange capacity for weak acids. They can relieve the load on the strong anion exchanger by removing the strong mineral acids, and the alkali used for regeneration then neutralizes these adsorbed acids, making the regeneration nearly 100 percent efficient.

Typically strong-base exchangers involve the removal of alkalinity from water by substitution for chloride ions. This process for the reduction of alkalinity without the use of acids is regenerated with sodium chloride brine and simplifies chemical handling.

The most common anion exchangers used in wastewater treatment involve the hydroxide form, with caustic soda being used for regeneration. The spent regenerant requires careful disposal, since it contains a large amount of unused acid plus calcium sulfate. The use of hydrochloric acid would avoid calcium sulfate precipitation, but may not be as cost-effective. For strong-base resins, the selectivity preference ranking for common anions is:

SO^{-2}
I^{-}
NO_3

CrO_4^{2-}
Br^-
Cl^-
OH^-

For example, the selectivity of anion exchange indicates that SO_4^{2-} has a preference over Cl^-.

Stabilization System

Stabilization treatment systems are generally designed to limit or reduce the ultimate release of hazardous constituents from a waste.[8,19] Typically, this is accomplished by reducing the solubility of the hazardous constituents, reducing the exposed area that may allow migration of the contaminants, or detoxifying the contaminants themselves. These treatment techniques also improve the handling characteristics of the waste for transport on-site or to an off-site TSD facility. Stabilization techniques designed to limit the solubility or mobility of hazardous constituents are particularly applicable to RCRA hazardous wastes containing heavy metals. Wastes that have undergone this type of treatment still must be disposed of on the land, but not necessarily in hazardous waste landfills.

In order to reduce the ultimate volume of waste for disposal, it is usually desirable to dewater the wastes initially before subjecting them to the solidification process. Solidification is widely practiced in the disposal of hazardous waste liquids and sludges. Most processes incorporate the waste into a solid matrix using a binding agent or polymers. Solidification may also include the addition of an absorbent to produce a liquid-free waste that can be easily handled in the field. Solidification and fixation processes are generally tailored to each waste on a case-by-case basis.

Common sorbents include fly ash, bottom ash, and cement kiln dust. The ideal sorbent should be inert and nondegradable. In selecting a sorbent, consideration should be given to the quantity required to eliminate free liquid, the compatibility with the waste, the sorbent contamination characteristics, and the binding properties of the sorbent. Acidic sorbents may solubilize metal hydroxides, release hydrogen cyanide, or produce hydrogen sulfide if improperly selected. Alkaline sorbents may release gases such as ammonia or carbon dioxide. Sorbents that contain carbon may create pyrophoric materials with hydrocarbon wastes.

Pozzolanic materials such as fly ash are capable of forming a solid mass when mixed with hydrated lime. Stabilization of waste using lime and pozzolanic materials requires that the waste be mixed with water as needed for an optimal consistency. Numerous treatment processes incorporate portland cement as a binding agent, along with pozzolanic materials, to improve the strength and chemical resistance of the solidified waste. Portland cement, which is a mixture of oxides of calcium, silica, aluminum, and iron is produced in high-temperature kilns from limestone and clay.

Additives that further enhance the performance of the pozzolan-cement system might include soluble silicates to reduce metals interference and emulsifiers for organic liquids. Pretreatment prior to stabilization, such as dewatering to reduce the waste volume or chemical treatment to scavenge toxic materials, may be beneficial to ensure more cost-effective containment of the hazardous waste.

Stabilization increases the volume of material for disposal, making it necessary to reduce the toxicity and other hazardous characteristics. Mixed wastes may require several pretreatment steps that might make the process cost-prohibitive. In any event, economic evaluations of the stabilization alternatives should be compared to determine the most feasible method.

The most significant cost associated with solidification of wastes is the price of the chemical additives. This price may vary considerably, based upon manufacturing costs at a particular location, the quantity to be used, the market demand, and the stability of the material. Solidification additives, e.g., portland cement, are widely used in the construction industry, and their pricing generally reflects the current state of construction activity. Transportation costs are often the second most costly part of solidification and can sometimes exceed the cost of the additives themselves. Bulk truck shipment is commonly used to transport the materials to the solidification site, where the geological and hydrogeological setting usually determines the feasibility of spreading the treated waste material on-site.

PHYSICAL TREATMENT

Physical treatment involves a wide variety of separation techniques that have been commonly practiced throughout industry for decades.[30] Whenever a waste containing liquids and solids must be treated, physical separation should be considered first because it is generally a cost-effective method and the least complicated solution to many waste management problems. Physical processes for the separation of liquids and solids include screening, sedimentation and clarification, centrifugation, flotation, filtration, sorption, evaporation and distillation, stripping, and reverse osmosis. Each of these processes involves the separation of suspended matter from a liquid phase and depends mainly on the quality and the characterization of the suspended solids relative to that liquid phase.

The tolerance levels for residual solids in the treated effluent are an important criteria in the selection of the most cost-effective treatment process. Large particles with high densities generally are much easier to remove than finely divided, low-density particles.

Screening

The initial solids-liquid separation step in wastewater treatment involves the use of bar racks, strainers, and/or screens for the removal of large solids such as plastics, wood, and paper. The fine solids that remain in the liquid phase may then require further physical treatment—and perhaps chemical or biological treatment as well.

Sedimentation

Sedimentation is the removal of suspended solids from liquids by gravitational settling. The velocity of the liquid must be reduced to the point that the retention time in the sedimentation vessel is sufficient for solids to settle by gravity. The settling rate is affected mainly by the size, shape, and density of the solid particle as well as by the density of the liquid phase. As the particles settle, they accelerate until the frictional drag on the surface against the liquid equals the weight of the particle in the liquid. Particles settle in liquids according to the following relationship:

$$F = \frac{g}{g_c}(d_1 - d_2)V \qquad (7.4)$$

where F = impelling force, lb
    g = acceleration due to gravity, ft/s^2
    d_1 = particle density, lb/ft^3
    d_2 = fluid density, lb/ft^3
    V = particle volume, ft^3
    g_c = dimensional constant, 32.17(lb)(ft)/(lbf)(s^2)

When solid particles settle through a liquid phase in free-fall, the liquid displaced by the particles moves upward and the space between the particles is sufficient so that the counterflow of the liquid does not cause friction. The particles settle as separate units with no apparent flocculation or interaction between the particles. The settling of washed sand in water would be an example of free-fall settling. As the settling particles fall in the vessel, they begin to form a solid-liquid interface and their previous free-fall velocity is diminished, as shown in Figure 7-2. As they become part of the sludge phase, these particles will slowly compact and their settling will be hindered. During hindered settling, the particles move close together in the liquid and thereby restrict the settling of neighboring particles to a relatively fixed position and at a uniform velocity. This group of particles settles as a single zone with a solid-liquid interface at the top of the zone between the clarified liquid and the settling particles. As this sedimentation process continues, the particles become a dense sludge layer. The compression settling rate within the sludge layer is greatly diminished because of the increase in the density of the fluid phase. These settling rates will also be directly proportional to the temperature of the liquid, since both the density and viscosity of the liquid are reduced with increasing temperature.

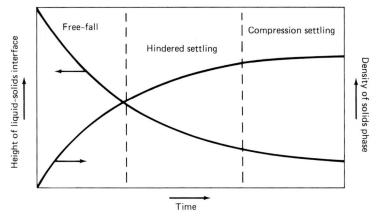

FIGURE 7-2
Stages of the settling of solids in liquids.

Clarification

Cost-effective and efficient clarifiers are often used to achieve more rapid gravity sedimentation and particle removal of solids from liquid wastes. Normally, the goal in clarification is to produce a clear liquid effluent rather than a dense, dewatered sludge. Large settling ponds can be used to clarify wastewater if sufficient land and other resources are available to support such an installation. These settling ponds are typically sized to contain several weeks' output of dilute aqueous systems. The residence time in the settling ponds must be sufficient to allow the solid particles to settle by gravity and collect on the bottom of the pond. The liquid overflow remaining after the removal of the solids then moves from the settling pond to undergo either discharge, recycling, or further treatment processing.

There are several types of clarifiers, all of which induce separation through gravity. These include sedimentation basins, solids contact units, and inclined-tube or -plate separators. The most commonly used sedimentation basin in the treatment of dilute aqueous liquids such as wastewater is the center-feed clarifier (Figure 7-3). This type of clarifier combines mixing, coagulation, flocculation, and subsequent clarification into a single unit. The liquid waste to be treated flows into the center of the clarifier, where it is mixed with chemicals that are added to enhance coagulation, flocculation, and sedimentation. In the mixing zone the solids concentration may be several orders of magnitude higher than in the other parts of the clarifier. This high solids concentration greatly increases the rate of destabilization reactions and desirable particle growth. Variable-speed mixers are used to control the coagulation and flocculation rates of the solids concentration in the free-fall and settling zones. These zones must have sufficient cross-sectional area to reduce the upward liquid ve-

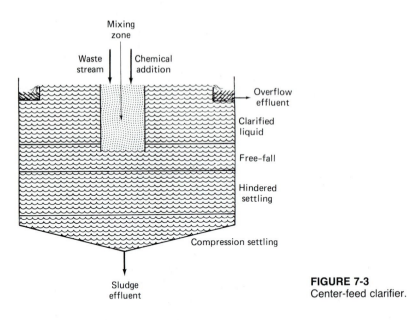

FIGURE 7-3
Center-feed clarifier.

locity and allow downflow of the solids. The cross-sectional area required for clarification A_c is given by the following:

$$A_c = 2\left(\frac{Q_E}{v_H}\right)$$

where Q_E = flow rate of the clarified effluent, ft³/h
$\quad v_H$ = solids velocity in hindered settling for solids-liquid clarification, ft/h

The sludge exits from the bottom of the clarifier with the aid of either a sludge blowoff pipe or a rake-and-pump system to facilitate removal of the solids. The treated aqueous effluent overflows and is withdrawn to be either discharged or to be sent to further treatment.

Solids contact units include slurry recirculation and sludge blanket clarifiers, which combine mixing, flocculation, and sedimentation in a single unit. These units maintain a high solids concentration, which greatly increases particle growth of the flocculated solids, thereby reducing the size of the equipment. In the slurry recirculation unit, the high volume of flocs is enhanced by the recirculation from the flocculation zone to the clarification zone. The sludge blanket clarifier maintains the flocculated solids in a central compartment, which results in a more uniform flow distribution than in standard clarifiers. As the larger flocs settle to the bottom, the fine flocs are removed from the liquid by contact with them. The flocculation and solids concentration in the reaction zone is controlled by variable-speed mixers. A solids balance must be carefully maintained between the incoming untreated solids-liquid phase and the effluent solids being removed from the bottom of the clarifier. For solids contact units to operate efficiently, large volumes of solids must be maintained within the clarification system.

In addition to the traditional clarifier design, other innovative clarifiers have been developed that are highly efficient and require less space for installation. These newer versions of clarifiers may be used where land is at a premium or more operational flexibility is desirable. Among them are clarifiers with inclined settling devices, where the liquid flows upward and the solids slide down the inclined plane or tube to the bottom.[28] The plane is inclined sufficiently to allow the sludge to settle in this manner.

The lamella separator, for example, contains inclined plates that are closely spaced, thereby creating more settling surface in a small volume to reduce the space requirements for installation of the unit. The lamella plates multiply the available settling surface by greatly shortening the settling distance. The coagulation and flocculation process in the lamella concentrates the accumulated sludge as it moves down the inclined surface.

The lamella is ideally suited for treatment of waste streams in either cramped locations or places where space is at a premium. It is also generally less costly to purchase and install and is easier to operate. Furthermore, it is readily adaptable to mobile installations, which could be advantageous in many hazardous waste management situations.

In addition to removal of low concentrations of solids from aqueous systems, sedimentation and clarification techniques may also be used for thickening or for removal of water from sludges with high solids content. The purpose of thickening is to increase the solids content of the sludge. The clarity of the water leaving the thickener is not as critical as in the clarification process because the liquid from a thickener will typically be recycled back to the clarification process. Gravity thickeners are similar to clarifiers, except that the thickeners generally require longer residence time to separate the liquids from the solids.

The cross-sectional area required for thickening A_T in a sedimentation basin is given by the following:

$$A_T = 1.5(Q_E + Q_B)\left(\frac{t_c}{h}\right) \tag{7.6}$$

where Q_E = flow rate of the clarified effluent, ft^3/h
$\quad\quad Q_B$ = flow rate of the bottoms effluent, ft^3/h
$\quad\quad t_c$ = time of transition from hindered to compression settling, h
$\quad\quad h$ = initial interface height of the hindered settling zone, ft

Centrifugation

Centrifuges are frequently employed in dewatering of waste sludges to 10 to 40 weight percent solids. The goal of dewatering is usually to produce a solid cake that has sufficient density, strength, and solids content to permit hauling as a solid waste to a final disposal site. This dewatering operation usually follows a conventional clarification and thickening of the solids. If the sludge is to be incinerated, it should be dewatered sufficiently to minimize the subsequent auxiliary fuel requirements for incineration. The centrate from the centrifuge usually contains finely divided suspended solids that may be recycled to the clarifier.

Centrifuges are used in dewatering applications because they are compact, have high throughput capacity, and are simple to operate. The use of gravitational forces in centrifugation greatly increases the separation efficiency when compared with conventional gravity clarification. This reduces the required retention time because the solid particles only have to settle a few inches instead of many feet, as in a clarifier.

Solid-bowl and basket centrifuges are the most commonly used types in dewatering sludges. The operation of the solid-bowl centrifuge is based upon Stokes' law:

$$v = \frac{2r^2(d_1 - d_2)g}{9\mu} \tag{7.7}$$

where v = settling velocity, ft/s
  r = particle radius, ft
  d_1 = particle density, lb/ft^3
  d_2 = liquid density, lb/ft^3
  g = acceleration due to gravity, ft/s^2
  μ = viscosity, lb/(ft)(s)

The g factor for centrifugation is in the 2000 to 3000 range versus a sedimentation g factor of 1, hence the dramatic difference between these operations for solids-liquid separation.

The most important design variables for centrifuges are bowl type, bowl rotational speed, and scroll speed. The retention time increases with increasing bowl length and diameter, producing drier solids and improving the clarity of the centrate, but at the same time increasing power requirements. Increasing bowl speed produces drier cake and clearer centrates, while increasing scroll speed increases throughput but also produces wetter solids and a poorer-quality centrate. Polyelectrolytes are often used to enhance the operation of centrifuges and are usually selected on a case-by-case basis to fit the sludge properties and the expected effluent requirements.

The solid-bowl centrifuge is flexible in its ability to balance the desirable cake dryness and the centrate quality over a broad range by changing the pool depth. Most solid-bowl centrifuges operate in the 1500 to 2500 r/min range. The conical section at one end of the bowl forms a dewatering beach over which the conveyor pushes the sludge for discharge through outlet ports. The centrate is removed through weirs or via skimmers. In a concurrent centrifuge, the sludge and the centrate leave the same end of the bowl. In a countercurrent centrifuge, the centrate and sludge leave at opposite ends.

A basket centrifuge involves a batch process for dewatering of slurries and pumpable sludges. The sludge or slurry enters through a feedline from the top of the centrifuge to a point near the bottom of the rotating drum or basket. The centrate is normally collected by simple overflow from a weir at the top of the bowl or from a perforated bowl which has a drum with holes similar to that of an automatic washing machine. The perforated drum requires a filter medium that is placed on the inside of the drum. The liquid passes by centrifugal force through the filter cake to the outside of the drum and is drained off. Basket centrifuges are used whenever a dry cake and the recovery of solids are desirable.

Flotation

Low-density solids and hydrocarbon solids may be separated from liquids by air flotation. The air is introduced into the waste liquid in the form of finely divided bubbles, which attach to the particles to be removed. The particles then rise to the surface for removal by skimming.

Henry's law describes the relationship for nonionizing gases of low solubility. It states that the concentration of dissolved gas in the liquid will be directly proportional to the partial pressure of that gas above the liquid surface:

$$X = \frac{P_i}{H} \tag{7.8}$$

where X = mole fraction of gas dissolved in liquid
P_i = partial pressure of gas in contact with liquid
H = Henry's constant

In flotation the microbubbles of air may become attached to the particles by contact or by actual formation at the solid-liquid interface. They may also become entrapped under larger particles or become an integral part of flocs. This potential for incorporation into floc structures encourages the use of polyelectrolytes, which can enhance flocculation of solid particles at the formation sites of the air bubbles.

The air-contacted particles, which have a specific gravity less than water, rise to the surface. Mechanical skimmers then remove the floating particles from the flotation unit, and the liquid is withdrawn from the bottom.

The air-to-solids ratio for a pressurized hazardous wastewater flotation system is given by

$$\frac{A}{S} = \frac{1.3X_a(fP - 1)}{X_S} \qquad (7.9)$$

where $\dfrac{A}{S}$ = air to solids ratio, mg/mg

X_a = air solubility in water, cm^3/l

f = dissolved air fraction, typically 0.5 to 0.8

P = inlet pressure, atm abs

X_S = concentration of suspended solids, mg/l

Some air flotation systems are designed to recycle a portion of the bottoms effluent back to the air pressurization tank, resulting in a modification of the air-to-solids ratio:

$$\frac{A}{S} = \frac{1.3X_a(fP - 1)R}{X_SQ_F} \qquad (7.10)$$

where R = flow rate of recycle, gal/day

Q_F = flow rate of wastewater feed, gal/day

Filtration

In filtration the liquid is passed through a porous medium to remove suspended solids. As this process occurs, the solids deposited add to the thickness of the porous medium. Sand filters have been commonly used as a final polishing step in treatment of wastewater to produce a high-quality effluent. The sand will "classify" in the filter, with the smallest particles rising to the top. As the treated wastewater flows down through the sand, the suspended solids form a mat on the upper portion of the filter bed. Backflow washing is used to periodically clean the bed, removing the layer of unwanted solids.

Multimedia filters offer greater operating flexibility, longer on-stream factors, and higher filtration rates than single-medium filters. The media selected should have different grain sizes and specific gravities. In this way, one of the media will rest on top of the other media after backwashing. The top, lighter medium provides a coarse filtration step, followed by the final polishing step through the heavier, bottom medium. Often ground anthracite (with specific gravity of 1.6 and grain size of 1 mm) and silica sand (with specific gravity of 2.6 and grain size of 0.5 mm) are used in multimedia filters. The anthracite allows longer filter runs at high rates by providing the coarse filtration step. The finer, heavier sand provides a final polish to the effluent. The addition of a third medium, such as garnet (with specific gravity of 4.5 and grain size of 0.3 mm) can further increase filtration efficiency.

The head loss from a bed of porous media with varying particle size is given by the Rose equation:[38]

$$h_L = \frac{1.067}{\phi} \frac{C_D}{g} D \frac{V^2_a}{\varepsilon^4} \sum \frac{x}{d} \qquad (7.11)$$

where h_L = head loss, ft
ϕ = particle shape factor
C_D = drag coefficient
g = acceleration due to gravity, ft/s^2
D = bed depth, ft
V_a = approach velocity, ft/s
ε = porosity
x = size distribution, weight fraction
d = particle diameter, ft

The drag coefficient C_D is defined by

$$C_D = \frac{24}{N_{Re}} \qquad \text{for } N_{Re} < 1$$

$$(7\text{-}12)$$

$$C_D = \frac{24}{N_{Re}} + \frac{3}{\sqrt{N_{Re}}} + 0.34 \qquad \text{for } 1 < N_{Re} < 10^4$$

The Reynolds number N_{Re} is defined as

$$N_{Re} = \frac{\phi\, d V_a}{v} \qquad (7.13)$$

where v is the kinematic viscosity in square feet per second.
For stratified beds with uniform porosity, the Rose equation becomes

$$h_L = \frac{1.067}{\phi} \frac{D}{g} \frac{V^2_a}{\varepsilon^4} \sum \frac{C_D x}{d} \qquad (7.14)$$

Vacuum filters, belt presses, and filter presses are often used for dewatering sludges and can produce filter cake with a solids content as high as 50 percent. The solids content of the filter cake is dependent on the slurry being dewatered. The rotary-drum vacuum filter system, which is commonly used for dewatering slurries and sludges and is shown in Figure 7-4, is a perforated cylindrical drum that rotates in a trough containing the solid-liquid phase to be dewatered. A vacuum is applied to the interior of the drum, and the separation is accomplished by drawing the liquid through a filter medium, normally a filter fabric. The solids on the fabric are then removed by means of a "doctor blade." As the initial solids collect on the filter medium, they will act as an additional filter for subsequent cake formation. Because of this phenomenon,

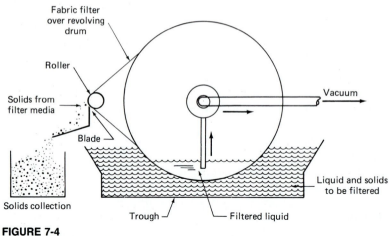

FIGURE 7-4
Rotary-drum vacuum filter.

it is desirable that the cake be formed gradually and that the vacuum be applied throughout the entire liquid-filtration step. This will enable water to be drawn through the filter cake and filter media to the inside of the drum and the filtrate to be removed.

The liquid level in the trough should be determined in conjunction with the rotary-drum cycle time that produces the desired cake thickness and solids content. Higher liquid levels generally produce thicker and lower-solids filter cakes than lower liquid levels, assuming all other variables remain constant. The filter media should be selected on the basis of the desired quality of the cake and the production rates. Thicker sludges will generally filter and release from the medium more readily than thin sludges. Large solid particles are also more desirable than fines because blinding of the filter media may occur if high levels of fines are present. The solids content of the filter cake may vary considerably, depending on the characteristics of the slurry being dewatered. Inorganic slurries offer the potential to dewater up to 70 percent solids, while biological sludges may only achieve a 25 percent solids level.

Coagulation and flocculation chemicals are often used in conjunction with vacuum filters, since large floc particles filter more readily and have less tendency to blind the filters. While the use of these chemicals requires an additional pretreatment step, it is normally cost-effective in maximizing the efficiency of the rotary-drum filter.

The yield for a vacuum filter is given by

$$Y = \frac{2 \, \Delta p W \alpha}{\mu R \theta} \tag{7.15}$$

where Y = filter yield, $lb/(h)(ft^2)$

Δp = vacuum pressure differential, lb/ft^2

W = weight of dry sludge solids per unit volume of filtrate, lb/ft^3

α = form time/cycle time

μ = filtrate viscosity, $lb/(s)(ft)$

R = filter cake specific resistance

θ = time for one drum revolution, s

W may be further defined as

$$W = \frac{\gamma}{[(1 - X)/X] - [(1 - X_c)/X_c]} \tag{7.16}$$

where γ = specific weight of water, $lb/ft3$

X = fraction of dry solids in sludge

X_c = fraction of dry solids in cake

Belt presses are continuous filters that utilize pressure to enhance dewatering. The conditioned sludge is fed onto a moving, fine-mesh, porous belt, where the initial drainage allows thickening to take place. This is the gravity drainage zone. This sludge then passes between two screens where pressure is applied and a partial dewatering occurs. Additional pressure is then used to further enhance the dewatering in the shear zone. The conditioned sludge is applied to the top of the belt media, which is usually a plastic or metal coarse-mesh fabric. Belt presses are particularly desirable for sludges that are difficult to dewater. The solids content in the cake will vary from 10 to 40 percent, depending upon the sludge being processed.

Plate and frame filter presses are commonly used to dewater sludges. This type of filter press consists of vertical plates held on a frame and pressed together. Between each plate is a filter medium, which is normally woven plastic. While liquids are passing through the filter medium, solids are being collected on the surface of the fabric. The slurry to be dewatered is fed to the filter press until the flow rate drops significantly. Then the flow to the unit is stopped, pressure is relieved, and the unit is opened to allow removal of the solid filter cake. Conditioning aids are generally used to shorten filter time and produce low-moisture filter cakes.

Drying beds are sometimes used to dewater sewage and industrial sludges whenever sufficient inexpensive land is available and the local climate is favorable for year-round operation of the beds. Drying beds offer the potential of lower operating costs and minimal maintenance requirements, which may offset the disadvantages of high land requirements, weather dependency, and potential odors that may affect air quality. The typical drying bed has drain tile that has been installed under sand-and-gravel filtration layers. The sludge for an effective dewatering operation using drying beds must have physical properties which allow the drainage of contained liquids without blinding the filter media. It is desirable that the sludge to be applied be as thick as possible to reduce the required drying time. The water drainage must be rapid and fairly complete.

An ultrafiltration polishing step to meet effluent guidelines or by-product criteria may be accomplished with cartridge filters, which may be tailored to the specifications of the finished product. These cartridge filters are usually expendable.

Sorption

The use of an adsorbent to remove a targeted substance from a solution is called *adsorption,* which is the physical adhesion of molecules or particles to the surface of a solid adsorbent without a chemical reaction. This contrasts with *absorption,* which involves the penetration of the molecules or particles into the solid absorbent. "Sorption" is a commonly used term that refers to both adsorption and absorption, since both may occur simultaneously in wastewater systems.

Adsorption The removal of organic and inorganic substances from aqueous waste with activated carbon is accomplished through adsorption of the chemical substances onto a carbon matrix.[4,27,35] In wastewater treatment, activated carbon is widely used to adsorb undesirable organic substances. It is used in either granular or powdered form, depending upon the application and the process economics. It is produced by controlled carbonization of high-carbon solids, followed by activation with steam or hot air. The effectiveness of activated carbon in removing these hazardous constituents from aqueous streams is directly proportional to the amount of surface area of the activated carbon, since adsorption is a surface reaction. Activated carbon usually has a total surface area in the range of 600 to 1000 m^2/g. It is porous, and the size of these pores is also important in determining the effectiveness of the adsorbent. The iodine number, which measures pores passing colloids larger than 1 mm, ranges from 650 to 1000 for activated carbon.

When activated carbon comes in contact with a water solution containing organics, adsorption of the organic solute occurs. Most adsorption is a physical process caused by van der Waals molecular forces, which are reversible. The adsorption equilibrium may be represented by the Freundlich isotherm:

$$\frac{x}{m} = kC^{1/n} \tag{7.17}$$

where x = mass of solute adsorbed, g
  m = mass of adsorbent, g
  k = empirical constant
  n = empirical constant
  C = equilibrium concentration of solute, g/l

The Langmuir isotherm is also used to describe this type of adsorption:

$$\frac{x}{m} = \frac{\alpha kC}{1 + kC} \qquad (7.18)$$

where α is the mass of the adsorbed solute required to saturate a unit mass of adsorbent.

Organic compounds that are less soluble in water are more likely to be adsorbed on activated carbon. Because of high investment and operating costs, the physical separation of these chemicals from aqueous streams is generally cost-effective only when the contaminants are present in very dilute quantities. Carbon adsorption is typically used to treat dilute aqueous streams with organics in the parts-per-million range. The carbon granules are placed in columns or vessels and operated until the effectiveness of the carbon columns reaches the point of diminishing return. Once the carbon has been spent, it must be regenerated. If the organic material is volatile, the carbon bed may be regenerated by the use of steam. More typically, however, the carbon is removed and then regeneration takes place in a furnace. In a large activated-carbon installation, the regeneration furnace is normally installed as part of the carbon unit. In smaller installations, the carbon is typically removed and returned to the supplier for reprocessing.

Absorption Gas absorption occurs when soluble components of a gas mixture are dissolved in a liquid. The absorption may be physical or it may also involve a chemical reaction with compounds in the liquid solution. Examples of absorption in the treatment of hazardous substances include the water absorption of ammonia or hydrogen chloride from air. The solute is normally recovered by stripping or distillation, and the absorbing liquid is recycled back to the absorber.

A packed tower is often used for gas absorption. It consists of a column with a gas inlet and distributor at the bottom, a liquid inlet and distributor at the top, a gas outlet at the top, and a liquid outlet at the bottom. The column is packed with saddles, rings, or other solid shapes to provide good liquid-gas contact for the absorption to occur in an efficient manner. It is desirable to have high porosities in the packed tower to ensure adequate flow of both liquid and gas without excessive pressure drop.

Evaporation and Distillation

The evaporation of liquids is widely used in many applications for hazardous waste management. All liquids exert a *vapor pressure*, which is a measurement of the volatility of the liquid. Liquids with high vapor pressure will evaporate readily, while those with low vapor pressure evaporate more slowly, even requiring the addition of heat to enhance the evaporation rate. The boiling temperature of a pure liquid has been reached when the vapor pressure of the liquid equals the atmospheric pressure. Soluble salts and other waste impurities in the liquid will decrease the vapor pressure and elevate the boiling point. As the liquid is evaporated, the waste solution will become more concentrated and eventually saturated with dissolved solids.

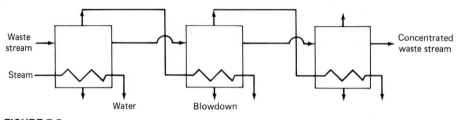

FIGURE 7-5
Multiple-effect evaporator.

Physical separation techniques are generally used before evaporation processes since separation reduces solids formation and maintains high heat transfer efficiencies. Evaporation produces a concentrated liquor that usually contains waste residue. By evaporating the solvent (often water or a valuable hydrocarbon), the volume of waste that must ultimately be breated or disposed of is greatly reduced.

Evaporation of liquids from hazardous wastes can be accomplished through single- and multiple-effect evaporators, distillation, steam stripping, or air stripping. Evaporators use steam tubes to heat the liquid waste to the boiling point. These steam tubes are generally submerged in the liquid to maximize heat transfer and promote efficient evaporation. The evaporator must have sufficient disengaging space to achieve the desired separation between the distillate and the liquid blowdown.

To conserve energy and enhance separation of volatile wastes from liquids, a multiple-effect evaporator, shown in Figure 7-5, may be used. The vapor from the first evaporator is fed to the tubes of the second evaporator, and the vapor from this second unit is fed to the third unit to produce the multiple effect. The vapor from the last tube in the series is condensed.

Distillation, the separation of two or more liquids by vaporization and condensation, is more effective on waste streams that require high-purity separation. Fractional distillation can produce a high-purity distillate and bottom streams that may be recycled or marketed. Depending upon the market potential for components of liquid waste streams, distillation may be a logical operation for separation into high-purity substances that can make this form of waste treatment an attractive business venture.

Stripping

Air stripping may be used to remove low concentrations of hazardous substances dissolved in water.[7,32] Stripping towers may be induced-draft towers, similar to cooling towers, with countercurrent flow of the upward air-solvent gas and the downward water-solvent liquid. The gas-liquid system will develop an equilibrium based upon Henry's law. The equilibrium waste in an air mixture will be

$$Y_W = \frac{P_W}{P_T} \frac{M_W}{M_A} \tag{7.19}$$

where Y_W = weight ratio of waste in air
P_W = partial pressure of the waste
P_T = atmospheric pressure in the tower
M_W = waste molecular weight
M_A = air molecular weight, 29

The air-waste streams may then undergo further treatment such as inciner-ation or carbon adsorption.

Steam stripping involves the injection of live steam directly into the liquid waste, as shown in Figure 7-6, to volatilize and separate the lighter compo-nents. Steam stripping is effective in separating low concentrations of volatile organic compounds. Stripping will remove volatile contaminants from an aque-ous waste stream and make them a part of the vapor from the treatment pro-cess. The overhead from a steam stripper will contain water along with the volatile organic components of the waste, requiring a condenser for further separation.

Reverse Osmosis

By the process of osmosis, a solvent flows through a semipermeable mem-brane from a dilute to a more concentrated solution.[21] The solvent normally flows in the direction that will reduce the concentration of the stronger solu-tion. The *osmotic pressure* of the solution is that pressure which when applied to the solution, will just prevent the passage of the solvent through the semipermeable membrane. In reverse osmosis, a differential pressure that ex-ceeds the osmotic pressure is applied to the membrane, causing the solvent to flow from the stronger to the weaker solution. The reverse osmosis process

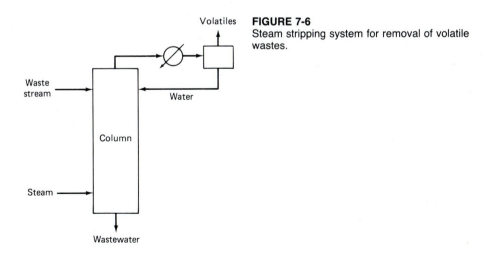

FIGURE 7-6
Steam stripping system for removal of volatile wastes.

has application in concentration of aqueous salt wastes to produce concentrated brines and high-purity water; in this case, a semipermeable membrane and hydrostatic pressure are used.

In the design of a reverse osmosis unit, the production of water, the water flux through the membrane, depends upon the membrane characteristics and the operating conditions of the system according to[25]

$$F_W = K(\Delta p - \Delta \pi) \tag{7.20}$$

where F_W = water production, gal/(day)(ft^2)
$\quad K$ = mass transfer coefficient, gal/(day)(ft^2)(psi)
$\quad \Delta p$ = feed and product water pressure difference, lb/in^2
$\quad \Delta \pi$ = feed and product water osmotic pressure difference, lb/in^2

The water production will gradually decrease over the life of the membrane because of a gradual and permanent densification of the membrane structure.

The following case study illustrates the use of physical and chemical processes to treat oil and gas drilling wastes. It is adapted from an actual case history.[42]

CASE STUDY
Oil-Field Waste Treatment with a Mobile System

Treatment and disposal of drilling muds and hazardous wastes has become a growing concern in the oil and gas industry. Concerns for environmental protection as well as rising trucking costs are both influencing a search for more effective and economic methods. Out of that has come the development of a mobile system for economical and environmentally effective cleanup of oil fields. The system includes equipment that is capable of being set up on a location within a matter of hours and is versatile enough to accommodate ever-changing oil-field conditions.

Development of the Technology

Mobile systems are needed to move into abandoned sites onshore to clean up the drilling-waste reserve pit after the drilling rig has left. The wastes in the reserve pit must be disposed of in an acceptable manner. The liquid waste must be separated into two products—clear water, which is discharged into the environment, and a relatively dry, nonleaching mud cake, which can be conveniently landfilled on or off location.

A process was developed to achieve the separation of solids from liquids in the waste using neutralization, solids precipitation, coagulation, and flocculation. The neutralization was necessary to achieve removal of heavy metals and other contaminants. The pH was reduced to precipitate contaminants, while the reactive solids were neutralized electrochemically. After neutralization, the particles began to settle because there were no electric charges to hold them in suspension. Several hours were necessary to achieve adequate settling.

The clear water on the surface still contained heavy metals and other contaminants that did not precipitate at a lower pH. During a second phase, the pH was raised to neutral, causing metal precipitation as well as precipitation of other contaminants. Thereafter, the water could be safely discharged into the environment.

During the neutralization process, coagulation was also occurring. Coagulation was achieved by adding a positively charged ion to the wastewater stream to attract the negatively charged particles. Tiny layers of heavy platelets were thus formed to promote settling, but they were small and their settling was hindered.

Because of the need for high flow rates during the treatment, a flocculation step was added. In flocculation the small layers of platelets were turned into large heavy solids that settled quickly. The addition of an organic flocculant to the waste stream created the flocculation necessary to achieve consistently high production rates. The polymer selected was positive, negative, or neutral, depending on the charge of the waste stream particles. The reactive sites on the polymer attracted the coagulated particles to form heavy popcorn-shaped solids.

Process Flow

The process consisted of mud dewatering, solids control, and water treatment, as shown in Figure 7-7. The process flow began from the reserve pit, with pH-adjustment chemicals added in line. The pH-adjusted waste slurry was then fed directly into the decanter centrifuge where polymer addition and dewatering occurred.

FIGURE 7-7
Process for oil-field waste treatment.

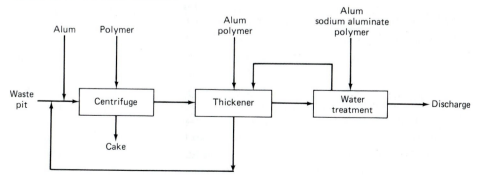

The decanter-type centrifuge was chosen for this dewatering application because it is very adaptable to a continuously varying solids feed from a large reserve pit. The variable-solids feed was used because of an inability to mix and agitate the entire pit. The centrifuge required chemical adjustments whenever the feed drastically changed, but the adaptability of the centrifuge meant that minor changes in feed required little if any chemical change.

The decanter centrifuge was a mud-dewatering unit specially designed to receive about 35 percent solids. The centrifuge operated at about 1650 r/min. The influence solids feed of about 35 percent by weight produced mud cake that was normally 70 percent solids or higher.

The chemistry in the decanter centrifuge operation involved slight pH adjustment of mud fed into the centrifuge where the polymer flocculant was added. The heavy drilled solids and barites were removed easily in the centrifuge, producing a clear centrate, while bentonite clay would not centrifuge as well. The centrate from the bentonite-type flow invariably contained some solids. The centrifuge had two discharge points, one to take the mud cake and the other the centrate. The solid mud-cake product formed from the centrifuge was conveyed and stacked around the site, pending later disposal. The centrate, which had fairly low solids, normally 3 to 5 percent, flowed into the thickener or solids control unit where additional chemicals and polymers were added.

The sludge thickener was a small mud tank with a series of mixers and baffles to reduce channeling through the bottom of the tank and to promote optimum removal of solids from the tank. The solids settled to the bottom of the unit, while the water overflowed and was moved to the final treatment unit. The influent for this unit ranged from 5 to 15 percent solids. Optimum flow rates were achieved at lower influent solids, while lower production was noted at higher influent solids.

The overflow was usually solids-free. The solids in the underflow of the thickener flowed back into the mud feed line before reaching the pH-adjustment point. Adding these solids in the mud line yielded benefits with residual polymer and pH adjustment. The light solids which would not centrifuge initially were reintroduced into the mud stream with the heavy slurry from the pit. Because of the flocculation characteristics of the polymer, these solids were of particle size much larger than normal. The more polymer added, the stronger the flocculated particle. These solids and the heavy mud slurry centrifuged more easily and chemical consumption was optimized.

The midrange solids were effectively treated and entered two separate treatment phases. The settled solids in the first bay were fed back into the decanter centrifuge, while the overflow contained in a surge tank was less than 1 percent solids and was treated through the water treatment unit in preparation for discharge. The water treatment unit effectively treated an influent feed of maximum 1.5 percent solids by weight and was completely self-contained and mobile.

In this treatment unit, the solids were floated instead of being allowed to sink, as was the process in the previous unit. Adjustment of pH was necessary to achieve coagulation and to begin solids removal. All pH adjustment was accomplished automatically with the use of meters that controlled the pumps feeding the pH-adjustment chemicals. After pH adjustment, an electric current was passed through the water by a series of electrodes; the electrolysis produced micrometer-size bubbles. Many of the bubbles and solid particles adhered to each other or to the solids, and the bubbles remained in very close proximity. The wastewater and bubbles were then mixed with an organic coagulant, a long-chain polyacrylamide. The polymer, the solids, and the bubbles were trapped in the floc particle, causing the particle to pop to the surface. The waste mixture flowed into a final large tank where the turbulence was relatively low and still more bubbles were added by electrolysis. The large tank provided a settling time which allowed flotation to occur.

The settling time in the basin, with very low turbulence, was about 25 minutes. The solids were skimmed off the basin with a chain-driven skimmer. The skimmings were pumped to the thickener unit where residual chemicals in the skimmings were utilized to begin treatment of the centrate, thus eliminating possible residual chemicals in the discharge. As the skimmings were removed, the water flowed continuously under a series of baffles and into the clear well where it was ready for off-site discharge.

Operating Results

Each unit was equipped with a complete laboratory to perform all state tests required for discharge. The water discharged was pumped to a nearby ditch or waterway. Discharge analysis was performed on composite samples every 12 hours. This analysis was recorded in log books kept on the location. Table 7-1 indicates a typical influent and discharge analysis. The influent at this location had a high oil content, but that was reduced to lower levels in the discharge. The system effectively removed 98 percent of all contaminants in the waste stream. Though there was no appreciable reduction in chlorides through the system, all other heavy-metals contaminants were reduced to within discharge limitations.

TABLE 7-1
WATER SAMPLE COMPARED WITH END PRODUCTS—WATER AND MUD CAKE

	Influent water	Effluent water	Solids leachability
pH	11.1	6	
Chlorides, mg/l	462	394	
COD*, mg/l	1981	98	
TSS†, mg/l	50	9	
Chromium, mg/l	0.29	0.05	0.05
Zinc, mg/l	2.3	0.65	0.75
Oil and grease, mg/l	330	0.044	1.5

*COD = chemical oxygen demand.
†TSS = total suspended solids.

The receiving body for the discharge was also monitored to ensure that no detrimental effects occurred in the waterway. Monitoring the receiving body included both visual and analytical inspection to ensure continual optimum performance. The mud-cake product was also thoroughly analyzed to ensure that no harmful effects would result from land-spreading it. Previous research on various types of drilling muds, including both water-based and oil-based muds, indicated very little leaching of the heavy metals, chromium or zinc, or oil and grease. The oils in oil muds remained with the cake because of the polymers used during the treatment process.

The process was pronounced environmentally sound and eminently successful.

BIOLOGICAL TREATMENT

Biological treatment can be an efficient, cost-effective way to remove hazardous substances from contaminated wastewater and groundwater, landfill leachate, and contaminated soil.[2,5,18,22,24,41] The microbes for biological treatment may be classified as *heterotrophic* or *autotrophic,* depending upon their source of nutrients. Heterotrophs use organic and autotrophs inorganic matter. Microorganisms may be further categorized according to their utilization of oxygen. In aerobic processes, oxygen molecules are required to decompose organic matter for the energy bacteria need to grow and multiply. Anaerobic microbes use oxygen that is combined chemically with other elements, such as nitrates, carbonates, or sulfates; anerobes also require the absence of any free oxygen molecules. *Facultative microbes* can use aerobic processes if oxygen molecules are present, but they can also use anaerobic processes.

The aerobic organisms are most commonly used to treat industrial waste streams, particularly wastewater. Anaerobic systems are usually confined to the treatment of strong organic waste or organic sludges from the aerobic process.

A typical growth pattern for microorganisms, shown in Figure 7-8, repre-

FIGURE 7-8
Stages in the life cycle of a community of microorganisms.

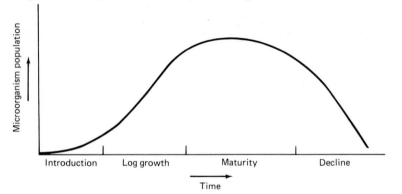

sents a life-cycle curve for the biological system. There are several stages involved in a microorganism's life cycle:

Introduction phase: The microbes are introduced and become acclimated to their new environment.

Log-growth phase: The microbial rate of fission is maximized through optimal growth conditions.

Maturity phase: The microbial rate of fission becomes limited because of the declining availability of one or more critical conditions.

Decline phase: The microbial population experiences a rapid and steady decline because the environment has now become less desirable for growth.

Bacteria reproduce by fission, with the parent cell splitting into new cells. If there is an adequate nutrient supply, this reproduction process will occur rapidly and organic substances will break down into less toxic chemicals or may be completely destroyed. The ability of bacteria to consume organics is measured by *biochemical oxygen demand (BOD)*, which is the quantity of oxygen utilized by microorganisms in the aerobic oxidation of organics at 20°C.

Microorganisms will grow if provided the proper conditions. They need a carbon and energy source, which may come from sunlight, a reduced inorganic compound, or an organic compound. They need nutrients such as nitrogen, phosphorus, and trace metals. Aerobic organisms need a source of oxygen. Some organisms can use oxidized inorganics such as nitrates as a substitute for oxygen. The temperature and pH must be controlled and substances that are toxic to the organisms must be removed.

Collectively, the cellular materials contain a wide variety of elements. Many proteins, when used as enzymes, require trace concentrations of metals. As a result, elements must be present as nutrients for organisms to grow. Other organisms, because they are not able to synthesize some of the required intracellular organics, must be supplied with both the inorganic nutrients and the organic intermediates needed for growth.

Many people assume that the treatment of hazardous waste with biological processes is not possible; they reason that hazardous materials are toxic to living organisms, and since microorganisms are living organisms, biological treatment is not a viable alternative. It is true that hazardous organics may be toxic to some or all members of a given microbial consortium when present above some critical concentration. The existence of such a critical toxic concentration is dependent upon the compound, its concentration, its exposure route, and the makeup of the microbial consortium. But a substance that is hazardous for one group of organisms may be a valuable food source for another group. Hazardous organics can be treated biologically provided that the proper organism distribution can be established. It is only by viewing biological treatment systems as a dynamic population of microbes whose composition is subject to various selection pressures that proper systems can be designed, maintained, and corrected when problems arise.

Biodegradability is system-specific. Unless the proper microbial consortium can be both developed and maintained, a compound may not degrade in that system. The aerobic process may need other physical and chemical treatment in order to achieve the desired results. In any event, biological systems can lower the cost of downstream processes by reducing organic load. Leachates and highly contaminated wastewaters can be treated with conventional process technology that provides adequate mixing, oxygen supply, nutrient addition, and temperature and pH control. Biological treatment of contaminated soils offers the same promise.

While a microbial community that is resistant to moderate levels of heavy metals can be developed, the accumulation of metal precipitates on the biomass may severely inhibit their activity. As a result, a pretreatment system to remove metal contaminants may be desirable. Treatment efficiency can be adversely impacted if the salt content is greater than 2 percent.

If the organics are biodegradable and if the desirable organisms can be enriched and maintained in the microbial community, then the system can be designed so that the toxin is maintained below toxic levels. If the toxin is nonbiodegradable, microbial strains that are resistant to the toxin must be enriched. If the concentration of organics fluctuates above the toxic limit or the flow rate varies greatly, the performance of the biological system could deteriorate. Because biological processes are sensitive to load variations, use of storage vessels to hold the contaminated material before introducing it to the biological system could reduce the possibility of upset.

Nitrogen and phosphorus are common nutrients that are added to a biological system, since lack of these elements in sufficient quantities in an inorganic form will severely retard biological activity.

Most of the organisms capable of treating hazardous substances grow well in the 6 to 8 pH range. Adjustment of the pH of soils and pH control in biological reactors treating wastewaters may be required if the pH is affected by either the biological activity or the hazardous material supply. Many hazardous organics are readily degraded aerobically, but because the depth of oxygen penetration in soils is limited, the rate and extent of biological detoxification is also limited. Aeration may sometimes be needed in biological treatment of leachates and other heavily contaminated wastewaters.

Temperature is a significant factor in biological treatment of hazardous wastes. Psychrophilic (cold), thermophilic (heat), and mesophilic (moderation) microbes require different temperatures for maximum growth. The temperature effect for the combined microbial community, shown in Figure 7-9, influences life-cycle tendencies similar to those shown in Figure 7-8, except that the decline is more pronounced because of the sensitivity of microbes to higher temperature ranges. For short-term variations in temperature, the rate of removal of organics is directly proportional to temperature until some maximum is reached, at which point it becomes inversely proportional. The impact of long-term changes in temperature is not as clear because the characteristics of the microbial consortium may vary with temperature. As a result, the rate and extent of removal of organics may vary with temperature much more than would be expected from short-term considerations.

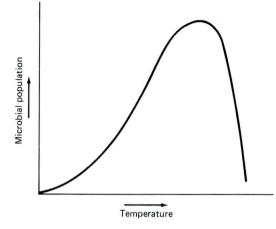

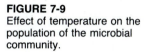

FIGURE 7-9
Effect of temperature on the population of the microbial community.

The microbial consortium that develops is, of course, strongly influenced by the treatment process selected. If a biodegradable toxin is allowed to accumulate, an essential member of the microbial consortium may be eliminated from the seed culture. The biological treatment of leachates and wastewaters containing hazardous materials, as illustrated in Figure 7-10, should include equalization and storage, pH adjustment, chemical precipitation and clarification, biotreatment, and then final polishing with activated carbon and sludge handling. In some instances, treatment of the exhausted gas must be considered. The design of the unit operations and processes requires experimental studies.

The two most common technologies for suspended-growth biological systems are the *continuous flow system (CFS)* and a time-stepped batch process

FIGURE 7-10
Biological treatment system for liquid hazardous waste.

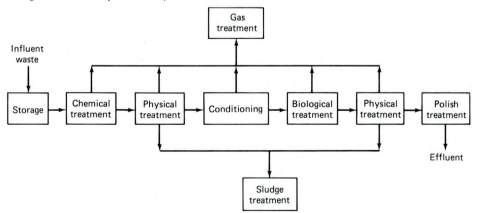

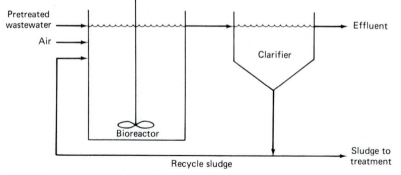

FIGURE 7-11
Continuous-flow biological reactor system.

called the *sequencing batch reactor (SBR)*. A CFS, shown in Figure 7-11, begins with pretreated water entering a stirred bioreactor for organism growth and accompanying substrate removal. The suspension passes from the bioreactor to a clarifier, where the biomass is separated from the treated liquid effluent, which may undergo further treatment. The bottoms of the clarifier are returned to the bioreactor to maintain the desired biomass concentration. Biomass in excess of that required for proper operation of the bioreactor flows to sludge processing.

An SBR system, shown in Figure 7-12, is a time-oriented, stepped process that accomplishes in a single vessel essentially the same process accomplished in CFS.[22] For the continuous treatment of wastewater, the SBR should be preceded by the pretreatment of leachates and highly contaminated wastewaters. A typical SBR system uses a cyclical process that includes fill, react, settle, draw, and idle steps. Often an SBR system uses two parallel reactors so that as one tank is filling, the other tank is completing the remaining periods of the cycle.

During the fill stage the pretreated leachate or wastewater enters the vessel containing acclimated biomass. Aerobic or anerobic reactions initiated during

FIGURE 7-12
Operation of a sequencing batch biological reactor system.

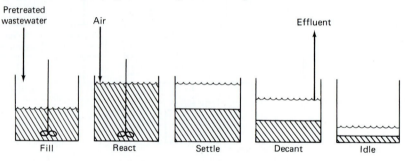

the fill are continued in the reaction stage. The time for reaction must be sufficient to meet the desired effluent requirements. The biomass is then allowed to settle for a predetermined period of time by shutting down the mixing and aeration equipment. The treated, clarified effluent is then removed during the draw stage. During idle, the liquid flow is switched into the other reactor, beginning a new cycle.

The time for each stage in the SBR operation can be related to a corresponding time in a CFS operation. Because treatability studies are imperfect and because leachates and highly contaminated wastewaters change character with time, the SBR single-reactor flexibility offers an excellent treatment alternative to the conventional CFS.

Aerobic Systems

The objective of aerobic systems is to develop microbes which will convert a wide variety of organic compounds to new cell material for removal by conventional separation techniques and to nonhazardous substances such as carbon dioxide and water. Some organics may not be degraded in a particular environment, while others are only partially degraded and are converted to other secondary organics. This understanding of the biodegradability of organics is applicable to all organics, whether or not they are classified as hazardous compounds. Aerobic processes generally take place according to the following reaction.

$$\text{Organics} + O_2 \rightarrow CO_2 + H_2O + \text{other products} + \text{energy}$$

The "other products" in this process are dependent upon the type of organics and other nutrients present as well as upon the extent of biological activity.

Aerobic oxidation is usually a first-order kinetic reaction:

$$\frac{-dc}{dt} = kc \tag{7.21}$$

where dc/dt = rate of bioreaction, lb moles / [(ft^3)(s)]
k = bioreaction rate constant, l/s
c = concentration of biodegradable substance, lb moles / ft^3

Rearranging, we get

$$\frac{C}{C_o} = e^{-kt} \tag{7.22}$$

where C_o = C at t = o.

The solids retention time in a bioreactor is given by

$$t_s = \frac{V_b}{R_b} \tag{7.23}$$

where t_s = solids retention time, days
  V_b = solids capacity of bioreactor, lb
  R_b = solids production rate in bioreactor, lb/day

The dissolved molecular oxygen concentration must be maintained at least at 2 pounds of O_2 per pound of solids destroyed. If the oxygen content is too low, portions of the solids may become anaerobic and adversely affect the biological destruction.

Many contaminated leachates, wastewaters, and soils may be treated by aerobic process.[23,31] The aerobic biological process selected must allow proper conditions—e.g., oxygen, pH, and temperature—to be established so that the required organism will have a competitive edge. The majority of the biological treatment systems are aerobic bioreactors that rely on aeration to support microbial growth. Several types of these aerobic systems include aerated lagoons, trickling filters, and rotating biological contactors.

Aerated Lagoons   Aeration lagoons are often used in hazardous waste treatment.[11] Sufficient oxygen should be furnished to maintain dissolved oxygen throughout the entire 8- to 12-foot depth. Aerated lagoons require ample land for a 1- to 2-month retention time. They usually are rectangular, with a length-to-width ratio of 2 to 1. Several lagoons may be installed and should be arranged so that either parallel or series operation is possible. Dikes forming the lagoon usually are sloped 1 to 3 or less, and riprap or other suitable protection is used to avoid destruction from wave action. The outside slopes should be vegetated to avoid erosion. The lagoon bottom and sides should be provided with a liner and have a freeboard of at least 3 feet. Concrete pads must be furnished under each aerator to protect the bottom from erosion. Stabilization ponds may be provided for the final effluent.

Aerated lagoons for treatment of industrial waste commonly have floating or platform-mounted mechanical aeration units. Complete mixing and adequate aeration are essential. Aerators should be spaced to provide uniform blending for dispersion of dissolved oxygen and suspension of microbial solids.

Organic treatment depends on suspended microbial communities developed within the basin, since there is no provision for settling and returning activated sludge. BOD removal is a function of retention time, temperature, and the waste biodegradability and nutrient content:

$$\frac{B_e}{B_i} = \frac{1}{1 + kt}$$

(7-24)

$$k_t = k_{20}D^{T-20}$$

where B_e = effluent BOD, mg/l
$\quad B_i$ = influent BOD, mg/l
$\quad k$ = BOD removal rate constant, per day
$\quad t$ = detention time, days
$\quad T$ = temperature, °C
$\quad D$ = temperature coefficient

The value of k relates to degradability of the waste organics, temperature, and completeness of aeration mixing. For example, at 20°C, k values range from 0.3 to over 1.0. D is a function of biodegradability, with 1.035 the most common value. Oxygen uptake relates to BOD removal by the relationship

$$\text{lb of oxygen/day} = A \text{ (lb of BOD removed/day)} \qquad (7.25)$$

The values of A are determined by testing the particular wastewater to be treated. Values of A range from 0.5 to 2.0, with 1.0 being typical.

Trickling Filters In trickling-filter systems, primary effluent is sprayed over a bed of crushed rock, or other medium, coated with biological films. The major components of the trickling bed are the filter medium, underdrain system, and rotary distributor. The filter medium provides a surface for biological growth and voids for passage of liquid and air. The preferred medium is 3 to 5 inches in diameter. The underdrain system carries away the effluent and permits circulation of air through the bed. The underdrainage system, with provision made for flushing, the effluent channels, and the effluent pipe are designed to permit free passage of air. A rotary distributor provides a uniform hydraulic load on the filter surface. The most prevalent kind is driven by the reaction of the wastewater flowing out of the distributor nozzles.

The biological layer shown in Figure 7-13 consists of microbes that are aerobic to a depth of only 0.1 to 0.2 mm. The zone next to the medium is anaerobic. Microorganisms near the surface of the bed, where food concentration is high, are in the log-growth phase, while the lower zone of a bed is in a state of starvation. Dissolved oxygen extracted from the liquid layer is replenished from the surrounding air. As a wastewater passes through the trickling filter bed, the microbial growths remove an appreciable amount of the organic materials for use as food substances. As wastewater passes over microbial growths, an appreciable amount of the organic material is removed along with molecular oxygen. Aerobic processes occur and the oxidized organic and inorganic end products are released into the moving water film. The wastewater passes through a filter, while the organic materials are retained for several hours as they undergo bio-oxidation.

Rotating Biological Contactors Wastewater flows through a rotary biological contactor which consists of multiple plastic disks mounted on a horizontal

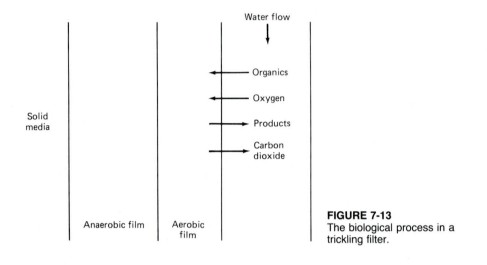

Water flow

Organics

Oxygen

Solid media

Products

Carbon dioxide

Anaerobic film

Aerobic film

FIGURE 7-13
The biological process in a trickling filter.

shaft. The shaft at right angles to the wastewater flow rotates, with about 40 percent of the total disk area being submerged. The bioabsorption and bio-oxidation processes that occur are similar to those of a trickling filter. A multistage rotary biological contactor consists of two or more stages connected in series to achieve the desired BOD removal. Recycle is not employed and the microbial growths sloughing from the contactor are removed by a final clarifier. Microbial activity is significantly reduced when the wastewater temperature drops, so in cold climates the disks must be covered for protection.

Advantages of the rotary biological contactors are their low energy requirements, their ability to handle shock loads, and the high degree of nitrification they provide. The principal design parameter for rotary disks is the wastewater flow per area of disk which is the hydraulic loading in gallons per day per square foot.

Anaerobic Systems

Anaerobic microbes require combined oxygen rather than molecular oxygen in order to function properly. Organic compounds generally undergo anaerobic conversion according to the following reaction:

$$\text{Organics} + \text{combined oxygen} \rightarrow CO_2 + CH_4 + \text{other products} + \text{energy}$$

The "other products" in anaerobic processes are dependent upon the type of organics and other nutrients present, the extent of biological activity, and the elements in combination with the oxygen source. Anaerobic systems require a narrower pH range than do aerobic systems, typically 6 to 8 for efficient methane production and lesser amounts of carbon dioxide. Oxygen sources which are nitrates result in nitrogen, and sulfates form hydrogen sulfide under anaerobic processes. Except for the type of oxygen source, the operational parameters are similar for both anaerobic and aerobic systems.

Anaerobic bioreactors are enclosed agitated vessels that operate with a methane and carbon dioxide gas cap. The influent, containing a high concentration of organics, is fed into the bioreactor. The gas is withdrawn for combustion and heat recovery or other utilization. The digested sludge is either recycled or dewatered. A supernatant liquid is removed from discharge or further treatment. Anaerobic digestion is typically carried on at 90 to 95°F for 15 to 20 days.

In designing a sludge digester, one must be aware of the many factors that will affect the digester volume; they include the nature of the fresh incoming sludge, the digested sludge produced, the digestion time required, the storage capacity for digested sludge, the supernatant liquor produced, and the gas that results.

For a batch system, the digester sludge volume required may be determined by the following relationship:

$$V_s = \left[V_1 - \tfrac{2}{3}(V_1 - V_2) \right] t$$

where V_s = total sludge volume, ft^3
V_1 = fresh incoming sludge, ft^3/day
V_2 = digested sludge produced, ft^3/day
t = required digestion time, days

QUESTIONS

1 Discuss and contrast distillation, steam stripping, and multiple-effect evaporation for liquid hazardous waste management.
2 Discuss the removal of organics from an aqueous waste stream using activated carbon adsorption.
3 Discuss two techniques that could be used for dewatering sludge.
4 Discuss the use of cement or lime to stabilize or solidify hazardous constituents in a waste.
5 Describe a chemical neutralization process.
6 Describe a heavy metal precipitation process.
7 Describe a process for the reduction of hexavalent chromium to trivalent chromium.
8 Describe the oxidation of sodium cyanide to produce nonhazardous products.
9 Discuss the following processes for the biological treatment of organics in aqueous waste streams:
   (a) Trickling filter
   (b) Anaerobic digestion
   (c) Rotating biological contactor
10 What treatment processes might be considered for removing color from wastewater?
11 How might you reduce the problem of hydrogen sulfide odors in wastewater?
12 Distinguish between coagulation and flocculation in industrial wastewater treatment.

PROBLEMS

1 Calculate the cross-sectional area and the clarifier diameter for clarification and thickening of hazardous industrial wastewater in a conventional clarifier. The maximum effluent-water flow rate is expected to be 35,000 gal/h. Based upon batch laboratory settling tests, the wastewater contains a maximum of 3000 mg/l of suspended solids, with a design sludge concentration of 12,000 mg/l. The initial interface height of the hindered settling zone is 2 feet, and the time to achieve transition from hindered to compression settling is 0.75 hour. The solids velocity in the hindered zone is 3.2 ft/h.

2 An industrial wastewater treatment plant requires a primary clarifier to process a peak loading of 1,850,000 gallons of wastewater per day, with a peak overflow rate of 1900 gal/(day)(ft^2). The peak weir loading is 28,000 gal/(day)(ft). Determine the clarifier diameter and the weir loading.

3 A wastewater from a plating shop contains 150 mg/l of zinc. The plating shop is relatively small, generating an average daily flow of 60,000 gallons. For this wastewater, the zinc is removed by hydroxide precipitation at the optimal pH of 9.5. The theoretical residual zinc remaining in solution is 0.3 mg/l; the secondary drinking water standard for zinc is 5 mg/l. The wastewater after being treated with caustic is sent through a clarifier with a desired overflow effluent concentration of 2 mg/l. The underflow has 2 percent solids.

(a) Determine the quantity of the underflow sludge requiring disposal.

(b) Often the assumption is made in clarifier design that the effluent concentration is 0 mg/l. If such an assumption is made, what would be the underflow daily rate? What percentage error results from this assumption versus the information provided in the problem?

4 Calculate the cubic feet of oxygen that may be dissolved in 20 pounds of water at an oxygen pressure of 1 atmosphere and a temperature of 20°C. The reciprocal of Henry's constant under these conditions is

$$0.033 \times 10^{-6} \frac{\text{lb mol O}_2}{(\text{lb mol H}_2\text{O})(\text{mmHg})}$$

5 Air flotation will be used to remove suspended solids from industrial wastewater containing 220 mg/l suspended solids and flowing at a rate of 450,000 gal/day. Laboratory tests have determined that 0.065 mg air per milligram of solids produces optimal air flotation with this wastewater. The flotation tank will operate at 10°C, and the solubility of air in water at this temperature is 22.8 ml/l. The fraction of air dissolved is 0.6. The flotation tank overflow rate is 1.9 gal/(min)(ft^2). Calculate the system pressure and the area of the flotation tank.

6 A centrifuge is to be used to dewater a conditioned waste sludge from a primary treatment operation. The conditioned sludge has 9 percent dry solids and a 1.12 specific gravity. The centrifuge can process sludge at a rate of 19,000 gal/day, with 93 percent solids removal, producing a cake with 22 percent dry solids. Determine the centrate and centrifuged cake production rates. Assume 8.34 lb/gal for the centrate.

7 A sand filter is to be used to remove suspended particles from a wastewater stream. The sand bed is 28 inches deep, has a 2.6 gal/(min)(ft^2) filtration rate, and will op-

erate at 60°F. The sand has a 2.7 specific gravity, a 0.8 shape factor, and a 0.44 porosity. Sieve analysis gave the following data:

Tyler sieve size	Sand retained, wt %	Mean sand diameter, ft
12–16	0.7	0.00395
16–24	9.5	0.00280
24–32	29.1	0.00198
32–42	37.2	0.00140
42–48	15.6	0.00107
48–65	6.4	0.00083
65–100	1.5	0.00059

Assuming uniform bed porosity, determine the head loss for the clean sand filter.

8 A rotary vacuum filter will be used to dewater a conditioned waste sludge. Laboratory tests on representative sludge samples have produced a filter yield of 5.18 lb/(h)(ft^2) at the anticipated operating temperature and vacuum. The sludge feed rate will be 75,000 gal/day, contain 3.5 weight percent dry solids, and have a 1.05 specific gravity. Determine the filter drum area to dewater the sludge.

9 Granular activated carbon will be used to treat an industrial wastewater that contains hydrocarbons. The wastewater total organic carbon (TOC) content is 0.380 gm/l. Determine the Freundlich isotherm constants using laboratory batch test data for the wastewater:

m, g/l	C_o, g/l	C_e, g/l
0.50	0.380	0.311
2.28	0.380	0.109
3.40	0.380	0.047
4.40	0.380	0.021
5.28	0.380	0.010

10 A wastewater stream contains residue ammonia that must be removed prior to discharge from an air-ammonia stripper. The stripper operates at 740 mmHg pressure and 20°C. Develop the coordinates for the stripper equilibrium curve. The partial pressure of 50-ppm ammonia in water at 20°C is 0.030 mmHg.

11 Determine the membrane area for a reverse osmosis unit to remove the minerals from 150,000 gallons of treated effluent per day. The membrane mass transfer coefficient is 0.0375 gal/(day)(ft)(psi) at 25°C. The feed and product water pressure differential is 335 psi. Their osmotic pressure difference is 40 psi. The anticipated minimum operating temperature is 15°C. The membrane area required at 15°C is estimated to be equal to 1.45 of the membrane area required at 25°C.

12 (a) A wastewater with a BOD concentration of 120 mg/l is sent to a 5-foot-deep trickling bed filter. Calculate the hydraulic loading on the bed if the BOD loading is 14 pounds of BOD per 1000 ft^3 per day.

(b) If the 5-foot-deep trickling filter is loaded at a rate of 40 pounds of BOD per 1000 ft³, calculate the required recirculation ratio to provide a hydraulic load of 18 mg/acre/day with a wastewater with a BOD of 120 mg/l.

13 Determine the primary clarifier and secondary clarifier sludges produced in a trickling filter plant that processes wastewater with 1300 lb/day of suspended solids and 1105 lb/day of BOD_5 (5-day biochemical oxygen demand). The primary clarifier before the trickling filter removes 37 percent of the BOD_5 and 67 percent of the suspended solids. The primary clarifier, trickling filter, and final clarifier plant remove 96 percent of the BOD_5 from the influent to the operation. The specific gravity of the primary clarifier sludge is 1.02, with 4.5 percent dry solids. The specific gravity of the secondary sludge from the final clarifier is 1.03, with 5.5 percent dry solids. Biological solids are produced at a rate of 0.36 lb per pound of BOD_5 removed.

14 The volume of an anaerobic sludge digester is to be determined for activated sludge in a wastewater treatment plant. The incoming fresh sludge contains 4400 pounds of dry solids per day, which represents 4 percent of the sludge. The wet sludge has a 1.02 specific gravity and has volatile solids that are 68 percent of the dry solids. During digestion at 90°F, 65 percent of the volatile solids is destroyed. The digested sludge has a 1.04 specific gravity and contains 7 percent dry solids. The sludge in the digester occupies 40 percent of the volume; gas and fluids take up the remaining 60 percent. The sludge residence time is 27 days and the sludge digestion time is 24 days at 90°F.

BIBLIOGRAPHY

1 *Alternatives to Hazardous Waste Landfills,* U.S. Environmental Protection Agency, Hazardous Waste Engineering Research Laboratory, Cincinnati, Ohio, 1986.

2 Bailey, J. E., and D. F. Ollis: *Biochemical Engineering Fundamentals,* 2d ed., McGraw-Hill, New York, 1986.

3 *Betz Handbook of Industrial Water Conditioning,* Betz Laboratories, Trevose, Penn., 1980.

4 Bhattacharyya, D., and C. Y. R. Cheng: "Activated Carbon Adsorption of Heavy Metal Chelates from Single and Multicomponent Systems," *Environmental Progress,* vol. 6, no. 2, 1987.

5 Blackburn, J. W.: "Prediction of Organic Chemical Fates in Biological Treatment Systems," *Environmental Progress,* vol. 6, no. 4, 1987.

6 Borup, M. B., and E. J. Middlebrooks: *Pollution Control in the Petrochemicals Industry,* Lewis Publishers, Chelsea, Mich., 1987.

7 Byers, W. D.: "Control of Emissions from an Air Stripper Treating Contaminated Groundwater," *Environmental Progress,* vol. 7, no. 1, 1988.

8 Campbell, K. M., et al.: "Stabilization of Cadmium and Lead in Portland Cement Paste Using a Synthetic Seawater Leachant," *Environmental Progress,* vol. 6, no. 2, 1987.

9 Clark, J. W., W. Viessman, Jr., and M. J. Hammer: *Water Supply and Pollution Control,* 3d ed., IEP, New York, 1977.

10 Dawson, G. W., and B. W. Mercer: *Hazardous Waste Management,* Wiley, New York, 1986.

11 Dienemann, E. A., et al.: "Rapid Renovation of a Sludge Lagoon," *Environmental Progress,* vol. 6, no. 3, 1987.

12 *Directory of Commercial Hazardous Waste Management Facilities,* U.S. Environmental Protection Agency, Office of Solid Waste, Washington, 1987.

13 Eckenfelder, W. W., Jr.: *Principles of Water Quality Management,* Van Nostrand Reinhold, New York, 1980.

14 Eckenfelder, W. W., Jr., and D. L. Ford: *Water Pollution Control,* Jenkins Publishing, Austin, Tex., 1970.

15 Edwards, B. H.: *Emerging Technologies for the Control of Hazardous Wastes,* Noyes Data Corp., Park Ridge, N.J., 1983.

16 Fair, G. M., J. C. Geyer, and D. A. Okun: *Water and Wastewater Engineering,* Wiley, New York, 1968.

17 Gehm, H. W., and J. I. Bregman: *Handbook of Water Resources and Pollution Control,* Van Nostrand Reinhold, New York, 1976.

18 Grady, C. P. L., Jr., and H. C. Lim: *Biological Wastewater Treatment,* Marcel Dekker, New York, 1980.

19 *Handbook for Stabilization/Solidification of Hazardous Waste,* U.S. Environmental Protection Agency, Hazardous Waste Engineering Research Laboratory, Cincinnati, Ohio, 1986.

20 *A Handbook on Treatment of Hazardous Waste Leachate,* U.S. Environmental Protection Agency, Hazardous Waste Engineering Research Laboratory, Cincinnati, Ohio, 1987.

21 Hess, M. C., et al.: "Wastewater Concentration by Seeded Reverse Osmosis: A Field Demonstration in the Electric Power Industry," *Environmental Progress,* vol. 7, no. 1, 1988.

22 Irvine, R. L., and A. W. Busch: "Sequencing Batch Reactors—An Overview," *J. Water Pollut. Control Fed.,* vol. 51, no. 235, 1979.

23 Irvine, R. L., S. A. Sojka, and J. F. Colaruotolo: "Enhanced Biological Treatment of Leachates from Industrial Landfills," *Hazardous Waste,* vol. 1, no. 123, 1984.

24 Irvine, R. L., and P. A. Wilderer: *Standard Handbook for Hazardous Waste Treatment and Disposal,* McGraw-Hill, New York, in print.

25 Kaup, E. C.: "Design Factors in Reverse Osmosis," *Chem. Engr.,* April 1973.

26 Kemmer, F. N.: *The Nalco Water Handbook,* McGraw-Hill, New York, 1979.

27 Ku, Y., and R. W. Peters: "Activated Carbon Polishing Treatment," *Environmental Progress,* vol. 6, no. 2, 1987.

28 Maimoni, A.: "Lamella Settlers: Material Balances and Clarification Rates," *Environmental Progress,* vol. 7, no. 2, 1988.

29 Merrill, D. T., et al.: "Field Evaluation of Arsenic and Selenium Removal by Iron Coprecipitation," *Environmental Progress,* vol. 6, no. 2, 1987.

30 Metcalf & Eddy, Inc.: *Wastewater Engineering: Treatment Disposal Reuse,* McGraw-Hill, New York, 1979.

31 Opatken, E. J., H. K. Howard, and J. J. Bond: "Stringfellow Leachate Treatment with RBC," *Environmental Progress,* vol. 7, no. 1, 1988.

32 Pearson, D. E., and A. R. Bowers: "An Air Stripping Method for Treatment of Electroplating Solutions," *Hazardous Waste and Hazardous Materials,* vol. 5, no. 1, 1988.

33 Peavy, H. S., D. R. Rowe, and G. Tchobanoglous: *Environmental Engineering,* McGraw-Hill, New York, 1985.

34 Perry, R., and D. Green: *Perry's Chemical Engineering Handbook,* 6th ed., McGraw-Hill, New York, 1984.

35 Peters, R. W., and Y. Ku: "Seeding the Metal Hydroxide/Metal Sulfide Reactor with Activated Carbon," *Environmental Progress,* vol. 6, no. 2, 1987.

36 *Principles of Industrial Water Treatment,* Drew Chemical, Boonton, N.J., 1981.

37 Reynolds, T. D.: *Unit Operations and Processes in Environmental Engineering,* PWS Publishers, Boston, 1982.

38 Rose, H. E.: "Further Researches in Fluid Flow through Beds of Granular Material," *Proc. Inst. Mech. Engrs.,* vol. 160, 1949.

39 Ulrich, G. D.: *A Guide to Chemical Engineering Process Design and Economics,* Wiley, New York, 1984.

40 Weast, R. C.: *Handbook of Chemistry and Physics,* 51st ed., Chemical Rubber, Cleveland, Ohio, 1971.

41 Weber, A. S., and M. R. Matsumoto: "Feasibility of Intermittent Biological Treatment for Hazardous Waste," *Environmental Progress,* vol. 6, no. 3, 1987.

42 Wentz, C. A., Jr., and C. M. Shiver: "Cleanup of Oilfield Wastes in an Environmentally Acceptable Manner," IADC/SPE Drilling Conference, New Orleans, February 1983.

43 Yurteri, C., and M. D. Gurol: "Removal of Dissolved Organic Contaminants by Ozonation," *Environmental Progress,* vol. 6, no. 4, 1987.

THERMAL PROCESSES

INTRODUCTION

Most hazardous wastes consist of carbon, hydrogen, and oxygen, with halogens, sulfur, nitrogen, and heavy metals also possibly present. While other elements may be involved, they usually exist only in small trace quantities and should not be a major consideration in applying incineration technology to the thermal destruction of hazardous waste.

The structure of the molecule generally determines how hazardous an organic substance is to human health and the environment. If the waste molecules can be destroyed or reduced to carbon dioxide, water, and associated inorganic substances, the organics should be rendered harmless. For these reasons, thermal destruction has generally become recognized as a preferred treatment technology in the management of hazardous wastes.[6,8] Incineration is a particularly desirable disposal technology when dealing with large quantities of organic hazardous wastes, since it ensures highly efficient destruction of most organic wastes, while at the same time producing only minimal quantities of undesirable air emissions, which can be controlled.[15,20] This technology has already greatly reduced the demand for hazardous waste landfills and should diminish the creation of additional Superfund sites for future generations. The problems of landfilling hazardous wastes are being increasingly recognized and dealt with in the United States, but the ever-present potential for landfill leakage and release of hazardous materials into the environment will be a legacy that will continue to haunt us for many generations to come. All concerned parties should be looking to thermal destruction as a preferred technology in hazardous waste treatment.[5,12]

ADVANTAGES AND DISADVANTAGES OF INCINERATION

Incineration offers a number of potential advantages over other waste treatment technologies and certainly over landfill operations. Incineration is an excellent disposal technology for all substances that have high heat-release potential. Liquid and solid hydrocarbons are particularly adaptable to incineration. The bulkier the materials to be incinerated, the greater the reduction in volume of wastes, and any significant reduction in volume of these problem wastes makes their management simpler and less subject to uncertainty.

Incineration offers detoxification of all combustible carcinogens, mutagens, and teratogens. Numerous other hazardous wastes detoxified by incineration included pathological wastes, which may otherwise result in disease transmission, as well as substances that are biologically active and may adversely affect other treatment processes. Another advantage of incineration is the reduction of leachable wastes from landfills and the elimination of long-term odors that might be emitted into the atmosphere surrounding the landfill. Incineration offers the opportunity to better manage potential air emissions at a central location as opposed to widely dispersed landfill locations.[19] From a regulatory perspective, a centralized operation is much easier and less costly to monitor and control. Further, industry and regulators alike have more experience in dealing with products of incineration as opposed to dealing with the complexities of organic hazardous waste in landfills. Another advantage of incineration is the potential energy recovery of the heat released and recovery of valuable by-products that can either be reused, recycled, or marketed.

While incineration of hazardous waste offers many potential advantages, it also has its drawbacks. The initial capital investment is higher than that for many other treatment technologies, certainly higher than that for landfilling. Incineration technology has evolved from open-pit burning in garbage dumps to use of highly efficient and sophisticated incinerators equipped with downstream apparatus to greatly limit both the quantity and type of air emissions. But these same improvements in incinerator technology have also resulted in higher investment costs for the new facilities and have increased the complexity of incinerator operations well beyond the capability of the traditional trash-and-refuse management business. Furthermore, the control of incineration technology requires highly trained operators. In order to ensure compliance with rules and regulations, qualified supervisory and operating personnel must be recruited for the incineration facility.

The actual operation of hazardous waste incineration is much more complex than other treatment technologies because of the variance in the waste composition and the severe operating conditions required to achieve desirable thermal destruction efficiencies. Incineration equipment has high maintenance requirements and must be carefully selected and maintained to ensure reliable operations, even under the most adverse climactic and process conditions.

The incineration of hazardous waste can potentially impact human health and the environment in a number of ways. The emission of odors, particulates, and hazardous gaseous substances must be controlled so as to keep these undesirable air pollutants from being emitted into the atmosphere.[11,17] The formation of potential air pollutants, such as hydrogen chloride, carbon monoxide, sulfur dioxide, nitrogen oxides, heavy metals, and other ash particulate matter, can have serious adverse impacts. Both process wastewater and runoff storm water must be effectively managed in order to ensure their containment and subsequent treatment. Processes that control air emissions create neutralization products that contain dissolved solids, abrasive suspended solids, and heavy metals, all of which could result in adverse environmental impacts. These factors must be subjected to risk assessment based upon experience and adaptability of technologies. The variations in the composition and volume of the waste feedback to be processed at the facility must also be considered.

In addition to these potential economic and technical concerns, the siting of hazardous waste incinerators has become a highly controversial issue.[21] While most people recognize the need to greatly reduce our historic reliance on landfills for hazardous waste disposal, there is a general reluctance on the part of most citizens to allow incineration operations to be sited in or near their communities, or even in their states. There must be a successful resolution of these siting problems or future generations will be faced with an ever-increasing occurrence of Superfund hazardous waste sites.

THE CHEMISTRY OF INCINERATION

Incineration is the controlled high-temperature oxidation of primarily organic compounds to produce carbon dioxide and water. Additional inorganic substances, such as acids, salts, and metallic compounds, will also be produced from the wastes. A thorough understanding of the chemistry of these processes is necessary to effectively apply incineration technology to the destruction of hazardous wastes.[22]

Incineration processes for management of hazardous wastes are highly complex and require control of the kinetics of chemical reactions under non-steady-state reaction conditions.[1,3,7,14,16] All of the mechanisms of heat transfer—including conduction, convection, and radiation—will take place among solids, liquids, and gases under high-temperature reaction conditions involving high rates of heat release. The complexities of these combined chemical and heat-transfer considerations are further complicated by fluid mechanics involving laminar and turbulent flow systems. Another factor that must be considered in incineration operations is the frequent and somewhat unpredictable shifting in the chemical and physical composition of the hazardous waste itself that is being fed into the incineration system. These variations will require sophisticated equipment if processes are to be controlled within desirable parameters during the day-to-day plant operation.

The chemistry of incineration represents a combustion process applied to the destruction of unwanted hazardous substances. It should be noted that the chemistry of combustion and the chemistry of incineration are interchangeable. Both "combustion" and "incineration" are used to define a thermal oxidation process. The distinction between combustion and incineration lies in the application of the chemistry and its relation to the desirable effects of resource conversion versus the destruction of undesirable substances. For example, combustion typically takes a valuable material, like coal, and oxidizes that material in the presence of a flame to produce a desirable end product— energy—and also undesirable waste products—air pollutants and a solid ash waste. On the other hand, incineration takes an undesirable waste—such as a hydrocarbon—and thermally destroys that waste to produce desirable air emission products—such as carbon dioxide and water—and energy of combustion; but undesirable air pollutants and a solid ash residue are also produced.

All combustion and incineration of organic substances is a highly complex sequence of reactions that ultimately result in similar final products. When an alkane is incinerated with air, the products of combustion are carbon dioxide and water. An example of this type of reaction for ethane, a relatively simple alkane, is shown in the following equation:

$$2C_2H_6 + 7O_2 \rightarrow 4CO_2 + 6H_2O$$

Aromatic hydrocarbons are incinerated in a manner similar to alkanes as shown by the combustion of toluene according to the following reaction:

$$CH_3 - C_6H_5 + 9O_2 \rightarrow 7CO_2 + 4H_2O$$

The incineration of mixtures of hazardous substances such as ethane and toluene commences as the temperature of the waste and air mixture is elevated to allow the oxidation reaction to occur spontaneously. The heat of combustion, which is the amount of heat released by complete combustion of the hazardous substance, will generally result in a high rate of heat release, and the phenomenon of burning will be observed. As the chemical bonds between the various elements of the reacting mixtures are broken, free radicals are formed to then produce the complete combustion products of carbon dioxide and water.

THERMODYNAMICS IN INCINERATION

There are two laws of thermodynamics that directly relate to all incineration technology.[18] The first law of thermodynamics states that although energy assumes many forms, the total quantity of energy is constant; when energy disappears in one form, it will reappear simultaneously in other forms. In other words, in any incineration process, the output of the system and surroundings must always equal the input into the system and surroundings. A simplistic way of looking at the first law of thermodynamics is that you cannot ever get something for nothing.

But the first law of thermodynamics, which states that energy must be conserved, imposes no restriction on the direction of energy transformations. The second law of thermodynamics is an expression of the fact that any process consisting solely of heat transfer from one temperature region to another forces that heat transfer to flow from the region of higher temperature to the region of lower temperature.

TABLE 8-1
ENTHALPY OF AIR, STEAM, AND VARIOUS GASES RELATIVE TO 60°F
(expressed in Btu/lb)

Temp., °F	H_{air}	H_{H_2O}	H_{CO_2}	H_{N_2}	H_{O_2}
500	106.79	1259.22	99.1	110.1	99.5
600	131.69	1307.12	124.5	135.6	123.2
700	156.87	1355.72	150.2	161.4	147.2
800	187.38	1405.02	176.8	187.4	171.7
900	208.21	1455.32	204.1	213.8	196.5
1000	234.36	1506.42	231.9	240.5	221.6
1100	260.81	1558.32	260.2	267.5	247.0
1200	287.55	1611.22	289.0	294.9	272.7
1300	314.56	1665.12	318.0	326.1	298.5
1400	341.85	1719.82	347.6	350.5	324.6
1500	369.37	1775.52	377.6	378.7	350.8
1600	397.17	1832.12	407.8	407.3	377.3
1700	425.08	1890.11	438.2	435.9	403.7
1800	453.24	1948.02	469.1	464.8	430.4
1900	481.57	2007.17	500.1	493.7	457.3
2000	510.07	2067.42	531.4	523.0	484.5
2100	538.72	2128.70	562.8	552.7	511.4
2200	567.52	2189.92	594.3	582.0	538.6
2300	596.45	2252.60	626.2	612.3	566.1
2400	625.52	2315.32	658.2	642.3	593.5
2500	654.70	2377.80	690.2	672.3	621.0

All incineration processes operate in conformance with the first and second laws of thermodynamics. Temperature is the driving force for the transfer of heat energy. The rate of heat transfer will be proportional to the temperature difference between the two media. The quantitative units of energy are based upon the temperature changes of a unit mass of water. For example, the *calorie* is defined as that quantity of heat that must be transferred to one gram of water to increase its temperature one degree Celsius. In a similar manner, the *British thermal unit (Btu)* is the amount of heat required to raise the temperature of one pound of water one degree Fahrenheit.

The term "enthalpy," which is the total energy of a substance at one temperature relative to the energy of the same substance at a different temperature, is a relative term that must be related to a base temperature point, as shown in Table 8-1. The incineration temperature may be calculated by the heat of the reaction and the properties of the products generated, as well as by the quantity of excess air in the incinerator.

The *net heating value (NHV)* of the hazardous waste mixture may be determined, assuming complete heat release of the incoming heating value. Usually 60°F is used as a reference temperature because heating value data for the hazardous waste components are readily available and may be used in the relationship

$$NHV_{mixture} = \sum_{i=1}^{\infty} X_i NHV_i \qquad (8.1)$$

In order to approximate the incineration temperature, several simplifying assumptions may be made:

1 The stoichiometric air requirement for any hydrocarbon waste is 0.01 ft³ air per British thermal unit. Using air at 60°F, this requirement becomes 7.5×10^{-4} lb air/Btu.
2 The heat capacity of the excess air (EA) is 0.3 Btu/(lb)(°F).
3 Adiabatic conditions exist in the incineration.

The NHV for the waste mixture becomes

$$NHV = (1 + 7.5 \times 10^{-4} NHV)(0.3)(t - 60)$$
$$+ (EA)(7.5 \times 10^{-4})(NHV)(0.3)(t - 60) \qquad (8.2)$$

Rearranging,

$$t = 60 + \frac{NHV}{(0.3)[1 + (1 + EA)(7.5 \times 10^{-4})(NHV)]} \qquad (8.3)$$

HEAT TRANSFER

The heat transfer objectives in hazardous waste incineration should include:

Maximization of the heat transfer rates, compatible with economic factors
Utilization of heat exchange whenever practical
Minimization of heat loss to the surroundings by the use of insulation

When optimizing heat transfer in incineration processes, all of these objectives may be desirable.

The three modes of heat transmission that interact in the thermal destruction of hazardous waste are conduction, convection, and radiation.[10,13] *Conduction* is the transfer of heat from one element to another by means of a temperature gradient, but without displacement of the adjacent elements themselves. Conduction involves the transfer of energy from one molecule to another adjacent molecule. Conduction heat transfer will always be supplemented by convection when dealing with gaseous and liquid phases. When solid particles are present, some of the heat energy will be transferred by radiation as well as by conduction.

Convection is the transfer of heat by the mixing motion of one fluid with another. Natural convection is a result of motion caused by variations in density resulting from temperature differentials. In forced convection, motion is typically enhanced by some external mechanical means such as fans or pumps.

In *radiation*, heat transmission results from transfer between particles not in physical contact with each other, but at different temperatures. The particle with the higher temperature will radiate more energy than it will absorb, and the cooler particle will absorb more than it radiates.

Since incineration operations involve all three modes of heat transmission to some extent, it is necessary to understand their mechanisms, as well as the principles of fluid flow, in order to understand the relationship of these modes of heat transfer.

The mechanism of heat transfer for thermal conduction through homogeneous solids can be expressed by

$$Q = -kA \frac{dt}{dx} \tag{8.4}$$

where Q = rate of heat conduction along the x axis.
  A = cross section of the path normal to the x axis.
$-dt/dx$ = temperature gradient along that path
  k = thermal conductivity, which is a physical property of the substance

Heat loss by the conduction mechanism will increase proportionally with the refractory surface area and the incineration temperature. Heat loss by conduction can be significantly decreased with improved insulation—for instance, with increased thickness of refractory brick.

Heat transfer by convection is related to the properties of the convection medium and the geometry of the system. The generation equation of the convection of heat is given by

$$Q = hA(T_2 - T_1) \tag{8.5}$$

where Q = heat transmission by convection
  h = film coefficient of heat transfer
  A = area of heat transfer surface
  T_1 = ambient temperature
  T_2 = temperature at the interface

Whereas conduction and convection heat transfer are affected primarily by temperature differences, the radiation mode of heat transfer increases with the level of temperature. As a result, at low temperature levels, conduction and convection represent a major contribution to heat transfer, while at higher temperatures, radiation becomes the controlling factor. When a particle is heated, radiant energy is emitted at a rate that is primarily dependent upon the temperature of the particle and its color and texture. Heat loss due to radiation can be expressed by the following equation:

$$Q = 0.174 \, A\varepsilon \left[\left(\frac{T_2}{100} \right)^4 - \left(\frac{T_1}{100} \right)^4 \right]$$

where Q = quantity of heat transferred

$\quad\quad \varepsilon$ = emissivity, which varies with color and texture of the particles

$\quad\quad A$ = area of the heat transfer surface

$\quad\quad T_1$ = absolute temperature of the lower temperature element

$\quad\quad T_2$ = absolute temperature of the higher temperature element

Since all three modes of heat transfer will be present in an incineration system, each of them must be a design consideration in achieving the desired thermal destruction of the hazardous waste. It should be noted that because of the high temperatures involved, radiation and conduction are more significant in heat transfer within incineration systems than is the mechanism of convection.

THE DESIGN OF AN INCINERATING SYSTEM

The thermal destruction of hazardous waste involves the controlled exposure of the waste to elevated temperatures, typically above 1600°F. When properly designed and operated, thermal destruction systems offer the opportunity to destroy hazardous organic wastes and significantly reduce their volume.

All hazardous waste incineration systems are normally governed by RCRA or TSCA regulations. These regulations typically specify a minimum destruction temperature that must be maintained for a required residence time in the presence of excess oxygen. Hazardous waste incineration normally occurs during the flow of hot, turbulent substances within a refractory-lined incinerator. The design of the incinerator plays a key role in ensuring adequate destruction of the waste. There are many factors of incinerator design that can significantly affect the thermal destruction of hazardous waste, including the following:

1 *Temperature*: In any thermal destruction process, the temperature is probably the most significant factor in ensuring proper destruction of the hazardous waste. The destruction and removal efficiency in any incineration operation depends upon the incinerator temperature. The threshold temperature that will ensure destruction of the waste and at the same time allow for cost-effective operation must be achieved. The *threshold temperature* has been defined as the temperature of operation to initiate thermal destruction of hazardous waste.

2 *Residence time*: The volume of the incinerator determines the residence time for any given flow rate. This time interacts with the thermal destruction temperature to ensure compliance with destruction and removal efficiency (DRE) regulations. Sufficient residence time must be allowed in order to achieve DREs, as well as to assure conversion to desirable incinerator products. In other words, the products of incomplete combustion must remain at the designed incinerator temperature long enough to ensure their conversion to carbon dioxide and water. Unless these desirable combustion products are realized, additional downstream processing will be necessary to ensure compliance with air emission standards.

3 *Turbulence*: The degree of turbulence may be used effectively to attain desirable DREs and lessen the severity of operating temperature and residence time requirements. The configuration of the incinerator will affect its ability to destroy hazardous wastes. The selection of pumps, blowers, and baffles should be based upon the type of waste to be incinerated and the desired DREs. Heat transfer and fluid flow should both be considered in the turbulence requirements for the design of the thermal destruction unit.

4 *Pressure*: Most hazardous waste incineration operations are designed to operate at slightly negative pressure to reduce fugitive emissions. Since air leaks will occur in these low-pressure systems, enclosure designs with adequate seals are normally not an important consideration. However, thermal destruction systems, which operate at positive elevated pressures, require nonleaking incinerators. Pressurized systems require high-temperature seals that are crucial to trouble-free operation.

5 *Air supply*: The incineration operation involves the reaction of combustible components with air. Normally air provides the oxygen for the incineration process. Typical incineration operations require sufficient oxygen to ensure complete combustion. Normally, products of incomplete combustion are undesirable and result only if constrained by residence time, temperature, or lack of sufficient air. To overcome this potential problem, the thermal destruction unit must have sufficient oxygen or air supply to ensure that products of hydrocarbon combustion ultimately result in carbon dioxide and water.

6 *Materials of construction*: Most incinerators are constructed with selected materials to allow continuous trouble-free operation over a wide range of hazardous wastes and destruction conditions. These materials of construction can range from ordinary steel to exotic alloys. A well-defined range of chemical and physical properties of the wastes to be incinerated is desirable to ensure proper selection of materials of construction that will provide a long operating life for the incinerator and minimize potential maintenance problems.

7 *Auxiliary features*:There are numerous additional features that must be considered in planning effective thermal destruction. The feed systems must be properly designed to incorporate the types of hazardous wastes that have been identified by market surveys. Afterburners may be needed to ensure proper DRE capability. Further downstream treatment is usually necessary to neutralize and remove undesirable destruction products such as mineral acids. Ash removal could play a key role in the thermal destruction of solid or semi-solid wastes.

Thermal destruction systems for hazardous waste must be insulated with refractory materials to effectively operate at high temperatures. The main purpose of refractory materials is to contain within the unit the heat released from the incinerator process. Proper containment of this energy is desirable for optimal vaporization and combustion of incoming hazardous waste. The selection of the refractory should normally be based upon stable physical and chemical properties at the elevated temperatures of incinerator operation. Incinerators must operate with heating and cooling cycles that could result in severe thermal stress.

The erosion and abrasion characteristics of the wastes being incinerated can cause considerable wear on the incinerator refractory. Also, incinerator refractory materials may be subjected to chemical reactions between hazardous wastes and their destruction products. Hence, the refractory materials must be versatile and able to withstand physical and chemical attack.

Refractory materials should offer adequate containment of combustion products, while protecting the processing unit from thermal stresses as well as from abrasion, erosion, and corrosion at high temperatures. The refractory must, of course, be capable of maintaining its strength properties under high-temperature conditions. Chemical corrosion could destroy the refractory cement or harm the integrity of the insulation. During heating and cooling, the thermal expansion of the refractory must be compatible with other materials of construction. Otherwise, expansions and contractions of the refractory would be harmful to the incinerator.

Proper refractory selection also helps provide a safe and healthy work environment for the employees. It can be used to greatly reduce the potential of employee injury from burns and heat exposure. The refractory also plays a key role in allowing continuous operation of the incinerator and reducing potential downtime for maintenance.

A wide range and variety of refractory materials have been developed for incineration systems. The most commonly used refractories are shown in Table 8-2; they include fireclay, alumina, silica, chromium, magnesite, and other oxides. Refractory materials are typically supplied in a dry form and mixed with water prior to their installation. They are applied in place by gunning, pouring, or troweling.

The ideal castible refractories provide a smooth, contiguous surface with the desirable physical and chemical properties for low maintenance incineration. These castible refractories can be supplied in lightweight form to act as insulators or in denser materials for high mechanical strength and abrasion resistance. The dense castible refractories, which have relatively low amounts of trapped air, are generally poor insulators. On the other hand, the lightweight castible refractories have excellent insulating properties.

Based upon predetermined criteria to ensure quality installation, the castible refractory must be mixed with water and then cured. The water must be added in accordance with the instructions of the manufacturer. Insufficient water will result in a dry mixture that will not properly flow into its castible form and thereby create voids. The voids may adversely affect the refractory performance. On the other hand, excessive water addition will result in a castible refractory that is too fluid and is unable to hold the desired shape through the subsequent curing operation.

All castible refractories can be placed in either regularly or irregularly shaped areas where they have been cast in place. Large areas requiring refractory such as refractory kilns are normally gunned in place. Once the refractory has been applied, it must be properly heat-cured in order to allow the ceramic bond to set. The degree of this bonding determines the strength. Improper cur-

TABLE 8-2
PROPERTIES OF SELECTED REFRACTORY MATERIALS

| Type | Brick classification | Weight percent | | | Temperature limit, °F | Density, lb/ft³ | Modules of rupture, psi | Cold crushing strength, psi | Thermal Expansion ambient to 1800°F, % |
		Silica (SiO₂)	Alumina (Al₂O₃)	Titania (TiO₂)					
Fireclay	Super duty	40–56	40–44	1–3	3185	140/145	730/1975	1830/7325	0.6
	High duty	51–61	40–44	1–3	3175	120/145	610/3660	1830/8550	0.6
	Medium duty	57–60	25–38	1–2	3040	120/145	975/3050	2075/7325	0.5–0.6
	Semisilica	72–80	18–26	1–2	3040	115/125	365/1100	1220/3660	0.7
High aluminum	45–48%	44–51	45–48	2–3	3245	135/160	1220/1950	3050/7325	0.4–0.5
	60%	31–37	58–62	2–3	3295	140/160	730/2200	2200/8550	0.6
	80%	11–15	78–82	3–4	3390	155/180	1340/3660	4880/10975	0.7
	90%	8–9	89–91	0.4–1	3500	165/190	1465/4275	4880/10975	0.7
	Mullite	18–34	60–78	0.5–3	3360	145/165	1220/4275	4275/10975	0.7
	Corundum	0.2–1	98–99	Trace	3660	170/200	2200/3660	6100/10975	0.8
Silica	Super duty	95–97	0.1–0.3 + lime	—	—	105/118	610/1220	1830/4275	1.3
	Conventional	94–97	0.4–1.4 + lime	—	—	105/118	730/1465	220/4880	1.2
	Lightweight	94–97	0.4–1.4 + lime	—	—	60	—	—	—
Silicon carbide	Bonded	—	—	—	3360	145/165	2440/4880	3050/18300	0.5
Insulating	1600°F	—	—	—	—	36	85/125	110/135	Low
	2300°F	—	—	—	—	46	120/200	135/230	Low
	2800°F	—	—	—	—	59	200/365	205/370	Low
	3000°F	—	—	—	—	60	490/730	975/1220	Low
Chrome	Fired	—	15–34*	—	—	185/205	855/1590	2440/4880	0.8

*Plus Cr_2O_3 (28–38); MgO (14–49); Fe_2O_3 (11–17).

ing can result in reduction of the refractory's mechanical strength, erosion and abrasion resistance, or chemical resistance to corrosion. Refractories are usually cured with a combination of air and heat at a predetermined temperature over a measured period of time. The heat curing is generally initiated at relatively low temperatures. These temperatures are then gradually elevated until they reach the actual temperature of normal operation for the incineration. In some instances, heat curing involves maintaining temperatures that are elevated above the normal operating conditions of the incinerator. These curing parameters are ultimately based upon the recommendations of the refractory manufacturer and then optimized according to experience with the actual operating conditions at the facility.

Firebrick is also used in many incineration systems. This material may be either a dense brick that is normally placed in direct contact with the hot incinerator stream or a lightweight insulating firebrick that generally must be protected when used in a system that would be subject to abrasion and erosion. Since many hazardous waste systems contain high particulate components, insulating firebrick is generally protected with a dense firebrick to allow long-term, trouble-free operation. This combination system provides the advantage of a well-insulated system, coupled with high abrasion resistance. The mortar for the firebrick should be carefully selected to ensure its compatibility with both the brick and the incinerator.

Firebrick generally requires anchors to hold it in place, both during and after its installation. It should be noted that these refractory and insulating systems may also be necessary downstream from the primary incineration equipment. These applications are generally at lower temperatures but could involve moist or even wet systems that accelerate chemical attack of the ceramic protection.

STOICHIOMETRY

Stoichiometric incineration of carbon involves use of the exact amount of oxygen required for complete combustion to produce carbon dioxide. Actual incineration conditions generally require excess oxygen to be present to ensure the formation only of products of complete combustion (POCs). Products of incomplete combustion (PICs) will result from insufficient oxygen. Excess air must be provided to ensure conversion of the waste to POCs and not to PICs. For example, a highly volatile, clean, hydrocarbon waste would probably require much less air than would a heavy hydrocarbon sludge that contained high levels of solids. Incineration of sludges and solids may require as much as 2 to 3 times excess air above stoichiometric equivalents. But an extreme of excess air should be avoided, since it involves increased fuel for heat requirements, reduced residence time for the hazardous wastes, and increased volumes of air emissions.

The incineration of halogenated organics results in the formation of halogen acids, which require further treatment to ensure environmentally acceptable air emissions from the incineration process. Chlorinated organics are the most common halogenated hydrocarbons found in hazardous waste. The incineration of chlorinated hydrocarbons with excess air results in the formation of carbon dioxide, water, and hydrogen chloride, according to the following reaction for the incineration of dichloroethane:

$$2C_2H_4Cl_2 + 5O_2 \rightarrow 4CO_2 + 2H_2O + 4HCl$$

This by-product hydrogen chloride must be removed before the carbon dioxide and steam can be safely exhausted into the atmosphere. Usually hydrogen chloride is removed by water, caustic, or lime scrubbing. However, HCl may also be removed during the combustion operation itself through the use of dry sorbents such as lime. The sorption of HCl in water will produce hydrochloric acid, which is highly corrosive and requires proper selection of materials of construction.

Should the hazardous waste being incinerated contain halogens such as fluorides or bromides, other operational problems may result. For example, hydrogen fluoride upon contact with water becomes hydrofluoric acid, a highly corrosive acid that could cause major and severe problems in downstream systems. On the other hand, hydrogen bromide will not produce as severe a corrosion problem as either HF or HCl, but even trace amounts of HBr have the potential to produce colorful exhaust emissions.

Hazardous waste may contain either organic or inorganic sulfur compounds. When these wastes are incinerated, sulfur dioxide is normally produced as with the destruction of ethyl mercaptan, as illustrated in the following reaction:

$$2C_2H_5SH + 9O_2 \rightarrow 4CO_2 + 6H_2O + 2SO_2$$

The sulfur dioxide produced by the incineration of sulfur-containing wastes must be dealt with in compliance with local air quality standards. Normally an alkaline scrubber system containing either lime or caustic is used to remove sulfur dioxide, which is not highly soluble in water.

Occasionally organic phosphorus compounds will be present in the hazardous waste. With excess air, incineration of organic phosphorous compounds will produce phosphorous pentoxide, which reacts readily with water to form phosphoric acid. A water or wet alkaline scrubber should effectively remove this potentially hazardous air quality emission.

TSCA INCINERATION STANDARDS
Regulations for Liquid PCBs

Under the Toxic Substances Control Act, incineration of liquid PCBs must be approved by EPA and is subject to the following combustion criteria:

1 The liquids introduced must be maintained for a 2-second dwell time at 1200° ± 100°C and 3 percent excess oxygen in the stack gas.

2 Alternatively, the liquids introduced must be maintained for a $1\frac{1}{2}$-second dwell time at $1600° \pm 100°C$ and 2 percent excess oxygen in the stack gas.

The EPA has interpreted these conditions to further require a liquid PCB DRE $\geq$ 99.9999 percent.

3 Combustion efficiency shall be at least 99.99 percent, computed as follows:

$$\text{Combustion efficiency} = \frac{C_{CO_2}}{C_{CO_2} + C_{CO}} \times 100 \tag{8.7}$$

$$\text{where } C_{CO_2} = \text{concentration of carbon dioxide}$$

$$C_{CO} = \text{concentration of carbon monoxide}$$

4 The rate and quantity of PCBs which are fed to the combustion system must be measured and recorded at regular intervals of no longer than 15 minutes.

5 The temperatures of the incineration process must be continuously measured and recorded. The combustion temperature of the incineration process should be based on either direct (pyrometer) or indirect (wall thermocouple–pyrometer correlation) temperature readings.

6 The flow of PCBs to the incinerator must stop automatically whenever the combustion temperature drops below the temperatures specified, i.e., 1200 or 1600°C.

7 Monitoring of stack emission products must be conducted when an incinerator is first used for the disposal of PCBs, and the following exhaust emissions must be monitored:

Oxygen (O_2)
Carbon monoxide (CO)
Oxides of nitrogen (NO_x)
Hydrogen chloride (HCl)
Total chlorinated organic content
PCBs
Total particulate matter

8 The flow of PCBs to the incinerator must be stopped automatically when there is a failure of monitoring operations, the PCB rate and quantity measuring and recording equipment fails, or excess oxygen falls below the percentage specified.

9 Scrubbers must be used for HCl control during PCB incineration.

Regulations for Nonliquid PCBs

Under the Toxic Substances Control Act, an incinerator used for incinerating nonliquid PCBs, PCB articles, PCB equipment, or PCB containers must meet the following requirements:

1 Mass air emissions from the incinerator must be no greater than 0.001 g PCB per kilogram of the PCB introduced into the incinerator, i.e., DRE ≥ 99.9999 percent.

2 An incinerator for nonliquid PCBs must comply with the same other rules as those for liquid PCBs.

RCRA INCINERATION STANDARDS

An incinerator burning hazardous waste must be designed, constructed, and maintained so that when operated it will meet the following performance standards under the Resource Conservation and Recovery Act:

1 An incinerator burning hazardous waste must achieve a destruction and removal efficiency (DRE) of 99.99 percent for each principal organic hazardous constituent (POHC) designated for each waste feed. DRE is determined for each POHC from the following equation:

$$\text{DRE} = \frac{(W_{in} - W_{out})}{W_{in}} \times 100\% \qquad (8.8)$$

where W_{in} = mass feed rate of one principal organic hazardous constituent (POHC) in the waste stream

W_{out} = mass emission rate of the same POHC present in exhaust emissions prior to release to the atmosphere

2 An incinerator burning hazardous waste and producing stack emissions of more than 1.8 kg/h (4 lb/h) or hydrogen chloride must control HCl emissions such that the rate of emission is no greater than the larger of either 1.8 kg/h or 1 percent of the HCl in the stack gas prior to its entering any pollution control equipment.

3 An incinerator burning hazardous waste must not emit particulate matter in excess of 180 mg per dry standard cubic meter (0.08 grains per dry standard cubic foot) when corrected for the amount of oxygen in the stack gas according to the formula:

$$P_c = P_m \frac{14}{21 - Y} \qquad (8.9)$$

where P_c = corrected concentrations of particulate matter

P_m = measured concentration of particulate matter

Y = measured concentration of oxygen in the stack gas, using the Orsat method for oxygen analysis of dry flue gas

The Trial Burn

On May 19, 1980, the U.S. Environmental Protection Agency published regulations under the authority of the Resource Conservation and Recovery Act for hazardous waste incinerators. Owners and operators of incinerators were henceforth required to demonstrate the performance of the facility by means of a trial burn. As a consequence, industry and control agency personnel have become involved in planning, conducting, and interpreting the results from trial burns. The key considerations in a trial burn are the regulatory limits that must be achieved, the permit conditions that result from the burn, and the extent of sampling and analysis activities required.[9]

Regulatory Limits The trial burn provides regulatory agencies with data that will allow them to issue an operating permit. Consequently, the trial burn is directed to testing the plant to show that it achieves the RCRA limits under the desired plant operating conditions. These RCRA limits are:

1 A destruction and removal efficiency (DRE) of greater than 99.99 percent for all subject principal organic hazardous constituents (POHCs)
2 A particulate emission of less than 180 mg per dry standard cubic meter (corrected to 7 percent O_2)
3 Hydrogen chloride (HCl) emissions of less than 4 lb/h or greater than 99 percent removal efficiency

The trial burn involves testing at conditions that meet the plant's operating needs while meeting these three RCRA limits. It may be necessary to test at more than one operating condition in order to satisfy all three needs. EPA recommends three or more runs at any one set of operating conditions, with varying conditions or with different waste feed characteristics.

In addition to the above standards, regional and state permit officials may add their own individual trial burn and permit conditions, which may be more stringent than the federal standards.

Operating Permit Operating conditions imposed by a permit should allow the plant to incinerate the types and quantities of waste they expect to handle, at the necessary feed rates and within an acceptable range of operating conditions. The permit conditions need to provide the plant with the desired flexibility, within limits that are reasonably achievable. Based on the trial burn results, the operating permit may specify certain criteria such as:

Maximum concentration of certain POHCs in waste feed
Maximum waste feed rate and/or maximum total heat input rate
Maximum air feed rate or maximum flue gas velocity
Minimum combustion temperature
Maximum carbon monoxide content of stack gas
Maximum chloride and ash content of waste feed

Sampling and Analysis The primary objectives of the sampling and analysis program are to quantify POHC input and output rates to determine whether DRE requirements are met, to measure input and output rates of chloride, and to determine stack effluent particulate concentrations.

Each test run in the trial burn includes sampling and analysis of the waste feeds and the stack effluent for the POHCs. Analysis results, along with waste feed rates and stack gas flow rates measured during each run, are used to calculate the DREs. Usually samples of ash and scrubber waters are also taken and analyzed for the POHCs.

Planning a Trial Burn   The probability for success of a trial burn is enhanced by well-conceived planning. The major objectives of the planning process should be to select trial burn conditions that provide the plant adequate operating flexibility, to ensure that the trial burn will be conducted in a manner acceptable to regulatory agencies, and to make the trial burn cost-effective.

In order to gain flexibility, the trial burn should be designed to include many different operating conditions. Important considerations are the key operating parameters that affect permit conditions. Test conditions should represent the worst-case conditions under which the incinerator is expected to operate, and therefore needs to be permitted to operate. The conditions selected may include any or all of the following:

Waste containing hardest-to-burn POHC
Highest concentrations of all POHCs selected
Maximum waste feed rates
Maximum air flow rate for combustion gas or minimum residence time
Maximum CO level in stack gas
Minimum combustion temperature
Minimum hydrocarbon heating value of waste
Maximum thermal input, Btu/h
Minimum O_2 level in stack gas
Maximum Cl content of waste feed
Maximum ash content of waste feed
Minimums or maximums on other operating conditions, e.g., scrubber water flow rate and pH

Obviously, it is very difficult to achieve all of the above operating conditions. In fact, some of the conditions are almost direct opposites, e.g., maximum air flow rate but minimum O_2 in stack gas. The first six items in the above list are probably the most important and may be achievable in one set of operating conditions that also includes some of the other conditions. If so, one trial burn of three runs at those conditions may suffice. If not, additional runs that include the other conditions may be necessary. Of course, operating conditions which result in permit conditions most favorable to each individual facility will have to be determined on a case-by-case basis.

The major problem with the worst-case conditions is that they maximize the chance of failure to meet RCRA requirements. Since the plant wants to pass the trial burn, the exact conditions must be carefully selected, balancing operating needs against increasing chance of failure. Plant operating experience is very important in these decisions.

POHCs for the trial burn should be selected during development of the trial burn plan. In addition to the regulatory criteria, the maximum flexibility of operating conditions under the permit and ease of sampling and analysis during the trial burn should be taken into account. Ideally, all trial burn POHCs should be selected from either the volatile or semiviolatile group. This minimizes the number of sampling trains used in the field and simplifies the analysis.

Pretesting or Miniburns Preliminary testing and miniburns can be extremely valuable in helping to select operating conditions for the actual trial burn and in providing some indication of the results to be expected. Pretesting should be done at least 2 months before the scheduled trial burn in order to complete all analyses, evaluate the results, and make whatever changes are required.

The following types of miniburns may be useful:

1 The hardest-to-burn POHC, at high concentration, can be used in a miniburn that is conducted at the lowest temperature and the highest CO level. If the results show a DRE exceeding 99.99 percent, then it is likely that a 99.99 percent DRE will be achieved, regardless of any other operating conditions.

2 At high chloride input rates, a well-designed scrubber will not usually fail the 99 percent removal, even at minimum conditions. A pretest could verify that presumption.

3 Achieving the particulate limit causes problems more frequently than does achieving DRE. A pretest with EPA Method 5 will help identify any problems and help in selecting conditions for the trial burn. The pretest can also uncover specific sampling and analysis problems that may not be readily apparent.

4 Mist carried over from a recirculating scrubber solution or alkaline scrubbers can have a drastic impact on particulate emission measurements, especially if the scrubbers are not equipped with efficient mist eliminators. It may be advisable to conduct a preliminary particulate test well in advance of the actual trial burn to identify possible problems.

Conducting a Trial Burn The incinerator facility operator is responsible for conducting the trial burn itself. Facilities must provide the types and quantities of waste needed and operate the plant during the trial burn at the conditions under which they desire to be permitted. Because EPA recommends three or more runs under any one set of operating conditions, the quantities of waste required for the burn are substantial, and each run may take 4 to 8 hours of plant operating time.

Though the facility itself is responsible for conducting the burn, the specialized sampling and analyses required in the process of the test are frequently beyond the capability of the incinerator staff, and often the owner/operator will decide to use an experienced contractor to conduct the tests. At times even facilities having the capabilities to run the tests themselves will opt to use a contractor because of the specialized nature of the methods and the fact that the trial burn may be only a one-time need.

COMMERCIAL APPLICATIONS OF HAZARDOUS WASTE INCINERATION

Many hazardous wastes are incinerated in industrial boilers and furnaces. The combustion of high-Btu-content hazardous waste liquids in industrial boilers has replaced use of fossil fuels in 5 to 10 percent of applications in industrial practice. But the combustion of hazardous wastes in boilers is limited by the amount of chlorine in the waste stream, since most industrial boilers do not utilize scrubbers for hydrogen chloride. The more common types of commercial hazardous waste incinerators will now be discussed.

Liquid Injection Incineration

The most common incinerator method for hazardous waste disposal is based on liquid injection. Horizontal, vertical, and tangential units are used. The majority of the incinerators for hazardous wastes inject liquid hazardous waste at 50 to 100 psig through an atomizing nozzle into the combustion chamber. These liquid incinerators vary in size from 1 million to 300 million Btu of heat release per hour. An auxiliary fuel such as natural gas or fuel oil is typically used as a supplemental combustion source. Incinerator temperatures usually range between 1500 and 3000°F. The liquid wastes, which must be converted to a gas prior to combustion, are injected, atomized into fine droplets, and then incinerated. An ideal droplet size is in the 40- to 100-μm range and is obtained with atomizers or nozzles. Efficient destruction of liquid hazardous wastes requires minimizing unevaporated droplets and unreacted vapors. Temperature, residence time, and turbulence should be optimized to increase destruction efficiencies. Typical residence times are 0.5 second to 2 seconds.

A high degree of turbulence is desirable for achieving effective destruction of the organics in the hazardous waste. Depending upon whether the liquid incinerator flow is axial, radial, or tangential, additional fuel burners and separate waste injection nozzles can be arranged to achieve the desired temperature, turbulence, and residence time. Vertical units are less likely to experience ash buildup. Tangential units have a much higher heat release and generally superior mixing.

Rotary Kiln Incineration

The rotary kiln is often used in hazardous waste disposal systems because of its versatility in processing solid, liquid, and containerized wastes. Waste is incinerated in a refractory-lined rotary kiln, as shown in Figure 8-1. The shell is mounted at a slight incline from the horizontal plane to facilitate mixing the waste materials with circulating air. The kiln accepts all types of solid and liq-

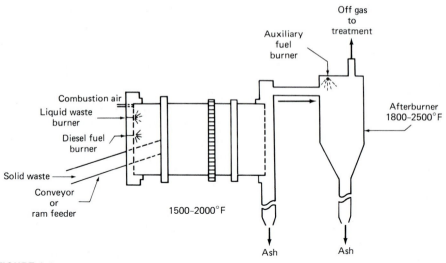

FIGURE 8-1
Rotary kiln for hazardous waste incineration.

uid waste materials. Solid wastes and drummed wastes are usually fed by a conveyor system or a ram. Liquids and pumpable sludges are injected through a nozzle. Noncombustible metal and other residues are discharged as ash at the end of the kiln.

Rotary kilns are typically 5 to 12 feet in diameter and range in length from 10 to 30 feet. Rotary kiln incinerators usually have a length-to-diameter ratio (L/D) of between 2 and 8. Rotational speeds range from 0.2 to 1 in/s, depending on the kiln periphery. High L/D ratios, along with slower rotational speeds, are used for wastes requiring longer residence times. The feed end of the kiln has airtight seals to adequately control the initial incineration reactions.

Residence time for solid wastes is based on the rotational speed of the kiln and its angle. The residence time to volatilize waste is controlled by the gas velocity. The solids retention time in the incinerator can be estimated from the following, where the coefficient 0.19 is based on limited experimental data:

$$\theta = \frac{0.19L}{NDS} \tag{8.10}$$

where θ = retention time, min
 L = kiln length, ft
 N = kiln rotational velocity, r/min
 D = kiln diameter, ft
 S = kiln slope, ft/ft

Drums and cartons of hazardous waste may be fed directly into the kiln but are often shredded prior to being introduced. Rotary kiln systems typically include secondary combustion chambers or afterburners to ensure complete destruction of the hazardous waste. Operating temperatures range from 1500 to 2800°F, and 1800 to 3000°F in the secondary combustion chamber or afterburner. Liquid wastes are often injected into the secondary combustion chamber. The volatilized and combusted wastes leave the kiln and enter the secondary chamber, where additional oxygen is available and high NHV liquid wastes or fuel may be introduced. The waste is destroyed at the desired DRE in the secondary chamber. Both the secondary combustion chamber and the kiln are usually equipped with an auxiliary fuel firing system for startup.

Advantages of the rotary kiln include its ability to handle a variety of wastes, its high operating temperature, and the continuous mixing of incoming wastes. Kilns can operate under oxygen-deficient or starved-air conditions to pyrolyze the wastes. The combustible off-gases can be incinerated in the secondary combustion chamber to reduce the particulates in the kiln gases. But rotary kilns have high capital and operating costs and require trained personnel. Maintenance costs can also be high because of the abrasive characteristics of the waste and exposure of moving parts to high incineration temperatures.

Other high-temperature industrial furnaces that are used to burn hazardous wastes include cement kilns, which are capable of achieving or exceeding the RCRA destruction standards for hazardous waste incineration. Cement plants can save energy by incinerating liquid wastes. Hydrochloric acid generated from chlorinated hydrocarbon wastes is neutralized by the lime in the kiln, slightly lowering the alkalinity of the cement products.

Fluid-Bed Incineration

Fluid-bed incineration for hazardous waste offers an environmentally acceptable alternative to landfill techniques.[2] High-temperature processes involving fluid beds have been used in industrial technology for many years. Initially this technology was utilized in coal gasification and was later extended to the application of catalytic cracking at petroleum refineries. Many subsequent processes have adopted fluid-bed technology because it offers a high degree of turbulence and a large heat-transfer area for mixing the hazardous waste, oxygen, and the hot fluid-bed medium. The intimate mixing in the bed and the large surface area available on the inert bed material provide a high degree of incineration with low excess-air levels and a minimal temperature gradient through the bed. The residence time of fluid-bed incineration is in a high range—from 5 to 8 seconds or more at a temperature of 1400 to 1600°F and a slight positive pressure. This long residence time ensures an efficient DRE for the organic waste and produces an inert ash that is normally suitable for nonhazardous waste land disposal. Fluid-bed incinerators offer several potential advantages, including high DREs, uniform temperatures, by-product neutralization, and low maintenance costs. The bed height and diameter are limited by the state of the design technology.

Bubbling Fluid-Bed Incineration

Bubbling fluidized-bed incinerators, as shown in Figure 8-2, have a granular bed of sand, which is stirred by passing air through the bed at a rate sufficiently high to cause the bed to expand and fluidize. Preheating of the bed is accomplished by a burner. The waste flows directly into the sand. Continuous exposure of the waste to the heated sand results in highly efficient incineration. Bed depths usually range from about 2 to 8 feet. The bed depth should be maintained at a minimum value consistent with complete combustion and minimum excess air.

Circulating Fluid-Bed Incineration

Circulating fluid-bed technique, as shown in Figure 8-3, extends the bubbling fluidized bed through increased turbulence and throughput per unit area. Circulating fluid beds employ high air velocities and circulation of solids to create a highly turbulent incineration zone and allow for sufficient residence time to

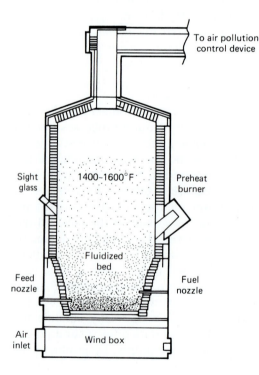

FIGURE 8-2
Bubbling fluidized bed for hazardous waste incineration.

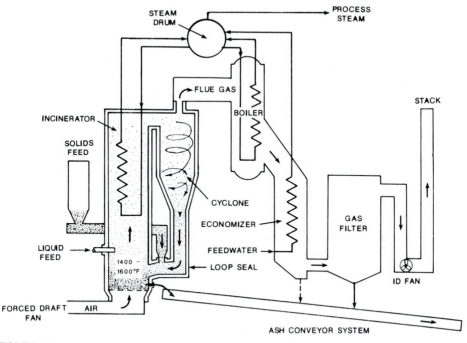

FIGURE 8-3
Circulating fluid-bed incinerator for hazardous waste.

adequately destroy the undesirable waste.[4] The solids from the circulating bed are separated from the off-gases with a cyclone and are returned to the incinerator. Temperatures in circulating fluid beds are fairly uniform throughout the length of the bed—in the range of 1400 to 1600°F. These temperatures are lower than in either rotary kilns or bubbling fluid beds but are still capable of achieving desirable destruction and removal efficiencies within the regulatory limitations of RCRA.

It is anticipated that in the future thermal destruction will be one of the preferred techniques for the management of hazardous waste disposal. The following case study illustrates the complex issues of incinerating hazardous waste. It is based on an actual case history of an innovative incinerator on an oceangoing vessel.

CASE STUDY
Vulcanus, **the Oceangoing Incinerator**

Prior to the passage of the Marine Protection, Research, and Sanctuaries Act (MPRSA) in 1972, it was common practice to dump chemical wastes directly into the ocean. With the prohibition of such disposal methods by MPRSA, alternative technologies for chemical waste disposal had to be developed. Land-based incineration, deep-well injection, and landfill methods have been primarily used in the United States. However, at-sea incineration technology was developed in Europe, more than two decades ago, and several incineration vessels are in use.

Background

Ocean incineration was developed in 1967 by Dr. Sobringer, a German engineer and specialist in combustion processes. Dr. Sobringer started a company that purchased a coastal tanker and converted it to a seagoing incinerator. This ship was used to burn chlorinated waste, making HCl, which was subsequently condensed and put into the sea where it is diluted and neutralized. Since 1967, several European countries such as the Netherlands and Belgium have used various ship incinerators on a larger scale to dispose of chlorinated organic waste.

Although there was no conclusive evidence to indicate that there had been any spills caused by the ship incinerators or any adverse effects on seawater or marine life, for the safety of marine life and the ship incinerator itself, the U.N. Intergovernmental Maritime Consultative Organization (I.M.C.O.) called for an international convention in October 1978 in London to prepare action leading to the regulation of ship incineration. The regulatory guidelines adopted by the I.M.C.O. at that conference dealt only with liquid organic waste incineration, since there had not been a successful demonstration of solid waste incineration at sea.

Subsequent Developments in the United States

A United States company with a multimillion dollar investment in the ocean incineration business is Chemical Waste Management Corporation. CWM owns two ships, the *Vulcanus I* and the *Vulcanus II*. For years EPA considered allowing *Vulcanus II* and its sister ship to incinerate waste in the Gulf of Mexico, but Gulf coast residents feared toxic slicks and fish kills, and regulatory delays have idled the incineration vessels.

Chemical Waste Management has to date conducted three test burns in United States waters. The first officially sanctioned at-sea incineration was performed aboard *Vulcanus II* in the Gulf of Mexico from October 1974 through January 1975. Four shiploads, with 4000 metric tons each of toxic chlorinated organic wastes, were incinerated at federally approved incineration sites 143 nautical miles south of Cameron, Louisiana. These sites were beyond the continental shelf, in water depths of 3000 to 6000 feet, outside all major shipping lanes, and well beyond commercial shrimping and fishing depths. The burns were monitored by EPA, the National Oceanic and Atmospheric Administration (NOAA), and the National Aeronautics and Space Administration (NASA).

The wastes were a mixture of mostly trichloropropane, trichloroethane, and dichloroethane. The first two shiploads were each incinerated under an EPA research permit, and the second two shiploads were burned under an EPA special permit. Composition of waste feeds was similar during the two research burns, with both containing 63 percent chlorine, 29 percent carbon, 4 percent hydrogen, 4 percent oxygen, and traces of heavy metals. Combustion efficiencies, or the percentage of hydrocarbons combusted, ranged between 99.92 and 99.98 percent.

The second at-sea incineration operation took place from March to April 1977 under an EPA permit. Chlorinated organic wastes were destroyed by the *Vulcanus II* in an incineration area located 130 miles south of Sabine Pass, Texas. The burn was monitored by a team of scientists and engineers under contract to EPA. Average feed rate was 22 metric tons per hour; a combustion efficiency of 99.95 percent was achieved.

The third incineration at sea of chlorinated organic wastes occurred from July 14 to September 2, 1977, again on board the *Vulcanus II,* which was under contract to the U.S. Air Force. The operation was carried out in three consecutive burns, the first under an EPA research permit and two under an EPA special permit, at a designated area in the Pacific Ocean, approximately 200 miles west of Johnston Atoll. These burns were monitored by a team of scientists under contract to the EPA. All burns were successfully completed with an average feed rate of 14.5 metric tons per hour. Destruction efficiencies for 2,4-D and 2,4,5-T were greater than 99.99 percent.

The Ship

The *Vulcanus* is a converted cargo ship of 4768 deadweight metric tons, with a waste tank capacity of 3505 cubic meters, or 800,000 gallons. Waste is burned in the two incinerators that have a combined maximum feed rate of 25 metric tons per hour.

Figure 8-4 presents the general arrangement of the incineration ship. The *Vulcanus* is equipped with extensive auxiliary processing systems to handle and incinerate hazardous waste. The incineration plant, liquor cargo pumps, and electric propulsion motors are located aft, with the accommodations and chemical analysis laboratory located forward, to achieve the maximum separation between the incinerator and the ship personnel. This arrangement not only increases the safety of the people aboard the vessel but also reduces the potential for chemical contamination of the crew and of the laboratory that monitors the incinerators' performance. The ship has diesel-electric generators that provide electric power to both the propulsion motors and to the incineration plant.

The deckhouse is located forward of the cargo areas and incinerators for the purpose of locating personnel away from the incinerator plume, heat, and po-

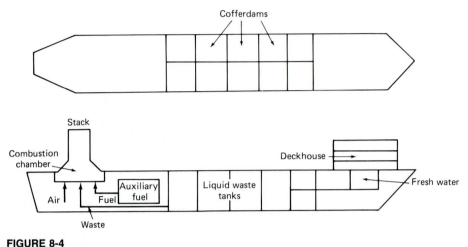

FIGURE 8-4
General arrangement of the *Vulcanus*.

tential chemical contamination. In addition, the *Vulcanus* is capable of continually steaming into the wind to keep the plume away from the vessel and crew. The forward deckhouse contains accommodations for all personnel. The chemical analysis laboratory for plume and waste samples is on the main deck level, aft of the crew accommodations. The lab has a separate entrance to the main deck and to the interior passageways of the deckhouse, so that chemical samples need not enter the main deckhouse.

Showers and change-of-clothing facilities are also provided immediately aft of the deckhouse on the main deck level. This area includes lockers for crew clothing and work gear, so that crew members can deposit dirty or contaminated gear at the entryway rather than having to enter the accommodations area to disrobe. This also prevents crew members from storing dirty gear in their own quarters. The shower facilities also provide emergency first-aid showers for anyone who may be accidentally contaminated. Medical supplies and hospital equipment are provided on board to provide emergency care for chemical-related injuries and sickness.

The cargo containment area is located in the midsection of the vessel. Waste storage has been divided into several enclosed containers to prevent an accidental spill or leak. The cargo tanks are stiffened by external structures. All tanks have smooth internal surfaces to simplify tank cleaning and to minimize the possibility of contamination and corrosion. Some structural stiffening has been provided by cofferdam spaces between the tanks, which separate incompatible cargoes. All cargo tanks have been epoxy-lined and contain double bottoms and wing tanks.

The incinerators and auxiliaries are located aft, along with the incinerator machinery room, the incinerator control room, an equipment room used to store special plume-monitoring devices, the propulsion motors, and the cargo pumproom. Adequate space for research and testing desired by EPA is provided on and below deck. Personnel can walk from the deckhouse to the incineration area via a passageway on top of the deck.

Three liquid injection incinerators are located aft. One of the incinerators is located on the ship's centerline, with the two other incinerators located outboard of the centerline. The feed system to the appropriate incinerator and auxiliary equipment, such as combustion air blowers and combustion monitors, is located near the incinerators. The cylindrical combustion chambers are lined with heat-resistant refractory bricks.

Liquid wastes can be transferred into the epoxy-lined cargo tanks using shoreside pumps and dockside loading gear at the terminal. The liquid wastes are fed into the preheated incinerators via uncoated extra-heavy steel pipes and cargo pumps. The waste feed and transfer system has been arranged so that the incinerators can receive waste from any cargo tank. The incineration processes have been designed to incinerate hazardous wastes with two incinerators simultaneously. The combined maximum feed rate for two incinerators has been rated at approximately 25 metric tons per hour.

The Process

The process is one of liquid injection; a mixture of combustible liquid waste and air flows into the chamber where incineration takes place. The exposed liquid surface area is maximized to promote destruction efficiency; the surface area is increased by atomizing the liquid flow with special nozzles.

Good atomization can be achieved at 100 to 150 psig. The *Vulcanus* liquid injection incinerators operate at a temperature of approximately 2300°F and residence time of 0.5 second, a somewhat higher temperature than that achieved in land-based incinerators. The high temperatures at which the *Vulcanus* incinerators operate causes the waste to break down into carbon dioxide, water, and hydrogen chloride.

The sea, which is slightly alkaline, neutralizes the acid when it comes in contact with the water; hence at-sea incinerators do not require scrubbers to remove the acid. This neutralization of hydrogen chloride with seawater instead of with scrubbers means lower costs for disposal of wastes at sea than is the case with land incineration.

Transportation Considerations

Hazardous waste must be transported to the *Vulcanus* by truck, train, or barge, and the transporters must operate under EPA rules that require each transporter of hazardous wastes to obtain an EPA identification number, comply with the manifest system, deliver the total quantity of hazardous waste to the specified treatment, storage, and disposal (TSD) facility, and keep records during the entire time the waste is being transported. Additional precautions and contingency plans are initiated in case of the accidental release of hazardous waste. These include cleaning up a hazardous waste spill and contacting the National Response Center. Even with these regulatory restrictions young wives and senior citizens in Philadelphia protested Chemical Waste Management transport and storage of hazardous waste for at-sea incineration in the *Vulcanus*.

Another environmental concern was the loading of the hazardous waste onto the incinerator ship at the seaport. The *Vulcanus II* system requires the pumping of liquid waste directly into the ship from tank truck, railcar, or barge, creating the possibility of a waste spill into the water near the ship. Also, because the *Vulcanus II* has large tanks to hold the waste until it is destroyed, the ship is a potential risk to the marine environment if it should have a collision, run aground, or sink.

These are the problems facing CWM, but they pertain to any potential at-sea incineration system. All ocean-based incinerator ships must have a land-based support network. The waterfront network for incinerator ships necessarily includes storage tanks, waste processing and handling equipment, a laboratory for the analysis of waste and incinerator residue, a cargo-transfer terminal, and an inland transportation system to deliver the hazardous waste.

As the liquid waste arrives at the TSD facility, it is placed in storage prior to being loaded on the incinerator ship. The liquid wastes are blended to optimize the combustion and transfer processes. The blended wastes include the liquid wastes received and the decontamination rinse from containers, trucks, tankers, and rail tank cars. Solid waste received by the on-shore facility is shredded and stored in large bulk containers until transport to the incinerator ship or to other land-based incinerators. It is necessary to shred or otherwise dispose of the liquid containers or contaminated drums. In turn, the ash from ocean incineration is transported back to the land-based network to be ultimately disposed of in a TSD facility. The plans for the land-based facility for the *Vulcanus* incinerator include a TSD facility on the waterfront; it is this part of the plan that draws major criticism of the ocean incineration system.

In locating and constructing the land-based network, a site must be selected where the potential environmental impact is minimal, transportation is convenient and cost-effective, and the geography and topography are amenable. Local building regulations pertinent to the specific location must be followed. In accordance with the criteria specified by federal regulations, the design must meet safety, health, and environment criteria, including contingency planning in case of major or minor releases of chemical wastes that have the potential for reaching the soil, air, or water. Public participation should be encouraged throughout the siting process.

In the United States, a survey of the existing terminal facilities found 139 ports and 1221 terminal docks, piers, or wharves with sufficient water depth to accommodate an incinerator ship. These facilities are concentrated at various locations on the east, west, and gulf coasts. A large majority of these facilities are privately owned and are located in the states of Texas, Louisiana, New

Jersey, New York, and California. These terminals are all technically feasible, but the major determinant for handling hazardous waste at these locations has been compliance with regulations and public acceptance.

Opposition to Ocean Incineration

To many people, burning hazardous waste at sea, removed from the population, seems like a perfect answer to destroying a large part of the nation's liquid hazardous wastes. But despite the fact that the U.S. Environmental Protection Agency officials have declared the incineration technology environmentally sound, commercial permits for ocean incineration of hazardous waste have not been approved because of public opposition. The groups opposing incineration have accused EPA of supporting ocean incineration simply because it is available, not necessarily because it has proved safe to human health and the environment. Questions have been raised by critics about whether incineration at sea will actually reduce the threat of toxic wastes to human health and the environment. State and local government officials, environmental groups, land-based incineration companies, and business and civic organizations have all raised objections to ocean incineration.

The potential for spills at sea has been another concern. Though there are similar risks in moving wastes on land, either to a land-based incinerator or to a port for transfer to a ship, a spill in the ocean can be more dangerous than a spill on land because containment and cleanup are much more difficult, if not impossible. On the other hand, the incineration ships that have operated in Europe since 1969 have never had an accident.

In March 1985, EPA estimated the probability of a spill from an ocean incineration ship such as the *Vulcanus* is only 1 per 1200 operating years, based on experience of other oil and chemical tankers. For a large spill, the risk is about 1 in 2400 years. Furthermore, EPA pointed out that the annual capacity of the *Vulcanus* is only about 0.01 percent of the 550 million metric tons of petroleum and hazardous materials already carried by ships and barges in the Gulf of Mexico each year.

A number of the general arguments and criticisms raised against the ocean *Vulcanus* are listed below. Many of these concerns can be mitigated with the proper application of technology.

- The *Vulcanus* exhaust stacks cannot be sampled to accurately determine gas flow, gas composition, or particulate emissions.
- The liquid feed rates of the hazardous liquid wastes and combustion air to the incinerators needs to be more accurately measured. The liquid feed rate to the incinerators should be measured by checking the level in the feed tanks in rolling seas.
- There is a need for improved measurement of incineration temperature profiles. Analytical measurements that are accurate to only two or three sig-

nificant figures cannot be used to calculate destruction efficiencies to 99.99 percent or 99.9999 percent.

• Measurement of the destruction of compounds in the liquid waste ignores incomplete oxidation and chemical recombination that create products of incomplete combustion, which may be more toxic than the original wastes. For example, the incomplete incineration of chlorinated hydrocarbons could produce chlorinated dioxins and dibenzofurans.

• Land-based incinerators that burn chlorinated hydrocarbons are equipped with scrubbers and sorbents to limit the amount of hydrogen chloride, organic compounds, and particulate matter exhausted as air emissions. Ocean incinerators are not equipped with these pollution control devices needed to protect the marine environment.

• The ship's incinerators cannot ensure complete destruction of hazardous wastes because of short stacks, low residence time, and lack of secondary combustion chambers. The short residence time of the *Vulcanus* incinerators is inadequate compared with the 2-second residence times required for PCBs under TSCA.

• Land-based incinerators can be kept under close surveillance by the public, while shipboard inspections can be compromised.

• Unburned wastes and PICs emitted from incinerators could adversely impact marine life, and later human health. Organic emissions may become attached to the microlayer on the ocean surface skin, which supports marine organisms at the bottom of the food chain.

In response to these concerns, both EPA and CWM claim that tests in Europe and the United States have demonstrated that the *Vulcanus* meets and even exceeds EPA destruction efficiency requirements. Particulate air emissions are limited because solids and metals in the waste are minimized by analytical controls. Dioxins and dibenzofurans are minimized and essentially eliminated with proper operating conditions. Even if trace amounts of toxic PICs are released, these environmental risks should be compared with the other disposal alternatives in current use. Hydrochloric acid emissions are neutralized and buffered rapidly by the ocean, with minimal environmental impact. The ship continually steams into the wind to keep the acid plume astern and away from the crew.

In response to the criticism that the residence time of the *Vulcanus* incinerators is insufficient, EPA claims that incinerators should be regulated by performance rather than by design. EPA has allowed shorter residence times for some land incinerators that have shown they could meet the desired destruction requirements.

Only liquid toxic wastes have been accepted for ocean incineration by both the Intergovernmental Maritime Consultative Organization and the Environmental Protection Agency. The complete combustion of these wastes yields carbon dioxide, water, and hydrogen chloride. Solid wastes have not been approved for ship incineration, nor have aqueous and nonaqueous salts that contain heavy metals. Waste streams for ocean incineration are limited to parts-per-million concentrations of heavy metals.

Ocean incineration wastes to date are composed mainly of waste streams from the organic chemical and pesticide industries and the petroleum refining industry. In any event, the portion of the total hazardous wastes that can be considered for ocean incineration must be determined on economic grounds; many wastes are not to be considered because they can be recycled at less expense, have excessive water content, or are located too far from port for economical transportation to an incineration ship.

NEED FOR OCEAN INCINERATION IN THE UNITED STATES

There are many factors that are stimulating demand and creating an urgent need for more capacity for liquid waste incineration:

- Waste generators worried about potential long-term liabilities are turning to destruction methods such as incineration instead of simply transporting off-site.
- Amendments to the Resource Conservation and Recovery Act passed in 1984 severely limit the disposal of liquid hazardous wastes in landfills, and EPA has restricted burning of such wastes in industrial boilers and furnaces.
- Leaking landfills will create more Superfund sites in the future, and remediation of these sites will require more incineration capacity.

While the overall demand for incineration capacity will grow in the foreseeable future, at-sea incineration offers the following advantages over its land-based counterparts:

- Public opposition to siting hazardous waste management facilities on shore is the critical factor in the search for new facilities.
- It is difficult to site a land-based incineration facility because of the not-in-my-backyard syndrome.
- Expensive scrubbers and secondary combustion units are not required for ocean incineration.

An economic evaluation of a somewhat typical ocean incineration process would be instructive in determining the relative advantages of adopting at-sea incineration as one response to needs in hazardous waste management. Such an evaluation is presented below; it has been based on the following assumptions:

1 The system is in compliance with United Nations Intergovernment Maritime Consultative Organization and EPA incineration ship guidelines.

2 Waste liquids to be incinerated have a 6000 Btu/lb average heating value.

3 The liquid wastes are readily pumpable and free of heavy metals.

4 The incineration ship is a converted tanker that can carry 12,000 metric tons of liquid wastes and incinerate up to 71 metric tons per hour.

5 Transportation to the incineration site is at the rate of 15 knots, with a 2-knot burning speed.

6 There is a 15 percent return on capital employed and a 10 percent return on operating costs after taxes.

Item	Capitalized costs
Tanker acquisition	$ 435,000
Incinerator equipment	2,000,000
Tanker rehabilitation	1,102,000
Shipyard engineering	112,000
Tanker construction	6,113,000
Subtotal	9,762,000
Administrative costs	390,000
Engineering consultants	160,000
Inspection and certification	65,000
Total	$10,377,000

As can be seen, a substantial capital cost is required to convert a tanker into an incineration ship. And the annual operating costs for an incinerator ship working in the Gulf of Mexico are estimated to be nearly as great as the original capital cost:

Operational item	Annual cost
Crew	$4,352,000
Ship fuel	284,000
Incinerator fuel	4,152,000
Insurance	311,000
Maintenance	730,000
Total	$9,829,000

These operating costs are based on incineration in the EPA-approved burn area, with wastes being picked up from Mobile, New Orleans, and Houston. The total cost for ocean incineration varies from $38 to $57 per metric ton for a converted tanker, to $80 to $90 for the *Vulcanus,* to $181 to $212 for land-based incineration. These economic comparisons clearly favor ocean incineration as the preferred method for incineration of hazardous wastes.

When compared with land-based incineration, incineration at sea seems like an excellent solution to destroying liquid hazardous wastes. Threats to human health would be limited by remoteness from people. In addition, the not-in-my-backyard syndrome and site-selection problems would be eliminated. Further, ocean incineration of hazardous wastes costs less than land-based incineration, making it both economically and environmentally viable.

However, despite these potential benefits, the *Vulcanus* faces a doubtful future in this field.

QUESTIONS

1 Discuss the two laws of thermodynamics that relate to incineration of hazardous wastes.
2 Discuss the three modes of heat transfer in a rotary kiln.
3 What are the significant properties of refractory materials related to hazardous waste incineration?
4 Discuss the reactions of carbon, ethyl mercaptan, chlorobenzene, and air in a hazardous waste incinerator.
5 Discuss and contrast incineration of hazardous waste with both stoichiometric and excess air.
6 Describe a rotary kiln hazardous waste incinerator.
7 Why is the rotary kiln the most common hazardous waste incinerator for solids?
8 Why are there more hazardous waste liquid incinerators in commercial use than any other type of incinerator?
9 What destruction and removal efficiency must be achieved in the United States in hazardous waste incinerators under RCRA? under TSCA?
10 Define destruction and removal efficiencies in terms of a principal organic hazardous constituent fed to an incinerator.
11 Describe a bubbling fluidized-bed hazardous waste incinerator.
12 Describe a circulating fluidized-bed hazardous waste incinerator.
13 The incineration of liquid hazardous wastes at sea has been successfully demonstrated in Europe. Why has this technology not been successfully transferred to the United States?

PROBLEMS

1 An incineration process produces 22.53 pounds of steam that generates 40,000 Btu, which is all absorbed by the steam. The steam enters the incinerator as liquid water at 60°F. What is the exit steam temperature?
2 A hydrocarbon liquid waste at 60°F is incinerated with a heat release of 800,000 Btu. The resulting incineration products are 200 pounds of steam and 1000 pounds of carbon dioxide. What is the resulting incineration temperature?
3 If the hydrocarbon waste mixture in Problem 2 enters the incinerator in the vapor phase rather than as a liquid, what should the incineration temperature be? At 60°F the heat of vaporization of water is 1059.6 Btu/lb.
4 Calculate the heat loss through a 6-inch refractory brick wall that is 20 feet high and 10 feet wide, when the inner and outer surface temperatures are 1500 and 150°F, respectively. The average thermal conductivity for the refractory brick is 1.2 Btu/(h)(ft^2)(°F/ft).
5 What is the heat loss by convection of an incinerator surface that is 15 feet long and 10 feet wide, when the interface temperature of the incinerator is 130°F? The ambient temperature is 80°F, and the film coefficient for the liquid organic waste is 2 Btu/(h)(ft^2)(°F).
6 What is the heat transferred by radiation between a 1000°F metal tube that is 20 feet long and 6 inches in outside diameter? The tube is in an enclosed chamber of refractory brick at 1900°F. The refractory brick chamber is 6 feet in diameter and has an emissivity of 0.8.

7 A liquid waste at 77°F containing 25 weight percent toluene in water is to be incinerated with stoichiometric air. A later test is performed with 50 percent excess air. Calculate the incinerator operating temperature for each of these cases, using the simplified approach given in the Equation (8-3). Assume NHV for toluene is 17,600 Btu/lb and the heat of vaporization of water at 77°F is 1051 Btu/lb.

8 A hazardous waste mixture of phenol, toluene, and trichlorobenzene is incinerated with 50 percent excess air at 2040°F and a 2-second residence time. The waste feed and the stack emission rates are shown below:

	Feed rate, lb/h	Emission rate, lb/h
Trichlorobenzene	1050	0.163
Toluene	1162	0.108
Phenol	425	0.026

Are the DREs in compliance?

9 Waste C_6H_5Cl is fed into a hazardous waste incinerator at a rate of 1850 lb/h, with 60 percent excess air. Assuming complete incineration of the chlorobenzene and that air is 21 percent oxygen and 79 percent nitrogen, quantify the products from the incinerator.

10 A hazardous liquid waste vertical incinerator is designed to operate at 2192°F with an incineration gas flow rate of 7500 scfm at 60°F. The dimensions of the rectangular incinerator are 8 feet wide, 10 feet deep, and 30 feet high. Determine the actual incineration gas flow rate using Charles' law, the incinerator volume required for a 2-second residence time, and the actual incinerator residence time.

11 A hazardous waste rotary kiln incinerator is 30 feet long, 11 feet in diameter, and has a slope of 0.012 ft/ft of length with a rotational velocity of 1.3 r/min. Determine the average residence time for the kiln solids. Estimate the minimum kiln rotational velocity if the average solids residence time must be at least 70 minutes.

BIBLIOGRAPHY

1 Bonner, T., et al.: *Hazardous Waste Incineration Engineering,* Noyes Data, Park Ridge, N.J., 1981.

2 Brunner, C. R.: *Design of Sewage Sludge Incineration Systems,* Noyes Data, Park Ridge, N.J., 1980.

3 Brunner, C. R.: *Incineration Systems,* Van Nostrand Reinhold, New York, 1984.

4 Chang, D. P. Y., et al.: "Evaluation of a Pilot-Scale Circulating Bed Combustor as a Potential Hazardous Waste Incinerator," *JAPCA,* vol. 37, no. 3, 1987.

5 Dellinger, B., et al.: "Incinerability of Hazardous Wastes," *Hazardous Waste and Hazardous Materials,* vol. 3, no. 2, 1986.

6 *Directory of Commercial Hazardous Waste Management Facilities,* U.S. Environmental Protection Agency, Office of Solid Waste, Washington, 1987.

7 Freeman, H. M., *Incinerating Hazardous Wastes,* Technomic Publishing, Lancaster, Penn., 1988.

8 Freeman, H. M.: *Innovative Thermal Hazardous Organic Waste Treatment Processes,* Noyes Data, Park Ridge, N.J., 1985.

 9 Gorman, P., R. Hathaway, D. Wallace, and A. Trenholm: "A Practical Guide to Trial Burns for Hazardous Waste," *JAPCA*, vol. 37, no. 1, 1987.
10 Kern, D. Q.: *Process Heat Transfer*, McGraw-Hill, New York, 1950.
11 Klicius, R., A Finkelstein, and D. Hay: "The National Incinerator Testing and Evaluation Program: Air Pollution Control Technology Assessment Results," *Hazardous Waste and Hazardous Materials*, vol. 5, no. 1, 1988.
12 Lee, C. C., G. L. Huffman, and D. A. Oberacker: "An Overview of Hazardous/Toxic Waste Incineration," *JAPCA*, vol. 36, no. 8, 1986.
13 McAdams, W. H.: *Heat Transmission*, 3d. ed., McGraw-Hill, New York, 1954.
14 Niessen, W. R.: *Combustion and Incineration Processes*, Marcel Dekker, New York, 1978.
15 Oppelt, E. T.: "Incineration of Hazardous Waste," *JAPCA*, vol. 37, no. 5, 1987.
16 Perry, R., and D. Green: *Perry's Chemical Engineering Handbook*, McGraw-Hill, New York, 1984.
17 Shields, E. J.: *Pollution Control Engineer's Handbook*, Pudvan, Northbrook, Ill., 1985.
18 Smith, J. M., and H. C. VanNess: *Introduction to Chemical Engineering Thermodynamics*, 3d. ed., McGraw-Hill, New York, 1975.
19 Theodore, L., and L. Buonicore: *Air Pollution Control Equipment*, CRC Press, Boca Raton, Fla., 1987.
20 Theodore, L., and J. Reynolds: *Introduction to Hazardous Waste Incineration*, Wiley, New York, 1987.
21 Visalli, J. R.: "A Comparison of Dioxin, Furan and Combustible Gas Data from Test Programs at Three MSW Incinerators," *JAPCA*, vol. 37, no. 12, 1987.
22 Weast, R. C.: *CRC Handbook of Chemistry and Physics*, 51st ed., Chemical Rubber Company, Cleveland, Ohio, 1971.

CHAPTER 9

TRANSPORTATION OF HAZARDOUS WASTES

INTRODUCTION

The public has become increasingly aware of the environmental and health damage that can result from accidents involving the transportation of hazardous wastes. At the same time, state and local officials are aware that they do not fully understand the complexity of the risks to public safety posed by transportation of hazardous materials. Moreover, there is a pervasive feeling that federal programs do not take special local circumstances into account, and local officials are increasingly asking for federal help in establishing regulatory, enforcement, and emergency response programs that meet their specific needs.[1]

The federal regulatory system governing the transportation of hazardous materials was developed over the past century with substantial industry involvement. The existing regulations promulgated by the U.S. Department of Transportation (DOT), EPA, and other federal agencies are extensive.[2,4] They cover all aspects of the transportation of hazardous wastes: classification of the wastes, engineering specifications for containers, communication requirements such as container and vehicle labeling, handling and operating requirements for each mode of transport, safety requirements for shippers and carriers, worker safety, and environmental protection.[3,5]

EARLY FEDERAL REGULATIONS

The first federal law regulating the transportation of hazardous materials, passed in 1866, covered shipments of explosives and flammable materials. An 1871 statute made it a criminal act to transport specific hazardous materials on passenger vessels in U.S. navigable waters.

After the Civil War, rail shipments of explosives were regulated by uncodified statutes and contractual obligations, based on English common law,

230

between shippers and carriers. Common carriers were granted a public charter to operate and were obligated to provide service to anyone upon reasonable request, for reasonable cost, and without unjust discrimination. Carriers could, however, prescribe conditions under which certain freight would be accepted. Shippers were required to identify the hazards of a dangerous commodity, use adequate packaging, and provide a clear warning to the prospective carrier.

The Interstate Commerce Commission (ICC) was established in 1887 primarily to regulate interstate rail transport, but its regulatory authority was gradually extended to other modes of transport. Until the formation of the Department of Transportation in 1966, ICC was the primary regulatory agency with authority over interstate transportation of hazardous materials.

THE DEPARTMENT OF TRANSPORTATION (DOT)

In 1966, authority to regulate the transportation of hazardous materials was transferred from the ICC, the Department of the Treasury, and the Civil Aeronautics Board to a new federal agency, the Department of Transportation (DOT). Separate modal administrations, shown in Figure 9-1, were retained to preserve organizational continuity. Although the DOT secretary had responsibility for all safety standards regulating the transportation of hazardous materials, each modal unit was allowed to promulgate independent regulations. Legislation pertaining to the transportation of hazardous materials passed in 1970, but DOT was unable to implement the 1970 statute because Congress refused to approve DOT requests for additional staff.

THE CONSOLIDATION OF REGULATIONS GOVERNING THE TRANSPORTATION OF HAZARDOUS WASTES

Persistent administrative and organizational difficulties in the early 1970s led DOT to seek the passage of legislation that would consolidate regulatory authority over hazardous materials. However, little was done until 1973, when a cargo jet carrying several tons of hazardous materials crashed. Inquiry into the accident showed that there was a general lack of compliance with existing requirements because of the complexity of the rules, the fragmentation of federal surveillance and enforcement authorities, and lack of industry familiarity with the regulations at the working level.

In 1975, the Hazardous Materials Transportation Act (HMTA) was passed. The intent of the law was to improve regulatory and enforcement activities by providing the secretary of transportation broad authority to set regulations applicable to all aspects of the transportation of hazardous materials.

Table 9-1 lists the hazardous materials that are subject to federal regulation. Many of the classes of materials listed had been established long before the HMTA was passed. The early regulations focused on materials that are likely

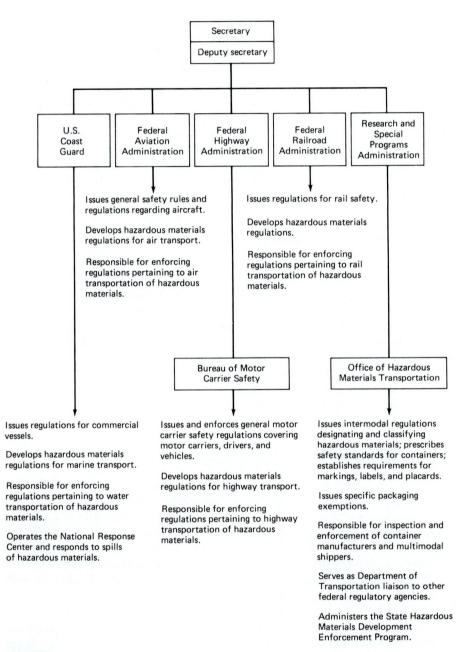

FIGURE 9-1
U.S. Department of Transportation functions that are applicable to transportation of hazardous substances.

TABLE 9-1
DEPARTMENT OF TRANSPORTATION HAZARD CLASSES

Hazard class	Definition	Examples
Flammable liquid	Any liquid having a flash point below 100°F.	Ethyl alcohol, gasoline, acetone, benzene, dimethyl sulfide
Combustible liquid	Any liquid having a flash point at or above 100°F and below 200°F.	Ink, fuel oil
Flammable solid	Any solid material, other than an explosive, liable to cause fires through friction or retained heat from manufacturing or processing or which can be ignited readily, creating a serious transportation hazard because it burns vigorously and persistently.	Nitrocellulose, phosphorus, charcoal
Oxidizer	A substance, such as chlorate, permanganate, inorganic peroxide, or a nitrate, that yields oxygen readily to stimulate the combustion of organic matter.	Potassium bromate, hydrogen peroxide solution, chromic acid
Organic peroxide	An organic compound containing the bivalent —O—O— structure and which may be considered a derivative of hydrogen peroxide where one or more of the hydrogen atoms have been replaced by organic radicals.	Urea peroxide, benzoyl peroxide
Corrosive	Liquid or solid that causes visible destruction or irreversible alterations in human skin tissue at the site of contact, including liquids that severely corrode steel.	Bromine, soda lime, hydrochloric acid, sodium hydroxide solution
Flammable gas	A compressed gas that meets certain flammability requirements.	Butadiene, engine starting fluid, hydrogen, liquefied petroleum gas
Nonflammable gas	A compressed gas other than a flammable gas.	Chlorine, xenon, neon, anhydrous ammonia
Irritating material	A liquid or solid substance which on contact with fire or when exposed to air gives off dangerous or intensely irritating fumes.	Tear gas, monochloroacetone

233

TABLE 9-1
DEPARTMENT OF TRANSPORTATION HAZARD CLASSES *(Continued)*

Hazard class	Definition	Examples
Poison A	Extremely dangerous poison gases or liquids belong to this class. Very small amounts of these gases or vapors of these liquids, mixed with air, are dangerous to life.	Hydrocyanic acid, bromoacetone, nitric oxide phosgene
Poison B	Substances, liquids or solids (including pastes and semisolids), other than poison A or irritating materials, that are known to be toxic to humans. In the absence of adequate data on human toxicity materials are presumed to be toxic to humans if they are toxic to laboratory animals.	Phenol, nitroaniline, parathion, cyanide, mercury-based pesticides, disinfectants
Etiologic agents	A viable microorganism, or its toxin, which causes or may cause human disease. These materials are limited to agents listed by the Department of Health and Human Services.	Vibrio chloerae, clostridium botulinum, polio virus, salmonella, all serotypes
Radioactive material	A material that spontaneously emits ionizing radiation having a specific activity greater than 0.002 microcuries per gram (μCi/g).	Thorium nitrate, uranium hexafluoride
Explosive	Any chemical compound, mixture, or device, the primary or common purpose of which is to function by explosion, unless such compound, mixture, or device is otherwise classified.	
Class A	Detonating explosives.	Jet thrust unit, explosive booster
Class B	Explosives that generally function by rapid combustion rather than detonation.	Torpedo, propellant explosive
Class C	Manufactured articles, such as small arms ammunition, that contain restricted quantities of class A and/or class B explosives, and certain types of fireworks.	Toy caps, trick matches, signal flare, fireworks
Blasting agent	A material designed for blasting, but so insensitive that there is very little probability of ignition during transport.	Blasting cap
ORM (other regulated materials)	Any material that does not meet the definition of the other hazard classes. ORMs are divided into five substances:	

234

TABLE 9-1
DEPARTMENT OF TRANSPORTATION HAZARD CLASSES *(Continued)*

Hazard class	Definition	Examples
ORM-A	A material which has an anesthetic, irritating, noxious, toxic, or other similar property and can cause extreme annoyance or discomfort to passengers and crew in the event of leakage during transportation.	Trichloroethylene, carbon tetrachloride, ethylene dibromide, chloroform
ORM-B	A material capable of causing significant damage to a transport vehicle or vessel if leaked. This class includes materials that may be corrosive to aluminum.	Calcium oxide, ferric chloride, potassium fluoride
ORM-C	A material which has other inherent characteristics not described as an ORM-A or ORM-B but which make it unsuitable for shipment unless properly identified and prepared for transportation.	Castor beans, cotton, inflatable life rafts
ORM-D	A material such as a consumer commodity which, although otherwise subject to regulation, presents a limited hazard during transportation due to its form, quantity, and packaging.	Consumer commodity not otherwise specified, such as nail polish, small arms ammunition.
ORM-E	A material that is not included in any other hazard class but is subject to the requirements of this subchapter. Materials in this class include hazardous wastes and hazardous substances.	Kepone, lead iodide, heptachlor, polychlorinated biphenyls

Source: U.S. Department of Transportation.

to cause immediate injury to carrier personnel and the public if they are unexpectedly released during transport. The present classification is more comprehensive.

It is estimated that 264 million metric tons of hazardous materials are generated each year in the United States. Of these, 96 percent are disposed of on-site. Most of the waste that is shipped off-site for disposal or treatment is transported by truck over distances less than 100 miles. In 1981, EPA estimated that over 14,000 generators produced hazardous wastes and that there were 12,367 transporters of such materials. In 1984 legislation was passed that extended the scope of existing regulations to include small-quantity generators of hazardous wastes. Because most small-quantity generators ship their waste to off-site facilities, the number of shipments regulated has increased.

The transportation of these materials wastes is regulated by both HMTA and the Resource Conservation and Recovery Act of 1976. Subtitle C of RCRA, which is administered by EPA, is the primary federal statute governing hazardous wastes. Under RCRA, EPA is directed to establish certain standards for transporters of hazardous materials and to coordinate regulatory activities with DOT. (See Chapter 4.) It is responsible for developing regulations covering the following:

Identification, listing, and labeling

Record keeping

Generators, transporters, and owners and operators of treatment and disposal facilities

Permit requirements for all facilities involved in the production and transportation of hazardous materials

Tracking of the movement of hazardous wastes (through the manifest system, described later in this chapter)

States are authorized to administer and enforce their own hazardous waste programs if their regulations are consistent with and at least as stringent as federal programs. EPA would declare a state policy inconsistent with federal standards if the program unreasonably restricted the free movement of hazardous materials across state lines or if the implementation of the program resulted in restrictions on the treatment, storage, or disposal of hazardous materials. HMTA specifically allows DOT to preempt inconsistent state and local requirements.

DOT and EPA Coordination

RCRA explicitly states that EPA regulations gover ing transporters of hazardous materials must be consistent with the DOT regulations established under HMTA. In February 1980, EPA adopted DOT regulations for labeling, marking, and placarding; for using proper containers; and for reporting discharges. In May of that year, DOT amended its hazardous materials regulations to make them applicable to hazardous wastes and to incorporate additional requirements for the transportation of hazardous wastes.

EPA Regions

The Environmental Protection Agency is responsible for administering environmental protection regulations, including the regulations governing the transportation of hazardous wastes for 10 regions (see Figure 9-2). EPA has adopted DOT regulations for communication, for packaging, and for reporting discharges. However, the EPA system for identifying and classifying hazardous wastes is different from the DOT system, and shippers and carriers of hazardous wastes must understand both classification systems.

The Nuclear Regulatory Commission

On the federal level, the Nuclear Regulatory Commission is involved, along with DOT and EPA, in regulating the transportation of hazardous waste. In that role, NRC regulates the receipt, possession, use, and transfer of by-product and source of special nuclear materials. NRC also sets standards for the design and performance of packages used to transport high-level radioactive materials and conducts inspection of its licensees. Other NRC regulations require advance notification to the states of certain shipments and provide for physical security measures. DOT reserves to itself regulatory authority over the design and performance of packages used to ship low-level radioactive materials and over the transportation of high-level materials.

DEFINITION OF GENERATORS (SHIPPERS) AND TRANSPORTERS (CARRIERS)

DOT considers a shipper to be an entity that performs any of the functions listed in 49 Code of Federal Regulations, Parts 172 and 173, such as labeling or packaging. EPA calls an entity fitting the DOT description of a shipper a waste "generator," and defines a generator as "any person, by site, whose act first causes a hazardous waste to become subject to regulation"—for example, any person who removes hazardous sludges and residues in vehicles or vessels that have carried products or raw materials, or who hires another party to remove and dispose of sludges and residues, or who takes a vehicle or vessel to a central facility for cleaning. EPA regards all parties involved in the transportation of hazardous waste as generators and believes that they can be held jointly and severally liable if regulations are violated.

Under DOT regulations, a carrier is also considered a generator if the carrier imports hazardous wastes into the United States, mixes hazardous wastes with different DOT descriptions, or is responsible for discharge of hazardous wastes or commercial chemical products occurring during transport. In the lat-

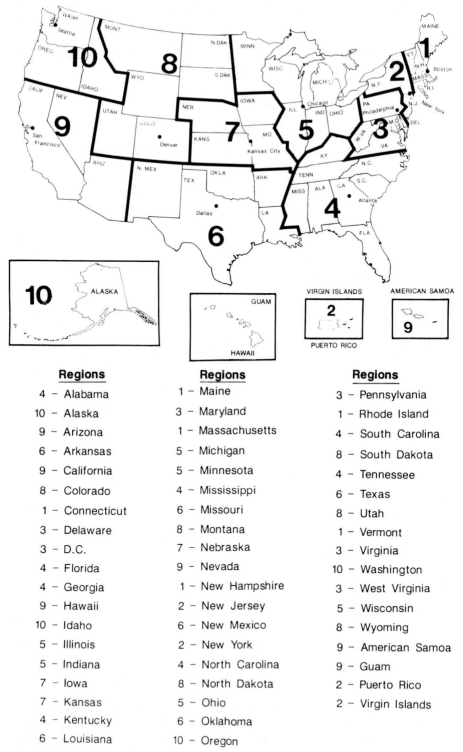

Regions	Regions	Regions
4 – Alabama	1 – Maine	3 – Pennsylvania
10 – Alaska	3 – Maryland	1 – Rhode Island
9 – Arizona	1 – Massachusetts	4 – South Carolina
6 – Arkansas	5 – Michigan	8 – South Dakota
9 – California	5 – Minnesota	4 – Tennessee
8 – Colorado	4 – Mississippi	6 – Texas
1 – Connecticut	6 – Missouri	8 – Utah
3 – Delaware	8 – Montana	1 – Vermont
3 – D.C.	7 – Nebraska	3 – Virginia
4 – Florida	9 – Nevada	10 – Washington
4 – Georgia	1 – New Hampshire	3 – West Virginia
9 – Hawaii	2 – New Jersey	5 – Wisconsin
10 – Idaho	6 – New Mexico	8 – Wyoming
5 – Illinois	2 – New York	9 – American Samoa
5 – Indiana	4 – North Carolina	9 – Guam
7 – Iowa	8 – North Dakota	2 – Puerto Rico
7 – Kansas	5 – Ohio	2 – Virgin Islands
4 – Kentucky	6 – Oklahoma	
6 – Louisiana	10 – Oregon	

FIGURE 9-2
The regions of the U.S. Environmental Protection Agency. (*Source:* U.S. Environmental
Protection Agency.)

ter cases, the transporter-generator is responsible for cleanup of the discharge, as well as any resulting pollution such as contaminated soil or water.

If a generator or transporter accumulates hazardous wastes for more than 90 days, an RCRA storage facility permit must be obtained. However, if a transport vehicle, vessel, tank, or container is used only for neutralizing corrosive wastes, a facility permit is not required. In addition, transfer facilities that store manifested shipments of hazardous wastes for 10 days or less are not required to obtain a permit.

REGULATIONS GOVERNING GENERATORS OF HAZARDOUS WASTES

Generators of hazardous wastes are responsible for complying with all DOT legislation regulating the transportation of hazardous materials as well as regulations promulgated by both DOT and EPA specifically covering hazardous wastes. The regulations cover three major areas: preparation for transport, including identification and notification and packaging; compliance with manifest requirements; and record keeping and reporting. Table 9-2 summarizes the requirements, indicates the agency responsible for compliance, and provides a reference to the Code of Federal Regulations.

Preparation for Transport

Most pretransport requirements are DOT regulations that apply to all hazardous materials. They include identifying and classifying wastes according to the DOT Hazardous Materials Table; determining whether the wastes are prohibited from certain modes of transport or whether special shipping requirements must be met; and complying with all packaging, marking, labeling, and placarding requirements. The following focuses on DOT regulations as they pertain to hazardous wastes and discusses relevant EPA requirements.

EPA Identification and Notification   Generators of waste must first determine whether their wastes are hazardous according to EPA criteria. A waste is considered to be hazardous if it satisfies all of the following conditions:

It is a solid waste as defined by the EPA.

It is listed as a hazardous waste by the EPA or is a mixture that contains a listed waste or exhibits one of the four EPA characteristics of a hazardous waste—ignitability, reactivity, corrosivity, or EP toxicity.

It is not explicitly excluded from regulation.

Once it has been established that a waste is hazardous, generators are required to obtain an EPA identification number by submitting EPA Form 8700–12 to the agency. Generators are also responsible for seeing that any entities that will eventually handle the waste (e.g., transporters or owner-operators of treatment, storage, or disposal facilities) have EPA identification numbers.

TABLE 9-2
EPA AND DOT HAZARDOUS WASTE TRANSPORTATION REGULATIONS

Required of	Agency	Code of Federal Regulations
Generator/shipper		
1. Determine if waste is hazardous according to EPA listing criteria	EPA	40 CFR 261 and 262.11
2. Notify EPA and obtain I.D. number; determine that transporter and designated treatment, storage, or disposal facility have I.D. numbers	EPA	40 CFR 262.12
3. Identify and classify waste according to DOT Hazardous Materials Table and determine if waste is prohibited from certain modes of transport	DOT	49 CFR 172.101
4. Comply with all packaging, marking, and labeling requirements	EPA	40 CFR 262.32 (b),
	DOT	49 CFR 173, 49 CFR 172, subpart D, and 49 CFR 172, subpart E
5. Determine whether additional shipping requirements must be met for the mode of transport used.	DOT	49 CFR 174–177
6. Complete a hazardous waste manifest	EPA	40 CFR 262, subpart B
7. Provide appropriate placards to transporter	DOT	49 CFR 172, subpart F
8. Comply with record-keeping and reporting requirements	EPA	40 CFR 262, subpart D
Transporter/carrier		
1. Notify EPA and obtain I.D. number	EPA	40 CFR 263.11
2. Verify that shipment is properly identified, packaged, marked, and labeled and is not leaking or damaged	DOT	49 CFR 174–177
3. Apply appropriate placards	DOT	49 CFR 172.506
4. Comply with all manifest requirements (e.g., sign the manifest, carry the manifest, and obtain signature from next transporter or owner/operator of designated facility)	DOT EPA	49 CFR 174-177 40 CFR 263.20
5. Comply with record-keeping and reporting requirements	EPA	50 CFR 263.22
6. Take appropriate action (including cleanup) in the event of a discharge and comply with the DOT incident reporting requirements	EPA DOT	40 CFR 263.30-31 49 CFR 171.15-17

Source: U.S. Environmental Protection Agency.

In addition, EPA requires generators to mark all containers of hazardous wastes with a capacity of 110 gallons or less with a statement indicating that federal law prohibits improper disposal of such wastes.

Generators of hazardous wastes that produce less than 100 kg of waste per month are exempt from EPA regulation.

DOT Identification and Classification   In the DOT system of classification of hazardous materials, hazardous wastes are ORM-E (other regulated material, class E; see Table 9-1, which lists all the DOT hazard classes). It is important to correctly classify hazardous waste according to the DOT system because regulations covering hazard communication and packaging of a hazardous material correspond to the class of the material.

First, it must be determined whether a hazardous waste is listed in the DOT Hazardous Materials Table in 49 Code of Federal Regulations, Part 172. If it is not, the characteristics of the waste must be identified, using DOT hazard class definitions. Note that the four criteria used by EPA to determine whether a waste is hazardous are broader than the DOT criteria. For example, a "reactive" waste according to EPA could be either an irritating material, such as tear gas, or an explosive. An "ignitable" waste according to EPA might be either a flammable material or a combustible material.

All generators and carriers of hazardous materials not classified as ORM-E, including small-quantity generators, must comply with appropriate DOT regulations covering marking, labeling, and placarding. These "hazard communications" furnish essential information about the cargo that can be used by emergency response personnel should an accident occur.

ORM-E materials are not subject to DOT labeling and placarding requirements but are instead accompanied by a document called a *hazardous waste manifest*.

DOT requires shippers (generators) to mark all packages with a capacity of 110 gallons or less with a proper shipping name, including a United Nations–North American (UN/NA) identification number. This is done so the contents of a package can be identified if it is separated from its shipping papers. Requirements for intermodal portable tanks, highway cargo tanks, and rail tank cars specify that the UN/NA number be displayed on a placard or an orange rectangular panel. There is a single UN/NA number for all hazardous wastes in the "Hazardous Waste n.o.s." (not otherwise specified) category—UN/NA 9189.

Packages containing ORM materials or hazardous liquids are subject to additional marking requirements. For example, packages containing liquid hazardous materials must be marked THIS SIDE UP or THIS END UP.

Labels are symbolic representations of the hazards associated with a particular material. Labels are required for most packages containing hazardous materials and must be printed on or affixed to a spot near the marked shipping name. Examples of DOT labels are shown in Figure 9-3. Like labels, placards offer symbolic representations of the hazards of a given cargo. They are placed on the ends and sides of motor vehicles, railcars, and freight containers. Figure 9-4 shows some sample placards. Placards are particularly important in case of accident because they are highly visible.

Packaging DOT regulations that pertain to the packaging of all hazardous materials are discussed below. Two special rules that apply to hazardous wastes are (1) an open-head drum, rather than a closed-head drum, may be

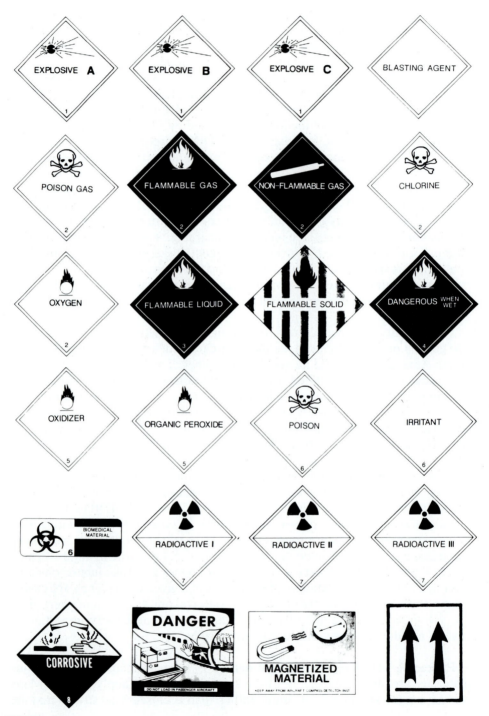

FIGURE 9-3
DOT labels for hazardous materials packages.

FIGURE 9-4
DOT placards for hazardous substances. (*Source:* U.S. Department of Transportation.)

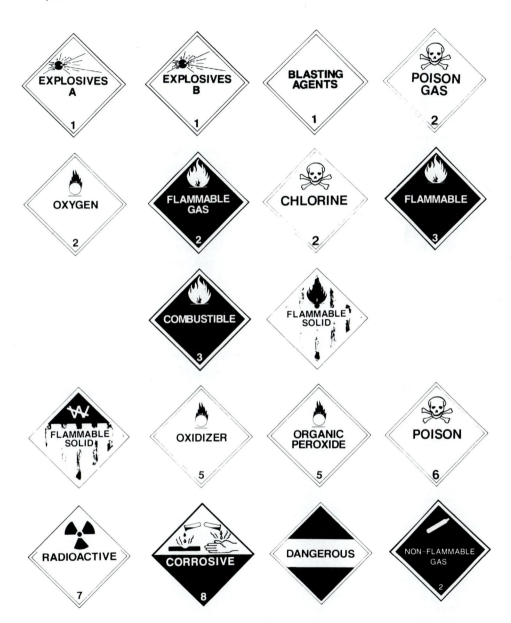

used for wastes containing solids or semisolids, and (2) hazardous wastes may be shipped in used packaging that has not been reconditioned or tested.

Manifest Requirements

The manifest system (which is discussed in detail in Chapter 4) was established by RCRA to ensure that hazardous wastes designated for delivery to off-site treatment, storage, or disposal facilities actually reach their destination. Hazardous waste management in the United States covers hazardous wastes from ''cradle to grave'' (Figure 9-5). A manifest is a form that contains information about a specific hazardous waste and accompanies a shipment from generation point to ultimate destination. A sample manifest form is shown in Figure 9-6. Like DOT shipping papers, manifests provide information about the nature of the shipment that can be used by emergency response personnel when accidents or incidents occur. The only significant difference between a manifest and a DOT shipping paper is that a manifest lists the EPA identification numbers of the generator, transporter, and designated facility. DOT regulations specify that an EPA manifest may be used in place of a DOT shipping paper.

Generators are responsible for originating and signing manifest forms. They

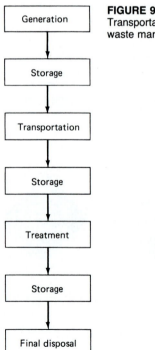

FIGURE 9-5
Transportation, storage, and handling in the hazardous waste management system.

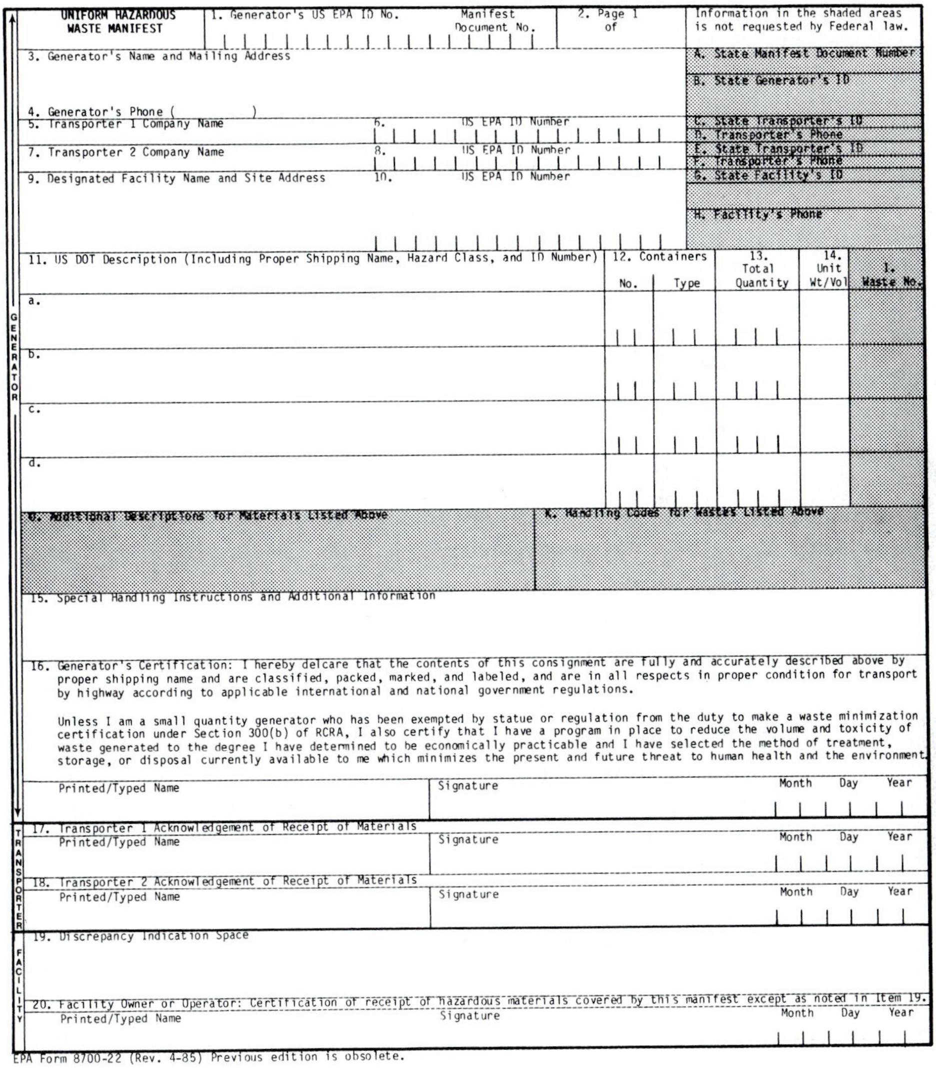

UNIFORM HAZARDOUS WASTE MANIFEST	1. Generator's US EPA ID No.		Manifest Document No.	2. Page 1 of	Information in the shaded areas is not requested by Federal law.
3. Generator's Name and Mailing Address					A. State Manifest Document Number
					B. State Generator's ID
4. Generator's Phone ( )					
5. Transporter 1 Company Name	6.	US EPA ID Number			C. State Transporter's ID
					D. Transporter's Phone
7. Transporter 2 Company Name	8.	US EPA ID Number			E. State Transporter's ID
					F. Transporter's Phone
9. Designated Facility Name and Site Address	10.	US EPA ID Number			G. State Facility's ID
					H. Facility's Phone

11. US DOT Description (Including Proper Shipping Name, Hazard Class, and ID Number)	12. Containers		13. Total Quantity	14. Unit Wt/Vol	I. Waste No.
	No.	Type			
a.					
b.					
c.					
d.					

J. Additional Descriptions for Materials Listed Above	K. Handling Codes for Wastes Listed Above

15. Special Handling Instructions and Additional Information

16. Generator's Certification: I hereby delcare that the contents of this consignment are fully and accurately described above by proper shipping name and are classified, packed, marked, and labeled, and are in all respects in proper condition for transport by highway according to applicable international and national government regulations.

Unless I am a small quantity generator who has been exempted by statue or regulation from the duty to make a waste minimization certification under Section 300(b) of RCRA, I also certify that I have a program in place to reduce the volume and toxicity of waste generated to the degree I have determined to be economically practicable and I have selected the method of treatment, storage, or disposal currently available to me which minimizes the present and future threat to human health and the environment.

Printed/Typed Name	Signature	Month Day Year

17. Transporter 1 Acknowledgement of Receipt of Materials		
Printed/Typed Name	Signature	Month Day Year

18. Transporter 2 Acknowledgement of Receipt of Materials		
Printed/Typed Name	Signature	Month Day Year

19. Discrepancy Indication Space

20. Facility Owner or Operator: Certification of receipt of hazardous materials covered by this manifest except as noted in Item 19.		
Printed/Typed Name	Signature	Month Day Year

EPA Form 8700-22 (Rev. 4-85) Previous edition is obsolete.

FIGURE 9-6
The hazardous waste manifest. (*Source:* U.S. Environmental Protection Agency.)

must also obtain the signature of the transporter, retain one copy of the form for their records, and give the remaining copies to the transporter.

Record Keeping and Reporting

Generators are required by EPA to keep a copy of each signed manifest for 3 years whether or not a signed copy is returned to the generator by the designated treatment, storage, or disposal facility. Records of all test results, waste analyses, etc., as well as copies of all reports submitted to EPA, must also be kept for at least 3 years.

Biennial reports must be submitted to EPA by all generators who ship their wastes off-site. The report describes all shipments initiated by the generator during a given time period. In addition, if a generator does not receive a signed copy of a manifest from the designated treatment, storage, or disposal facility within 45 days of the date the waste was accepted by the initial transporter, an exception record must be filed with EPA. Exception reports help EPA to determine whether a waste has been properly disposed of.

REGULATIONS GOVERNING TRANSPORTERS OF HAZARDOUS WASTES

Transporters of hazardous wastes are also regulated by both EPA and DOT. The regulations applicable to transporters include notification requirements, manifest requirements, rules governing record keeping, and cleanup regulations. Some states have developed their own permit and registration programs for transporters of hazardous wastes.

Notification Prior to Transport

All transporters of hazardous wastes are required to obtain an identification number from EPA and to follow DOT regulations governing hazard communication. DOT regulations prohibit all transporters from accepting hazardous materials that have not been properly identified, packaged, marked, and labeled. Special requirements for leaking containers have been established by the DOT for each mode of transport.

Generators are responsible for following DOT and EPA pretransport requirements. If a generator has not affixed the appropriate placard to a shipment, the generator must supply the transporter with the necessary placard and the transporter must affix it. Generators are responsible for placarding railcars, highway cargo tanks, intermodal tanks, and certain freight containers.

Manifest Requirements

EPA regulations prohibit transporters from accepting hazardous waste shipments from a generator without a manifest. Transporters who accept manifested hazardous wastes are required to sign and date the manifest, return a signed copy of the manifest to the generator, and ensure that the manifest accompanies the waste to its destination. When the shipment is delivered to the next transporter or to its designated facility, the initiating transporter must obtain a signature from the accepting transporter or the operator of the facility. A transporter is responsible for a hazardous waste shipment until the manifest is signed by a receiving facility. If a hazardous waste shipment cannot be delivered to the facility designated on the manifest, the transporter must ask the generator for further instructions. Special requirements for bulk shipments by water and rail have been established.

Record Keeping

Transporters must keep a copy of each signed manifest, or shipping papers that may be used in place of manifests for bulk shipments, for 3 years. This applies to shipments of hazardous wastes outside the United States.

Discharges and Cleanup

A discharge of hazardous waste is defined as "the accidental or intentional spilling, leaking, pumping, pouring, emitting, emptying, or dumping of hazardous waste into or on any land or water." EPA regulations require all transporters to take immediate action in the event of a discharge. Such action may include notifying local authorities or initiating interim measures such as diking an area to contain the wastes. DOT immediate-notification requirements for incidents involving hazardous materials are applicable to discharges of hazardous wastes. Notice is given by calling the National Response Center, which is operated by the U.S. Coast Guard. Both EPA and DOT have included provisions in their regulations authorizing federal, state, or local government officials to permit the immediate removal of hazardous wastes by transporters who do not have EPA identification numbers and are without a manifest. EPA has also exempted all persons involved in treatment or containment activities taken during an immediate response to the discharge of hazardous wastes or materials from requirements governing facility permits.

After the emergency, all normal regulations for the final disposition of the wastes must be followed. EPA has established a procedure for rapidly issuing identification numbers to emergency response personnel and to shippers or carriers who need to transport hazardous wastes following an unanticipated release. A provisional identification number may be obtained by telephoning the appropriate EPA regional office.

EPA regulations require that transporters clean up all discharges that occur during transport and take any actions required by appropriate government officials for mitigating the effect of the discharge on human health or the environment. DOT regulations do not contain a comparable provision for other hazardous materials.

Finally, DOT requirements for written incident or accident reports must be met. For discharges of hazardous wastes, transporters are required to attach a copy of the manifest to the DOT reporting form and provide an estimate of the quantity of wastes removed from the scene, the name and address of the facility to which the wastes were taken, and the manner of disposition of any wastes that were not transported elsewhere.

CONTAINERS FOR HAZARDOUS MATERIALS

Ensuring the safe transportation of hazardous materials is a complex activity. The accidental release of hazardous materials poses serious threats to human safety and property and to the environment. Consequently, the regulations governing the construction and use of hazardous waste containers are stringent.

Most of the estimated 180 million annual shipments of hazardous materials reach their destinations safely because hazardous materials transportation is heavily regulated and because industry wants to ensure that its products reach customers intact. Over 30,000 different hazardous materials are covered by DOT regulations (see Table 9-1). These materials, essential to the economy of the United States, are shipped by air, highway, railroad, and water under regulations that reflect the different histories and operating characteristics of the various means used to transport them. Hazardous products are transported in bulk by vessels, tank cars, tank trucks, and intermodal portable tanks, and in smaller lots in containers such as cylinders, drums, barrels, cans, boxes, bottles, and casks. Packagings of widely varying specifications have been developed by industry to order to match the strength and integrity of the containers to the characteristics and hazards of the materials.

The Research and Special Programs Administration (RSPA) of DOT is responsible for issuing regulations covering all hazardous materials containers except bulk marine containers, which are regulated by the U.S. Coast Guard, and containers for high-level radioactive material. It is also responsible for establishing technical standards for the design and testing of the containers it has regulatory authority over.

The major packaging issues that must be faced by RSPA are as follows:

The types and severity of tests necessary for accurately determining the level of protection provided by a given container

The development of new packaging materials

The influence of international commerce and standards on U.S. packaging designs

The frequency of discharge accidents or incidents and the effects of these incidents on container regulation

DOT requires that containers used for shipping hazardous materials be so designed and constructed that if an incident occurs under normal transportation conditions:

There will be no significant release of the hazardous materials to the environment.

The effectiveness of the packaging will not be substantially reduced during transport.

There will be no mixture of gases or vapors in the package which could, through any spontaneous increase of heat or pressure, or through an explosion, significantly reduce the effectiveness of the packaging. In addition, packaging materials and contents must ensure there will be no significant chemical reaction among any of the materials in the package. Closures must prevent leakage, and gaskets must be used that will not be significantly deteriorated by the contents of the container.

The classification of a hazardous substance affects packaging, marking, labeling, and placarding. Many commonly transported materials are listed in the DOT regulations, and shippers need only locate the listing to be guided to the required packaging. If the material is not listed, however, the shipper must determine if it is hazardous and classify it according to definitions in the regulations.

Reconditioned Drums as Hazardous Waste Containers

Hazardous wastes are often accumulated in drums and containers. Historically, these waste drums have been stored to eventually corrode and pose a threat to human health and the environment. EPA has drum and container regulations to better manage industry practices in handling hazardous wastes. Under these regulations, all hazardous wastes must be placed in drums and containers that are in good condition. The hazardous wastes must be compatible with the drum or container. Inspections must be periodically carried out to assess containers being used to store the hazardous wastes. Any wastes in drums that are either damaged or leaking must be recontainerized.

The drum reconditioning industry uses the hazardous waste industry as a potential source of drums, but there is a long-term risk in supplying used drums to reconditioners. TSD facilities should be cautious in selecting a drum reconditioner without assurance of the firm's capability and financial strength. And the drum reconditioners must be assured of compatibility of hazardous waste drums with their reconditioning process.

Drum reconditioning offers yet another integration potential for the hazardous waste management industry. Yet the question of marketplace acceptance of reconditioned drums remains. The marketplace is generally suspicious of drums from hazardous waste facilities, and this stigma will be hard to overcome.

BULK TRANSPORT
Highway Transport

Table 9-3 summarizes information on bulk transportation of hazardous materials by road, rail, and water. Cargo tanks are the main carriers of bulk hazardous materials over the roads. Cargo tanks are usually made of steel or alu-

TABLE 9-3
BULK SHIPMENTS OF HAZARDOUS MATERIALS

	Highway	Rail	Water
Containers regulated by DOT	Most	All	All
Inspection or testing frequency	Upon manufacture	Upon manufacture plus every 5–10 year	Yearly
Fleet size	130,000 cargo	115,600 tank cars	4909 tank barges
Number of operators	260,000	26,000	45,000
Size of load, gallons	4000–12,000	10,000–30,000	300,000–600,000

Source: Office of Technology Assessment.

minum alloy but can be constructed of other materials, such as titanium, nickel, or stainless steel. They range in capacity from about 4000 to 12,000 gallons. Federal road weight laws usually limit motor vehicle weights to 80,000 pounds gross. Some states, however, allow higher gross weights, and in those states cargo tanks can have capacities larger than 12,000 gallons. Table 9-4 lists the commodities that cargo tanks of different specifications can carry.

The bulk trucking business differs from rail or water bulk transport in that there are many more small carriers, including interstate and intrastate carriers. The quality of the equipment varies within each of these groups, but generally the large private interstate transporters have the newest tankers and the small intrastate private carriers have the older equipment.

The useful life of a cargo tanker used to transport fuels can easily exceed 20 years; and cargo tanks generally go through a succession of owners. Large private interstate carriers, primarily large petrochemical companies, have the resources to purchase new equipment and maintain it well. They use their trucks around the clock 6 to 7 days a week. After 8 to 10 years, when maintenance

TABLE 9-4
CARGO TANKER SPECIFICATIONS

Cargo tanker specification no.	Commodities carried
MC-306 (MC-300, 301, 302, 303, 305)	Combustible and flammable liquids of low vapor pressure
MC-307 (MC-304)	Flammable liquids and poison B materials with moderate vapor pressures
MC-312 (MC-310, 311)	Corrosives
MC-331 (MC-330)	Liquefied compressed gases
MC-338	Refrigerated liquefied gases

Source: 49 Code of Federal Regulations, Parts 172.101 and 178.315–178.343.

becomes uneconomical because of downtime for repairs, the cargo tanker is sold to a smaller company, with fewer resources. The second-tier owner uses the tanker until it becomes uneconomical to do so and then sells the truck to yet another owner.

Cargo tanks carrying certain corrosives have much shorter life spans than tankers carrying noncorrosives. It is often desirable for a carrier to obtain backhauls; then a tanker that has carried a corrosive commodity must be cleaned between loads. Such cleaning subjects the tank to additional wear, exacerbating the effects of the corrosive and further shortening the life span of the tank.

Most truck transport of hazardous materials in intrastate commerce involves delivery of gasoline, fuel oil, and propane. MC-306 tank trucks make over 40,000 daily deliveries to retail service stations in every locality in the country. This large volume is the primary reason that truck transportation of gasoline is responsible for more deaths, injuries, and property damage than transportation of all other hazardous materials combined. Many of the worst incidents are the result of tank truck rollovers.

Many of the most serious discharges of hazardous materials during bulk transport over the highway are caused by vehicle accidents, the result of driver error and/or equipment failure. The number of accidents could thus be reduced by both improving equipment safety and providing driver training. The Insurance Institute for Highway Safety (IIHS) has recommended that tachographs be standard equipment on all large trucks. IIHS also recommends that speed limiters be placed on trucks and better braking systems be employed, and that recapped tires not be allowed on front wheels.

Rail Transport

Rail shipments account for about 5 percent of the tonnage of hazardous materials transported annually. All rail containers must be of the proper specification, regardless of the origin, destination, or duration of the trip or characteristics of the shipper or carrier. About 80 percent of annual rail shipments of hazardous materials involve tank cars, which have useful lives of 30 to 40 years. Since 1970, the capacity of tank cars for carrying hazardous materials has been limited to 34,500 gallons, or 263,000 pounds gross weight.

The two major classifications of rail tank cars are pressure and nonpressure (for transporting both gases and liquids). Both categories have several subclasses, which differ in such things as test pressure, presence or absence of bottom discharge valves, type of pressure relief system, and type of thermal shielding. Ninety percent of tank cars are made of steel; aluminum is the second most common material used.

Tables 9-5 and 9-6 list the common classes of rail tank cars of both categories. Approximately 66 percent of the rail tonnage consists of chemicals, and 23 percent consists of petroleum products. The commodities most often

TABLE 9-5
PRESSURE RAIL CARS

Class	Material	Insulation	Test pressure	Relief valve setting	Notes
DOT 105	Steel, aluminum	Required	100	75	No bottom outlet or washout; only one opening in tank; chlorine
			200	150	
			300	225	
			400	300	
			500	375	
			600	450	
DOT 112	Steel	None	200	150	No bottom outlet or washout; anhydrous ammonia
			340	225	
				280	
			400	300	
				330	
			500	375	
DOT 114	Steel	None	340	255	Similar to DOT 105; optional bottom outlet; liquefied petroleum gas
			400	300	

Source: Office of Technology Assessment.

shipped by rail are flammable liquids and corrosive materials (DOT-hazard classes), each accounting for about 25 percent of the tonnage.

In the mid-1970s, a series of derailments occurred. One serious derailment involved the puncture of flammable pressurized tank cars by the couplers of adjoining cars. The ignited material venting from the punctured car impinged on other derailed tank cars carrying flammable gas, simultaneously heating and expanding their contents beyond the capacity of safety relief devices and weakening the tank shells. The resulting explosions and fires caused enormous damage.

TABLE 9-6
NONPRESSURE RAIL CARS

Class	Material	Insulation	Test pressure	Relief valve setting	Notes
DOT 103	Steel, aluminum, stainless steel, nickel	Optional	60	35	Optional bottom outlet; whiskey
DOT 104	Steel	Required	60	35	Similar to DOT 103
DOT 111	Steel, aluminum	Optional	60	35	Optional bottom outlet and bottom washout
DOT 111A	Steel, aluminum	Optional	100	75	Hydrochloric acid

Source: Office of Technology Assessment.

Recommendations made in the late seventies by the National Transportation Safety Board (NTSB) and the Federal Railroad Administration (FRA) led DOT to mandate installation of top and bottom shelf couplers that would be less likely to disengage and puncture adjacent cars. For flammable gas, anhydrous ammonia, and ethylene oxide tank cars, DOT also required installation of head shields as further protection against coupler damage, as well as additional thermal protection to prevent rapid overheating if a neighboring tank car were on fire.

After the retrofits of the DOT 112 and 114 tank cars were completed, the number of railroad accidents involving disastrous releases of flammable gases decreased dramatically. A 1981 study by the Railway Progress Institute showed that the frequency of head punctures for retrofitted tank cars decreased by 95 percent from the preretrofit rate, and the frequency of thermal ruptures dropped by 93 percent. Experience since that study has shown that while the shelf couplers tend to keep the cars more securely attached to one another, which results in more car derailments per accident, they have continued to prevent punctures and ruptures. All rail tank cars carrying hazardous materials are now being fitted with shelf couplers.

During the same period that DOT 112 and 114 tank cars were being retrofitted, FRA increased the number of over-the-rail inspections of railcars. There are about 183,000 tank cars, approximately 63 percent of which are used for hazardous materials. FRA performed 39,000 tank car inspections in 1982 and 31,000 in 1983, about twice the number of annual inspections performed in 1978 and 1979. This practice has undoubtedly contributed to the reduction in number of rail accidents.

Water Transport

The largest bulk containers for water transport are ships, tankers, and tank barges; together they account for about 91 percent of all marine shipping of hazardous materials. Tank barges range in capacity from 300,000 to 600,000 gallons, and tankers can be 10 times larger. About 8 percent of marine shipments of hazardous materials are carried by dry cargo barges, which can hold either bulk or nonbulk containers. More than 90 percent of the tonnage in bulk marine transport consists of petroleum products and crude oil. Chemicals, such as sulfuric acid, fertilizers, sodium hydroxide, alcohols, benzene, and toluene, constitute most of the remainder.

Marine shipments typically involve very large quantities, and fewer trips are required to move a given amount of product by water than by the other modes. Bulk marine shippers and recipients are generally large companies, well aware of the potential liability they assume with each shipment. Because of the substantial economic investment these shipments represent, the companies expend the necessary resources to ensure safe transport. In addition, the vessels travel slowly. For all these reasons, the water mode is statistically the safest, both in absolute numbers of accidents and spills per ton-mile, although when a spill does occur, the damage can be enormous.

All vessels carrying bulk hazardous materials are subject to federal regulations. Records kept by the government list every vessel in commerce in U.S. waters and every shipment of commodities to or from every port in the United States. Moreover, the captains and operators of bulk marine vessels are tested and certified by the U.S. Coast Guard. Tanker captains and operators must demonstrate to the Coast Guard familiarity with the general arrangement of cargo tanks and with suction and discharge pipelines and valves, and be able to operate pumps and other equipment. In addition, they must demonstrate knowledge of pollution laws and regulations, procedures for discharge containment and cleanup, and methods for disposal of sludge and waste materials from cargo and fueling operations. Because many spills occur during loading and unloading, shippers generally provide special training to those who load and unload barges and tankers.

The Coast Guard also regulates tank barges and tankers. All new vessels to be used to transport bulk hazardous cargoes must meet the design requirements of 46 Code of Federal Regulations. New vessels are inspected and certified by the Coast Guard or by the American Bureau of Shipping. Federal regulations require that all existing tankers which carry hazardous cargoes be inspected semiannually, and an additional midterm inspection means that the effective time between inspections is actually 12 months. Moreover, some major shippers conduct their own inspection of bulk vessels before each loading. This high frequency of inspections may partly explain why the bulk water mode for transportation of hazardous materials has the best safety record.

NONBULK TRANSPORT

Small packages represent only a small proportion of the hazardous substances tonnage by rail and water, about half the highway traffic, and virtually all air transport. Correspondingly, nonbulk packages constitute a small percentage of the incidents reported in the Hazardous Materials Information System in the rail and water modes but comprise about 80 percent of the containers cited in highway releases and all the containers cited in air transportation releases.

Materials used in nonbulk packaging include fiberboard, plastic, wood, glass, fiberglass, and metal. Combination containers or packages within packages—for example, glass bottles in fiberboard boxes—are often used for transport of hazardous materials. Composite packagings, such as plastic-lined steel drums, may be made of two or more materials. Most containers can be used for a multitude of products, although custom packaging may be designed for a particular commodity. Free-standing single units such as steel drums and cylinders for compressed gases are also widely used.

Factors related to the transportation system itself understandably influence container design. For example, products that are used only in small unit quantities often are packaged in those unit quantities, and many containers that will be transported on trucks and railcars are designed to facilitate loading, unloading, and efficient use of vehicle space. The type of handling equipment available is also a consideration. The 55-gallon steel drum, for example, is about the largest unit that can fit through a normal doorway and can be handled by a single person.

More than 60 percent of hazardous materials releases involving small packages can be attributed to human errors such as improper packing, bracing, loading, or unloading. These accidents have happened even with well-designed packages, and the greatest opportunity to reduce the frequency of spills may come from programs to address factors other than the containers themselves.

Analysis of hazardous materials violations also supports a need for shippers to improve operations and procedures. A 1983 survey of states participating in a DOT enforcement training program identified the following as the most common hazardous materials violations found during roadside inspections of motor carriers:

Failure to display the correct placard
Failure to block or brace hazardous materials containers
Leaking discharge valves on cargo tanks
Improperly described hazardous wastes
Inaccurate or missing shipping papers
Excessive radiation levels in the cab of the truck

In addition, a 1979 report issued by the National Transportation Safety Board cited a number of reasons for noncompliance with the hazardous materials regulations. These reasons included the complexity of the regulations, economic pressures, lack of available training for inexperienced personnel, and the fact that industry personnel often are unaware of the regulations.

STATE AND LOCAL REGULATION

The entry of state governments into the field of hazardous materials transportation safety began in earnest in the early 1970s. A series of episodes involving radioactive materials prompted states to call for more vigorous efforts to monitor and control the shipment of hazardous materials.

Licensing, registration, and permit requirements enable state and local governments to monitor and obtain information from shippers and carriers operating within their jurisdictions. However, a general distinction can be made between registration programs designed to identify shippers and carriers and the permitting or licensing programs, usually intended to obtain assurances of fitness and more detailed information about company operations. Fees from all such programs are often used to cover only the administrative costs of processing application forms. However, they may also be used to generate funds for emergency response and enforcement activities.

State and local requirements vary, with some focusing on specific types of hazardous materials, while others are broader in scope. Information requested from shippers and carriers may include the types of materials they handle, origins and destinations of shipments, routes followed, miles covered in a given year, proof of insurance coverage, vehicle inspection dates, and drivers employed. Thirty-four states (shown in Table 9-7) require transport companies carrying hazardous wastes to register and pay a fee on a per vehicle or per company basis. Fees imposed range from a low of $3 up to $500 and may be good for one trip only or for as long as a year. Some states also require special driver training or certification, vehicle registration, and inspection and proof of liability insurance.

Information obtained through permit, licensing, or registration requirements may be used to target enforcement activities, plan emergency response programs, and develop regulations. For example, emergency response personnel would use data on the types of materials they are likely to encounter to develop appropriate training programs. Driver or carrier information is important to enforcement officials for identifying individuals or firms with poor performance records. Regulatory agencies interested in providing industry with information on new or amended regulations must know the location of shippers and carriers of hazardous materials.

Notification Requirements

Notification requirements have been established by numerous local governments and by transportation facilities such as bridge and tunnel authorities. The vast majority of these requirements apply to truck transport. Requirements (Table 9-8) include notification prior to shipment, periodic summaries, and reports on individual shipments filed after the trip. Prenotification is required by 23 state and 77 local regulations; 14 call for periodic reporting, and 22 concern individual trip reports. Transportation facilities almost universally require some type of prenotification to arrange for escorts and notify emergency response agencies; these requirements generally focus on radioactive materials in addition to other hazardous materials, such as explosives and flammable materials. States and municipalities have tended to regulate spent fuel and high-level radioactive wastes, although some also include other radioactive materials.

Routing Requirements

Routing is an important tool for local governments for preventing or reducing the consequences of hazardous materials accidents. Increasing numbers of cities, counties, and townships are adopting ordinances requiring hazardous materials carriers to use designated routes. Carefully made routing decisions restrict hazardous materials shipments to the safest routes, often interstate highways and beltways, providing a low-cost prevention measure that local police can enforce without additional equipment or training. On the other

TABLE 9-7
STATES WITH PROPOSED OR EXISTING HAZARDOUS WASTE TRANSPORTATION REGISTRATION AND FEE REQUIREMENTS

State	Company registration	Company fee	Years covered	Vehicle registration	Vehicle fee	Vehicle inspection	Driver training certification/registration
Alabama	Yes	$250	3				
Arizona	Yes						
Arkansas	Yes	$100/$50*	5				
California	Yes	$200	1	Yes	$50 each	Yes	Yes
Colorado	No						
Connecticut	Yes	$500	1	Yes		Yes	Yes
Delaware	Yes	$50	1	Yes			
Florida	No						
Georgia	No						
Idaho	Yes	$20					
Illinois	Yes	$100	1	Yes			
Indiana	Yes	$100	1	Yes	$10 each	Yes	
Iowa	No						
Kansas	Yes	$250	1				
Kentucky	Yes	$25	1	Yes			
Louisiana	No						
Maine	Yes	$100	1	Yes	Yes		
Maryland	Yes		1	Yes	$50/trailer		Yes
Massachusetts	Yes	$100	1	Yes	$200 each	Yes	Yes
Michigan	Yes	$500	1	Yes	$200 each		
Minnesota	No						
Mississippi	No						
Missouri	Yes		1	Yes	$20/$100		
Montana	Yes	$25	1		$5 each		
Nebraska	No						
Nevada	Yes						
New Hampshire	Yes	$100	1	Yes			Yes

TABLE 9-7
STATES WITH PROPOSED OR EXISTING HAZARDOUS WASTE TRANSPORTATION REGISTRATION AND FEE REQUIREMENTS *(Continued)*

State	Company registration	Company fee	Years covered	Vehicle registration	Vehicle fee	Vehicle inspection	Driver training certification/registration
New Jersey	Yes		1	Yes	$50		Yes
New Mexico	No						
New York	Yes		1	Yes	$500		
North Carolina	Yes	$25	One time			Yes	
North Dakota	Yes						
Ohio	Yes	$25		Yes	$3 each		
Oklahoma	Yes				$15 each		
Oregon	Yes	$125	1	Yes		Yes	
Pennsylvania	Yes	$125/$200*	1/2				
Rhode Island	Yes		1	Yes	$25 each	Yes	Yes
South Carolina	Yes						Yes
South Dakota	No						
Tennessee	Yes	$300	1				
Texas	Yes	$25	One time				
Utah	No						
Vermont	Yes		1	Yes	$10/unit		
Virginia	Yes	$80/$120†	10				
Washington	No						
West Virginia	No						
Wisconsin	Yes	$400	2				Yes
Wyoming	No						
District of Columbia	No						

*Separate fees required by different state regulatory bodies.
†$80 for in-state and $120 for out-of-state companies.
Source: Office of Technology Assessment.

TABLE 9-8
HAZARDOUS SUBSTANCES COVERED BY NOTIFICATION REQUIREMENTS IN 1985

	Spent fuel and/or high-level waste	Other radioactive materials	Hazardous wastes	Other hazardous materials
State				
Arkansas	...	...	X	X
California	X	...	...	...
Colorado	...	...	X	...
Connecticut	X	X	...	...
Florida	X	X	...	...
Georgia	X	X	X	X
Illinois	...	...	X	X
Louisiana	...	...	X	...
Maine	...	X	X	...
Massachusetts	X	...	X	...
Michigan	X	X	...	...
Mississippi	X	X	...	...
Nevada	X	X	...	...
New Hampshire	...	...	...	X
New Jersey	X	X	...	...
New Mexico	X	X	...	...
North Carolina	X	...	...	...
Ohio	X	X	...	...
Oregon	...	...	...	X
Rhode Island	X	X	X	...
South Carolina	X	X	...	...
Tennessee	X	...	...	...
Vermont	X	X	...	...
Virginia	X	X	X	...
Total	17	14	9	5
Local				
Chickasaw, Al	...	...	X	...
Phoenix, AZ	...	...	X	X
Tempe, AZ	...	...	...	X
Tucson, AZ	X	X	...	...
Morro Bay, CA	X	X	...	...
New London, CT	X	X	...	...
Garden City, GA	B	X	...	...
Lawrence, KS	B	X	...	...
Covington, KY	X	X	X	X
Kenner, LA	...	...	...	X
Kent County, MD	X	...	...	...
Prince George's County, MD	X	X	...	...
Newton, MA	X	...	...	...
Ypsilanti, MI	B	X	...	...
Missoula, MT	X	X	...	...
Binghamton, NY	X	...	...	...
Geneva, NY	X	X	...	...

TABLE 9-8
HAZARDOUS SUBSTANCES COVERED BY NOTIFICATION REQUIREMENTS IN 1985 *(Cont.)*

	Spent fuel and/or high-level waste	Other radioactive materials	Hazardous wastes	Other hazardous materials
Local				
Ithaca, NY	X	X	...	...
Jefferson County, NY	X	X	...	X
New York, NY	X	X	...	...
Rockland County, NY	X	X	...	...
St. Lawrence County, NY	X	X	...	...
Syracuse, NY	X	X	...	...
Tompkins County, NY	X	X	...	...
Vestal, NY	X	X	...	...
Yates County, NY	X	...	...	...
Facilities				
Golden Gate Bridge, CA	X	X	...	...
Delaware Memorial Bridge, DE	X	X	X	X
Francis Scott Key Bridge, MD	X	X	...	X
Harry W. Nice Memorial Bridge, MD	X	X	...	X
John F. Kennedy Memorial Highway, MD	X	X	...	X
Susquehanna River Bridge, MD	X	X	...	X
William Preston Lane, Jr., Memorial Bridge, MD	X	X	...	X
Massachusetts Turnpike Authority, MA	X	X	...	...
Blue Water Bridge, MI	B	B	...	X
Mackinac Bridge, MI	X	X	...	X
Garden State Parkway, NJ	X	X	...	...
Newark International Airport, NJ	X	X	...	X
New Jersey Turnpike, NJ	X	X	...	X
Bayonne Bridge, NY	X	X	...	X
George Washington Bridge, NY				
Expressway	B	X	...	...
Lower level	B	X	...	...
Upper level	X	X	...	X
Geothals Bridge, NY	X	X	...	X
Holland Tunnel, NY	B	X	...	...
Kennedy International Airport, NY	X	X	...	X
La Guardia Airport, NY	X	X	...	X
Lincoln Tunnel, NY	B	X	...	...

Note: B = ban on transportation.
Source: Office of Technology Assessment.

hand, routing requirements may lengthen and complicate trips for truckers and sometimes bring local governments into conflict with each other or with federal regulations governing interstate commerce. The trucking industry has challenged some local routing ordinances, claiming that they interfere with interstate commerce.

The hazardous materials guidelines include procedures for analyzing risks associated with the use of alternative routes within a jurisdiction. The risk assessment is based on the probability of a hazardous materials accident and the consequences of such an accident measured in terms of the population or property located inside the potential accident impact zone. Other factors, such as emergency response capabilities and proximity to sensitive ecological areas or populations that may be unable to evacuate themselves, may be applied when a risk analysis does not indicate that one alternative is clearly superior to the others. The guidelines suggest that such factors should be selected by consensus, reflecting community priorities.

Right-to-Know Laws

Many states and municipalities have passed legislation, commonly referred to as right-to-know laws, requiring the release of information on the hazards associated with chemicals produced or used in a given facility. These laws have been adopted because some manufacturers have been unwilling to comply with requests for information because of concerns about protecting trade secrets or other information considered to be proprietary.

The majority of state right-to-know laws address both community and employee access to information about workplace hazards. (See Table 9-9.) The requirements of right-to-know laws most relevant to hazardous materials planning and emergency response include providing public access to information on hazardous materials present, conducting inventories or surveys, establishing record-keeping and exposure reporting systems, and complying with container labeling regulations for workplaces. OSHA now requires chemical manufacturers and importers to prepare Material Safety Data Sheets for all hazardous materials produced or used. Some states and localities specifically require that copies of MSDSs be made available to a state agency or local fire chief as part of their community right-to-know programs.

Good Samaritan Laws

Governmental entities and industry are concerned that they may be held responsible for emergency response activities that result in damages. Good Samaritan laws have been enacted by at least 38 states to relieve the burden of potential liability for persons who assist during a hazardous materials transportation accident.

TABLE 9-9
STATES WITH RIGHT-TO-KNOW LAWS IN 1985

State	Community access	Worker access
Alabama	. . .	X
Alaska	. . .	X
Arizona	. . .	. . .
Arkansas	. . .	X
California	. . .	. . .
Colorado	. . .	. . .
Connecticut	X	X
Delaware	X	X
Florida	X	X
Georgia	. . .	. . .
Hawaii	. . .	. . .
Idaho	. . .	. . .
Illinois	X	X
Indiana	. . .	. . .
Iowa	X	X
Kansas	. . .	. . .
Kentucky	. . .	. . .
Louisiana	X	X
Maine	X	X
Maryland	X	X
Massachusetts	X	X
Michigan	. . .	X
Minnesota	. . .	X
Mississippi	. . .	. . .
Missouri	X	. . .
Montana	X	X
Nebraska	. . .	. . .
Nevada	. . .	. . .
New Hampshire	X	X
New Jersey	X	X
New Mexico	. . .	. . .
New York	. . .	X
North Carolina	X	X
North Dakota	X	X
Ohio	. . .	. . .
Oklahoma	. . .	. . .
Oregon	X	X
Pennsylvania	X	X
Rhode Island	X	X
South Carolina	. . .	. . .
South Dakota	. . .	. . .
Tennessee	X	X
Texas	X	X
Utah	. . .	. . .
Vermont	X	X
Virginia	. . .	. . .
Washington	X	X
West Virginia	X	X
Wisconsin	. . .	X
Wyoming	. . .	. . .

HAZARDOUS SUBSTANCES EMERGENCY RESPONSE

Hazardous materials are transported over the nation's vast system of highways, rails, waterways, and airlanes, necessitating emergency response capabilities at all levels of government.

When transportation accidents involving hazardous materials do occur, local policy officers and fire fighters are usually the first officials to appear at the site. How they respond depends on whether they have received emergency response training for those types of accidents. Moreover, should any injuries result from exposure to toxic materials, medical personnel respond appropriately only if they have had training in the treatment of such injuries.

There are approximately 1.2 million fire fighters nationwide, 85 percent of whom are volunteers and the remaining 15 percent paid employees of municipal, county, or local governments. Federal, state, and local government and law enforcement officials and approximately 400,000 basic emergency medical technicians also assist victims of hazardous materials accidents, depending on the scale and location of the accident and the materials involved.

For example, in December 1981, a tank truck carrying 40,000 pounds of toluene diisocyanate (TDI) skidded off the New York State Thruway and overturned, spilling some of its contents. The truck was heated and insulated in order to keep the TDI in a liquid state. When the truck overturned, TDI spilled and congealed on exposure to the cold ground, contaminating the area around the tank truck as well as the clothing of two state troopers who had been called to the accident. Upon the officers' return to their warm car, some of the TDI that had adhered to their shoes and pants vaporized, and they inhaled the toxic fumes. TDI enters tissue cells and irritates eyes, nose, and throat, and when inhaled in large quantities, damages the lungs. As a result of their exposure, both of these officers suffered permanent respiratory damage and have been unable to return to police work. It follows that those officials who may enforce hazardous materials transportation regulations as part of their regular duties must also be familiar with the dangers posed by the materials in case of an accident.

Developing hazardous materials emergency response capabilities so that communities feel adequately protected is a formidable task. A survey of 3107 local emergency management organizations (Table 9-10) indicated that transportation accidents involving hazardous materials are major concerns of local governments.

EPA has established an environmental response team based in Edison, New Jersey, that has provided various degrees of management or technical support for the more than 500 incidents since 1978. The Environmental Emergency Response Unit is a highly specialized technical team that is available to provide on-site assistance. In addition, the Coast Guard operates and maintains teams on the Atlantic, Pacific, and Gulf coasts for emergency response activities. These teams have sophisticated equipment for containing, skimming, and removing oil. The Coast Guard also operates the National Response Center for the DOT as the point of contact for transportation releases of hazardous materials. During hazardous materials emergencies, scientific advice is provided

TABLE 9-10
HAZARDS PERCEIVED AS SIGNIFICANT BY LOCAL JURISDICTIONS (3107 Surveyed)

Hazard	Number of jurisdictions
Nuclear attack	3107
Hazardous materials, highway incident	2791
Winter storm	2569
Flood	2206
Hazardous materials, rail incident	2188
Tornado	2162
Hazardous materials, stationary incident	2026
Urban fire	1877
Wildfire	1519
Hazardous materials, pipeline incident	1509

Source: Office of Technology Assessment.

to the Coast Guard by the National Oceanic and Atmospheric Administration's special hazardous materials group in Seattle, Washington.

State and Local Emergency Response

State authority for hazardous materials emergency response is fragmented. It may rest with the office of the state fire marshall or state departments of health, transportation, environment, radiological affairs, or civil defense, or some combination of these. Just as the statutory authority for emergency response varies from state to state, so does the interest emergency response generates within the state government. States that are highly industrialized and heavily traveled with hazardous materials—that is, those that have a large number of waste disposal facilities or chemical industries—are more likely to encourage and support the development of emergency response capabilities.

State, regional, and local plans should outline specific responsibilities, coordinate on-site activities, and appoint a response leader to reduce the confusion at the accident site and provide a clear chain of authority for response activities and information dissemination to the media. Fire, police, and other government agencies, including emergency management and public works departments that may participate in emergency response, should be part of the planning process. Simulations of emergency situations provide an opportunity to test these plans and discover organizational problems prior to an actual hazardous materials accident.

Industry has contributed to many local emergency response activities, but questions remain regarding emergency response on private property, such as a company facility or a railroad right-of-way. Advance arrangements between special industry response teams and existing public emergency response networks are necessary. Formal mutual aid agreements among independent industry response teams and communities are a means of achieving coordinated and comprehensive response capabilities. Such agreements allow neighboring communities to share equipment, fire and police department personnel, emergency medical services, and private sector resources.

During the planning stage, participating response agencies should identify equipment requirements and procedures to ensure adequate communication and isolation of radio frequencies for emergency use. Liability issues are a concern for governmental entities, which may be held responsible for emergency response activities that result in damages. Good Samaritan laws can relieve the burden of potential liability for qualified emergency responders who assist during a hazardous transportation accident.

Providing accurate reports to the press and public is another necessary part of coordinated emergency response activities. At many accidents, particularly severe ones, the media become a part of the response process and are an important public information source. The first media contact can determine how the incident is perceived by the public and can help maintain public calm and cooperation.

The same factors that influence state emergency response development also operate at the local level, and communities with emergency response capabilities have set up a wide variety of response systems. In rural communities, responsibility for hazardous materials emergency response usually lies with the fire or police department. In major metropolitan and urban areas, many public safety officers, primarily fire fighters and emergency service organizations, have developed or are developing special competence to respond to hazardous materials accidents. These areas are usually transportation hubs and major manufacturing centers (Figure 9-7) that handle large movements of industrial raw materials, gasoline, and fuel oils. Many of these teams are located in regions where there are heavy concentrations of chemical plants and transportation corridors, as shown in Figure 9-8.

Industry Emergency Response

Over the past decade, manufacturers of hazardous substances have evaluated their safety programs and often have taken steps to address public concerns. The involvement of industry in hazardous emergency response ranges from technical assistance to specialized response teams.

Many large petrochemical and chemical manufacturers maintain company emergency response teams for both their facilities and transportation accidents. A team may respond to a report of an accident involving a company product or, under formal agreements, may request another participating company closer to the incident to respond. Industry teams are instructed to defer to the local on-scene commander at an accident, so that the emergency response effort remains coordinated.

Emergency Response Equipment

Emergency response equipment represents the primary line of protection and defense in handling hazardous materials. The equipment must be adapted to a

FIGURE 9-7
Public hazardous materials response teams. (*Source:* Office of Technology Assessment.)

FIGURE 9-8
Chemical manufacturing and handling facilities. (*Source:* Office of Technology Assessment.)

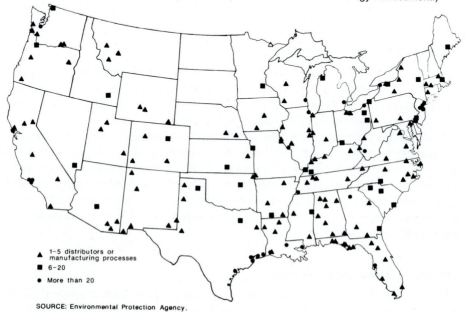

▲ 1–5 distributors or
manufacturing processes

■ 6–20

● More than 20

SOURCE: Environmental Protection Agency.

particular hazard and be made of materials that are resistant to the hazardous chemical. It must protect those areas and functions of the human body susceptible to the hazard.

The lack of useful information on the appropriate type of personal protective equipment and procedures for its use is a major concern for local governments and emergency service personnel. Fire fighters and hazardous materials response teams currently rely on fire service literature, manufacturers' information, and accumulated personal expertise when selecting chemical protective gear. However, if a community identifies the hazardous materials manufactured, stored, and transported through its jurisdiction, equipment selection can be made based on this information.

The appropriate choice among the varieties of equipment offered and the numerous operating procedures available depends on the hazardous materials being handled, and those responsible for equipment purchase are faced with difficult and expensive options. The factors to be considered prior to purchasing protective clothing include the initial cost of the clothing, chemical protection capabilities of the construction material, ease of use, maintenance of the clothing, and durability.

Personal protective equipment is currently made of a variety of materials that differ in terms of chemical resistance and durability. Butyl rubber, polyvinyl chloride, and vitron are the three most common materials used. Butyl rubber is resistant to gas permeation and can be used with almost anything except chlorinated, aliphatic, or aromatic solvents. Polyvinyl chloride is considered excellent for use with acids and bases, and is also good for use with most organics except chlorinated and aromatic solvents. However, it allows some permeation by organics and retains some absorbed material. Vitron is resistant to most organics, including chlorinated hydrocarbons and solvents—with the exception of oxygenated solvents, such as alcohols, aldehydes, ketones, esters, and ethers.

THE HAZARDOUS WASTE TRANSPORTATION INDUSTRY

The hazardous waste transportation industry has grown out of the waste hauling industry, which historically has been involved in the disposal of refuse, trash, and various liquid wastes. Small, local waste haulers could easily enter the hazardous waste transportation field with minimal up-front capital at risk. The ease of entry and withdrawal from this type of business has meant that the hazardous waste transportation industry is dominated by small operators. These small businesses have experienced rapid turnover because of low pay and transient personnel. These heretofore loosely regulated haulers have been involved in many of the environmental abuses attributed to hazardous waste management. Most of these local haulers are only now coming under federaljurisdiction through the EPA identification number system.

As controls and enforcement in the cradle-to-grave RCRA management system become more stringent, it is anticipated that this industry will become better managed. Reliable, financially sound companies are becoming more common in hazardous waste transportation. Another factor in the evaluation of the industry is the fact that hazardous waste generators are becoming more deeply involved in transporting their own wastes. By delivering their wastes to the TSD facility, the generator has greater control and assurance that this vital link of the cradle-to-grave system will be managed properly. Even when generators do not furnish their own transportation, they select outside transporters who offer them a high degree of quality assurance in addition to being cost-effective. Generators who do not select reliable transporters will be leaving themselves at risk with long-term disposal liabilities.

In a similar fashion, TSD facilities often use their own system of transportation to bring generator-produced wastes to the disposal site. With their own transportation, the TSD facility should achieve better quality control and assurance, again greatly reducing their risks in long-term liability.

Outside transporters of hazardous wastes who provide their services to either generators or TSD facilities will continue to be an important part of the cradle-to-grave management system. However, the risk of long-term liability will force that segment of the hazardous waste transportation industry to become more responsive to regulations. These developments should encourage mergers that will impact on the transportation industry in the future. Generators and TSD facilities will vertically integrate to satisfy strategic goals and financial objectives, and the entrance of new untried transporters into hazardous waste management will be increasingly difficult without assured markets, adequate regulatory experience, and the financial stability to mitigate long-term liabilities.

QUESTIONS

1 Discuss the functions of the Department of Transportation as they relate to hazardous substances.
2 Contrast the shipment of hazardous substances by land, water, and air.
3 Why is there a cradle-to-grave management system for hazardous waste?
4 Describe the different types of waste haulers.
5 Discuss the manifest system for the disposal of hazardous wastes.
6 What is the reasoning behind Good Samaritan laws?
7 Discuss the characteristics or dangers of hazardous waste that relate to placards.

BIBLIOGRAPHY

1 Dawson, G. W., and B. W. Mercer: *Hazardous Waste Management,* Wiley, New York, 1986.
2 49 Code of Federal Regulations, Parts 101–179, July 1, 1987.
3 *Hazardous Materials Transportation Guide,* Bureau of National Affairs, Washington, 1984.
4 *RCRA Orientation Manual,* U.S. Environmental Protection Agency, Office of Solid Waste, Washington, 1986.
5 *Transportation of Hazardous Materials,* U.S. Congress, Office of Technology Assessment, Washington, July 1986.

10

GROUNDWATER CONTAMINATION

INTRODUCTION

Groundwater is a vast resource found in aquifers beneath the surface of the earth. Numerous sources of surface water such as lakes, rivers, and streams are highly visible, but they make up only a small part of the fresh water on the earth, for groundwater composes 96 percent of the world's total freshwater resources. For years the general population has taken availability of uncontaminated groundwater for granted. Few people have worried that our water resources had finite limits and could be depleted or lost because of contamination and waste. But people who live today in semiarid regions of the United States are increasingly aware of the lowering of the groundwater table and of declines in their water supply. Because groundwater is the source of approximately 20 percent of our nation's domestic, agricultural, and industrial water supply—indeed in many regions of the United States it is the only dependable supply—it must be protected.[3,6]

Groundwater is stored primarily in aquifers, which are geological formations of permeable saturated zones of rock, sand, or gravel. Aquifers are recharged as atmospheric precipitation seeps into the ground or as surface waters drain into them. Aquifer recharge rates depend upon a number of factors, including the depth of groundwater below the surface as well as the depth and type of sources above the aquifer. In many regions of the United States, recharge areas are near the surface and may be significantly affected by agricultural, residential, or industrial activities. Once groundwater is contaminated by the refuse of such activities, it becomes difficult and sometimes impossible to restore it to its initial quality.

While only a small amount of the nation's groundwater is generally believed to be contaminated at this point, the contamination is significant because it is often near heavily populated areas where groundwater is being increasingly relied upon for a variety of uses. Practices and activities that have caused this pollution were begun many years ago, long before groundwater contamination came to the attention of the general public. Though most of the current attention of the news media and government regulatory authorities has focused on sources of pollution such as landfills, surface impoundments, and waste piles, many other sources of hazardous and nonhazardous substances have also contributed to the contamination of groundwater in the United States.

The solution to this growing problem is not an easy one. Because groundwater is not directly accessible, once it becomes contaminated there are major difficulties both in monitoring the conditions and in cleaning them up.[1] Groundwater restoration is an unpredictable, complex, and expensive process.

As even more incidents of groundwater pollution are discovered across the United States, and as the public becomes increasingly aware of the magnitude of the potential problem, public concern is being translated into demands for expanded protection of this vital natural resource.

EFFECTS OF GROUNDWATER CONTAMINANTS ON HUMAN HEALTH

Whether the presence of chemical contamination in groundwater results in a problem for human health and the environment depends upon many site-specific criteria—for example, the hydrogeology of the site, the groundwater use patterns, the degree of human exposure, the availability and quality of the alternative water supplies, and the feasibility of corrective remediation.

Many organic chemicals once thought safe for human contact may actually present serious and substantial health risks, even in low concentrations. Most organics have not been tested exhaustively for their mutagenic, teratogenic, or carcinogenic properties. For toxic compounds that do not show those properties, exposures should be kept below dosage limits based on laboratory data that include a safety factor, usually of a value ranging from 10 to 1000.

It is known that acute exposure to high concentrations of many organic compounds can cause nausea, dizziness, tremors, blindness, or other health problems. Lower concentrations may cause skin eruptions or impair the central nervous system. Cancer is also a possible outcome, though there is often a long latency between time of exposure and emergence of the cancer.

It is not possible to predict with certainty the effects of drinking water contaminated with organic compounds, but it is known that some people have been exposed to chemically contaminated drinking water for extended periods of time. It is known too that some factors—such as individual smoking and alcohol consumption habits—compound the risk, but such variables cannot be accurately assessed when attempting to determine the effects of groundwater contamination on human health.

HISTORICAL USES AND ABUSES

Groundwater is available everywhere, being one of the most common substances on earth and one of our most widely used resources. From 1950 to 1980 total groundwater withdrawals in this country increased from 34 to 89 billion gallons per day. These withdrawals are expected to increase in the future as our domestic, agricultural, and industrial needs for water continue to grow. Historically, groundwater has been readily available as a low-cost commodity in states such as California, Texas, Nebraska, Kansas, Arizona, Idaho, Florida, and Arkansas. Each of these states utilizes groundwater in the more arid regions, in the regions where drinking water supplies cannot easily be provided by surface water sources. Groundwater is, in fact, the drinking water source of 48,000 community water systems and about 12 million individual water wells across the country. Almost all rural households depend upon groundwater for their drinking water supply. Additionally, 34 of the nation's 100 largest cities rely in part upon groundwater for their drinking water sources.

The advantages of groundwater as a drinking water source are easily named: (1) it is widely available, (2) it is available in large quantities, (3) it is of generally high quality, and (4) it experiences minimal quality fluctuations. The disadvantages of groundwater as a drinking water source are just as easily listed: (1) it can have high concentrations of mineral ions and (2) once it becomes polluted, cleanup is difficult.

Until recently, the general public viewed drinking water that was drawn from groundwater sources as being pristine and unspoiled. People believed that the soil bound and held chemicals that were applied or spilled on the surface. Now we know that groundwater, once thought to be safe from contamination, is a threatened resource. Nearly one-third of our larger public water systems have detected the presence of synthetic chemicals in their groundwater sources, and more than 4000 water wells have been closed or affected by chemical contamination.

The sources of contamination are many and varied. As the use of organic chemicals has grown in our economy, so has the potential for groundwater contamination, simply because these chemicals are transient and will migrate through soil and into groundwater. Many heavy metals and other potentially toxic inorganic chemicals also have the potential to contaminate groundwater. Some of the more troublesome contaminants include organic solvents, gasoline, pesticides, and nitrates.

Historical waste disposal practices are the greatest threat of groundwater contamination in the United States. In this country, landfill disposal of hazardous chemicals was long the acceptable environmental practice. There are

19,000 abandoned and uncontrolled hazardous waste sites in the United States; preliminary studies at almost one-half of these sites have found some degree of groundwater contamination at 40 percent of them.

Many types of waste disposal facilities such as industrial and municipal landfills, storage lagoons, and surface impoundments were constructed and operated for years without adequate planning or safeguards to protect the environment. Many of them pose the potential threat of long-term pollution from persistent organic and inorganic chemicals.

There are 93,000 landfills in the United States to dispose of nonhazardous and household wastes. Most of these landfills represent existing or potential sources of groundwater contamination, since the overwhelming majority produce leachate, which drains from the landfill into the groundwater below.

There are more than 180,000 surface impoundments in this country which receive both hazardous and nonhazardous wastes from industries and municipalities. Many of these impoundments—planned, designed, and sited without meaningful safeguards for protecting groundwater—are located over aquifers that are used for drinking water.

Septic systems are used by nearly one-third of our households, discharging waste filled with pathogens and nitrates as well as organic solvents and oils. The improper use of pesticides, herbicides, and fertilizers, though greatly benefiting our agricultural economy, also poses the potential for groundwater contamination. Our nation's roads and highways are constructed and improved with petroleum-based hydrocarbon products, and these same highways are treated with deicing compounds during the winter. All of these substances, though of great benefit to our transportation system, are also potential groundwater contaminants.

Underground storage tanks such as those for gasoline and diesel oil, as well as aboveground storage tanks and pipelines, have the potential to leak and contaminate groundwater. There are about 10 million underground storage tanks presently in place in the United States; approximately 2.3 million of them are used to store gasoline. Many of these tanks, which were installed in the 1950s and 1960s, are subject to corrosion and fractures that result in leakage.

THE HYDROLOGY OF GROUNDWATER

Water occurs in two distinctly different zones below the surface of the earth, as shown in Figure 10-1.[4,8,13] The uppermost, or unsaturated, zone extends from the land surface to depths ranging from very shallow in humid areas to hundreds of feet in some of the more arid regions of the United States. The cavities in this zone contain both water and air, which is why it is called the *unsaturated zone*. Below this unsaturated zone is another zone with interconnected cavities containing only water. This zone is referred to as the *saturated zone*. The water table is the upper part of the saturated zone, where water occurs under a pressure equal to atmospheric. A capillary fringe, which is maintained by the strong surface tension of water, occurs in the saturated zone just

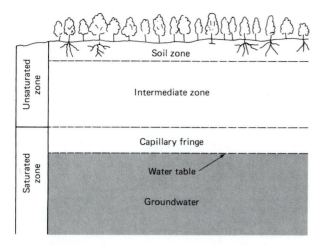

FIGURE 10-1
Groundwater zones.

above the water table level. All water that is below the water table is generally referred to as *groundwater;* this is the water that is discharged through springs and wells.

When rainfall occurs, part of that precipitation percolates downward through the unsaturated zone to the saturated zone. After reaching this confined aquifer, the water continues to move downward, as shown in Figure 10-2, into areas known as *recharge areas* because they are where the groundwater recharge occurs. The water continues to move downward and laterally across the hydraulic gradients prevailing in the groundwater system and eventually flows into the discharge areas. Slow groundwater movement, combined with the large volume of groundwater aquifers, results in detention times of many years, making the annual renewal rate of groundwater very small. Groundwater is a dependable, long-term water resource that is insulated from short-term fluctuations in precipitation. However, once an aquifer becomes polluted, it may be centuries before the contaminants are flushed from the system.

The direction and velocity of groundwater flow are important in understanding groundwater contamination. The driving force influencing the movement of groundwater is the *hydraulic head,* which is a measure of the total energy of the water at a given location. Since groundwater moves very slowly, kinetic energy may be neglected and the hydraulic head then becomes the sum of pressure and elevation heads. As groundwater moves from one point to another, friction must be overcome, resulting in a head loss over the distance traveled. This loss divided by the distance is called the *hydraulic gradient.* The hydraulic gradient is always negative, since water flows in the direction of decreasing hydraulic head. The rate of groundwater flow is directly proportional

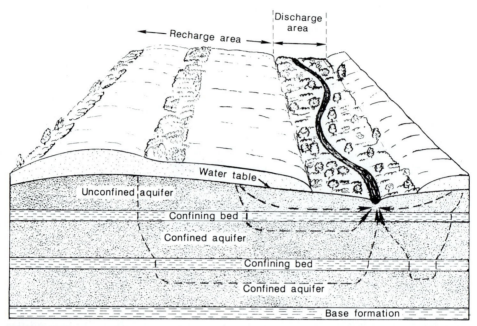

FIGURE 10-2
Groundwater movement.

to the hydraulic gradient. The sum of the pressure head and the elevation head is the vertical distance from a reference datum plane to the water level in the well. By measuring the depth to water from the top of the well casing and subtracting the height of the well casing above a given datum, one can determine the hydraulic head relative to the stated datum.

The capability of geological formations to transmit water is referred to as *permeability,* or *hydraulic conductivity.* Those saturated geological formations whose permeability is great enough to supply water in a usable quantity to a well or spring are referred to as *aquifers.* Intervening geological layers between aquifers are referred to as *confining beds,* which have low permeability. Because the permeability of aquifers is normally several orders of magnitude times that of confining beds, the aquifers function as pipelines that transmit groundwater from recharge areas to discharge areas. Within groundwater systems where the aquifers and confining beds are horizontal, the confining beds impede the vertical movement of the groundwater. As a result, much of the groundwater lateral movement tends to occur in the shallowest aquifers.

Hydraulic conductivity, a measure of an aquifer's ability to conduct water under the influence of a hydraulic gradient, is defined as the volume of water that will move through a unit area in unit time. Hydraulic conductivity has units of velocity and is a property of both the porous medium and the fluid flowing through it. The higher the conductivity, the better the aquifer conducts water. The *storage coefficient* is a dimensionless quantity expressing the volume of water released per volume of aquifer. Large pressure changes over extensive areas are usually required to produce substantial yields in confined aquifers.

Specific yield is defined as the volume of water that a saturated soil will yield per unit volume of aquifer under the influence of gravity. It represents the ratio of the volume of water released from the aquifer by gravity to the total volume of the aquifer. For an unconfined aquifer, it is essentially equal to the storage coefficient. Unconfined sandy aquifers typically have specific yields in the range of 0.10 to 0.30. Water flowing to or from an aquifer, of course, changes the storage volume of the aquifer. This change in volume equals the specific yield times the change in volume of the aquifer over a period of time.

An example will illustrate the effect of porosity on the storage of groundwater. If an aquifer has a specific yield of 0.2, is 1000 meters by 1000 meters in areal extent, and declines 3 meters because of pumping, the amount of water release is

$$0.2 \times 1000 \times 1000 \times 3 = 0.6 \times 10^6 \text{ m}^3$$

Conversely, if the contents of a surface lagoon containing 0.6×10^6 cubic meters of water and measuring 1000 meters by 1000 meters by 1 meter deep were to reach the groundwater, the water table would rise 3 meters.

Darcy's law states that the rate of flow of water through sand beds is directly proportional to the head loss over the bed and inversely proportional to the thickness of the bed, as stated in the following equation:

$$\frac{Q}{A} = -K\frac{\Delta H}{\Delta X} \tag{10.1}$$

where Q = flow rate, ft^3/h
A = cross-sectional area perpendicular to the flow direction, ft^2
K = hydraulic conductivity, ft/h
ΔH = hydraulic head loss over the distance, ΔX, ft/ft

Aquifers are usually complicated with heterogeneous soil properties, making the mathematics of groundwater movement relatively sophisticated, involving as it does the unsteady-state numerical solution of partial differential equations. This requires a three-dimensional model of the hydrogeologic properties of the aquifer that may be costly and time-consuming to construct. The study of groundwater aquifers should begin with a well-conceived field program to define the hydrogeology. With adequate hydrogeological data, an appropriate predictive approach can be chosen, ranging from simple water table maps to unsteady-state, three-dimensional numerical models.

Characterization of contamination leaching from a waste disposal site involves groundwater movement of all species of substances dissolved in the groundwater. Prediction of the movement of chemicals in groundwater is complicated by geochemical reactions as well as hydrologic dispersion phenomena. Estimating the transport of dissolved chemical species in groundwater requires the simultaneous solution of groundwater flow equations with geochemical transport equations.

The degree of contamination depends upon the temperature and distance of the source from the water production well, well spacing, pumping rate, aquifer volume, aquifer porosity, and the properties of the material in the aquifer. The contaminant being pumped flows from the source to the production well by various paths and at rates determined by the hydraulic gradients and properties of the aquifer. Contaminants entering the aquifer near the production well, where gradients are steepest, travel to the production well quickly compared with contaminants entering the aquifer some distance upstream or downstream. The groundwater pumped at any given time consists of water that entered the aquifer at different points, times, and temperatures. The aquifer integration of these factors usually results in a more uniform, buffered groundwater contamination level than may be identified at the contaminant source.

THE CHEMISTRY OF CONTAMINATION

Dissolved constituents in groundwater are generally only a small fraction of the total weight of the water. Concentrations of ions are commonly reported in parts per million or in milligrams per liter, which are almost the same if the concentration of dissolved solids is low and the specific gravity of the water is nearly 1.0. Groundwater concentrations are often expressed in equivalents per million (epm), which is calculated by dividing parts per million by the equivalent weight of the ion under consideration. The *equivalent weight* is equal to the atomic weight divided by the valence. The sum of the cations and the sum of the anions expressed in equivalents per million will each equal half of the total groundwater concentration.

The hydrogen-ion concentration is expressed as the pH, which is the reciprocal of the logarithm (base 10) of the hydrogen-ion concentration in moles per liter. An alkaline water has a pH greater than 7.0, which indicates a preponderance of hydroxyl ions. An acidic water has a pH of less than 7.0, which indicates a preponderance of hydrogen ions. The pH of pure water at 25°C is 7.0.

When material goes into solution in water, the water's pH is usually changed. Most groundwater has pH values between 5.0 and 8.0. Water as rain or snow contains only small quantities of dissolved mineral matter. Once on the earth, however, it begins to react with the minerals of soil and rocks. The amount and character of the mineral matter dissolved by precipitation depend upon the chemical composition and physical structure of the rocks, temperature, pressure, duration of contact, materials already in solution, pH, and redox (oxidation-reduction) potential. Water is assisted as a solvent by carbon dioxide from the atmosphere or by organic processes.

The ability of groundwater to conduct an electric current is called its *electrical conductance,* or *electrical conductivity,* which is a function of temperature, type of ions present, and concentration of various ions. Pure water has a conductance of 0.055 S (siemens) at 25°C. Rainwater will usually range from 5.0 to 30 S, ocean water from 45,000 to 55,000 S, and normal groundwater from 30 to 2000 S.

Most chloride in groundwater comes from entrapped seawater, solutions of minerals, evaporation of precipitation, and solution of fallout from the atmosphere. Most nitrate in groundwater is derived from organic sources or from agricultural chemicals.[5,7] Dissolved gases occurring in groundwater include oxygen, nitrogen, carbon dioxide, hydrogen sulfide, methane, nitrogen oxides, sulfur dioxide, and ammonia. These gases are commonly derived from the atmosphere and from decaying organic matter. In general, the solubility of a gas in water varies inversely with temperature and directly with pressure.

THE PROCESS OF CONTAMINATION

The sources of toxic chemicals that can potentially contaminate groundwater include industrial and municipal landfills, septic tanks, mining and agricultural activities, and "midnight dumping." Contaminants in surface waters can also, depending on the geology and hydrology of the area, cause pollution in an aquifer.[10,11] Storm-water runoff and leaky sewer lines carrying the liquid refuse of automotive service stations, dry cleaning establishments, and printing shops are all contributors to local groundwater contamination.

In all cases, the threat of contamination to groundwater depends on the specific geologic and hydrologic conditions of the site, and the complexity of the hydrogeologic conditions will always make prediction of the extent of groundwater contamination difficult. The hydrologic flow and the soils must be evaluated, since a pit sited on a thick clay layer is more secure than an unlined pit in sandy soil.[12]

Chemicals pass through several different hydrologic zones as they migrate through the soil to the groundwater system. As noted before, the pore spaces in the unsaturated zone are occupied by both air and water. Flow in this zone for liquid contaminants is downward by gravity. The upper region of the unsaturated zone is important for pollutant attenuation. Some chemicals are retained by adsorption onto organic material and chemically active soil particles. These adsorbed chemicals will decompose through oxidation and microbial activity. Below this soil zone, the pore spaces are also unsaturated, and as chemicals percolate through this zone, oxidation and aerobic biological degradation continue to take place. In the capillary zone, spaces between soil particles may be saturated by water rising from the water table. Chemicals which are lighter than water will "float" on top of the water table in this zone and move in different directions and rates than dissolved contaminants.

Once dissolved contaminants reach the water table, they may flow in both horizontal and vertical directions, depending on the hydraulic gradients. All pore spaces between soil particles below the water table are saturated, and the lack of dissolved oxygen in the saturated zone limits the oxidation of chemicals. Groundwater flow is laminar, with minimal mixing occurring as the groundwater moves. Dissolved chemicals in the saturated zone will flow with the groundwater in a flow rate governed by hydraulic gradient and hydrostatic head. The flow system consists of the recharge downflow and the discharge upflow.

Because groundwater involves laminar flow, dissolved chemicals will follow groundwater and form distinct plumes. Plumes of contaminated groundwater may be up to several miles downstream of the pollution source, though groundwater pollution is usually a local phenomenon, occurring in an area less than a mile long and a half mile wide, with the plume moving at the average rate of less than 1 foot a day.

The shape and size of a contaminant plume depends upon the local hydrogeological setting, groundwater flow, the characteristics of the contaminants, and geochemistry. Since chemicals attenuated in the soil react with constituents of the aquifer, it is difficult to accurately predict the movement and fate of chemicals in groundwater. Volatile organic chemicals in groundwater are extremely mobile. In addition, solubility, adsorption characteristics, and degradation affect mobility. The density of the contaminant is important in the shape and movement of the plume. Lighter chemicals will tend to flow on top of the water table, while the heavier contaminants will sink to the bottom. Slightly soluble materials may result in multiphase flow.

The actual movement of a contaminated groundwater plume can be highly complex because of intergranular permeabilities in the subsurface environment. Permeability changes are fairly common in geological formations that were formed by river deposits, and these varying permeabilities can greatly affect the shape and the rate of movement of the contaminant plume. This hydrogeologic condition is further complicated by unique flow patterns that may develop with different pollutants. For example, a dense pollutant such as an inorganic compound tends to create a plume that migrates to the base of the aquifer. Pollutants such as hydrocarbons that are lower in density than water will tend to float near the top of the saturated zone of the aquifer. Additionally, individual pollutants will move through the subsurface at different rates relative to the groundwater movement because of the interaction of biodegradation, ion exchange, sorption, and desorption. As a result, the levels of maximum concentration of the individual pollutants throughout the groundwater plume will vary considerably.

Variations in operating practices at waste disposal facilities can cause multiple contamination plumes to flow independently away from the site. Pumping from wells can also affect groundwater flow and alter the movement of a contaminant plume. The solution and dissolution of chemicals in the plume as a result of contaminant interactions with geological strata in its path will cause fluctuation in contaminant concentration. These factors which influence movement of groundwater and contaminants within aquifers are complex, requiring extensive investigation over time.

DETECTION OF GROUNDWATER CONTAMINATION

In order to assess the impact of hazardous waste on groundwater quality, a rigorous study must be made of the whole subsurface area, including both the unsaturated and saturated zones. It should be noted that many of the analytical techniques that are applicable to surface water will not necessarily apply to groundwater testing. For example, the collection methods for obtaining a representative groundwater sample are much more difficult and expensive than those for sampling surface water. The subsurface of the soil is a complex geological system where the physical, chemical, and biological changes can occur within relatively short distances. Additionally, these chemical and biological parameters that have traditionally indicated pollution of surface water may not provide an accurate portrayal of groundwater quality.

For a well-conceived groundwater study, considerable planning must take place before the initiation of any fieldwork.[9] All existing geologic and hydrogeologic information should be collected and interpreted. Once this information has been studied, plans can be made regarding the type and the magnitude of groundwater investigation that is needed.

The potential concentration levels of contaminants, the time available for monitoring, and the general geologic region of consideration will all influence the selection of sampling procedures. If the groundwater monitoring program is to take place in a large regional area, one may use existing water wells, springs, or even streams, should these systems be compatible with the desired parameters. Often, time is the critical element in sampling contaminated groundwater, and existing sample locations are the only practical alternative. On the other hand, if the possible contamination source is a single, well-defined location such as a landfill or if the contaminated concentrations appear to be very low and sensitive to analytical techniques, monitoring wells will usually be necessary. Both the number and location of the monitoring wells should be well planned and will depend on the goal of the monitoring, the aquifer characteristics, and mobility of the pollutants in the aquifer.

An initial step in the hydrogeologic investigation of a site is the collection and review of soils, geologic, and groundwater reports; examination of test boring data; study of well logs and records; and analysis of water-quality data. As a result, it can be known whether a site overlies an important aquifer, its depth and flow, the water quality, and the presence of other water zones. A site visit is also desirable to gather visual information.

Exploratory test wells are generally required before geologic, hydrologic, and geochemical conditions can be defined. The number and depth of these borings will depend on specific geohydrologic information requirements and the disposal area. The goal of the investigation should be to provide sufficient data to make an accurate prediction of the movement of the plume and its contaminant concentration.

If the geology is fairly homogeneous, low in permeability, and uniformly sloping, four to six borings extending to bedrock should be sufficient. Test wells into the uppermost aquifer should provide data on the water-table slope and background water quality for preliminary conclusions concerning the contamination. Since most geologic formations are not homogeneous, the flow of groundwater may vary considerably at the site. If more than one aquifer is to be investigated, more wells must be drilled at appropriate spacings.

All groundwater monitoring programs must include background sampling. On rare occasions it may be possible to sample the groundwater quality of a region as it was before the potential source of contamination was introduced. While this is highly desirable, it will probably be possible only at new facility sitings. The more normal situation is that the potential pollution source is already in place and the objective of background sampling is simply to collect, for comparative purposes, a groundwater sample that has a high probability of being out of the influence of the pollution source. For example, a monitoring program for detecting pollution near an existing landfill should involve the siting of a background well that is up-gradient from the landfill and at least three down-gradient wells that are perpendicular to the known groundwater flow pattern; it is also necessary, of course, to penetrate the entire thickness of the saturated zone of the aquifer under study. This monitoring plan should be applicable to virtually any point source of potential pollution. Should the pollution already have occurred, then the principal objective of the monitoring plan should be to define the contaminated plume. A reasonable initial approach to determine the extent of plume contamination would be to commence the four-well program described above for point-source contamination. It should be noted that once results of the initial sampling program have been determined, additional wells will probably be necessary to better define the contamination plume.

Design and Installation of Monitoring Wells

Monitoring wells provide early warning of groundwater contamination. Monitoring can reveal not only which pollutants are present and at what concentrations but also the areal and vertical distribution of these pollutants within the contaminated plume. Properly designed monitoring networks can also aid in determining the effectiveness of engineered groundwater protection.

Under nonpumping conditions, the water-table configuration will generally follow the land surface topography, and monitoring wells should be situated downslope from the site, between it and the nearest natural discharge point. However, when the influence of a nearby pumping well extends beneath the site, groundwater flow will be toward that well, preventing detection of contamination in downslope monitoring wells. In that case, sampling the production wells themselves might be all that is required to detect contamination.

There are instances where groundwater monitoring wells may not be needed at all. If the objective is merely to determine the presence of a particular pollutant in a drinking water supply, a simple and inexpensive approach would be to collect a sample at the drinking water tap. If the objective is to sample only a small portion of an aquifer, a determination of groundwater quality can be made with a single monitoring well, though this technique represents a major disadvantage in trying to obtain an accurate description of groundwater and is normally taken with monitoring wells that are expensive and difficult to install. On the other hand, if the objective is to define both the horizontal and vertical distribution of a contaminant and to predict its eventual fate, then it will be necessary to obtain sample cores, install monitoring wells, and add specialized sampling equipment, all of which will drastically increase both the complexity of the monitoring and its cost.

Geological faults and the general heterogeneous nature of the subsurface environments make locating sampling points a complicated and unpredictable science when trying to intercept and measure the pollutant plume. Since hydrogeologic conditions are site-specific, it is impossible to predetermine standard locations for groundwater sampling sites that will be uniformly applicable.

Depending upon the location, the groundwater monitoring wells may intercept fractured zones that may or may not be hydraulically interconnected to the source of contamination. When locating monitoring wells in highly fractured regions, there will always be the potential of drilling into a dry pocket and of then moving only a few feet away and drilling into a plentiful supply of groundwater. The irony of all this is that either of these wells may or may not be hydraulically connected to a nearby source of pollution. And there is also always the possibility of intercommunication between the geological layers and subsequent misinterpretation of results because of the sample mixture.

The horizontal location of a groundwater monitoring well in relation to the suspected pollution source will determine whether or not the contaminated groundwater plume will be intercepted. Furthermore, the vertical location of the well screen will also affect the reliability of the samples collected. Should the well screen be located either above or below the zone of contamination, groundwater samples will probably indicate no contamination unless the well is pumped sufficiently to change the groundwater plume flow pattern. On the other hand, if the well screen has not been properly sealed from the other zones, the groundwater samples may be representative of a composite of several zones, some of which may be contaminated. There is the further potential that the groundwater monitoring wells may provide an undesirable connection between several independent groundwater zones.

Once the locations of the wells in the groundwater monitoring program have been determined, the next step is to properly design and construct the wells in order to provide satisfactory access to the groundwater interval to be studied. Without properly designed monitoring wells and proper installation, it becomes more difficult to collect reliable samples for subsequent interpretation in the monitoring program.

The diameter of the casing for groundwater monitoring wells should be sufficient to allow the sample pump to be placed in the well at the desired depth. Generally the hole drilled for the casing should be at least 2 inches larger than the casing itself to ensure an adequate cement seal between the exterior casing wall and the geological formation. Should the casing or the drill holes be significantly larger than necessary, that alone could contribute to inaccuracies in the data. The sampling procedure could also be complicated by very low formation permeabilities that would greatly reduce the water level in the casing.

The intake of a monitoring well should be specific for the depth to be studied. The screen or other openings in the well should permit water to enter the well or casing only at the specified depth range. It is important that these monitoring wells be constructed in such a way as to sample only from one specific layer, without undesirable interconnection to the other layers.

When sampling for contaminants that are less dense than water, it is highly desirable to sample near the top of the saturated zone within an aquifer. The well screen should be placed near the anticipated position of the water table, with allowance of several feet both above and below this water level to account for future fluctuations.

The screen portion of the well which allows the groundwater to enter the casing must be properly constructed and developed to avoid subsequent sampling problems. These well screens should have a sufficient open area to permit the easy inflow of water into the casing from the groundwater formation.

The groundwater sampling equipment, including the well casings, should be constructed of materials that are unlikely to contaminate the groundwater-quality parameters that are being studied; yet at the same time, the equipment must be cost-effective. From the perspective of obtaining quality sample data, the use of polytetrafluoroethylene is highly desirable because it is inert to virtually all inorganic contaminants and will not be adversely affected by most organic contaminants. Stainless steel (316) also represents a low contamination potential. Polyvinyl chloride, polyethylene, and polypropylene are relatively inert for inorganic contaminants but may be adversely affected by organic materials. While galvanized and carbon steels may offer some cost saving over these other more exotic materials, the potential for cross contamination by steel components may severely affect the quality of the data obtained from the monitoring wells.

In most situations it is probably realistic to compromise some data accuracy in return for reasonable cost trade-offs. This is particularly true with regard to the material of construction for the well casing. For example, it might be reasonable to use monitoring wells that have been cased with less expensive and readily available PVC pipe. In any event, the materials of construction should be carefully selected, and the analytical laboratory should be aware of the exact nature of the materials used in the monitoring wells and associated equipment.

Considerable care should be given to the preparation of the casing and well screens prior to the installation. Both the casing and the well screens should be washed with a detergent and rinsed thoroughly with uncontaminated water. All of the sample casing and equipment should be well protected from contamination during shipment to and subsequent installation at the site by packaging in polyethylene.

It is important to select a qualified, experienced driller to actually drill the hole and set the casing. The driller should be familiar with the geographic area and preferably have experience with the geological formations that are expected to be encountered during the drilling of the well.

Well Development

The process of cleaning the face of the borehole and the formation around the well screen to permit representative groundwater to flow into the monitoring well is called *well development*. The development of the well is a necessary process to remove residual drilling mud, formation clays, and other fines. Unless proper well development occurs, the plugging action of these residual materials will substantially reduce the permeability of the formation and retard the movement of the groundwater into the well screen. The residual materials could also ostensibly interfere with the chemical analysis of the groundwater samples.

The well development process should include vigorous agitation of natural formation water in the vicinity of the screen in order to remove the clay and silt fines. There are several methods that are suitable for the development of monitoring wells, including use of a surge block, an air lift, or a bailer; another method is "surging the pump."

A surge block is a round plunger that is moved up and down inside the well casing to agitate the water in the monitoring well. Surge blocks are commonly used with cable tool drilling rigs. The air lift involves pumping compressed air down a pipe inside the well casing to blow the water out of the monitoring well. A bailer can be used inside the well casing in a manner similar to a surge block. Bailers have the added advantage of removing fines each time they are brought to the surface and dumped. Surging a pump is done by starting and stopping it so that water flows back and forth through the screen, thereby removing the fines.

Collection of Groundwater Samples

Even after the monitoring well has been properly located and constructed, special precautions are necessary during the sampling process to ensure that the sample being taken from the well is representative of the groundwater at that location. A groundwater sample from a monitoring well that indicates the presence of contamination may verify the existence of contamination as long as the integrity of the well is intact and the sampling procedure is done in a reliable manner. The sample cannot be contaminated or otherwise altered by the sampling and handling procedures because erroneous information will then be produced by the monitoring program. It should be understood that the composition of the water inside the well casing and outside near the well screen is probably not representative of the overall groundwater quality at the sample site. The well should be pumped or bailed until it has been thoroughly flushed of standing water and contains representative water from the aquifer. A common procedure is to pump or bail the well, prior to collecting the representative groundwater sample, until about 5 borehole volumes have been removed. This procedure is dependent upon many factors, including the characteristics of the well, the hydrogeology of the aquifer, the type of sampling equipment, and the parameters being sampled. In any event, it is essential that all the standing water within the well bore be completely exchanged with fresh groundwater.

One must be aware that the instability of many physical, chemical, and biological factors will greatly affect the validity of any sample. Groundwaters in the saturated zone are usually well insulated and therefore subject to minimal temperature fluctuations. This must be contrasted with surface conditions where there are significant temperature fluctuations. These temperature changes have the potential to greatly influence many aspects of water quality. The reaction kinetics of slow processes related to well-insulated groundwater may double for some processes with each 10°C rise in temperature. These elevated temperatures could also affect microbial growth much as do chemical reaction kinetics.

Frequency of sampling at a disposal site is determined on the basis of groundwater flow rates, historical variations in selected chemical parameters, distance from the source, geologic setting of the monitoring well, the characteristics of the formations affected, and the water-table depth. Because of the generally slow movement of groundwater, sampling greater than quarterly is rarely justified. However, more frequent analysis may be desirable to establish trends.

Should the potential pollutant source be located above the water table, it will probably be necessary to sample the unsaturated zone. Since most pollutants can be sorbed to soil in the unsaturated zone, a false groundwater reading showing no contamination may be observed, even though significant pollutants may be moving slowly through the unsaturated zone toward the groundwater.

Recording of Samples and the Chain of Custody

Because of the substantial expenditures involved in groundwater sampling, it is important that accurate and detailed information be recorded during the sampling procedures. Furthermore, the chain of custody of the samples themselves must be properly recorded in order to provide references for unforeseen legal actions.

The following represent the type of information that should be recorded during the groundwater sampling program:

Sample description: Type of water and volume
Source: Well number and location
Identification of the sampler
Date and time of sampling
Laboratory sampling number
Well data: Total depth, depth to water table, pumping schedule
Preservatives used
Sampling appearance: Color, turbidity, and sediment
Reason for sampling

There are several guidelines that should be followed regarding chain of custody of the sample: As few people as possible should handle the sample; custody transfers should be recorded for each individual sample; and all these records should be kept in a field logbook maintained in a neat and orderly manner.

Collection of Subsurface Solids Samples

If groundwater monitoring confirms an absence of contamination, it does not necessarily preclude a contamination problem at the site. In order to fully assess site contamination it is desirable to sample subsurface soils in both the saturated and unsaturated zones in addition to obtaining groundwater samples. Because of sorption and physical impediments, some pollutants move very slowly downward through the earth toward the water table. This is particularly true in the unsaturated zone. The degree of attenuation and movement of the contaminants will vary greatly, but many of these potential pollutants might not actually be detected in the groundwater for long periods of time. These contaminants represent long-term pollution problems for groundwater, and it is imperative that their behavior in the subsurface be determined.

Microbial populations could cause biological changes in the contaminants near the surface of the site but may not be present as the pollutants proceed downward toward the groundwater. By carefully sampling the interior of the cores from the saturated zone, the aquifer microbes can be determined.

It is important that the core samples be processed as soon as possible, ideally in the field. However, if this is impractical, the core should be retained in the core barrel, placed in a sterile polyethylene bag, sealed, and then transported to the analysis laboratory.

CONTROL AND MITIGATION OF GROUNDWATER CONTAMINATION

There are several technologies for controlling the migration of contaminated groundwater plumes. Groundwater pumping involves extraction of contaminated water to either treat the plume or alter the direction of flow. Groundwater pumping techniques have been shown to be most effective for plume management at sites where the aquifers have high permeability and where the contaminants have a high degree of mobility with the groundwater. Subsurface drains can collect liquid discharges by gravity flow. Barriers with low permeability can be used to divert groundwater flow from a waste disposal site or to contain leachate leaking from a waste site. Leachate plumes may also be treated by in situ biological and chemical treatment processes that have been specifically designed to remove the contaminants of the plume. Biodegradation processes which destroy the hazardous contaminants and chemical treatment which neutralizes and renders the contaminants harmless both offer considerable potential for in situ treatment of hazardous waste.

The following case study is illustrative of the type of pollution problems that may occur from improper management of surface lagoons that contain agricultural chemical wastes. The remediation techniques used in this case study to contain the potential pollutants are applicable to the protection of groundwater in many other instances. The material is adapted from a case study by the U.S. Environmental Protection Agency.[2]

CASE STUDY
Sampling and Remediation after a Spill

Large surface impoundments containing pesticide and fertilizer wastewater were located on the property of an agricultural chemical products manufacturer. The facility opened in the early 1950s; seepage and overflow through the dikes occurred several times thereafter. Then, during a 100-year rainstorm in 1980, in order to prevent dike failure about 3.5 million gallons of fertilizer wastewater containing 2400 mg ammonia was discharged into a slough leading to the nearby bay.

Background

The existing 100-acre pond system on the 140-acre site in northern California was built primarily in the late 1950s and early 1960s. There were about 56 acres of pesticide wastewater ponds and 32 acres of fertilizer wastewater impoundments. Seepage through the dikes and overflow of the ponds occurred several times during subsequent years because of cracks in the dikes and heavy winter rainstorms. In response to these problems, the company repaired and upgraded the dikes during the early 1970s by widening and adding clay covers to various sections to increase their structural strength and to prevent slumping and seepage. These modifications were not intended to increase overall capacity. Until 1980, most of the releases of wastewater were of small volume, under 100 gallons, and were reported to the California Regional Water Quality Control Board (WQCB).

In February 1980 a heavy, 100-year rainstorm filled the ponds close to their capacity. A representative of the company called the WQCB on February 20,

1980, to report that the waste ponds were on the verge of topping the dikes and to request permission to discharge some of the water in order to relieve the pressure on the dikes. There were several alternatives:

1 To allow topping of all ponds, which might have resulted in a 40-million-gallon discharge from complete dike failure
2 To discharge controlled amounts to the sewer system
3 To discharge only the least hazardous wastewater, thus providing additional pond capacity into which the more toxic wastes could be transferred

WQCB believed the latter alternative to be the most desirable and allowed the company to lower the fertilizer pond level by releasing 3.5 million gallons to the adjacent slough, which emptied into the bay. Following the discharge, a cease-and-desist order was issued to prevent future releases.

Site Description

The site is shown in Figure 10-3. The manufacturing facility occupied about 140 acres and could be divided into two areas separated by street X. The area southeast of street X consisted of chemical manufacturing, storage facilities, and offices on 40 acres. The remainder of the property was to the northwest of street X and contained an evaporation and wastewater treatment pond system and the fertilizer plant.

The evaporation pond area was dissected by numerous ditches and natural sloughs through which surface runoff passed from the east to the bay. The main slough for the other drainageways was located north of the fertilizer plant. Many of these former sloughs and drainage ditches influenced the layout and configuration of the 16 existing dikes. With the development of the fertilizer plant and the evaporation pond system, surface drainage across the site had been diverted into ditches that were built to flow directly into creek X, which then drained into the bay. The bay area was used by residents for recreation, navigation, and industrial water supply. In addition, it was the habitat for waterfowl and migratory birds, fish, and shellfish.

The soils in the site area were characterized as silty clays, typically consisting of very poorly drained soils in saltwater marshes and tidal areas where there was regular inundation by high tides. The depth from the surface of a typical profile was approximately 5 feet. These Reyes series soils were more commonly known as "bay mud." Except for the pond locations on site, the bay mud in the area was overlain by a fill material which ranged in thickness between 3 and 10 feet. West of street X, the uppermost soil unit beneath the treatment and evaporation ponds was a dark-gray silty clay that was rich with organic matter and was highly pervious. The thickness of the bay mud, which underlay the organic silty clay in the area west of street X, ranged from 2.5 feet below the east side of the fertilization pond to 34 feet below the south end of the site. The bay mud was not present east of street X. In this area, the fill was

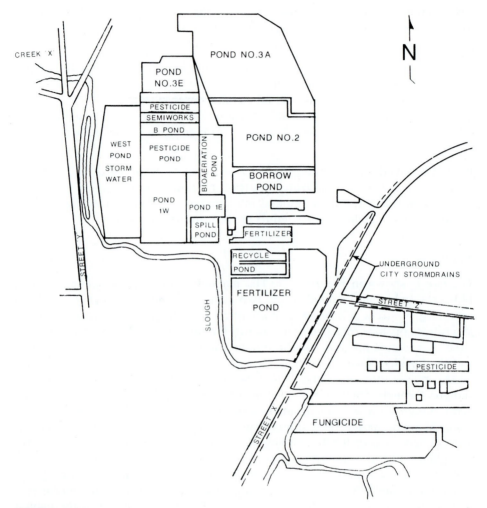

FIGURE 10-3
Agricultural chemical manufacturing facility.

directly underlain by alluvium and the soil type was described as "urban land." Below the bay mud was older bay mud, which was darker in color and stiffer in texture than the later bay mud. The thickness of the older bay mud ranged between 2 and 6 feet. The elevation in the vicinity of the site was at or near sea level, and the slope was less than 1 percent. The soil was extremely moist and had a permeability between 1.4×10^{-4} and 4.5×10^{-5} cm/s.

The site was situated with numerous other industrial facilities on the outskirts of the city. The bay-shore areas to the southwest and those that surround the city had been used for industrial purposes for at least 80 years. Directly to the northwest of the site, creek X was fed by another creek and the marshy areas to the north before entering the bay.

Hydrogeology of the Site

The site was located along the eastern shore of the bay. The entire bay area was a drowned river valley within a northwest-trending structural trough formed in Franciscan bedrock. The bay was formed when a block of bedrock tilted toward the east. The uplifted western edge of the block formed hills, and the downdropped eastern edge created the depression that is now the bay. Subsequent to the downdropping of the block, material eroded from the eastern hills and was deposited in alluvial fans to form the gently sloping plain that bordered the eastern shoreline of the bay where the site was located.

Four major geologic units occur beneath the site area. These have been listed according to relative age, with the youngest appearing first:

Bay mud: Clayey sandy silt and silty clay with organic matter and shells
Old bay mud: Stiff silty clay with sand and fine gravel
Estuary deposits and alluvium: Silty and sandy clays with interbedded gravels and gravel lenses
Franciscan bedrock: Sandstones and siltstones

Because the site was located near an inundated zone, in an area that was nearly level, the underlying subsurface conditions reflected even minor fluctuations that occurred in the bay water level.

The texture of the alluvium was variable, ranging from brown and grayish-brown silty clays to silty sands with fine gravel lenses. This variability reflected two processes that had taken place during the formation of the alluvial fans in the site area. The first process reflected the gradual erosion of the hills and slow deposition of the eroded sediments. Deposition of the coarser gravel and sands generally occurred in the upper part of the fan, while the silts and clays were deposited along the outermost flat-lying portions. The second process involved runoff flowing through channels across the fan surface, transporting and sorting sediments, and storms carrying coarse sediment.

The estuary deposits consisted of brownish-gray to gray silty clays and clayey silts deposited in the quiet, shallow marine environment of the early bay. These clays were often calcareous and contained shell fragments. The estuary sediments at the site also contained an alluvial component because of the site's proximity to present and past bay shorelines. A shallow, near-shore environment received a large influx of alluvial sands and silts, which were reworked by tidal currents and benthic organisms.

The bedrock material underlying the alluvial-estaurine sequence consisted of sandstones and siltstones of the Franciscan formation. It occurred at a depth of 273 feet at the northeast corner of the fertilizer pond, increasing in depth to the northwest and the bay.

The alluvial deposits, consisting primarily of sands and silts with occasional gravel, constituted the principal shallow water-bearing strata. The estuarine deposits consisted mainly of clays, organic clays, and silts that had low permeabilities. Therefore, potential groundwater development for drinking water sources and industrial uses within the site area was limited. Within the site area, there was only one deep well that was completed in the sand and gravel zones between depths of 100 and 170 feet and was used for industrial purposes. Within a 2-mile radius of the site, there were only two privately owned wells registered for domestic use. Both wells were located northeast of the site and were completed in sands and gravels at depths between 175 and 240 feet.

The site location could be hydrologically characterized as a regional discharge area. The principal source of recharge in the area were the hills to the southeast of the site. The predominant direction of groundwater flow at the site was from the southeast to the northwest.

The water table was generally shallow over the site area, ranging between 2 and 8 feet below the ground surface. The height of the groundwater table within the site area was greatly affected by the established network of drainage ditches and by the existing surface impoundments. The water table tended to be higher in the vicinity of both the drainage ditches and surface impoundments.

Within the sediments underlying the site, six main water-bearing zones had been identified, based on the interpretation of available geophysical logs and drill-hole data. Four of these zones were within 200 feet of the ground surface. All six zones were continuous over the site and had higher permeabilities than the intervening silty clay strata. The uppermost zone A consisted of placed fill and the underlying younger bay-mud deposits. Potential usage of groundwater within this zone was limited because of the low permeability of the younger bay-mud deposits.

Five remaining zones existed at depths below this uppermost unit and consisted primarily of sand-silt-gravel mixtures that were confined by clay strata. These units will be discussed in order of increasing depth.

Zone C consisted of several large discontinuous sandy lenses within a silty clay sequence. This zone extended from 20 to 90 feet below sea level (BSL). The groundwater in zone C was moderately brackish, and on the basis of chemical analysis, it was not considered potable.

Zone B was relatively continuous under the site between elevations of 100 and 130 feet BSL. The water within this zone was fresh and considered potable. The estuarine clay layer bounding these zones was relatively impermeable and acted as a barrier to downward migration of contaminants.

Zone D was also relatively continuous and occurred between elevations of 140 and 200 feet BSL. Like zone B the water contained within this unit was considered potable, and the zone was expected to be protected from downward migration of contaminants by the confining clay acquiclude.

Waste Disposal History

The entire evaporation pond area, which included the wastewater treatment pond system and the fertilizer plant, was within a former tidal marsh. Prior to the development of the evaporation pond system, the area was traversed by numerous ditches and natural sloughs. Examination of a topographical map of the area indicated that the northern and eastern portions of the area were once pasture and farmland. In addition, a trash dump was located in the northwest corner of the site and extended into the area that was occupied by pond 3A (Figure 10-3).

The fertilizer plant and evaporation pond systems were constructed during the late 1950s and early 1960s. Preconstruction preparation of the plant area involved the removal of several feet of soft marsh deposits, followed by placement of compacted fill onto the underlying younger bay mud. The plant foundation was then constructed in the placed fill. There were several parts of the facility in the western portion of the site that were supported by piles because of the thicker marsh deposits there. The ground surface throughout the plant area was at an elevation of 10 to 11 feet above sea level.

The facility's pond boundaries were formed by dikes that were initially constructed with soils excavated from adjacent marsh area. The initial elevation of these structures was between +8 and +10 feet, and they were probably less than 10 feet wide at the base. Subsequent to their original construction, the dikes were gradually enlarged, using borrow fill materials of varying composition. In September 1980, all perimeter dike embankments had been widened to at least 20 feet at the base at an elevation equal to the planned maximum pond level, which was 11 feet above sea level for the majority of the ponds. In addition, the pond side of all exterior dikes was given additional height to provide a minimum of 2 feet of freeboard against overflow by wind-generated waves, and the height and thickness of the dikes were increased to permit higher pond levels and to improve their stability and leakage resistance.

At that point, the disposal/evaporation pond system occupied 100 acres of land and had a total capacity of 150 million gallons. The system was divided into six areas according to type of waste:

Area 1 comprised the fungicide ponds and consisted of 45 acres of evaporation ponds and bioaeration for treatment and disposal of wastewater containing sodium salts and fungicide intermediates with trace amounts of carbamate fungicide and solvents.

Area 2 comprised the pesticide ponds and consisted of 11 acres, with the "pesticide pond" and other ponds used for disposal of process wastes containing salts, some heavy metals, and pesticides.

Area 3 comprised the fertilizer ponds and consisted of 21 acres of recycle, evaporation, and borrow ponds holding wastewater that contained ammonium chlorides, sulfates, and nitrates.

Area 4 contained the storm-water pond, an 11-acre pond for storm-water runoff from the agricultural chemical manufacturing areas. Constituents of storm-water runoff were low concentrations of materials contained in process waste streams from the various manufacturing areas.

Area 5 contained the emergency spill pond, which covered about 1 acre and was available for spill containment.

Area 6 held the solid wastes, approximately 13,000 cubic yards of material from the bottom of an old evaporation pond; this area was situated near ponds 3E and 3A (Figure 10-3).

Description of Contamination

The surface and groundwater contamination from the evaporation pond system was controlled by (1) the thickness and permeability characteristics of the natural sediments and the dikes and liners that confined the ponds, (2) the pond levels of the system, (3) the local area weather conditions, and (4) the hydraulics of the groundwater zone near the surface. Although the evaporation pond system at the site had performed relatively well over the years, there were incidents which suggested that leakage had occurred. There were two dike areas in particular that were cause for concern. One area was located along the west dike of the west pond and near the east and west dikes of the fertilization pond. In the first case, wastewater seepage was pumped from the adjacent drainage ditch, collected, and returned to the pond. In the case of the fertilization pond, ammonia-contaminated wastewater was detected in the sloughs that ran along the pond's south and west dike boundaries and within the storm drain along the east dike of the pond. Ammonia contamination was limited to the pipe bedding material along the storm drain.

The potential hazard of lateral wastewater leakage was not considered serious because the groundwater flow was away from populated areas and the low permeability of the underlying bay muds inhibited waste migration. However, the integrity of the site became a critical concern in February 1980. During the period from February 20 to 22, intense rainfall threatened the pond system. Either a controlled release had to be maintained or the dikes would be topped and completely breached. If the latter was allowed to occur, the spill could be as much as 40 to 50 million gallons. Once contacted about the emergency, the WQCB staff quickly decided that they should discharge the water containing ammonia to the bay rather than release the pesticide-contaminated pond water. As a result, 3.5 million gallons of ammonia-containing liquid waste was discharged from the fertilizer evaporation ponds.

Biological studies were subsequently conducted by the State Regional Water Quality Control Board and the Department of Fish and Game to determine the effect of the ammonia-based spill on marine life in the bay. Results revealed no evidence of widespread fish kill due to the release. Rapid dilution had minimized any potential damage.

The WQCB's response to the spill incident was an enforcement action ordering that the waste evaporation ponds be upgraded to preclude any recurrence of the discharge. The company retained a consultant to conduct a site study to:

Define the groundwater regime and water quality across the site and possible presence of contamination in subsurface soils

Evaluate the permeability and stability of the perimeter dikes surrounding the ponds.

Evaluate the permeability of the pond bottoms

A report was submitted in October 1980 to the WQCB for improving the overall integrity of the evaporation pond system.

The hydrogeologic study identified two usable sand-gravel aquifers beneath the site area. These units were similar to zones B and D in the area's hydrogeology. The two water-bearing units were horizontally continuous and occurred at approximate depths of 130 and 175 feet, respectively. Direction of flow of these water-bearing zones was from southeast to northwest. They were confined by a low-permeability silty clay material that acted as a barrier, inhibiting downward migration of contaminants.

Contamination, with the exception of manganese, was absent within these two zones. The two most shallow water-bearing zones, A and C, both contained nonpotable water that was brackish and exceeded federal drinking water standards. Several constituents were detected in high concentrations in these zones: total dissolved solids (TDS), sulfate, chloride, heavy metals (lead, arsenic, cadmium, and selenium), and lindane (one occurrence in zone A). Concentrations of ammonia, carbamate fungicide, tetrahydrophthalic acid, and tetrahydrophthalimide were also detected, although not in quantities that exceeded EPA limits. The areal distribution of ammonia, fungicide, and arsenic concentrations in the groundwater samples are shown in Figures 10-4 and 10-5. Generally, higher concentrations of these substances were found around the treatment and evaporation ponds than were found in samples taken east of street X; particularly high concentrations were found in samples taken from the northwest corner of the site. It was therefore established that the uppermost two water-bearing zones contained poor-quality water, which was initially nonpotable because of its high salt content. The lower two aquifers had high artesian heads, indicating that the silty clay layer confining them was impermeable and was inhibiting vertical leachate movement.

The hydrogeologic investigation indicated that downward movement of contaminants would be greatly retarded by the impermeable muds underlying the site, as well as by the upward artesian pressure from the deeper aquifers. Lateral movement in the upper water-table zone could occur toward the bay, away from the populated area. The area of highest parameter concentrations appeared to be in the near-surface zone at the northwest corner of the site, where landfilled materials influenced soil permeability. This area northwest of pond 3A was historically a trash dump. Two former sloughs had originally passed beneath the dikes in the northwest area of the sites. The permeable fill material in the sloughs allowed rapid movement of fluids through this corner area.

Laboratory soil chemical tests were conducted on soil samples collected at 18 locations in the site area. The soil samples were composites which incorporated the upper 10 feet of each boring, typically in two depth increments of 0 to 5 and 5 to 10 feet.

Ammonia was present in nearly all samples tested, with the higher concentration (115 mg) occurring in a storage area for fertilizers. The areal distribution of ammonia concentrations in soil samples collected on site is shown in Figure 10-6.

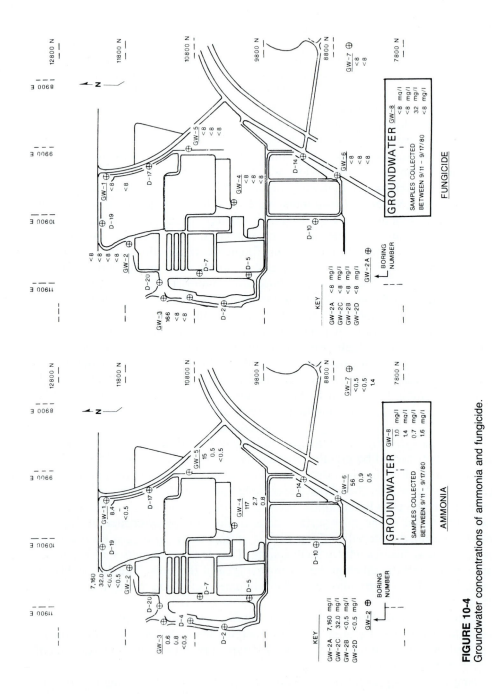

FIGURE 10-4
Groundwater concentrations of ammonia and fungicide.

294

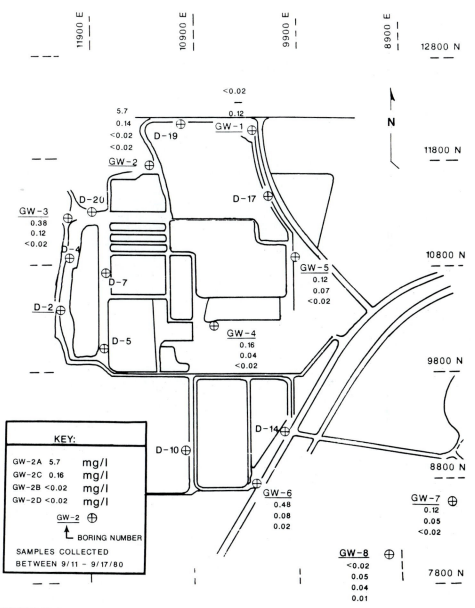

FIGURE 10-5
Concentrations of arsenic in groundwater versus the EPA limit of ≤ 0.05 mg/l.

Carbamate fungicide was detected in soils around the west pond, the borrow pond, and along the northern boundary of the site. The highest level found was 0.135 ppm, which occurred in the area of the borrow pond.

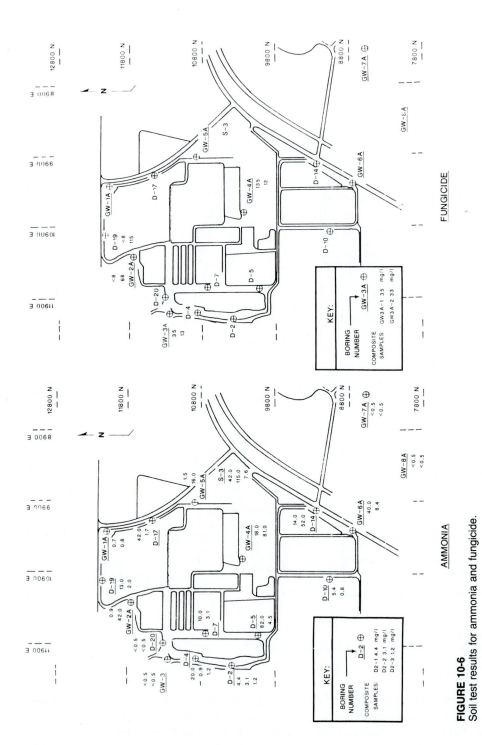

FIGURE 10-6
Soil test results for ammonia and fungicide.

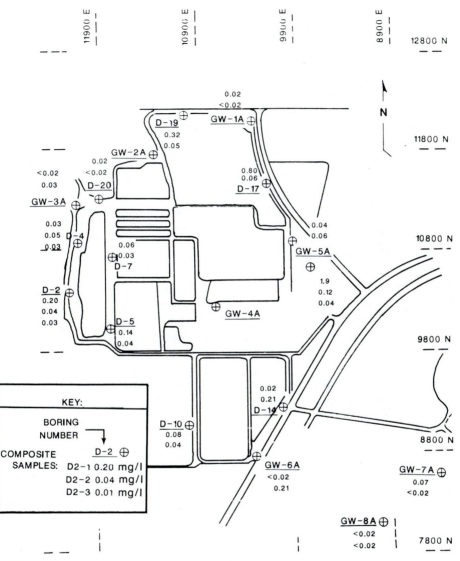

FIGURE 10-7
Concentrations of arsenic in soil versus the EPA limit of ≤ 5.0 mg/l.

Arsenic was detected at most sampling locations, although no samples exceeded EP toxicity limits. The highest concentrations were found in the borrow pond area shown in Figure 10-7.

According to the analytical results, the upper 10 feet of soils in the evaporation pond area contained some significant concentrations of certain organic compounds, ammonia, and arsenic.

The potential for contamination in the evaporation pond area could be controlled by proper design of the thickness and permeability characteristics of the dikes and liners that confined the ponds and the hydraulics of the pond system. Even with well-designed and constructed perimeter dikes and liners and well-planned operating procedures, there were still three factors over which there was minimal control—i.e., thickness and permeability of natural sediments, local area weather conditions, and the hydraulics of the near-surface groundwater zone.

There were several reasons for potential problems in dike integrity at the site. Many of the perimeter dikes bounding the ponds were originally built using highly organic and peaty materials from marsh areas immediately adjacent to the dikes. These soils are typically quite permeable because of the open framework produced by the decaying organic constituents. In addition, the dike material experienced shrinkage from drying and later from traffic over the dikes which were used as roadways. This shrinkage produced cracks within the dikes that could have become conduits for leakage. After the original construction of the evaporation pond system, perimeter dikes adjacent to the drainage ditch were blanketed with a clay layer, as shown in Figure 10-8, that was intended to improve stability and reduce leakage into surrounding site area. Clay blanketing necessitated trenching down into the bay muds to create an acceptable seal. The resulting instability might then have caused the dikes to fail in the direction of the trenches. To avoid this, only very short sections of the dikes were trenched and blanketed at a time, minimizing the time a trench section remained open. This procedure helped prevent dike failure but created many more interfaces in the clay, thereby increasing the potential of a poor seal within the clay lining. As a result, some sections of the clay experienced leakage problems.

FIGURE 10-8
Schematic cross section through the dike, showing seepage barrier.

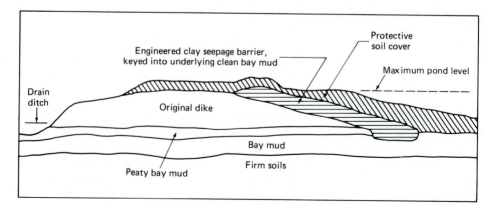

The Site Response

To increase the capacity and integrity of its pond system following the February 1980 release and subsequent cease-and-desist order, the company undertook two major site response actions:

About 75 million gallons of wastewater was pumped out of the fertilizer and pesticide ponds and trucked to approved landfills.

The dikes were reinforced by increasing their thickness and height and by adding a cutoff wall along the northern, western, and southern dikes of the west pond in 1980, around the fertilizer pond and pond 2 in 1982, and along two sides of the borrow pond in 1983.

The first response action undertaken at the site was the removal and disposal of 75 million gallons of wastewater from the surface impoundment system. The disposal operation was a straightforward pumping-and-hauling operation. Wastewater was pumped into 5400-gallon tank trucks and shipped to approved disposal facilities. The disposal operation took place over the summer and fall of 1980 at a rate of over 100 truckloads per day; it was completed on October 16, 1980. The different wastewater types—e.g., fertilizer and pesticide wastewater—were disposed of at different facilities according to their hazard classification.

The second response action involved erection of an underground ASPHEMIX wall to reinforce the dikes. It was of innovative design, and the choice of materials resulted from the interplay of several factors. Past experience with embankments consisting of clay materials had a major influence on the selection of a wall composed of a material that was not clay. The material selected was a combination of asphalt emulsion, sand, cement, and water. The exact proportion of each constituent that was used in the mixture was determined through laboratory compatibility testing of various asphalt mixtures and existing pond fluids. Testing was performed over a period of 2 to 3 months. The asphalt mixture used around the different ponds was essentially the same, with slight variations depending upon the fluid contained within the pond.

The parameters involved in the structural design of the ASPHEMIX barrier wall were wall width, depth, length, and linear configuration. The depth to which the wall extended below the surface, the length, and its linear configuration were all dependent upon the pre-existing dikes, the geologic conditions, structures at the site, and the locations of the area in need of repair. The width or thickness of the ASPHEMIX wall was not dependent upon dike conditions but rather was predetermined by the width of the beam used for wall installation.

Construction of an ASPHEMIX barrier wall required the use of one crane-suspended I beam, which was connected to a vibrator, as shown in Figure 10-9. The ASPHEMIX material was installed much like a grout curtain, with side-by-side injections. The 80-ton crane was used as a pile driver to vibrate the specially designed, 17-foot-long I beam into the ground and through the bay mud below; the ASPHEMIX was injected as the beam was withdrawn. The beam was locked in a guide frame for positioning purposes and stabilized by a hydraulic foot that provided guidance and aided in keeping the inserted beam vertical. The ASPHEMIX material was mixed and contained within a small plant at the rear of the beam rig and was injected through a set of nozzles located at the base of the beam. At the completion of each wall panel, the rig was moved along the direction of the wall. Every injected panel was overlapped to ensure continuity of the completed wall. This process was repeated until the wall was complete. All wall installations required the use of one beam rig.

The first ASPHEMIX wall at the facility was installed during the summer of 1980, along the north, west, and south boundaries of west pond. Operations began in the northeast corner of the pond and progressed southward and around to the southeast corner, where the wall terminated. The wall, as shown in Figure 10-10, was 2000 feet in length and 10 inches in width and extended to an average depth of 17 feet, passing vertically through the center of the dike along the outside of the clay seepage barrier.

Preconstruction site-preparation activities were often necessary. These activities most frequently involved widening the dike structures to enable the ASPHEMIX rig to move along the top of the dike. Dike reinforcement involved extending the dike width to a minimum of 25 feet. This widening process was often selective because of the fact that some dike areas already had a

FIGURE 10-9
Schematic diagram of the ASPHEMIX injection beam rig.

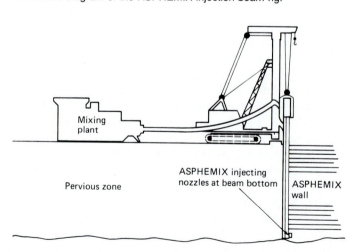

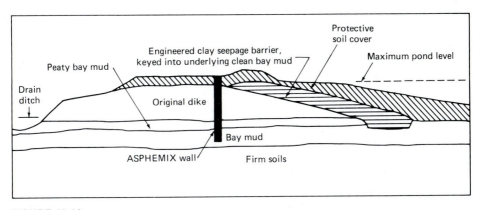

FIGURE 10-10
Schematic cross section through the dike showing the ASPHEMIX wall and seepage barrier.

minimum width of 25 feet. When the installation process was complete and the rig equipment removed, the dikes were then built up to meet dike height requirements. Consolidation of the earthen material because of the weight of the equipment caused some lowering of the top elevation of the dike.

The actual wall installation process involved a great deal of testing and visual monitoring to ensure an effective barrier. The two most important and critical features of the completed ASPHEMIX wall were the alignment of the beam-injected panels and the uniform composition of the ASPHEMIX across the wall. Verticality and precise alignment of the ASPHEMIX panels were of great concern during and after installation, because without precise alignment the chances that gaps or windows would remain within the wall were greatly increased. During installation along the west pond, a leveling device was used to measure the angular displacement of the beam as it was driven into the ground.

In addition to beam verticality, there were several other parameters relating to the character of the ASPHEMIX operation that required close monitoring during installation. Five tests were performed on the asphalt mixture to ensure uniformity in asphalt content, fluid content, stockpile moisture content, aggregate particle size, and mix consistency. The mix-consistency and stockpile-moisture-content tests were conducted as required—for example, if material was acquired from a new source or the appearance of the mix was slightly different from what it should have been. The other tests (fluid content, asphalt content, and aggregate particle size) were conducted twice daily.

The barrier wall installed around the exterior portions of west pond terminated at the pond's southeast corner. The wall did not continue along the southern sides of pond 1W (Figure 10-3) and the spill pond because these dike areas contained clay liners and there was no evidence of leakage problems.

The dry season of 1981 passed without any additional work being performed at the pond site, since prior to any further installation, it was necessary that the ASPHEMIX wall technique be approved by the WQCB. The time lapse between wall installations was primarily due to the fact that WQCB did not receive the site response plans from the company for review until March 30, 1981, and was not able to complete its review by April 12, as requested by the company in order to meet the 1981 dry season schedule. The technique finally was approved in December 1981. At that point, final plans were made to continue the wall along the east side of the fertilizer pond.

Installation of that wall began on July 15, 1982, and was completed on September 25, 1982. The total time taken for completion was approximately 6 weeks, the same time as that taken to erect the wall along the west pond. Although the same amount of time was necessary for the two installations, there were differences between the two operations and differences between the walls themselves. The fertilizer pond's east side wall was 2929 feet in length, 17 feet in depth, and about 10 inches in width. The wall extended from the southeast corner of the fertilizer pond, along the railroad track for approximately 2200 feet, and then shifted west toward the southeast corner of the borrow pond, where it ended. The approach taken during the design stages of the second wall were slightly different from those taken during the design of the west pond wall. In erecting the second wall, in 1982, the facility management took command of the structural design and played a major role in the design of its composition, arranging, in agreement with their contractor, for additional compatibility testing on various asphalt mixtures. During the design of the west pond wall, the ASPHEMIX testing had been performed exclusively by the contractor.

Operations along the east side of the fertilizer pond were somewhat more complicated than those for the first installation because of the presence of power lines, storage facilities, pipeways, and railways. Detailed wall design and construction planning were critical in anticipating and avoiding problems and delays that could have been caused by these structures. Several facilities were relocated, and underground pipeways and railways were moved. The entire fertilizer plant's power was shut off twice so that power lines could be relocated. Despite the extra construction activities necessary during the second installation and the additional 1000 linear feet of area to cover, the second installation was completed in the same amount of time as the first. The difference in completion time between the two operations was primarily due to the fact that during the fertilizer pond installation, both contractor and facility management were working with the experience gained from the west pond operation.

After the completion of the east side, installation activities began along the fertilizer pond's west side. The west side wall was 1173 feet in length, 17 feet in depth, and 10 inches in width. It extended from the northwest corner of the spill pond to the southwest corner of the fertilizer pond. An ASPHEMIX wall was not installed along the south side of the fertilizer pond since seepage problems were never observed along the south dike and studies showed the clay liner there to be intact.

All testing and monitoring procedures in erecting the wall on the west side were similar to those undertaken during installation along the east side, but there was one considerable difference between these two operations. During the west side installation, approximately two-thirds of the distance down to the southwest corner of the fertilizer pond where the wall was to end, the vibrated-beam rig was relocated at the southwest corner and proceeded thence along the dike in a northerly direction. This change in direction was necessary because of the presence of an aerial power line that ran perpendicular to the line of installation. Subsequent to the change in direction, the rig moved northward to meet and connect with the segment installed earlier. Other than the power line, there were no further complications. The completion of the east wall ended the construction activities undertaken in 1982.

Construction activities on the last wall commenced on July 1, 1983. The wall was 4000 feet long, 17 feet deep, and 10 inches wide and extended from the southeast corner of the borrow pond, following the dike areas north and then east to the northwest corner of west pond. With the completion of that wall, the potential for further contamination problems at the facility was effectively ended.

ATTEMPTS AT REGULATION OF GROUNDWATER CONTAMINATION

In spite of the importance of groundwater as a national resource, until very recently little was done to prevent its contamination by organic chemicals. Many groundwater supplies of drinking water are now closed because of high concentrations of chlorinated hydrocarbons and other toxic organic chemicals. Contamination by even low levels of many volatile organic compounds is enough to render a supply unpotable for reasons of long-term health risks. Whole segments of important aquifers have become degraded and may essentially be lost forever as sources of drinking water.

Only in the early 1970s did the government and the public become aware that many waste disposal landfills were creating groundwater contamination problems. Since that time, federal legislation—essentially under the Safe Drinking Water Act, FIFRA, RCRA, and the Hazardous and Solid Waste Amendments—and EPA regulations have been drafted and enacted to address the problem. (See Chapters 3 and 4.)

States have since used a wide variety of techniques to protect groundwater quality. State regulations include setting water quality standards to ensure safe drinking water supplies, requiring discharge permits, and imposing land use controls. Many states have also established funds to clean up hazardous waste sites, and a large number actively monitor the groundwater that is near hazardous waste land disposal facilities and contaminated sites that have been previously identified.

Local governments have also taken action to prevent and mitigate groundwater contamination. Local zoning has been used to regulate residential and commercial development over groundwater recharge areas. Restrictions in the density of septic tank systems have also been used on a local basis to protect groundwater.

QUESTIONS

1 Define the following terms:
   (a) Recharge areas
   (b) Water table
   (c) Hydraulic conductivity
   (d) Unsaturated zone
   (e) Groundwater
   (f) Saturated zone
   (g) Capillary fringe
   (h) Permeability
   (i) Aquifers
   (j) Confining beds
2 Describe significant sources of groundwater contamination.
3 Choose a hazardous waste and diagram the pathways by which it could eventually endanger human health.
4 How would you determine the three-dimensional distribution of a hazardous pollutant in groundwater?
5 Discuss the effect of temperature on water quality of groundwater samples.
6 How would you plan a monitoring system for detecting contaminants at a leaking landfill?
7 What design criteria should be considered for the intake of a groundwater monitoring well?
8 What are the considerations in the selection of materials of construction for groundwater sampling equipment?
9 Why should well development be performed in testing groundwater?
10 Discuss the handling of sample cores from the field to the laboratory.
11 What groundwater sample records should be retained?

PROBLEMS

1 A valley with uniform cross-sectional area and impermeable sides and bottom contains groundwater flowing through coarse sand. There is a decrease in the hydraulic head of 0.1 meter per 100 meters in the valley aquifer. The hydraulic conductivity is 200 m/day and the aquifer is 60 meters high and 3000 meters wide. Estimate the flow rate of groundwater through the valley.
2 A landfill is leaking hazardous leachate into an aquifer and endangering a nearby river that is 13,000 feet away. The aquifer is unconfined with a hydraulic conductivity of 700 ft/day and a 0.2 effective flow porosity. Two monitoring wells between the landfill and the river have been placed 3000 feet apart. The groundwater depths from the tops of the well casings are 60 and 63 feet, respectively. The path of the groundwater plume is directly from the landfill to the river. What is the groundwater velocity and how long will it take for the leachate to travel from the landfill to the river?

BIBLIOGRAPHY

1 Canter, L. W., and R. C. Knox: *Groundwater Pollution Control,* Lewis Chelsea, Mich., 1985.

2 *Case Studies 1-23: Remedial Response at Hazardous Waste Sites,* U.S. Environmental Protection Agency, Washington, 1984.

3 D'Itri, F. M., and L. G. Wolfson: *Rural Groundwater Contamination,* Lewis, Chelsea, Mich., 1987.

4 Driscoll, F. G.: *Groundwater and Wells,* Johnson Division, St. Paul, Minn., 1986.

5 Fairchild, D. M.: *Groundwater Quality and Agricultural Practices,* Lewis, Chelsea, Mich., 1987.

6 Heath, R. C.: *Groundwater Regions of the United States,* U.S. Department of the Interior Geological Survey, Washington, 1984.

7 Logan, T. J., J. M. Davidson, J. L. Baker, and M. R. Overcash: *Effects of Conservation Tillage on Groundwater Quality,* Lewis, Chelsea, Mich., 1987.

8 Page, G. W.: *Planning for Groundwater Protection,* Academic, Orlando, Fla., 1987.

9 Scalf, M. R., J. F. McNabb, W. J. Dunlap, R. L. Cosby, and J. Fryberger: *Manual of Groundwater Sampling Procedures,* National Water Well Association, Worthington, Ohio, 1981.

10 Shields, E. J.: *Pollution Control Engineer's Handbook,* Pudvan, Northbrook, Ill., 1985.

11 Travis, C. C., and E. L. Etnier: *Groundwater Pollution,* American Association for the Advancement of Science, Westview, Boulder, Colo., 1984.

12 Walton, W. C.: *Groundwater Pumping Tests—Design and Analysis,* Lewis,Chelsea, Mich., 1987.

13 Walton, W. C.: *Groundwater Resource Evaluation,* McGraw-Hill, New York, 1970.

CHAPTER 11

LANDFILL DISPOSAL

INTRODUCTION

Historically, landfill has been the most commonly practiced method for disposal of waste materials in the United States.[5] Prior to more restrictive regulations, landfill was generally the method of choice of disposal, even of hazardous wastes. Economics have favored landfill operations because of low initial costs. However, when all short-term and long-term costs are considered, landfill may not be the most economic means of disposal after all.

Refuse, trash, and garbage are biodegradable in a sanitary landfill. For this reason, municipal landfills that have accepted only sanitary wastes should not present severe long-term threats to human health and the environment. But disposal of chemical substances in a landfill is an entirely different matter. Because of their persistence, many hydrocarbons and synthetic chemicals require further treatment before disposal if they are to be rendered harmless.[3]

Legislation and regulations are now in place to ensure minimal adverse impact on human health and the environment from future landfill design, construction, and operation. However, there are numerous landfills currently operating or abandoned that were not designed under these more stringent regulations. Many of these older landfills have now become Superfund sites that must be remediated at tremendous costs to all concerned parties.[6,7]

The following case study illustrates an example of poor landfill management and planning by government and industry alike.

CASE STUDY
Tragedy at Love Canal

Niagara Falls, New York, is a city of natural endowments stemming from a strait of water that connects Lake Erie to Lake Ontario. Flowing north at a rate of 0.5 million tons per minute, the Niagara River widens in its channel near Niagara Falls and then breaks into rapids before taking its famous 186-foot drop. Then the river cascades into rapids that are higher and swifter than any other in the continental United States.

Industrial History of the Area

The area surrounding Niagara Falls was a major gateway for western expansion in the nineteenth century because of its strategic location at the juncture of lakes Erie and Ontario. The development of hydroelectric power and the harnessing of this energy brought industrial growth to the region in 1890. Because the direct current that was generated could not be transferred long distances, energy-intensive industries were developed in clusters within blocks of the power source.

William T. Love developed a plan in 1892 to build a canal that would connect the upper and lower levels of the Niagara River. The canal was to be about 7 miles long. Love intended to build a city and industrial complex to use the power generated near this canal. Construction began in 1893, but the development of alternating current ended Love's plan and left two sections of the canal unfinished, each one-quarter mile long.

But though alternating-current transmission ended work on the canal, it allowed further expansion of industry in the region. Once power became available in larger amounts at less cost, industry began to specialize in products and processes that were energy-intensive. The electrochemical, abrasive, and graphite industries, highly dependent on electrical power, were attracted to the area.

Niagara Falls became the center for these industries, especially emerging chemical companies. At the turn of the century the major chemical produced was sodium hydroxide, a product of the electrolysis of sodium chloride. But electrolysis of this salt also produced chlorine, an undesirable by-product when produced in large quantities. Research in the 1930s began to address alternative uses for the excess chlorine. This led to the development of chlorinated organic chemicals and related solvents used in products such as plastics, fire retardants, plasticizers, pesticides, and other industrial intermediates.

During that period, manufacturers and government did not recognize, or even consider, the environmental effects of chemical products and by-products. No one thought that the benefits from pesticides such as DDT and endrin and from chlorinated organics such as 2,4,5-T, chlorinated solvents, and chloroform would be balanced by disastrous environmental effects. This lack of foresight has resulted in numerous long-term liabilities. The story of the canal in Niagara Falls provides just one graphic illustration.

The Canal Becomes a Landfill...

In the 1930s, Hooker Chemical and Plastic Corporation, whose processes included the manufacture of pesticides, plasticizers, and caustic, began landfilling the north quarter-mile section of Love's canal (Figure 11-1) with their waste residues. At that time, the surrounding terrain was meadowland and orchards, with a small cluster of homes only 30 feet from the ditch. Workers often used neighborhood garden hoses for washing themselves when they accidentally came in contact with the scalding sludges they were landfilling into the canal. By 1947 many companies were using the canal as a chemical waste dump site, and the city itself deposited fly ash there. The United States Army may even have deposited a large quantity of biological warfare agents and residues in Love Canal, although the Pentagon has denied this accusation. In 1952 the canal was closed and capped by Hooker Chemical.

...And Then a School Is Built

In 1953, city officials ordered Hooker Chemical to sell the city the canal land for a new school. Hooker filed disclaimers citing the possible dangers of building over the landfill, but the Niagara Falls School Board and the city were determined; the canal was a prime location for an elementary school. After being threatened with eminent domain proceedings, Hooker sold the entire canal strip to the city for $1.

FIGURE 11-1
Love Canal, Niagara Falls.

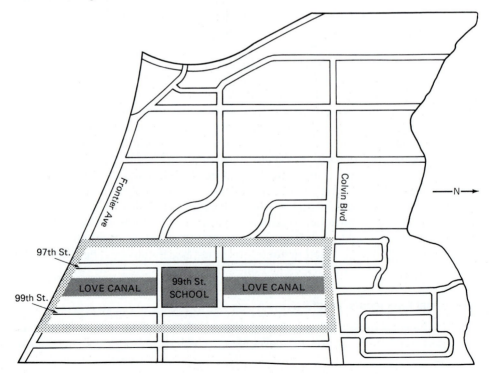

The school was constructed and young families began to settle along land neighboring what had been the dump site. Part of the site was converted into a park, where children soon found playing could be a painful experience. Finding chunks of phosphorous, they would throw them against rocks to see the brilliant explosions and trails of sparks. In 1958, three children were burned by exposed residues that had migrated to the surface. Though they were aware of the incident, Hooker issued no public warnings.

That same year, a mother near Love Canal gave birth to her third child, one born with a damaged heart, bone blockages of the nose, deformed ears, and a cleft palate. Before she was 2, the child was diagnosed as being mentally retarded and as having an enlarged liver. She had a double row of teeth on the bottom gum line. But it was believed that these problems were a quirk of nature. Then in 1974, this same family awoke to discover that their swimming pool had risen 2 feet out of the ground. When the pool was removed from the ground, the cavity immediately began to fill with yellow-, blue-, and orchid-colored groundwater. This water was so caustic that nearby redwood fence posts simply collapsed from chemically induced rot.

Another neighborhood family had spent years battling a black sludge that first began to seep into their basement in 1959. They tried various ways of stopping the seepage and finally put a hole into the basement wall to see what was on the other side. A large quantity of black liquid, full of hazardous waste, poured into the room through the hole in the cinder blocks of the basement wall. The true nature of the Love Canal tragedy was only beginning to come to light.

The Aftermath

Large quantities of toxic halogenated compounds were detected in the city sewer systems. The presence of these chemicals should have caused immediate alarm, but governmental agencies remained inactive and secretive, even as local residents raised fears for their health.

Eight months after the swimming pool incident, state employees began testing air samples from basements in the area. The results showed the air to be well above the threshold-limit values for some toxic substances. Health surveys in the neighborhood produced startling data; spontaneous abortions were 250 times above normal; blood tests showed increases in liver damage from detoxification of toxic substances; birth defects were high, including club feet, deafness, and mental retardation.

High levels of industrial chemical wastes were found in groundwater tests, including 11 suspected carcinogens such as benzene, chloroform, and trichloroethylene. Hooker Chemical released information that 200 tons of trichlorophenol had been placed in the landfill; in all, 22,000 tons of chemical wastes had been deposited over the years in Love Canal.

By 1976, puddles of chemicals were starting to surface in the backyards of many residents. Their complaints to the city brought no action, for the city did not want to upset Hooker; the firm employed 3000 local workers and was planning to build a $17 million headquarters in downtown Niagara Falls. Finally, in

1977, the city admitted that a problem existed but claimed they could not fix the responsibility. The Niagara Falls city manager stated that the site may be displeasing to the eyes and nose but it was not a crisis situation. It was only when the New York state government became involved and documented adverse health impacts that the citizens began to be heard.

In early 1978, the state ordered the county health commissioner to cover the exposed chemicals, erect a fence around the site, and ventilate the contaminated basements. The county health officer installed two fans in the basements of the two worst-contaminated basements and erected a wooden snow fence around the canal; the fence was broken down within 3 days. On August 2, 1978, the state, at a public meeting, recommended the closing of the 99th Street School and evacuation of all pregnant women and infants living nearby. But there were no funds available to help these people relocate, and they could not afford to make mortgage payments on a vacant house.

Anguished protests on behalf of the citizens of the Love Canal area finally brought results. In 1978, with the aid of EPA, 237 families were evacuated. Many of these people suffered from the direct effects of chemical exposure, including irritability, dizziness, nausea, weakness, fatigue, insomnia, and numbness. They also suffered from the psychological effects of living in a tragically dangerous environment without the financial means to relocate. The local suicide, divorce, and crime rates rose substantially, and there was general distrust of the environment, government, and industry in general.

The initial regulatory solution proposed by the state for Love Canal was to stop the uncontrolled leaching, prevent future leaching, and cover the canal. An engineering firm was hired to assess the situation and prepare remedial plans. The city of Niagara Falls and the Niagara County Board of Health were ordered to implement the plan for the southern portion of the canal, subject to approval by the State Department of Environmental Conservation. The plan was to turn Love Canal back into a quiet neighborhood, using over $20 million of state and federal money to accomplish the feat.

This remedial plan called for the installation of a tile drain to divert leachate to a trench system. The leachate would be pumped from wells to a holding tank, treated to remove organic toxic wastes, and finally emptied into the municipal sanitary sewer system. The canal itself was to be covered with an 8-foot clay cap to prevent rainfall from entering. Although the project plan contained recommendations for further studies to discover whether the bedrock and underground wastes had been adversely affected, the proposal was generally optimistic. It was predicted that homes across the street from those directly abutting the canal would become habitable upon completion of the work.

During that primary election period of 1978, the governor of New York continued to show his concern for the Love Canal residents. Taking advantage of a speaking engagement in Buffalo, he visited the 99th Street School in Niagara Falls to reaffirm all promises made to the residents. The citizens were assured that communications between an interagency task force and the residents would improve. The most positive sign to residents was the establishment of an office in the school for the Love Canal Homeowners Association. This office was crucial for the collection of relevant information and coordination of the citizen activities.

The citizens subsequently wrote a forceful statement criticizing the remedial plan, the interagency task force, and, by implication, the governor. As a result, a large public meeting was called; the governor returned to listen to the concerns of the many people who felt particularly endangered by the planned site work. The Niagara Falls residents were paying dearly for the wonders of modern technology, and they wanted compensation of one form or another. But government bureaucracy was slow to respond, though the state of New York did file suit against Hooker Chemical for $635 million.

When in 1980 a study was released to the public which reported evidence of chromosome damage, President Carter ordered the evacuation of 700 families from the Love Canal area. The state opposed the evacuation and refused any compensation until the federal government furnished the bulk of the expenses.

Meanwhile, Hooker claimed the disposal techniques they had used were neither careless nor outmoded. Indeed, their disposal techniques had, from the beginning, apparently conformed to the standards for hazardous waste management that were now being adopted by the Carter administration.

What was harder to defend was the series of decisions which allowed construction on and around the disposal site. These were decisions that Hooker had repeatedly warned against. They were pushed through by local governmental agencies, especially the Niagara Falls School Board, which was so strapped for cash and desperately in need of a place to build a school to handle increased enrollment that it knowingly procured land with chemicals beneath it. Hooker had escorted school board members to the site to witness the drilling of core samples. Waste chemicals were found in two of those cores, no more than 4 feet beneath the surface. When the city had persisted in the sale, Hooker appended a deed disclaiming responsibility for any injuries that might result from the buried wastes.

The responsibility and the liability for the Love Canal predicament was now shifted to the Niagara Falls Board of Education. This effectively delayed the EPA cleanup program under the Superfund act, which held that no industry could be made responsible for compensating victims or instituting cleanup until all other legal remedies had been exhausted. In 1983, the Congressional Office of Technology Assessment voiced doubts about the habitability of Love Canal, stating it could not be certain that it would ever be safe to live near Love Canal.

Finally, an out-of-court settlement was reached between 1345 residents of the Love Canal neighborhood and Occidental Petroleum, which had become the parent company of Hooker Chemical in 1968. The residents had sued for health and property damages as a result of the toxic wastes buried in the dump by Hooker between 1942 and 1953. The proposed settlement cost Occidental between $5 million and $6 million. Insurance paid the remainder of the $25 million settlement. This action resolved most of the claims against Occidental, though the company maintained, "The settlement isn't an admission of any negligence on the part of Occidental and should not be interpreted as such."

LANDFILLS AS DISPOSAL SITES

Many domestic generators have sent their hazardous wastes off-site for landfill disposal, since this was normally the least expensive alternative available.[10] Generators were encouraged to landfill wastes by attractive economics and by the shortsighted influence of government, industry, the general public, and special interest groups. More recently, all concerned parties have come to realize that the low initial costs of landfilling are merely a small portion of the true costs to human health and the environment.[1,2,9,12] As was seen in the Love Canal case study, many of the sites once acceptable for landfills or surface impoundments for hazardous wastes have now become Superfund sites.[4] This is costing taxpayers and consumers hundreds of billions of dollars more than what it would have cost to properly treat and incinerate the hazardous wastes in the first place.

But landfills are today's reality, and while significant cost increases are beginning to close the economic gap that has historically favored landfilling as a primary method of waste management, the lower initial costs are expected to continue to provide in the near future a somewhat attractive alternative to other treatment and disposal techniques. In dealing with that reality, federal and state governments have moved to bring landfilling of hazardous wastes under strict regulation. It is hoped that such regulation will bring to an end the abuses of the environment and the threat to human health posed by landfilling in the past; moreover, it is hoped that such regulation will circumvent the use of sanitary municipal landfills as a depot for hazardous wastes whenever relatively small, unnoticeable quantities of such waste can be incorporated into that disposal network.

A hazardous waste landfill that follows today's restrictive regulations is a highly engineered TSD facility that has been carefully planned and constructed so as to ensure efficient, long-term operation. The landfilling process is based on the efficient use of space. Solid wastes are typically disposed of by spreading layers of the wastes across one unit of the landfill site and then compacting those layers to reduce their volume. The layers are covered with soil each day so as to minimize human health and environmental problems. Drums or other containers of hazardous wastes are typically disposed of in a similar manner, by layering the containers and covering them with soil or other material.

Optimal use of the landfill capacity is necessary in order to ensure the long-term operational life of the TSD facility. Proper management of space may result in an extension of landfill life; on the other hand, improper utilization can reduce the life of the landfill and adversely affect the long-term economics of the project.

Landfilling includes many factors that must be considered in the overall cost of disposal of hazardous waste:

Capital investment costs in the planning, design, and construction stages
Operational and maintenance costs during active service life
Closure costs at the end of the active service life
Maintenance and security costs for the postclosure period
Long-term liability costs, which may occur at any time

In order to obtain a true picture of disposal costs for landfilling hazardous wastes, an accounting must be made for all of the above factors. These individual cost segments should be analyzed through appropriate risk and probability assessment and should then be discounted over the life of the project to obtain a true overall cost for the disposal of hazardous wastes. Even the most sophisticated, properly constructed and operated landfill will eventually leak, to the detriment of human health and the environment. As a result, it is difficult to envision an economic situation that would favor landfill for long-term disposal of hazardous wastes that could otherwise be destroyed. Clearly, landfill technology should be applicable only for disposal of residual wastes that have no alternative treatment or incineration potential.

DEVELOPING A NEW FACILITY

A new landfill project will have several phases over its lifetime that must be considered at the outset:

- Selection of the site
- Development of an engineering plan and design
- Construction of the facility
- Operation of the facility throughout its active life
- Closure of the facility
- Postclosure monitoring and security

Public participation and comment is both desirable and necessary in developing each of these phases in order to assess local viewpoints and to ensure compliance with the regulation and permit process. Effective communication between all concerned parties—including the TSD facility owner, industry, government, and the general public—is necessary from the very beginning. The burden of open communication rests mainly with the owner of the TSD facility, who must establish a high level of confidence in the performance of the facility in order to overcome any inherent distrust on the part of the public.

Siting a Landfill

Since siting a hazardous waste landfill anywhere in the United States will provoke a great deal of controversy, the long-term goals of any new landfill project must address the needs of the local population and ensure protection of human health and the environment. Many years ago, siting a landfill was predominantly a project requiring geological and engineering expertise, with a relatively minor amount of input and discussion from the general public. However, in the present regulatory climate, the needs of the local community or neighboring residents must be satisfied as an integral part of the landfill project.

Under RCRA Subtitle D, solid waste disposal facilities should consider the following factors when setting minimal technical standards to ensure protection of human health and the environment:

- Groundwater
- Floodplains
- Surface water
- Air quality
- Operational safety
- Disease transmission
- Impact on food-chain cropland
- Endangered species

In order to minimize the risk to human health and the environment, landfill criteria must address all of these concerns, and the decision about the siting of any landfill must be based on due consideration of each factor.

Groundwater quality could be adversely impacted by leachate leaking from a hazardous waste landfill; the location and quality of nearby underlying aquifers must be considered in site selection. Hazardous waste landfills must be located outside historic floodplains. Map overlays can be used during the early stages of site selection to eliminate floodplains from consideration.

Other siting concerns should include the proximity of surface waters and potential storm-water runoff problems that may be associated with the landfill site. The site must offer the capability of collecting and controlling all surface water and storm-water runoff so that it will not adversely impact property that is adjacent to the landfill site. A series of dikes, ponds, and other impoundments may be necessary to protect adjacent property.

The air quality in the vicinity of a hazardous waste landfill must be monitored and controlled to ensure compliance with applicable air quality standards and to minimize objectionable odors near the site. Since protection of existing air quality will be a major issue in the site selection process, considerable time and resources should be spent in order to adequately address this issue. Conditions may warrant the installation of a gas recovery system in order to conserve energy and minimize emission odors from the landfill.

Without proper safeguards, the operation of hazardous waste landfills can make for a dangerous work environment. These hazardous materials must be handled and segregated so as to minimize adverse working conditions. While some of these safety measures can be achieved simply by compliance with

OSHA regulations, managerial philosophy in regard to health and safety will impact heavily on the work environment.

Careful identification of incoming hazardous wastes will greatly minimize concerns about disease transmission. Infectious medical and biological wastes must be properly characterized and treated prior to entering the landfill so as to minimize their volume and potential for cross-contamination with other hazardous wastes.

Landfarming is commonly practiced by many industries in the United States. It involves the spreading of hazardous wastes on the land and incorporating these wastes into topsoil where they undergo biological degradation. This biological degradation of hydrocarbon wastes has been used extensively by the petroleum industries. Halogenated hydrocarbons, on the other hand, are more difficult to biodegrade and therefore are potential problems in landfarming operations, as are wastes contaminated by EP toxicity metals, which require more specialized treatment techniques and cannot be landfarmed. Careful management of landfarms, including testing and monitoring, is necessary to ensure that hazardous waste constituents will not be introduced into crops that will enter the human food chain.

The issue of endangered species must be considered in the siting process on a case-by-case basis. Overlays are useful in avoiding a siting adverse to an endangered species.

Besides this concern with RCRA siting criteria, other considerations that should enter into landfill site selection include the topography and hydrogeology of an area. Generally, limestone and crystalline rock are not as desirable as alluvial bedrock or sedimentary formations. The base of the landfill should be well above the saturated zone. Landfill sites ideally should be in climates that have low rainfall and high surface evaporation rates. They should also be located away from water supply wells. The landfill site topography should be selected to prevent standing water from forming on flat land and at the same time prevent erosion and runoff from sites that have excessive sloping. Ideal topography for a site should incorporate slopes of more than 1 percent and less than 10 percent to accomplish these goals. Slope restrictions such as these are necessary to ensure physical integrity at the landfill and at the same time adequately contain the hazardous wastes.

The permeability of the soil at the site will generally be the major factor that will affect the rate of contaminant transport through the soil once the landfill has begun leaking. Soil texture plays an important role in permeability characteristics. Fine-grained soils like clay have a large specific surface area per unit weight, which results in lower leachate penetration. An ideal native soil in the vicinity of the landfill should have a permeability that does not exceed 1×10^{-7} cm/s. This low permeability is based upon existing state regulations for landfill liners for nonhazardous wastes. It should be noted that this permeability goal probably will not be met because most native soils exceed the optimum value.

The pH of the soil is also a consideration for a number of reasons. The solubility of metals is inversely proportional to the soil acidity. Conversely, soils absorb organics in direct proportion to their acidity. Since these characteristics for metals and hydrocarbon confinement tend to offset each other, a soil pH in the range of 7 to 8 is generally recognized to balance reductions in heavy metals while still maintaining the potential of biodegradation of organic constituents in leachate.

Other factors to be considered in site selection include normal prevailing wind direction, proximity of the waste generators, accessibility for both truck and rail transportation, availability of soils for cover material, and size and complexity of the required landfill.

Designing a Landfill

One of the major objectives in designing a landfill should be to reduce environmental and health risks to reasonable levels that will mitigate local, regional, and national concerns. A properly designed and constructed landfill should incorporate proven technology to guard against the release of contaminants into air, surface water, and groundwater, reducing environmental concerns over its entire operating and postclosure life.

One begins with the assumption that it is virtually impossible to design and operate a landfill with absolute assurance that it will never fail. Even the most sophisticated barriers have a finite life expectancy for leak prevention. The forces of nature, which are often unpredictable, may contribute to leaking landfills. Secure postclosure facilities might still be subject to human intrusion, which could ultimately expose the environment to materials that have been landfilled.

Well-engineered landfills do have the potential to delay leaks for a sufficient time to allow the landfill wastes to become less harmful, and in this way they do reduce the risk to both human health and the environment. However, it should be noted that many organic and inorganic hazardous wastes have such a high degree of persistence that landfills can at best merely delay the ultimate risk to human health and the environment.

Proper landfill design can be most effective when it is considered as an integral part of the site selection process. In that way, the potential for future operational problems will be greatly diminished. As has been said, the underlying assumption should be that eventually the landfill will leak, and the design goal should be to mitigate all eventual leachate contamination. By building adequate safeguards into the original site selection process, this goal can be accomplished.

While many geological and engineering problems can be minimized through effective landfill designs, proper planning in the site selection process will greatly reduce the risk that may accompany design problems. Once the site has been selected, the definitive landfill design can proceed. While there are many aspects of landfill design that need to be considered, the major components that must be addressed include the following:

- Type and volume of hazardous and nonhazardous wastes to be landfilled
- Life expectancy of the landfill during its active operating period
- Topography and soil characteristics at the site and in its vicinity
- Climatic conditions throughout the year
- Surface water and groundwater in the vicinity
- Collection and treatment of surface runoff
- Soil cover requirements for individual containment cells
- Anticipated quality and volume of leachate
- Selection of leachate collection and treatment systems
- Monitoring of groundwater and surface water during operation and beyond
- Selection of venting systems for gaseous products
- Selection of flexible membrane liners and other impermeable liners
- Closure and postclosure plans
- Alternative uses during the postclosure period
- Effect on human health and the environment

Both hazardous and nonhazardous wastes that will be landfilled must be identified and quantified by a market survey. This data can then be used in relation to information established in the site selection process—the area's size, climate, geology, topography—to determine the life expectance of the landfill and the need for unique design considerations. Landfill capacity should be based primarily upon the volume of compacted wastes to be handled, the requirements of soil cover, and the ultimate operating life of the TSD facility.

The proper design of a landfill ensures an operation that protects the public from leachate, fires, odors, insects, and rodents. There are numerous technologies and techniques that are available to minimize the risk to the environment and human health. All residues that must be landfilled should be studied in order to optimize the properties of the waste and minimize its ability to migrate should the landfill begin to leak.

From a design and engineering perspective, the hydrogeological characteristics of the site are the first important parameters to be considered. These characteristics include the proximity and quality of the groundwater and its depth flow rates and the withdrawal rates of the nearby users of that resource. Major geological features of the site, including faults, should be identified; these features should be seriously considered in devising plans to reduce the risks of leakage from the landfill. The landfill should also be designed in such a way as to prevent runoff from either storm water or accidental spills.

The site topography, along with surface water and climatic conditions and soil characteristics, must be incorporated into the landfill design. A major concern might be potential contamination of a nearby aquifer should the TSD facility begin to leak. The possibility of leachate from the landfill contaminating an underground aquifer will always exist. Should the leachate escape from the landfill, a contaminated groundwater plume could develop that would adversely affect the health of nearby residents who may be using the local aquifer as a drinking water source. In order to monitor the landfill site for possible leakage, the general site requirements should include observation wells in aquifers and surface monitoring on land and waterways that are in the vicinity of the landfill site. Sufficient monitoring devices up-gradient from the site are necessary to provide baseline data for later comparison with down-gradient monitoring.

The individual containment cells must be properly sized, and appropriate quantities of soil cover must be made available to minimize leachate formation and transport through the landfill.

Wastes which may be either reactive or water soluble will tend to migrate downward through the landfill as leachate. The amount of leachate produced in a landfill is highly dependent on the amount of water that infiltrates through the soil cover and the hazardous waste layers. This quantity of leachate could be further increased if the hazardous wastes have substantial moisture content. The leachate from this water migration will contain a wide variety of chemical and biological constituents. Because of the variety and complexity of hazardous wastes that may be landfilled, it is difficult to predict all of the chemical reaction products that may be produced in a TSD facility. For example, both organics and inorganics may be subject to oxidation, reduction, combination, and decomposition reactions involving landfill constituents. Complicating these reactions is the biological activity occurring on-site that will differ from landfill to landfill. The landfill pH and temperature will be important parameters in determining both the biological and chemical reaction rates; as such they can help determine both the rate of production and the complexity of the hazardous leachate produced. The use of sorbents, cement, and other types of fixation materials should minimize the release of hazardous material from landfills.

In order to protect against leakage from the landfill, any leachate must be collected and treated so as to render it environmentally safe. Proper design of the leachate collection system is necessary to ensure that it can handle the anticipated volumetric flow of contaminated liquids. The surface runoff, which would be primarily from rainfall, must also be collected. The treatment of all surface runoff and underground leachate must then be designed so as to permit their discharge in an environmentally acceptable manner.

Based upon the present state of technology, a well-designed landfill for hazardous wastes, as shown in Figure 11-2, should include a double-liner and drainage system that will handle all types and quantities of leachate that are produced. The selection of membrane and other impermeable liners should be made to ensure uninterrupted long-term landfill operation.

While a wide variety of materials is available for containment in hazardous waste landfill construction, synthetic membranes are generally considered to offer the best long-term containment of leachate. The chemical and physical

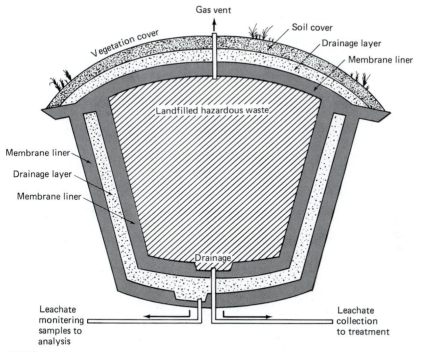

FIGURE 11-2
Secure, double-lined landfill after closure.

properties of these synthetic liners should be weighed carefully in order to ensure both long life and cost-effectiveness of the liner system. Flexible membrane liners are typically polymers or compounds with additives to improve their physical and chemical properties. These properties of liners in landfill service are functions of molecular weight, molecular weight distribution, chemical structure, copolymer or additive enhancement, and the degree of cross-linking.

Physical characteristics should include tensile strength, elongation, tear strength, modulus of elasticity, and hardness. These physical properties may also be indicative of the chemical resistance of the polymer. Environmental-stress crack resistance can be used to measure the long-term resistance of the polymer to the chemical properties of the leachate. Ultraviolet degradation of the landfill liner must be effectively controlled to ensure long life.

There have been numerous studies that have evaluated a wide variety of polymers as flexible membrane liners for landfills. The most widely used membrane liners for landfill applications (see Table 11-1) include polyolefins, chlorinated and chlorosulfonated polyolefins, and compounds based upon polyvinyl chloride. Many of the more recent landfill installations have made use of black polyethylene with high environmental-stress crack resistance. Based

TABLE 11-1
CHARACTERISTICS OF FLEXIBLE MEMBRANE LINERS

Polymer	Range of costs	Advantages	Disadvantages
Butyl rubber	Medium	Low vapor permeability; thermal stability	Swells with hydrocarbons; difficult to install and repair
Chlorinated polyethylene	Medium	Good tensile strength and elongation; resistant to organics	Swells with aromatic hydrocarbons
Chlorosulfonated polyethylene	Medium	Good resistance to acids and alkalis; easy to seam	Poor resistance to oil
Neoprene	High	Resistant to oils, abrasion, and mechanical damage	Difficult to install and repair
Polyvinyl chloride	Low	Good resistance to inorganics; easy to seam	Attacked by organics
Polyethylene	Medium	Good resistance to oils and chemicals; resistant to weathering	Subject to puncture and tear propagation

upon present technology, this type of liner is probably the most cost-effective solution to the selection of flexible membrane liners for landfills that contain hazardous wastes.

Under RCRA Subtitle C, landfills must be underlain with two liners that will prevent the leakage of liquids within the space between the liners themselves. In other words, these liners must have physical strength in order to resist failure from pressure gradients and chemical resistance to leachate exposure as well as to withstand a broad range of ambient conditions. Additionally, stresses generally associated with liner installation and subsequent daily operations must be managed. The base for the liner must be designed to prevent failure from forces caused by ground settlement or uplift. Liner selection, based upon options outlined in Table 11-1, must consider the service life desired, compatibility tests with leachate and other products, the site conditions, the operating temperatures throughout the year, and those regulatory requirements that affect landfills. Clay is commonly used as a subbase for flexible membrane liners. The clay must be covered with a porous material like sand to allow leachate to flow into the collection system. While soil liners are generally unacceptable as a primary liner for hazardous waste landfills, they can provide a desirable backup defense for preventing leachate migration. A leak detection system placed between the double liners will alert the landfill operator to potential problems and allow their mitigation.

A leachate collection and removal system must be installed above the top liner. A riser pipe extending from the sump to the ground surface facilitates the removal of leachate. This riser pipe allows the leachate to be pumped to the surface for subsequent treatment and disposal. The leachate collection system must remain operational during the entire 30-year postclosure period. The material of construction for the leachate collection and monitoring system must also have high chemical resistance to the anticipated constituents in the leachate.

Groundwater and surface water must be accurately monitored to provide early warning systems for developing problems. While much of this is covered by federal and state regulations, the monitoring should be planned and implemented to effectively reduce concerns of local residents. The groundwater monitoring system should consist of piezometers that have been strategically located in and around the landfill site, carefully selected to minimize the effect of geological faults and other stratigraphic abnormalities and to provide both up-gradient and down-gradient information. The up-gradient monitoring furnishes baseline contamination levels from sources other than the landfill site. The down-gradient monitoring then gives information to be compared with the up-gradient background data, yielding an accurate assessment of possible groundwater contamination from the landfill. This monitoring will be necessary in both the operational and postclosure periods of the landfill.

The final cover for the landfill must minimize infiltration of surface water, prevent runoff contamination, and generally maintain the integrity of the hazardous waste landfill over the entire postclosure period. The use of an impermeable liner followed by a drainage layer and soil cover that can be properly vegetated is recommended for the landfill closure. The configuration shown in Figure 11-2 utilizes the same flexible membrane liner material that was originally chosen for the landfill during its active operational period to ensure the compatibility of the liners. Typically, flexible membrane liners are 20 to 100 mils thick. Preliminary laboratory testing is recommended to determine the most cost-effective membrane liner thickness. Usually sand or other porous material is used between the flexible membrane liner and the soil cover. This middle layer transports rainfall that has penetrated the ground cover for treatment prior to discharge. The top layer should be quality soil that is at least comparable to the topsoils in the vicinity of the landfill site. This top layer must be at least 2 feet thick and capable of supporting vegetation that will help prevent erosion of the soil cover. The erosion rate of the top soil must not exceed 2 tons per acre per year. This final landfill cover should have perimeter slopes with surface drainage control of runoff so as not to damage vegetation in the vicinity of the site.

Such closure and postclosure operating plans must be incorporated in the original landfill design. Proper planning greatly reduces the possibility of later adverse environmental problems. The goal should be to provide a site during the postclosure period that is environmentally acceptable to the local community. Care must be taken so as to avoid disastrous postclosure situations such as that at Love Canal.

OPERATING A LANDFILL

The appearance of the landfill to both area residents and visitors can be enhanced by good housekeeping practices and proper landscaping. Highways leading into the landfill should be well maintained during all climatic conditions. As wastes are disposed of in a landfill, they should be covered and compacted by equipment; potential odors should be reduced by application of sufficient soil cover that has been adequately compacted on the disposed wastes. This daily cover will allow the formation of units that will reduce the potential for fires throughout the landfill.

Efficiently and effectively operated and carefully monitored through a postclosure period, landfills can safely continue to fill this country's vast need for disposal of the end products of our cradle-to-grave waste management system.

The following case study explores the heap-leaching process used in gold mining. It demonstrates the effective use of landfilling in mining operations that use a hazardous chemical technology and require complex liner systems to protect the environment. It is adapted from a study by the U.S. Environmental Protection Agency.[8,11]

CASE STUDY
Heap Leaching of Gold

Since the surge in precious metal prices in the 1970s, gold has been an attractive investment in the domestic metal mining industry. Because of the low capital investment and fast payout, the production of gold by heap leaching is widely used. This method permits operators to process relatively low-grade ores, waste rock, and discard tailings from previous mining activities. Currently, the United States has about 80 active heap-leach operations, most of which are located in Nevada. The others are scattered throughout California, New Mexico, Colorado, South Dakota, Idaho, and Montana.

Comparison of Processes

The percolation and leaching with cyanide of relatively coarse, low-grade gold ore piled on an impervious surface was first suggested in 1969. This heap-leaching method has since proved itself in the processing of ores containing free, disseminated, submicrometer particles of gold in porous host rock. Heap-leaching facilities have been developed that range in size from small, intermittent and batch operations to large, well-capitalized facilities capable of the continuous processing of up to 20,000 tons of ore per day. In 1984, 524,553 troy ounces of gold was recovered from 19,857,613 tons of ore treated by cyanide heap leaching (see Table 11-2). By comparison, 1,136,504 troy ounces of gold was recovered from conventional cyanidation extraction in vats, tanks, and closed containers. The estimated average ore grades recovered, based on these figures, are 0.03 ounce of gold per ton of ore by heap leaching and 0.09 ounce of gold per ton of ore by conventional cyanidation.

The low capital investment and operating costs of heap leaching have made it an increasingly attractive method for recovery of gold. The capital costs of heap leaching are 20 to 36 percent of those required for conventional cyanidation, and operating costs are 40 to 55 percent of the conventional process. Average production costs are about $290 per ounce, and many operations are below $200 per ounce. Heap-leaching facilities also entail a shorter startup period, and the process can be applied on a small scale. The efficiency of heap leaching, however, is less than that of conventional cyanidation, which uses an agitated leach. The conventional process achieves about 90 percent recovery, while heap-leaching recoveries range from 50 to 85 percent.

The Chemistry of Heap Leaching

The heap-leaching process, shown in Figure 11-3, sprays an alkaline cyanide solution over ore that has been stacked on a sloped, impermeable pad. Gold is dissolved in the solution and flows off the pad to a lined impoundment. The pregnant solution is pumped from the impoundment to a recovery process, where the gold is removed. The barren solution with makeup sodium cyanide and lime is returned to the ore to complete a closed loop. After the leaching is completed, the residue is rinsed with fresh water, drained, and either left on the pad or hauled to a disposal site.

Cyanide is the only commercially proven lixiviant used in heap leaching. The cyanidation reaction proceeds in two stages, with most of the gold being dissolved by the first reaction:

$$2Au + 4CN^- + O_2 + 2H_2O \rightarrow 2Au(CN)_2^- + H_2O_2 + 2OH^-$$

TABLE 11-2
DOMESTIC GOLD PRODUCTION FROM CYANIDE PROCESSING

| | Extraction in tanks | | Heap leaching | |
Year	Ore treated, short tons	Gold recovered, troy ounces	Ore treated, short tons	Gold recovered, troy ounces
1980	7,869,153	483,113	3,910,427	120,142
1981	7,023,836	648,334	8,875,392	264,408
1982	7,616,036	710,688	12,294,232	391,033
1983	11,317,285	1,086,205	16,178,533	499,403
1984	12,063,871	1,136,504	19,857,613	524,553

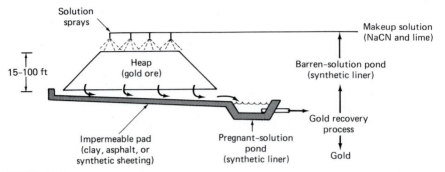

FIGURE 11-3
Conceptual flow diagram of a gold heap-leach operation.

Additional gold is then dissolved by a second reaction:

$$4Au + 8CN^- + O_2 + 2H_2O \rightarrow 4Au(CN)_2^- + 4OH^-$$

The rate of the cyanidation reactions depends on the concentration of cyanide and the alkalinity of the solution. The optimum pH is 10.3.

Sodium cyanide (NaCN) is used as the source of cyanide by all heap-leach operations. Lime (CaO) or caustic (NaOH) is used to maintain the alkalinity of the leach solution in a pH range of 9 to 11. The presence of cyanides in the ore will require greater quantities of cyanide to be added to the leaching solution. Cyanicides include realgar (As_2S_2), orpiment (As_2S_3), and stibnite (Sb_2S_3), which react rapidly with cyanide and inhibit dissolution of gold; carbonaceous materials that absorb dissolved gold; metal ions, such as Fe^{2+}, Fe^{3+}, Ni^{2+}, Cu^{2+}, Zn^{2+}, and Mn^{2+}, which retard cyanidation; acids that hydrolyze cyanide; and organics that consume the dissolved oxygen necessary for the reaction. The caustic or lime required is also determined by ore mineralogy. If acid-forming constituents are present, more caustic or lime will be required to maintain the high pH for the cyanidation reaction.

Precious metal recovery usually is accomplished by either carbon adsorption or precipitation. Typically, the dissolved gold is recovered from the pregnant solution on-site.

Design and Operation of a Heap Leaching Facility

Heap-leach operations are typically zero-discharge facilities. The heap-leach operation as shown in Figure 11-4, begins with the ore being stacked in engineered heaps on sloped, impermeable pads. A weak alkaline cyanide solution is then sprayed over the ore. The solution percolates through the heap and dissolves the gold, then flows over the pad to a lined collection ditch. The ditch carries the gold-bearing cyanide solution to a lined pregnant-solution pond. Next the pregnant solution is pumped to a recovery plant, where the gold is removed by carbon adsorption, followed by stripping and electrowinning or by precipitation with zinc followed by filtration. The barren solution is then pumped to a lined holding pond with additional NaCN and lime. From the barren pond, the solution is recycled to the heap.

The heap must be built with ore that is uniformly permeable and yet able to maintain its structural stability when it has been wetted. Old tailings with poor permeability or poor structural strength because of the presence of clays can be heap-leached following agglomeration. The agglomeration process involves crushing ore particles to a −1-inch or finer size, treating the ore with 5 to 10 pounds of portland cement per ton of ore, wetting it with water or a strong cyanide solution to achieve 8 to 16 percent moisture, and then mechanically tumbling and curing the mixture. Agglomeration causes the clay and fine particles to adhere to coarser particles present in the ore, and this prevents these fines from segregating in the heap and causing impermeable zones and solution channeling. If cyanide is used during agglomeration, the leaching process is initiated before the ore is stacked on the pad; this method may reduce leach cycle time and increase metal recovery. The cement added during agglomeration also aids in maintaining the alkaline pH necessary for cyanide leaching.

The leach pad is sloped so that pregnant solution is directed to a lined col-

FIGURE 11-4
Flow diagram of a heap-leach operation.

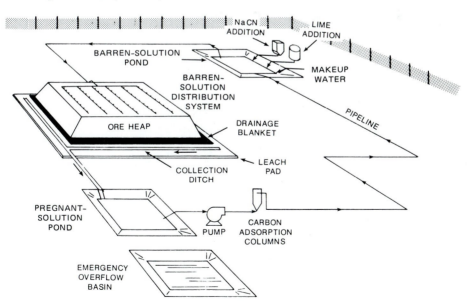

lection ditch situated along the one or two downgrade sides of the pad. Pads are constructed with asphalt or polyethylene liners over clays, as shown in Figure 11-5.

The pads must be nearly impermeable at 1×10^{-7} cm/s or less. They must also be capable of providing structural support for the heap without suffering damage from deflection because of the weight of the ore or equipment traffic.

Pad construction involves clearing the area, grading and compacting the subbase, installing the liner, and placing a layer of gravel or ore over the liner to provide both drainage and protection. Smaller pads cover less than an acre, whereas the largest individual pads cover up to 50 acres.

The barren solution is piped to the heap by plastic pipe, then sprayed over the surface through sprinkler heads, which distribute the solution to minimize evaporation. The sprinklers are usually placed on 40-foot centers over the top of the heap. The application rate is 0.005 gal/(min)(ft²). This operation is mon-

FIGURE 11-5
Typical construction of heap-leach pads.

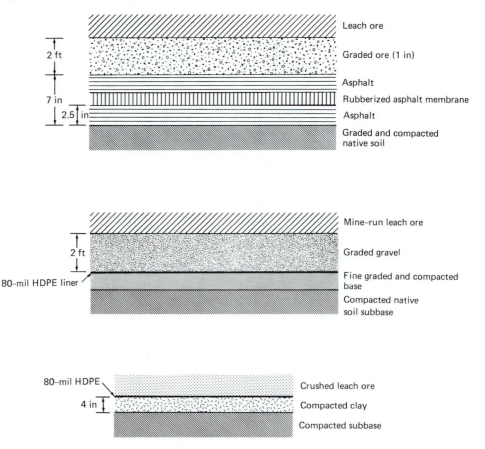

itored to ensure that the sprinklers are functioning, that they do not become stuck in one position, and that no ponding of solution occurs on the surface, which would indicate that the application rate was too high or that a zone of low permeability existed.

Moisture content in run-of-mine ore is typically 5 to 10 percent by weight. The solution applied to a fresh heap percolates through the ore, flowing over ore particles and into cracks and crevices by capillary action. Sufficient solution must be applied to saturate the heap and overcome its storage capacity before any solution will drain from the heap. The moisture content is typically in the range of 10 to 15 percent by weight at saturation.

One operation may be used by way of example: one facility held 20-foot-high heaps that contained about 90,000 tons of mine-run ore. Initial break-through of solution occurred about 18 hours after solution application began at 0.005 gal/(min)(ft^2), and a steady-state flow was achieved after about 72 hours). Two hundred fifty thousand gallons were required to saturate the heap. When heaps were idled over winter and releached in the spring, the same storage capacity was noted.

The volume of pregnant solution leaving the heap under steady-state leaching conditions is a function of the area of the top of the heap, the solution application rate, and the evaporation rate. A small heap having 40,000 square feet of the surface area, for example, could generate a maximum of 200 gal/min while a 50-acre heap could achieve a flow of 4000 gal/min under steady-state conditions. The pH of the pregnant solution is usually lower than that of the barren spray because of the neutralization that occurs in the heap. However, for agglomerated ore, the pH of the pregnant solution may be the same as or higher than that of the barren spray because of the cement used as a binder.

The free-cyanide content is lower in the pregnant solution because some cyanide volatilizes at the surface of the heap. Cyanide at 1 pound per ton of solution percolating through the heap is also tied up in metal complexes, destroyed by cyanicides present in the ore, bound by carbon present in the ore, or otherwise consumed. The amount of cyanide added should equal its consumption in the heap. Consumption varies from 0.1 to 0.3 pound of NaCN per ton of ore, while lime addition to the barren liquid is typically at a rate of 0.03 pound per ton of ore.

The dimensions of the pregnant-solution pond are a function of the size of the heap and the climate. These ponds are typically 10 to 20 feet deep and have steep slopes. An emergency overflow basin is usually situated immediately downgrade from the pregnant-solution pond to provide emergency containment of any overtopping of the pond.

The pregnant solution is pumped to the gold recovery process, and the barren solution is then sent to a pond, which may be about half the size of the pregnant-solution pond and have a total residence time of 3 days or more. The barren-solution pond is also constructed with synthetic liners placed over compacted earth. The barren solution is treated with cyanide and lime before being pumped back to the heap.

Solution application often must be curtailed or halted during the winter in northern climates because of ice formation. Heating the barren solution to allow leaching to continue during mild winter conditions can extend the leaching season.

Precious metals in the pregnant solution are recovered either by adsorption on activated carbon or by zinc-dust precipitation.

The carbon adsorption process involves three unit operations:

Absorption of gold from the pregnant solution onto activated carbon in a series of countercurrent tanks

Elution of gold with a hot caustic cyanide solution, then regeneration of the stripped carbon by steam or thermal reactivation

Recovery of gold from the concentrated cyanide solution by electrowinning, followed by refining to produce bullion

The zinc-dust precipitation process involves four major process steps:

Clarification of the pregnant solution to achieve efficient precipitation
Vacuum deaeration to remove dissolved oxygen and carbon dioxide
Addition of powdered zinc to precipitate the gold
Filtration of the precipitates and return of the barren solution to the heap

Assuming a 1-ppm gold content in the pregnant solution, the carbon absorption method produces an ounce of gold at a cost of about $7.50. The zinc-dust precipitation method has production costs in the same general range as carbon absorption.

The Valley Leach Process

The valley leach method, shown in Figure 11-6, is used in steep terrain where normal heaps cannot be constructed. The major difference between the two methods is that a pregnant-solution pond is not constructed in the valley leach system. Instead, a containment dike is built by using compacted waste rock at the downhill limit of the heap and a liner is then placed over the upstream face of the dike and the pad area above it. The heap is built behind this dike. The

FIGURE 11-6
Typical cross section of a valley leach heap.

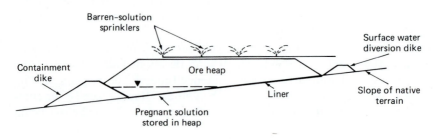

pregnant solution is stored internally in the heap and contained by the dike and liner; it is removed through pipes passed through the containment dike. A valley leach system requires a durable ore for stability and a high-integrity liner because of the hydraulic head from the pregnant solution.

Residue Disposal and Site Closure

The heap-leach residue, the barren ore remaining, is either left on the pad or hauled away. At closure, the residue can range from 1 to 50 acres in surface area and can be 16 to 200 feet in height.

Standard industry practice has been to allow the residue to drain for 1 or more days, during which time no solution is applied. The heap is then rinsed with fresh water for several days. Nevada requires rinsing the residue heap until the pH reaches 8 or lower and cyanide content of 0.2 ppm or less has been achieved in the rinse water. The barren solution remaining is allowed to evaporate to dryness or is treated with cyanicide. No discharge is permitted.

Leach residue on pads is disposed of by loading it into trucks and hauling it, presumably over a short distance, to a dump area. The residue is dumped on top of the disposal pile, cascading over the outer face of the pile and spreading out in a thin layer that dries rapidly. Free cyanide left in the residue volatilizes and escapes to the atmosphere or is destroyed by ultraviolet radiation.

At closure, any solution remaining in the pregnant and barren ponds will be evaporated to dryness. Collection ditch liners and other exposed liner material around the heap will be removed and placed in the empty impoundment. The impoundment liner will then be folded over on itself and buried in place.

The application of a clay or synthetic cap over a waste disposal unit is required in the closure of any hazardous waste facility. The purpose of this cap is to prohibit infiltration of rainfall or surface-water run-on and thereby to preclude formation of leachate. During the postclosure period of a heap-leaching operation, only the leach residue remains as a potential source of cyanide contamination through leachate generation. Capping the residue pile reduces this potential. But although capping can reduce the potential for leachate formation by limiting infiltration, it also reduces the rate of natural degradation of cyanide left in the heap-leach residue. Because the cap limits natural aeration of the heap, it reduces volatilization of any free cyanides present. It also prevents photodecomposition due to ultraviolet radiation.

Capping of leach heaps can also be an expensive proposition. Heaps are constructed with steep (1 to 1) side slopes, which are usually dictated by the natural angle of repose of the ore. Heaps are stacked as steeply as possible to maximize the use of pad area. Such steep slopes cannot be capped. The slopes have to be reduced to at least 3 to 1 for capping to be possible. The cost of slope modification varies with the original size and height of the heap. For example, regrading a 1-acre heap having 1 to 1 slopes and a height of 15 feet would require movement of 1700 cubic yards of material at a cost of about $2500. After slope modification, the surface area of the heap would be 1.4 acres. Application of a cap consisting of 3 feet of earth would require 6800 cubic yards of cap material. Assuming a suitable source could be found near the site, the cap could cost about $36,000. A large heap covering 50 acres and having a height of 100 feet would require the regrading of 550,000 cubic yards of material. The modified heap would require capping to be placed over 67 acres at a total cost of $1.8 million.

Postclosure Monitoring and Maintenance

Pregnant- and barren-solution ponds are fenced and signs are posted to warn of the presence of cyanide. Because the presence of surface water is a strong attraction to passing animals, especially in arid regions, freshwater ponds are often constructed to provide an attractive alternative drinking water source for animals.

   After the closure of heap-leach operations, the leach residue is the only potential source of cyanide contamination, assuming that the process-solution ponds have been removed as required. Leach sites in typically arid climates have less potential for long-term impacts than leach operations where significant precipitation or surface water flows are present. Monitoring requirements are also less in the dry areas. Monitoring of groundwater wells installed at the time of closure is continued through the postclosure period, typically over a period of 30 years. As an alternative, the monitoring of wells used during the active life of the operation can continue through the postclosure period if such wells are available. In addition to the monitoring of groundwater, maintenance of the monitoring system and of other controls such as caps and fencing is also required. The annual cost of maintaining such systems is usually estimated to be 1 to 5 percent of their capital costs. The cost of monitoring groundwater varies with the number of wells, the required samples, the number of duplicates, and the analytical parameters. During this period, RCRA Subtitle C requires monitoring wells to be sampled semiannually. Quadruplicate samples to be analyzed for groundwater contamination indicators such as total organic carbon, specific conductance, and pH are taken from each well. The cost of this monitoring will vary widely and will depend primarily on the number of wells. For example, the cost to monitor a relatively small site having eight wells around the heap would be about $6400 per year for analytical services, plus the costs of reporting and record keeping.

Cyanide Content of Process Solutions

During the heap-leaching operation, sodium cyanide is typically added to the barren solution to maintain a concentration of about 1 pound of NaCN per ton of solution, or about 200 ppm. The pH is maintained between 9 and 11 in the barren-solution pond by the addition of lime or caustic. The barren-solution pond may hold hundreds of thousands of gallons of this solution. Under these conditions, the cyanide present is mostly free cyanide, as required in the leaching reaction. The pregnant-solution pond contains lesser concentrations of free cyanides because of the destruction and complexation that occur in the heap. However, a significant concentration of free cyanide is still present, and these impoundments represent the greatest source of free cyanide at a leach operation. Failure of the containment system, liner failure, or overtopping of the pond would be disastrous in that free cyanide in an alkaline solution would be released, harming the environment and endangering human health.

Cyanide Content of Leach Residue

Cyanide in leach residue occurs in combinations of various metallic-cyanide complexes and free-cyanide ions. The complexes that are formed in a heap are determined by the mineralogy of the ore and range from complexes that are strongly bound and stable, to those that are moderately bound and likely to dissociate with time, to those that dissociate easily:

Strong metal complexes	Moderately strong metal complexes	Weak metal complexes
$Fe(CN)_6^{4-}$	$Cu(CN)_2^-$	$Zn(CN)_4^{2-}$
$Co(CN)_6^{4-}$	$Cu(CN)_3$	$Cd(CN)_3^-$
$Au(CN)_2^-$	$Ni(CN)_4^{2-}$	$Cd(CN)_4^{2-}$
	$Ag(CN)_2^-$	

As metallic-cyanide complexes dissociate, they form free cyanide. Depending on the pH, the free cyanides may be released to the atmosphere or leached with water. If the pH of the heap leach is less than 9, most of the free cyanide formed will be released to the atmosphere as HCN. If the pH is greater than 9, the free cyanide will remain in solution. Low concentrations of soluble free cyanides are amenable to biodegradation, but high concentrations of free cyanide are not easily biodegraded. This could result in cyanide contamination in runoff or in liquids percolating to groundwater.

During gold heap leaching, an alkaline pH (9 to 11) is maintained, but after completion, the heap leach piles are usually rinsed with fresh water and the pH approaches a more neutral 7 to 9. If the heap is not rinsed or if rinsing is inadequate, the solution remaining in the interior of the heap may retain its alkalinity. Thus, the interior of such heaps may be potential sources of unknown amounts of free cyanide for long periods of time.

Several environmental factors influence the rate of degradation of cyanide in heap leach residue. Intermittent rainfall and higher temperatures will both increase the release of cyanide and degradation within the heap. When leach residue is spoiled off the pad, the amount of aeration and the amount of sunlight reaching the residue increases, both of which enhance degradation. As leach residues are aerated, they become more neutral and less alkaline through absorption of carbon dioxide from the atmosphere.

Toxicity of Cyanide

The toxicity of cyanide varies widely with the form of the cyanide. HCN has been shown to be the most toxic, while many metallic-cyanide complexes are far less toxic. The toxicity of metallic-cyanide complexes in the aquatic environment varies with the stability of the complexes. Those that dissociate readily to release free cyanide, such as zinc and cadmium cyanide complexes, are highly toxic. Others such as copper, nickel, and silver cyanide complexes exhibit moderate dissociation and are less toxic. Iron and cobalt complexes are tightly bound and are considered to be nontoxic.

Cyanide in the form of HCN is a respiratory or cellular asphyxiant that prevents tissues from utilizing oxygen. The central nervous system, which is the tissue most sensitive to oxygen deficiency, can be adversely affected from exposure to HCN.

Cyanide is absorbed by humans through the skin, mucous membranes, and inhalation. Inhalation of cyanide fumes can be rapidly fatal, depending on concentration. Alkali salts are toxic only upon ingestion. The nonvolatile cyanide salts seem to be nontoxic systemically, as long as they are not ingested and the formation of hydrocyanic acid is prevented. Exposure to small amounts of cyanide compounds over long periods of time may cause loss of appetite, headache, weakness, nausea, dizziness, and irritation of the upper respiratory tract and eyes.

Free-cyanide concentrations of 0.05 to 0.10 mg/l can be fatal to many fish, and levels as low as 0.01 mg/l have had adverse effects on some fish species. EPA has established an ambient concentration of 0.005 mg/l as the criterion level to protect freshwater and marine aquatic life and wildlife.

Cyanide toxicity to aquatic organisms would be due mainly to HCN derived from dissociation, photodecomposition, and hydrolysis of cyanide compounds. Thus, both the free-cyanide concentration, which produces the toxic effects, and the total cyanide concentrations, which have the potential to release free cyanides as HCN through degradation, have been shown to be toxins of concern.

Migration of Cyanide

Cyanide from leach residues can migrate through release to air, groundwater, surface water, and soil. The principal transport process for free cyanide in mining wastes is through volatilization of HCN to the atmosphere. The alkalinity of leach residues is reduced near the surface through absorption of carbon dioxide, which decreases the pH of the residue and increases the volatilization of cyanide in the form of HCN.

The secondary transport process for free cyanide and soluble metallic-cyanide complexes is leaching. Zinc and cadmium cyanide complexes are more soluble than other metallic cyanide complexes. In areas of a heap where the pH remains above 9, free cyanide remains in solution and can be transported to surface water and groundwater through rainwater runoff and percolation. Instances of fish, deer, and bird kills have occurred after rainstorms, floods, or other surface water releases from leach residues; kills have also resulted when wildlife gain access to the surface impoundments.

Free cyanides have the potential to migrate through saturated and unsaturated soils, but transport may be limited by complexing between the soils and the cyanide compounds. Transport may also be affected by sorption onto clays or organics in the soil. Low levels of cyanides can be degraded by microbes. Transport of cyanides can occur in sandy soils or soils low in organic content. Migration is limited in soils heavy with hydrous metal oxides and in soils with a high clay or a high organic content.

Cyanide Destruction

During the closure and postclosure periods, the heap-leach residue is the only potential source of cyanide contamination. Process solutions in the barren- and pregnant-solution ponds would have been evaporated to dryness or treated to destroy cyanide and then released. The current practice at most sites is to rinse the heap-leach residue with fresh water. The rinse may continue until a cyanide concentration of 0.2 mg/l or a pH of ≤ 8 has been achieved for the leachate. The time to complete this rinsing operation rarely exceeds a week.

A treatment option could use an oxidizing cyanicide with the rinse solution at the time of closure. The addition of a cyanicide would help to reduce cyanide left in the leach residue that could escape to the environment. A variety of processes have been demonstrated to be effective in destroying cyanide or in removing it from the solution. These treatments include natural degradation, evaporation, alkaline chlorination, oxidation with hydrogen peroxide, and adsorption on ferrous sulfide. The first three are the cyanide reduction and destruction processes associated with heap-leach residue.

The form of the cyanide present in heap-leach residue depends on the mineralogy of the ore. The most likely types of cyanide species to be present are listed, in the order of increasing stability, in Table 11-3. The stability of the species is important in determining an effective treatment and the quantity of reagent required.

Natural degradation and evaporation are the most common methods of destroying any cyanide left in the residue following the water rinse. When exposed to air, HCN vaporizes from cyanide solutions, especially if the pH is below 10.5. The effectiveness of natural degradation depends on the species of cyanide present, pH, temperature, bacterial metabolism, photodegradation, and aeration. If sufficient time is allowed, natural processes will return heap-leach material to acceptable conditions. Because most heap-leach operations

TABLE 11-3
CYANIDE COMPLEXES LIKELY TO BE PRESENT IN HEAP-LEACH RESIDUE

Term	Form of cyanide
1. Free cyanide	CN^-, HCN
2. Simple compounds	
Readily soluble	NaCN, KCN, $Ca(CN)_2$, $Hg(CN)_2$
Relatively insoluble	$Zn(CN)_2$, $Cd(CN)_2$, CuCN, $Ni(CN)_2$, AgCN
3. Weak complexes	$Zn(CN)_4$, $Cd(CN)_3$, $Cd(CN)_4$
4. Moderately strong complexes	$Cu(CN)_2$, $Cu(CN)_3$, $Ni(CN)_4$, $Ag(CN)_2$
5. Strong complexes	$Fe(CN)_6$, $Co(CN)_6$

are located in arid regions, evaporation plays a major role both in removing solution from the heap and in determining if any leachate will be formed.

The alkaline chlorination process for cyanide destruction is a proven technology. This process destroys all cyanide except iron cyanide and the more stable metallic-cyanide complexes. Chlorine, calcium hypochlorite, and caustic can be used in solution to treat heap-leach residue. The oxidation of cyanide by calcium hypochlorite occurs in two stages:

$$2NaCN + Ca(OCl)_2 + 2H_2O \rightarrow 2CNCl + Ca(OH)_2 + 2NaOH$$

$$CNCl + 2NaOH \rightarrow NaCNO + NaCl + H_2O$$

As an example, in one facility 84,000 tons of agglomerated tailings were heap-leached in 15-foot stacks. During the 6 months of operation, about 105,000 pounds of NaCN was applied to the heaps. About 70 percent of the NaCN applied was consumed during leaching by the cyanicides in the ore. Most of the cyanide remaining was removed by the freshwater rinse during the postclosure operations. About 12,000 pounds of NaCN remained in the entrained solution in the leached tailings. Almost all of the cyanide was present as free cyanide. Over the course of the 15-month study, the moisture content in the heap decreased from 14.4 to 13.1 percent. The water-soluble residual cyanide content decreased from 0.58 to 0.11 g/l. The decrease in cyanide was due to natural degradation, as no treatments were applied during this period.

Tests indicated that treating the leach residue with 0.5 gram of calcium hypochlorite solution per liter immediately after leaching was effective in destroying the cyanide left in the heap. Consumption of the hypochlorite was 0.6 pound per ton of leach residue. This treatment was reported to be quick and effective but was expensive in terms of reagents and personnel needed.

Another example for hypochlorite treatment of heap-leach residue involved a hypochlorite solution that was flushed through heap-leach residue, as fresh water recirculated through the system. In 1 month, the cyanide concentration in the solution decreased from 300 to 3.4 ppm. A year later, the cyanide content ranged from 0.2 to 0.01 ppm.

A third example involved operation of a heap-leach facility that incorporated post-leach cyanide destruction using hypochlorite. The operating permit required cyanide destruction and a 24-hour-average free-cyanide concentration not exceeding 0.2 mg/l in the rinse solution leaving the heap; no single sample was to exceed 1.0 mg/l. To meet this limit, the leach residue was treated with an alkaline chlorine solution that was prepared on-site. The process heaps were leached with alkaline cyanide solution for 20 days and then treated for cyanide destruction for 6 days before being off-loaded to a spoil disposal area on site. Chlorine was consumed at the rate of 4000 lb/day, with 1000 ppm free-chlorine concentration; 8000 pounds of lime per day was required to maintain the high pH that was necessary. After treatment with chlorine, the leach residue was excavated and hauled to the disposal site, where it was spread in 1- to 2-foot layers. This allowed further oxidation and volatilization of any remaining cyanide and chlorine.

An evaluation was made of the cost of installing and operating an alkaline chlorination system for cyanide destruction during the postleaching rinse. The cost of this system, estimated for a range of processing rates, is shown in Figure 11-7. The system could produce 200 to 350 gal/min of alkaline chlorine solution, a volume sufficient for application over 0.9 acre to 1.6 acres at a rate of 0.005 gal/(min)(ft^2). Heaps with much larger surface areas and solution flow rates are common. To treat a large 20-acre heap would require that the capacity of the alkaline chlorination system be increased by a factor of 20 to allow

FIGURE 11-7
Capital and annualized costs of a cyanide neutralization system at a gold heap-leaching facility.

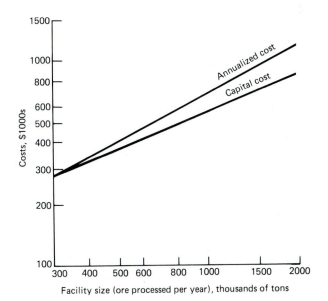

for treatment of the entire heap at one time. As an alternative, a smaller system could be used to apply the treatment solution at a slower rate for a longer period of time, or at the same rate in sequential applications over small portions of the heap.

In case of multiple-use pads, the system would be in constant use over the life of the operation. At sites with single-use pads, however, such a system may be applicable only at closure. In addition, at operations having single-use pads, the leach residue would not be excavated and spread out so that additional oxidation of cyanide and chlorine could take place. If cyanide destruction occurs only at closure, the existing process solution ponds, distribution system, and lime-addition facilities could be used. In this case, only the capability of adding chlorine would have to be provided.

All of the essential elements of the solution-handling system necessary to effect cyanide destruction by alkaline chlorination of heap-leach residue during closure are already present at each operation. Solution storage reservoirs, pumps, distribution pipes, and lime-addition equipment used during leaching operations could also be used during alkaline chlorination. Calcium hypochlorite would replace cyanide in the flow scheme. Thus, the cost of this treatment represents only the cost of the reagents and the personnel to operate the system.

Waste Management Alternatives

A number of waste management alternatives can be applied to minimize the potential for cyanide contamination from heap-leach operations. These include alternative liner construction, oxidation of cyanide during post-leaching flushout, and use of reagents other than cyanide. Most heap-leach operations are relatively small, and the only sources of potential contamination are the heaps and the two solution ponds. After cessation of operations, only the heaps remain as potential contamination sources since the process ponds must be emptied during closure.

The EPA policy regarding active heap-leach piles and leaching liquors has been that these materials do not represent wastes but rather are raw materials used in production. Only the leach liquor that escapes from the production process and abandoned heap-leach piles is considered waste material. This EPA regulatory position has influenced alternative management practices.

The applicability of an alternative management practice is determined primarily by the four phases during the life of the heap-leach site:

Preoperations phase, which includes site characterization, engineering design, and establishment of operational parameters—all to satisfy permit requirements—and construction of the facility

Operations phase, which covers the leaching cycle for gold extraction, varying from several months to many years.

Closure, which covers the period immediately following cessation of leach-ing, when the site is brought to a stabilized condition that is to be maintained throughout the postclosure period

Postclosure, which is the period following site closure, during which time the site must be monitored and maintained, usually for 30 years under RCRA

Improved management practices can be employed in each of these phases to prevent or mitigate seepage from the heaps, leach residue, and solution ponds:

Phase	Management practice
Design	Installation of a system of French drains beneath the pad and solution-pond liner to allow leakage detection; construction of pregnant- and barren-solution ponds with RCRA double-liner system
Operations	Use of alternative lixiviants like thiourea to eliminate potential for cyanide con-tamination; installation of groundwater monitoring wells
Closure	Flushing of heap with hypochlorite solutions to destroy residual cyanide; recontouring of the heap and installation of an impermeable cap
Postclosure	Long-term maintenance of heaps; monitoring of groundwater and surface water; maintenance of site security

French Drains under Leach Pads In the design and construction of the leach pads, one alternative management process could involve installation of a system of French drains beneath the leach pad. Pads are currently constructed of compacted clays, asphalt, and synthetic liners. Placement of a drainage sys-tem with leachate detection and collection capabilities between the subbase of native soils and the leach pad would allow determination if the integrity of the pad has been breached.

The drain systems beneath the leach pads, as shown in Figure 11-8, would be individually monitored to determine leakage. A layer consisting of about 12 inches of free-draining gravel would be placed between the clay leach pad and the compacted subbase. This drainage layer would have a 5 to 6 percent grade. Slotted, 2-inch, Schedule 40 PVC pipe would be installed in the gravel along the two downgrade sides of the pad. Seepage through the pad would flow pref-erentially through the gravel along the surface of the compacted native soil subbase to the slotted collection pipes and then to a collection sump accessed by a manhole. The sump would be periodically checked for the presence of seepage. If any seepage was found, it could be pumped from the sump to the pregnant collection pond. If leakage was severe, the pad could be taken out of service.

The use of French drains would allow immediate detection of leakage through the pad. Such a system could be placed beneath liners constructed of clay, asphalt, or synthetic materials. The drain system would have to be con-structed so that it could support the weight of the heap without failing and so that it would not compromise the integrity of the leach pad as a result of de-flection or settlement of the drain blanket during the loading of the pad with

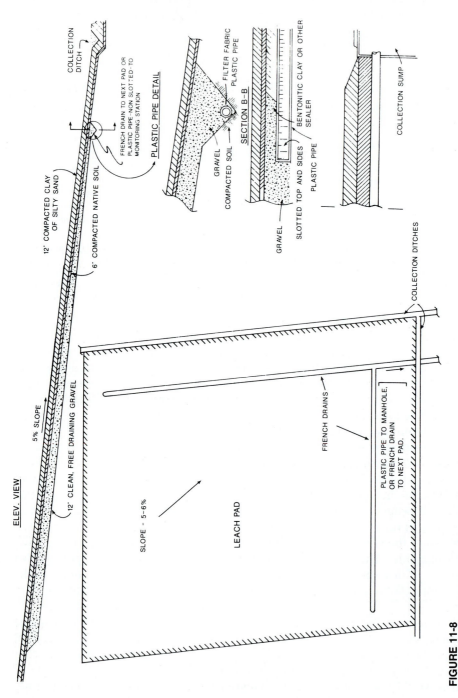

FIGURE 11-8
Design of French drains under a heap-leach pad.

ore. Such a system could only be placed during the construction of the pad; it could not be retrofitted to heaps during the operational phase.

Table 11-4, a comparison of estimated costs, shows that a French drain system about doubles the cost of the design without French drains.

Double Liners for Process-Solution Ponds The standard practice in the heap-leach industry has been the use of a single synthetic liner (see Figure 11-9) in the pregnant- and barren-solution ponds. Some operations have constructed process ponds with double liners and leak detection. Because release of leach solutions represents a loss of valuable product to the operator, the goal of no release is as important from a production as from an environmental viewpoint. Most incidents of cyanide release at heap-leach operations have involved failure of the solution-process pond. It follows that a double-liner system with leachate detection and collection for process-solution ponds should be a desirable safeguard.

Table 11-5 presents an economic comparison of the single-liner system with the double-liner system illustrated in Figure 11-10. The double liner estimates assume two layers of 40-mil high-density polyethylene separated by a leachate detection and collection system, with a drainage blanket placed between the liners. This leachate detection and collection system, installed in the bottom of

TABLE 11-4
CONSTRUCTION COST COMPARISON FOR A FRENCH DRAIN SYSTEM WITH A HEAP-LEACH PAD*

		French drain system	
Construction item	Unit cost, $/unit	Not included	Included
Direct costs			
Clear site	$0.29/yd^2$	$ 2,900	$ 2,900
Remove and stockpile 6 in of topsoil	$1.45/yd^3$	2,500	2,500
Remove 12-in layer of soil	$1.45/yd^3$	—	5,000
Purchase and place 12 in of gravel	$16.16/yd^3$	—	53,900
Install drain pipe	1.72/ft	—	930
Install 18-in sump	23.05/ft	—	50
Level base	$0.44/yd^2$	4,400	4,400
Compact base		410	410
Haul clay for 6-in lift	$7.81/yd^3$	13,300	13,300
Place clay layer	$1.34/yd^3$	2,300	2,300
Add moisture and compact	$1.21/yd^3$	2,060	2,060
Construct 2d and 3d lifts		35,300	35,300
Subtotal direct costs		$63,170	$123,050
Indirect costs†		$20,200	$ 39,400
Total cost		$83,400	$162,000
Pad cost/ft^2		$ 0.93	$ 1.80

*The pad is 300 feet × 300 feet.
†Indirect costs include engineering, design, and contingencies and are assumed to be 32 percent of direct costs.

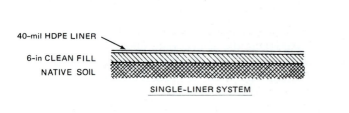

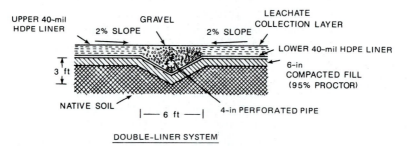

FIGURE 11-9
Cross sections of a single- and double-liner system for a process-solution pond.

TABLE 11-5
COMPARISON OF CONSTRUCTION COSTS OF PROCESS-SOLUTION PONDS WITH
SINGLE AND DOUBLE LINERS

Construction item	Unit cost, $/unit	Liner system	
		Single	Double
Direct costs			
Pond excavation	0.97/yd3	$12,600	$ 12,600
Anchor trench excavation	2.99/yd^3	210	420
Backfill of anchor trench	0.96/yd^3	70	130
Drain excavation	2.99/yd^3	—	240
Placement of 6-in clay bed	1.17/yd^3	1,060	1,080
Primary liner (40-mil HDPE)	0.55/ft^2	28,300	28,600
Secondary liner (40-mil HDPE)	0.55/ft^2	—	29,300
Drainage blanket (HDPE)	0.25/ft^2	—	12,300
2-in Schedule 40 slotted drain	1.72/ft	—	410
Sump and 2-in connector	—	—	460
Gravel backfill for drain	9.31/yd^3	—	480
Subtotal direct costs		$42,200	$ 86,000
Indirect costs*		$13,500	$ 27,500
Total cost		$55,700	$113,500

*Indirect costs include engineering, design, and contingencies and are estimated to be 32 percent of direct costs.

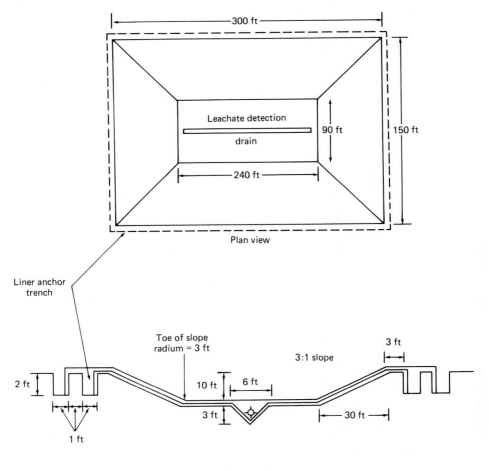

FIGURE 11-10
Design of a process-solution pond using a 40-mil HDPE double-liner system for leak detection.

the pond, consists of perforated pipes in the drainage blanket leading to a sump that can be accessed to determine failure in the upper liner and can be used to remove leachate if failure does occur.

Alternative Lixiviants Cyanide is the only lixiviant currently used at commercial precious metal heap-leach operations. Because of the toxicity associated with cyanide, suitable substitutes for cyanide should be evaluated. The development of alternative lixiviants to replace cyanide in heap-leach operations is still at the laboratory or pilot-scale testing stage. Thiourea has received considerable attention and examination, but its use would require some additional development prior to application on a commercial scale.

Thiourea dissolves in water to yield an aqueous form that is stable in acidic solutions. It reacts with certain transition metal ions to form stable cationic complexes. Extraction of gold by thiourea requires a pH of the leach solution between 0.5 and 2.0, as opposed to the alkaline pH of 9 to 11 that is necessary for cyanide leaching. Experimental results indicate that the leaching ability of thiourea is significantly reduced at a pH above 2.0. Sulfuric or nitric acids can be used to acidify the leach solution.

The thiourea reaction with gold also requires the presence of a condensed-phase oxidant, usually a ferric iron compound. In cyanide leaching, the oxidant is gaseous atmospheric oxygen. A comparison of the dissolution reactions for cyanide and thiourea leaching follow:

$$2Au + 4NaCN + \tfrac{1}{2}O_2 + H_2O \rightarrow 2NA[Au(CN)\,\overline{_2}] + 2NaOH \qquad \text{(cyanide)}$$

$$2Au + 4TU + Fe_2(SO_4)_3 \rightarrow [Au(TU)\,\overset{+}{_2}]_2SO_4 + 2FeSO_4 \qquad \text{(thiourea)}$$

The effectiveness of thiourea leaching is controlled by the amount of thiourea in solution, the leaching time, and the amount of trivalent iron present. One of the main advantages of thiourea is that it can leach gold from ore in a matter of hours instead of the days required for leaching with cyanide. Another advantage is that thiourea does not form complexes with cations present in the ore as readily as does cyanide.

One major problem with thiourea leaching is that the reagent cost is approximately 25 percent more than that of cyanide leaching. Another problem is the amount of reagent consumption through oxidation, which can be excessive if not controlled. Also, the intermediate product of oxidation of thiourea can coat the ore particles and prevent fresh thiourea from reacting with the available gold. The addition of sulfur dioxide gas can control the oxidation intermediates. Thiourea leaching also requires a very acidic environment that may have to be neutralized during closure.

Thiourea can be an alternative commercial lixiviant for precious metals heap leaching if the oxidation is controlled to reduce reagent cost and consumption. Because thiourea leaches gold more rapidly from ore than cyanide, this faster leaching rate can offset the reagent cost differential.

Leachate Detection

Gold heap leaching involves three primary operational units that may have a direct environmental impact on surrounding soils, geology, and groundwater quality: the barren-solution pond, the heap-leaching pad, and the pregnant-solution pond. The primary environmental concerns are the cyanide and the heavy metals associated with the leaching operation.

All heap-leaching operations have common design features, including solution collection systems, synthetic liners in the barren-solution pond, heap-leaching pad liners, and synthetic liners in the pregnant-solution pond. These design features limit solution losses and fluid balances as an integral part of the operation and reduce the potential for soil and groundwater contamination.

The monitoring of soil and groundwater is necessary to detect and assess leachate production resulting from the gold heap operation and to characterize the pathways for contaminant transport. The monitoring system can be used to determine the need for the implementation of corrective actions. A groundwater monitoring program requires a fundamental understanding of the surrounding geology and hydrogeology and the operational characteristics of the gold heap-leaching facility. This understanding can be gained from a study of:

Existing geologic and topographic maps
Historical precipitation records
Surface and groundwater characteristics
Characteristics of the ore
Nature, history, and location of the leaching operation
Location and design of the solution ponds and leach pads

In the establishment of monitoring well locations and screen depths, consideration should be given to identifying background water quality, transport pathways, environmentally sensitive areas, local and regional receptors, and the water-bearing zones. The approximate number and location of monitoring wells will depend on the number, size, and complexity of the gold heap-leaching process units and the characteristics of the surrounding surface and subsurface environments. Gold heap-leaching operations are located in the arid west, where effects on the hydrogeologic system may take several years to detect. High evapotranspiration rates may retard the downward transport of released contaminants and cause them to be confined primarily to the vadose zone, where detection monitoring is often difficult and expensive to implement and maintain.

A typical monitoring network consists of several wells located down-gradient from the solution ponds and heap-leaching pad. In addition, at least one well must be located up-gradient in an area that would be affected by potential contaminant migration. The number and the complexity of the well network is site-specific. Figure 11-11 shows an example of a leachate detection system.

The depth of monitoring wells depends on the depth and characteristics of the underlying aquifer and the vertical spread of potential contaminants. At gold heap-leaching operations, the depth of wells probably will vary from 25 to 300 feet. However, in the arid regions of the southwest, such wells are frequently deeper.

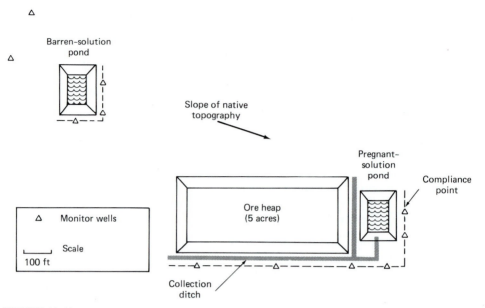

FIGURE 11-11
Detection monitoring system at a small heap-leach operation.

Well diameters may vary from 2 to 6 inches and will be a function of the flow rates and depth of the aquifer and proposed sampling methods. The well is typically 4 inches in diameter and placed in a 6- to 8-inch annulus. Drilling methods are determined on the basis of the geologic formation to be penetrated, the depth and size of the hole, and the potential for contamination as a result of the drilling itself. Methods and materials used during well construction should be selected so as not to interfere with groundwater quality.

The cost for installing a monitoring well system at a gold heap-leaching operation will vary greatly from site to site. The primary factors that influence costs are the size of the operation and the complexity of the hydrology. The characteristics of the groundwater, the extent of contamination, the availability of supplies and equipment, and local wage rates will also affect the cost. Installation costs include the costs of drilling, well materials, crews, and equipment—all of which will be affected by the conditions under which the well system must be installed. The principal factors are the diameter, depth, and components of the well; the drilling specifications; the geologic structure; the sampling requirements; and site access.

Based on the site shown in Figure 11-5 and an assumed $50 per foot for well installation, the cost of installing a system of 11 wells to average depths of 150 feet can be estimated to be $82,500. Consultant fees for a qualified hydrogeologist could be $20,000. Analytical costs based upon annual, quadruplicate sampling would be about $14,000, plus the costs of reporting and record keeping. These costs could have considerable variability because of site-specific conditions. If the monitoring system eventually indicates the presence of contamination, additional monitoring probably will be required at significant additional cost.

QUESTIONS

1 Describe technical project considerations in the design of a hazardous waste landfill.

2 What are the major development phases for a new landfill?

3 Why are treatment and incineration of hazardous wastes generally more desirable than landfilling those wastes?

4 Diagram a hazardous waste landfill with a double-liner and drain system.

5 Discuss the factors that could influence leachate generation and the potential detrimental impact on water resources at the landfill site.

6 Name and discuss the properties of the polymers most commonly used in flexible-membrane liners for landfills.

7 Discuss the elements of a leachate control system.

BIBLIOGRAPHY

1 Bennett, G. F.: "Air Quality Aspects of Hazardous Waste Landfills, *Hazardous Waste and Hazardous Materials,* vol. 4, no. 2, 1987.

2 Brown, K. W., and K. C. Donnelly: "An Estimation of the Risk Associated with the Organic Constituents of Hazardous and Municipal Waste Landfill Leachates," *Hazardous Waste and Hazardous Materials,* vol. 5, no. 1, 1988.

3 Dawson, G. W., and B. W. Mercer: *Hazardous Waste Management,* Wiley, New York, 1986.

4 Deegan, J., Jr.: "Looking Back at Love Canal," *Environmental Science and Technology,* vol. 21, no. 5, 1987.

5 *Directory of Commercial Hazardous Waste Management Facilities,* U.S. Environmental Protection Agency, Office of Solid Waste, Washington, 1987.

6 Higgins, T. E., J. R. Dunckel, and B. G. Marshall: "Avoiding Land Disposal of Hazardous Waste—Some Case Studies," *JAPCA,* vol. 37, no. 11, 1987.

7 *Landfill and Surface Impoundment Performance Evaluation,* U.S. Environmental Protection Agency, Office of Solid Waste and Emergency Response, Washington, 1983.

8 PEI Associates, Inc.: "Gold/Silver Heap Leaching and Conceptual Management Practices to Control Cyanide Releases," draft report to the EPA Water Engineering Research Laboratory, Cincinnati, Ohio, September 1986.

9 Siegenthaler, C.: "Hydraulic Fracturing—A Potential Risk for the Safety of Clay-Sealed Underground Repositories for Hazardous Wastes," *Hazardous Waste and Hazardous Materials,* vol. 4, no. 2, 1987.

10 Sittig, M.: *Landfill Disposal of Hazardous Wastes and Sludges,* Noyes Data, Park Ridge, N.J., 1979.

11 Versar, Inc.: "Quantities of Cyanide-Bearing and Acid-Generating Wastes Generated by the Mining and Beneficiating Industries, and the Potentials for Contaminant Release," draft report prepared for the U.S. Environmental Protection Agency, Office of Solid Waste, Washington, June 27, 1986.

12 Wood, J. A., and M. L. Porter: "Hazardous Pollutants in Class II Landfills," *JAPCA*, vol. 37, no. 5, 1987.

INJECTION WELL DISPOSAL

INTRODUCTION

The underground injection of hazardous liquid wastes has been widely practiced in the United States for many years.[2,5] Generally, this disposal technique has placed the materials in well-confined geological formations that are deep below the surface of the earth. With proper planning, injection well disposal does not present an unreasonable risk to human health and the environment. The hazardous materials that have been injected into these geological formations remain securely in place unless they are disturbed.

The major environmental concern regarding underground disposal of hazardous wastes is the potential contamination of drinking water.[1,4] For this reason, legislation was drafted under the Safe Drinking Water Act of 1974 to protect underground drinking water sources from the contamination that may be caused by the disposal of hazardous liquids in injection wells.

INJECTION WELL CLASSIFICATIONS

Within the underground disposal control program, the U.S. Environmental Protection Agency established five classifications for injection of the various types of liquid wastes: classes I, II, III, IV, and V.[3]

Class I wells are those used by generators of hazardous waste or operators of hazardous waste management facilities to inject fluids into a formation which is beneath the lowermost formation containing an underground source of drinking water within one-quarter mile of the well bore. Industrial and municipal injection disposal systems frequently make use of Class I wells.

Class II wells are those used to inject fluids which have been brought to the surface in the course of conventional oil or natural gas production; these fluids may be commingled with waste waters from gas plants as an integral part of production operations, unless those waters are classified as a hazardous waste at the time of injection. Class II wells are also used for enhanced recovery of oil or natural gas and for storage of hydrocarbons which are liquids at standard temperature and pressure.

Class III wells are those used to inject fluids for the extraction of minerals, including mining of sulfur by the Frasch process, in situ production of uranium or other metals, and solution mining of salts or potash.

Class IV wells are those used by generators of hazardous or radioactive waste and operators of hazardous waste management facilities or of radioactive waste disposal sites to inject hazardous or radioactive waste into or above a formation that has an underground source of drinking water within one-quarter mile of the well bore.

Class V injection wells are those not identified in classes I, II, III, or IV, including:

* Air conditioning return flow wells used to return to the supply aquifer the water used for heating or cooling in a heat pump.
* Cesspools which have an open bottom and receive wastes. This does not apply to single-family residential cesspools nor to nonresidential cesspools which receive solely sanitary wastes and have the capacity to serve fewer than 20 persons a day.
* Cooling water return flow wells used to inject water previously used for cooling.
* Drainage wells used to drain surface fluid, primarily storm runoff, into a subsurface formation.
* Dry wells used for the injection of wastes into subsurface formations.
* Recharge wells used to replenish the water in an aquifer.
* Saltwater intrusion barrier wells used to inject water into a freshwater aquifer to prevent the intrusion of saltwater into the fresh water.
* Backfill wells used to inject water and sand, mill tailings, or other solids into mined-out portions of subsurface mines.
* Septic system wells used to inject the waste or effluent from a septic tank of a multiple dwelling or a business establishment. This does not apply to single-family residential septic system wells which are used solely for the disposal of sanitary waste and have the capacity to serve fewer than 20 persons a day.
* Subsidence control wells used to inject fluids into a non-oil- or gas-producing zone to reduce or eliminate subsidence associated with the over-draft of fresh water.
* Radioactive waste disposal wells other than those regulated as Class IV wells.
* Injection wells associated with the recovery of geothermal energy for heating, aquaculture, or electric power.

• Wells used in solution mining processes such as stope leaching.
• Wells used to inject spent brine, after extraction of halogens or their salts, into the same formation from which it was withdrawn.
• Injection wells used in experimental technologies.
• Injection wells used for in situ recovery for lignite, coal, tar sands, and oil shale.

The rules and regulations of this underground injection control program are administered by the U.S. Environmental Protection Agency, but in many instances, EPA has delegated the administration of this program to the states, as shown in Table 12-1. (Whenever applicable, the state agency that is responsible for program administration is also noted in the table.)

CLASS I INJECTION WELLS

Class I well must meet certain criteria and standards of the EPA underground injection control program. All Class I wells should be sited to inject into a formation which is beneath the lowermost formation containing an underground source of drinking water within one-quarter mile of the well. The wells should be cased and cemented to prevent the movement of fluids into or between underground sources of drinking water. The following factors should be considered for determining the casing and cementing requirements:

• Depth to the injection zone
• Injection pressure, external and internal pressure, and axial loading
• Hole size
• Size and type of all casing strings
• Corrosiveness of injected and formation fluids
• Temperature
• Lithology of injection and confining intervals
• Type of cement

All Class I injection wells, except those municipal wells injecting noncorrosive wastes, must inject fluids through tubing with a packer or fluid seal set immediately above the injection zone. The tubing, packer, and fluid seal should be designed for the expected service. The tubing or packer design should take into account the following factors:

• Depth of setting
• Characteristics of injection fluid, including chemical content, corrosiveness, and density
• Injection pressure
• Annular pressure
• Rate, temperature, and volume of injected fluid
• Size of casing

Appropriate logs must be kept and tests conducted during the drilling and construction of Class I wells. These logs and tests should include:

TABLE 12-1
STATES THAT ADMINISTER UNDERGROUND INJECTION CONTROL PROGRAMS FOR
WASTE MANAGEMENT

State	Well classification	Administering agency	Effective date
Alabama	II	State Oil and Gas Board	Aug. 2, 1982
	I, III, IV, V	Department of Environmental Management	Aug. 25, 1983
Alaska	II		May 6, 1986
Arizona			June 25, 1984
Arkansas	I, III, IV, V	Department of Pollution Control and Ecology	July 6, 1982
California	II	Division of Oil and Gas	March 14, 1983
	I, III, IV, V		June 25, 1984
Colorado	I, III, IV, V		June 25, 1984
Florida	I, III, IV, V	Department of Environmental Regulation	March 9, 1983
Idaho	I, II, III, IV, V	Department of Water Resources	July 22, 1985
Illinois	I, III, IV, V	State Environmental Protection Agency	March 3, 1984
	II	Department of Mines and Minerals	March 3, 1984
Indiana	I, II, III		June 25, 1984
Iowa			June 25, 1984
Kansas	I, III, IV, V	Department of Health and Environment	Dec. 2, 1983
	II	Corporation Commission Department of Health and Environment	Feb. 8, 1984
Kentucky	I II, III		June 25, 1984
Louisiana	I, II, III, IV, V	Department of Natural Resources	March 23, 1982
Maine	I, II, III, IV, V	Department of Environmental Protection	Sept. 26, 1983
Massachusetts	I, II, III, IV, V	Department of Environmental Quality Engineering	Dec. 23, 1982
Michigan	I, II, III		June 25, 1984
Minnesota	I, II, III, IV		Dec. 30, 1984
Mississippi	I, III, IV, V	Department of Natural Resources	Sept. 26, 1983
Missouri	II	Department of Natural Resources	Dec. 2, 1983
Montana	I, II, III		June 25, 1985
Nebraska	II	Oil and Gas Conservation Commission	Feb. 3, 1983
	I, III, IV, V	Department of Environmental Control	June 26, 1984
Nevada	I, II, III		June 25, 1984
New Hampshire	I, II, III, IV, V	Water Supply and Pollution Control Commission	Oct. 21, 1982
New Jersey	I, II, III, IV, V	Department of Environmental Protection	Aug. 15, 1983
New Mexico	II	Energy and Minerals Department, Oil Conservation Division	March 7, 1982
	I, III, IV, V	Water Quality Control Commission	Aug. 10, 1983
New York	I, II, III		June 25, 1984

TABLE 12-1
STATES THAT ADMINISTER UNDERGROUND INJECTION CONTROL PROGRAMS FOR
WASTE MANAGEMENT *(Continued)*

State	Well classification	Administering agency	Effective date
North Dakota	II	Industrial Commission	Sept. 24, 1983
	I, III, IV, V	Department of Health	Oct. 5, 1984
Ohio	II	Department of Natural Resources	Sept. 22, 1983
	I, III, IV, V	Department of Natural Resources and state Environmental Protection Agency	Jan. 14, 1985
Oklahoma	I, III, IV, V	Department of Health	July 24, 1982
	II	Corporation Commission	Dec. 2, 1981
Oregon	I, II, III, IV, V	Department of Environmental Quality	Oct. 9, 1984
Rhode Island	I, II, III, IV, V	Department of Environmental Management	Aug. 15, 1984
South Carolina	I, II, III, IV, V	Department of Health and Environmental Control	July 24, 1984
South Dakota	II	Department of Water and Natural Resources	Dec. 7, 1984
Tennessee	I, II, III		June 25, 1984
Texas	I, III, IV, V		Feb. 7, 1982
	II	Railroad Commission	May 23, 1982
Utah	I, III, IV, V	Department of Health, Division of Environmental Health	Feb. 10, 1983
	II	Department of Natural Resources, Division of Oil, Gas and Mining	Nov. 7, 1982
Vermont	I, II, III, IV, V	Department of Water Resources and Environmental Engineering	July 6, 1984
Washington	I, II, III, IV, V	Department of Ecology	Sept. 24, 1984
Wisconsin	I, II, III, IV, V	Department of Natural Resources	Nov. 30, 1983
Wyoming	I, III, IV, V	Department of Environmental Quality	Aug. 17, 1983
	II	Oil and Gas Conservation Commission	Dec. 23, 1982

- Deviation checks on all holes constructed; these checks are run by first drilling and then enlarging a pilot hole. Such checks should ensure that vertical avenues for fluid migration, in the form of diverging holes, are not created during drilling.
- Resistivity, spontaneous potential, and caliper logs as may be needed before the casing is installed to protect underground sources of drinking water.
- A cement bond, temperature, or density log after the casing is set and cemented.
- Resistivity, spontaneous potential, porosity, and gamma-ray logs for intermediate and long strings of casing intended to facilitate injection; these are needed before the casing is installed.

• Fracture-finder logs and a cement bond, temperature, or density log for intermediate and long strings of casing; these are needed after the casing is set and cemented.

For new Class I wells, information concerning the injection formation should include the fluid pressure, temperature, fracture pressure, other physical and chemical characteristics of the injection matrix, and physical and chemical characteristics of the formation fluids. The pressure during injection should not initiate or propagate fractures in the injection zone. In no case should the injection pressure initiate fractures in the confining zone or cause the movement of injection or formation fluids into an underground source of drinking water.

Injection between the outermost casing protecting underground sources of drinking water and the well bore is prohibited. Unless an alternative to a packer has been approved, the annulus between the tubing and the long string of casing should be filled with an approved fluid that has been pressurized.

Monitoring requirements for Class I wells include the following:

• Analysis of the injected fluids to yield representative data for their characteristics.

• Continuous records of injection pressure, flow rate, and volume, and the pressure on the annulus between the tubing and the casing.

• Type, number, and location of wells to be used to monitor any migration of fluids into underground sources of drinking water.

• Parameters to be measured and frequency of monitoring.

• Demonstration of mechanical integrity at least once every 5 years during the life of the well. This demonstration should be performed to ensure there is no significant leak in the casing, tubing, or packer and no significant fluid movement into an underground source of drinking water. These tests should be based upon the annulus pressure or the fluid pressure.

Class I injection wells for the disposal of hazardous wastes typically will pump these liquid wastes into limestone or sandstone formations that are located 2000 feet or more beneath the earth's surface. These injection zones are confined typically between impermeable layers of shale or clay formations. These confining layers prevent the liquid wastes from migrating upward and contaminating groundwater sources that are being used for drinking water.

A thorough understanding of the geology in the vicinity of the site is necessary prior to developing a Class I injection well. Once the geological considerations have been defined, the construction of the hazardous waste disposal well may then proceed in accordance with the design illustrated in in Figure. 12-1. A large-diameter hole should be drilled to a level below all known groundwater aquifers and then the steel casing cemented in place. A second, smaller-diameter hole should then be drilled to penetrate the desired zone for waste injection, and the intermediate steel casing should be cemented in place.

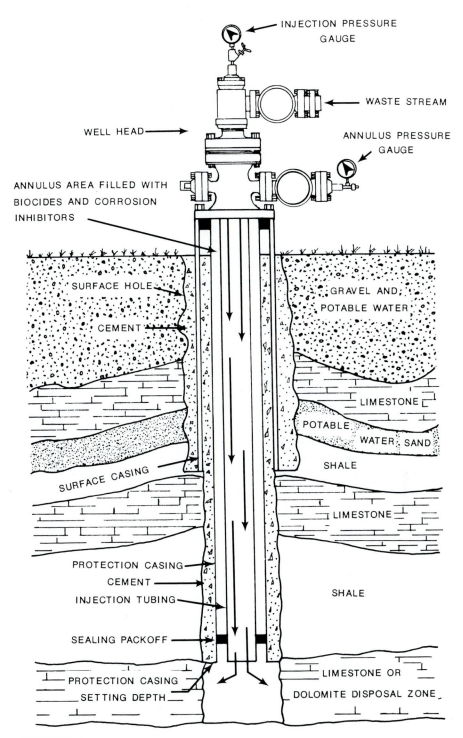

FIGURE 12-1
Design of a hazardous waste disposal well.

This second steel casing will be perforated at the injection zone. The annular space between the waste injection tubing and the intermediate casing should then be filled with a noncorrosive, inert fluid that is sealed in the annular space above the injection zone. Monitoring devices will be installed to detect differential pressure changes between the injected well fluids and the inert, annular fluid. Any change in these relative pressures will alert the operator that wastes are leaking into the annulus and will automatically trigger a shutdown of the disposal well.

Certain hydrogeological considerations must be satisfied before the appropriate government authorities will grant a permit for a Class I well. The injection well should be located in an area that is free from earthquakes. The geological formation near the disposal location should not contain faults. The operator must give assurance that the disposed waste will not migrate upward to the surface of the earth or into groundwater zones. Geochemically, it must be demonstrated that the hazardous liquid wastes to be injected are compatible and nonreactive with the geological formation that will become the injection zone.

Once the disposal well is in use, the entire operation is subjected to continuous monitoring under U.S. Environmental Protection Agency and state regulations. This monitoring for mechanical failures is necessary to provide an early warning signal of potential problems. When there is a mechanical failure of a disposal well, that well must be immediately shut down and an environmental damage assessment performed. The cause of the failure must be determined and the problem corrected. Following correction of the problem, the operator must demonstrate again the mechanical integrity of the well before being allowed to restart the operation.

There have been a number of incidences of leaking wells that have cast doubt on the safety of Class I wells. Because of the potential for leaking wells to contaminate groundwater, this segment of the hazardous waste management industry will face ever-increasing EPA regulations and enforced compliance. It is much more difficult to monitor and quantify problems in belowground disposal well than to assess air and surface damage potential to human health and the environment. With even the best of monitoring capabilities, evidence is inconclusive, and there is a continued need to find better assessment techniques.

As improved processes for the treatment and incineration of hazardous wastes are developed, it would seem more prudent to either destroy the wastes or make them less harmful prior to disposal rather than to rely on deep-well injection of toxic liquids. Because of the complexity of this issue, destruction of wastes rather than deep-well disposal should be the method increasingly preferred by industry, government, and general public alike.

The following case study illustrates complexities with respect to placement and operation of a Class I injection well.

CASE STUDY
Deep-Well Injection of Treated Effluent

Process operations typically produce large quantities of contaminated wastewater that must either be reused, treated prior to discharge, or disposed of in an environmentally acceptable manner. Organics can be separated from the wastewater and either reused or treated in the overall plant process. However, some of the inorganic constituents remain as an environmental problem that must be managed to protect human health and the environment. This case study highlights the complexity of deep-well injection disposal as an integral part of such an operation.

An Inorganic Wastewater Treatment System

The inorganic wastewater treatment system in a new plant was to be designed to pretreat and dispose, by deep-well injection, of the excess inorganic wastewater that could not be reused. These inorganic waste streams would originate primarily in the secondary water treatment unit and the low-pressure steam system. Distillate from the multiple-effect evaporator was also to be discharged via the deep well on an intermittent basis.

The inorganic treatment system was based on maximum reutilization of the wastewater and disposal of the excess water that could not be utilized, along with the water that was too high in salt concentration. Several inorganic wastewater streams from the secondary water treatment system, used for backwashing filters or for rinsing regenerated ion exchange resins, would be sufficiently high in quality to be reused as feed to the primary water treatment unit. For instance, the wastewater resulting from the backwash of the gravity filters in secondary water treatment unit was to be collected in the backwash pit and pumped to the raw water storage pond to be reused as feed to the primary water treatment unit. Other inorganic wastewater streams would also collect in the backwash pit; these would come from the backwashing and rinsing of the ion exchange resins. In each of the four ion exchange systems (sodium zeolite softeners, mixed-bed polishers, low-pressure condensate polishers, and high-temperature condensate polishers), the resins would need to be regenerated regularly with the appropriate solutions. The residual brine would be removed by a rinse solution of high-quality water (softened water for the zeolite softeners and demineralized water for the polishers) before the ion exchange equipment was brought back on-line. The portion of the rinse water with a low salt concentration would flow to the backwash pit for recycle to the primary water treatment system. The portion with high salt concentration was to be disposed of by deep-well injection.

The low-pressure steam system would require a blowdown of approximately 275 gal/min to prevent the buildup of dissolved solids and impurities in the steam system. The majority (125 to 175 gal/min) of this inorganic waste stream was to be reused as makeup to the quench system in the wastewater treatment process. The excess (100 to 150 gal/min) that could not be reused within the facility was to be disposed of via deep-well injection.

Chemical addition to the low-pressure-boiler feedwater system and high-pressure-boiler feedwater system would be necessary to minimize corrosion rates and prevent scaling in the boilers and steam system. The boiler feedwater chemical treatment for the high-pressure steam system would utilize sodium phosphates, hydrazine, and morpholine as additives. Chemical treatment for the low-pressure steam system would utilize sodium sulfite, morpholine, and trisodium phosphate. Residual traces of these chemicals would be present in the blowdown from the low-pressure steam system, and that wastewater was also to be disposed of by deep-well injection.

The evaporator distillate from the multiple-effect evaporator would contain low concentrations of light organic compounds. For this reason, the distillate would be used primarily as makeup to the cooling water system. However, under extremely cold winter conditions when the cooling tower evaporation rates precluded normal makeup, the volume of distillate that could not be stored in the cooling-tower surge pond was also to be disposed of via deep-well injection. Under normal winter conditions, deep-well disposal of the evaporator distillate would not be needed.

The remaining inorganic wastewater streams would be the brine solutions resulting from regeneration of the various ion exchange resins. The waste brine solution from the zeolite softeners (75 gal/min) would have cation and anion concentrations of 15,000 ppm each. The brine solution resulting from regenerating the polishing resins (18 gal/min) would have cation and anion concentrations of 12,000 ppm each. These brine solutions could not be reused within the plant and were to be disposed of via deep-well injection.

The deep-well pretreatment system was designed to process the excess inorganic wastewater to prevent the loss of permeability in the injection zone. The deep well had to comply with EPA regulations for underground injection control to protect drinking water. The maximum design flow rate was 400 gal/min, with a normal winter flow rate of 223 gal/min and a normal summer flow rate of 199 gal/min. The pretreatment system would include two levels of filtration and pH adjustment. The final product water injected would have a pH adjusted to between 5.0 and 6.0 and a maximum particle size of no greater than 10 μm. The filtration package included three pressure sand filters in parallel. The final processing step included measurement and adjustment of the pH, since core testing had shown that calcium carbonate precipitated in the formation water of the injection zone at a pH of 8.4.

Feasibility Studies

A study was prepared to determine the feasibility of disposing of inorganic and organic wastewater streams in certain geological formations located at the gasification plant site. The potentially acceptable geologic strata for deep-well disposal as well as the storage capacity and the radius of influence for the acceptable injection zones were estimated. Additional recommendations were sought for drilling a test well, for preinjection treatment to prevent well clogging and precipitation, and for monitoring of the deep-well system. A conceptual design and cost estimate for the system were also provided.

To determine the geological and hydrological characteristics of the various formations, a core testing program was conducted to assess the chemical compatibility of the inorganic and organic waste streams with the cores and the formation waters. Cores from three possible well locations—in A, B, and C formations—were tested. In the early stages of planning, deep-well disposal of untreated process cooling tower blowdown was considered to be an attractive plant design option. When it became evident from the core tests that injection of untreated organic wastewater streams was not acceptable, additional tests were initiated to evaluate the feasibility of pretreatment for the organic and inorganic systems. Nearly all the testing was done on the organic stream because of its complex chemical composition.

The geochemical compatibility of the wastewater streams and the formation waters were tested to determine whether precipitation would occur or if gases would evolve as a result of chemical or physical interaction. The tests and computer simulations showed that reactions were likely to take place when the wastewater streams contacted the formation water. During the two experimental simulations in which the organic wastewater stream was added to the formation water, the pH dropped from 8.8 to 7.3 while the wastewater was being added, and then rose to 8.5 after the water addition was completed. The rise in pH was attributed to CO_2 evolution from the wastewater stream. Small concentrations of ammonia were also detected and probably were a result of the liquid interactions. No precipitation occurred during these simulations.

However, when both wastewater streams were mixed with the formation water at a pH of 8.4, a calcium carbonate precipitate formed. This precipitate was governed by the carbonate-bicarbonate equilibrium. When the pH was reduced to 7 in subsequent tests, no precipitate formed. On the basis of these chemical compatibility tests, pH control was recommended, along with additional pretreatment methods for the organic waste stream.

Laboratory tests were carried out to determine core permeability changes due to injection of the organic wastewater stream. The test apparatus used was a constant-head triaxial permeability system. The cores were confined in rubber sleeves and kept under a hydrostatic head throughout the tests to prevent the test fluid from bypassing the cores. The permeability characterizations were made using distilled water, then the simulated formation brine, and then the organic wastewater stream. These tests were also made in conjunction with various pretreatment schemes to minimize changes in permeability for the cores. The tests showed that there was minimal loss of permeability for the core when comparing distilled water with simulated formation water. However, the organic stream consistently reduced the permeability of the core even when the organic stream had been prefiltered and pretreated. The two mechanisms believed to cause this core plugging were the passage of colloidal matter through the filters and the interaction of dissolved organic matter with the core matrix. In addition, it was found that once the cores were plugged, the permeability could not be restored through back-flushing with water. This core testing program concluded that extensive pretreatment would be required for the organic wastewater stream before it could be injected into a deep well.

Design of the Treatment System

It was originally anticipated that the only pretreatment required for the organic wastewater stream would be filtration. However, because of the severe loss in permeability for the filtered organic wastewater stream, various additional pretreatment schemes were studied, including:

Coagulation using acidification
Coagulation using polyelectrolytes
Coagulation using ferric chloride
Coagulation using aluminum sulfate
Activated carbon absorption

The acidification tests proved to be ineffective because the effluent settled slowly and incompletely. Although the acidification promoted coagulation and settling, the process was insufficient to prevent the core from plugging. Pretreatment with polyelectrolytes was also found to be ineffective in precipitating the suspended and colloidal matter in the organic wastewater stream. Cationic, neutral, and anionic polyelectrolytes were tested and found to be ineffective. Ferric chloride and aluminum sulfate were tested as coagulants but also proved to be ineffective for clarifying the wastewater. Neither coagulant promoted settling and the solutions remained colored after they were filtered, indicating that colloidal material and dissolved organic matter remained. The filtrates continued to cause a significant decrease in permeability when injected into a core sample.

Activated carbon provided the best results, removing the colored organic matter along with the colloidal particles when tested under acidic conditions using 1 to 3 percent activated carbon and a 60-minute contact time. Although activated carbon pretreatment was adequate to allow deep-well injection of the organic waste stream, economic analysis indicated that the cost of activated carbon and a carbon regeneration facility was too high, eliminating this as a method of pretreatment. Thus all pretreatment systems, with the exception of activated carbon, proved to be ineffective in treating the organic wastewater stream; though activated carbon absorption was an effective treatment, it was found to be economically unacceptable.

The inorganic wastewater stream was found to require only coarse filtration and pH adjustment prior to being disposed of by deep-well injection. The inorganic wastewater stream consisted of 220 gal/min of low-pressure steam blowdown, along with brine solutions from the regeneration of the softening and demineralizer resins. Pretreated, it could be injected into the A, B, and C zones.

On the basis of these tests, it was recommended that only the inorganic waste stream be disposed of through deep-well injection.

Proposed Location of the Injection Well

A test well was to be drilled to obtain specific information to verify the results of the study. The test well was to be used to:

Log the lithology of the rock encountered

Obtain rock cores of the injection zone and upper and lower confining units for identification and laboratory testing

Perform drill-stem tests to obtain the hydraulic characteristics of the injection zone and upper and lower confining units

Obtain in situ water samples from the injection zone for water-quality testing

Perform simulated injected tests to determine the hydraulic characteristics of the injection zone

Determine operating injection pressures and volumes

An important aspect of the test well from an economic standpoint was that upon completion of a successful and acceptable test, the test well could be converted to an actual operating well. Ideally, the location of the injection well should be within the boundaries of the proposed plant site and in close proximity to the final waste stream discharge point and pretreatment facilities. However, the location of the injection well was actually dependent on the characteristics of the subsurface units designated as the primary injection zones and associated confining units. The lithology, depth, and thickness of the injection zone and associated confining units were considered in determining the location of the well.

A Injection Zone The optimum location for a well based on lithology, depth, and thickness in the A injection zone could be anywhere within the boundaries of the proposed plant site. In this general area, the depth to the top of the A injection zone was 4350 feet, measured from ground surface. The total thickness of the injection zone was 400 feet, with an effective thickness of 250 feet. The upper confining unit thickness in this area was 250 feet, with a lower confining unit thickness of 200 feet.

On the basis of a review of the geophysical logs and strip logs in this area, it was found that the lithology of the A injection zone—i.e., alternating beds of sandstone and shale—essentially remained consistent, with a greater sandstone-to-shale ratio in the area immediately below the proposed plant site.

B Injection Zone The optimum location for a well in the B injection zone, based on lithology, depth, and thickness, was found to be 10 to 15 miles west southwest of the proposed plant site. In this general area, the depth to the top of the B injection zone was 6150 feet, measured from ground surface. The total thickness of the injection zone was 225 feet, with an effective thickness of 160 feet. The upper confining unit thickness in this area was 130 feet, with a lower confining unit thickness of 200 feet.

On the basis of a review of the geophysical logs and strip logs in this area, it was found that the B injection zone, consisting of sandstone with some shale and dolomite, thickened toward the center of the region and the sandstone-to-shale ratio also increased in that general direction.

C Injection Zone   The optimum location for a well in the C injection zone, based on lithology, depth, and thickness, was found to be approximately 15 to 20 miles west southwest of the proposed plant site, in the same general location as that of the B zone well. In this area, the depth to the top of the C injection zone was 7000 feet, measured from ground surface. The total thickness of the injection zone was 180 feet, with an effective thickness of 60 feet. The upper unit thickness in this area was 100 feet, with a lower confining unit thickness of 120 feet.

On the basis of a review of the geophysical logs and strip logs in this area, it was found that the lithology of the C injection zone—i.e., sandstone with some shale and limestone—thickened toward the center of the region and the sandstone-to-shale ratio also increased in that general direction.

Conceptual Design and Estimated Costs of the Test/Operating Well

The conceptual design of the injection well included assumptions based on data that were incomplete and could be determined only by test drilling and/or the constructing the injection well itself. The major assumptions on which the design was based included:

The injection rate would be 220 to 600 gal/min.

The primary injection zone would be in A or B formations.

The injection fluid would not be corrosive to steel or concrete. Actually, studies were continuing in this regard and adjustments could be incorporated in the steel composition and the type of grout employed in areas subject to contact with the injected fluid.

No pumping (reverse cycle), or pumping not to exceed the higher injection rate, would be required. (Injected wells are often designed to allow for reverse withdrawal pumping at double the injection rate to assist in well cleaning. Since most formation cleaning at this site would be of a chemical nature, the design incorporated a pump with a capacity of only 600 gal/min.)

A leakage monitoring system would be required.

The location of the injection well would be within the immediate vicinity of the proposed plant site. The cost estimates would vary depending on final well location.

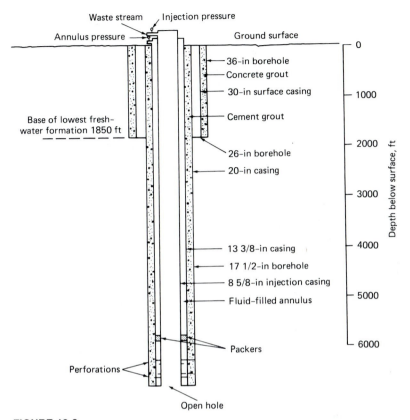

Waste stream   Injection pressure

Annulus pressure

Ground surface

0

36-in borehole
Concrete grout

30-in surface casing

1000

Cement grout

Base of lowest fresh-
water formation 1850 ft

2000

26-in borehole

20-in casing

3000

Depth below surface, ft

13 3/8-in casing

4000

17 1/2-in borehole

8 5/8-in injection casing

Fluid-filled annulus

5000

Packers

6000

Perforations

Open hole

FIGURE 12-2
Design of the injection well for the A and B formations.

The anticipated well design is shown in Figure 12-2, and related costs are included in Table 12-2 (A zone) and Table 12-3 (B zone). One size well was assumed for both injection rates and depth, because the limiting interior diameter was predicated on placement of downhole tools and a pump for borehole maintenance. The nominal 8-inch-diameter interior casing would allow placement of a pump capable of discharging about 550 gal/min from 3000 feet of depth, which would be suitable for most well treatment processes.

The well was designed with 30-inch surface casing set to rock and a secondary 20-inch casing set through the lowest freshwater aquifer. Both upper strings of casing were to be cemented from the bottom to the surface. A 17½-inch hole, to accept 13⅜-inch casing, would be drilled into the confining formation and the casing again grouted from the lowest aquifer bottom to the top. A pilot hole would be drilled initially and reamed to the proper size after testing and logging operations were concluded. Testing would include drill-stem tests in the A and B formations for permeability determinations, electric

TABLE 12-2
FORMATION A INJECTION WELL COST ESTIMATES

		Casing costs			
Diameter, in	Length, ft	Interval, ft	Wt/ft, lb	Cost/100 ft	Total
8⅝	4180	0–4180	32	$ 957	$ 40,000
13⅜	4180	0–3000	68	2100	63,000
		3000–4180	85	3220	38,000
20	1850	0–1000	106	3500	35,000
		1000–1850	133	4353	37,000
30	200	0–200	158	6000	12,000
Subtotal					$225,000
Taxes, freight, and handling					20,000
Total					$245,000

Drilling and testing costs		
Mobilization-demobilization	SC*	$ 50,000
Drill 36-in hole, 0–200 ft	$ 80/ft	16,000
Install 30-in-diameter casing, 0–200 ft	$ 5/ft	1,000
Drill 26-in hole, 200–1850 ft (1650 ft)	$ 70/ft	115,500
Install 20-in-diameter casing, 0–1850 ft	$2.50/ft	4,700
Drill 17½-in-hole, 1850–4200 ft (2350 ft)	$ 50/ft	116,500
Install 13⅜-in-diameter casing, 0–4200	$ 1/ft	4,200
Drill 12¼-hole, 4200–4600 ft (400 ft)	$ 30/ft	12,000
Install 8⅝-in casing, 0–4200 ft	$ 1/ft	4,200
Install packer at 4200 ft and monitoring fluid	SC	5,000
Well development	$150/h	5,000
Drill-stem tests	SC	50,000
Electric logging		16,900
Standby time for tests/logging	$150/h	15,000
Test pumping	SC	15,000
Provide and install type 304 heavy-duty 8⅝-in stainless steel screen	$185/ft	74,000
Hydraulic fracturing, 400 ft		30,000
Total		$535,000

		Cementing costs	
Casing O.D., in	Drill hole diameter, in	Grout volume in sacks	Cost (estimated)
13⅜	17½	2700	$ 40,000
20	26	2650	25,000
30	36	750	10,000
Total			$ 75,000
Subtotal†			$ 855,000
20% contingencies‡			$ 171,000
Total estimated costs			$1,026,000

*SC = service cost.
†Casing plus drilling and testing plus cementing costs.
‡Includes miscellaneous purchases and services.

TABLE 12-3
FORMATION B INJECTION WELL COST ESTIMATES

Casing costs

Diameter, in	Length, ft	Interval, ft	Wt/ft, lb	Cost/100 ft	Total
8⅝	5900	0–4000	32	$ 1000	$ 40,000
		4000–5900	36	1211	23,000
13⅜	5900	0–3000	68	2000	60,000
		3000–5900	85	3207	93,000
20	1850	0–1000	106.5	3500	35,000
		1000–1850	133	4353	37,000
30	200	0–200	158	6000	12,000
Subtotal					$300,000
Taxes, freight, and handling					25,000
Total					$325,000

Drilling and testing costs

Mobilization-demobilization	SC*	$ 50,000
Drill 36-in hole, 0–200 ft	$ 80/ft	16,000
Install 30-in-diameter casing, 0–200 ft	$ 5/ft	1,000
Drill 26-in hole, 200–1850 ft (1650 ft)	$ 70/ft	115,500
Install 20-in casing, 0–1850 ft	$2.50/ft	4,700
Drill 17½-in hole, 1850–5900 ft (4050 ft)	$ 50/ft	203,000
Install 13⅜-in casing, 0–5900 ft	$ 1/ft	5,900
Drill 12¼-in hole, 5905–6080 ft (175 ft)	$ 30/ft	5,300
Install 8⅝-in casing, 0–5900 ft	$ 1/ft	5,900
Install packer at 5900 ft and monitoring fluid	SC	5,000
Well development	$ 150/h	5,000
Drill-stem tests	SC	50,000
Electric logging	Estimated	17,700
Standby time for testing/logging	$ 150/h	15,000
Test pumping	SC	20,000
Provide and install type 304 heavy-duty 8–⅝-in stainless steel screen	$ 185/ft	35,000
Hydraulic fracturing, 175 ft		25,000
Total		$580,000

Cement costs

Casing O.D., in	Drill hole diameter, in	Grout volume in sacks	Cost (estimated)
13⅜	17½	4000	$ 60,000
20	26	2650	30,000
30	36	750	10,000
Total			$ 100,000
Subtotal†			$ 1,005,000
20% contingencies‡			$201,000
Total estimated costs			$ 1,206,000

*SC = service cost.
†Casing plus drilling and testing plus cementing costs.
‡Includes miscellaneous purchases and services.

and radioactivity logs for lithologic and porosity evaluation, and special tests to verify cement and casing placement.

After the 13⅜-inch casing had been placed and cemented, the A or B zone would be drilled to 12¼-inch diameter. Costs included providing and installing a stainless steel wire screen in the event the formation was not sufficiently competent. Costs for hydraulic fracturing to increase the permeability of the A or B formation were also included.

The final step of casing installation was to be placement of the 8⅝-inch-diameter injection string from the top of the A or B zone to the surface. The bottom of the casing was to be sealed to the 13⅜-inch casing with a packer, and the annulus filled with a fluid for leakage monitoring. To reduce the possibility of undetected downhole failures of the well structure, monitoring devices were to be installed to inform the operator of the behavior of the system. Pressure in the outer casing–injection casing annulus would be monitored to detect any changes that might indicate leakage through the injection casing or outer casing–injection packer. The purpose of this measurement was to determine the security of the injection tube, the packer, and the well-head system, and to ensure that fluid entering the injection tube flowed out the bottom of the tube and did not leak into the annulus. The monitoring system would consist of three separate but integrated components—a fluid filled annulus, a packer seal, and a pressure monitoring device.

The annulus between the 8⅝-inch casing and the 13⅜-inch casing was to be filled with a rust-inhibitor fluid under pressure. This fluid pressure was to be continuously monitored, and any change in pressure would be indicative of a possible leak in the injection system.

In addition to the various testing techniques noted above, a period of well development and testing would be required to evaluate the injection capabilities after construction. Sufficient surface water containment would be required for storage of the brine produced during this testing period.

Well and Formation Testing Procedures

A comprehensive series of well and formation tests were undertaken during and following drilling and completion of the test well. The recommended testing procedures outlined below were designed to provide information regarding the three potential injection zones, while utilizing only a single test well and minimizing the cost of the testing program.

The tests were designed to provide qualitative and quantitative information regarding the potential injection zones and their confining units in the immediate vicinity of the test well site. Information gathered during this testing program would be used to provide:

Stratigraphic correlations between the test well and other wells drilled into the same formations

Data for estimation of formation properties such as permeability, porosity, and effective thickness

Information needed for the ultimate design and construction of an operational injection well

Examination of the response of the injection zone during actual liquid injection

The recommended testing included geologic logging of the borehole, laboratory analyses of core samples, geophysical borehole logging, drill-stem testing, chemical analyses of formation water samples, and pumping and injection tests.

Geologic Logging   Geologic logging, in conjunction with borehole geophysical logging, would result in a visual log of the stratigraphy at the test well site. This information would be used to correlate stratigraphic units between the test well and other wells drilled into the same formations, and also to provide local information regarding depths and effective thickness of the potential injection zones and their confining units.

During the test well drilling, the drill cuttings and core samples would be examined and an accurate log of the observations maintained. Also, observations would be recorded about drilling rate and performance, the presence and the flow of the formation fluids, the loss or alteration of drilling fluids, and the presence of fractured zones. Geologic logging would be conducted for the total depth of the hole.

Core Analyses   Laboratory analyses of core samples would provide preliminary quantitative measurements of the permeabilities and porosities of the injection zones and their confining units. Such measurements referred only to primary matrix properties rather than secondary porosity and permeability resulting from fractures, joints, and solution activities, though secondary properties were often more important than primary properties in controlling fluid flow through reservoir rocks. Nevertheless, the results of the laboratory analyses of core samples could be used to compare and contrast primary formation properties for the strata encountered in the test hole, and to enable correlations based on primary formation properties between the test well and other wells drilled into the same formations.

Selected core samples would be taken from each of the potential injection zones, as well as from the confining units overlying and underlying each potential injection zone. Core plugs would be cut at least every 10 feet over the length of the core, and at every distinct change in lithology. The core plugs would be submitted to a commercial laboratory for core analysis.

Geophysical Logging   The borehole geophysical logs would provide quantitative and semiquantitative information on a variety of lithologic parameters, including stratigraphic correlations, rock porosity, location of fractured zones, and formation fluid properties such as density, viscosity, and temperature. The major purpose of borehole geophysical logging in the present study was to supplement the results of core analyses, to refine the stratigraphic correlations and locations of formation boundaries, to guide the design of the operational disposal well, and to determine the effectiveness of the cement bond in the casing-formation annulus.

After each injection zone was drilled through, an appropriate suite of logs would be run, followed by formation testing. The types of logs to be run on each injection zone would depend in part on the expected nature of the injection zone as inferred from available log data of oil and gas wells in the area. The logs to be run would include some or all of the following: spontaneous potential, resistivity, induction, natural gamma, neutron, sonic velocity, formation density, caliper, and temperature.

Drill-Stem Tests   The drill-stem tests would provide water samples from each potential injection zone for chemical analyses, direct measurement of the initial static pressure in each potential injection zone, and data to calculate the formation permeability and skin effect for each zone.

After each of the potential injection zones was drilled and logged, the drill-stem test (DST) tool would be run and tests conducted over several intervals of the injection zone. At least three standard double shut-in drill-stem tests would be conducted in each injection zone. The lengths of flowing and shut-in periods for each test was to be selected in consultation with the DST service company, making use of previous DST results from other wells in the same formation where possible. Care was to be taken in testing the formation because of the possible presence of nitrogen gas. The system would be equipped with a pressure release valve to avoid the possibility of a blowout.

Pumping Tests   At least one pumping test of 3 to 7 days' duration would be conducted on each potential injection zone. The tests would provide data from which formation properties could be evaluated and would allow the collection of formation water samples with minimal contamination by drilling fluids. The formation properties determined from the pumping tests could be compared with those determined from subsequent injection tests to detect any changes in injection efficiency due to such factors as plugging of the injection zone by suspended or precipitated solids, or fracturing of the injection zone due to fluid injection at high pressure.

Following the drill-stem tests on a particular potential injection zone, a temporary screen or perforated casing would be set, the zone packed from above, and the aquifer pumped at a constant rate of 200 to 400 gal/min for 3 to 7 days. During the pumping period and the subsequent recovery period following cessation of pumping, the surface pressure would be monitored frequently. The formation fluid would be pumped to the surface during the pumping test to be stored in a holding pond for use in a subsequent injection test.

Injection Tests   A short-term injection test would be the most direct method of determining the feasibility of injection into a particular zone. Such a test might identify potential difficulties or inefficiencies in the injection procedure and provide data from which formation properties and potential changes in those properties could be determined. The test could identify the minimum fracture pressure of the formation, or the maximum injection pressure possible without fracturing the formation.

The injection test would include a series at constant rates, as shown below, each followed by a period of recovery:

Injection rate, gal/min	Time interval, h
100	18
Shut in	6
200	18
Shut in	6
400	18
Shut in	6
600	18
Shut in	6
800	18
Shut in	6
400	18
Shut in	6
200	18
Shut in	6
100	18
Shut in	6

The testing would be observed and field records maintained for data plots, and minor changes in recommended rates and intervals of injection. During each injection and shut-in period, the surface pressure was to be recorded frequently.

General Test Schedule

A general schedule for the recommended test procedures has been outlined below:

1 Drill through the A formation, coring selected intervals
2 Geophysically log the entire borehole
3 Set a temporary screen opposite the A injection zone, pack off the zone, and conduct DST, pumping, and injection tests
4 Pull the temporary screen and drill through the B formation, coring selected intervals of the formations
5 Geophysically log the borehole from the bottom of the A formation to the new bottom of the hole
6 Set a temporary screen opposite the B injection zone, pack off the zone, and conduct DST, pumping, and injection tests
7 Pull the temporary screen and drill through the C formation shale, coring selected intervals of the C formations
8 Geophysically log the borehole from the bottom of the B formation to the new bottom of the hole

9 Set a temporary screen opposite the C injection zone, pack off the zone, and conduct DST, pumping, and injection tests

10 Analyze all available data and prepare specifications for converting the test well into an operational injection well

Reservoir Evaluation

On the basis of geologic and geophysical reservoir evaluation, it was found that the A, B, and C formations each comprised potential injection zones. The A formation had the most desirable cost-effective reservoir characteristics for a potential injection zone, followed, in decreasing order of desirability, by the B and C injection zones.

Deep-well injection of the inorganic demineralizer and zeolite softener effluent at 200 gal/min into the A or B injection zones was technically feasible. The pretreatment of this waste stream should include coarse filtration to remove solids and pH adjustment to prevent precipitation.

Deep-well injection of the organic cooling tower blowdown effluent at 400 gal/min should be precluded unless no other feasible technical and economic means of disposal were available. This conclusion was based on the injection of the organic waste stream into either the A or the B injection zones would involve suspended solids and dissolved organic concentrations. These parameters could cause irreversible well plugging, and the economic consideration of such a system would preclude its feasibility.

Well Location and Cost Estimates

The ideal location for an injection well penetrating the A zone was found within a 5-mile radius of the proposed plant site. The estimated costs for the drilling, testing, and completion of injection wells in the A and B injection zones were $1,026,000 and $1,206,000, respectively. These costs were based on the assumption that the well would be near the proposed plant site.

Reservoir Analysis

The radial motion and dispersion of the interface between the injected waste stream and the formation fluid, and of the increase in formation pressure due to waste stream injection, led to the following conclusions:

Radial movement of the interface was controlled by formation (thickness and porosity) and operational (injection rate and duration) parameters which were known, so that predictions of interface movement should be reasonably accurate.

The radius of influence for a single injection well was estimated to be of the order of a few thousand feet. This radius of influence would be directly proportional to the injection rate and inversely proportional to the formation thickness and porosity.

Dispersion was not expected to significantly influence interface motion.

The increase in formation fluid pressure due to injection could be significant. For a high rate of injection at 600 gal/min into a relatively thin formation of 100 feet, the pressure increase in the immediate vicinity of the well could exceed 1000 psi after 25 years of continuous injection. However, a pressure increase of only a few hundred psi was more likely at the recommended injection well site and would depend on actual formation properties encountered.

Recommendations

On the basis of all these studies, it was recommended that the concept of a deep-well injection system be pursued and that the following actions be implemented:

1 The permit application for deep-well injection should be submitted to the local authorities prior to any test drilling.

2 An injection well should be drilled to penetrate through the three potential injection zones.

3 Sufficient electrical and nuclear logs and core samples should be obtained to provide quantitative information to determine the physical properties of the potential injection zones.

4 Samples of formation fluids with emphasis on the A injection zone should be obtained and analyzed. This should include downhole temperature and viscosity determinations.

5 Pilot injection tests should be conducted using water and simulated treated effluents to determine pressure versus flow rate relationships prior to effluent waste disposal operations.

6 Fluid and formation pressure increases should then be reevaluated.

CLASS II INJECTION WELLS

Class II wells, which are used for disposal of wastes from oil and gas production and storage, have been generally accepted and used throughout the petroleum industry for many years. They represent a low initial cost method of disposal when compared with either landfilling, treatment, or incineration. The annular injection of oil and gas wastes offers significantly lower costs of disposal than treating on-site or hauling off-site. When properly managed, Class II wells will protect aquifers and can be implemented quickly once the proper permit has been obtained. The surface casing is drilled to a depth below all freshwater aquifers prior to its being cemented in place. The intermediate casing, which is drilled into the zone for waste injection, is also cemented in place. The steel casing then permits the installation of a bottom hole plug, followed by perforation of the casing in the zone where injection is to be accomplished.

Since this Class II disposal technique is normally only applicable to dry holes, it allows the waste fluids to be injected into any geological zone that might be acceptable for disposal without damaging human health and the environment. This allows the injection of water, brines, drilling fluids, drilled solids, drill-stem test fluids, and other wastes that may be present in the surface mud pits. Rules and regulations regarding disposal of oil and gas wastes vary from state to state, with record keeping, reporting, and inspections being requirements of the permit process. The lack of a uniform federal policy on this issue has meant considerable variance in state regulations of the oil industry.

Generally, however, it is minimally required by the regulatory authorities that Class II wells must inject into a formation which is separated from any drinking water source by a confining zone that is free of known open faults or fractures. All Class II injection wells must be cased and cemented to prevent movement of fluids into or between underground sources of drinking water. The casing and cement used in the construction of each newly drilled well should be designed for the life expectancy of the well. The following factors should be considered in determining casing and cementing requirements:

- Depth to the injection zone
- Depth to the bottom of all drinking water sources
- Estimated injection pressures

In addition, parameters that may be considered include:

- Formation fluids
- Lithology of injection and confining zones
- External pressure, internal pressure, and axial loading
- Hole size
- Size and grade of all casing strings
- Class of cement

The above requirements do not apply to existing Class II wells located in existing fields if the casing and cementing were in compliance when drilled and well injection will not result in the movement of fluids into an underground source of drinking water and create a significant risk to human health. Appropriate logs and tests should be conducted during the drilling and construction of new Class II wells. The results relating to drinking water sources and the adjacent confining zones should be interpreted. The injection and adjacent formations should be checked for hole deviation by first drilling a pilot hole and then enlarging the pilot hole to ensure that vertical diverging holes for fluid movement were not created during drilling. Logs and tests for surface casing intended to protect underground sources of drinking water include electric and caliper logs before the casing is installed and a cement bond, temperature, or density log after the casing is set and cemented. Logs are also needed for intermediate and long strings of casing intended to facilitate injection—including electric, porosity, and gamma-ray logs before the casing is installed and fracture-finder logs and cement bond, temperature, or density logs after the casing is set and cemented.

For new Class II wells, information concerning the injection formation should include the fluid pressure, estimated fracture pressure, and physical and chemical characteristics of the injection zone.

Class II injection wells must be operated so the pressure during injection does not initiate new fractures or propagate existing fractures in the confining zone adjacent to the sources of drinking water. In no case should the injection pressure cause the movement of injection or formation fluids into an underground source of drinking water. Injection between the outermost casing protecting underground sources of drinking water and the well is prohibited. Monitoring requirements include the characterization of injected fluids at frequent time internals, observation of injection pressure, flow rate, and cumulative volume at least weekly for produced fluids disposal, monthly for enhanced recovery operations, daily during the injection of liquid hydrocarbons and injection for withdrawal of stored hydrocarbons, and daily during the injection phase of cyclic steam operations.

CLASS III INJECTION WELLS

Class III wells are those used in connection with the recovery of minerals—that is, in mining processes. All new Class III wells should be cased and cemented to prevent the migration of fluids into or between underground sources of drinking water, unless there is substantial evidence against contamination of underground sources of drinking water. The casing and cement used in the construction of each newly drilled well should be designed for the life expectancy of the well. The following factors must be considered in determining and specifying casing and cementing requirements for Class III wells:

- Depth to the injection zone
- Injection pressure, external pressure, internal pressure, axial loading
- Size and grade of all casing strings (wall thickness, diameter, nominal weight, length, joint specification, and construction material)
- Corrosiveness of injected fluids and formation fluids
- Lithology of injection and confining zones
- Type and grade of cement

Appropriate logs and other tests should be conducted during the drilling and construction of new Class III wells. The results of the logs and tests should be based upon the function, depth, and construction of the well and the availability of similar data in the area of the drilling site. Deviation checks should be conducted on all holes where pilot holes and reaming are used, unless the hole will be cased and cemented by circulating cement to the surface. Where deviation checks are necessary, they should be conducted at frequent intervals to ensure that vertical avenues for fluid migration in the form of diverging holes were not created during drilling. Where the injection zone is a formation which is naturally water-bearing, information concerning the injection zone should include the fluid pressure, fracture pressure, and physical and chemical characteristics of the formation fluids.

Where the Class III injection formation is not water-bearing, fracture pressure must be determined. Where the injection will be into a formation which contains water with less than 10,000 mg/l total dissolved solids, monitoring wells should be completed into the injection zone and into any underground sources of drinking water above the injection zone which could be affected by the mining operation. These wells must be located to detect any excursion of injection fluids, process by-products, or formation fluids outside the mining area or zone. If the operation could be affected by subsidence or catastrophic collapse, the monitoring wells should be located so that they will not be physically affected.

Where the injection will be into a formation which does not contain water with less 10,000 mg/l TDS, monitoring wells are not necessary in the injection stratum. Where the injection wells penetrate a drinking water source in an area subject to subsidence or catastrophic collapse, an adequate number of monitoring wells should be completed into the drinking water source to detect any movement of injected fluids, process by-products, or formation fluids into that drinking water source. The monitoring wells should be located outside the physical influence of subsidence or catastrophic collapse.

In determining the number of wells, their location, construction, and frequency of monitoring, the following criteria should be considered:

- Population relying on the drinking water source affected
- Proximity of the injection to drinking water points of withdrawal
- Local geology and hydrology
- Operating pressure and determination of whether a negative pressure gradient is being maintained
- Characteristics and volume of the injected fluid, the formation water, and the process by-products
- Injection well density

The operating requirements for Class III wells must ensure that the injection pressure does not initiate new fractures or propagate existing fractures in the injection zone. In no case should injection pressure initiate fractures in the confining zone or cause the migration of injection or formation fluids into an underground source of drinking water. It is also required that the injection not occur between the outermost casing protecting underground sources of drinking water and the well bore.

Frequent monitoring of Class III wells should be used to characterize the injected fluids. Semimonthly monitoring of injection pressure and flow rate or daily metering and recording of the injection and production fluid volumes are required. Mechanical integrity must be demonstrated every 5 years during the life of wells used for salt solution mining. Monitoring of the fluid level in the injection zone and water quality parameters in the monitoring wells should be done semimonthly.

CLASS IV AND CLASS V INJECTION WELLS

The use of Class IV injection wells for disposal of hazardous waste is rapidly being phased out because such disposal can endanger groundwater sources that are used for drinking water. Permits for new Class IV injection wells have become extremely difficult, if not impossible, to obtain from regulatory authorities.

The Class V injection well category contains a wide range of specialty applications for disposal of liquid wastes. The permitting process for Class V wells is usually decided on a case-by-case basis with the appropriate regulatory authorities.

QUESTIONS

1 Discuss the environmental concerns of deep-well disposal of hazardous liquid wastes.
2 Diagram a hazardous waste injection well and discuss its operation.
3 Describe the five classes of injection wells covered under the EPA underground injection well program.
4 How could treatment systems affect the site selection for an injection well?
5 How could geochemical considerations influence waste treatment prior to injection disposal?
6 What factors should enter into determination of the feasibility of a hazardous injection well?

BIBLIOGRAPHY

1 Canter, L. W., and R. C. Knox: *Groundwater Pollution Control*, Lewis, Chelsea, Mich., 1985.
2 Dawson, G. W., and B. W. Mercer: *Hazardous Waste Management*, Wiley, New York, 1986.
3 *Directory of Commercial Hazardous Waste Management Facilities*, U.S. Environmental Protection Agency, Office of Solid Waste, Washington, 1987.
4 Driscoll, F. G.: *Groundwater and Wells*, 2d ed., Johnson Division, St. Paul, Minn., 1986.
5 Powers, P. W.: *How to Dispose of Toxic Substances and Industrial Wastes*, Noyes Data, Park Ridge, N.J., 1976.

CHAPTER 13

PROCESS SELECTION
AND FACILITY SITING

SELECTING THE PROCESS

The decisions made in the selection and procurement of hazardous waste control technologies are generally based, at least in part, upon economics.[9] Government regulations and the adaptability of process technology are also considerations, as are public relations and geographic location. And the decision can, in the end, be largely influenced by subjective political reasons.

At least one survey has shown that compliance with government regulations is the major consideration in choosing a hazardous waste management technology (Table 13-1).[8]

Hazardous waste activities of other firms may provide insight into what is being done within an industry as well as what needs to be done to be competitive. Information based upon competitive activities is generally accessible and

TABLE 13-1
SELECTION CRITERIA FOR HAZARDOUS
WASTE MANAGEMENT TECHNOLOGY

Criteria	Weighting
Government regulations	0.4
Economics	0.3
Public relations	0.2
Process technology	0.1
Total	1.0

Source: University of North Dakota Survey.

can lead to a shortened learning curve for a company that needs to achieve regulatory compliance.

The adaptability of various process technologies to specific hazardous wastes should help define the limitations of any proposed waste treatment system. This critique should be done early in the decision-making process in order to ensure the selection of an appropriate technology that is compatible with the waste stream to be controlled.[3,4,5]

A survey should be made of the various waste streams that will be managed by the facility. Then the most cost-effective and environmentally safe manner of managing these wastes should be determined. The waste streams should be characterized using the sampling and analytical technologies that were described in Chapter 5 to determine the degree to which the wastes are hazardous and to quantify their potential threats to human health and the environment. Since the operation of the facility must be cost-effective, these waste characterizations will provide important information in ultimately determining how best to manage each individual stream. If the generator is producing on-site waste, the criteria in Chapter 6 should be initially utilized to determine the feasibility of waste elimination or reduction. If the wastes can be eliminated or reduced significantly, subsequent treatment processes either become unnecessary or are reduced in scope. These highly desirable alternatives must be carefully considered in trying to arrive at reasonable technical and economic solutions to hazardous waste management. It should be noted that successful elimination of hazardous wastes on-site negates the need for the TSD facility and the subsequent regulatory procedures related to facility siting. Elimination or significant reduction of these wastes works to the benefit of all concerned parties.

If after exploring the various alternatives for waste reduction and elimination, the generator is still left with hazardous waste, then the treatment alternatives shown in Figure 13-1 should be systematically explored. Each of the RCRA and TSCA wastes shown in the figure requires additional treatment prior to final disposal. The physical, chemical, and biological treatment processes discussed in Chapter 7 should then be considered. Many inorganic wastes can be treated by either neutralization processes or physical and chemical treatment techniques. These types of processes are desirable solutions because they are both cost-effective and well-known technologies that can be implemented on virtually any scale that the generator or TSD facility can accommodate on-site. It is also true that the proponents of the not in my backyard (NIMBY) position are more likely to be receptive to the siting of a TSD facility based upon physical, chemical, and biological treatment because there are no exhausts or smokestacks that represent point sources of air emissions.

Many low-concentration effluents and other wastewaters can usually be managed with modest capital and operating costs to treat these waste streams prior to discharge into municipal sewers. Even strong acids and alkalis can be neutralized to effectively eliminate their being characterized as a hazardous waste under the RCRA corrosivity criteria. Heavy metals are virtually impos-

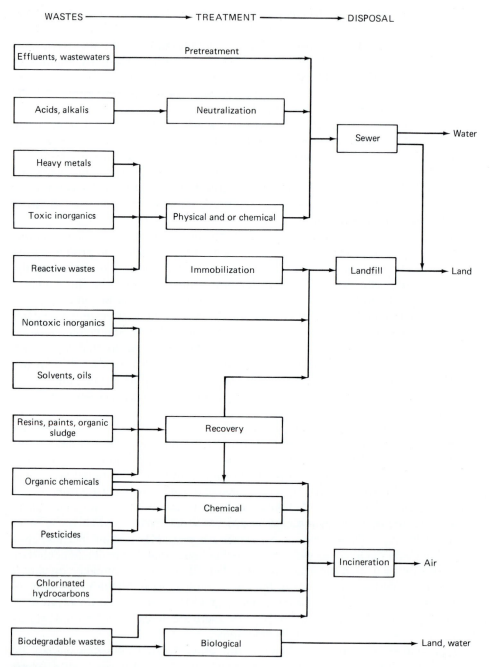

FIGURE 13-1
Treatment and disposal alternatives for industrial wastes.

sible to destroy, so they must be managed by immobilization techniques. Once heavy metals have undergone a suitable fixation process so that they have become nonleachable, these wastes can then be landfilled. Reactive wastes must be carefully handled prior to undergoing physical and chemical process treatment that will make them environmentally acceptable.

Should the inorganic waste streams contain sufficient quantities of metals and other potentially valuable resources, their recovery through physical and chemical separation techniques is highly desirable. The potential for recovery must be studied on a case-by-case basis and will relate to the estimated value of the quantities available and the acceptance of the recovered waste in the marketplace as well as to the perception of the general public regarding the recycling and reuse of such a waste product. For example, even a chemically pure waste by-product may carry a stigma in the public imagination that will require considerable time, money, and effort to overcome.

Organic wastes offer considerable recovery potential with separation techniques such as distillation or extraction to recover valuable hydrocarbon streams that can subsequently either be used for energy or recycled back into the chemical process industries. It should be noted that these organic recovery processes will still produce a concentrated but probably significant volume of hazardous waste that eventually must be destroyed or landfilled.

The ultimate destruction of hazardous wastes that cannot be either eliminated or recovered involves incineration or biological treatment. Incineration is a preferred method of getting rid of hazardous waste because it eliminates the potential future problems that might be created by landfill disposal and other interim hazardous waste management processes. While today incineration in the United States lags its utilization in Europe, it is apparent that this desirable ultimate disposal technique will become more widely practiced here in the future. Biological treatment also offers the potential for complete destruction of a hazardous waste. The development of specialized microbes for highly efficient destruction systems eliminates the need for subsequent landfill disposal. Future hazardous waste management disposal strategies are expected to emphasize the more desirable alternatives of biological treatment and incineration in the selection of process technology.

Ultimate disposal of products from hazardous waste management facilities will inevitably affect the air, water, or land. There is simply no way to avoid the ultimate placement of by-products of wastes from our societal needs and technological creativity in our air, water, and/or land. As we developed environmental legislation and promulgated regulations, we merely shifted the emphasis on ultimate disposal from one media to another.

SITING THE FACILITY

While greater emphasis is now being placed upon waste elimination or reduction, there will always remain the need for residue TSD facilities. The NIMBY sentiment in the United States has greatly restricted the ability to site TSD facilities on the land. Even the most well-conceived, environmentally safe hazardous waste disposal facility creates emotional responses from groups of concerned citizens and national environmental organizations. While many people in the United States now realize the need for well-managed hazardous waste disposal facilities, the siting question remains an extremely difficult issue for developers of TSD facilities.

Obtaining an RCRA permit for a hazardous waste TSD facility is a difficult, laborious, costly, and time-consuming effort.[1] It typically takes 3 to 4 years to process an RCRA permit for a hazardous waste incineration facility. There is a major backlog in RCRA permit applications for incinerators. Unless the NIMBY sentiment can be overcome, this backlog is expected to grow in the future. Historically, industry has been reluctant to communicate in an open forum its plans for future facilities, including hazardous waste disposal operations. This lack of communication, which, on one hand, is a desirable strategy to follow to protect competitive advantages, must, in the case of siting TSD facilities, now change in order to allow local communities greater participation and enlightenment in the complex technical issues of hazardous waste disposal.

There are numerous criteria that must be considered in connection with siting a TSD facility. The waste characteristics and the volume of the waste should be the first of any well-conceived site selection criteria. Regarding the site itself, its topographic geology and hydrogeology are factors that need to be addressed. The local climate, particularly rainfall and temperature ranges, will affect the operation of the treatment processes at the TSD site. It will be necessary to protect air quality as well as local groundwater. TSD facilities should never be located in floodplains, or in areas where severe earthquakes might damage the facility. The facility should also be in an area where strict security can be implemented and maintained. Care should be taken so as not to adversely impact the local ecology and to protect local endangered species. Areas of low population density that have appropriate zoning and offer local community support are, of course, the most desirable locations when it comes to siting a hazardous waste TSD facility.

An ideal hazardous waste TSD facility site should:

Conform with the land use planning and zoning of the local area
Be easily accessible in all weather conditions to the type of vehicle and other transportation modes that can be expected during operation of the facility
Have secure safeguards against any potential air, surface water, and groundwater pollution
Be selected with adequate regard for the sensitivities of the local community residents.
Be located where the operation will not unreasonably impact upon environmentally sensitive resources
Be large enough in scale to accept and process hazardous wastes during the life of the operation of the facility
Be cost-effective end economically profitable, while complying with the rules and regulations applicable to the facility

There is a natural fear associated with any hazardous waste facility siting. This fear provokes opposition to siting of any new facility as well as resistance even to using existing facilities to dispose of hazardous wastes. The siting process must be perceived by the public as fair, open, and equitable; otherwise continued NIMBY opposition can be expected.

A well-planned and organized facility siting program must include ample opportunities for public participation. This public participation can range from public meetings with small groups of individual citizens and local government officials to open hearings that may be required by government regulations. Scientific and local citizen advisory committees may also be helpful in achieving full public participation. News releases and interviews with the news media should be encouraged. Surveys to assess public opinion can also provide additional input to the decision-making process. Tours of comparable facilities elsewhere that would be models for the proposed facility to be sited locally would be helpful in alleviating concerns. The potential technological risk of the facility should be compared with other risks that are experienced by local citizens and the community on a daily basis. This will help create a public awareness of the relative risk of the facility in their backyard. Another point that needs to be made is that the facility itself is being considered to solve an even bigger national environmental problem. By openly involving the public, problems created by emotion can be reduced at the outset, and the final decision on facility siting can be made on the more rational basis of technical and economic feasibility.

Facility siting should incorporate the protection of human health and the environment, the protection of property values in the local community, and the general acceptance of the hazardous waste TSD facility by the community. Local citizens must be convinced that a TSD facility is needed, that all reasonable steps will be taken to make it compatible with the environment, and that the facility location represents an equitable solution to a much larger problem.

While there will never be unanimous approval and acceptance in the siting of a hazardous waste TSD facility from local citizens, the vast majority of people in the Unites States are supportive of establishing environmentally acceptable facilities to clean up our environment and protect our health. They realize that there are major long-term disadvantages if proper facilities are not built and hazardous waste disposal continues through existing techniques that are not environmentally acceptable. The NIMBY syndrome disregards a national crisis, and most local communities and the citizens do not subscribe to such a narrow sentiment. The public at large, when made aware of the need for these facilities, will usually accept the reasonable risks associated with siting the facility in their vicinity. There are economic benefits to an environmentally acceptable hazardous waste TSD facility. Local jobs are created, and it is not unreasonable for the local community to expect significant tax proceeds from the facility.

Many lessons in how to successfully site a hazardous waste TSD facility in the United States can be learned from the following case study about such a facility siting in Alberta, Canada. This case is an example of how the risk of such a facility was not simply mitigated but how the operation turned into a desirable business enterprise for a local community.[6]

CASE STUDY
Alberta Sets an Example

The siting of a hazardous waste treatment facility near Swan Hills, Alberta, Canada, generated disbelief, curiosity, and amazement among waste managers whose own experience has generally brought them up against the NIMBY— not in my backyard—syndrome, against citizens and politicians who may agree that waste handling facilities are necessary for the maintenance of a clean and safe environment but who feel that those facilities should be located "somewhere else." Alberta's siting program was successful; but it was not without hard work, long hours, and a sensitive approach to the broad spectrum of waste management. The approach was reflected in the implementation plan to involve the public to the fullest extent; to integrate the theoretical and practical procedures for waste collection, treatment, and disposal; and to continue the government's role as facilitator to ensure that responsible pollution control resulted in maintenance of environmental quality and human health.

The system established in Denmark has long been an enviable example of proper waste management. Collection, transfer, treatment, and disposal operations there are controlled and effective. The addition of recycling and resource recovery to the scheme has resulted in an integrated network where industry and the public participate. Setting such a system as a goal in Alberta allowed the government, municipalities, waste generators, and the public to assess their requirements and define local, regional, and provincial programs.

The Alberta Program

The departments of Environment and Social Services and Community Health, in conjunction with municipal and private operators, plan and manage the disposal of municipal waste in Alberta through a system of transfer stations and regional sanitary landfills. The special, or hazardous, waste management system is an extension of an already-functioning program. The basis of the special waste operation is public understanding of the need for waste handling facilities and the citizen's role in ensuring that the waste is not indiscriminately dumped. Public information, local involvement, and participation in the decision-making process have been key factors in the success of an integrated waste management system. This system begins with the householder and small generator; includes municipal waste collection, transfer, and disposal in a sanitary landfill; encompasses recycling, reuse, and resource recovery; utilizes a controlled transportation network; and provides a treatment and disposal plant for those organic and inorganic wastes which cannot be safely disposed of elsewhere.

The component in this system which has received the most attention has been the treatment and disposal facility. Its siting brought together the theory, skills, and practical application of environmental science, ecology, hydrogeology, land use planning, sociology, process technology, and political science. It involved a wealth of research and the cooperation of every level of government, industry, and society.

Beginnings of the Site Selection Process

On March 12, 1984, the minister of environment announced the location for the development of an integrated special waste treatment and disposal facility (Figure 13-2). Environmental requirements had been satisfied, and general support had been gained from the people of the nearest town, Swan Hills. This announcement was the culmination of an intensive provincewide site selection and public information program begun in 1980 by the government of Alberta. It was unprecedented in North America that a facility site such as this had been offered by citizens and then selected on the basis of environmental and social acceptability.

The announcement not only marked the completion of a major siting program, it also served as a new direction in public involvement, technology assessment, site preparation, facility construction, transfer station planning, and special waste system management. Many government agencies were involved and the private sector was an active participant in the building, ownership, and operation of the facility. The Alberta Special Waste Management Corporation (a provincial Crown corporation) was established to oversee the system and ensure both continued human health and safety and the protection of the competitive position of Alberta's industry.

A chronicle of the development of Alberta's waste management system begins with reference to 1979 when the need was identified to assess the management options for special waste in the province of Alberta. At that time, a private waste handling firm proposed to construct and operate a treatment plant in an industrial community near Edmonton. So forceful was the public opposition to this proposal that the minister of environment placed a moratorium on all off-site development of waste handling facilities until a management strategy could be devised by the government.

Immediately, the Hazardous Waste Management Committee was formed, consisting of representatives from government and the public, to consider a management program and to provide recommendations to the minister. The key recommendations of the committee's final report were:

Albertans had an obligation to develop a waste management plan.
A system to treat special waste should be established.
The government of Alberta should maintain a leadership role.

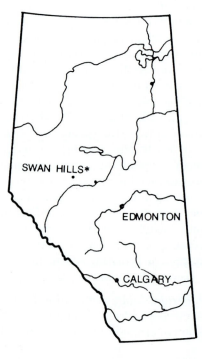

PROVINCE OF
ALBERTA

* Hazardous waste treatment
and disposal facility site

FIGURE 13-2
Location of the provincial facility.

The report prepared by the committee formed the basis for public hearings convened, upon request of the provincial cabinet, by the Environment Council of Alberta. The E.C.A. is a Crown agency with the mandate to conduct independent assessments of environmental needs and programs at the request of the provincial government. Under this general direction, the E.C.A. was given the assignment of determining the public view on the Hazardous Waste Management Committee report. The council was also charged with investigating the types and amounts of wastes in Alberta, storage and treatment options available, and criteria that might be used to site a treatment facility.

Following a series of public hearings held at 16 locations throughout the province, the E.C.A. presented its recommendations in 1981. Among these was the recommendation that the government begin a site selection process. To proceed with site selection, a hazardous waste team was established. The team consisted of representatives from government and the public, including the public representatives from the original committee. To work in conjunction with this team, the Department of Environment assigned staff, and this group, as a task force, developed and implemented the site selection process which resulted in North America's first integrated waste treatment facility.

Local Participation in the Program

In mid-1980, after the Hazardous Waste Management Committee report was released and while the Environmental Council of Alberta compiled its public hearing reports, Alberta initiated its community involvement program. Before any activity was undertaken to start the physical siting program, a meeting was held with the directors of the province's regional planning commissions. These planning commissions were involved in matters of regional concern and had a responsibility to advise and participate in matters of land use, servicing, and long-range planning.

Following a presentation of the intent of the hazardous waste management program and an explanation of the siting plans for the province, the directors of the commissions endorsed the program and encouraged the task force to contact municipal bodies throughout the province. The planning commissions continued to be involved and were included in all regional activities. Periodic briefings were held in the commission offices, particularly later in the program once candidate sites had identified themselves.

From this beginning, awareness of the program spread, and the task force held meetings with regional development associations and municipal councils across the province. The meetings were introductory only, held to explain the widespread nature of the waste management program. No specific details were available; no work had yet been done to define suitable sites for any type of waste handling facility. Upon invitation, any municipality, special interest group, or body had access to the available information and could host a meeting to discuss the situation. During 1981, every county, municipal district, improvement district, and special area in Alberta asked for and received a briefing session wherein they were given general information on the criteria which might be used in a plant siting program. This amounted to a total of over 120 community meetings throughout the province.

Awareness spread rapidly during the border-to border information program, and the task force was gratified to find that there was considerable interest and support in the efforts of the government to manage wastes and establish a system for safe collection, transportation, treatment, and disposal of special wastes. Upon completion of the circuit of introductory meetings, local authorities then had the option to go no further in the program or to request a detailed regional analysis of their area. This request had to be in written form and signed by the county manager. Invitations to assess the suitability for a plant site were received from 52 of a possible 70 jurisdictions in the province. Studies were undertaken by the government at no charge to the municipality, but with the condition that all reports be presented and explained at an open public meeting or a council meeting to which the public had been invited. Local committees were established in each municipality, and they had full access to all government information and updates on the program.

With this basic understanding of waste treatment and control, 25 percent of the areas studied requested further consideration as a possible host community for the waste treatment plant. Environmental constraints and public opposition caused others to drop or be dropped from consideration, typically for reasons based on fear of:

Effects on health, especially that of children
Effects on livestock and crops
Pollution of water and air
Decrease in land values
Risk from plant explosion
Transportation risk
Influx of undesirable waste-producing industries near the plant
Creation of additional industrial development zones in the area
The possibility of the area's becoming a dump for other jurisdictions

Municipalities that invited further study and consideration as a host community perceived the development of a plant in a positive light. Some of the potential benefits envisioned were:

Improved local and regional waste management practices
Opportunity for local citizen involvement in the regulatory process
Optimum environmental protection
Employment in the plant and with service firms
Local benefits from a broader tax base and diversification

In the end, the list of potential sites was narrowed to five communities; those sites were then subjected to detailed drilling to test the suitability of the local geology, and the communities entered a program of intensive seminar sessions. A series of three seminars was offered to help the public fully understand the background of the program, the reasons for the development of a waste management system, the technology available, and the type of operation that would be introduced should their area be chosen for the plant site.

To assess public support, the five areas held referendums and the results reflected well on the efforts of the government to quell fears, raise awareness, and allow the public to participate in the program. With unprecedented large voter turnout, the two major contenders voted 79 and 77 percent in favor of hosting the plant. With such a strong indication of public acceptance, and proven environmental suitability, the cabinet chose the site near Swan Hills for development of the hazardous waste treatment plant. The actual selection of the specific location for the facility followed that announcement.

Specific Site Selection

The essence of site selection was the elimination of all areas which did not fit the chosen criteria. Base maps, overlain with a series of data maps displaying color-coded siting criteria, were used. A provincial perspective of Alberta was initially developed to provide an overview of potentially suitable regions. Broad-based maps at 1:1,000,000 were used for information on water systems, geology, soils, habitat, forestry, and historical resources. More refined regional assessments were then based on maps at 1:250,000 and coincided with transportation and resource inventory materials. These provided excellent detail for presentation of data on a scale which delineated individual land holdings. This scale also matched that used by the provincial land survey, which served as an accurate base-map grid. Data were derived from government and research agencies, and much use was made of the Canada Land Inventory. All data were readily available but had never been compiled in such a way as to present a total picture of environmental suitability for industrial development.

Over the base map, which provided the legal grid, river systems, towns, and transportation routes, all other criteria were separately color-displayed. As each sheet was placed over the base map, areas of constraint compounded to give an overall view of blank or constraint-free locations. This approach provided a comprehensive representation of all criteria which may affect a particular tract of land. Using graphics in this way not only presented data in the context of related activities but provided a vehicle by which public comment could contribute to the planning process. Public participation was encouraged in producing the package and adding local refinements to the mapping. Attempts were made not to present perfect finished graphics to the public but in fact to allow individuals to assist with development of draft maps during the actual discussions.

Guided by the need to protect environment quality and preserve cultural values, officials developed siting criteria for the delineation of lands which could be considered as candidate locations for a waste treatment plant site. Four general categories of constraints were defined: physical, biological, land use, and human. This order followed a natural progression from the stable natural environment, to the variables of ecology, to human activities related to biophysical limitations. Social and cultural values were related directly to the opportunities provided by environmental conditions.

These criteria were then delineated as follows:

Physical constraints
  Geology
  Hydrogeology
  Surface water
  Topography
  Seismic activity potential
Biological constraints
  Forestry
  Soils
  Wildlife
  Birdlife
Land use constraints
  Agriculture
  Federal land
  Provincial Crown land
  Resource extraction
Human constraints
  Recreation areas
  Archaeological/historical sites

Physical constraints were established to ensure that any waste treatment plant site was capable of containing a spill or leak. Alberta was fortunate in that glaciation had left behind a dense, stable layer of till which, in many areas, was gravel-free and highly impermeable. All areas with significant gravel or sand, fractures, or groundwater recharge were ruled out. To avoid possible contamination of water, all locations adjacent to bodies of surface water or aquifers were similarly deleted. Steep slopes were avoided because of instability and difficulties of site preparation and construction and potential problems of runoff containment. Alberta's geology, though not prone to seismic activity, did allow some tectonic movements, and induced activity was evident in areas of enhanced oil recovery.

Regions with rich soil, commercial timber, and important game and bird habitats were all avoided. Alberta has a rich mosaic of prime farmland, valuable grazing reserves, ecological preserves, and vast tracts of renewable and nonrenewable resource extraction. Land with potential for productivity was eliminated from consideration. All federally owned land was eliminated, including national parks, Indian reservations, and military zones. Transportation corridors were noted for future access.

The preservation of cultural values was the most important human resource criteria. Historic sites considered of great worth to the cultural fabric of the province were eliminated from further consideration.

Following the mapping exercise, data were returned to each municipal council. Local public input was invited, and the community could then choose constraint-free lands for further consideration. These areas were then assessed in more detail. Up to this point, all work had been depicted graphically. Site-specific studies were then begun to:

Confirm all data used in the mapping

Gather information on site conditions of terrain, surface water and ground-water, soils, vegetation, and geology

Install a series of monitors to provide data on long-term conditions and changes in the environment

Within 2 years of the program initiation, the five candidate sites were selected to undergo detailed hydrogeological assessment. All sites proved to be environmentally suitable prior to the final siting announcement in March 1984.

The site then chosen for the facility was 12.5 miles northeast of the town of Swan Hills, which was 125 miles northwest of Edmonton in central Alberta. This was an area of dense glacial deposits overlain by muskeg and forest. Climatic conditions reflected the high elevation and latitude, with long, cold winters and short, warm summers. The site was within a vast tract of government-owned land and had no neighboring land users. The main activities in the area were oil and gas exploration and lumbering.

The site consisted of 320 acres of land, of which 23 acres made up the development site. A 0.5-mile buffer zone surrounded the property and ensured that all plans for adjacent land were first reviewed by the government and by neighboring land users.

Construction of the Facility

In a government policy statement issued in January 1982, it was announced that the treatment facility would be built, owned, and operated by the private sector, to the extent practical. Following this announcement, a request for proposals was issued.

Nineteen firms from several different countries responded; the competition was eventually reduced to a list of four firms which all had expertise in waste management. A committee of experts from Europe, England, the United States, and Canada reviewed the applications and chose Chem-Security Limited.

Site development plans were reviewed by the Crown, and technological input was gained through an international project team. The fully integrated plant was expected to accept all of the organic and inorganic wastes from Alberta generators. The treatment and disposal processes would consist of high-temperature incineration, physical-chemical treatment, secure landfill, and deep-well injection for treated residues. No wastes from outside Alberta were to be accepted.

The Crown owned the property on which the plant was to be built and held a reservation on the surrounding buffer zone. Also, all utilities were provided to the site, including electric power, natural gas, water, and telephone. Access roads to the site were to be realigned and rebuilt whenever necessary.

Establishment of an integrated waste management system in Alberta, including a network of collection and transfer stations, the authorization of all off-site hazardous waste handling facilities, and the establishment of a strong database for ambient environmental conditions surrounding the facility site, was to be regulated by the Crown.

As part of a long-term monitoring program, groundwater and surface water quality test wells were placed on and around the site, and water samples were submitted to laboratory analysis to determine chemical and metal content. Air monitors recorded weather conditions and air quality on-site and regionally. Samplings of soil, vegetation, and small mammals identified natural conditions and served as a baseline for future monitoring programs. The government regulatory agencies set the emission standards with which the plant had to comply.

Construction of a hazardous waste treatment plant is, in itself, a major achievement. However, in order to move waste materials efficiently through the province, a system of local waste collection facilities and regional transfer stations was also planned. Wastes would be delivered directly to these sites by the generator. At the transfer station, wastes were to be sorted, bulked where possible, and transported directly to the treatment plant at Swan Hills. Such a system would facilitate waste management at the regional level and would provide for the monitoring and regulation of hazardous waste movement.

Public Participation Experience

It is impossible to describe Alberta's site selection program without a full discussion of the public involvement which went hand in hand with the physical site assessment. Community involvement had been a cornerstone in the hazardous waste treatment facility siting program. The process of providing information to the citizens of Alberta was begun well before the site selection program was implemented.

The term "hazardous waste" creates strong emotional feelings. It can arouse deep-seated angers, frustrations, fears, and reactions against any level of government, industry, and progress in the modern world. Irrational reactions can cause illness, depression, arguments, alarm, and widespread panic. Fear of the unknown or distrust of pollution control programs can bring about vociferous opposition to hazardous waste facility siting plans. This has also been a popular issue with the news media, which has been known to promulgate misinformation.

Citizen awareness and participation in the decision-making process is an approach which can result in calm, two-way communication between the people and the government, and permit an understanding of why a management system is needed, how it can be implemented, and what the undesirable and desirable impacts may be. The approach taken by the task force assigned to the program in Alberta was one of complete and open disclosure of all information gathered and derived for the siting process. Before any step was implemented, the public was made aware of the government's intentions. No studies were confidential, and no test results were kept from public scrutiny.

Understanding the subject of hazardous waste is difficult for the layperson, particularly if it is introduced suddenly and out of context. Recognizing this potential problem area was a major breakthrough in structuring an approach to the community involvement program. Hazardous waste was presented as a small, but important, part of the total regional waste stream, and by showing the local waste management practices and problems, this special waste came to be perceived as a familiar, local, and expected part of the waste produced by any household, community, or industrial park.

Associating hazardous waste management with waste reduction, exchange, and recycling also helped put the problem into perspective. Options for taking previously hazardous wastes out of the system and recycling them as products or feedstock for other processes made environmental and economic sense. A display of how a network of waste management facilities might operate in the province proved effective in bringing all aspects of municipal, industrial, and hazardous waste into focus. Graphic and printed materials, audiovisuals, and other communications tools enhanced a personal approach and helped the varied audiences understand their role in developing an effective waste collection, transfer, transportation, treatment, and disposal network.

THE INTEGRATED SYSTEM

Economic and environmental success in a TSD facility depends upon the input of waste at every level of generation. An "integrated" system accentuates the interdependence of waste handling facilities which collect and transfer the wastes to the treatment plant. Consequently, a treatment facility cannot be planned, built, or operated without consideration of this network of regional facilities. Plant operations require a continuous feedstock. However, the treatment plant has a remote location from local and regional waste management collection and transfer stations which deal directly with the public, small generators, and industry.

Origins of all components of the waste stream and their introduction into the system at a collection or transfer station and movement to the plant for treatment and disposal must be considered in system planning in order to rationally site the collection and transfer stations. Successful waste management must encompass all levels and all facets of collection, exchange, recycling, transfer, treatment, and disposal.

Technological options for waste handling are dependent upon waste type, amount, location, and operating costs. Not so well defined is the approach to public understanding of a waste management program, attitudes toward management techniques, local requirements, both real and perceived, and levels of participation necessary for the facility to operate effectively. The greater the level of public participation during program planning, the higher the level of awareness of environmental issues pertaining to waste, and the greater the local acceptance in recycling, waste separation, and disposal of hazardous wastes.

QUESTIONS

1 What criteria should be used in selecting treatment technology for hazardous waste?

2 What factors should enter into decisions regarding siting a hazardous waste facility?

3 How would you attempt to mitigate a not-in-my-backyard situation for hazardous waste management?

BIBLIOGRAPHY

1 Boomer, B. A., and A. R. Trenholm: "Common Deficiencies in RCRA Part B Incinerator Applications," *JAPCA*, vol. 37, no. 3, 1987.

2 Dawson, G. W., and B. W. Mercer: *Hazardous Waste Management*, Wiley, New York, 1986.

3 Fuller, W. H., and A. W. Warrick: *Soils in Waste Treatment and Utilization*, volume II, *Pollution Containment, Monitoring, and Closure*, CRC Press, Boca Raton, Fla., 1985.

4 Grisham, J. W.: *Health Aspects of the Disposal of Waste Chemicals*, Pergamon, New York, 1986.

5 Long, F. A., and G. E. Schweitzer: *Risk Assessment at Hazardous Waste Sites*, American Chemical Society Symposium Series, Washington, 1982.

6 McQuaid-Cook, J.: "The Development of a Special Waste Management Program in Alberta, Canada," paper given at 3d International Symposium on Operating European Hazardous Waste Management Facilities, Odense, Denmark, September 1986.

7 Peirce, J. J., and P. A. Vesilind: *Hazardous Waste Management*, Ann Arbor Science, Ann Arbor, 1981.

8 *RCRA Orientation Manual*, U.S. Environmental Protection Agency, Office of Solid Waste, Washington, 1986.

9 Smith, M. A., F. M. Lynn, and R. N. L. Andrews: "Economic Impacts of Hazardous Waste Facilities," *Hazardous Waste and Hazardous Materials*, vol. 3, no. 2, 1986.

CHAPTER 14

SITE REMEDIATION

INTRODUCTION

Releases of hazardous substances have occurred at uncontrolled sites throughout the United States.[3] Groundwater and surface water have been contaminated, drinking water supplies have been lost, and people have been evacuated or in some instances permanently relocated. The general public has become worried and angry about acute and chronic toxic threats to their health and their environment, about the loss of natural resources, and about adverse effects on the value of their homes and property.

Before there was any federal legal authority, site cleanup typically involved temporary stopgap measures that attempted to solve immediate and threatening problems. When a hazardous spill occurred—such as from a ruptured pipeline, a leaking storage tank, or an accident involving a railcar full of chemicals—it was cleaned up by private parties, usually the owner or operator directly involved with the spill. Polluted sites that resulted from long-term leaks or seepage were also cleaned up on an as-needed basis by the owner or operator. However, if the responsible parties did not clean up their spills, state and local governments were called upon to remediate the problem. The ability of state and local governments to cope with the complexities of chemical spills and contamination varied greatly, as did funding for expensive long-term cleanup, particularly at abandoned dump sites. State funds were usually unavailable for this purpose, and states also lacked the legal authority to force the responsible parties to undertake long-term cleanup activities. Furthermore, state and local governments usually did not have the necessary technological expertise to adequately define either the problem or the solution at the contaminated site.

In 1976 the Resource Conservation and Recovery Act (RCRA) established a system to track hazardous wastes from the generator through ultimate disposal. The main objective of RCRA was to prevent future problems from being created by hazardous substances. RCRA did not address the cleaning up of historic problem sites. The federal government did have the authority under RCRA to force responsible parties to take necessary cleanup actions during emergency situations; however, when the responsible parties would not take appropriate action, there was no provision in RCRA that allowed the federal government itself to respond directly and clean up the site.

Incidents during the late 1970s helped to make the public and Congress more aware of the potential dangers of large-scale disposal of hazardous substances as well as of the risks entailed in the transportation and handling associated with their use in commerce. There was need for a mechanism to respond to emergency situations and, even more, to the long-term dangers created by site contamination.

THE SUPERFUND LAW

The Comprehensive Environmental Response, Compensation and Liability Act (CERCLA) of 1980 became law to fill in the gaps in site remediation that had not been addressed by other environmental legislation.[7] The purpose of CERCLA was "to provide for liability, compensation, cleanup and emergency response for hazardous substances released into the environment and the cleanup of inactive hazardous waste disposal sites." CERCLA filled the gap to protect human health and the environment by authorizing federal action in response to threats from any hazardous waste source, including abandoned hazardous waste sites. CERCLA, or the Superfund law, provides both response and enforcement mechanisms.[4] Response typically involves removal and remedial actions, while enforcement gives EPA the authority to force responsible parties to undertake cleanup or to recover cleanup costs when the responsible parties themselves do not or cannot undertake remediation. The federal government may also respond directly to environmental threats, and these federal responses may be financed by the trust fund created under CERCLA. Initially the trust fund was supported by taxes on producers and importers of petroleum and 42 basic chemicals. In its first 5-year period, this Superfund collected about 1.6 billion dollars, with 86 percent of that money coming from industry and the remainder from federal government appropriations. In 1986 the Superfund Amendments and Reauthorization Act (SARA) greatly expanded the money available to remediate Superfund sites.

CERCLA effectively revised the National Contingency Plan (NCP), which provided federal authority to respond to the problems of abandoned or uncontrolled hazardous waste disposal sites as well as to certain incidents involving hazardous substances. The NCP defines three types of responses for incidents involving hazardous substances; any of these three may be carried out by EPA through its remedial response program:

Immediate removal, which requires a prompt response to prevent immediate and significant harm to human health or the environment. Immediate removals must be completed within 6 months.

Planned removal, which is expedited when some response, not necessarily an emergency response, is required. The same 6-month limitation also applies to planned removal.

Remedial response, which requires additional time and money. It is intended to achieve a site solution that is a permanent remedy for the particular problem involved.

Immediate removals originate from an emergency involving hazardous substances. These emergencies might include fires; explosions; direct human contact with a hazardous substance; human, animal, or food chain exposure; or contamination of drinking water sources. An immediate removal involves cleaning up the hazardous site to protect human health and life, containing the hazardous release, and minimizing the potential for damage to the environment. For example, a truck, train, or barge spill could involve an immediate removal determination by EPA to get the spill cleaned up. On the other hand, an inactive hazardous waste site may need only immediate containment and storage, which could allow well-planned cleanup to take place later. Immediate removal responses may include activities such as sample collection and analysis, containment or control of the release, removal of the hazardous substances from the site, provision of alternative water supplies, installation of security fences, excavation of threatened citizens, or general deterrent of the spread of the hazardous contaminants.

A planned removal involves a hazardous site that does not present an immediate emergency. Under Superfund, EPA may initiate a planned removal if the action will minimize damage or risk and is consistent with a more effective long-term solution to the problem. Planned removals are carried out by EPA if the responsible party is either unknown or cannot or will not take timely and appropriate action. The state in which the cleanup site is located must be willing to match at least 10 percent of the costs of the removal action as well as agree to nominate the site in question for the National Priority List.

In 1984 an EPA study characterized the types of threats posed by hazardous sites where removal actions had been taken. Threats to human health were identified at 87 percent of the removal sites in the study. Both human health and the environment were threatened at 75 percent of the sites studied. The most common health threats were the potential for direct physical contact with hazardous substances and contamination of drinking water. Soil contamination was the most common environmental threat. As shown in Table 14-1, PCBs, pesticides, and heavy metals were the hazardous substances most often found at the removal sites. Typical remedial actions which were taken to eliminate

TABLE 14-1
SUBSTANCES MOST OFTEN FOUND IN REMOVAL ACTIONS

Substance	Percent of removal actions
PCBs	23.3
Pesticides	13.9
Heavy metals	13.9
Unspecified organics	9.3
Toluene	8.5
Cyanide	6.9
Benzene	5.4
Paints	5.4
Caustic soda	4.7
Acids	4.7
Ethyl benzene	3.9
Trichloroethylene	3.9
Xylene	3.9
Information not available	6.2

Source: U.S. Environmental Protection Agency.

the threats to human health and the environment varied greatly according to the conditions at the site. These remedial actions ranged from installing security fence, to excavating and transporting contaminated soil off-site, to placing leaking drums of hazardous substances in special containers, to installing temporary barriers or ditches, to controlling migration of hazardous substances after a spill.

At many contaminated sites, the remediation cannot be achieved by simply removing leaking drums or excavating contaminated topsoil.[8] Uncontrolled methods of disposal and handling of hazardous substances through the years have created extensive contaminated groundwater and other subsurface media. These contaminated sites represent complex remediation problems that are generally defined and handled as remedial response situations under the National Contingency Plan.

EPA has a designated office in each region for discussing matters pertaining to Superfund. The mailing addresses for each EPA regional office are given in Table 14-2. All concerned parties are encouraged by EPA to utilize these offices for Superfund-related matters.

PRELIMINARY SITE ASSESSMENT AND INSPECTION

EPA involvement usually begins with the identification of a potential hazardous waste site; the initial information can come from a variety of sources, including local citizens and officials, state environmental agencies, the site owners themselves, or simply from awareness of potential problems associated with particular industries. Once EPA has learned of the existence of a potential hazardous waste site, that site must be screened in order to evaluate the potential for adverse impact on human health and the environment.

EPA has developed an inventory system called the Emergency and Remedial Response Information System (ERRIS) to document all of the sites in the United States that may be candidates for remedial action. This is a continuing program that identifies sites as information about them becomes available. The growth in the number of ERRIS sites has been dramatic and is expected to continue for the foreseeable future as additional abandoned and contaminated sites are discovered.

The identification from the ERRIS list of those sites that pose the greatest threat to human health and the environment has been a difficult task. A preliminary assessment is typically the first step in identifying the potential for

TABLE 14-2
EPA REGIONAL SUPERFUND OFFICES

U.S. Environmental Protection Agency Office of Emergency and Remedial Response (WH-548E) 401 M Street, SW Washington, DC 20460	U.S. Environmental Protection Agency Region 6 Hazardous Waste Management Division 1201 Elm Street Dallas, TX 75270
U.S. Environmental Protection Agency Region 1 Waste Management Division John F. Kennedy Building Boston, MA 02203	U.S. Environmental Protection Agency Region 7 Waste Management Division 726 Minnesota Avenue Kansas City, KS 66101
U.S. Environmental Protection Agency Region 2 Office of Emergency and Remedial Response 26 Federal Plaza New York, NY 10278	U.S. Environmental Protection Agency Region 8 Waste Management Division One Denver Place 999 18th Street Denver, CO 80202-2413
U.S. Environmental Protection Agency Region 3 Hazardous Waste Management Division 841 Chestnut Building Philadelphia, PA 19106	U.S. Environmental Protection Agency Region 9 Toxics and Waste Management Division 215 Fremont Street San Francisco, CA 94105
U.S. Environmental Protection Agency Region 4 Waste Management Division 345 Courtland Street, NE Atlanta, GA 30365	U.S. Environmental Protection Agency Region 10 Hazardous Waste Division 1200 6th Avenue Seattle, WA 98101
U.S. Environmental Protection Agency Region 5 Waste Management Division 230 South Dearborn Street Chicago, IL 60604	

hazards from a particular site. The primary objectives of the preliminary assessment are to determine if there is immediate danger to persons living or working near the site and whether or not a site inspection is necessary. Samples for environmental analyses are generally not taken during the preliminary site assessment. Following the preliminary assessment, EPA or the appropriate state agency might determine that an immediate threat to residents or employees at the site requires a removal action. Otherwise, on the basis of the preliminary assessment the site is classified by EPA into one of the three following categories:

There is no further action needed, since there is no threat to human health or the environment.

Additional information is required to complete the preliminary assessment.

Inspection of the site is necessary.

By the end of 1984, 11,700 sites had been the subject of preliminary assessments, and approximately one-third of them had received an actual site inspection. Site inspections require sampling to determine the types of hazardous substances that are present and to identify the extent of contamination and its migration. The actual site inspection includes preparation of a work plan and an on-site safety plan and can take up to 6 months to complete. On the basis of this site inspection, EPA then makes one of the following determinations:

An immediate removal action is necessary.

No further action is required.

Additional information is needed.

The site poses a significant but not immediate threat.

THE HAZARD RANKING SYSTEM (HRS) AND THE NATIONAL PRIORITY LIST (NPL)

If it is determined that the site poses a significant threat, EPA then uses its Hazard Ranking System (HRS) to measure the relative risk posed by a site. Based upon this ranking system, sites that warrant the highest priority for remedial action then become part of the National Priority List (NPL).

The HRS is a procedure for ranking facilities in terms of the potential threat based upon containment of the hazardous substances, route of release, characteristics and amount of the substances, and likely targets. The methodology of the HRS provides a quantitative estimate that represents the relative hazards posed by a site and takes into account the potential for human and environmental exposure to hazardous substances. The HRS score is based on the probability of contamination from three sources or routes— groundwater, surface water, and air—on the site in question. The HRS determines the potential hazards presented by a site relative to other sites by assigning three scores to the hazardous site:[5]

• S_M is the potential for harm to humans or the environment from migration of a hazardous substance into groundwater, surface water, or air; it is a composite of scores for each of the three routes.

• S_{FE} is the potential for harm from substances that can explode or may be flammable.

• S_{DC} is the potential for harm from direct contact with hazardous substances at the site.

The score for each of these hazard modes is obtained by considering a set of factors that characterize the potential of the facility to cause harm, as shown in Table 14-3. Each factor is assigned a numerical value according to prescribed criteria. This value is then multiplied by a weighting factor, yielding the factor score. The factor scores are then combined: scores within a factor category are added together and then the total scores for each factor category are multiplied together. S_M is a composite of the scores for the three possible migration routes:

$$S_M = \frac{1}{1.73}\sqrt{S^2_{gw} + S^2_{sw} + S^2_a} \tag{14.1}$$

where S_{gw} = ground water route score

S_{sw} = surface water route score

S_a = air route score

Use of the HRS requires considerable information about the site and its surroundings, the hazardous substances present, and the geology to the aquifers. If data are missing for more than one factor in connection with the evaluation of a route, then that route score becomes 0, and there is no need to assign scores to factors in a route that will be set at 0.

The factors that most affect an HRS site score are the proximity to a densely populated area or source of drinking water, the quantity of hazardous substances present, and the toxicity of those hazardous substances. The HRS methodology has been criticized for the following reasons:

There is a strong bias toward human health effects, with only slight chance of a site in question receiving a high score if it represents only a threat or hazard to the environment.

Because of the human health bias, there is an even stronger bias in favor of highly populated affected areas.

The air emission migration route must be documented by an actual release, while groundwater and surface water routes have no such documentation requirement.

The scoring for toxicity and persistence of chemicals may be based on site containment which is not necessarily related to a known or potential release of the toxic chemicals.

TABLE 14-3
RATING FACTORS FOR HAZARD RANKING SYSTEM

Hazard mode	Category	Groundwater route	Surface water route	Air route
Migration	Route characteristics	Depth to aquifer of concern	Facility slope and intervening terrain	
			1-year 24-hour rainfall	
		Net precipitation		
		Permeability of unsaturated zone	Distance to nearest surface water	
		Physical state	Physical state	
	Containment	Containment	Containment	
	Waste characteristics	Toxicity/persistence	Toxicity/persistence	Reactivity/incompatibility
		Quantity	Quantity	Toxicity
				Quantity
	Targets	Groundwater use	Surface water use	Land use
		Distance to nearest well/population served	Distance to sensitive environment	Population within 4-mile radius
			Population served/distance to water intake downstream	Distance to sensitive environment
Fire and explosion	Containment	Containment		
	Waste characteristics	Direct evidence		
		Ignitability Reactivity Incompatibility Quantity		

Targets	Distance to nearest population
	Distance to nearest building
	Distance to nearest sensitive environment
	Land use
	Population within 2-mile radius
	Number of buildings within 2-mile radius
Direct contact	
Observed incident	Observed incident
Accessibility	Accessibility of hazardous substances
Direct contact	
Observed incident	Observed incident
Accessibility	Accessibility of hazardous substances
Containment	Containment
Toxicity	Toxicity
Targets	Population within 1-mile radius
	Distance to critical habitat

Source: U.S. Environmental Protection Agency.

A high score for one migration route can be more than offset by low scores for the other migration routes.

Averaging of the route scores creates a bias against the site that has only one hazard, even though that one hazard may pose an extreme threat to human health and the environment.

EPA provides quality assurance and quality control for each HRS score to ensure that these site evaluations are performed on a consistent basis. These HRS scores range from 0 to 100, with a score of 100 representing the most hazardous site. Generally, HRS scores of 28.5 or higher will place a site on the NPL. Occasional exceptions have been made in this priority ranking to meet the CERCLA requirement that a site designated by a state as its top priority be included on the NPL.

When EPA places a hazardous waste site on the NPL, it also issues a summary description of the site and its threat to human health and the environment. The summaries that follow are based on some typical examples from EPA files.

EPA Summary of Conditions at the East Bethel Demolition Landfill (September 1985)

The East Bethel Demolition Landfill covers about 6 acres in East Bethel Township in north-central Anoka County, Minnesota. The surrounding area is populated with farms and new single-family homes. Approximately 3400 people live within 3 miles.

In the late 1960s, the landfill operated as a dump. In October 1971, the Minnesota Pollution Control Agency (MPCA) issued a permit to the Sylvester Brothers Development Company to operate a sanitary landfill on the site. Later the landfill began to accept only demolition waste. MPCA files indicate that the equivalent of approximately 4400 drums of hazardous industrial wastes and contaminated soils were buried in the landfill in 1974.

The landfill is located on the Anoka Sand Plain, a shallow sand aquifer which provides drinking water to a few residents in the area. The aquifer is contaminated with organic compounds, including chloroform and 1,1,1-trichloroethane, as well as arsenic, according to analyses conducted by a consultant to East Bethel Demolition Landfill. The majority of residents use a deeper aquifer. A relatively impermeable material is between these two aquifers, which are approximately 1000 feet south of the landfill.

EPA Summary of Conditions at the Idaho Pole Company (October 1984)

Idaho Pole Company, which has been in operation since 1946, treats wood products with pentachlorophenol (PCP) on a 10-acre site in Bozeman, Gallatin County, Montana. Groundwater in the area is very shallow and flows to the north-northwest, where it discharges into Rocky Creek. About 1250 people living within 3 miles of the site use groundwater as a source of drinking water.

It was known that any hazardous material leaking onto the ground during the wood-treatment process could contaminate groundwater because of the highly permeable soils and the shallow groundwater. An even greater concern was that wastewater discharged onto the surface at the facility could rapidly infiltrate the groundwater; the facility had, in fact, a history of surface water problems associated with its discharges.

In 1978, the state investigated a complaint concerning PCP in Rocky Creek. At that time, a ditch, originating at the Idaho Pole plant and running from the plant for about 200 to 300 yards before entering Rocky Creek, contained large quantities of PCP. While minute quantities were noted at the mouth of the ditch and Rocky Creek, large quantities had collected on the rocks and vegetation along and in the ditch. Stains high on the sides of the ditch and on vegetation indicated that discharge had been much greater in the past.

In August 1983, EPA collected samples at the old Bozeman landfill, which neighbors the Idaho Pole property. The results showed that a considerable amount of PCP was migrating from the plant. A state sample showed even higher PCP concentrations at the landfill.

In 1984 the state issued a compliance order requiring Idaho Pole to take measures to eliminate discharges into Rocky Creek and to prevent the future placement of wastes in locations where they were likely to pollute state waters. But when Idaho Pole started work to comply with the order, they discovered that because of leaking pipes and tanks and a deteriorated main pumphouse sump, soil contamination at the facility was more extensive than anyone had realized. Therefore, to halt the movement of PCP into groundwater, Idaho Pole, working in conjunction with the state, constructed an interceptor trench running the length of the property boundary.

EPA Summary of Conditions at the University of Minnesota Rosemount Research Center (October 1984)

The University of Minnesota operated a 4-acre disposal site in Rosemount, a rural area in Dakota County, Minnesota. About 9600 people use wells within 3 miles of the site as a source of drinking water.

Between 1960 and 1973, the university buried or incinerated gaseous, liquid, and solid chemical laboratory wastes on the site. A year before they closed the facility, the university detected volatile organic chemicals and heavy metals in monitoring wells and soil on the site. New monitoring data collected by the state in 1984 indicated that the contamination was spreading. As a result, the state began an enforcement action against the university, and because of the contamination, began supplying bottled water to 28 families in Rosemount.

EPA REMEDIAL ACTION

EPA remedial actions may be taken only at those sites that are on the NPL. This ranking helps ensure that the Superfund dollars are used in the most cost-effective manner and where they will yield the greatest benefit.

EPA and the state work in close consultation to determine their appropriate roles in Superfund remedial work. Once these roles have been defined, the investigators can begin to collect and analyze the data necessary to justify remedial action and to support the development of alternatives in the subsequent feasibility study.

Before a remedial action can be taken at a site, a number of questions must be answered:

What are the contaminants and how much contamination is present? How large is the surface area of the contaminated site? What is the size of the contaminated groundwater plume? Where is its exact location and in what direction is it moving?

Based upon the alternatives available, what is the best way to clean up the site? How should these alternatives be implemented? What products will they yield? How long will it take to complete the implementation and what will it cost?

What level of protection is adequate? In other words, how clean is clean?

The answers to the first two sets of questions require scientific and engineering background that is supported by extensive sampling of the contaminated site area. The last question cannot be answered objectively; rather it is a subjective question, and oftentimes political.

The identification and quantification of risks to human health and the environment from uncontrolled and highly complex hazardous waste sites is difficult. Humans face daily exposures to toxic chemicals wherever they are—at home, in the workplace, and through the general environment—and it is difficult to attribute the cause and effect of exposure to toxic chemicals to any single source. Risk assessment and site cleanup will usually have to proceed on the basis of very limited knowledge for determining the precise level of cleanup necessary. There is simply not enough technical and health-related information available to know precisely what the level of cleanup at any specific site should ultimately be. The selection of appropriate cleanup technologies and the ultimate evaluation of cleanup performance remains somewhat of an art rather than a science. Restoring sites to pristine or background levels or requiring the use of best available technology is probably not practical or economical based on a rational cost-benefit analysis.

An ideal remedial cleanup should provide complete and total protection of human health and the environment from the remediated site contamination. However, complete protection is neither technically feasible nor affordable. There will always be some level of risk remaining at a remediated site. For example, the amount of a hazardous substance in soil at the site could be reduced to less than 1 ppb, but practical technology may not be available to achieve this low level of contamination. Even if the technology is available, it may be prohibitively expensive and not justifiable, if one considers the total funding available to remediate all of the sites on the NPL.

The questions of concern are first posed during an initial site investigation. The scope of this remedial investigation will vary, depending upon which one of the three types of remedial action is involved, i.e., initial remediation, source control, or off-site measures. Typically, remedial investigations involve a sequence of activities that might include visiting the site to define the boundary conditions, prepare a site map, and study the hydrogeology, groundwater, surface water, soils, and air quality, as well as to identify, even in a preliminary way, the appropriate remedial technology.

A feasibility study is often conducted simultaneously with the remedial investigation of the project. This feasibility study includes the development of alternatives based upon the established objectives for the cleanup, identification of possible technologies, and design of site-specific methods for the remedial action itself.[6] During the feasibility study these alternatives are analyzed in great detail and recommendations are made based upon the most cost-effective approach to achieve the desired results. Also included in this analysis is the development of a preliminary design of the recommended alternative and its review by the people living in the affected area.

Initial remedial measures could include construction of fences, stabilization of dikes or waste impoundments, temporary provisions for alternative water supplies, and removal of aboveground drums of storage tanks that are leaking hazardous substances. When substantial concentrations of hazardous substances remain on-site and existing dikes to retard the migration are inadequate, it may be necessary to pursue source control actions. These source control actions might include installation of grout curtains or trenches, closure of surface impoundments, capping of contaminated areas, and excavation of contaminated soil or buried waste. When source control measures are inappropriate or will not effectively reduce migration of hazardous substances from the site, it may be necessary to include a permanent provision for alternative water supplies, control of a contaminated aquifer, dredging of contaminated river sediments, or perhaps even relocation of the affected population.

The following examples of remedial alternatives are based upon EPA information.

Drake Chemical Site

Drake Chemical is ranked 394th on the NPL. The site, located in Lock Haven, Pennsylvania, was operated for approximately 30 years as a chemical manufacturing facility. The owner filed for bankruptcy in 1981, after being charged several times with violating environmental and health and safety regulations. The major contaminant present was a herbicide, fenac, although a human carcinogen, beta-naphthylamine, was also detected at the site. There was contamination of the buildings on-site and of the groundwater, surface water, and soil.

According to EPA plans, the first phase of the remedial action will be to control the flow of a contaminant stream leaking from a lagoon on-site through a closed municipal park to a creek south of the site. A pipe will be installed to collect the leachate stream, and contaminated sediments will be placed in a lined lagoon on-site. The second phase of the remedial action will address conditions at the remainder of the site, including groundwater, sludge, and buildings.

Highlands Acid Pit Site

The Highlands acid pit site is listed 424th on the NPL. During the 1950s, an unknown quantity of industrial waste was buried under sand at the 6-acre site, which is located 16 miles east of Houston, Texas. In addition to soil contamination, investigations at the site detected the presence of relatively small amounts of metals and volatile organic chemicals in groundwater. The selected remedy includes excavating to a depth of 8 feet to remove the buried waste and installing a groundwater monitoring system. The remedy does not cover the slight contamination of groundwater that has already occurred, because that does not present a perceptible health risk, and including it in the remedy would result in much higher cleanup costs.

Tysons Dump Site

The Tysons dump site is ranked twenty-fifth on the NPL. The site, located about 15 miles northwest of Philadelphia, Pennsylvania, is a former quarry that was used by several private companies to dispose of various industrial and municipal wastes. The site is located just over one-half mile from a municipal drinking water intake on the Schuylkill River, and is also adjacent to a residential area. Contamination of groundwater, surface water, and soil is present at the site. The principal contaminant is 1,2,3-trichloropropane.

The remedial work at Tysons dump will be split into at least two phases. The first phase of the remedial action will include excavating contaminated materials and transporting them to an RCRA-permitted landfill for disposal, improving a treatment system installed earlier at the site by EPA to remove hazardous substances from the water, and continuing operation of the on-site treatment system for approximately 5 years, or until groundwater contamination is eliminated. The second phase will address the remainder of the off-site contamination.

The case study given below highlights problems associated with the current regulatory approach to establishing cleanup levels.

CASE STUDY
The Seymour Site

The Seymour Recycling Corporation (SRC) site in Seymour, Indiana, was one of the first major cleanup actions conducted under Superfund. Although land disposal sites are the most common operation requiring cleanup, the Seymour case illustrates how a processing or treatment facility can also create substantial problems. Over a 10-year period, SRC established and operated a facility where large amounts of hazardous waste were sent for recycling and treatment. Eventually, authorities discovered that these wastes were not well managed. By 1978 the state of Indiana found it necessary to file a lawsuit to get SRC to clean up an estimated 40,000 drums of waste in various states of decay, leakage, and disarray.

In 1980, after SRC had ceased operations, EPA became involved through the Clean Water Act. EPA estimated that total cleanup costs would be $25 million. Throughout 1980 EPA took legal actions against a number of generator and transporter parties, spent more than $700,000 removing some wastes for incineration, and hired contractors to investigate the groundwater. Two companies whose wastes were at SRC voluntarily spent slightly more than $1 million to remove their drums and place them in a commercial land disposal facility.

In 1981, EPA took the position that Superfund should not be used at the Seymour site because the site did not present an emergency. Moreover, the state maintained it did not have the resources to cover the matching funds required under Superfund. As a result, EPA pursued an enforcement strategy based on getting responsible private parties, chiefly the generators of the wastes, to pay for cleanup.

During 1982 and 1983, two important events took place. EPA reached a settlement with some of the companies that had used the site. Those companies agreed to spend as much as $15 million for surface cleanup, and EPA agreed to eliminate their responsibility for future subsurface cleanup. The cost of groundwater cleanup was estimated at $15 million; $5 million toward those costs was collected from some of the parties involved. A major issue raised at that time was whether it is technically possible and administratively reasonable to make a distinction between surface and subsurface cleanup.

At the same time, the SRC site was evaluated to determine its eligibility for placement on the NPL. The site received a high score because of the observed release of hazardous substances into both surface water and groundwater. The HRS scoring of the site, results of various studies, and the need to supply alternative drinking water to residents suggested that a potentially large, costly groundwater cleanup might be required, but it was not clear what the extent of groundwater contamination was, what the difficulty and costs might be, what cleanup goals would be used, and what effect the surface cleanup would have on the groundwater problem. Nor was it clear whether groundwater cleanup was to be delayed until the responsible parties agreed to pay for it or whether Superfund monies would be used.

The surface cleanup, completed early in 1984, reflected the fundamental approach used from the beginning. The surface cleanup consisted of removing wastes and contaminated soil from the site and sending them elsewhere for land disposal. It was at best a shortsighted solution; the issue of problems associated with land disposal sites that have received removed wastes becomes increasingly important as problems with the technical soundness of any regulatory control over hazardous waste land disposal facilities become more and more evident.

The Seymour site illustrates the concept of impermanent cleanups leading to high future costs. About $12 million has been spent thus far at Seymour for initial responses involving site containment and waste removal, surface cleanup, and many studies and investigations, including the ongoing groundwater work. Nevertheless, permanent cleanup has not yet been achieved. Future actions will be required, probably including groundwater cleanup, removal or treatment of contaminated soil, cleanup of land disposal sites that have received wastes from Seymour, and continuing water treatment. Altogether, future spending for this site is likely to surpass what has already been spent.

CONTAINMENT AND TREATMENT TECHNOLOGIES

The technical solutions to the cleanup of Superfund sites involve either long-term containment systems or expeditious treatment to destroy the waste or render it harmless. Containment technologies represent only interim solutions; inevitably, barrels, drums, impoundments, and landfills will eventually leak, posing a renewed threat to human health and the environment. Additionally, any leachate formed by the contact of water with the hazardous waste must be collected and treated.

The better containment systems for control of hazardous waste sites require that a number of technologies be combined to produce a low probability of failure. There are numerous containment technologies that can be applied to hazardous waste sites on a case-by-case basis. The application depends a great deal on factors such as topography, erosion potential, surface and groundwater flow patterns, and expected rainfall. The advantages, disadvantages, and limitations of these containment technologies have been summarized in Table 14-4.

Groundwater barriers prevent the off-site migration of contaminated water by physically restricting horizontal groundwater flow. These barriers have become the principal means for containment of contaminated plumes that threaten aquifers. Normally these barriers, used in combination with groundwater pumping or capping of the contaminated site, must be attached or made contiguous with another low-permeability geological layer such as bedrock or clay in order to restrict vertical migration of contaminants. The use of barriers is therefore limited to sites where such geological layers are available and accessible or where the bedrock is not heavily fractured. These barriers should have permeabilities of a maximum of 1×10^{-7} cm/s in order to effectively reduce groundwater flow through the containment region, though groundwater barriers will never be completely impermeable, even under ideal construction conditions.

The major types of groundwater barriers include:

Slurry wall, which is a fixed underground physical barrier formed by pumping a cement and bentonite slurry into a trench and allowing the slurry to set in place

TABLE 14-4
SUMMARY OF CONTAINMENT TECHNOLOGIES

Technology	Advantages	Disadvantages	Limitations
Groundwater barriers			
Slurry wall	Most versatile, best-understood barrier technology; inexpensive; low operation and maintenance.	Requires excavation; requires area to mix backfill; difficult to verify continuity of slurry or backfill; difficult to key to bedrock.	Must tie to impervious zone; not impermeable.
Grout curtain	Minimal site disturbance; no excavation required; low operation and maintenance.	Chemicals in grout compromise site safety and pose environmental problems; difficult to verify continuity of wall; limited applicability; expensive compared with other barriers.	Must tie to impervious zone; not 100% impermeable.
Vibrated beam	Special slurries improve containment; no chemical compatibility; no excavation required; low operation and maintenance.	Very sensitive to construction quality; difficult to verify continuity of wall; difficult to key to bedrock; relatively new technology.	Can have no obstructions in soil; must tie to impervious zone; not impermeable.
Sheet pile	No excavation required; low operation and maintenance.	Expensive; difficult to key to bedrock.	Must have loosely packed soils; limited to about 50 feet; must tie to impervious zone; not impermeable; chemical involvement with piling material.
Block displacement	No underlying impervious zone needed.	Still under development.	Complex design requirements limit site conditions.

TABLE 14-4
SUMMARY OF CONTAINMENT TECHNOLOGIES *(Continued)*

Technology	Advantages	Disadvantages	Limitations
Groundwater pumping	Proven and well understood; can function for very long periods; high design flexibility; high reliability; useful in many situations; effectiveness can be verified.	May require expensive modeling; long-term operation and maintenance required; performance sensitive to design; collected liquid must be treated.	Useful up to 10 meters; will not affect contaminants in unsaturated zone or contaminants that do not flow; site conditions may complicate use and performance.
Subsurface drains	Proven and well understood; low operations and maintenance; superior to wells under certain conditions; less sensitive to design than wells; conceptually simple.	Less flexibility than wells; susceptible to clogging; excavation required; collected liquid must be treated; difficult to install beneath waste site.	Cost effective only in shallow applications.
Runon/runoff controls	Proven and well understood; inexpensive; effective; only conceptual design required.	Periodic inspection and maintenance required.	May not be able to handle abnormal storms.
Surface seal/caps	Inexpensive compared with excavation and removal; may be used as an interim measure where surface infiltration is a problem.	Periodic inspection and maintenance required.	Difficult for very large sites; subject to potential failure without proper design, installation, and maintenance.
Solidification and stabilization	High short-term effectiveness; waste material (e.g., fly ash, kiln dust) can be used as a pozzolan.	Extensive testing may be required; many processes still developmental.	Long-term integrity uncertain; not useful for many organics.
Encapsulation	Improves effectiveness of land disposal.	Still developmental.	Long-term integrity uncertain; requires solidification of bulk wastes.

Grout curtain, which is formed by injecting a cement or sodium silicate grout into the ground at well points

Vibrated beam, which is a technique that enhances the performance of slurry walls

Sheet pile, which is constructed by driving webbed or ribbed sections of steel sheet piling into the ground, each of these sections being interlocked to restrict groundwater flow through the barrier

Block displacement, which involves the placement of a fixed underground physical barrier beneath a large mass of earth

Groundwater pumping involves a series of wells to remove groundwater for treatment or to contain the plume. While groundwater pumping techniques are proven technology, the application must be tailored to the cleanup site; the specific requirements of the site dictate the number of wells, the location depth, and the pumping rate. As the pumping system is shut down, the groundwater flow patterns usually return to the original conditions. As a result, groundwater pumping systems have to be operated for long periods of time unless the contaminant source has been either eliminated or rendered harmless through treatment.

Subsurface drains are normally constructed by placing tile or perforated pipe in a trench, covering with gravel or sand, and then backfilling with soil or clay. These drains are then used to collect the leachate as well as to lower the water table for the dewatering of the site. Subsurface drains represent a proven technology that has had many applications other than hazardous waste management. These drains are normally inexpensive to install and operate, but they are not as versatile as wells and therefore are more sensitive to errors of design and construction.

Surface water must normally be controlled, both to prevent the contaminated water from leaving the cleanup site and to prevent off-site contaminated water from entering. Dikes, dams, terraces, downpipes, and vegetation cover are used in conjunction with other technologies. Contaminated water from these runoff control systems will probably require additional treatment prior to final discharge.

Surface seals are low-permeability barriers placed over a site to prevent surface water infiltration, prevent contact with contaminated materials, and control fugitive emissions from the cleanup site. The types of materials that might be used for surface seals include soil, clay, asphalt, concrete, and plastic membranes. Generally soil and vegetation compatible with the region are used to cover these surface sealant materials.

Solidification, storage, and chemical fixation technologies are used to reduce the potential for leachate production by binding the waste in a solid matrix through physical and chemical processes. The hazardous wastes are mixed with the binding agent and allowed to cure into a solid material. This stabilized waste is then usually capped, contained, or land-disposed.

Encapsulation is a process where the wastes are enclosed within a stable water-resistant material. The encapsulated wastes must then be placed in a landfill or similar disposal site. As long as the encapsulation material remains intact, there is little risk of potential leakage.

Numerous treatment technologies are available to remediate contaminated sites.[1,9] The major technologies to perform these remediation processes are physical, chemical, and biological treatment and thermal destruction processes. Generally, treatment processes are specific to the type of hazardous waste to be controlled. Table 14-5 presents a summary of these technologies. Most of them have been used at Superfund sites, and based upon these experiences, many could be adapted to a broad variety of cleanup sites. None of these technologies, however, is universally adaptable to all Superfund sites because of the complexities and variability of hazardous wastes.

Physical treatment processes will not destroy hazardous wastes. Rather, they change the hazardous wastes, through concentration or phase changes, to a more convenient form for disposal. Most physical treatment operations generally produce two separate streams. One of these streams is typically a nonhazardous liquid or solid material that may be easily disposed of. The other stream produced by physical treatment is usually a reduced volume of concentrated hazardous waste that must then undergo additional treatment or thermal destruction. Otherwise it must be placed in a hazardous waste landfill. Typically, the removal of inorganics such as heavy metals during remedial site work will produce a sludge or solid that must be sent to a landfill for disposal. Stripping will produce volatile compounds that may then be destroyed by thermal techniques or treated prior to discharge into the atmosphere. While carbon adsorption is expensive, it may still be the most cost-effective way to remove trace quantities of organics from aqueous systems.

During chemical treatment, hazardous wastes may be rendered harmless, either by destroying the constituents or by changing them chemically. Neutralization and precipitation are widely used chemical treatment techniques to remove inorganic wastes from aqueous streams. Both of these processes are capable of producing hazardous sludges that then must be disposed of in an environmentally acceptable manner. Other chemical treatment techniques include wet air oxidation, which involves a combination reaction that occurs in the liquid phase through the addition of oxygen at high pressure and elevated temperatures. Chemical oxidation involves the addition of an oxidant such as ozone or potassium permanganate.

Biological treatment utilizes microorganisms to biodegrade waste contaminants; the resulting product is then disposed of. Biological treatment systems are usually highly sensitive to changes in temperature, oxygen content, and the loading of toxic contaminants to the system.

Thermal treatment processes use high temperatures as the principal mechanism to destroy hazardous wastes. During incineration, organic molecules are oxidized when they are burned at very high temperatures. Other high-temperature thermal destruction techniques are under development to provide higher thermal destruction and removal efficiencies for hazardous wastes. Incineration has been successfully demonstrated both on and off Superfund sites.

TABLE 14-5
SUMMARY OF PHYSICAL, CHEMICAL, AND BIOLOGICAL TREATMENT AND INCINERATION PROCESSES

Process	Advantages	Disadvantages	Limitations
Physical treatment			
Carbon absorption	Applicable to many organics that do not respond to biological treatment; high degree of flexibility in operation and design; high degree of effectiveness.	Regeneration or disposal of spent carbon required; pretreatment may be required for suspended solids, oil, grease; high operation and maintenance cost.	Many inorganics and some organics are poorly absorbed.
Flocculation, sedimentation, and filtration	Low cost	Generates sludge for disposal	
Stripping	Well understood and demonstrated.	Air controls may be required.	Applicable only to relatively volatile organic contaminants.
Flotation	Well understood and demonstrated; inexpensive.	Generates sludge for disposal.	
Reverse osmosis	High removal potential.	Generates sludge for disposal; pretreatment to remove suspended solids or adjust pH may be required; expensive.	Variability in waste flow and composition affects performance.
Chemical treatment			
Neutralization/precipitation	Wide range of application; inexpensive.	Hazardous sludge produced.	Complexing agents reduce effectiveness.
Ion exchange	Can recover metals at high efficiency.	Generates sludge for disposal; pretreatment to remove suspended solids may be required; expensive.	Resin fouling; removes some constituents but not others.

TABLE 14-5
SUMMARY OF PHYSICAL, CHEMICAL, AND BIOLOGICAL TREATMENT AND INCINERATION PROCESSES *(Continued)*

Process	Advantages	Disadvantages	Limitations
Wet air oxidation	Good for wastes too dilute for incineration or too concentrated or toxic for biological treatment.	Oxidation not as complete as thermal oxidation or incineration; may produce new hazardous species; extensive testing is required; high capital investment; high level of operator skills required; may require posttreatment.	Poor destruction of chlorinated organics; moderate efficiencies of destruction.
Chlorination	Essentially complete destruction; well understood and widely used in other applications.	Specialized for cyanide.	Interfering waste constituents may limit applicability or effectiveness.
Ozonation	Can destroy refractory organics; liquids, solids, mixes can be treated.	Oxidation not as complete as thermal oxidation or incineration; may produce new hazardous species; extensive testing is required; high capital investment; high operation and maintenance.	
Reduction	High destruction.	Specialized for chromium.	Interfering waste constituents may limit applicability or effectiveness.
Permeable treatment beds	Limited excavation required; inexpensive.	Still developmental; periodic replacement of treatment media required; spent treatment medium must be disposed of.	Best for shallow plumes; many reactants treat a limited family of wastes; effectiveness influenced by groundwater flow variations.

Chemical injection	Excavation not required; no pumping required.	Still developmental; extensive testing required.	Best for shallow plumes; need fairly homogeneous waste composition.
Biological treatment			
Conventional	Applicable to many organic waste streams; high total organic removal; inexpensive; well understood and widely used in other applications.	May produce a hazardous sludge which must be managed; may require pretreatment prior to discharge.	Microorganisms are sensitive to oxygen levels, temperature, toxic loading, inlet flow; some organic contaminants are difficult to treat; flow and composition variations can reduce efficiency.
In situ biodegradation	Destroys waste in place.	Limited experience; extensive testing may be required; containment also required.	Aeration is difficult to depths over 2 ft; many common organic species are not easily biodegraded; needs proper combination of wastes and hydrogeological characteristics; proper mix of contaminants, organisms, and nutrients is necessary; organisms may plug pores.

TABLE 14-5
SUMMARY OF PHYSICAL, CHEMICAL, AND BIOLOGICAL TREATMENT AND INCINERATION PROCESSES *(Continued)*

Process	Advantages	Disadvantages	Limitations
Incineration			
Conventional incineration	Destroys organic wastes.	Disposal of residue required; test burn may be required; skilled operators required; expensive.	
On-site incineration	Destroys organic wastes; transportation of wastes not required.	Disposal of residue required; on-site feedstock preparation required; test burn may be required; skilled operators required; expensive.	Mobile units have low feed rate.

The problems created by hazardous substance disposal received considerable public attention during the 1970s and the 1980s . Incidents such as the following case illustrate the problems with the creation and subsequent remediation of sites that have been contaminated with hazardous wastes.[2]

CASE STUDY
Superfund Remediation at CMI

Hazardous substances were stored in drums, containers, and tanks at a bankrupt metal reclamation and chemical manufacturing facility in Baltimore, Maryland. Off-site migration of these substances threatened to contaminate a tributary of the Patapsco River and presented a risk of explosion and release of toxic vapors that threatened the health and safety of residents in the surrounding area.

Background

Chemical Metals Industries (CMI), owned by L & M Associates, Inc., operated a precious metal reclamation facility and was a manufacturer of copper sulfate. They filed for bankruptcy in August 1981.

The site was investigated in September 1981 by the Maryland Office of Environmental Programs (OEP) and the U.S. Environmental Protection Agency (EPA). The CMI facility had consisted of two sites, separated by a block containing 20 occupied residences. Site 1 (Figure 14-1) was the location of an old gasoline station. It was enclosed by an 8-foot cinder-block wall, where approximately 1500 drums were found. The drums were filled with chemicals, including caustic, organic solvents, and cyanide. The drums were damaged and piled haphazardly on the site.

Site 2 was enclosed by a dilapidated fence and contained the metal reclamation plant. About 50 drums and containers marked as acids and oxidizers were found in the plant building (see Figure 14-2). The laboratory and storage area of the building contained small quantities of chemical reagents along with various heavy metals. In the yard were 15 aboveground storage tanks containing liquid and solid wastes. The yard also contained approximately 100 drums of wastes from the metal reclamation operation. Many of these deteriorated drums were leaking. Some were near an open storm drain that led to the municipal sewer system. A storage vault containing various solid wastes was also found at site 2.

Materials stored at CMI were wastes that had accumulated from two manufacturing processes. One process involved production of copper sulfate and copper hydroxide. The other process involved reclamation of precious metals from waste chemical solutions and printed circuit boards. For example, gold from circuit boards was dissolved in aqua regia and then neutralized, causing the metals to precipitate out of the solution.

Remediation Efforts

An October 1981 EPA report agreed with the conclusion of the state that conditions at CMI justified emergency response action. The agency outlined three major threats: (1) formation and release of hydrogen cyanide vapors from leaking drums; (2) off-site migration of contaminated surface water from leaking drums, affecting walkways, streets, and the Patapsco River; and (3) a fire danger that threatened nearby residences and the environment with the release of toxic vapors and water runoff from fire-fighting efforts. To stabilize the site and reduce these threats, EPA proposed to secure the drums; assess the integrity of the aboveground storage tanks; and inventory, sample, analyze, categorize, and dispose of all wastes.

The principal cause of concern was the threat of explosion and fire presented by the improper storage of incompatible materials in an area next to

FIGURE 14-1
The CMI facility.

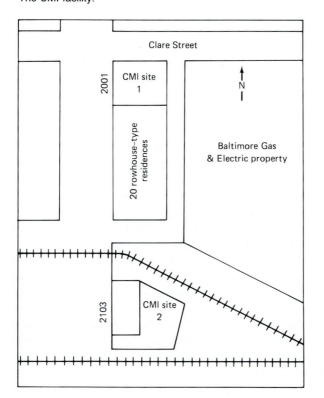

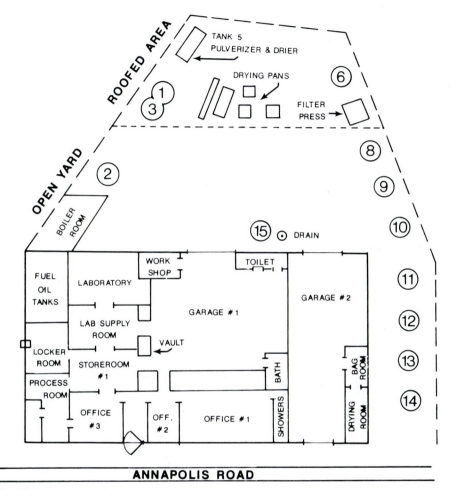

FIGURE 14-2
Site 2 at the CMI facility.

occupied residences. Most of the contamination was confined to drums, tanks, debris, and surface soils. An estimated 100 tons of contaminated debris and surface soil was located on sites 1 and 2. It appeared from the initial investigations that the surface contamination resulted mainly from the contents of deteriorated drums and tank spills onto the ground. Acid fumes were detected in the soil and EP toxicity tests at site 1 also indicated excessive cadmium levels. Leaking drums stacked near an open storm drain at site 2 posed a threat of contaminated runoff into the drain system. The surface runoff from the CMI sites eventually fed into Glynns Falls, a tributary of the Patapsco River.

Monitoring wells were used to determine subsurface contamination. On site 2 a bluish-green water was observed in several monitoring wells. It was subsequently found to contain high levels of copper sulfate, with the highest concentration being in the center of the site. Gasoline was found in one well on site 1 at a depth of 8 feet.

Contamination of the air was a major concern at CMI because cyanide was found close to strong acids, which could produce toxic hydrogen cyanide gas. This concern was underscored by reports from neighbors of noxious odors from the sites. Several fuming drums were observed during early site investigations. The initial analysis of air samples by EPA showed cyanide concentrations in excess of 30 ppm. This led to a cessation of all site activity while investigators attempted to confirm these results. When they failed to confirm the initial results, the investigators consulted with the detector manufacturers and learned that high concentrations of nitrogen dioxide gas from the degradation of nitric acid at the site may have caused the erroneous cyanide reading. Investigators eventually determined that the fumes came from the mixture of water with the acids in the leaking drums.

On October 19, 1981, EPA authorized an emergency response action at CMI, to be funded under CERCLA, making the CMI the first Superfund site in Maryland. EPA was given final authority over all actions taken at CMI. EPA headquarters pledged $58,000 to pay for staging and initial response action costs. Then EPA made an oral demand upon CMI's bankruptcy receiver for cleanup funding; this was followed by a written demand. The receiver responded that no such funds were available.

The emergency response action covered about 7 weeks, from mid-October to mid-December 1981. J & L Industries of Baltimore was hired as the primary contractor for the cleanup. Workers first removed a large amount of trash and debris from the two sites. A 35-ton crane was used to move the haphazardly piled drums about so they could be sampled and analyzed. The 2000 drums found at the two sites were classified as full, partially full, or empty. Empty drums were subclassified as salvageable or unsalvageable. Salvageable empty drums were removed by a chemical company, and unsalvageable empty drums were crushed and removed by a scrap metal dealer. Partially full and full drums were subclassified according to their contents: acid, base, solvent, and cyanide. Cyanide drums were taken to a licensed disposal facility. Solvents went to a cement kiln for use as a low-grade fuel. Acids and bases were taken to a nearby chemical treatment and disposal facility.

Three underground tanks at site 1 were pumped and their contents disposed of. The tanks were then cut open, filled with cement grout, covered, and capped with clay. Four monitor wells were installed at site 1; then the site was graded, capped with clay, covered with topsoil, and seeded.

At site 2 the contents of the 15 aboveground liquid storage tanks were sampled and analyzed. Bulk liquid acids and bases were removed by a vacuum truck. The storage tanks were dismantled and removed. The exteriors of a building and several walls left standing at the site were sandblasted; the interior of the building was cleaned with detergents and disinfectants. Zirconium powder found in a vault in the building was removed and burned under controlled conditions. Four monitor wells were then installed at site 2, and the site was graded and paved with asphalt.

The Contractors

Ecology and Environment served as the on-site technical assistance team for the CMI remediation effort under its 3-year contract with EPA Region III. It was responsible for coordinating various special projects, sampling, documentation, and planning. J & L Industries was hired as the general contractor for the cleanup. That firm was selected by EPA because of its experience and proximity to CMI. J & L oversaw the removal and disposal of all drums, tanks, bulk liquids, and contaminated soil and debris, subcontracting with the Delaware Container Company for disposal of solvents. J & L hired Delaware Container because of past work experience and because of the company's proximity to CMI. J & L also subcontracted with Clean America of Baltimore to pump out bulk liquids at CMI and transport them to appropriate disposal facilities. Clean America was hired primarily because it had the vacuum trucks and experience that were needed to do the job.

EPA hired several companies to treat and dispose of various substances. It hired Chem-Clear, a chemical waste treatment and disposal facility in Baltimore, to dispose of the acids and bases from CMI. A time and materials contract was used with Chem-Clear, which was selected because of its expertise in the field, the technical capabilities of its facility, and its proximity to CMI. EPA hired CAMAX Corporation to remove and dispose of all nonzirconium materials from the vault and laboratory area at site 2. EPA also hired Martel Laboratory Services, Inc., of Baltimore to analyze samples from CMI for RCRA disposal capability and precious metal content and to monitor well samples for groundwater contamination. Martel was selected because it was located nearby and had the capacity to perform prompt analyses, while state and federal labs in the region were handicapped by a large backlog.

T & A Excavating, Inc., was hired to do the final site cleanup, including removing the building from site 1, grading and sodding that area, grouting the underground tanks at site 1, clay-capping the tank area, and grading and paving site 2.

Two Browning Ferris Industries (BFI) facilities were used by J & L, Chem-Clear, and Delaware Container for disposal. BFI's proximity and capability to receive these wastes were major reasons for its selection. All nonliquid hazardous substances from CMI, including sludges from Chem-Clear and Delaware Container work, were disposed of at BFI's Solley Road facility. Nonhazardous solid wastes such as debris and some empty decontaminated drums were disposed of at BFI's sanitary disposal facility. BFI had an open disposal contract with Chem-Clear and Delaware Container for their sludges. J & L had a contract with BFI to dispose of contaminated soil and debris, and

EPA had a separate contract with BFI for disposal of the nonhazardous materials.

EPA had several local firms perform designated removal work under formal or informal agreements in exchange for the materials removed. Abbey Drum Company in Baltimore removed about 600 empty uncontaminated drums from sites 1 and 2 at no charge and was allowed to keep them. Included in this number were 51 drums loaned to CMI by Robinson Chemical Company, which Abbey returned to Robinson as a favor. Spectron, Inc., removed stainless steel tanks from site 2 in exchange for the tanks. Finally, Klaff Metals of Baltimore, a scrap metal dealer, agreed to remove over 400 empty uncontaminated, unsalvageable drums and uncontaminated debris. All of these firms were selected because they were willing and able to remove these materials quickly and at no charge to EPA or the state.

Project Costs and Funding

The emergency response action at CMI cost $340,343.42, as shown in Table 14-6. Most of the CMI project was funded directly under authority of CERCLA, although the state of Maryland and the city of Baltimore contributed substantial funds and services. A total of $199,143.42 in direct costs was funded under CERCLA, with most of that amount going to J & L Industries, the general contractor ($152,289.17), followed by Chem-Clear ($25,435.25), T & A Excavating ($15,000), Clean America ($4989), and Williams Mobile offices ($1430).

The state of Maryland spent an estimated $103,500 in personnel and equipment. Personnel who spent time on the project included chemical and civil engineers, a biologist, a geologist, well drillers, investigative staff, and a lawyer. Maryland also provided such support equipment as a well-drilling rig, a van and a four-wheel drive vehicle, respirators, an MSA self-contained breathing apparatus, and monitoring equipment. The state also paid for some of the costs incurred by T & A in capping the sites. The U.S. Coast Guard agreed to reimburse some costs—fencing the sites and placing sorbent barriers to prevent runoff—incurred by the state during the initial response to the CMI site before authority was switched to EPA and funding to CERCLA.

Baltimore provided 24-hour site security for part of the project's duration, a 35-ton crane for moving drums, a civil defense van, fire equipment, a recharging self-contained breathing apparatus, plus the time of personnel from the fire department, bomb squad, and health department and the mayor's representative. These goods and services totaled $7700.

The cost of the EPA special projects team for the CMI case came to $30,000.

FINANCIAL CONSIDERATIONS

In each case where the need for remedial action has been established, EPA must decide whether to use its enforcement authority to engage the responsi-

TABLE 14-6
COST OF THE EMERGENCY RESPONSE ACTION AT CMI

Task	Quantity	Expenditure	Unit cost	Funding source	Period of performance
Oversight of all removal and disposal work		$147,789.17		CERCLA	10/19/81–12/18/81
Disposal of contaminated soil and debris	100 tons	4,500.00	$45/ton	CERCLA	10/19/81–12/18/81
Treatment and disposal of bulk liquids, acids, and basics	19,500 gal	25,435.25	1.30/gal	CERCLA	10/24/81–12/18/81
Pumping and transport of bulk liquids	19,500 gal	4,989.00	0.25/gal	CERCLA	10/24/81–12/18/81
Grading, sodding, and capping sites 1 and 2		15,000.00		CERCLA	11/27/81–12/18/81
Mobile office rental	1	1,430.00		CERCLA	10/20/81–12/18/81
Work plan, safety protocol, chemical analysis		30,000.00		CERCLA	10/19/81–12/18/81
State of Maryland equipment and personnel		103,500.00		Maryland	9/2/81–12/18/81
City of Baltimore equipment and personnel		7,700.00		Baltimore	10/19/81–12/18/81
Total		$340,343.42			9/2/81–12/18/81

ble party or parties in the cleanup operation or to conduct a Superfund-financed remedial action with the possibility of later cost recovery. The need for timely remedial site response and the likelihood of securing a responsible party to finance the cleanup are important considerations in the EPA decision-making process. Ideally, EPA would like to secure a responsible party to finance the cleanup whenever possible, because that preserves the Superfund monies for use at other sites.

If EPA determines that an enforcement action is appropriate at a Superfund site, the first enforcement activity undertaken is an attempt to identify potentially responsible parties. Once EPA has identified all of the potentially responsible parties at the site, notification letters are sent to these parties to inform them of their potential liability and of the opportunity for them to take appropriate response actions. If the responsible parties decide to negotiate, it may be possible to reach an agreement that specifies the actions needed to be taken. Typically, before these negotiations begin EPA will prepare a draft enforcement document that details the suggested site remedy and the proposed terms of settlement. This document then becomes the basis for the negotiations between EPA and the responsible party. If EPA and the responsible parties reach a negotiated settlement, the scope and terms of the remedy will generally be spelled out in a consent administrative order or consent decree. A *consent administrative order* is a written agreement signed by EPA and the responsible parties specifying the actions to be taken by both sides. A *consent decree* is a more formal document that must be signed by a federal district court judge. Consent decrees are usually issued when there are a large number of responsible parties or the terms of the settlement are highly complex.

If the negotiations are unsuccessful and no settlement is reached, EPA is left with the alternatives of filing a civil suit against the responsible parties, issuing an administrative order requiring the responsible parties to take certain cleanup steps, or conducting a Superfund-financed response and then attempting to recover the costs. Before EPA initiates a civil suit, a determination must be made about whether the response action can be delayed without increasing the threat to human health or the environment. When the remedial response must be taken immediately at the site, EPA will respond immediately and later sue the responsible parties to recover expenditures from the Superfund.

The last step in remedial response involves defining the selected remedy in a bid package and formally advertising this package to allow contractors to bid on the work. Following award of the contract, the plan design is then implemented and the remedial action is completed in accordance with plan.

There is rarely a fair, equitable solution to the problem of how to allocate cleanup costs for abandoned hazardous waste sites. The following case study will help illustrate the dilemma that faces EPA, industry, and the general public in trying to assess the responsibility for these major environmental disasters.

CASE STUDY
Who Pays the Bill?

Once upon a time there was a well-intentioned young man who bought some land in the country near a growing town. On this land he started a waste disposal operation to service the needs of nearby industries. Since he was providing a valuable and necessary service for these industries, he became affectionately known to everyone in the region as "the wastekeeper." He was very conscientious and endeavored to manage his waste disposal business at least as well as, if not better than, anyone else in the region. For many years he accepted and disposed of the waste from companies in the area. Thanks in part to its thriving industries, the town grew into a city and eventually annexed the wastekeeper's land as part of a growing metropolitan area. After 40 years of faithfully serving the community, the wastekeeper decided to retire; as a result, he shut down his waste disposal operation. Many years following his retirement, the wastekeeper died peacefully from natural causes. What should be the end of the story is now only the beginning.

Several years after the wastekeeper died, neighbors near his disposal site began to discover that their well water had a bad odor and was unfit to drink. The neighborhood summoned help from the government authorities; people with knowledge of waste disposal came to study the well water problem. This study revealed that the old disposal site was leaking, that the leachate was contaminating neighborhood wells, and that it posed a threat to both human health and the environment. The authorities mandated that the site be cleaned up and that the three identifiable companies whose wastes had been transported and disposed of at the site pay for the cleanup. Though it was very difficult for the companies to accept responsibility for the disposal of the wastes they had delivered to the wastekeeper and paid for many years ago, they agreed to comply with the order to pay for the site cleanup.

The government authorities then hired a prestigious architectural and engineering consulting firm, which identified the nature and extent of the contamination problem and recommended the most cost-effective response. It was estimated by this A/E firm that adequate cleanup of the site could be accomplished for $5 million—$3 million to clean up the on-site contaminant sources and an additional $2 million to clean up the off-site contamination. All three companies agreed that the cleanup work was necessary and that the cost estimates were reasonable. However, they were uncertain about how to allocate and share these costs in a equitable manner. The concern centered on the types and quantities of wastes that they had sent to the wastekeeper and how these specific wastes were now impacting the total cost of the cleanup operation.

The wastes had varied greatly in quantity and degree of toxicity:

	Chemical	Amount disposed, lb
Company 1	Liquid death	100,000
Company 2	Wastewater sludge	4,000,000
Company 3	Sanitary refuse	30,000,000

Because these wastes had been disposed over a long period of time and had been commingled at the disposal site by the wastekeeper, there was no way to distinguish separate locations where the individual wastes had been deposited. However, sampling and analyses of the contaminated well water in the neighborhood revealed that only contaminants from the liquid death wastes were actually polluting the drinking water.

Each company had its own suggestions for equitable cost sharing. The first company, the firm that had disposed of liquid death with the wastekeeper, wanted to keep it uncomplicated by merely using a quantitative basis for cost apportionment. The second company thought that the first company should pay for most of the on-site cleanup and certainly all of the off-site cleanup involving the contaminated well water. The third company believed their responsibility was minimal because all of their wastes were merely trash and refuse typical of sanitary municipal landfill disposal.

After considerable discussion among the government and the companies, it became obvious that each company would be unhappy, no matter what settlement was finally negotiated.

The dilemma that the case of the wastekeeper illustrates is typical of the difficult decisions faced by the EPA in assessing responsibility for the cleanup of many Superfund sites. Neither CERCLA nor the regulations promulgated by EPA under Superfund recognize degree of hazard in the shared liability for site cleanup. Certainly, each party that has used the site for disposal should have some share in the liability and associated costs for remediating the hazards posed by the contaminated site.

Court settlements for the cleanup costs of abandoned waste sites now indicate that any waste generator can be made a potentially responsible party and be held liable for a disproportionate share or even all of the total cleanup costs for the site. This concept of "joint and several liability" need not recognize either the quantity or the degree of risk to human health or the environment. In other words, waste generators will never be completely relieved of potential long-term liability for the wastes until the wastes have been completely and finally destroyed or otherwise rendered harmless. The enforcement of CERCLA regulations should therefore reduce the number of abandoned hazardous waste sites in the future, since generators will select only responsible TSDs in the cradle-to-grave waste management system.

QUESTIONS

1 How does the EPA Hazard Ranking System interact with the National Priority List of CERCLA sites?
2 Discuss the feasibility study for Superfund site mitigation.
3 Compare the following approaches to mitigation of abandoned hazardous waste sites:
  (a) Physical removal and disposal
  (b) Physical removal and physical/chemical treatment prior to disposal

  (c) Biological degradation and disposal
  (d) Fixation or immobilization
  (e) No restoration
4 Describe the three types of responses for incidences involving hazardous substances under the Superfund remedial response program.
5 Describe the methodology for prioritizing Superfund sites.
6 Justify your best estimate for the cost of cleaning up uncontrolled hazardous waste sites in the foreseeable future.
7 An independent medical laboratory landfilled 1000 pounds each of botulinum toxin A, tetanus toxin, diphtheria toxin, and, 2,3,7,8-tetrachlorodibenzo-*p*-dioxin. Why is it likely that field mice in the vicinity of this landfill site will have a short life expectancy?
8 How would you clean up the 10,000 to 15,000 objects that have already been discarded in outer space?

BIBLIOGRAPHY

1 Bennett, G. F., F. S. Feates, and I. Wilder: *Hazardous Materials Spills Handbook,* McGraw-Hill, New York, 1982.
2 *Case Studies 1-23: Remedial Response at Hazardous Waste Sites,* U.S. Environmental Protection Agency, Washington, March 1984.
3 Dawson, G. W., and B. W. Mercer: *Hazardous Waste Management,* Wiley, New York, 1986.
4 40 Code of Federal Regulations, Part 300, Appendix A, July 1, 1987.
5 Hallstedt, P. A., M. A. Puskar, and S. P. Levine: "Application of the Hazard Ranking System to the Prioritization of Organic Compounds Identified at Hazardous Waste Remedial Action Sites," *Hazardous Waste and Hazardous Materials,* vol. 3, no. 2, 1986.
6 Shields, E. J.: *Pollution Control Engineer's Handbook,* Pudvan, Northbrook, Ill., 1985.
7 U.S. Congress, *Superfund Strategy,* Office of Technology Assessment, Washington, April 1985.
8 Wagner, K., et al.: *Drum Handling Manual for Hazardous Waste Sites,* Noyes, Park Ridge, N.J., 1987.
9 Wagner, K., et al.: *Remedial Action Technology for Waste Disposal Sites,* Noyes, Park Ridge, N.J., 1986.

PRIORITY POLLUTANTS

Priority pollutant	Type of chemical substance
Acenaphthene	Aromatic
Acenaphthylene	Aromatic
Acrolein	Organic
Acrylonitrile	Organic
Aldrin	Pesticide
Anthracene	Aromatic
Antimony	Metal
Arsenic	Metal
Asbestos	Mineral
Beryllium	Metal
Benzene	Aromatic
Benzidine	Substitute aromatic
Benzo[a]anthracene	Aromatic
3,4-Benzofluoranthane	Aromatic
Benzo[k]fluoranthane	Aromatic
Benzo[ghi]perylene	Aromatic
Benzo[e]pyrene	Aromatic
e-BHC-α	Pesticide
b-BHC-β	Pesticide
r-BHC (lindane)-γ	Pesticide
g-BHC-Δ	Pesticide
bis(2-chloroethoxy)methane	Chlorinated ether
bis(2-chloromethyl)ether	Chlorinated ether
bis(Chloromethyl)ether	Chlorinated ether
bis(2-Chlorolsopropyl)ether	Chlorinated ether
bis(2-Ethylhexyl)phthalate	Phthalate ester
Bromoform	Chlorinated alkane
4-Bromophenyl phenyl ether	Chlorinated ether

Priority pollutant	Type of chemical substance
Butyl benzyl phthalate	Phthalate ester
Cadmium	Metal
Carbon tetrachloride	Chlorinated alkane
Chlordane	Pesticide
Chlorobenzene	Chlorinated aromatic
Chlorodibromonethane	Chlorinated alkane
Chloroethane	Chlorinated alkane
2-Chloroethyl vinyl ether	Chlorinated ether
Chloroform	Chlorinated alkane
2-Chlorophenol	Phenol
4-Chlorophenyl phenyl ether	Chlorinated esther
2-Chlorophythalene	Chlorinated aromatic
Chromium	Metal
Chrysene	Aromatic
Copper	Metal
Cyanide	Miscellaneous
4,4-DDD	Pesticide
4,4-DDE	Pesticide
4,4-DDT	Pesticide
Dibenzo[*a,h*]anthracene	Chlorinated aromatic
1,3-Dichlorobenzene	Chlorinated aromatic
1,4-Dichlorobenzene	Chlorinated aromatic
3,3-Dichlorobenzidene	Substituted aromatic
Dichlorbromothane	Chlorinated alkane
Dichlorodifluromethane	Chlorinated alkane
1,1-Dichloroethane	Chlorinated alkane
1,2-Dichloroethane	Chlorinated alkane
1,1-Dichloroethylene	Chlorinated alkane
2,4-Dichloro phenol	Phenol
1,2-Dichloropropane	Chlorinated alkane
1,2-Dichloropropylene	Chlorinated alkane
Dieldrin	Pesticide
Diethyl phthalate	Phthalate ester
2,4-Dimethyl phenol	Phenol
Dimethyl phthalate	Phthalate ester
Di-*n*-Butyl phthalate	Phthalate ester
4,6-Dinitro-o-cresol	Phenol
2,4-Dinitrophenol	Phenol
2,4-Dinitrotoluene	Substituted aromatic
2,6 Dinitrotoluene	Substituted aromatic
Di-N-Octyl phthalate	Phthalate ester
1,2-Diphenyl hydrazine	Substituted aromatic
A-Endosulfan-α	Pesticide
B-Endosulfan-β	Pesticide
Endosulfan sulfate	Pesticide
Endrin	Pesticide
Endrin aldehyde	Pesticide
Ethylbenzene	Aromatic
Fluoranthene	Aromatic
Fluorene	Aromatic
Haphthalene	Aromatic
Heptachlor	Pesticide

Priority pollutant	Type of chemical substance
Heptachlor epoxide	Pesticide
Hexachlorobenzene	Chlorinated aromatic
Hexachlorobutadiene	Chlorinated alkane
Hexachlorocyclopentadiene	Chlorinated alkane
Hexachloroethane	Chlorinated alkane
Indeno[1,2,3-c,d]pyrene	Aromatic
Isophorone	Organic
Lead	Metal
Mercury	Metal
Methyl bromide	Chlorinated alkane
Methyl chloride	Chlorinated alkane
Methylene chloride	Chlorinated alkane
Nickel	Metal
Nitrobenzene	Substituted aromatic
2-Nitrophenol	Phenol
4-Nitrophenol	Phenol
n-Nitrosodimethylamine	Organic
n-Nitrosodi-N-propylamine	Organic
n-Nitrosodiphenylamine	Organic
Para-chlor-meta-cresol	Phenol
PCB-1016	Chlorinated biphenol
PCB-1221	Chlorinated biphenol
PCB-1232	Chlorinated biphenol
PCB-1242	Chlorinated biphenol
PCB-1248	Chlorinated biphenol
PCB-1254	Chlorinated biphenol
PCB-1260	Chlorinated biphenol
Pentachlorophenol	Phenol
Phenanthane	Aromatic
Phenol	Phenol
Pyrene	Aromatic
Selenium	Metal
Silver	Metal
2,3,7,8-Tetrachlorodlbenzo-p-dioxin	Chlorinated organic
1,1,2,2-Tetrachloroethane	Chlorinated alkane
Tetrachloroethylene	Chlorinated alkane
Thallium	Metal
Toluene	Aromatic
1,2-trans-Dichloraoethylene	Chlorinated alkane
1,2,4-Trichlorobenzene	Chlorinated aromatic
1,1-Trichloroethane	Chlorinated alkane
1,1,2-Trichloroethane	Chlorinated alkane
Trichloroethylene	Chlorinated alkane
Trichlorofluoromethane	Chlorinated alkane
2,4,6-Trichlorophenol	Phenol
Vinyl chloride	Chlorinated phenol
Zinc	Metal

HAZARDOUS WASTES FROM NONSPECIFIC SOURCES

Industry and EPA hazardous waste no.	Hazardous wastes from nonspecific sources	Hazard code*
Generic:		
F001	The following spent halogenated solvents used in degreasing: tetracloroethylene, trichloroethylene, methylene chloride, 1,1,1-trichloroethane, carbon tetrachloride, and chlorinated fluorocarbons; all spent solvent mixtures/blends used in degreasing containing, before use, a total of 10 percent or more (by volume) of one or more of the above halogenated solvents or those solvents listed in F002, F004, and F005; and still bottoms from the recovery of these spent solvents and spent solvent mixtures.	(T)
F002	The following spent halogenated solvents: tetrachloroethylene, methylene chloride, trichloroethylene, 1,1,1-trichloroethane, chlorobenzene, 1,1,2-trichloro-1,2,2-trifluoroethane, ortho-dichlorobenzene, trichlorofluoromethane and 1,1,2-trichloroethane; all spent solvent mixtures/blends containing, before use, a total of 10 percent or more (by volume) of one or more of the above halogenated solvents or those listed in F001, F004, or F005; and still bottoms from the recovery of these spent solvents and spent solvent mixtures.	(T)
F003	The following spent nonhalogenated solvents: xylene, acetone, ethyl acetate, ethyl benzene, ethyl ether, methyl isobutyl ketone, *n*-butyl alcohol, cyclohexanone, and methanol; all spent solvent mixtures/blends containing, before use, one or more of the above nonhalogenated solvents, listed in F001, F002, F004, and F005; and still bottoms from the recovery of these spent solvents and spent solvent mixtures.	(I)

Industry and EPA hazardous waste no.	Hazardous wastes from nonspecific sources	Hazard code*
F004	The following spent nonhalogenated solvents: cresols and cresylic acid, and nitrobenzene; all spent solvent mixtures/ blends containing, before use, a total of 10 percent or more (by volume) of one or more of the above non-halogenated solvents or those solvents listed in F001, F002, and F005; and still bottoms from the recovery of these spent solvents and spent solvent mixtures.	(T)
F005	The following spent nonhalogenated solvents: toluene, methyl ethyl ketone, carbon disulfide, isobutanol, pyridine, benzene, 2-exthoxyethanol, and 2-nitropropane; all spent solvent mixtures/blends containing, before use, a total of 10 percent or more (by volume) or one or more of the above non-halogenated solvents or those solvents listed in F001, F002, or F004; and still bottoms from the recovery of these spent solvents and spent solvent mixtures.	(I,T)
F006	Wastewater treatment sludges from electroplating operations except from the following processes: (1) sulfuric acid anodizing or aluminium; (2) tin plating on carbon steel; (3) zinc plating (segregated basis) on carbon steel; (4) aluminum or zinc-and-aluminum plating on carbon steel; (5) cleaning/stripping associated with tin, zinc, and aluminum plating on carbon steel; and (6) chemical etching and milling of aluminum.	(T)
F019	Waste treatment sludges from the chemical conversion coating of aluminum.	(T)
F007	Spent cyanide plating bath solutions from electroplating operations.	(R,T)
F008	Plating bath residues from the bottom of plating baths from electroplating operations where cyanides are used in the process.	(R,T)
F009	Spent stripping and cleaning bath solutions from electroplating operations where cyanides are used in the process.	(R,T)
F010	Quenching bath residues from oil baths from metal heat-treating operations where cyanides are used in the process.	(R,T)
F011	Spent cyanide solutions from salt bath pot cleaning from metal heat-treating operations.	(R,T)
F012	Quenching wastewater treatment sludges from metal heat-treating operations where cyanides are used in the process.	(T)
F024	Wastes, including but not limited to, distillation residues, heavy ends, tars, and reactor cleanout wastes from the production of chlorinated aliphatic hydrocarbons, having carbon content from one to five, utilizing free radical catalyzed processes. (This listing does not include light ends, spent filters and filter aids, spent dessicants, wastewater, wastewater treatment sludges, spent catalysts, and wastes listed in Appendix C.)	(T)
F020	Wastes (except wastewater and spent carbon from hydrogen chloride purification) from the production or manufacturing use (as a reactant, chemical intermediate, or component in a formulating process) or tri- or tetrachlorophenol, or of intermediates used to produce their pesticide derivatives. (This listing does not include wastes from the production of hexachlorophene from highly purified 2,4,5-trichlorophenol.)	(H)

Industry and EPA hazardous waste no.	Hazardous wastes from nonspecific sources	Hazard code*
F021	Wastes (except wastewater and spent carbon from hydrogen chloride purification) from the production or manufacturing use (as a reactant, chemical intermediate, or component in a formulating process) of pentachlorophenol, or of intermediates used to produce its derivatives.	(H)
F022	Wastes (except wastewater and spent carbon from hydrogen chloride purification) from the manufacturing use (as a reactant, chemical intermediate, or component in a formulating process) of tetra-, penta-, or hexachlorobenzenes under alkaline conditions.	(H)
F023	Wastes (except wastewater and spent carbon from hydrogen chloride purification) from the production of materials on equipment previously used for the production or manufacturing use (as a reactant, chemical intermediate, or component in a formulating process) of tri- and tetrachlorophenols. (This listing does not include wastes from equipment used only for the production or use of hexachlorophene from highly purified 2,4,5-trichlorophenol.)	(H)
F026	Wastes (except wastewater and spent carbon from hydrogen chloride purification) from the production of materials on equipment previously used for the manufacturing use (as a reactant, chemical intermediate, or component in a formulating process) of tetra-, penta-, or hexachlorobenzene under alkaline conditions.	(H)
F027	Discarded unused formulations containing tri-, tetra-, or pentachlorophenol or discarded unused formulations containing compounds derived from these chlorophenols. (This listing does not include formulations containing hexachlorophene synthesized from prepurified 2,4,5-trichlorophenol as the sole component.)	(H)
F028	Residues resulting from the incineration or thermal treatment of soil contaminated with EPA hazardous waste nos. F020, F021, F022, F023, F026, and F027.	(T)

*Hazard code definitions
C = Corrosivity
E = EP toxicity
H = Acute hazardous waste
I = Ignitability
R = Reactivity
T = Toxic waste

APPENDIX

HAZARDOUS WASTES
FROM SPECIFIC SOURCES

Industry and EPA hazardous waste no.	Hazardous Wastes	Hazard Code*
Wood preservation		
K001	Bottom sediment sludge from the treatment of waste-waters from wood preserving processes that use creosote and/or pentachlorophenol.	(T)
Inorganic pigments		
K002	Wastewater treatment sludge from the production of chrome yellow and orange pigments.	(T)
K003	Wastewater treatment sludge from the production of molybdate orange pigments.	(T)
K004	Wastewater treatment sludge from the production of zinc yellow pigments.	(T)
K005	Wastewater treatment sludge from the production of chrome green pigments.	(T)
K006	Wastewater treatment sludge from the production of chrome oxide green pigments (anhydrous and hydrated).	(T)
K007	Wastewater treatment sludge from the production of iron blue pigments.	(T)
K008	Oven residue from the production of chrome oxide green pigments.	(T)
Organic chemicals		
K009	Distillation bottoms from the production of acetaldehyde from ethylene.	(T)
K010	Distillation side cuts from the production of acetaldehyde from ethylene.	(T)

Industry and EPA hazardous waste no.	Hazardous Wastes	Hazard Code*
K011	Bottom stream from the wastewater stripper in the production of acrylonitrile.	(R,T)
K013	Bottom stream from the acetonitrile column in the production of acrylonitrile.	(R,T)
K014	Bottoms from the acetonitrile purification column in the production of acrylonitrile.	(T)
K015	Still bottoms from the distillation of benzyl chloride.	(T)
K016	Heavy ends or distillation residues from the production of carbon tetrachloride.	(T)
K017	Heavy ends (still bottoms) from the purification column in the production of epichlorohydrin.	(T)
K018	Heavy ends from the fractionation column in ethyl chloride production.	(T)
K019	Heavy ends from the distillation of ethylene dichloride in ethylene dichloride production.	(T)
K020	Heavy ends from the distillation of vinyl chloride in vinyl chloride monomer production.	(T)
K021	Aqueous spent antimony catalyst waste from fluoromethanes production.	(T)
K022	Distillation bottom tars from the production of phenol/acetone from cumene.	(T)
K023	Distillation light ends from the production of phthalic anhydride from naphthalene.	(T)
K024	Distillation bottoms from the production of phthalic anhydride from naphthalene.	(T)
K093	Distillation light ends from the production of phthalic anhydride from orthoxylene.	(T)
K094	Distillation bottoms from the production of phthalic anhydride from orthoxylene	(T)
K025	Distillation bottoms from the production of nitrobenzene by the nitration of benze.	(T)
K026	Stripping still tails from the production of methyl ethyl pyridines.	(T)
K027	Centrifuge and distillation residues from toluene diisocyanate production	(R,T)
K028	Spent catalyst from the hydrochlorinator reactor in the production of 1,1,1-trichloroethane.	(T)
K029	Waste from the product steam stripper in the production of 1,1,1-trichloroethane.	(T)
K095	Distillation bottoms from the production of 1,1,1-trichloroethane.	(T)
K096	Heavy ends from the heavy ends column from the production of 1,1,1-trichloroethane.	(T)
K030	Column bottoms or heavy ends from the combined production of trichloroethylene and perchloroethylene.	(T)
K083	Distillation bottoms from aniline productions.	(T)
K103	Process residues from aniline extraction from the production of aniline.	(T)
K104	Combined wastewater streams generated from nitrobenzene/aniline production.	(T)

Industry and EPA hazardous waste no.	Hazardous Wastes	Hazard Code*
K085	Distillation or fractionation column bottoms from the production of chlorobenzenes.	(T)
K105	Separated aqueous stream from the reactor product washing step in the production of chlorobenzenes.	(T)
K111	Product washwaters from the production of dinitrotoluene via nitration of toluene.	(C,T)
K112	Reaction by-product water from the drying column in the production of toluenediamine via hydrogenation of dinitrotoluene.	(T)
K113	Condensed liquid light ends from the purification of toluenediamine in the production of toluenediamine via hydrogenation of dinitrotoluene.	(T)
K114	Vicinals from the purification of toluenediamine in the production of toluenediamine via hydrogenation of dinitrotoluene.	(T)
K115	Heavy ends from the purification of toluenediamine in the production of toluenediamine via hydrogenation of dinitrotoluene.	(T)
K116	Organic condensate from the solvent recovery column in the production of toluene diisocyanate via phosgenation of toluenediamine.	(T)
K117	Wastewater from the reactor vent gas scrubber in the production of ethylene dibromide via bromination of ethene.	(T)
K118	Spent adsorbent solids from purification of ethylene dibromide in the production of ethylene dibromide via bromination of ethene.	(T)
K136	Still bottoms from the purification of ethylene dibromide in the production of ethylene dibromide via bromination of ethene.	(T)
Inorganic chemicals		
K071	Brine purification muds from the mercury cell process in chlorine production, where separately prepurified brine is not used.	(T)
K073	Chlorinated hydrocarbon waste from the purification step of the diaphragm cell process using graphite anodes in chlorine production.	(T)
K106	Wastewater treatment sludge from the mercury cell process in chlorine production.	(T)
Pesticides		
K031	By-product salts generated in the production of MSMA and cacodylic acid.	(T)
K032	Wastewater treatment sludge from the production of chlordane.	(T)
K033	Wastewater and scrub water from the chlorination of cyclopentadiene in the production of chlordane.	(T)
K034	Filter solids from the filtration of hexachlorocyclopentadiene in the production of chlordane.	(T)
K097	Vacuum stripper discharge from the chlordane chlorinator in the production of chlordane.	(T)

Industry and EPA hazardous waste no.	Hazardous Wastes	Hazard Code*
K035	Wastewater treatment sludges generated in the production of creosote.	(T)
K036	Still bottoms from toluene reclamation distillation in the production of disulfoton.	(T)
K037	Wastewater treatment sludges from the production of disulfoton.	(T)
K038	Wastewater from the washing and stripping of phorate production.	(T)
K039	Filter cake from the filtration of diethylphosphorodithioic acid in the production of phorate.	(T)
K040	Wastewater treatment sludge from the production of phorate.	(T)
K041	Wastewater treatment sludge from the production of toxaphene.	(T)
K098	Untreated process wastewater from the production of toxaphene.	(T)
K042	Heavy ends or distillation residues from the distillation of tetrachlorobenzene in the production of 2,4,5-T.	(T)
K043	2,6-Dichlorophenol waste from the production of 2,4-D.	(T)
K099	Untreated wastewater from the production of 2,4-D.	(T)
K123	Process wastewater (including supernates, filtrates, and washwaters) from the production of ethylenebisdithiocarbamic acid and its salt.	(T)
K124	Reactor vent scrubber water from the production of ethylenebisdithiocarbamic acid and its salts.	(C,T)
K125	Filtration, evaporation, and centrifugation solids from the production of ethylenebisdithiocarbamic acid and its solids.	(T)
K126	Baghouse dust and floor sweepings in milling and packaging operations from the production or formulation of ethylenebisdithiocarbamic acid and its salts.	(T)
Explosives		
K044	Wastewater treatment sludges from the manufacturing and processing of explosives.	(R)
K045	Spent carbon from the treatment of wastewater containing explosives.	(R)
K046	Wastewater treatment sludges from the manufacturing, formulation, and loading of lead-based initiating compounds.	(T)
K047	Pink/red water from TNT operations.	(R)
Petroleum refining		
K048	Dissolved air flotation (DAF) float from the petroleum refining industry.	(T)
K049	Slop oil emulsion solids from the petroleum refining industry.	(T)
K050	Heat exchanger bundle cleaning sludge from the petroleum refining industry.	(T)
K051	API separator sludge from the petroleum refining industry.	(T)
K052	Tank bottoms (leaded) from the petroleum refining industry.	(T)

Industry and EPA hazardous waste no.	Hazardous Wastes	Hazard Code*
Iron and steel		
K061	Emission control dust/sludge from the primary production of steel in electric furnaces.	(T)
K062	Spent pickle liquor generated by steel finishing operations of facilities within the iron and steel industry (SIC Codes 331 and 332).	(C,T)
Secondary lead		
K069	Emission control dust/sludge from secondary lead smelting.	(T)
K100	Waste leaching solution from acid leaching of emission control dust/sludge from secondary lead smelting.	(T)
Veterinary pharmaceuticals		
K084	Wastewater treatment sludges generated during the production of veterinary pharmaceuticals from arsenic or organoarsenic compounds.	(T)
K101	Distillation tar residues from the distillation of aniline-based compounds in the production of veterinary pharmaceuticals from arsenic or organoarsenic compounds.	(T)
K102	Residue from the use of activated carbon for decolorization in the production of veterinary pharmaceuticals from arsenic or organoarsenic compounds.	(T)
Ink formulation		
K086	Solvent washes and sludges, caustic washes and sludges, or water washes and sludges from cleaning tubs and equipment used in the formulation of ink from pigments, driers, soaps, and stabilizers containing chromium and lead.	(T)
Coking:		
K060	Ammonia still lime sludge from coking operations	(T)
K087	Decanter tank tar sludge from coking operations.	(T)

*Hazard code definitions
C = Corrosivity
E = EP toxicity
H = Acute hazardous waste
I = Ignitability
R = Reactivity
T = Toxic waste

LISTING OF EPA HAZARDOUS WASTES FROM COMMERCIAL CHEMICAL PRODUCTS, INTERMEDIATES, AND RESIDUES

Hazardous waste no.	Chemical abstracts no.	Hazardous substance
P023	107-20-0	Acetaldehyde, chloro-
P002	591-08-2	Acetamide, n-(aminothioxomethyl)-
P057	640-19-7	Acetamide, 2-fluoro-
P058	62-74-8	Acetic acid, fluoro-, sodium salt
P066	16752-77-5	Acetimidic acid, n-[methylcarbamoyl)oxy]thio-, methyl ester
P002	591-08-2	1-Acetyl-2-thiourea
P003	107-02-8	Acrolein
P070	116-06-3	Aldicarb
P004	309-00-2	Aldrin
P005	107-18-6	Allyl alcohol
P006	20859-73-8	Aluminum phosphide (R,T)
P007	2763-96-4	5-(Aminomethyl)-3-isoxazolol
P008	504-24-5	4-α-Aminopyridine
P009	131-74-8	Ammonium picrate (R)
P119	7803-55-6	Ammonium vanadate
P010	7778-39-4	Arsenic acid
P012	1327-53-3	Arsenic oxide As_2O_3
P011	1303-28-2	Arsenic oxide As_2O_3
P011	1303-28-2	Arsenic pentoxide
P012	1327-53-3	Arsenic trioxide
P038	692-42-2	Arsine, diethyl
P036	696-28-6	Arsonous dichloride, phenyl-
P054	151-56-4	Aziridine
P013	542-62-1	Barium cyanide
P024	106-47-8	Benzenamine, 4-chloro-

Hazardous waste no.	Chemical abstracts no.	Hazardous substance
P077	100-01-6	Benzenamine, 4-nitro-
P028	100-44-7	Benzene, (chloromethyl)-
P042	51-43-4	1,2-Benzenediol, 4-[1-hydroxy-2-(methyl-amino)ethyl]-, (R)-
P046	122-09-8	Benzeneethanamine, α,α-dimethyl-
P014	108-98-5	Benzenethiol
P001	81-81-2	2H-1 Benzopyran-2-one, 4-hydroxy-3-(3-oxo-1-phenylbutyl)-, and salts
P028	100-44-7	Benzyl chloride
P015	7440-41-7	Beryllium dust
P016	542-88-1	*bis*(chloromethyl) ether
P017	598-31-2	Bromoacetone
P018	357-57-3	Brucine
P021	592-01-8	Calcium cyanide
P022	75-15-0	Carbon bisulfide
P022	75-15-0	Carbon bisulfide
P095	75-44-5	Carbonic dichloride
P023	107-20-0	Chloroacetaldehyde
P024	106-47-8	*p*-Chloroaniline
P029	544-92-3	Copper cyanide
P030		Cyanides (soluble cyanide salts), not otherwise specified
P031	460-19-5	Cyanogen
P033	506-77-4	Cyanogen chloride
P034	131-89-5	2-Cyclohexyl-4,6-dinitrophenol
P036	696-28-6	Dichlorophenylarsine
P037	60-57-1	Dieldrin
P038	692-42-2	Diethylarsine
P041	311-45-5	Diethyl-*p*-nitrophenyl phosphate
P040	297-97-2	O,O-Diethyl O-pyrazinyl phosphorothioate
P043	55-91-4	Diisopropyl fluorophosphate (DEP)
P004	309-00-2	1,4:5,8-Dimethanonaphthalene, 1,2,3,4,10,10-hexachloro-1,4,4a,5,8,8a-hexahydro-, (1α,4α,4aβ,5α,8α,8aβ)
P060	465-73-6	1,4:5,8-Dimethanonaphthalene, 1,2,3,4,10,10-hexachloro-1,4,4a,5,8,8a-hexahydro-, (1α,4α,4aβ,5β,8β,8aβ)-
P037	60-57-1	2,7:3,6-Dimethanonaphth[2,3b]oxirane, 3,4,5,6,9,9-hexachloro-1a,2,2a,3,6,6a,7,7a-octahydro-, (1aα,2β,2aα,3β,6β,6aα,6aβ,7β,7aα)-
P051	72-20-8	2,7:3,6-Dimethanonaphth[2,3b]oxirane,octahydro-, (1aα,2β,2aα,3α,6α,7β,7aα)-
P044	60-51-5	Dimethoate
P045	39196-18-4	3,3-Dimethyl-1-(methylthio)-2-butanone, O-[(methylamino)carbonyl]oxime
P046	122-09-8	α, α-Dimethylphenethylamine
P047	534-52-1	4,6-Dinitro-*o*-cresol and salts
P048	51-28-5	2,4-Dinitrophenol
P020	88-85-7	Dinoseb
P085	152-16-9	Diphosphoramide, octamethyl-
P039	298-04-4	Disulfoton
P049	541-53-7	2,4-Dithiobiuret
P050	115-29-7	Endosulfan
P088	145-73-3	Endothal

Hazardous waste no.	Chemical abstracts no.	Hazardous substance
P051	72-20-8	Endrin
P042	51-43-4	Epinephrine
P101	107-12-0	Ethyl cyanide
P054	151-56-4	Ethyleneimine
P097	52-85-7	Famphur
P056	7782-41-4	Fluorine
P057	640-19-7	Fluoroacetamide
P058	62-74-8	Fluoroacetic acid, sodium salt
P065	628-86-4	Fulminic acid, mercury (2+) salt (R,T)
P059	76-44-8	Heptachlor
P062	757-58-4	Hexaethyltetraphosphate
P116	79-19-6	Hydrazinecarbothioamide
P068	60-34-4	Hydrazine, methyl-
P063	74-90-8	Hydrocyanic acid
P063	74-90-8	Hydrogen cyanide
P096	7803-51-2	Hydrogen phosphide
P064	624-83-9	Isocyanic acid, methyl ester
P060	465-73-6	Isodrin
P007	2763-96-4	3(2H)-Isoxazolone, 5-(aminomethyl)-
P092	62-38-4	Mercury, (acetato-O)phenyl-
P065	628-86-4	Mercury fulminate (R,T)
P082	62-75-9	Methamine, n-methyl-n-nitroso-
P016	542-88-1	Methane, oxybis[chloro-
P112	509-14-8	Methane, tetranitro-(R)
P118	75-70-7	Methanethiol, trichloro-
P050	115-29-7	6,9-Methano-2,4,3-benzodioxathiepen, 6,7,8,9,10,10-hexachloro-1,5,5a,6,9,9a-hexahydro-,3-oxide
P059	76-44-8	4,7-Methano-1H-indene, 1,4,5,6,7,8,8-heptachloro-3a,4,7,7a-tetrahydro-
P066	16752-77-5	Methomyl
P067	75-55-8	2-Methylaziridine
P068	60-34-4	Methyl hydrazine
P064	624-83-9	Methyl isocyanate
P069	75-86-5	2-Methyllactonitrile
P071	298-00-0	Methyl parathion
P072	86-88-4	α-Naphthylthiourea
P073	13463-39-3	Nickel carbonyl
P073	13463-39-3	Nickel carbonyl, (T-4)-
P075	54-11-5	Nicotine and salts
P076	10102-43-9	Nitric oxide
P077	100-01-6	p-Nitroaniline
P078	10102-44-0	Nitrogen dioxide
P076	10102-43-9	Nitrogen oxide NO
P078	10102-44-0	Nitrogen oxide NO_2
P081	55-63-0	Nitroglycerine (R)
P082	62-75-9	N-Nitrosodimethylamine
P084	4549-40-0	N-Nitrosomethylvinylamine
P074	557-19-7	Nickel cyanide
P085	152-16-9	Octamethylpyrophosphoramide
P087	20816-12-0	Osmium oxide
P087	20816-12-0	Osmium tetroxide

Hazardous waste no.	Chemical abstracts no.	Hazardous substance
P088	145-73-3	7-Oxabicyclo[2.2.1]heptane-2,3-dicarboxylic acid
P089	56-38-2	Parathion
P034	131-89-5	Phenol, 2-cyclohexyl-4,6-dinitro-
P048	51-28-5	Phenol, 2-4-dinitro-
P047	534-52-1	Phenol, 2-methyl-4,6-dinitro- and salts
P020	88-85-7	Phenol, 2, (1-methylpropyl)-4,6-dinitro
P009	131-74-8	Phenol, 2,4,6-trinitro-, ammonium salt (R)
P092	62-38-4	Phenylmercury acetate
P093	103-85-5	Phenylthiourea
P094	298-02-2	Phorate
P095	75-44-5	Phosgene
P096	7803-51-2	Phosphine
P041	311-45-5	Phosphoric acid, diethyl 4-nitrophenyl ester
P039	298-04-4	Phosphorodithioic acid, O,O-diethyl S-[2-(ethylthio)ethyl] ester
P094	298-02-2	Phosphorodithioic acid, O,O-diethyl S-[ethylthio)methyl] ester
P044	60-51-5	Phosphorodithioic acid, O,O-dimethyl S[2-(methylamino)-2-oxoethyl] ester
P043	55-91-4	Phosphorofluoric acid, bis(1-methylethyl)-ester
P089	56-38-2	Phosphorothioic acid, O,O-diethyl O-(4-nitrophenyl) ester
P040	297-97-2	Phosphorothioic acid, O,O-diethyl O-pyrazinyl ester
P097	52-85-7	Phosphorothioic acid, O-[4-[(dimethylamino)sulfonyl]phenyl] O,O-dimethyl ester
P071	298-00-0	Phosphorothioic acid, O,O-dimethyl O-(4-nitrophenyl) ester
P110	78-00-2	Plumbane, tetraethyl-
P098	151-50-8	Potassium cyanide
P099	506-61-6	Potassium silver cyanide
P070	116-06-3	Propanal, 2-methyl-2-(methylthio)-, O-[(methylamino)carbonyl]oxime
P101	107-12-0	Propanenitrile
P027	542-76-7	Propanenitrile, 3-chloro-
P069	75-86-5	Propanenitrile, 2-hydroxy-2-methyl-
P081	55-63-0	1,2,3-Propanetriol, trinitrate (R)
P017	598-31-2	2-Propanone, 1-bromo-
P102	107-19-7	Propargyl alcohol
P003	107-02-8	2-Propenal
P005	107-18-6	2-Propen-1-ol
P067	75-55-8	1,2-Propylenimine
P102	591-08-2	2-Propyn-1-ol
P008	504-24-5	Pyridinamine
P075	54-11-5	Pyridine, (S)-3-(1-methyl-2-pyrrolidinyl)-, and salts
P111	107-49-3	Pyrophosphoric acid, tetraethyl ester
P103	630-10-4	Selenourea
P104	506-64-9	Silver cyanide
P105	26628-22-8	Sodium azide
P106	143-33-9	Sodium cyanide
P107	1314-96-1	Strontium sulfide
P108	57-24-9	Strychnidin-10-one, and salts
P018	357-57-3	Strychnidin-10-one, 2,3-dimethoxy-
P108	57-24-9	Strychnine and salts
P115	10031-59-1	Sulfuric acid, thallium(I) salt
P109	3689-24-5	Tetraethyldithiopyrophosphate

Hazardous waste no.	Chemical abstracts no.	Hazardous substance
P110	78-00-2	Tetraethyl lead
P111	107-49-3	Tetraethylpyrophosphate
P112	509-14-8	Tetranitromethane (R)
P062	757-58-4	Tetraphosphoric acid, hexaethyl ester
P113	1314-32-5	Thallic oxide
P113	1314-32-5	Thallium(III) oxide
P114	12039-52-0	Thallium(I) selenite
P115	10031-59-1	Thalium(I) sulfate
P109	3689-24-5	Thiodiphosphoric acid, tetraethyl ester
P045	39196-18-4	Thiofanox
P049	541-53-7	Thioimidodicarbonic diamide
P014	108-98-5	Thiophenol
P116	79-19-6	Thiosemicarbazide
P026	5344-82-1	Thiourea, (2-chlorophenyl)-
P072	86-88-4	Thiourea, 1-naphthalenyl-
P093	103-85-5	Thiourea, phenyl-
P123	8001-35-2	Toxaphene
P118	75-70-7	Trichloromethanethiol
P119	7803-55-6	Vanadic acid, ammonium salt
P120	1314-62-1	Vanadium(V) oxide
P084	4549-40-0	Vinylamine, N-methyl-N-nitroso-
P001	81-81-2	Warfarin
P121	557-21-1	Zinc cyanide
P122	1314-84-7	Zinc phosphide (R,T)
U001	75-07-0	Acetaldehyde (I)
U034	75-87-6	Acetaldehyde, trichloro-
U187	62-44-2	Acetamide, N-(4-ethoxyphenyl)-
U005	53-96-3	Acetamide, N-9H-fluoren-2-yl
U112	141-78-6	Acetic acid, ethyl ester (I)
U144	301-04-2	Acetic acid, lead salt
U214	563-68-8	Acetic acid, thallium (1 +) salt
U232	93-76-5	Acetic acid, (2,4,5-trichlorophenoxy)-
U002	67-64-1	Acetone (I)
U003	75-05-8	Acetonitrile (I,T)
U004	98-86-2	Acetophenone
U005	53-96-3	2-Acetylaminofluorene
U006	75-36-5	Acetyl chloride (C,R,T)
U007	79-06-1	Acrylamide
U008	79-10-7	Acrylic acid (I)
U009	107-13-1	Acrylonitrile
U011	61-82-5	Amitrole
U012	62-53-3	Aniline (I,T)
U014	492-80-8	Auramine
U015	115-02-6	Azaserine
U010	50-07-7	Azirino(2',3':3,4)pyrrolo[1,2-a]indole-4,7-dione, 6-amino-8-[((aminocarbonyl)oxy)methyl]-1,1a,2,8,8a,8b-hexahydro-8a-methoxy-5-methyl-
U157	50-49-5	Benz[j]aceanthrylene, 1,2-dihydro-3-methyl-
U016	225-51-4	3,4-Benzacridine
U017	98-87-3	Benzal chloride

Hazardous waste no.	Chemical abstracts no.	Hazardous substance
U192	23950-58-5	Benzamide, 3,5-dichloro-N-(1,1-diethyl-2-propynyl)-
U018	56-55-3	Benz[a]anthracene
U094	57-97-6	Benz[a]anthracene, 7,12-dimethyl-
U012	62-53-3	Benzenamine (I,T)
U014	492-80-8	Benzenamine, 4,4'-carbonimidoylbis[N,N-dimethyl-
U049	3165-93-3	Benzenamine, 4-chloro-2-methyl-
U093	60-11-7	Benzenamine, N,N-dimethyl-4-(phenylazo)-
U328	95-53-4	Benzenamine, 2-methyl-
U353	106-49-0	Benzenamine, 4-methyl-
U158	101-14-4	Benzenamine, 4,4'-methylenebis[2-chloro-
U222	636-21-5	Benzenamine, 2-methyl-, hydrochloride
U181	99-55-8	Benzenamine, 2-methyl-5-nitro-
U019	71-43-2	Benzene
U038	510-15-6	Benzeneacetic acid, 4-chloro-α-(4-chlorophenyl)-α-hydroxy, ethyl ester
U030	101-55-3	Benzene, 1-bromo-4-phenoxy-
U035	305-03-3	Benzenebutanoic acid, 4-[bis(2-chloroethyl)amino]-
U037	108-90-7	Benzene, chloro-
U221	25376-45-8	Benzenediamine, ar-methyl-
U028	117-81-7	1,2-Benzenedicarboxylic acid, bis(2-ethylhexy) ester
U069	84-74-2	1,2-Benzenedicarboxylic acid, dibutyl ester
U088	84-66-2	1,2-Benzenedicarboxylic acid, diethyl ester
U102	131-11-3	1,2-Benzenedicarboxylic acid, dimethyl ester
U107	117-84-0	1,2-Benzenedicarboxylic acid, di-n-octyl ester
U070	95-50-1	Benzene, 1,2-dichloro-
U071	541-73-1	Benzene, 1,3-dichloro-
U072	106-46-7	Benzene, 1,4-dichloro-
U060	72-54-8	Benzene, 1,1'-(2,2-dichloroethylidene)bis[4-chloro-
U017	98-87-3	Benzene, (dichloromethyl)-
U223	26471-62-5	Bezene, 1,3-diisocyanatomethyl- (R,T)
U239	1330-20-7	Benzene, dimethyl- (I,T)
U201	108-46-3	1,3-Benzenediol
U127	118-74-1	Benzene, hexachloro-
U056	110-82-7	Benzene, hexahydro- (I)
U220	108-88-3	Benzene, methyl-
U105	121-14-2	Benzene, 1-methyl-2,4-dinitro-
U106	606-20-2	Benzene, 2-methyl-1,3-dinitro-
U055	98-82-8	Benzene, (1-methylethyl)- (I)
U169	98-95-3	Benzene, nitro- (I,T)
U183	608-93-5	Benzene, pentachloro-
U185	82-68-8	Benzene, pentachloronitro-
U020	98-09-9	Benzenesulfonic acid chloride (C,R)
U020	98-09-9	Benzenesulfonyl chloride (C,R)
U207	95-94-3	Benzene, 1,2,4,5-tetrachloro-
U061	50-29-3	Benzene, 1,1'-(2,2,2-trichloroethylidene)bis[4-chloro-
U247	72-43-5	Benzene, 1,1'-(2,2,2-trichloroethylidene)[4-methoxy-
U023	98-07-7	Benzene, (trichloromethyl)- (C,R,T)
U234	99-35-4	Benzene, 1,3,5-trinitro- (R,T)
U021	92-87-5	Benzidine
U202	81-07-2	1,2-Benzisothiazol-3-(2H)-one, 1,1-dioxide and salts
U203	94-59-7	1,3-Benzodioxole, 5-(2-propenyl)-

Hazardous waste no.	Chemical abstracts no.	Hazardous substance
U141	120-58-1	1,3-Benzodioxole, 5-(1-propenyl)-
U090	94-58-6	1,3-Benzodioxole, 5-propyl-
U064	189-55-9	Benzo[rst]pentaphene
U022	50-32-8	Benzo[a]pyrene
U197	106-51-4	p-Benzoquinone
U023	98-07-7	Benzotrichloride (C,R,T)
U085	1464-53-5	2,2'-Bioxirane (I,T)
U021	92-87-5	[1,1'-Biphenyl]4,4'diamine
U073	91-94-1	[1,1'-Biphenyl]-4,4'-diamine, 3,3'-dichloro-
U091	119-90-4	[1,1'-Biphenyl]-4,4'-diamine, 3,3'-dimethoxy-
U095	119-93-7	[1,1'-Biphenyl]-4,4'-diamine, 3,3'-dimethyl-
U027	39638-32-9	*bis*(2-chloroisopropyl) ether
U024	111-91-1	*bis*(2-chloromethoxy) ethane
U028	117-81-7	*bis*(2-ethylhexyl) phthalate
U225	75-25-2	Bromoform
U030	101-55-3	4-Bromophenyl phenyl ether
U128	87-68-3	1,3-Butadiene, 1,1,2,3,4,4-hexachloro-
U172	924-16-3	1-Butanamine, N-butyl-N-nitroso-
U031	71-36-3	1-Butanol (I)
U159	78-93-3	2-Butanone (I,T)
U160	1338-23-4	2-Butanone peroxide (R,T)
U053	4170-3-3	2-Butenal
U074	764-41-0	2-Butene, 1,4-dichloro- (I,T)
U143	303-34-4	2-Butenoic acid, 2-methyl-, 7-[(2,3-dihydroxy-2-(1-methoxyethyl)-3-methyl-1-oxobutoxy)methyl]-2,3,5,7a-tetrahydro-1-pyrrolizin-1-yl ester, lα(Z),7(2S, 3R), 7aα]]-
U031	71-36-3	n-Butyl alcohol (I)
U136	75-60-5	Cacodylic acid
U032	13765-19-0	Calcium chromate
U238	51-79-6	Carbamic acid, ethyl ester
U178	615-53-2	Carbamic acid, methylnitroso-, ethyl ester
U097	79-44-7	Carbamic chloride, dimethyl-
U114	111-54-6	Carbamodithioic acid, 1,2-ethanediylbis-, salts and esters
U062	2303-16-4	Carbamothioic acid, *bis*(1-methylethyl)-S-(2,3-dichloro-2-propenyl) ester
U215	6533-73-9	Carbonic acid, dithallium (1+) salt
U033	353-50-4	Carbonic difluoride
U156	79-22-1	Carbonochloridic acid, methyl ester (I,T)
U033	353-50-4	Carbon oxyfluoride (R,T)
U211	56-23-5	Carbon tetrachloride
U034	75-87-6	Chloral
U035	305-03-3	Chlorambucil
U036	12789-03-6	Chlordane
U026	494-03-1	Chlornaphazine
U037	108-90-7	Chlorobenzene
U039	59-50-7	p-Chloro-m-cresol
U041	106-89-8	1-Chloro-2,3-epoxypropane
U042	110-75-8	2-Chloroethyl vinyl ether
U044	67-66-3	Chloroform
U046	107-30-2	Chloromethyl methyl ether

Hazardous waste no.	Chemical abstracts no.	Hazardous substance
U047	91-58-7	beta-Chloronaphthalene
U048	95-57-8	o-Chlorophenol
U049	3165-93-3	4-Chloro-o-toluidine, hydrochloride
U032	13765-19-0	Chromic acid, calcium salt
U050	218-01-9	Chrysene
U051	8021-39-4	Creosote
U052	1319-77-3	Cresols (Cresylic acid)
U053	4170-30-3	Crotonaldehyde
U055	98-82-8	Cumene (I)
U246	506-68-3	Cyanogen bromide
U197	106-51-4	2,5-Cyclohexadiene-1, 4-dione
U056	110-82-7	Cyclohexane (I)
U057	108-94-1	Cyclohexanone (I)
U130	77-47-4	1,3-Cyclopentadiene, 1,2,3,4,5,5-hexachloro-
U058	50-18-0	Cyclophosphamide
U240	94-75-7	2,4-D, salts and esters
U059	20830-81-3	Daunomycin
U060	72-54-8	DDD
U061	50-29-3	DDT
U062	2303-16-4	Diallate
U063	53-70-3	Dibenz[a,h]anthracene
U064	189-55-9	Dibenzo[a,i]pyrene
U066	96-12-8	1,2-Dibromo-3-chloropropane
U069	84-74-2	Dibutyl phthalate
U070	95-50-1	o-Dichlorobenzene
U071	541-73-1	m-Dichlorobenzene
U072	106-46-7	p-Dichlorobenzene
U073	91-94-1	3,3'-Dichlorobenzidine
U074	764-41-0	1,4-Dichloro-2-butene (I,T)
U075	75-71-8	Dichlorodifluoromethane
U078	75-35-4	1,1-Dichloroethylene
U079	156-60-5	1,2-Dichloroethylene
U025	111-44-1	Dichloroethyl ether
U081	120-83-2	2,4-Dichlorophenol
U082	87-65-0	2,6-Dichlorophenol
U240	94-75-7	2,4-Dichlorophenoxyacetic acid, salts and esters
U083	78-87-5	1,2-Dichloropropane
U084	542-75-6	1,3-Dichloropropene
U085	1464-53-5	1,2:3,4-Diepoxybutane (I,T)
U108	123-91-1	1,4-Diethyleneoxide
U086	1615-80-1	N,N-Diethylhydrazine
U087	3288-58-2	O-O-Diethyl-S-methyl-dithiophosphate
U088	84-66-2	Diethyl phthalate
U089	56-53-1	Diethylstilbestrol
U090	94-58-6	Dihydrosafrole
U091	119-90-4	3,3'-Dimethoxybenzidine
U092	124-40-3	Dimethylamine (I)
U093	60-11-7	Dimethylaminoazobenzene
U094	57-97-6	6,12-Dimethylbenz[a]anthracene
U095	119-93-7	3,3'-Dimethylbenzidine
U096	80-15-9	α,α-Dimethylbenzylhydroperoxide (R)

Hazardous waste no.	Chemical abstracts no.	Hazardous substance
U097	79-44-7	Dimethylcarbamoyl chloride
U098	57-14-7	1,1-Dimethylhydrazine
U099	540-73-8	1,2-Dimethylhydrazine
U101	105-67-9	2,4-Dimethylphenol
U102	131-11-3	Dimethyl phthalate
U103	77-78-1	Dimethyl sulfate
U105	121-14-2	2,4-Dinitrotoluene
U106	606-20-2	2,6-Dinitrotoluene
U107	117-84-0	Di-n-octyl phthalate
U108	123-91-1	1,4-Dioxane
U109	122-66-7	1,2-Diphenylhydrazine
U110	142-84-7	Dipropylamine (I)
U111	621-64-7	Di-*n*-propylnitrosamine
U001	75-07-0	Ethanal (I)
U174	55-18-5	Ethanamine, *N*-ethyl-*N*-nitroso-
U155	91-80-5	1,2-Ethanediamine, *N,N*-dimethyl-*N'*-2-pyridinyl-*N'*-(2-thienylmethyl)-
U067	106-93-4	Ethane, 1,2-dibromo-
U076	75-34-3	Ethane, 1,1-dichloro-
U077	107-06-2	Ethane, 1,2-dichloro-
U131	67-72-1	Ethane, hexachloro-
U024	111-91-1	Ethane, 1,1'-[methylenebis(oxy)]*bis*[2-chloro-
U117	60-29-7	Ethane, 1,1'-oxybis- (I)
U025	111-44-4	Ethane, 1,1'-oxybis[2-chloro-
U184	76-01-7	Ethane, pentachloro-
U208	630-20-6	Ethane, 1,1,1,2-tetrachloro-
U209	79-34-5	Ethane, 1,1,2,2-tetrachloro-
U218	62-55-5	Ethanethioamide
U227	110-80-5	Ethanol, 2-ethoxy-
U359	79-00-5	Ethane, 1,1,2-trichloro-
U173	1116-54-7	Ethanol, 2,2'-(nitrosoimino)bis-
U004	98-86-2	Ethanone, 1-phenyl-
U043	75-01-4	Ethene, chloro-
U042	110-75-8	Ethene, (2-chloroethoxy)-
U078	75-35-4	Ethene, 1,1-dichloro-
U079	156-60-5	Ethene, 1,2-dichloro-, (E)-
U210	127-18-4	Ethene, tetrachloro
U228	79-01-6	Ethene, trichloro
U112	141-78-6	Ethyl acetate (I)
U113	140-88-5	Ethyl acrylate (I)
U238	51-79-6	Ethyl carbamate
U038	510-15-6	Ethyl 4,4'-dichlorobenzilate
U114	111-54-6	Ethylenebisdithiocarbamic acid, salts and esters
U067	106-93-4	Ethylene dibromide
U077	107-06-2	Ethylene dichloride
U359	110-80-5	Ethylene glycol monoethyl ether
U115	75-21-8	Ethylene oxide (I,T)
U116	96-45-7	Ethylene thiourea
U117	60-29-7	Ethyl ether (I)
U076	75-34-3	Ethylidene dichloride
U118	97-63-2	Ethyl methacrylate

Hazardous waste no.	Chemical abstracts no.	Hazardous substance
U119	62-50-0	Ethylmethanesulfonate
U120	206-44-0	Fluoranthene
U122	50-00-0	Formaldehyde
U123	64-18-6	Formic acid (C,T)
U124	110-00-9	Furan (I)
U125	98-01-1	2-Furancarboxyaldehyde (I)
U147	108-31-6	2,4-Furandione
U213	109-99-9	Furan, tetrahydro- (I)
U125	98-01-1	Furfural (I)
U124	110-00-9	Furfuran (I)
U206	18883-66-4	D-Glucopyranose, 2-deoxy-2(3-methyl-3-nitrosoureido)-
U126	765-34-4	Glycidylaldehyde
U163	70-25-7	Guanidine, N-methyl-N'-nitro-N-nitroso-
U127	118-74-1	Hexachlorobenzene
U128	87-68-3	Hexachlorobutadiene
U129	58-88-9	Hexachlorocyclohexane (gamma isomer)
U130	77-47-4	Hexachlorocyclopentadiene
U131	67-72-1	Hexachloroethane
U132	70-30-4	Hexachlorophene
U243	1888-71-7	Hexachloropropene
U133	302-01-2	Hydrazine (R,T)
U086	1615-80-1	Hydrazine, 1,2-diethyl-
U098	57-14-7	Hydrazine, 1,1-dimethyl-
U099	540-73-8	Hydrazine, 1,2-dimethyl-
U109	122-66-7	Hydrazine, 1,2-diphenyl-
U134	7664-39-3	Hydrofluoric acid (C,T)
U134	7664-39-3	Hydrogen fluoride (C,T)
U135	7783-06-4	Hydrogen sulfide
U096	80-15-9	Hydroperoxide, 1-methyl-1-phenylethyl- (R)
U136	75-60-5	Hydroxydimethylarsine oxide
U116	96-45-7	2-Imidazolidinethione
U137	193-39-5	Indeno[1,2,3,cd]pyrene
U139	9004-66-4	Iron dextran
U190	85-44-9	1,3-Isobenzofurandione
U140	78-83-1	Isobutyl alcohol (I,T)
U141	120-58-1	Isosafrole
U142	143-50-0	Kepone
U143	303-34-4	Lasiocarpine
U144	301-04-2	Lead acetate
U146	1335-32-6	Lead, bis(acetato-O)tetrahydroxytri-
U145	7446-27-7	Lead phosphate
U146	1335-32-6	Lead subacetate
U129	58-89-9	Lindane
U147	108-31-6	Maleic anhydride
U148	123-33-1	Maleic hydrazide
U149	109-77-3	Malononitrile
U150	148-82-3	Melphalan
U151	7439-97-6	Mercury
U152	126-98-7	Methacrylonitrile (I,T)
U092	124-40-3	Methanamine, N-methyl- (I)
U029	74-83-9	Methane, bromo-

Hazardous waste no.	Chemical abstracts no.	Hazardous substance
U045	74-87-3	Methane, chloro- (I,T)
U046	107-30-2	Methane, chloromethoxy-
U068	74-95-3	Methane, dibromo-
U080	75-09-2	Methane, dichloro-
U075	75-71-8	Methane, dichlorodifluoro-
U138	74-88-4	Methane, iodo-
U119	62-50-0	Methanesulfonic acid, ethyl ester
U211	56-23-5	Methane, tetrachloro-
U153	74-93-1	Methanethiol (I,T)
U225	75-25-2	Methane, tribromo-
U044	67-66-3	Methane, trichloro-
U121	75-69-4	Methane, trichlorofluoro-
U123	64-18-6	Methanoic acid (C,T)
U154	67-56-1	Methanol (I)
U155	91-80-5	Methapyrilene
U142	143-50-0	1,3,4-Metheno-2H-cyclobuta[cd]pentalen-2-one, 1,1a,3,3a,4,5,5,5a,5b,6-decachlorooctahydro-
U247	72-43-5	Methoxychlor
U154	67-56-1	Methyl alcohol (I)
U029	74-83-9	Methyl bromide
U186	504-60-9	1-Methylbutadiene (I)
U045	74-87-3	Methyl chloride (I,T)
U156	79-22-1	Methylchlorocarbonate (I,T)
U226	71-55-6	Methylchloroform
U157	56-49-5	3-Methylcholanthrene
U158	101-14-4	4,4'-Methylenebis(2-chloroaniline)
U068	74-95-3	Methylene bromide
U080	75-09-2	Methylene chloride
U159	78-93-3	Methyl ethyl ketone (MEK) (I,T)
U160	1338-23-4	Methyl ethyl ketone peroxide (R,T)
U138	74-88-4	Methyl iodide
U161	108-10-1	Methyl isobutyl ketone (I)
U162	80-62-6	Methyl methacrylate (I,T)
U163	70-25-7	*N*-Methyl-*N'*-nitro-*N*-nitrosoguanidine
U161	108-10-1	4-Methyl-2-pentanone (I)
U164	56-04-2	Methylthiouracil
U010	50-07-7	Mitomycin C
U059	20830-81-3	5,12-Naphthacenedione, (8Scis)- 8acetyl10[(3amino- 2,3,6- trideoxy)-α-L-lyxo-hexopyranosyl)oxy]-7,8,9,10-tetrahydro- 6,8,11-trihydroxy-1-methoxy-
U165	91-20-3	Naphthalene
U047	91-58-7	Naphthalene, 2-chloro-
U166	130-15-4	1,4-Naphthalenedione
U236	72-57-1	2,7-Naphthalenedisulfonic acid, 3,3'-[(3,3'dimethyl-(1,1'biphenyl)- 4,4'-diyl)]-*bis*(azo)*bis*(5-amino-4-4hydroxy)-, tetrasodium salt
U166	130-15-4	1,4-Naphthoquinone
U167	134-32-7	alpha-Naphthylamine
U168	91-59-8	beta-Naphthylamine
U026	494-03-1	2-Naphthylamine, *N,N'-bis*(2-chloromethyl)-

Hazardous waste no.	Chemical abstracts no.	Hazardous substance
U167	134-32-7	1-Naphthylenamine
U168	91-59-8	2-Naphthylenamine
U217	10102-45-1	Nitric acid, thallium (1+) salt
U169	98-95-3	Nitrobenzene (I,T)
U170	100-02-7	p-Nitrophenol
U171	79-46-9	2-Nitropropane (I,T)
U172	924-16-3	N-Nitrosodi-n-butylamine
U173	1116-54-7	N-Nitrosodiethanolamine
U174	55-18-5	N-Nitrosodiethylamine
U176	759-73-9	N-Nitroso-N-ethylurea
U177	684-93-5	N-Nitroso-N-methylurea
U178	615-53-2	N-Nitroso-N-methylurethane
U179	100-75-4	N-Nitrosopiperidine
U180	930-55-2	N-Nitrosopyrrolidine
U181	99-55-8	5-Nitro-o-toluidine
U193	1120-71-4	1,2-Oxathiolane, 2,2-dioxide
U058	50-18-0	2H-1,3,2-Oxazaphosphorin-2-amine, N,N-bis(2-chloroethyl)tetrahydro-,2-oxide
U115	75-21-8	Oxirane (I,T)
U126	765-34-4	Oxiranecarboxyaldehyde
U041	106-89-8	Oxirane, (chloromethyl)-
U182	123-63-7	Paraldehyde
U183	608-93-5	Pentachlorobenzene
U184	76-01-7	Pentachloroethane
U185	82-68-8	Pentachloronitrobenzene (PCNB)
U242	87-86-5	Pentachlorophenol
U186	504-60-9	1,3-Pentadiene (I)
U187	62-44-2	Phenacetin
U188	108-95-2	Phenol
U048	95-57-8	Phenol, 2-chloro-
U039	59-50-7	Phenol, 4-chloro-3-methyl-
U081	120-83-2	Phenol, 2,4-dichloro-
U082	87-65-0	Phenol, 2,6-dichloro-
U089	56-53-1	Phenol, 4,4'-(1,2-diethyl-1,2-ethenediyl)bis-, (E)-
U101	105-67-9	Phenol, 2,4-dimethyl-
U052	1319-77-3	Phenol, methyl-
U132	70-30-4	Phenol, 2,2'-methylenebis[3,4,6-trichloro-
U170	100-02-7	Phenol, 4-nitro-
U242	87-86-5	Phenol, pentachloro-
U212	58-90-2	Phenol, 2,3,4,6-tetrachloro-
U230	95-94-4	Phenol, 2,4,5-trichloro-
U231	88-06-2	Phenol, 2,4,6-trichloro-
U150	148-82-3	L-Phenylalanine, 4-[bis(2-chloroethyl)amino]-
U145	7446-27-7	Phosphoric acid, lead salt
U087	3288-58-2	Phosphorodithioic acid, O,O-diethyl-, S-methyl-, ester
U189	108-95-2	Phosphorous sulfide (R)
U190	85-44-9	Phthalic anhydride
U191	109-06-8	2-Picoline
U179	100-75-4	Piperidine, 1-nitroso-
U192	23950-58-5	Pronamide
U194	107-10-8	1-Propanamine (I,T)

Hazardous waste no.	Chemical abstracts no.	Hazardous substance
U111	621-64-7	1-Propanamine, N-nitroso-N-propyl-
U110	142-84-7	1-Propanamine, N-propyl- (I)
U066	96-12-8	Propane, 1,2-dibromo-3-chloro-
U149	109-77-3	Propanedinitrile
U171	79-46-9	Propane, 2-nitro- (I,T)
U027	39638-32-9	Propane, 2,2'-oxybis[2-chloro-
U193	1120-71-4	1,3-Propane sulfone
U235	126-72-7	1-Propanol, 2,3-dibromo-, phosphate (3:1)
U140	78-83-1	1-Propanol, 2-methyl- (I,T)
U002	67-64-1	2-Propanone (I)
U084	542-75-6	1-Propane, 1,3-dichloro-
U152	126-98-7	2-Propanenitrile, 2-methyl- (I,T)
U007	79-06-1	2-Propenamide
U243	1888-71-7	1-Propene, hexachloro-
U009	107-13-1	2-Propenenitrile
U008	79-10-7	2-Propenoic acid (I)
U113	140-88-5	2-Propenoic acid, ethyl ester (I)
U118	97-63-2	2-Propenoic acid, 2-methyl-, ethyl ester
U162	80-66-2	2-Propenoic acid, 2-methyl-, methyl ester (I,T)
U233	93-72-1	Propionic acid, 2-(2,4,5-trichlorophenoxy)-
U194	107-10-8	n-Propylamine (I,T)
U083	78-87-5	Propylene dichloride
U148	123-33-1	3,6-Pyridazinedione, 1,2-dihydro-
U196	110-86-1	Pyridine
U191	109-06-8	Pyridine, 2-methyl-
U237	66-75-1	2,4(1H,3H)-Pyrimidinedione, 5-[bis(2-chloroethyl)amino]-
U164	56-04-2	4-(1H)-Pyrimidinone, 2,3-dihydro-6-methyl-2-thioxo-
U180	930-55-22	Pyrrolidine, 1-nitroso-
U200	50-55-5	Reserpine
U201	108-46-3	Resorcinol
U202	81-07-2	Saccharin and salts
U203	94-59-7	Safrole
U204	7783-00-8	Selenious acid
U204	7783-00-8	Selenium dioxide
U205	7446-34-6	Selenium sulfide (R,T)
U015	115-02-6	L-Serine, diazoacetate (ester)
U233	93-72-1	Silvex
U206	18883-66-4	Streptozotocin
U103	77-78-1	Sulfuric acid, dimethyl ester
U189	1314-80-3	Sulfur phosphide (R)
U232	93-76-5	2,4,5-T
U207	95-94-3	1,2,4,5-Tetrachlorobenzene
U208	630-20-6	1,1,1,2-Tetrachloroethane
U209	79-34-5	1,1,2,2-Tetrachloroethane
U210	127-18-4	Tetrachloroethylene
U212	58-90-2	2,3,4,6-Tetrachlorophenol
U213	109-99-9	Tetrahydrofuran (I)
U214	15843-14-8	Thallium(I) acetate
U215	6533-73-9	Thallium(I) carbonate
U216	7791-12-0	Thallium chloride
U217	10102-45-1	Thallium(I) nitrate

Hazardous waste no.	Chemical abstracts no.	Hazardous substance
U218	62-55-5	Thioacetamide
U153	74-93-1	Thiomethanol (I,T)
U244	137-26-8	Thioperoxydicarbonic diamide, tetramethyl-
U219	62-56-6	Thiourea
U244	137-26-8	Thiuram
U220	108-88-3	Toluene
U221	25376-45-8	Toluenediamine
U223	26471-62-5	Toluene diisocyanate (R,T)
U328	95-53-4	o-Toluidine
U353	106-49-0	p-Toluidine
U222	636-21-5	o-Toluidine hydrochloride
U011	61-82-5	1H-1,2,4-Triazol-3-amine
U226	71-55-6	1,1,1-Trichloroethane
U227	79-00-5	1,1,2-Trichloroethane
U228	79-01-6	Trichloroethylene
U121	75-69-4	Trichlormonofluoromethane
U230	95-95-4	2,4,5-Trichlorophenol
U231	88-06-2	2,4,6-Trichlorophenol
U234	99-35-4	sym-Trinitrobenzene (R,T)
U182	123-63-7	1,3,5-Trioxane, 2,4,6-trimethyl-
U235	126-72-7	Tris (2,3-dibormopropyl) phosphate
U236	72-57-1	Trypan blue
U237	66-75-1	Uracil mustard
U176	759-73-9	Urea, N-ethyl-N-nitroso-
U177	684-93-5	Urea, N-methyl-N-nitroso-
U043	75-01-4	Vinyl chloride
U248	81-81-2	Warfarin, when present at concentrations of 0.3% or less
U239	1330-20-7	Xylene (I)
U200	50-55-5	Yohimban-16-carboxylic acid, 11,17-dimethoxy-18-[(3,4,5-trimethoxybenzoyl)oxy]-, methyl ester
U249	1314-84-7	Zinc phosphide, when present at concentrations of 10% or less

INDEX

INDEX